PRESSED

Public Money, Private Profit

A Cautionary Tale

Molly S. Henderson
Ed.D. Temple University

Christiaan A. Hart Nibbrig
M.S. Columbia University Graduate School of Journalism

Pressed

Copyright © 2019 Molly S. Henderson, Ed.D.

All rights reserved. No part of this publication may be reproduced or transmitted in any form or by any means, including informational storage and retrieval systems, without permission in writing from the copyright holder, except for brief quotations in a review.

ISBN-13: 978-1-0904-2957-5

For Alex with my deep love and respect.

CONTENTS

Acknowledgements 7
Dedication 9
Foreword 11
Preface 15
Commonly Used Acronyms in *Pressed* 19
Chapter One: Lights! Action! and the Bard 21
Chapter Two: Doing Good So You Can Do Well 27
Chapter Three: The Project 47
Chapter Four: The Project Grows 77
Chapter Five: Hurricane Shaub—Category 5 105
Chapter Six: It's All About the Hotel—Really 131
Chapter Seven: "Molly Is Toast" 161
Chapter Eight: Conestoga View 181
Chapter Nine: The DA Investigation 203
Chapter Ten: The Grand Jury 225
Chapter Eleven: The Relentless Press 245
Chapter Twelve: Finishing the Job 265
Epilogue: When Truth Does Not Matter 283
Endnotes 297

Appendices

  A: Totaro's Request for a Grand Jury 464
    1. Request for Grand Jury - February 2005 464
    2. Totaro's email - November 7th, 2005 467
    3. Notice of Submission - November 10th, 2005 468
    4. Totaro's Commonwealth's Affidavit -
       July 12th, 2006 470
  B: The 57 Questions: Questions and Topics for PSP,
     LCCCA, and RACL 478
  C: Newspaper Headline Examples And Article
     Count 2004–2007 490
  D: Lancaster County Board of Commissioners 2004-2007 496
  E: Why We Sold Conestoga View 501
  F: Pennsylvania County Nursing Homes 504
  G: Status of the Lancaster County Convention Center
     and Marriott Hotel Project as of 2018 506
  H: Documents found on Pressed the Book website 511

Timeline Related to Lancaster County Hotel and Convention Center Project 517

Bibliography 533

Index 539

ACKNOWLEDGEMENTS

To Laura rational Douglas, Anita encouraging Cava, Leslie Shakespeare Laird and Laurie reader Baulig, thank you for your ongoing candid help.

To the artist in *Pressed* who captured the likeness of our cast of characters with just a touch of whimsy. Thank you for sharing your gift.

Thank you to Patti Waldygo, my editor, who took a very complicated account and made it just complicated.

To Christiaan Hart Nibbrig whose knowledge of journalistic standards and research skills made this book possible.

DEDICATION

Lancaster County has natural beauty and fertile farmland. It is a joy to live here. A portion of the sale of each *Pressed* book will be donated to Lancaster County environmental and farmland preservation efforts.

FOREWORD

Political economists and geographers and urban sociologists have long identified the forces behind changing urban economic landscapes: coalitions of local developers, commercial-interests (with greater or lesser degrees of competitive antagonisms amongst themselves), and media forces, brokered by local politicians.[*] They have also documented a powerful trend, at least since 1980, toward a privatization of "the common" in the processes of urban restructuring undertaken in response to the urban crisis that had been brewing in the U.S. since the 1960's.[**] Suburbanization had created a problematic loss of tax bases for cities. The problem, which began to manifest itself in a classic form with the 1975 fiscal crisis of New York City, created an urban economic development challenge. The trend toward privatization emerged out of a general equation of economic development as business development. The general presumption was, in line with the Thatcher-Reagan revolution, the public would be best served by a boosting of private business interests as a way of rebooting urban economies.

Privatizations diverted resources from the public good and put them at the service, or even under the control, of private business groups in those attempted rebooting operations.

But the "business development" privatization strategy has never been the panacea its proponents promised for people in need and

---

[*] See Logan and Molotch, especially chapter 3. For an even broader theoretical perspective, see Harvey, 1985, especially chapter 5.

[**] Zukin 1995 discusses and offer cases studies of this privatization trend. She highlights the role of public-private partnerships and of bureaucratic (and, democratically speaking, opaque) governance instruments like Business Investment Districts in this process of privatization.

communities in stress. What privatization has mostly done is to deliver more livable urban areas for the more affluent and a consolidation of power and wealth for the most affluent. In contrast, for the non-affluent, often displaced by forces of gentrification, deprived of public goods (e.g., good public schools), and nickel-and-dimed for basic services, privatization has resulted in a degradation of their private and public lives and their prospects (Phillips-Fein, 2017). If inequality has increased in our country in general since 1980--with, arguably, disastrous political, civic, and human consequences--that is not only because of the doings on Wall Street but also because of the doings in the local Chambers of Commerce and Government in which deals have been brokered, different interests have been channeled into predictable streams of winners and losers, and the commonwealth has been reapportioned accordingly.

This has been the case just about everywhere.

In *Pressed*, Molly Henderson gives us an insider look at how a coalition of developers-media-industry-politicians promoted a Marriott Hotel and Convention Center economic development project in the City of Lancaster, Pennsylvania. Henderson served as a Lancaster County Commissioner during some of the time this project was being promoted and came to oppose the terms under which the project was being developed. *Pressed* is Henderson's own narrative of the reasons for her opposition and of the ensuing political tug of war. She documents a vigorous campaign against her in the local media outlets, the parent company of which was a partner in the development of the project, arguing that the purpose of the campaign was to discredit her personally and politically in order to weaken the force of her opposition to the project. She wrote *Pressed*, she tells her readers, in order to recover the honor and integrity she had seen the media campaign impugn, to give posterity a narrative of her own to counter-pose to local media narrative. While Henderson's defamation lawsuit against Lancaster Newspapers, Inc. failed in the courts, the legal process of discovery unearthed information which she includes, along with information she had from her own direct experiences, in her narrative.

As a detailed account of the words and deeds of the participants in the Marriott Hotel and Convention Center project in the City of Lancaster, *Pressed* is an important case study through which scholars can illustrate and/or further develop, or even test, their theories of urban politics, sociology, and economics. The question at hand is not whether local economic and cultural elites have and use power to benefit themselves: that in itself falls more in the category of an "evident truth" than of a theoretical hypothesis. The question is, rather, whether those traditionally entrusted with the public good (politicians and the press) work more to negotiate the public good with economic and cultural elites, or work more instead to subordinate the public good to those elites.

In *Pressed*, Henderson argues that those entrusted with the public good in Lancaster subordinated it to the private interests of the elites. I myself have co-authored a report on the Lancaster economy which tends to support that argument (Callari, Gentry, and Yost). Those who promoted the form of economic development the Marriott Hotel and Convention Center project represents would of course not agree with this assessment. Their argument has to be that they promoted the project for the public good. Which of these two views better captures reality is something the public can judge, and scholars can assess, on the basis of evidence. *Pressed* gives us the behind-the scenes-words and deeds that make the case for the view those entrusted with the public good betrayed it in Lancaster. Perhaps those who promoted the Marriott Hotel and Convention Center project will want to give their behind-the-scenes words and deeds narrative to support the case that they were promoting the public good. The citizens of Lancaster deserve as transparent and open a record of what happened, of how power was used, in their community as possible. More generally, scholars also deserve as transparent and open record as possible, for it is on that base that they can refine the theories that let people everywhere understand how their communities are planned.

> Antonio Callari
> Sigmund M. and Mary B. Hyman Professor
> Franklin and Marshall College
> Lancaster, Pennsylvania.

References

Callari, Antonio, Evan Gentry, and Berwood-Yost. 2015. *Lancaster Prospers? An Analysis of Census Data on Economic Opportunities and Outcomes.* Floyd Institute for Public Policy. Franklin and Marshall College.

Harvey, David. 1985. *The Urban Experience.* Baltimore and London. The Johns Hopkins University Press.

Phillips-Fein, Kim. 2017. "How the Rich Seized Control of New York City. Today's stark inequality is a consequence of the City's crisis in the 1970's." *The New Republic.* April 13, 2017

Logan, John R. and Harvey L. Molotch. 2007. *Urban Fortunes. The political economy of place.* Second Edition. 20th anniversary edition, with a new Preface. Berkeley, Los Angeles, and London. University of California press.

Zukin, Sharon. 1995. *The Culture of Cities.* Malden, Massachusetts and Oxford, UK. Blackwell Publishers.

PREFACE

The 99%, Occupy Wall Street, "The Deplorables" and so many others today feel left behind and cheated by a system that is saying "so long". They feel victimized – better than their circumstances- vassals of the moneyed elite and its political enablers. This arrangement has always existed in one form or another. Through crony capitalism, those in power grow their influence and wealth.

Politicians use billions of our tax dollars to build publicly financed stadiums, arenas, and convention centers in cities and counties across the United States. They promote these projects as silver-bullet solutions for "revitalizing" ailing local economies. It is a "build-it-and-they-will come" approach to local economic development. This, justified by the multiplier effect of spending in the community, is a consistently overrated rationale.

Almost always, the promises turn out to be empty. Rather than being the heralded panaceas, these projects become expensive millstones hung around the necks of citizen taxpayers, who wind up paying for them for years to come.

Yet not everyone loses money. In virtually every one of these plans, a very few individuals, politically connected members of the business inner circle, make tens, even hundreds of millions of dollars. Bankers, property owners, and law firms leverage key local officials, whom they support financially, and manage to legally siphon public money into their private accounts.

Pressed tells the unsavory story of the downtown Lancaster hotel and convention center project, one of the most expensive capital project in Lancaster County's history, and the tactics its proponents used to destroy any and all opposition. *Pressed* deconstructs the process and misuse of power, influence and wealth that was, and still is, being played out in the hundreds of millions of dollars in a small American city to accomplish their goal.

I am a progressive, not a naysayer, and want to see the City of Lancaster develop and prosper. I am writing this book to fully report what actually happened in Lancaster County, Pennsylvania, during my term as county commissioner from 2004 to 2008 and why it happened. *Pressed* is not a book of reminiscences. It is an important account that needs to be added to the public record. It is part of Lancaster history, and it deserves to be told.

One might ask, "Doesn't a 'public record' already exist of your term in office in the archives of Lancaster Newspapers, the newspapers of record in Lancaster County at the time?"

Yes, and no.

During my term, one of my fellow commissioners, Dick Shellenberger, and I became the subject of more than one thousand newspaper articles, columns, editorials, and pseudo letters-to-the-editor, nearly all of them harshly critical of us as commissioners.

The ostensible reason for the blizzard of press coverage was the improper hiring of an administrative staff member and the sale of the county-owned nursing home Conestoga View. As was later confirmed through sworn testimony, Lancaster Newspaper, Inc., orchestrated "crime of the century" coverage of staff hiring and the sale of Conestoga View. This continued nearly every day for more than two years. The real "crime" had been to question and oppose the Lancaster establishment, including Lancaster Newspapers, Inc., which has a financial interest in the convention center and hotel project. As a result, I spent over two years in a Kafkaesque snow globe world, in which nonstop "news" promoted the value of a building project that in reality would only hurt taxpayers.

Using the pages of Lancaster Newspapers and backed by the means, resources, and experience of those with community influence and economic power produced a well-choreographed public relations campaign against the commissioners. It worked.

The trail of falsehoods published in Lancaster Newspapers contributed to the downfall and disgrace of three county commissioners. In my opinion, the falsehoods also constituted libel, demonstrating a reckless disregard for the truth. The newspaper "coverage" amounted to an egregious misuse of the immense power of the press. This took place at a time just before the mass adoption of the smartphone and the tablet, when newspapers still remained the primary source of news and information in Lancaster County.

When I left office, I sued Lancaster Newspapers for libel, along with its publisher, top editors, specific reporters, and a columnist. This book discusses the case in detail, including discovery evidence that demonstrates the newspaper's agenda.

You will come to understand from their own words, in under-oath testimony, how the leadership of Lancaster Newspapers, Inc., working with the region's biggest industrialist, S. Dale High, and his top executives, planned and carried out a newspaper campaign to alter public opinion and complete their project. What had prompted the anger of Lancaster County's most powerful entities? What caused their attacks on an almost daily basis? Finally, why was there an investigation by the district attorney and a criminal grand jury?

I believe it had nothing to do with Conestoga View or hiring practices. The power elite was irate because the use of taxpayer money for the Lancaster County Convention Center and Marriott Hotel project was being challenged.

High and Lancaster Newspapers—equal "private" equity shareholders in the hotel portion of the project—stood to make tens of millions of dollars from it. High had already made millions. As commissioners, we had the position and the power to question the risky, taxpayer-dependent project. That threat to their project brought down the wrath of the Lancaster establishment.

This book explains how it happened.

Christiaan Hart Nibbrig researched this book and made sure that the footnotes and the text fully explained the political and journalistic context. Mr. Hart Nibbrig, an alumnus of the Columbia University Graduate School of Journalism, has reported extensively on the hotel and convention center project. He was also the founding editor and publisher of several newspapers, including the *Lancaster* (Pa.) *Post*, the

Mendocino County (Cal.) *Outlook*, and the *East Bay* (Cal.) *Observer*. Chris worked as a publishing analyst at *People* magazine and as a writer at *Time Daily*, *Time* magazine's online daily publication in the mid 1990s. He is the author of *A Thief in the Church*, a nonfiction account of an Old Order Mennonite who defrauded other Plain people of $65 million. He currently lives in California.

—Molly S. Henderson
2018

COMMONLY USED ACRONYMS IN *PRESSED*

1. **CCAP** – County Commissioners Association of Pennsylvania – elected representatives from each of the 67 counties of Pennsylvania.
2. **CRIZ** – City Revitalization and Improvement Zone - A state program administered by the Department of Community and Economic Develop, Governor's Office of the Budget, and the Department of Revenue. Its mission is to revitalize local business communities through redistribution of local tax revenue.
1. **CV** – Conestoga View- a nursing and rehabilitation center in Lancaster county owned by the county of Lancaster until 2005 when it was sold to Complete Healthcare Resources.
2. **FF&E** – fixtures, furniture and equipment.
3. **HACC** – Harrisburg Community College, a central Pennsylvania community college with branches in Dauphin, Lancaster, Lebanon, Adams and York counties.
4. **IFIP** – Infrastructure Facilities Improvement Program, a multi-year grant program that will provide money to certain issuers of debt in order to assist with the payment of debt service.
5. **IGT** – Intergovernmental Transfer Program, a method of moving funds from one governmental entity to another.
6. **LCCCA** – Lancaster County Convention Center Authority, a seven-member board
7. **PDCVB** – Pennsylvania Dutch Convention & Visitors Bureau, now known as Discover Lancaster! is a membership organization that markets and promotes tourism in Lancaster County.

8. **PKF** – Parnell Kerr Forster, international accounting firm that conducted the feasibility study on the hotel and convention center project. Now known as CBRE.
9. **PSP** – Penn Square Parents, a business partnership in Lancaster comprised originally Lancaster Newspapers, Inc., High Industries and Fulton Financial. Now made-up of Lancaster Newspapers, Inc. and High Industries, Inc.
10. **RACL** – Redevelopment Authority of the City of Lancaster whose purpose is to promote homeownership and prevent blight in the city of Lancaster.
11. **RKL** – Reinsel Kuntz Lesher, is a business and accounting consulting firm in Pennsylvania.
12. **TIF** – Tax Increment Financing is a public financing method that is used as a subsidy for redevelopment, infrastructure and other community improvements.

Chapter One

LIGHTS! ACTION! AND THE BARD

Faith, gentlemen, now I play a merchant's part,
And venture madly on a desperate mart.
—William Shakespeare, *Taming of the Shrew*, 1590

One Saturday evening my husband, Alex, and I traveled through pouring sleet to the Black Gryphon Restaurant outside of Elizabethtown for dinner and a "Pop-Up" Shakespearean production. The fare, of Welsh influence, was only fair. Welsh eating houses remain rare for a reason. Actually, the Welsh are not known for much, except the development of the long bow, which seriously annoyed the English around 1300. The real reason for our visit was the Shakespeare.

Six students in the theater department of Elizabethtown College presented seven scenes from Shakespeare's comedies and tragedies. They had no stage or sound system, no spotlights or costumes. The students just "popped-up" in the center of the room and did their rendition of a scene from *Macbeth*, *Hamlet*, or *As You Like It*. Though it wasn't a packed house, everyone—even while eating dinner—paid rapt attention. We had a lovely evening, enjoying their art.

The "Pop-Up" performances coincided with the touring exhibit of *The First Folio* of 1623 and the 400th anniversary of Shakespeare's death. Considered one of the most influential books ever written, *The First Folio* comprises the complete collection of Shakespeare's thirty-six plays. Elizabethtown College invited the public to view an original copy of the nearly four centuries old book at its library. I decided to go.

On Sunday afternoon, I drove up to Elizabethtown to see some significant history. Snow flurries blew sideways as a blustery wind whipped leaves everywhere. A fabulous fall day! Few students ventured out in the cold weather on the beautiful campus. When I turned the corner to approach the library, I read the large block letters engraved in granite over the doorway to the tasteful brick building: THE HIGH LIBRARY.

Lights! Action! and the Bard

The Merchants of Lancaster

In One Act

The Merchants of Lancaster was presented in late fall 2003 in Room 503, Lancaster County Court House, Lancaster, PA. The cast, as follows:

The Commissioners

County Commissioner, incumbent, soon-to-be chairman:	Howard Pete Shaub
County Commissioner-Elect, soon to be vice chair:	Richard "Dick" Shellenberger
County Commissioner-Elect, minority seat:	Molly S. Henderson

The Merchants

Industrialist, Real Estate Developer, Businessman:	S. Dale High
Lancaster Newspapers Inc., Chief Executive Officer:	John "Jack" Buckwalter
Fulton Bank, Chief Executive Officer:	Rufus Fulton

<u>Director:</u> Impromptu
<u>Costumes:</u> Traditional business attire of the period

<u>Scene:</u> *Early afternoon in the busy County Commissioners' Office, 5th floor of the Lancaster County Courthouse. A wooden table dominates the windowless conference room. Three high-backed swivel chairs on rollers, upholstered with shabby blue cloth, line each side of the table, with one at each end. Large glass walls enclose opposite ends of the room, so one can see whatever goes on outside or in. Although curtains can be drawn to cover the glass, today the curtains remain open at one side of the room, revealing the employees' active workstations.*

The commissioners and the merchants file into room 503. All appear cordial as they shake hands. They take seats at the table. Three commissioners on one side face the merchants across the table. Shaub sits across from Fulton at the far right. Shellenberger, in the middle chair, faces Buckwalter. Henderson takes the left seat opposite High. The purpose of the meeting is to review the status of the hotel and convention center project.

Shaub: [*Comfortable and smiling*] Hello, everyone. Thank you for coming. I'd like to introduce Molly Henderson and Dick

Shellenberger, who will join me on the Board of Commissioners in January. And Molly and Dick, I'd like to introduce Dale High of High Industries [*High appears reserved, smiles and nods to the commissioners*]; Jack Buckwalter, head of Lancaster Newspapers [*he smiles broadly and nods to the commissioners*], and Rufus Fulton, president of Fulton Bank [*he seems at ease, smiles and nods to the commissioners*].

Fulton: [*warmly*] Congratulations on your election.

Shellenberger: [*amicably*] We have a lot to learn. Everyone is being helpful.

Henderson: [*smiling*] Yes, thank you. It's nice to meet you. I've met Mr. Buckwalter previously at various functions in Lancaster. The paper was quite supportive when I worked at the city health department.

Buckwalter: [*easily*] You've got a lot on your plate here at the commissioners' office. It's a big county.

Shellenberger: [*matter-of-factly*] We're looking to streamline the office and be more efficient—run things more like a business.

High: [*pleasantly and calmly*] Yes, congratulations. There is a lot of work ahead for all of us.

Fulton: [*positively*] It looks like the baseball stadium is coming along. That's great for the community.

Shaub: [*upbeat and casual*] We're looking forward to so many things next year. There are a lot of ideas we've got going. There are many plans already underway that need to be finished—like the Safety Training Center, for one, and the Rail Trail.

Shaub: [*Now more serious, looking at Fulton, Buckwalter, then directly at High*] And another thing we need to not only finish, but just get started is the convention center project. [*tone more intense*] Where are we on this? The county has put the tax in place. The county has guaranteed the bond. What are you guys doing? When will you draw drawings?

[*The tension in the room immediately becomes palpable.*]

Fulton: [*Begins to study his pen on the table in front of him, moving it about slightly.*]

Buckwalter: [*Smiles slightly and begins looking down at the table—anywhere but at Shaub.*]

Shellenberger: [*ever the peacemaker, says gently*] Pete, there is a lot going on for this project. I'm sure everyone is working to get this thing moving.

Henderson: [*Listening closely and thinking it's time to put on her seatbelt. She says nothing, waiting for the apache* dance to begin between Shaub and High.*]

Shaub: [*Directly to High now, strictly, chastising*] Well, Dale? What is your plan? Life is too short to be dragging on like this. We need deliverables!

High: [*High raises his head, first with a quizzical look toward Shaub, then as one collecting his thoughts. High begins his response, directly to Shaub. High speaks in a low tone with a ridged jaw. His hands are on top of the table.*] Our organization has been working on this project for years.

Henderson: [*She sits directly across from High, her view fastened to the change in his appearance as he speaks. He quakes with rage, and mottled purple spots appear on his face. She is sure no one ever speaks to Mr. High in this manner.*]

High: [*Spittle collects in the corners of his mouth, as he speaks deliberately through clenched teeth. The tone and volume continue to decrease, as High's fury increases.*] We are moving forward. Pete, you don't know what you're talking about. You don't understand what is at stake here.

Buckwalter, Fulton, and Shellenberger—speechless—watch and listen, clearly embarrassed by the exchange.

Henderson: [*Her mother told her about apoplexy. She is glad she knows CPR.*]

Shaub: [*Still directly to High and unruffled by High's emotion.*] So. What is it, Dale? When will we have something?

Shellenberger: [*Attempts to diffuse the situation.*] Okay, there are many things to discuss as we go forward here. Let's take our time and get back to this later.

Shaub: [*Not letting go*] Dale, I repeat, when will we have some drawings?

Buckwalter and Fulton, agitated, shift in their chairs.

---

* apache—pronounced ah-PAHSH; a French dance, often violent, between a man and a woman.

High: [*Still furious, becomes dismissive of Shaub*] No one speaks to me this way or questions my methods. We will do this project. This meeting is over!

The merchants rise abruptly and file out, saying nothing.

Henderson: [*Remembering,* "I guess that's what Paul and Ron warned me about."]

Curtain

This was my first and last meeting with S. Dale High.

Clearly, I had entered in the middle of the action, my first glimpse of the dramatic catastrophe known as *the Lancaster County Convention Center Debacle!* To understand what was going on, we need to go back a little further and start at the beginning.

Chapter Two

DOING GOOD SO YOU CAN DO WELL

"You can give me a fish. You can teach me to fish.
But I know very well who owns the pond."
—Reverend Edward M. Bailey, Pastor,
Bethel AME Church, Lancaster, PA, August 6, 2003

The Power Brokers

"Welcome, my lord, how far off lies your power?"
—William Shakespeare, *Richard II*, 1595

It is a truism that if you want to get to the bottom of something, you "*follow the money.*" By following the money to power and influence in Lancaster County, you'll discover two names: Steinman and High. These two families—the Steinmans, especially—have shaped the culture and history of Lancaster County far more than any other since the birth of the place in the early 1700s.

Today, the average Lancastrian has no idea what a Steinman or a High might look like. While they are public figures, they haven't held elected office since the middle of the nineteenth century.[1] Still, the Steinmans and the Highs touch the lives of Lancastrians every day.

The Highs, who became prominent many years after the Steinmans, have had an immense impact in the region since the middle of the twentieth century. Not only are the Steinmans and the Highs two of Lancaster's wealthiest families, they have used that wealth to influence and control the Lancaster establishment for generations.[2]

A simple stroll through downtown Lancaster gives evidence of the families' imprint. The Steinman family owns virtually the entire first block of West King Street: Lancaster's central business district. The headquarters of Lancaster Newspapers, Inc., the Steinmans' newspaper company, occupies the five-story building as the centerpiece of the block. Steinman Park sits in the middle of the block, next to Steinman's Pressroom Restaurant.[3]

Across the street, we see the Lancaster Heritage Center.[4] The Steinmans helped establish that society and have been its main benefactor for more than a hundred years. On Penn Square, half a block from the newspaper headquarters, stands a 19-story, 300-room Marriott Hotel, indirectly co-owned by the Steinmans and the Highs.

At the Boys and Girls Clubs, historical societies, hospitals, museums, and schools, the biggest plaques invariably will prominently display the names Steinman and High on the lists of benefactors. Both families generously embody a noblesse oblige.

One of High's companies constructed the Old Town section of Lancaster, an upscale housing redevelopment near the city center.[5] High also developed several residential communities in the Lancaster area, including Greenfield Estates, Eastwood Village, Wedgewood Estates, and Willow Acres.

Leaving the city, we see more of the High family footprint. The sprawling High-owned, 600-acre Greenfield Corporate Center extends east of Lancaster, near the outlet malls that attract many thousands of Lancaster County tourists.[6] Here are the massive industrial yards and warehouses of High Steel Structures. The bridge across the Susquehanna River was built with High Steel. At Elizabethtown College, alma mater of current High patriarch S. Dale High, we'll find the High Center for Business. The college's main library, the High Library, is the central building on the campus. The Steinmans also have a visible presence at Elizabethtown with the Steinman Center for Communication and Art. Franklin & Marshall College, in Lancaster city, houses the Steinman College Center and the Caroline Steinman Nunan Arboretum.

This small sample revealing the physical presence of the Steinman and High families in Lancaster County only hints at their influence. They are everywhere.

Printing Money: The Steinmans

After arriving from Saxony in 1749, the German immigrants Christian and Anna Steinman began the long, successful family line in Lancaster. As would be the pattern until the 1980s, the family gave each Steinman male a substantial start in business. He would grow that business and the Steinman name in each successive generation. Beginning with a hardware store, then buying property and gaining ownership of coal and iron mines and newspapers, the following generations of Steinmans, through hard work and shrewd business sense, would accumulate property, means, and power.

Andrew Jackson Steinman (fourth-generation American), born October 10, 1836, became the most ambitious and brilliant of the Steinman men.[7] After attending Yale, he returned to Lancaster to practice law and involve himself in the community. AJ brought the Steinman family into the newspaper business.

On November 1, 1866, Steinman purchased a 50 percent interest in the *Lancaster Intelligencer*, a floundering publication of the Democratic Party. The *Lancaster Intelligencer* had begun as the Federalist *Lancaster Journal* in 1794, then changed hands, names, and political affiliations several times. It had a circulation of about 500 when AJ purchased it.[8] People considered the publication a Democratic "copperhead" newspaper. During this era, Democrats were the conservative party. "Copperheads" were Northerners who approved of slavery and opposed a war between the states. Prior to the Civil War, the newly formed Republican Party with Lincoln's leadership was considered the more progressive division. The two parties changed labels in the future.

Early Use of Power of the Press

Five days after AJ Steinman purchased his interest in the four-page, six-column newspaper, the *Intelligencer* published an editorial that said, "The old Democratic doctrine of manifest destiny had its origin in the proud consciousness of the superiority of the race of white men who dwelt in the United States."[9]

After brother George lost a congressional bid to Thaddeus Stevens in 1860, AJ Steinman continued the election animosity in his newspaper, the *Lancaster Intelligencer*. He mocked Stevens's relationship with Lydia Hamilton-Smith. Hamilton-Smith was Stevens's African American housekeeper and a businesswoman in her own right. Steinman's editorial opined in 1867:

> If Thaddeus Stevens insists on being buried side by side with the woman he is supposed to have taken to his bosom that is entirely a matter of taste. But why did he not purchase a lot in an African burying ground at once? There, no white man's bones would have jostled his own, and she who has long been his most intimate associate might have been gathered to his side without exciting public scandal.[10]

Steinman and the *Intelligencer* continued to attack Thaddeus Stevens. Stevens championed the 13th, 14th, and 15th Amendments to the United States Constitution. These laws emancipated African Americans from slavery, gave them citizenship, and granted the men the right to vote. After Stevens died in 1868, close to the election date, his name stayed on the ballot. The *Intelligencer* mocked the "corpse for Congress." Yet a dead Stevens still defeated his Democratic opponent.[11]

AJ Steinman filled the publisher's role in the partnership, handling the business side of the newspaper's operation. AJ, not being a journalist, rarely wrote editorials for the newspaper. He did, however, provide the editorial vision of the paper. The paper always remained AJ's and always functioned as an overtly political instrument. The *Intelligencer* called Republicans "radicals" during the first twenty years AJ Steinman owned the newspaper.[12]

In 1905, AJ Steinman and Charles Foltz purchased the buildings at 8-10 West King Street, a few doors from Steinman Hardware, for

$11,000. The next year, these properties were appraised at $17,000. Steinman and Foltz rented 10 W. King until 1923, when that space underwent a major renovation of the newspaper building.[13] By this point, the Steinmans owned the entire south side of the first block of West King Street.

The early twentieth century developed into a time of rapid newspaper growth. Cities bustled with people who needed entertainment but had very little money. The teeming masses could read, however. Print newspapers, broadsheets, and tabloids entertained the public. This was the age of William Randolph Hearst and Joseph Pulitzer and their newspaper "wars," stoking public sentiment with sensationalistic stories and selling millions of newspapers across the country, especially in New York.[14]

This "yellow journalism," with its hysterical headlines and purple prose, drew readers by the millions. Occasionally, as with Nelly Bly and H. L. Menken, it produced excellent journalism and social criticism.[15] Often, mere sensationalism passed for "news."

Around the turn of the nineteenth century and into the early twentieth, Lancaster became a vibrant, growing city. In 1890, its population consisted of about 32,000 residents. By 1900, 41,000 people lived there, and by 1920, 53,000.[16] Lancaster was booming.

In July 1909, AJ Steinman and Charles Foltz started the *Lancaster Morning Journal* to pair with their afternoon *Intelligencer*. The *Morning Journal* had a circulation of 2,700. In March 1915, Steinman purchased the *Lancaster Morning News*, increasing the morning circulation to a substantial 7,000 daily readers. They called the combined morning paper the *News Journal*.[17]

Before his death on November 17, 1917, Andrew Jackson Steinman—lawyer, iron and coal magnate, financier, newspaperman, and political activist—transferred ownership of his companies and properties to his four children. He was buried in the Steinman family plot at the Woodward Hill Cemetery. He left behind an enormous fortune and an array of profitable businesses. His half of the newspaper business went to his sons, John Frederick and James Hale Steinman. Like their father and his father and grandfather, the next generation of Steinman men would grow that fortune to even vaster dimensions.

The Monopoly Media Begins

When John Frederick and James Hale inherited the newspaper business and other enterprises from their father, Andrew Jackson Steinman, John was thirty-three years old, and James, thirty-one. The brothers operated Steinman Enterprises with stunning success from 1916 until James died in 1962 and John in 1980.

John supervised the production and circulation of the newspapers, while James directed the editorial and advertising end. James, as "Publisher," served as the public face of the newspaper business, and John took the role of "Co-Publisher." Wrote Steinman family biographer John Brubaker: "The sons treated the newspapers as a manufacturing enterprise instead of the political organ and business liability their father had inherited and never altered."[18]

In May 1921, the Steinman brothers bought out Foltz's 50 percent interest in the *Intelligencer* for $75,000.[19] The brothers also brought the accountant "Izzy" Buckwalter from Penn Iron over to the newspaper operations.

John oversaw and monitored the technological side of the newspaper business. With his leadership, the presses of Lancaster Newspapers always remained at the forefront of the latest technology. He demonstrated his approach to his employees in the 1920s, when he wrote "a friendly word" to type operators contemplating a strike:

> Use your reason, men. The employers must win—must, we say, because you know the eight-hour day (six days a week) is just, and the public is with us in it. For our money loss, we are insured. . . . Stick to your jobs, men, because by sticking you are doing the right thing.[20]

Soon the Steinman brothers faced a more serious challenge than a labor strike. In 1923, a New York–based publisher named Paul Block purchased the *Lancaster New Era*. Block already owned dozens of newspapers across the country, and he intended to fight for the Lancaster market.[21] Block immediately added a bit of splash to the *New Era* by including color comics, which the Steinmans' newspapers did not use.

The *New Era* had been founded in 1877 as a Republican (i.e., liberal) newspaper. When Block acquired the *New Era* in the mid 1920s, it became a competing afternoon paper to the Steinmans' morning *News Journal* and afternoon *Intelligencer*.

The Steinmans responded by lowering advertising rates and launching the weekly *Sunday News*. They also built the five-story headquarters on West King Street that still houses Lancaster Newspapers' offices today. The *Sunday News* emerged as an enormous success. With a jump in the *Intelligencer*'s circulation from 6,000 in 1923 to 30,000 in 1928, Block gave up. He sold the *Lancaster New Era* to the Steinmans for almost $1 million.[22]

By 1928, the Steinmans had complete control of the print newspaper market in Lancaster County with the only daily morning paper, now the *Intelligencer Journal*; the only daily afternoon paper, the *Lancaster New Era*; and the *Sunday News*. This print monopoly continues to this day.

The importance of the small-town newspaper in American society cannot be overstated. Newspapers provided information, news, entertainment, and culture. For most of the twentieth century, newspapers functioned as the thread connecting towns, counties, states, and the country together. In Lancaster County, the Steinmans owned the only spool. The Steinman family had absolute control over newspaper publishing for most of the twentieth century. They possessed true power.

Newspapers have several revenue streams: subscriptions, newsstand sales, display advertising, and classified advertising, including obituaries and legal notices. These revenues grow with the circulation. The revenues of all three Lancaster Newspapers benefited the Steinman family.

In the early 1950s, Lancaster Newspapers' co-publisher John Steinman expressed the brothers' sentiment toward the newspapers: "Like my father I was never a newsman—always a businessman. That's what I am now. The newspaper is and always has been a business—nothing more!"[23]

Media Moguls

"Sweet thou art now one of the greatest men in this realm."
—William Shakespeare, *Henry IV, Part II*, 1597

The Steinmans acted as major media players in other areas besides the newspaper monopoly in Lancaster. Beginning in 1923, when they purchased the WGAL radio frequency, the Steinmans became the most important force in Lancaster's booming radio business.[24]

Through WGAL radio (1490 AM and 101.3 FM), the Steinmans dominated the radio airwaves in Lancaster County during radio's golden age: the 1930s through the 1950s. They reaped huge advertising profits as a result. Their radio stations carried the popular shows of the day, including *Amos 'n Andy*, *Jack Benny*, and *George Burns and Gracie Allen*.

The brothers got into television very early. The first broadcast of WGAL-TV to the Lancaster audience aired in March 1949. WGAL became the fourth television station in the state of Pennsylvania. It was the first television station outside of Philadelphia and had the smallest market of any station in the country.[25]

The Steinmans expanded their television holdings by purchasing stations in Delaware, New Mexico, and Arizona. They held most of these radio and television stations into the 1970s, when they sold many of them to the Pulitzer Media Group. The Federal Communications Commission (FCC) forced the Steinmans to sell WGAL-TV in Lancaster on an anti-trust claim, so they sold it to the Pulitzer group in 1978. After getting rid of the television and radio stations, the Steinmans generated the largest amount of revenue from the newspapers.[26]

John Frederick Steinman died at age ninety-eight in 1980, leaving behind a daughter, Shirley. James Hale had three daughters: Louise, Caroline, and Beverly, known as "Peggy."[27]

The Next Generations

My Earliest Introduction to the Steinmans

At age ten, I thought that someone smoking a cigarette on a horse had to be a cowboy. *Wagon Train*, *Rawhide*, roll your own—the movies had it that way. This scene was different. This was no cowboy. It was a young woman on a tall, elegant black horse riding along the alley behind our house in Millersville. My two sisters and I, like most little girls, were horse crazy. (We repeatedly told our parents that we could keep a pony in the garage.) The horse came to a halt, and we slowly approached.

"May we pet him?" I asked.

"Yes, but don't spook him," she advised in a quiet voice.

We were thrilled! My older sister, Jane, asked the rider, "What's your name?"

She answered agreeably, "Peggy Steinman." She then trotted off, flicking her cigarette to the street.

I picked up the still-smoldering butt and put it out. That event, more than fifty years ago, is as clear to me as yesterday. It certainly made an impression on me.

Twenty Years Later

At age thirty, I occasionally saw the Steinmans at social occasions. My husband, Alex, was a new associate at the law firm of Hartman, Underhill, and Brubaker. During one of his first years there, Hale (Steinman) Ansberry worked as a summer law intern. Hale—bright, charming, and engaging—sometimes came over to our house to visit and have dinner. We enjoyed her company. During that time, the Steinmans reciprocated invitations.

One summer day, Hale's aunt Caroline Steinman Nunan invited us to a cookout. This would be my first venture out of the house after our son, Ander, was born in June. I had taken maternity leave from the hospital. The weather was miserably hot, and the day did not go well. I dressed in my best postpartum summer frock, and we started

Beverly (Peggy) Steinman – Owner of Steinman Enterprises and Chairman of Lancaster Newspapers, Inc.

out. Alex's mother stayed with Ander. We didn't even make it off the property before the first accident occurred. Alex started the car and had it in drive before I got in. The car pushed me forward and wedged me between the front bumper and the wall. I screamed, and a terrified Alex quickly reversed the Audi. It was a bruised and ominous start to the outing.

The cookout was casual and pleasant. On that fiercely hot day, we sat outside with many other guests at tables shielded from the sun by umbrellas. About mid-meal, I realized that I hadn't anticipated the day's timing well. I was nursing, and it was *that* time. The "letdown" reflex began, and two large milk blots saturated my dress. What to do? Well, of course, act like nothing was happening. Through my embarrassment, the Steinmans' ever-present decorum, and waving bees away, Alex and I finished our visit and went home. I remember we had popsicles for dessert. A day of terror and mortification made an indelible memory in my mind.

After Hale went back to law school and moved to Washington, D.C., our social interactions subsided. She later married another lawyer, Robert Krasne. They have since returned to Lancaster.

Twenty-Three Years Later

At age fifty-three, I never directly connected the Steinmans with the newspaper. Certainly, I knew they owned it, but my experiences with their family had occurred through social or civic events. As commissioner, I sat on the Board of the Heritage Center of Lancaster County, where Caroline Steinman Nunan was a champion. The

Steinmans are great supporters of farmland preservation, which our board of commissioners funded generously.

My daughter, Leslie, attended the same high school as Caroline Nunan's grandson Tom. Ever generous, the Steinmans donated a civic prize to the school. In eleventh grade, Leslie won the Steinman "Most Outstanding Citizenship" award at her school. Her plaque now hangs in our living room.

To me, the paper functioned as an entity separate from the family. The Steinmans were about giving to the community. I didn't realize the family was directly involved with the paper's content until it was revealed in Jack Buckwalter's deposition. Then I learned Peggy Steinman had requested that some "adjustments" be made in the paper during the convention center coverage.

Good Measure: HIGH

> ". . . a piece of work so bravely done, so rich, that it did strive
> In workmanship and value."
> —William Shakespeare, *Cymbeline*, 1609

High Industries markets itself with an unusual phrase: "Giving Good Measure since 1931."[28] "Good measure" means the welder gives the customer a strong, full-measure weld. The customer isn't cheated.

Today High Industries, a conglomerate that employs thousands in Lancaster County and several states, has moved beyond welding but still uses the identifiable "good measure" in its marketing.[29]

The Highs built their empire on an even more humble foundation than the Steinmans, who got their start with a thriving eighteenth-century hardware store. The High name rose to prominence about 150 years after the Steinmans.

In the depths of the Depression, 1931, Sanford H. High and his older brother, Benjamin, borrowed $7,500 to buy the welding shop where they worked.[30] Sanford wasn't a welder but knew the shop would be a good business opportunity.

Despite his inexperience in the field, Sanford High believed that welding had a great future. Giving up farming, he proved to be an excellent welder and businessman. The small shop in Lancaster grew steadily. High Welding began as a four-man shop that fixed appliances, repaired cars (bumpers, mostly), and made fuel tanks. Sanford had a natural talent with a blowtorch and a mask. In the early part of the twentieth century, welding technology quickly advanced.

Sanford High's business became one of the first to extensively use electric welding for its repair work. "We repaired anything from automobile fenders to extremely heavy castings," said Calvin G. High, Sanford's eldest son.[31]

Sanford High had a burning "big idea": welding bridges to repair them, instead of using rivets and bolts. In the first years of High Welding, he spent a lot of time lobbying Pennsylvania state highway officials to repair bridges with welding. In 1933, Sanford convinced the state to give High Welding a contract on a bridge in York County. Evidently, High's company did a good job, because the government work increased immediately.[32]

High Welding grew rapidly during the 1940s and the 1950s, adding bridge manufacturing and pipeline repair jobs to its bridge repair work. The company began fabricating and erecting structural steel in 1946, which opened up new business opportunities.

Needing more space, High moved the company, with his thirty employees, east of Lancaster City in 1955. High Welding then stopped its bridge-repair work and shifted to fabricating steel structures. In addition to bridges, the company built commercial structures and schools, always using the newest technologies in steel production.

The 1960s interstate road–building boom brought increased profits to High Welding. Throughout the region, High provided steel for innumerable bridge and road projects. In 1970, High got the 8,000-ton steel contract for the Columbia-Wrightsville Bridge via Route 30. One must drive on High steel to cross the Susquehanna River.

Sanford High's company kept growing. He built his second plant and soon expanded that. In 1971, with Sanford in his mid-sixties, High Welding changed its name to High Steel Structures.[33] The company diversified into real estate and construction but kept building bridges, bigger ones.

Sanford High died in December 1983 at age seventy-six. He was a marvel. His vision and work left an indelible mark on millions of people in the United States. He had taken a tiny shop in Lancaster and built one of the nation's largest steel companies. A technological innovator, he invented several new welding and steel-fabrication techniques. His business expansion left a permanent imprint in the Mid-Atlantic States. A historically important figure, Sanford High revolutionized road and bridge construction in the twentieth century.

Six years before he died, he turned his company over to his youngest son, S. Dale High, thirty-five. Everyone called him "Dale."

When Dale High came to work for High Welding in 1963, the company had sixty employees and gross revenues of about $1 million per year. By the time he turned over the presidency of the company in 2012, High Industries employed thousands and generated annual revenues of about a half-billion dollars.[34] Like the Steinman heirs, S. Dale High was given a great start in business, and he made the most of it.

When Dale took over High Steel, the company owned zero hotels. After his first ten years at the helm, the company had acquired eight.[35] The hotel he wanted to build on Penn Square became a heated issue between us.

Dale High was not a mechanic like his father. He was, however, a shrewd businessman, like Sanford—and an extraordinarily successful one. Headquartered at the High-owned Greenfield Corporate Center, Dale High expanded the family welding and steel business into construction, real estate development, management, concrete, hotels, food service, and worker placement divisions.[36]

S. Dale High – Principal, High Industries

Doing Good

"... 'Twere good you do so much for charity."
—William Shakespeare, *Merchant of Venice*, 1596

Both the Steinman and the High family have kept their businesses under family control. Steinman family members make up the majority of the board for "Steinman Enterprises." In addition, the family maintains complete control of the $85 million Steinman Foundation. The foundation has given young people hundreds of four-year scholarships totaling more than $2 million.[37] Dale High has remained chairman of High Industries since his retirement in 2012.[38] Again, like the Steinmans, the High family retains the leadership of the High companies and related boards. The "S. Dale High Family Council," made up of Dale, his wife, and three adult children, control all of the High entities: High Steel Structures, High Concrete Group, High Steel Service Center, High Associates, High Construction Company, High Hotels, and High Real Estate. The High Family Council also controls the High Foundation, a family nonprofit that seeks "to make a significant difference in the lives of those most in need in our community."[39]

Supporting Cast

"... Your trusty and most valiant servitor..."
—William Shakespeare, *Othello*, 1604

As the twentieth century ended, the Steinman-owned business interests remained powerful entities in Lancaster. These included Intelligencer Printing, eleven radio stations, Steinman Coal Company, the Pressroom Restaurant, and Lancaster Newspapers. The family's net worth is estimated to be in the hundreds of millions of dollars.

By the year 2000, Lancaster Newspapers' penetration of the Lancaster County market included:
The Intelligencer Journal—morning daily, circulation 45,000
The Lancaster New Era—evening daily, circulation 41,000
The Sunday News—Sunday, circulation 92,000

Lancaster Farming—weekly, circulation 54,000
The Ephrata Review—weekly, circulation 8,200
The Lititz Record—weekly, circulation 8,000
La Voz—a Spanish language weekly, circulation 10,000.

The Steinmans ran each newspaper as a separate publication, with separate editors and reporters, as well as its own circulation and advertising staff.[40]

The entire editorial and publishing staff of the *Intell*, the *New Era*, and the *Sunday News*—all of the reporters, the editors, the accountants, the ad execs, the pages, the publishers, and the presidents—worked out of the same building: 8 West King Street. The Steinmans owned the editorial staff's shared desks, computers, elevators, and lobbies.

Any twentieth-century newspaper publisher would envy the readership penetration of Lancaster Newspapers in Lancaster County, population 490,000.[41] The newspapers reached about half of the households in the 984-square-mile county. That level of saturation, with no competition, carried significant power and influence in Lancaster County. That power would be brought to bear on me in just a few years.

☙

In 1983, John M. Buckwalter, Izzy's son, became president and CEO of Lancaster Newspapers. Known to everyone as "Jack," Buckwalter was born in 1931 and raised and educated in Lancaster city.

Jack Buckwalter got his first job at Lancaster Newspapers at fifteen as a part-time messenger. He served two years in the army after Harvard, then returned to Lancaster to work full time at Lancaster Newspapers. He was employed there until his death in 2010.[42]

Buckwalter began working for the Steinmans in the advertising department as a "color coordinator," directly involved in sales. "My job in the advertising department was to generate color advertising," he said in 2010, about his early work with Lancaster Newspapers. When Jack became president and CEO of Lancaster Newspapers, he assumed the publisher's role. He took his lead on dealing with the editorial side from the Steinman brothers. The Steinmans, according to Buckwalter, believed that "editors

John (Jack) Buckwalter – Chairman of the Board of Lancaster Newspapers, Inc., 2004 – 2010; Representative for Lancaster Newspapers Inc., in Penn Square Partners

have the final say" about the content of the newspapers. "If it had anything to do with news, it stopped at their desks," Buckwalter said of the editors. "When it came to decision-making in the newsroom, the Steinmans generally stayed out. Much of the limited contact between news executives and editors took place in the elevators between floors."[43]

Buckwalter didn't quite follow the Steinman brothers' "church-state" separation between the publishing and editorial sides, as I found out after being elected Lancaster County commissioner. When it concerned the Steinmans' downtown hotel project, Jack Buckwalter had no problem weighing in editorially on behalf of the project.

Buckwalter was among the eighteen Lancaster business Brahmins—lawyers, doctors, industrialists—who lunched every Monday at the exclusive Hamilton Club, where Andrew Jackson Steinman had been one of the thirty-one charter members in 1889. Buckwalter's group called itself the "Wash Day Club." They named the gathering thus because their wives did laundry that day and had told the men not to come home for lunch.[44]

Buckwalter always carried a small handheld voice recorder and often pulled out his recorder to make a comment or a note. "That thing was never out of his clench," said Robert Mueller, one of Buckwalter's oldest friends.[45] He used that recorder to organize his many civic responsibilities, which included the Lancaster Alliance and its subsidiary, the Lancaster Campaign. Buckwalter, a founding member, and the group primarily focused on completing the downtown hotel and convention center project.

Doing Good So You Can Do Well

In 2004, the year Jack Buckwalter became chairman of the board of Steinman Enterprises— "chairman of everything," as he put it— Lancaster Newspapers remained strong and influential in Lancaster County.[46] This was just before the smartphone revolutionized how people got their daily news and information.[47]

At this time, 2004–2008, people walked around with cell phones, yes, but in just a few years, they were carrying computers in their pockets. By 2009, people didn't need newspapers to get information anymore. Yet during my years as Lancaster County commissioner, 2004 to 2008, the print form of Lancaster Newspapers still effectively functioned as the sole source of local news in Lancaster County. Lancastrians either got the *Intel* or the *New Era*, and everyone got the *Sunday News*. The Steinmans controlled all of these newspapers.

As chairman of Steinman Enterprises, Jack Buckwalter reported to the board of directors—the "Steinman ladies," as he called them.[48] The board then consisted of two of James Hale Steinman's daughters, Caroline Steinman Nunan and Beverly "Peggy" Steinman; and three granddaughters, Caroline Nunan-Hill and Louise Steinman Ansberry's daughters, Louise Diane Ansberry and Hale Krasne.

Buckwalter met with the Steinman ladies at quarterly luncheon meetings. He provided the agenda, covering issues related to the Steinman businesses and their many civic projects.

"The hotel convention center, obviously, was of interest to them, and we obviously wanted to keep them informed," said Buckwalter of those meetings. At one point, he brought all of the Steinman ladies out to High's Greenfield business complex to look at the colors of the hotel that would be attached to the downtown convention center.[49]

Dale High presided over an impressive array of businesses. The small welding shop Sanford High opened in 1931 had turned into Lancaster County's largest private employer by the turn of the twenty-first century. High Industries now comprised a half-a-billion-dollar conglomerate, with companies in steel manufacturing and fabrication, construction, property management, real estate, consulting, and hotels.

Nevin Cooley, CEO, President, High Industries, Lancaster, PA; Partner – Penn Square Partners

Nevin Cooley joined High in 1986 as vice president of development and acquisitions in the commercial real estate development division. I first came across Cooley in the 1980s when Lancaster General Hospital employed both of us. I worked as a registered respiratory therapist, and Cooley had the position of a hospital administrator from 1981 to 1986.[50]

Just as Jack Buckwalter represented the interests of the Steinmans on various local business boards, Nevin Cooley served as High's surrogate on many of the same boards of directors. Lancaster's most prominent businessmen and leading attorneys sat on these boards. Each group worked to stimulate, support, and recruit business in Lancaster City and County.

The Steinman and High families contribute significantly to enrich Lancaster County's economy and invest in culture, and they have for generations. Both families provide jobs for thousands of Lancastrians. Personally, and through proxy agents, such as Jack Buckwalter and Nevin Cooley, the Steinmans and Highs have acted in ways they believed were in the best interests of the community they love. For the most part, Lancaster remained a remarkably well-run, civilized community for very long time, helped by their influence.

Yet something happened. The downtown hotel and convention center project promised to make the Steinmans and Highs even richer and more powerful. That project is the crux of this book. With that project, many betrayed the community they had always served and misused the power they'd taken centuries to earn.

The E-Mail

On Monday, November 7, 2005, at 8:14 a.m., Donald Totaro, district attorney of Lancaster County, Pennsylvania, sent an e-mail to Thomas Myers, the county's human resources director. In the e-mail, Totaro asked Myers, "Tom," for the report Myers was writing on hiring an ex-county employee.

Here is Totaro's e-mail:

> Tom: I understand you are currently investigating the circumstances surrounding the hiring of Gary Heinke, and a final report is expected later this week. Once you have concluded your investigation, I would appreciate a copy of that report, along with copies of all relevant documentation.
>
> Thank you.
> Don Totaro

When Totaro did not receive Tom Myers's report by Thursday morning, seventy-two hours later, he filed a "Notice of Submission" with the Lancaster County Court of Common Pleas, requesting a criminal grand jury investigation into the Heinke hiring (see Appendix A).

And so, began an ordeal for me, for County employees, and for the entire community of Lancaster, Pennsylvania, that destroyed reputations and morale of so many. That ordeal is not the full story, though. The real story involves misuse of power to promote a project that greatly benefited an elite few at the expense of many.

However, to comprehend the scope of what they did to achieve their goal, we must backtrack a bit.

Chapter Three

THE PROJECT

"Build it, and they will come."
—*Field of Dreams*, film directed by Phil Robinson, 1989

"If you can look into the seeds of time, and say which grain will grow
And which will not,
Speak them unto me."
—William Shakespeare, *Macbeth*, 1605

"The art of taxation consists in so plucking the goose as to obtain the largest amount of feathers with the least amount of hissing."
—Jean-Baptiste Colbert, 1619–1683

Our story takes place in Lancaster County, Pennsylvania. Its natural beauty is unsurpassed in the state. Bordered on the west by the powerful Susquehanna River and the Mason-Dixon Line on the south, the county features rivers, streams, waterfalls, cliffs, mountain ridges, forests, nature preserves, glens and glades, valleys, and glorious green fertile farmland. In this truly magnificent place, one township is aptly named "Eden"; another, "Paradise."

The county—an industrious, working-class region—has a tradition of economic stability and "pride of place" appearance.

Each year, more than 8 million visitors flock to the area's historic sites and tour the Amish and Plain communities. Many hotels, motels, and bed & breakfasts are in the rolling countryside, outside the city. Approximately 20,000 people, about 10 percent of the county's workforce, worked in the tourism industry in 2004.

Democratic political consultant James Carville reportedly described Pennsylvania as "Philadelphia in the east, Pittsburgh in the west, and Alabama in the middle."[1] Politically, Lancaster County veers closer to Carville's "middle."

If Lancaster County looks much like small-town America, circa 1975 (or, in the case of the Plain people, *1875*), the City of Lancaster (population 55,000 in 2004) looks like many other contemporary small, struggling American cities.[2]

In the Beginning, a Law Was Created

The $200 million Lancaster County Convention Center and Marriott Hotel, the issue at the core of this book, began with one law.[3]

The Pennsylvania Third-Class County Convention Center Authority Act of 1994 authorized third-class counties to impose a "room rental tax" on all hotel and motel rooms to fund a county convention center and "promote tourism."[4] A third-class county in Pennsylvania has between 210,000 and 500,000 residents.[5] Lancaster County was a third-class county.[6]

The policy logic of the Convention Center Act proposed that taxpayer-funded convention centers would stimulate tourism and generate revenue for the county. According to the bill sponsors, this "circuit of economic activity" would benefit and more than offset the economic burden of the tax on hotel and motel owners.[7] It would also cover the built-in operating deficit of operating a convention center. "Build it, and they will come," as someone once said about a make-believe baseball park. That was the logic.

This law begat the Lancaster project.

Stevens & Lee

"I have neither the scholar's melancholy, which is emulation;
   nor the musician's which is fantastical; nor the courtier's, which is proud;
   nor the soldier's which is ambitious; nor the lawyer's which is politic..."
—William Shakespeare, *As You Like It,* 1599

The Project

Although Representative Caltagirone of Berks County sponsored the 1994 Convention Center Act, he did not write it. The powerful Berks County law firm Stevens & Lee drafted the act. I knew of Stevens & Lee's reputation within the Lancaster legal community as competent and very expensive.

Stevens & Lee, a perennial top-200 firm, comprises about 150 lawyers and 50 non-attorney associates and consultants.[8] Stevens & Lee markets itself as a "full-service" law firm. It provides a myriad of professional legal services but has largely built its practice on municipal and state government financial legal work.[9]

Stevens & Lee has represented local and state governmental entities throughout central Pennsylvania for many decades. These clients include counties, cities, countless boroughs, townships, and all varieties of municipal authorities—redevelopment, industrial development, housing, transportation, and convention centers.[10]

A swinging door has long existed between the private, for-profit Stevens & Lee law firm and the public sector. Those who joined Stevens & Lee after leaving the public sphere include:

- State senator/majority leader David "Chip" Brightbill (R)
- Michael B. Rosenstein—House Appropriations Committee, Health & Welfare Committee
- Robert C. Archibald—House Insurance Committee and Liquor Control Committee
- Timothea Kirchner—former Lancaster County administrator

With its "multidisciplinary," "vertically integrated" staff of attorneys, banking and insurance executives, accountants, health-care experts, and other business professionals, Stevens & Lee can handle any complex legal issue.

The moving force at the firm is managing partner Joseph M. Harenza.[11] Harenza, a one-man legal conglomerate, works in mergers, acquisitions, and capital formations. Harenza is every bit the "super lawyer"—a designation given through peer and professional recognition from the organization SuperLawyers.[12]

The firm reaches into the Pennsylvania legislature, not just to author laws and employ ex-legislators but to act as an influential lobbyist in Harrisburg. In addition to several major corporate clients, including

Fortune 500 companies, Stevens & Lee functioned as the registered lobbyist for High Industries—even during the critical early period of the Lancaster hotel and convention center's development.[13]

On its website, Stevens & Lee declares its role in writing the law that enabled the hotel room tax:

> Stevens & Lee was at the forefront of the 1994 legislation which allowed Pennsylvania's third-class counties to institute a hotel tax to generate funds to build convention centers, promote tourism and build their local economies. Our state regulatory and government affairs team with the help of our tax-exempt finance lawyers drafted, introduced and successfully lobbied the hotel tax legislation. Our tax-exempt finance lawyers assisted several convention center authorities in planning and financing their projects and our litigation team successfully defended the constitutionality of the hotel tax.[14]

Using the firm's own description, Stevens & Lee "drafted, introduced and successfully lobbied" the 1994 Convention Center Act. Then, the firm "assisted several convention center authorities in planning and financing" and "defended" the convention center tax in court. In other words, Stevens & Lee wrote a law that provided the firm with a number of new, built-in lucrative revenue streams. It billed the Lancaster County Convention Center Authority (LCCCA) more than $7 million for the Lancaster project alone, before being replaced in 2007. I knew that if Stevens & Lee were involved, money was being made.

From its inception, Stevens & Lee has embodied the idea of the "public-private" law firm. In Lancaster, Stevens & Lee represented one of the two "private" developers (High) as a lobbyist *and* represented the "public" Lancaster County Convention Center Authority *and* Lancaster County as solicitor for both. In my opinion, this private-public representation in the same project clearly amounted to a conflict of interest. The other private partner, Lancaster Newspapers, never explored it. This conflict was one of my concerns about the project, along with many others.

In the proposed Lancaster hotel and convention center project, I recognized that these three entities—High, Lancaster Newspapers, and Stevens & Lee—had exploited their access to powerful elites in

Harrisburg. They leveraged it to build a luxury hotel at the end of the Steinman's block on Penn Square.

The Hotel and Convention Center Project

"Thy sumptuous buildings and thy wife's attire
   Have cost a mass of public treasury."
            —William Shakespeare, *Henry VI*, Part II, 1590

Lancaster Newspapers gently introduced its readers to the downtown Lancaster hotel and convention center project on March 28, 1994, nine months *before* Governor Robert Casey signed the Third-Class County Convention Center Authority Act into law.

That afternoon, the *Lancaster New Era* reported in an article, "3% Hotel Tax Proposed to Fund Convention Centers," that the law might impact Lancaster County:

> Lancaster and other similar-sized Pennsylvania counties could impose a 3 percent hotel and motel room tax to fund convention centers, under legislation approved Tuesday by the House Tourism Committee.
>
> The bill is designed to help fund a $25 million project planned in Reading. But it could also provide a revenue option for Lancaster and other areas pursuing similar projects. . .[15]

The next morning the *Intelligencer Journal* reported the same news in "Hotel Room Tax Bill Goes to Pa. House." The *Intell* staff added only one word to the *New Era*'s report, essentially photocopying its "competitor's" copy: "The bill is *specifically* designed to help fund a $25 million project planned in Reading, but it could also provide a revenue option for Lancaster and other areas pursuing similar projects. . ."[16]

Lancaster County representative Katie True was on the Tourism Committee that passed the bill on to the full House. True didn't vote for the bill. "If this comes out that a lot of the hotels and bed-and-breakfast people are comfortable . . . and they want me to support it, I will support it," she said, after it got out of the committee. "But until that time . . . I'm very leery of it."[17]

Little Accountability

"Do thine own fortunes that obedient right
Which both thy duty owes and our power claims, . . ."
—William Shakespeare, *All's Well That Ends Well,* 1602

Several inherent problems exist with "public-private" developments such as convention centers. One is the lack of accountability in the construction and administration of the facility. Convention center authority boards of directors are selected by county or city officials from the areas where the centers will be built.[18] These boards are not elected and, after being appointed, operate autonomously without oversight.

Another problem with convention centers, even successful ones, is that most of the time they are vacant "big boxes" in the center of town. A busy month might have two conventions, lasting a total of eight days. On some days, the centers host private meetings. That means the building remains dark and empty three weeks every month. Most convention centers aren't that busy. The people who attend conventions don't travel to the city to see the sights. They come to attend the conference. The convention centers don't materialize as the economic generators their sponsors purport them to be.[19]

These multimillion-dollar, publicly financed convention centers come at the expense of other revitalization programs that have a more direct benefit to the "community." Public money going to a convention center doesn't go to a library, a school, or some other community need.

The most serious problem with these "partnerships" is that if the taxpayer-funded convention center cannot pay its debt service on the millions borrowed, the taxpayers must pay for any deficit. This last concern was the fundamental reason I opposed the downtown Lancaster project as a county commissioner. I had no problem with Dale High and the Steinmans building a convention center and a hotel. I did have a big problem with using mostly public money to do it. If the project failed, the taxpayers would have to bail it out. To me, the risks seemed daunting.

Penn Square Partners

"How now, Shylock! What news among the merchants?"
—William Shakespeare, *The Merchant of Venice*, 1596

The city of Lancaster, Pennsylvania, like many American cities, suffered terribly during the 1970s. The combination of manufacturing and retail job loss and "white flight" devastated local economies in every state. When the Park City shopping mall opened in 1971, just a few miles from the city center, it ripped the retail heart out of downtown Lancaster.

Lancaster's revitalization efforts, detailed in David Schuyler's excellent study *A City Transformed*, were spectacularly unsuccessful.[20] Until the renovations began in 2016, the Stalinesque Lancaster Square on North Queen Street remained a civic embarrassment for decades.

Location, Location, Location

"I summon up remembrance of things past."
—William Shakespeare, Sonnet 30, 1609

Watt and Shand Department Store
Circa 1950
Architect: C. Emlen Urban
Picture from Jennifer Stallings on Pinterest

The Watt & Shand department store, an impressive four-story landmark, sat right on Penn Square in the middle of Lancaster city. The building (really, a collection of buildings) had a beautiful Beaux-Arts façade with an elegant main structure, designed by highly regarded Lancaster architect C. Emlen Urban.[21] Watt & Shand was *the* department store in Lancaster County.

On one of my first independent adventures, at age twelve I rode the bus downtown to Watt & Shand to buy my mother an embroidered handkerchief for her birthday. Years later, I often met friends at the basement-level Rendezvous Restaurant for a lunch of tuna sandwiches. My fondest memory involves the elevator, operated by a dignified gentleman who asked, "Which floor, please?" after closing the cage doors. Pneumatic tubes carried messages from one department to another. It was fabulous. Sadly, by 1992, due to the opening of the Park City Mall, it was fading fast. In February 1992, the 115-year-old Watt & Shand department store was sold to the Bon-Ton company, a York-based department store.[22]

The Lancaster Alliance

"Now join your hands, and your hands your hearts."
—William Shakespeare, *Henry the VI*, Part III, 1595

In June 1993, twelve of Lancaster County's most prominent business figures formed an organization to "revitalize" downtown Lancaster. The nonprofit group called itself the "Lancaster Alliance." The stature of the founding members was impressive. The Lancaster Alliance charter members included:
- S. Dale High—High Industries
- John (Jack) M. Buckwalter—Lancaster Newspapers, Inc.
- Rufus A. Fulton—Fulton Bank
- William Adams—Armstrong World Industries, chairman
- John O. Shirk—Barley, Snyder, Senft & Cohen Attorneys (also Lancaster Newspapers' attorneys)
- Thomas Baldrige, executive director of the Lancaster Chamber of Commerce and Industry

Lancaster New Era reporter (soon to be editor in chief) Ernest J. "Ernie" Schreiber reported the new organization's founding: "The chief executives of 12 of Lancaster County's largest corporations have launched a new organization, the Lancaster Alliance, to help improve the economy and social conditions of Lancaster City."

The money-losing Bon-Ton store in the Watt & Shand building closed for good within three years.[23] Now, an enormous empty structure stood in the center of downtown Lancaster, right on Penn Square. This "hole in the ground" lay just a block from the other "hole" on Lancaster Square. The city was in trouble, and it showed. This truly represented a loss for all of us who had shopped there, for everything from wedding presents to school shoes. I still have a few of the sturdy white Watt & Shand boxes with the distinctive blue drawing of the building printed on the top. It brings back nice memories of a lovely place.

In late 1994, I made a major life decision to dip my toe into the political waters and serve the community in another capacity.

On Christmas morning 1994, just before I officially announced my candidacy for Lancaster County commissioner, the *Sunday News* ran a big article about my interest in flintlock rifles and shooting.

In "'This Book Changed My Life!' How the Civil War Sparked Molly Henderson's Interest in Muzzle Loading," Jack Hubley, the *Sunday News* Outdoors editor, wrote a long, flattering, and just a little patronizing story about my rifle hobby and life.[24]

Here's how Hubley opened the *Sunday News* article:

> SO, I'M SITTING in the living room of this immaculate, 19th-century stone farm house over near Millersville and I'm talking to Molly Henderson and at the same time I'm thinking, this just doesn't compute.
>
> She's this little sprite of a thing, as polished as the pegged pine boards on the floor. A couple of years my junior, she's a Penn Manor graduate with a doctorate in education. She teaches emergency medical procedures for the Red Cross.

I'll bet she was student council president. I'll bet she plays tennis. I'll bet she's never even touched a gun. . .

I couldn't have asked for better press on the eve of announcing a political campaign—a story about a woman who shoots guns in Second Amendment–supportive Lancaster County.

Two weeks later, on January 8, 1995, the *Sunday News* again ran a lengthy profile about me, this time focusing on my just-announced commissioner candidacy. Again, the piece was very positive.

In "DEMO JOINS BUMPER CROP IN RACE FOR COMMISSIONER," the *Sunday News* made me sound like a super-heroine:

> She is a public health educator, a horsewoman and a Civil War history buff.
>
> Last spring, she saved the life of a 6-year-old boy who was injured when an interior wall fell on him at a local grocery store. She wears a lot of hats. Last week, she threw one of them into the ring.
>
> Molly S. Henderson has officially joined former Lancaster City Council president Ron Ford in the Democrats' race for county commissioner.[25]

Two weeks after that article, the *Sunday News* ran more good press with "CANDIDATE HOLDS THANK YOU PARTY," a nice article about a party I held at my home for the many people who helped me in my run for county commissioner.[26] About ninety people attended the party, including fellow Democrat and commissioner candidate Ron Ford. So, as this illustrates, the press I got from Lancaster Newspapers back then was good to great.

In the May 1995 primary, I came in fourth of the seven Democrats and didn't get my name on the November ballot. In the election that fall, Democrat Ron Ford became a Lancaster County commissioner, as did a Republican silver-haired former professor named Paul Thibault.[27]

Thibault, the sitting county treasurer, had not been endorsed by the Lancaster County Republican Party when he won the election for commissioner. Yet he had the endorsement that counted—the Lancaster Alliance, whose powerful, wealthy members financed his campaign. Thibault's political action committee, "Friends of Paul Thibault," raised more than double the money of his opponents both times he ran for commissioner.[28]

Paul Thibault
Lancaster County Commissioner
1996 - 2004

HACC

"Educated men are so impressive."
—William Shakespeare, *Romeo and Juliet*, 1591

Meanwhile, the Watt & Shand building continued to languish, a stark symbol of the city's depressed condition. In June 1996, the Harrisburg Area Community College (HACC) board of trustees voted to buy Watt & Shand and move its campus downtown. HACC planned to preserve the facade and use the building as a main campus in Lancaster. The college anticipated more than $8 million in funding from the state to help it acquire the building.[29]

The prospect of HACC moving into Watt & Shand ignited fiery debates in Lancaster. Then mayor Janice Stork, an embattled Democrat, supported HACC's move into the building. The Economic Development Company of Lancaster and the EDC Finance Company also gave their support. Jack Buckwalter, Lancaster Newspapers' chairman and a founding member of the Lancaster Alliance, worked particularly hard to bring HACC downtown.

I thought a HACC campus in downtown Lancaster was a great idea. According to HACC'S 2016 official website, over 4,300 full- and part-time students attended classes at the site east of Lancaster city.[30] The students, the faculty, and the staff would bring energy—and dollars—to Lancaster city.

Not So Fast, HACC

Strong resistance erupted against the HACC plan. Former Lancaster city mayor Arthur E. "Art" Morris led the opposition. Lancaster Newspapers often quoted Morris about his objections to the plan, the main one being that the college would not pay property taxes.

"I have a number of concerns, but a significant one is the tax base of this city," said Morris to the *Intelligencer Journal* in the middle of the HACC debate.[31] Morris further stated in an interview at Penn Square, on July 24, 2001, "I opposed HACC coming here because economically it was not going to help the city. There is no buying power. The people that come to HACC are great people, but they don't have high income. They don't stay here and shop. They just go to a location, get an education, and leave. That's not the kind of economic development needed in the city. What we need is the kind of thing that is happening [the hotel and convention center project], and the only way to make it happen is to subsidize it."[32]

Morris had explored bringing a convention center to Lancaster when he served as mayor in the late 1980s.[33] He didn't raise his concern about taxes when the City of Lancaster took the Highs' and Steinmans' hotel *off* the property tax rolls in 2005, where it remains today. On that, the outspoken Morris kept silent.

In 1996, the Lancaster Alliance created a subsidiary organization, the Lancaster Campaign.[34] The next year the Lancaster Campaign hired renowned urban planner Bert Winterbottom to conduct a far-reaching study to develop a strategic revitalization plan for the city.[35] Winterbottom held several public meetings with the Lancaster community and did research for several months. He unveiled the results publicly in February 1998.

Charlie Takes Aim

> "He speaks plain cannon fire, and smoke and bounce;
> He gives bastinado with his tongue;
> Our ears are cudgell'd . . ."
> —William Shakespeare, *King John*, 1596

In 1997, Lancaster city held a mayoral election. Historically, neither party has consistently taken the helm of the city. The power swings back and forth between Democrats and Republicans. The Democrats ran Jon Lyons, a mellow lawyer. I volunteered for Jon by distributing fliers and knocking on doors. The Republicans put a stout, talkative local pharmacist and gun aficionado on the ballot: Charles W. "Charlie" Smithgall.

Smithgall had little political experience, but people knew him about town. He owned two branches of the busy Smithgall's Pharmacy, started by his grandfather. Charlie saw lots of people and talked with lots of people. Charlie was a talker.

Prior to being elected mayor, Charlie Smithgall had been known for his cannons. He collected antique firearms and owned more than 70 nineteenth-century cannons in operational condition.

Charles Smithgall –
Lancaster City Mayor
1998 - 2006

A Civil War reenactor, Smithgall appeared onscreen and acted as a consultant in the 1993 Civil War film *Gettysburg*.[36]

Every year at the Fourth of July concert in Long's Park, Smithgall blasted his cannons at the climax of Tchaikovsky's "1812 Overture." All of this—the cannons at Long's Park, the busy pharmacy, and the film—made Smithgall a very well-known man about town. When he ran for mayor, Smithgall had the public support of the entire Lancaster Republican political establishment. Congressman Joe Pitts, state senator

Gibson Armstrong, House Appropriations chairman John Barley, and the two of the Republican Lancaster County commissioners, Paul Thibault and Terry Kauffman, all backed Smithgall. Congressman Pitts and Senator Armstrong even held separate fundraisers for him.

On the HACC issue, similar to Art Morris, Smithgall was strongly opposed. Smithgall also objected to the loss of property tax revenue if the college occupied the former Watt & Shand building.[37] And, like Morris, Smithgall offered not a word of objection when the Steinmans' and Highs' "private" hotel was taken off the tax rolls. Smithgall, the mayor, as did the next mayor, Rick Gray, waived several hundreds of thousands of dollars that High Construction should have paid to the city for permit fees.

In March 1997, the state's Department of Community and Economic Development rejected HACC's multimillion-dollar request for funds to purchase the Watt & Shand building.[38] The historic building remained empty.

On election day, November 4, 1997, Charlie Smithgall trounced Jon Lyons. The city braced itself for Mayor Charlie Smithgall and his "whack-a mole" approach to city government.

Smithgall overtly aligned himself with the Lancaster Alliance and the Lancaster Campaign. Of the Winterbottom LDR study, Smithgall said to the *Lancaster New Era* in December 1997, weeks before taking office: "The [Lancaster] Campaign, through the study conducted by LDR International, they're going to come up with our vision. It's up to the mayor to implement it."[39]

In 1995, I had run in the May primary for county commissioner but came in fourth among the Democrats and didn't get my name on the November ballot. From 1995 until 1999, I stayed active in the Democratic Party, holding fundraisers and campaign events for Democrats, including state Representative Mike Sturla, the assemblyman who represented Lancaster city in the Pennsylvania legislature.[40] I worked full time for the American Red Cross as a public health educator and continued giving instruction in various health certification courses. Our son, Ander, was in middle school, and we brought our daughter, Leslie, home from Russia in July 1996, so I remained busy on the domestic front.

The Project

After the Harrisburg Area Community College deal died, Bon-Ton announced in December 1997 that the company planned to sell the Watt & Shand building on the open market.[41] Mayor-elect Smithgall said he couldn't live with the beloved Watt & Shand going to "some foreign investor." He set about finding a local buyer.[42]

Smithgall's first move after his inauguration in January 1998 was to appoint James Pickard, a former Pennsylvania secretary of commerce, as his special economic adviser. Smithgall charged Pickard with only one job: find a local buyer for Watt & Shand. Pickard did not take a salary for his task.[43]

Enter Penn Square Partners

After that, the details of who called the initial meeting remain vague. It was likely Smithgall. Sometime in the first two weeks of January 1998, a group of Lancaster businessmen, public officials, ex-public officials, and the new mayor gathered at the Greenfield Corporate Complex headquarters of S. Dale High. The topic of discussion focused on the Watt & Shand building.

Those attending the Greenfield meeting included Charlie Smithgall, Dale High, Jack Buckwalter, Rufus Fulton, Jim Pickard, and Art Morris.[44]

On January 18, 1998, the nearly 100,000 *Sunday News* subscribers opened their newspapers and found on the front page:

A BIG 3 WORKS TO BUY BON-TON

With S. Dale High in the picture, everything changes.

The deal isn't quite done yet, but when the county's best-known developer and the man at its helm stepped into Penn Square, the future of the Bon-Ton building suddenly looked a lot different. Along with Lancaster Newspapers Inc. and Fulton Financial Corp., High Real Estate Group is negotiating with the Bon-Ton to buy the city's landmark department store.

Smithgall got credit for the deal. "Charlie really got it off the dime. He really got it going," said Rufus Fulton, president of Fulton Bank, in the *Sunday News* article.

A month later, the "Big 3"—who called their partnership Penn Square Partners—officially bought the Watt & Shand building for $1.25 million.[45] This became a very lucrative investment.

"We're looking at all the options," said Dale High, the general partner of Penn Square Partners, to the *Lancaster New Era* on February 17, 1998. "We see it as a mixed-use building."

I felt hopeful. This could help the city. Our family lived in the city school district, and my husband's firm was downtown. I had been employed at several agencies in Lancaster and went out of my way to shop in the city. When my minivan needed repairs, I used K&W for tires or Smith's garage for service. We dined downtown and shopped at Central Market on Saturday mornings. Maybe a rejuvenated Watt & Shand building would turn things around.

Winterbottom Study Results

The day after Penn Square Partners (PSP) finalized the sale of the Watt & Shand building, February 18, the Winterbottom study was unveiled. Winterbottom examined three sections of Lancaster: downtown (including Lancaster Square and Penn Square), the North Prince Street area, and South Duke Street.

The *Intelligencer Journal* reported that "hundreds" were in attendance.[46] Winterbottom looked at a variety of things, including park enhancement, streetscape, city lighting, and sidewalk improvement.

Winterbottom's most noteworthy recommendation concerned a $6 to 7 million "conference center," to be built on Lancaster Square adjacent to the existing but downtrodden Brunswick Hotel.

"With upgrading of the [Brunswick] hotel," wrote Winterbottom in the report, "there is the opportunity to create a small, state-of-the-art conference center and additional hotel space."[47]

Toward the end of the report, Winterbottom wrote cryptically about the future of the Watt & Shand building. Three of the founding members of the Lancaster Alliance—the group paying

Winterbottom for his study—had just purchased the building the previous day:

> As this report is being written, the ownership of the Watt and Shand Building is being transferred from the current out-of-town owners to a small local group of owners at a fair price... Local private and public leadership must be prepared to support this project with their influence and their financial resources. This will not be an easy project.... While outright sale and development of the property is most desirable, the owners and the community must also be prepared to consider a variety of partnership arrangements that may involve other local investors, the City, the County and the State.[48]

"They Play—You Pay"

"... and let men say we be men of good government."
—William Shakespeare, *Henry IV*, Part I, 1597

In general, the art of government consists of taking as much money as possible from one class of citizens to give to the other.
—Francois Marie Arouet (Voltaire), 1694–1778

In 1998, the governor of Pennsylvania was Republican Tom Ridge, a buttoned-down, law-and-order, former assistant district attorney from Erie. With his straight-edge part on a full head of hair and solid approval ratings, Ridge was up for reelection in November. During the campaign, Ridge supported a controversial bill that proposed to raise the state's debt ceiling by $500 million. Of that money, $325 million would be used to build four new sports stadiums in Philadelphia and Pittsburgh. The balance—$175 million—would be chopped into chum and tossed to legislative districts whose representatives helped pass Ridge's "Stadium Bill."[49]

Several books describe the misuse of taxpayer money for projects such as those stadiums to be built in Philadelphia and Pittsburgh. *Field of Schemes* (2008) by deMause/Cagan explains how the great stadium schemes turn public money into private profit. *Public Dollars,*

Private Stadiums: The Battle over Building Sports Stadiums (2003) by Delaney/Eckstein recounts the battles over publicly financed stadiums in some of America's largest cities. It tells where the power resides and where the money goes. James Bennett wrote about this in *They Play, You Pay: Why Taxpayers Build Parks, Stadiums, and Arenas for Billionaire Owners and Millionaire Players* (2012). Even today, the taxpayers of Los Angeles are being coerced into a new stadium for the Rams football team. The residents and the taxpayers will not realize any benefit from this. In San Diego, California, voters rejected building a new stadium for the Chargers football team at the ballot box. The Chargers owners decided to take their ball and move to Los Angeles in 2017.

Lancaster County was in a good position to receive some of the Stadium Bill pork scraps. Representative John E. Barley, a Republican from southern Lancaster County, served as chairman of the powerful House Appropriations Committee.[50] Barley held influence over not just the six-member Lancaster Republican delegation, but with members of both houses of the state legislature and the governor. Appropriations affected every district in the commonwealth. In 1998, Senator Gibson E. "Gib" Armstrong represented much of Lancaster County and part of York County. Armstrong, a clean-cut ex-Marine and former investment adviser, chaired the Labor & Industry Committee. He also served on the important Rules Committee and the Finance Committee. In 1999, Armstrong chaired the Banking & Insurance Committee in the state senate. He retired in 2008 as Senate appropriations chairman.[51] On

Gibson Armstrong – PA State Senator, 13th District, Lancaster County; PA State Representative 100th District

multiple occasions, Senator Armstrong personally changed Pennsylvania law to specifically help the hotel and convention center project in Lancaster.[52]

My contact with Senator Armstrong to this point had occurred only twice. As a new college graduate, I first visited then Representative Armstrong about applying for possible jobs in public health in state government. My second meeting years later, with now Senator Armstrong, concerned the public health issue of teenage pregnancy. I urged him to support a comprehensive sex education initiative for both girls and boys. He looked at me and said sardonically, "Well, boys will be boys." This flippant disregard for such a serious widespread problem made me furious. Years later, we crossed paths again.

People anticipated that the Stadium Bill would pass the Senate easily, where Republicans held a majority. Yet votes wouldn't come as readily in the House. The GOP had a slim 104–99 majority in 1998. Ridge could not count on all Republicans to support his bill. Many of them saw the bill as a benefit only to the big cities of Philadelphia and Pittsburgh. Some objected to spending money on professional sports. Others argued that the $325 million could be used for things such as roads, schools, and public health.[53]

Governor Ridge needed Lancaster County's John Barley, the powerful House Appropriations chairman, to pass his bill. In exchange for whipping up votes, Ridge promised Barley a $15 million slice of the Stadium Bill "pork" for the "conference center" recommended by Winterbottom.[54] The $15 million would be a state "match," if the county could raise $15 million for a conference center. The $15 million "match" would come from the hotel room tax, written into Pennsylvania law by the Stevens & Lee law firm with the Third-Class County Convention Center Authority Act of 1994. The public subsidy "leftovers" of Ridge's sports arenas money eventually became the down payment for the Lancaster hotel and convention center project.

Let's Up the Ante . . .

"The commons hath he pill'd with grievous taxes . . ."
—William Shakespeare, *Richard II*, 1595

The history of the project gets very interesting at this point. On April 2, 1998, the *Intelligencer Journal*, in "Local Leaders Consider Taxing Tourists to Help City," addressed the levying of a 5 percent, not a 3 percent, hotel room rental tax in Lancaster County.[55]

The *Intell* begins: "Local legislators, the county commissioners and Lancaster Mayor Charlie Smithgall are considering imposing a countywide hotel/motel room tax to help pay for a proposed conference center in the city . . ."

Raising a legitimate concern about the proposal, Senator Gib Armstrong commented, "Let's check it out with some of the people in the hospitality industry. The hospitality industry has to be reassured."

Representative Barley echoed Senator Armstrong, "If I were a county commissioner, I wouldn't be interested in doing this unless I had the support of the affected community—the hotel people."

The sole Democratic House member from Lancaster, Representative P. Michael "Mike" Sturla, supported the hotel room tax right away. "If there's a proposal for a downtown convention center, I would certainly encourage it," Sturla said to the *Intell*.

Jim Pickard, Smithgall's adviser, also offered his endorsement of a room tax. "In Pennsylvania, with the exception of Lancaster and Harrisburg, virtually every major city in the state has a

P. Michael Sturla – PA House of Representatives, 96th District, Lancaster City, 1991 - 2018

room tax," Pickard said to the *Intell*. "It's only fair we ask our visitors to help pay. The residents of Lancaster won't be paying it." "*The residents of Lancaster won't be paying for it.*"[56] This statement turned out to be completely false.

All Aboard

> "Our business is not unknown to the senate;
> they have had an inkling this fortnight what we intend to do . . ."
> —William Shakespeare, *Coriolanus,* 1607

Ridge easily retained the governor's seat in November 1998, defeating Democrat Ivan Itkin. The Constitution Party got 10 percent of the vote. Its lieutenant governor candidate, Jim Clymer, later became a fierce opponent of the hotel and convention center project.

At the time when Ridge was reelected, the Stadium Bill still had not been brought before a vote in the General Assembly. The proportion of Democrats to Republican representatives was almost the same in the next legislature.

Around this time, the conference center (not yet called a "convention center") also mysteriously relocated from Lancaster Square to Penn Square, where Dale High, Lancaster Newspapers, and Rufus Fulton had just bought the Watt & Shand building. No explanation was given for the move down the block.

Representative Barley sounded sure that the Stadium Bill would pass and Lancaster would get funds for a convention center, but he wasn't as sure about the center's location. He said to the *Lancaster New Era* on November 24, 1998, "[The convention center] could be there [at Lancaster Square], could be Penn Square. It would be in the city."[57]

The *Sunday News* quoted Representative Mike Sturla's comments on the convention center before the stadium vote, "[The convention center] is a particularly palatable project because it's greased and ready to go."

Senator Armstrong sounded equally confident that Lancaster would get state funds for a convention center. "If the train is moving down the track," said Armstrong, "do you stand in front of it, or do you get on and hope it benefits your district?"[58]

Even with Ridge's popularity, proponents couldn't gather enough votes in the House to pass the Stadium Bill, and it was pulled from a vote. This caused only a temporary delay.

Representative John Barley remained confident after the vote was tabled and stated in the *Sunday News*: "The governor is more committed than ever. This will adequately fund projects in places like Lancaster, York and other areas."[59]

On February 2, 1999, after convincing passage in both houses, Governor Ridge's Stadium Bill became law. Philadelphia and Pittsburgh would get their stadiums, and Lancaster would get millions to build a convention center. The Lancaster County commissioners simply had to impose a new tax.

Lancaster Newspapers and the Project

"I am not furnish'd with the present money;
Besides, I have some business in the town.
—William Shakespeare, *Comedy of Errors*, 1589

Lancaster Newspapers put itself in an odd position with the proposed downtown hotel and convention center project. The Steinman family, through Lancaster Newspapers, Inc., was a limited partner in Penn Square Partners, the private operators of the proposed hotel. Lancaster Newspapers was an equal investor with general partner High Real Estate. When Penn Square Partners began, High and Lancaster Newspapers each had 44 percent, and Fulton Bank had 12 percent. (In 2008, Fulton withdrew from the partnership. Then High and Lancaster Newspapers each held a 50 percent equity stake.)[60]

As private investors, the Steinmans stood to make substantial profits from the overall project. The value of their many properties on West King Street and around downtown Lancaster would undoubtedly increase considerably with the new development.[61] And they would own 44 percent of a luxury hotel (later to be 50 percent).

Yet with its two daily and Sunday newspapers, Lancaster Newspapers functioned as *the* print source of information for Lancaster County. The Steinmans had a complete monopoly over the print market.[62] The newspaper still remained the primary means of getting local news. Lancaster Newspapers' involvement in the project meant that its reporters and editors would cover a project in which the Steinmans held a major financial stake. That is not merely the *appearance* of a conflict of interest; that *is* a conflict of interest.

After the Stadium Bill was signed, Lancaster Newspapers reported the Lancaster project as inevitable. When it became clear that the Lancaster County commissioners—Paul Thibault, Terry Kauffmann, and Ron Ford—would vote on the tax sometime after Labor Day, the coverage of the project became over-the-top biased on behalf of the project.

During the month of August 1999, Lancaster Newspapers published a flurry of articles that read more like advertisements for a coming entertainment event, rather than investigative analysis of a proposed $75 million taxpayer-financed project. Once the Stadium Bill passed, the project not only moved from Lancaster Square to Penn Square, but the size, scope, and cost of the project mushroomed. Winterbottom's "$6–7 million conference center" transformed into a $75 million hotel and convention center project! The project continued to grow.

Here are some of the Lancaster Newspapers' headlines as the September 1999 vote approached:

- ELSEWHERE IN PA., HOTEL ROOM TAX IS BOOSTING BUSINESS, *Lancaster New Era*, August 19, 1999 (1,136 words)

- CONVENTION CENTER, HOTEL PROPOSED AT PENN SQUARE WHY NEW HOTEL ROOM TAX IS A KEY PART OF CONVENTION CENTER PACKAGE, *Lancaster New Era*, August 19, 1999 (1,486 words)

- CONVENTION CENTER, HOTEL PROPOSED AT PENN SQUARE $75 MILLION PLAN TURNS EX-WATT & SHAND INTO LUXURY HOTEL AND SHOPS, WITH 14-STORY TOWER, *Lancaster New Era*, August 19, 1999 (1,734 words)

- CONVENTION CENTER/HOTEL PLAN WOULD HELP CITY, COUNTY, *Lancaster New Era*, August 20, 1999 (608 words)

- THE WATCH ON THE SQUARE: CONVENTIONAL WISDOM EXPERTS LIKE LANCASTER'S CHANCES AT MAKING A GO OF LUXURY HOTEL AND CONVENTION CENTER, *Sunday News*, August 22, 1999 (1,650 words)

- "PENN SQUARE COMPLEX IS HAILED AS 'EVERYTHING THE CITY NEEDS,'" *Lancaster New Era*, August 26, 1999, a few weeks before the vote on the room tax. (1,168 words)

These "articles" were not buried items deep inside the newspaper. They appeared on the front pages, often a thousand words or more, accompanied by an artist's flattering pastel four-color impressions of what the new "complex" might look like on a sparkling spring day. Lancaster Newspapers ran a hyped-up public relations campaign about the project. They featured little coverage about a tax that had the potential to adversely impact the county.

From 1995 until 1999, I stayed active in the Democratic Party, holding fundraisers and campaign events for Democrats, including state Representative Mike Sturla, the assemblyman who represented Lancaster city in the Pennsylvania legislature.[63]

Cleaning Up Lancaster

"And in thy best consideration check this hideous rashness."
—William Shakespeare, *King Lear*, 1605

In 1999, Lancaster couldn't compare to disease-ridden seventeenth-century London, but it was by no means a clean city.[64] In fact, from a public health standpoint, the city of Lancaster was dirty. People had major concerns about the sanitation of Lancaster's restaurants.

The city's approximately 400 eating and food-related establishments were not being regularly inspected, as required by city code—some hadn't been checked in two or three years. The *Sunday News* pressured Republican mayor Charlie Smithgall to release restaurant inspection reports, but he refused, saying he didn't want to ruin anyone's business.[65] That was a typical Smithgall response.

The health department, then called the Department of Health, Housing, and Sanitation, consisted of a single inspector. With the department's documentation and paperwork in disorder, the public's health was at risk. Smithgall responded by hiring me as director for the newly named Environmental Health and Protection Unit.[66]

In many ways, leading the Environmental Health and Protection Unit was the perfect job for me. It combined various aspects of my experience and education in public health. I had also just submitted a comprehensive curriculum on food safety to the state Department of Agriculture. Mine was one of three curricula approved by the state.

Immediately after being employed by the city, I hired more people to do the inspections. I made sure the staff was properly certified and up-to-date with food safety training and regulations. Smithgall wanted restaurants inspected twice a year, and our department made that happen.

During my first week on the job, my department faced one of the most memorable and challenging cases we ever had—Country Boy Meats. Located at 451 E. King Street, this grocery store and butcher shop had been cited and complained about for years.[67]

Our inspectors observed rancid turkey necks, fruit flies on decomposing produce, rusted cans, and out-of-date food. I personally entered a walk-in refrigerator to find two shopping carts filled with pig heads and the carcass of a recently shot deer hanging from the ceiling, staring at me and dripping blood onto lettuce below.

This was nauseating. It was illegal. The store had too many violations to count. The department revoked Country Boy's milk and meat license and issued an "order of abatement of nuisance." Country Boy Meats presented "an immediate danger to the public health," I said at the time.[68]

Being busy as head of public health, I didn't pay much attention to the convention center issue in 1999. Every day I worked throughout the city and often walked past the empty landmark. I felt sad to see it declining. Yet it did crop up in the news a lot, and I do remember something often being repeated in the newspapers.[69] The sponsors of the project—mainly, Nevin Cooley, the PSP spokesman from High—kept saying that the convention center and the hotel would be financially independent of each other. I knew Cooley from my work as a registered respiratory therapist at Lancaster General Hospital. Cooley had been a hospital administrator before working for High.

Cooley, as president of PSP, always said that the private partners would pay for the $45 million hotel and that the state grant of $15 million and $15 million from the room tax would pay for the $30 million convention center. The partners never came close to that capital investment, even after the project approached $200 million.[70]

Not everyone supported the project, even at that hyped-up early stage when it cost "only" $75 million. The same Lancaster County hotel and motel owners whom Representative Barley and Senator Armstrong said needed to support the project overwhelmingly opposed it.

The Hoteliers

More than 150 hotels and motels are spread out over Lancaster County, including 300-room hotels off major highways, quaint bed & breakfasts down unpaved country lanes, and every size of lodging establishment in between. All but one of these establishments was located outside of Lancaster city in 1999, and occupancy had plummeted at the downtown Brunswick (now the Hotel Lancaster). The overnight room demand occurred outside the city.[71]

The room tax imposed on Lancaster hotel and motel owners would supposedly either be absorbed or be passed along to their guests in the price-sensitive hospitality industry.[72] It seemed odd to me that competitors would collect money for their rivals—sort of like Ford giving money to Chevrolet. The new tax revenue would be used to construct the convention center and, after the center opened, would go toward paying the construction debt service charges. Twenty percent of the tax revenue would go to the Pennsylvania Dutch and Convention Visitors Bureau for the vaguely defined "tourism purposes."[73]

After the Stadium Bill passed in February 1999, talk of a downtown hotel and convention center heated up. The Greater Lancaster Hotel and Motel Association (GLHMA) strongly contested the proposed tax. The organization conducted a survey of its 58 members in August—yes or no—on the tax. As a result, 54 of 58 voted no; 3 abstained; and 1 voted in favor.[74] The hotel voting in favor happened to be a Hampton Inn owned by High Industries.

The hotel and motel owners got "lawyered up" and on September 10 sent a letter to the Lancaster County commissioners. The hotel and motel owners' attorney, Christopher Conner, advised the county commissioners that the proposed Lancaster tax did not agree with the 1994 Convention Center Act.[75]

"The [Convention Center] Act is not applicable to Lancaster," wrote Conner, pointing out that the law stipulated: "This Act shall not apply to a county which has an existing convention center which covers an area of more than 40,000 square feet."

Attorney Conner noted that nearby Lancaster Host Hotel had 72,000 square feet of convention center space. "It is clear from the Act," wrote Conner, "that the legislature did not intend that public financing and the imposition of a hotel room rental tax be used to construct a convention center that would compete with an existing convention center of more than 40,000 square feet."

In fact, five years earlier, before the Convention Center Act had passed and before he went to work for Stevens & Lee (the authors of the bill), Senator Chip Brightbill had spoken in support of the law. During the Senate debate of the bill, he said into the record:

> [T]his is a "may" bill, and it is a bill that is limited to third class counties with an exclusion of third class counties that already have a convention center of 40,000 square feet, or a third-class county that has a joint planning commission. . . What we are asking for here is very limited authority for two counties, basically Berks and Luzerne . . .
>
> —148 51 PA. LEGIS. J.-S. 2984-85 (1994) (statement of Senator Brightbill)[76]

We'll Just Fix Things Later

"This is really a no-brainer," said Charlie Smithgall to the *Intelligencer Journal* before the commissioners' vote. "I don't think it's going to be real hard to get the votes. This is such a big win for the city."[77]

On the morning of the hotel room tax vote, September 15, 1999, the Steinman-owned *Intelligencer Journal* editorialized:

> We also believe that the county commissioners should impose a room tax on hotels throughout the county to help pay to build the convention center and to promote tourism in both the city and county. . . .[78]

No one was surprised when the Lancaster County Board of Commissioners voted 3–0 to impose a 5 percent tax on all hotel and motel rooms in the county on September 15, 1999.

"We've helped set the stage. That's all government can do," said Commissioner Paul Thibault, the chairman of the board, to the *Lancaster New Era* after the vote. "It's now up to the private sector."[79]

Thibault was wrong. That was not all government could, or would, do for the hotel and convention center project. And Thibault himself would personally "do" much more. As for the project being "up to the private sector," Thibault was partly right about that. The project was all about the private sector, true, but most of the money to build the project—both the "private" hotel and the "public" convention center—would come from the public, more than 90 percent from the taxpayers.

On the day of the vote, Mayor Charlie Smithgall showed up inside the crowded commissioners' chambers, along with several other prominent project supporters, including former Lancaster mayor Art Morris and Lancaster campaign executive director Tom Baldridge. They all applauded after the commissioners' vote.

"I'm very pleased," clucked Smithgall, nearing the end of his second year in office. "The work is just beginning now."[80]

The Hotel Tax

". . . shall I not take mine case in mine inn
but I shall have my pocket picked?"
—William Shakespeare, *Henry IV, Part I*, 1597

The Lancaster County commissioners passed three separate ordinances—44, 45, and 46—that September morning. They established the room tax, a seven-member city-county "authority" to administer the tax revenue, and an "excise" tax.

The county ordinances were based on the 1994 Pennsylvania Third-Class County Convention Center Authority Act, authored by Stevens & Lee. At the time of the September 15 vote, seated just to the right of the Lancaster County commissioners, was county solicitor John Espenshade, a partner at the Stevens & Lee law firm.

These new taxes legislated and enacted by the Lancaster County Board of Commissioners underscored the power of the office, the office I would hold in four years. I believed that taxing Lancaster County businesses to subsidize their competition constituted a misuse of that power.

Both taxes took effect on January 1, 2000.

John Espenshade –
Attorney with Stevens & Lee; solicitor
for Lancaster County and Lancaster
County Convention Center

Chapter Four

THE PROJECT GROWS

But doth suffer a sea-change
Into something rich and strange.
—William Shakespeare, *The Tempest*, 1610

I served as director of the Environmental Health and Protection Unit in Lancaster city from 1999 to 2002 and was aware of the convention center plan, but restaurant inspections, hoarders, and rats had most of my attention. Even so, I noticed that a lot happened with the downtown hotel and convention center project. It kept inching forward.

Thus far, the hotel tax had been enacted in 1999 by the county commissioners, and the Lancaster County Convention Center Authority (LCCCA) board of directors was named. The county commissioners appointed four members to the first LCCCA board, and Mayor Smithgall, with the approval of the city council, appointed three.[1] To my knowledge, none of them had any hotel/motel or convention center background.

The LCCCA held its first board meeting in October. Its offices were in the Fulton Bank building, in the space leased and occupied by the law firm of Stevens & Lee. The LCCCA voted Pickard as chairman and the authority's acting executive director. The agenda had only one item—to appoint the authority's solicitor.

The seven members voted unanimously to hire the law firm of Stevens & Lee. The Stevens & Lee lawyer representing the LCCCA was John Espenshade, the same John Espenshade who worked as solicitor for the county of Lancaster. To review:

Stevens & Lee wrote the convention center law;

Stevens & Lee represented Lancaster County;

Stevens & Lee represented the Lancaster County Convention Center Authority; and

Stevens & Lee's chairman, Joseph Harenza, acted as the registered lobbyist for the Penn Square partner High Industries, in Harrisburg.

Lancaster Newspapers never mentioned this quadruple "conflict of interest" role played by the Stevens & Lee law firm.[2]

The hoteliers' attorney, Christopher Conner, warned the county commissioners in September that the room tax violated the 1994 Convention Center Act. The act did not allow the tax to be imposed if an existing 40,000 square feet or larger facility was located within the county, yet there was one. The Lancaster Host Resort and Convention Center had 74,000 square feet of convention center.[3] Conner threatened to sue.

Armstrong Law Change No. 1

A legal challenge was coming from the hotel and motel owners. This posed a threat to the project. Something had to change, so project supporter Senator Gib Armstrong ensured that it did. Armstrong, the chairman of the Senate Banking Committee, amended Pennsylvania state law to undermine the case the hoteliers had prepared to file.

Senator Armstrong tacked his amendment onto a bill that authorized funding for Flag Day. He slipped in one change to the 1994 Convention Center Act, which he introduced to be reenacted by the 1999 legislature.

The "Armstrong Amendment" changed only one sentence of the existing Convention Center Act. Instead of the rule prohibiting construction of a convention center if another center of "more than

40,000 square feet" existed within the county, Armstrong changed the Convention Center Act to read:

> *This subdivision shall not apply to a county which has an existing convention center owned by, leased by, or operated by an existing authority or the Commonwealth which covers an area of more than 40,000 square feet.*[4]

The 74,000-square-foot Lancaster Host Resort and Convention Center was privately owned, not "owned by, leased by, or operated by an existing authority or the Commonwealth." Armstrong's maneuver undermined the hotel owners' principal legal challenge to the Lancaster tax. They still sued, but this dealt a serious blow to their impending case.

When the act, with Armstrong's amendment, came up for a vote, most of Lancaster County's delegation did not vote for it. They bristled at the sly tactics Armstrong had used to introduce it. Only Armstrong, Representative Barley, and Lancaster's lone Democrat Sturla backed the amendment. All three were project supporters.[5]

Armstrong's amendment changed the 1994 Convention Center Act to specifically enable the Lancaster project and weaken the hotel owners' legal challenge. In Senator Armstrong and Representative Barley, Penn Square Partners clearly had forces to help them in Harrisburg. This misuse of power came from Lancaster County's most powerful elected representatives. It was far from the last time it happened.

On November 3, 1999, Governor Ridge signed the revised legislation. Two days later, he stood in downtown Lancaster, on Penn Square, with a big cardboard $15 million check representing the state's matching funds of the expected room tax revenues.[6] Flanking the smiling governor were Senator Gib Armstrong, Mayor Charlie Smithgall, and County Commissioner Paul Thibault. It was all show.

Robbing Peter to Pay Paul

"Is it not enough to break into my garden,
And, like a thief, come to rob my grounds…"
—William Shakespeare, *Henry VI*, Part II, 1590

In March 2000, thirty-seven Lancaster County hotel and motel owners filed a lawsuit naming the LCCCA and the city and county of Lancaster as defendants.[7] They filed the case in the Lancaster County Court of Common Pleas. The judge assigned to the case was Louis Farina.[8] The thirty-seven plaintiffs included the owner of the struggling Brunswick Hotel on blighted Lancaster Square, two blocks away from Penn Square. The Brunswick stood adjacent to the site where Winterbottom, in 1998, proposed a $6–7 million "small, state-of-the-art conference center." When the hotel owners filed their suit, the project's estimated cost had increased to more than ten times what Winterbottom had estimated. That number continued to grow.

The Armstrong Amendment neutered the hoteliers' best legal argument against the room tax: that there was an existing convention center of more than 40,000 square feet within the county. The hotel owners claimed that the room tax violated their due process and equal protection rights. They argued that the tax presented them with an unfair economic "burden," with little or no demonstrated economic "benefit" from projected spillover room bookings.

No Room at the Inn

The sponsors, PSP, Senator Armstrong, Commissioner Thibault, and Mayor Smithgall, made an unconvincing case. They argued that the convention center would attract so many visitors that the attached hotel (owned by PSP) would fill to capacity during the events. When convention center visitors couldn't get rooms at PSP's hotel, the extra room demand would "spill over" to accommodations outside the city. That was the "benefit" to the hotel owners miles and miles away in Ephrata or Elizabethtown and elsewhere in the county. It made no sense.[9]

The Project Grows

The hotel owners also argued the "Armstrong Amendment" amounted to "special legislation," specifically drafted to circumvent the existing Convention Center Act. The misuse of official power by Senator Armstrong clearly aimed to benefit the Lancaster project.

The hotel and motel owners asked the Court for an immediate cessation of the tax and a refund of all taxes collected.

"Let it alone, thou fool; it is but trash."
—William Shakespeare, *The Tempest*, 1611

Trash collection also fell within the purview of my job as director of the Lancaster Environmental Health and Protection Unit.

In the late 1990s, the city's trash problem became intolerable. We received complaints about dogs eating from open garbage containers, backyards and apartments full of trash, hoarders, and rats.

The first difficulty in dealing with trash was the city's physical, street-by-street layout: all swirls and curves, narrow one-ways, and pinched little alleys. Picking up the trash in such a maze would be difficult enough for a single trash hauler, but Lancaster had dozens of independent trash haulers using inadequate pickup trucks with homemade wooden walls on the truck beds. Trash pick-up service was random and sometimes nonexistent for certain streets.

Of the approximately 3,500 people in 1999 who didn't have trash collection service, some threw their refuse in public dumpsters, in other people's cans, in their backyards and front yards, or even in the living room. The situation resembled the TV show *Hoarders*.[10]

One day the department received an anonymous call about a possibly deserted house with no recent activity, except for daily Meals-on-Wheels deliveries.

When another inspector and I arrived at the huge three-story townhouse, we had to double-check the address. The outside looked great, freshly painted and in good repair. Was it the wrong address? The picture didn't make sense. We knocked on the door, and an older woman wearing a long, dingy nightgown opened it and invited us into the vestibule. Immediately, we could see—and smell—that this was a serious situation.

Overflowing trash bags filled the first floor, leaving little room to walk. The plumbing didn't work, so they'd put jars of human waste on the windowsills. We asked to see the second floor. As we sidestepped up the stairs, cockroaches appeared on the walls and began to crawl on this unfortunate woman's arms and neck. Not only was this house a public health disaster, it was a serious fire hazard. I must confess that I felt too terrified to see what was on the third floor. I exited to the safety of the front sidewalk, where I hopped up and down to shake off any insects and immediately called the Lancaster County Office of Aging.[11]

The Office of Aging knew about the elderly siblings and had tried for years to help them. Their trust fund took care of the *outside* of the house, giving the appearance that all was well.

Working with the fire marshals and the Lancaster County Office of Aging, we got the entire house completely cleared of debris, got the plumbing up to code, hired an exterminator on an ongoing basis, and brought the electric and heating systems up to code. As a result, the brother and sister were able to remain in their home.

In March 2000, about six months after I'd been hired as public health director, Mayor Smithgall announced that on April 1st, the city would pick up all trash the citizens left outside on the curb—including appliances, furniture, tires, or anything that wouldn't fit into a plastic bag. "It's city cleanup day, and that's no April fool," was the tagline from Smithgall's office for the one-day event.[12]

The "one-day" cleanup lasted weeks. Mountains of garbage and old, rusting appliances lined the streets of Lancaster, block after block. One house had piled up twenty mattresses on the sidewalk. The cleanup cost the city hundreds of thousands of dollars. We arranged a special deal with the Lancaster County Solid Waste Management Authority to help the city and enlisted prisoners from the county jail to help remove the refuse.

I came up with a proposal to solve the trash-hauling problem.[13] I designed the plan to preserve the business of the private haulers currently working in the city—a Smithgall condition—and to ensure that all city residents had a trash hauler. City residents would be billed for trash services through their sewer and water bills. The proposal did not reduce a single hauler's net number of customers.

The Project Grows

Yet the trash haulers didn't exactly embrace the idea. The Lancaster County Independent Trash Haulers Association, representing about a dozen Lancaster city haulers, said it would prevent them from soliciting business outside their assigned areas. They also objected to losing certain current customers, who would be re-apportioned under the plan, although the number of customers would remain the same or grow.

The "great trash debate" between the city and the trash haulers lasted for more than a year. Mayor Smithgall was unable to endorse or support the plan. He just sat straddling the fence. Some of the trash haulers had operated in Lancaster for decades, and Smithgall simply didn't want to disappoint them. I was his popular health chief, though, and my plan made sense. The Board of Health, the city council, and the newspaper supported the plan. It would organize the chaotic trash-hauling situation, clean up the city, and save the taxpayers money.

The City Council, which then had a 4–3 Democratic majority, approved the plan in October 2000 and planned to implement it after the first of the year. Smithgall, afraid of the haulers, announced on December 23, 2000, that the trash plan would be delayed for one year, until January 2002, after the next city council election.

"We can't be ready. We can't implement it," Smithgall said to the *Lancaster New Era*.[14]

"But mice and rats, and such small deer,
Have been Tom's food for seven long years . . ."
—William Shakespeare, *King Lear*, 1605

During this time the trash piled up, and rats became yet another public health concern in the city of Lancaster.

One day in the fall of 2000, I arrived at my office at Southern Market Center and saw a lunch-size brown paper bag on my desk. One of the inspectors had left it there, with a note taped to it: "We have a problem."

Inside the bag was the headless body of a recently alive pet parakeet, "Pierre" (not his real bird name). It seems Pierre had been perched peacefully in his cage, waiting for breakfast in a city kitchen, when a Norwegian rat, a hardy fellow from the Old Country, climbed up the pole and squeezed its little rodent body into the cage and dined on poor Pierre, beginning with the pitiable parakeet's head. (Ed. note: Unconfirmed sources say Pierre tasted "like *poulet*.")

Although reports of rat sightings went up tenfold after the great trash cleanup of 2000, Mayor Charlie Smithgall seemed unconcerned. "Look," he told me one day, "if there was a rat problem, they'd be showing up in the sewers. We don't see them in the sewers. There ain't no rat problem."

Tell that to Pierre.

The news that the city's restaurants were finally being professionally inspected was very well received by the public. Lancaster Newspapers had covered the Country Boys saga and other inspections during my first year on the job, and the press coverage remained uniformly positive about the health department and me.

After I'd held the position for one year, on October 29, 2000, the *Sunday News* published a complimentary editorial about me for its massive Sunday audience.

> What a difference a year makes. Since Molly Henderson took over Lancaster's new Environmental Health and Protection Unit last October, restaurant inspections have been on the front burner—the first time in years. Nearly every one of the nearly 400 establishments licensed to sell food in the city has been inspected not just once, but twice.[15]

In December 2000, Judge Farina opened the hotel owners' case against LCCCA and the county and the city. The original thirty-seven plaintiffs had dwindled to eleven.[16] Many had dropped out due to legal costs; others felt concerned about opposing the powerful project sponsors. The Brunswick withdrew from the litigation without comment. The trial lasted ten days, sporadically scheduled during the Christmas holiday season. It finished on January 13, 2001. Three weeks later, Judge Farina released his decision. The hotel owners lost on all counts.

Wrote Farina in the 43-page opinion:

Plaintiffs simply cannot prove that the tax has produced any direct burden in and of itself. . . . Plaintiffs simply cannot carry their heavy burden to prove the hotel tax unconstitutional.[17]

The eleven plaintiff hotel owners quickly appealed to the state's Commonwealth Court, where they argued,

The County Ordinances, the City Ordinance and the Armstrong Amendment, facially and as applied to the Plaintiffs, constitute arbitrary, capricious, irrational and unreasonable regulations and legislation which violates Plaintiffs' substantive due process rights as secured by the Fourteenth Amendment to the Constitution of the United States . . .[18]

A year later, in January 2002, the Commonwealth Court sent the case back to Judge Farina in Lancaster.

The appellate court was pointedly critical of Farina:

Although the trial court acknowledged the necessity of considering the private hotel's impact on (hoteliers) in conducting a benefit and burden analysis, the trial court deemed the increased competition from the hotel to be irrelevant. This does not make sense. Because the additional competition is a burden on (hoteliers) that would not exist without the room tax and the convention center, the increased competition most definitely is relevant to the benefit and burden analysis.[19]

The LCCCA hired well-known Philadelphia lawyer Richard Sprague to handle the next phase of the case. Sprague had a statewide reputation and petitioned to have the case heard at the State Supreme Court. The state's highest court agreed to hear the case on an expedited basis.

The hotel owners made the same claims they had in the initial litigation: the tax was a burden and had no benefit for them. They also argued that the growth in the project's size and cost changed the "burden" enough to reverse Farina's decision.

Attorneys for both sides—the LCCCA and the hotel owners—submitted briefs before the Pennsylvania State Supreme Court in May 2002.

"The hoteliers should not, in effect, be permitted to destroy this important economic stimulus project by delaying it, when they cannot succeed on the merits of their challenges," the 50-page LCCCA brief read in part.

Eight weeks later, in July 2002, the State Supreme Court affirmed Farina's original decision.[20]

The case wasn't finished. The Supreme Court sent the lawsuit back to the appellate Commonwealth Court for an "expeditious review." Among the issues the appellate court would determine was whether the "Armstrong Amendment" amounted to "special legislation"—a law specifically written to aid only the Lancaster County project.

A month later, the Commonwealth Court returned another victory for the LCCCA and the project's sponsors. It was a 7–0 unanimous decision.

"Hey, we are the clear winners and they are clear losers," LCCCA chairman James O. Pickard said contemptuously to the *Lancaster New Era* after the Commonwealth Court decision.[21]

The "clear losers" did not give up. The same eleven plaintiffs filed another suit. The hotel and motel owners argued that the room tax would depress demand for their rooms and negatively impact occupancy rates. The coming "luxury" hotel was estimated to book 15,000 of the 30,000 new room nights per year. Splitting up the remaining 15,000 rooms did not produce enough of a "benefit" for subsidizing the competitor downtown hotel. Much of the common space that the "private" hotel and convention center would use—kitchens, hallways, lobbies—would be paid for by the LCCCA.[22] The Lancaster hotel and motel owners were undeniably being forced to directly subsidize their competition.

The Project Grows

According to Rodney Gleiberman, the owner of the Continental Inn and one of the plaintiffs,

> The project had unquestionably changed. It was much bigger and much more expensive. And when one of the judges on the appeals court suggested, during open oral arguments, that we file a second lawsuit arguing that fact—that it was a completely different project than the one Farina looked at—that is exactly what we did.[23]

" . . . the be all and end all."
—William Shakespeare, *Macbeth*, 1605

The Lancaster County hoteliers emerged as the first real opponents of the hotel and convention center project. Leading up to the vote on the room tax, all three Lancaster Newspapers reported on the project as kind of a "magic bullet." It would completely revitalize downtown Lancaster and give a major boost to the larger county economy.

For months, in article after article, often with pastel artistic renderings, Lancaster Newspapers touted the coming "luxury" hotel and convention center as the panacea for Lancaster's economic woes. "PENN SQUARE COMPLEX IS HAILED AS 'EVERYTHING THE CITY NEEDS' STRONG PRAISE FROM CROWD OF NEARLY 300," screamed an above-the-fold *Lancaster New Era* banner headline weeks before the commissioners voted on the room tax.[24]

Like Gleiberman, many hotel owners had operated their inns for generations in Lancaster County. When they challenged the tax, the newspaper coverage of them turned vicious. The innkeepers were the first to get hit with a full assault from Lancaster Newspapers.

On December 22, 2002, the *Sunday News* published a front-page story that reported on a press conference held by several Lancaster County and city officials.[25] Soon after the hoteliers filed their second lawsuit, commissioners Thibault and Ford, Mayor Smithgall, and LCCCA chairman Pickard called a press conference. Its purpose was to express official outrage at the new suit and to announce the intention of counter-suing the hotel owners for filing a frivolous lawsuit. Richard Sprague again represented the county and LCCCA.

In a front-page article, Pickard described a letter Sprague had written to the hotel owners' attorney. "We're drawing a line in the sand. All right, guys, we've gone far enough," Pickard declared. "Now it will cost you dough. It's all-out war."[26]

Commissioner Thibault said: "This extremism has got to come to an end," adding that some hotel owners had a "war to the death mentality. They won't stop until they've killed this project that will be a benefit to them and everyone else in the county."

Democratic commissioner Ron Ford said of the hotel and motel owners, "[They] are holding the people of Lancaster County hostage to their own self-interest."

Mayor Charlie Smithgall, who earlier had called the hotel owners "economic terrorists," chimed in, saying he wanted to hold the hotel and motel owners accountable for the "serious economic harm" they were bringing to the city.[27]

Mike Sturla, Lancaster's Democratic state assemblyman, said to the *Intelligencer Journal* in the December 22 article: "If this [hoteliers' lawsuit] is nothing more than a delay tactic to hold up the project long enough so it goes away, then they're doing a disservice to everyone. They should let it be known that their objective was for it to die on the vine, not truth, justice and the American way."

In an amicus curiae ("friend of the court") brief sent to the Supreme Court on behalf of the project sponsors, Lancaster city councilman John Graupera wrote, "[T]he actions of the hoteliers are not defensible."[28]

Lancaster Newspapers prominently published these statements vilifying the hotel owners. The Lancaster County public read that the "hoteliers" were Public Enemy Number One.

Despite the hotel owners' resolute efforts, their lawsuits did not stop the hotel and convention center project from proceeding.

The Project Creeps Forward

"To-morrow, and to-morrow, and to-morrow
creeps in this petty pace from day to day . . ."
—William Shakespeare, *Macbeth*, 1605

When the room tax went into effect in January 2000, the LCCCA began purchasing properties around the proposed project site. In March, the LCCCA bought four old, rundown buildings bordering the Watt & Shand site, for $539,900. One of the properties had been the former home and office of Thaddeus Stevens, the Reconstruction congressman despised by AJ Steinman in the nineteenth century.[29]

The LCCCA now held its monthly public meetings in the City Council chambers at the Southern Market Center. Pickard presided over them, and they soon exploded in testy exchanges between the chairman and a few members of the public. Pickard resented, and prohibited, questions from the public. He refused to answer or allow board members to answer questions.

The *Intelligencer Journal* gave Pickard space to explain the LCCCA's policy regarding answering questions from the public:

> We wish to clarify what the public comment section of the agenda is for—and will add this above point of clarification to all of our agendas. We also wish to clarify what the "public comment" portion of the agenda is NOT: It is not a question and answer session. It is not an opportunity for plaintiffs or defendants in a lawsuit to conduct discovery. The Authority has complied with all the requirements of Sunshine Act and welcomes public input and comment during our meetings. It is not the intention of the Authority to avoid being responsive to legitimate questions, but the lawsuit filed by the hoteliers has had a chilling effect on our ability to respond. We have been advised by our legal counsel that it is inappropriate to respond to questions or comments from the public that impact the pending litigation. . . . [Emphasis in original.][30]

At each LCCCA public meeting, the board would "pay the bills," by approving the monthly invoices from various consultants, lawyers, and contractors. The LCCCA paid hundreds of thousands of dollars each month to project advisers from the tax money the LCCCA received from Lancaster hotel and motel owners. One of the bills discharged each month was $52,500 to the "master developer" of the project, High Construction.[31] The board, led by Pickard and stocked with people appointed by Smithgall and Thibault, rubber-stamped these invoices. By 2002, they had spent millions, and the project's financing remained far from secure—while not a spade of dirt had been turned.

Convention Center Management

An important marker in the hotel and convention center's development began in January 2001. That month, the LCCCA sent out "Requests for Proposals" to various firms to manage the convention center once it was built.[32]

Two market studies commissioned earlier, one by the Lancaster Campaign and the other by the LCCCA, recommended a single manager for both the hotel and the convention center, rather than a separate one for each building.[33] The LCCCA had chosen three finalists for the convention center manager contract: Global Spectrum Corp., Interstate Hotels, and Spectacor Management Group (SMG).

Interstate, based in Pittsburgh, had no experience managing convention centers but did manage several hundred hotels. The other two firms had extensive convention center experience, including, in Spectacor's case, managing the Philadelphia Convention Center, among others.[34]

". . . doth protest too much"
—William Shakespeare, *Hamlet*, 1600

The debate over whether a "common manager" should oversee both the hotel and the convention center became *the* news of the summer of 2001. The private sponsors—Penn Square Partners—wanted Interstate to manage both entities and said that if Interstate weren't selected, they would pull out of the project. In July 2001, PSP hired Interstate to manage their "private" hotel.[35]

The Project Grows

Opponents of a single manager for the convention center, including the hotel and motel owners, objected on "conflict of interest" grounds. A company managing both entities would face conflicts when booking events that might be profitable to the privately-owned hotel but not to the other hotels in the county.

In late spring of 2001, the LCCCA asked the Tourism Advisory Task Force, formed the previous year, for advice on the manager question. The nine-member task force consisted of people from the LCCCA board and the Pennsylvania Dutch & Convention Center Visitors Bureau.[36] On August 15, the Tourism Advisory Task Force recommended separate management and endorsed Spectacor as the center's manager.

"One candidate emerged above all others—way above all others: SMG [Spectacor]," said task force member Harvey Owen to the *Intelligencer Journal*. Owen, a retired trade show and convention center veteran with three decades of industry experience, added, "It was the unanimous choice of three industry consultants. (With SMG), there will be no conflict of interest. There will be no perception of a conflict of interest."[37]

On August 19, the *Sunday News* declared the following to its 100,000 subscribers with this banner headline stacked across the front page:

DOWNTOWN HOTEL TEETERS ON BRINK // PARTNERS IN WATT & SHAND BUILDING WILL PULL OUT IF CONVENTION CENTER AUTHORITY TAKES ADVICE OF TOURISM TASK FORCE FOR SEPARATE MANAGEMENT AND FACILITIES [38]

In the same August 19 *Sunday News*, in a signed open letter that greatly exceeded the letter-to-the-editor word limit, the three Penn Square Partners wrote:

> Despite the naysayers, Penn Square Partners persisted by investing substantial time, effort and money to promote this vision for a better Lancaster. The opponents chose to litigate and undermine the collaborative efforts proposed by Penn Square Partners and the authority. Their sole goal was to delay,

postpone and destroy the project and the corresponding benefits to the community.

If the authority board accepts the recommendation from the task force, Marriott will require the hotel to compete directly with the convention center for meeting and ballroom business.... It is the authority's fiduciary responsibility to create a structure that optimizes the long-term economic viability of the convention center. To recommend otherwise is shortsighted, narrowly focused and only beneficial to the self-interest of a few hoteliers in the community.... Penn Square Partners will not be party to a structure that endangers the economic feasibility of the hotel and convention center project. It would be a greater disservice to the project and the community to proceed under the task force's recommendation.[39]

Pickard and the LCCCA board had not voted on the management issue by August 22, 2001. That night, at a crowded LCCCA public meeting, three leading national hospitality consultants spoke, endorsing Spectacor. Most of the Lancaster establishment supported Interstate. Speaking on behalf of Interstate, Mayor Smithgall pronounced, "I don't care if [Spectacor] is the most spectacular convention center manager in the world. I think it's better to have Interstate manage it than to have nothing."[40]

The Management Vote

"Comparisons are odorous."
—William Shakespeare, *Much Ado about Nothing*, 1599

The LCCCA scheduled a vote on September 12, 2001, for a manager for the convention center. The Lancaster debate even attracted the notice of national press group Knight-Ridder, which early on the morning of September 11 ran this story through its wire service: "Lobbying Intense as Lancaster, Pa., Convention Center Vote Nears."

As the vote nears on an operator for the planned Lancaster County Convention Center, the people who will be making that decision are reading letters and e-mails and answering their telephones. "I have never in my life received as much information about how I should vote on anything as I have in the last couple of weeks," said Paul E. Wright, one of seven appointed Convention Center Authority board members expected to cast their vote Wednesday morning. . . . [41]

Another story later that morning eclipsed all other news stories that day. Yet as world-changing as the September 11th Twin Towers terrorist attacks were, they apparently weren't important enough to postpone the vote for a manager of an unbuilt hotel and convention center in Lancaster, Pennsylvania. The very next morning, September 12, with the country still in shock, the Lancaster County Convention Center Authority held its scheduled meeting.

If holding a non-essential meeting on the morning after the terrorists' attacks pushed the bounds of decency, the comments of Penn Square Partners' general partner S. Dale High completely trampled them.

Before the LCCCA board voted, people on both sides of the management debate lined up at the microphone to make statements during the "public comment" portion of the meeting. Hundreds of people had shown up in the Southern Market Center that mild September morning.

Robert Butera, the industry executive and president of the Philadelphia Convention Center, spoke on behalf of Spectacor. Butera said that Interstate operating both facilities amounted to a "direct subsidy" to Penn Square Partners for their hotel.

Then Dale High took his turn at the microphone. High looked like an unimposing, mild-mannered man. However, the president of High Industries and the general partner of Penn Square Partners was a county heavyweight, and people shut up and listened.

"This is not a matter of taking our ball and going home," said High of his threat to leave the project if Interstate wasn't selected. Then S. Dale High took decency down a couple of notches. "As we saw with the Twin Towers, these things can be taken away from us in a day."[42]

The board rejected the Task Force's recommendation and on September 12, 2001, voted 5–1 (one absent) that Interstate would manage both the convention center and the hotel.

"I'm very disappointed the way this process has worked out. I have thought that I had a gun to my head," said board member W. Garth Sprecher, who voted for Interstate.[43]

Public Health Work

"And I will see what physic the tavern affords."
—William Shakespeare, *Henry VI*, Part I, 1591

Back in March 2001, the *Sunday News* had reported that the city of Lancaster would make restaurant inspection reports available to the public.[44] This idea had my full support from the time I took the job. From March 2001 on, the restaurant inspection reports were among the most-read and best-liked regular features in all of the Lancaster newspapers.

It was my responsibility to have food industry businesses comply with state and local codes. The goal was to educate owners about food safety and keep their business open—not to close them. It was a step-by-step process that worked well for the patrons, the owners, and the city overall.

Molly S. Henderson, Lancaster County Commissioner, 2004 - 2008

The position of director of public health in Lancaster City was truly one of my favorite in my career. It brought together my public health and education backgrounds. There are so many interesting and sometimes funny and tragic stories to be told. From baby mice born on a pizza at a deli to desperate families forced to leave condemned properties, I never knew what challenge or adventure would arise each day. The job required knowledge and common sense. My colleagues were talented and worked together well. The fire marshals and the housing inspectors were essential to us. We relied on one another. I felt that we made a positive impact each day for the residents of Lancaster.

The Project Grows

The 2003 Election

"But I do prophesy th' election."
—William Shakespeare, *Hamlet*, 1600

Shortly before I left my job as public health director in Lancaster, in April 2002, Ron Ford, the Democrat on the Lancaster County Board of Commissioners, announced his retirement.[45] It is customary for the Democrat to serve only two terms as county commissioner. This is so that other Democrats get public service experience in a region where precious few opportunities for the minority party exist. According to state law, there must be minority party representation on the board of county commissioners.

I read this front-page news about Ford one morning while passing a newspaper kiosk near a McDonald's I was inspecting. At that moment, I decided to run for Lancaster County commissioner. I thought I could win. Since running for commissioner in 1995, I had stayed active in the Democratic Party, holding fundraisers and doing grassroots work. I had remained "plugged in" from my years of working with the city's health department. I felt that my experience would be very useful to the county.

We conducted a beautiful campaign.[46] The campaign team couldn't have been better. One of my "coaches," my political mentor and friend Helen Moyer, served as the honorary co-chair of the campaign.[47] In January 2003, Helen threw me a campaign kick-off brunch, which was attended by, among others, Representative Mike Sturla, Commissioner Ron Ford, and the three Lancaster City Council Democrats. Ron Ford was my other honorary co-chair.[48] Barbara Humphrey coordinated the campaign plan.[49]

The *Sunday News* gave Helen Moyer's kick-off brunch prominent front-page coverage on January 12, 2003. In the article, Helen Colwell Adams wrote, "Moyer said even if she weren't a friend of Henderson's, she would still be working for her. 'She's highly qualified with education and experience,' Moyer said. 'She will be able to handle the job.'"[50]

The persuasive article highlighted my decades as a Lancaster County and state committeewoman and my work within the party. The newspaper favorably covered my service at the city's health department as well. The public seemed happy to know their restaurants were regularly and professionally inspected and which ones were clean. I felt very pleased with the *Sunday News* coverage.

My job during the campaign was to knock on doors and talk with the voters personally. No one would outwork me, I knew that. Always diligent, the end of every day I sat down at my desk and, by hand, answered each letter written to me during the campaign.

People generally had very positive reactions when I knocked on their doors. (Once a naked man did answer the door, but I excused myself and went on my way.) Most people felt glad to learn that I handled restaurant inspections for the city. A typical exchange would go something like this:

Me: "Hi, I'm Molly Henderson, and I'm running for Lancaster County commissioner. You may know me as the director of the city's health department; we did the restaurant inspections."
Voter: "Oh, yes, . . . I love those! I read 'em all the time."

Then we would chat about the election and discuss issues that were important to them.

I faced two Democratic opponents in the May 2003 primary. Bill Saylor, my opponent in the 1995 race, again sought the commissioner's seat. Also running was Jon Price, a legislative analyst and Clay Township supervisor.

The Democratic Party endorsed all three candidates going into the May primary. It was a very difficult time for me to be interviewed. My mother, Wanda DeHart, had just died, and I had to fly back and forth to Florida, where she had lived. I felt sad and was under a lot of stress.

On the GOP side, two-term Republican commissioner chairman Paul Thibault announced he would not seek a third term. The Republicans—oddly, to my mind—endorsed only one candidate for the May primary election, even though seven Republican candidates filed papers to run for the two GOP positions on the November ballot.[51]

The Republican Party chose not to endorse the incumbent commissioner, Howard "Pete" Shaub. Shaub had proved to be a difficult coworker in the commissioners' office.[52] He didn't merely alienate his fellow commissioners, but also raised the hackles of the secretaries, the department heads,

96

the staff, and virtually everyone in the courthouses. The GOP apparently considered this too much bad behavior, so it declined to endorse the volatile Shaub.

The GOP endorsed Richard "Dick" Shellenberger, a tall, pleasant political novice with no elected office experience.[53] Shellenberger, born and raised on a Lancaster County farm, owned the Eatery, a family-style restaurant. A fundamentalist Christian, Shellenberger wore his faith on his sleeve. Unlikely as it seems, he and I became closely allied. Dick Shellenberger lost his courageous battle with Mesothelioma in January 2019. I was honored to speak at his funeral.

Howard "Pete" Shaub – Lancaster County Commissioner, 2000 - 2006

2003 Campaign Issues

The hotel and convention center was not initially a major issue of the 2003 campaign. Normally, a Lancaster County commissioner's race deals with issues such as property taxes, parks, prisons, and, most important, farmland preservation.

I didn't particularly follow the convention center issue. I didn't have a strong opinion one way or the other when the room tax was implemented, but it did seem strange for the county to "tax" hotel owners in order to help their competitors. When the campaign began, I expected to address the usual county-related issues.

I basically supported the project when the campaign began. My stated "on the record" position during the primary was:

> The community accepted this project years ago. Dozens of revitalization projects —public and private— are based upon its completion.... To ensure that project lenders provide rigorous

financial discipline, commissioners must insist that the hotel must be self-supporting and the center's debt is owed only by the authority and not county-guaranteed.[54]

I accepted that the project would be built and was thinking about other issues. Then two things happened that turned my attention more closely to the convention center and hotel issue: (1) Someone on my campaign staff alerted me that the LCCCA was spending millions of dollars on consultants for the project; and (2) the cost of the project had grown dramatically. Furthermore, the consultants didn't seem to be doing much to earn the exorbitant sums they were being paid.[55]

The other change in the project was the idea that Lancaster County would guarantee a $40 million bond issued by the LCCCA.[56] The Convention Center Authority wanted more money, and it wanted the county to co-sign a loan for it. I didn't think that sounded like something the county ought to do for this project.

When the sponsors first pitched the project to the public, during the delirious summer of 1999, they said the convention center portion would cost $30 million. Now, in early 2003, they claimed that construction had increased $25 million to $55 million. The LCCCA wanted to issue bonds on the municipal market. The LCCCA bond would then be remarketed by a bank for purchase by investors.[57]

By using the county to guarantee the bond, the LCCCA could take advantage of Lancaster County's "AAA" bond credit rating.[58] With this arrangement, if the LCCCA failed to make its debt payments, the taxpayers of Lancaster County would be responsible for those payments.

At the time of the May 20, 2003, primary, *all* of the candidates for Lancaster County commissioner supported the hotel and convention center project. Despite beautiful weather, voter turnout amounted to only 21 percent of the county's Republicans and Democrats. People cast a total of 49,630 ballots on election day.[59]

The Commissioner Candidates for November 2003–7 for Three Spots

When the Republican votes were tallied, Shellenberger won, and Shaub got second place and his name on the November ballot.[60]

On the Democratic side, I won, beating Bill Saylor by almost 1,500 votes. Jon Price lagged 300 votes behind Saylor. I now had to essentially "run" against the other Democrat for the third seat. I thought I'd make it on through the general election. Then something out of the ordinary happened.

Shortly after the primary, a Lancaster lawyer named James Clymer decided to enter the commissioner's race.[61] Clymer needed the signatures of 1,500 registered voters on his petition before July 1, 2003, to qualify for the November ballot. He submitted more than 3,000 by the deadline.[62] Clymer ran on a single issue: opposition to the convention center.

Clymer was not a political novice. He'd served for several years as the national chairman of the Constitution Party. He ran for Pennsylvania lieutenant governor on the U.S. Taxpayers Party ticket in 1994. In that election, Clymer received about 16 percent of the votes—not bad for a minor party candidate. He ran as the Libertarian candidate for auditor general in 1992 and once again for auditor general in 1998. He received more than 10 percent of the vote statewide.[63]

Jim Clymer was somewhat soft-spoken but articulate, gracious, and smart, and he adamantly opposed using taxpayer money to build a convention center. He considered the idea of a $40 million county bond guaranty unacceptable. The project, particularly the bond issue, became the main issue for the rest of the campaign.

"In business, you don't just go out and start a new project without looking at what's happening in other places," Clymer said during the campaign. "Convention centers are failing all over the place. What does this city have that will make a difference? We don't even have air service."[64]

A Visit to a Foreign Land

". . . hoist by your own petard . . ."
—William Shakespeare, *Hamlet*, 1600

After the primary, the candidates generally take a small break before the fall campaign. Ander, my son, had been away the year after high school as an exchange student to Taiwan. Rotary International sponsors this fabulous worldwide program. Parents are not supposed to have much contact with their child during the year. At the end of the program, parents are encouraged to visit the host family and country. So, after the primary, when school had let out, the time was right to travel. We went to Taipei, Taiwan's capital.

Leslie, Alex, and I flew into the middle of the 2003 SARS*** epidemic. Actually, because I was a registered respiratory therapist, it didn't particularly worry me. Everyone, including us, wore masks—everywhere. When you entered a building or a store, an attendant flashed an infrared thermometer beam at your brow to detect a fever. The upside to this: no one was around. Taiwan is a densely crowded island, but all of the locals stayed home. We went to museums, parks, and restaurants with never a wait.

"There was never yet philosopher
That could endure the toothache patiently."
—William Shakespeare, *Much Ado about Nothing*, 1599

It's always something. On our second day, I cracked my canine tooth on a Tootsie Pop. It was orange flavored, my favorite. Anything hot, cold, or even just air sent searing pain up through my upper jaw and into my sinuses. We had five more days to visit. Ander advised, "Mom, one of the Rotary members is a dentist. He's a great guy. I'm sure he can help you. He uses laughing gas."

I grumbled, "No, I don't think it will work. I'll wait until I'm home to see my good U.S. dentist." That day I called Lancaster and

---

** Severe acute respiratory syndrome—a viral respiratory infection spread by close contact with other people.

arranged to be in the dentist's chair an hour after we arrived home at the end of the week.

As I sat in the chair with a blue bib on, head back, and mouth gaping, waiting for relief, the hygienist came in. She explained, "Mrs. Henderson, I'm sorry, but Dr. Botto has been called away on an emergency. His new associate, Dr. Suling Chen, just here from Taiwan, will be right in to help you."

To this day, you cannot tell which tooth was repaired, and I have never eaten another Tootsie Pop—even an orange one.

Enter Resolute Harper

> ". . . nor shrinking from distress, but always resolute, in most extremes."
> —William Shakespeare, *Henry VI*, Part I, 1591

Jim Clymer brought with him to the 2003 county commissioner campaign probably the wildest card in Lancaster County at the time: Ronald Preston "Ron" Harper, Jr.

Harper, a very talented investigator, cut quite a character. My understanding was that he did opposition research for the Senate Republicans. He called himself an independent journalist, and he lived up to that calling. He wrote and posted stories on his deliberately unpolished, frequently brilliant website, 5thEstate.com. Harper's investigations and online stories often scandalized the powerful in Lancaster County.[65]

An example of Harper's work concerned Representative John Barley, the influential House Appropriations chairman who helped steer some Stadium Bill pork to the project. Barley resigned in 2002, after Harper hounded him out of office. Harper supposedly had evidence of bad behavior by Barley and planned to leverage it.

As a political operative, Harper specialized in what might be called *oppositional activism*, getting under the skin of opponents. He functioned as an unofficial member of Clymer's campaign.[66]

The Fall Campaign

"A horse, a horse, my kingdom for a horse!"
 —William Shakespeare, *Richard the III*, 1592

I had a potentially dangerous encounter with Harper during the fall campaign. Every year, after Labor Day, several Lancaster County boroughs and townships hold annual fall parades. There, political candidates can meet voters. The candidate sits in a car, rides a scooter, or walks the parade route and waves and smiles. It's part of running for office. Having grown up in Millersville, I decided to march in that parade.[67]

The night before the Millersville parade, I attended the Lancaster County Democratic Fall Banquet. It was jam-packed with candidate speeches and enthusiastic encouragement all around. Bill Saylor, my Democratic running mate, also attended. At the end of the banquet, around 10:30 p.m., I spoke with Saylor, telling him I would be riding a horse in the Millersville Parade the next morning. I hadn't informed anyone else of this. (Bill lived along the main parade route.)

I arrived on horseback the next morning—a bright, sunny, perfect fall day. Before the parade began at 7:00 a.m., I saw Harper at the staging area with a placard. The sign read, "Hey, Molly, get off your high horse!"

I alerted parade security and said, "I have an eight-hundred-pound animal here. There are kids and older folks along the street, and we do *not* want a problem." I stepped off, all the while watching for Harper.

At the halfway mark of the parade in front of the post office, a police officer informed me that Harper was waiting about three blocks down with a video camera. Perhaps he wanted to catch me looking foolish or weak in some way by spooking the horse. Looking down from the saddle, I again warned the officer about the danger to the crowds.

Down three blocks, across the street from Harper, at 326 N. George Street, stood a Millersville University frat house. The frat brothers had been drinking and by 9:00 a.m. were already drunk. Sure enough, when I rode past the big pink Victorian frat house, about ten young men, majoring in beer, began running about, hollering, whistling, and yelling at me. My normally even-tempered horse soon became agitated. Luckily, my son, Ander, had accompanied me. Some of the frat boys knew Ander from high school and stopped their foolishness. Harper likely captured this very dangerous stunt on camera. How did Harper know I would be riding a horse in the Millersville Parade? And guess who owned the pink Victorian?

The November Election—2003

Because of Clymer's entrance into the race, the convention center bond became the main issue in the county commissioners' race. Every candidate opposed the county's backing the $40 million bond. My position, which I repeated quite often, was: "I am very much in favor of the convention center, but I do not support the county backing of the bond. The convention center must be self-supporting."

The Republicans also disapproved of the bond. Shellenberger said, "I am behind the convention center; however, I am opposed to the county insuring the bond." Shaub also went on the record against the county bond guaranty and declared he would not vote for it.

"With this bond issue, the taxpayers of Lancaster County are basically being asked to use their wallets as an insurance policy in case the convention center tanks," Clymer said.[68]

Lancaster mayor Charlie Smithgall supported the county bond guaranty. Smithgall, using worst-case estimates from the LCCCA's financial adviser, chuckled that even if the convention center tanked and the guaranty kicked in, the cost per Lancaster County taxpayer would be "$2.66, less than a Happy Meal."[69] Yet, it actually cost the taxpayers a lot more than that.

"I see them lay their heads together to surprise me."
—William Shakespeare, *Henry VI*, Part II, 1590

On October 29, six days before the election, lame duck commissioners Paul Thibault and Ron Ford passed Ordinance Number 73, guaranteeing the $40 million LCCCA bond issue. Shaub (who told people he was doing so reluctantly) voted against the ordinance.[70]

I felt good on Election Day, November 4, 2003. I voted mid-morning at my Lancaster Township precinct. Early that evening, I received the news that I'd been elected Lancaster County commissioner. I was at the Lancaster County Democratic headquarters with Alex, Leslie, and my dad. Ander was away at college in New York City. My mother would have been beaming. I remember standing on a wobbly folding chair in my high heels and giving a little acceptance speech about Ginger Rogers dancing backward.

We went home and had a little champagne, and I fell asleep that night knowing I would be on the Lancaster County Board of Commissioners. I didn't realize storm clouds were already gathering around our board.

Chapter Five

HURRICANE SHAUB– CATEGORY 5

Why, now blow wind, swell billow, and swim bark!
The storm is up, and all is on the hazard.
—William Shakespeare, *Julius Caesar*, 1599

Ronald Ford – Lancaster County Commissioner, 1996 - 2004

Storm Advisory

I had a lot to learn prior to taking office the first week of January 2004.[1]

Lancaster County, the fourth-largest employer in the county, had an annual budget of about $250 million.[2] Most of its approximately two thousand employees were not elected.[3] So, the people who ran the county were already in place when my term began. A new administration did not customarily purge the staff on arrival.

During this time, outgoing commissioners Paul Thibault and Ron Ford invited me to lunch. We met at the Bird's Nest, a quiet downtown Lancaster restaurant. We didn't talk about the convention center bond they'd just passed or any other issue. Thibault and Ford had called the meeting for the sole purpose of warning me about Pete Shaub.[4]

Thibault and Ford were gracious and respectful to me and also respectful of the Office of Lancaster County Commissioner. They spoke bluntly about Shaub: Pete was trouble.

Thibault described several examples of Shaub acting on his own, without proper board authorization. He spoke of Shaub's temper tantrums and frequent berating of staff. Shaub's interpersonal style went beyond abrasive; it was often abusive, according to the commissioners.

Thibault advised, "Pete's always saying there is no 'I' in 'the word *team*.' But," Thibault noted wryly, "if you look hard, there is a 'me' in there somewhere."

The Clouds Collect

"The ambitions ocean swells and rages and foam,
To be exalted with the threatening clouds."
—William Shakespeare, *Julius Caesar*, 1599

Although we'd gone to the same high school, one year apart, I remember Pete Shaub only vaguely from those days. He played on the soccer team. Our paths did not cross.

As an adult, I rarely encountered him. As an active Democrat, I didn't share many of Shaub's social or political views.[5]

A 1972 graduate of Penn Manor High School, Howard E. "Pete" Shaub, Jr., was born in 1954 in Willow Street, in the southern part of Lancaster County. He was one of six children of third-generation professional auctioneers Howard and Kathy Shaub.[6]

After Penn Manor, Shaub went to East Stroudsburg University, in the northeastern part of Pennsylvania, where he received a bachelor's degree in political science in 1976. After college, Shaub served in the marines from 1976 to 1979. He always wore his marine's pin on his suit lapel.

The same year he graduated from college, Shaub married Shendra "Shendy" Landis, also an East Stroudsburg alumnus. The Shaubs had two children, Jason and Jessica, who were in their early twenties when I took office in 2004.[7]

After the marines, Shaub was employed as an auctioneer for several years in the family business, Shaub Family Auctioneers. While we were in office, on several occasions I worked at benefit auctions with Pete. He called, and I clerked. I kept track of the bidding numbers. He was quite good, and his delivery had a clear musical cadence. He spoke and engaged the crowd, reminding them to be generous because the auction benefited charity.

When Shaub left the auction block, he moved into the construction field, where he worked for the next eighteen years as a project executive for a noted Lancaster company: Wohlsen Construction. At Wohlsen, he oversaw large projects.[8]

Shaub, like me, had not held a publicly elected office prior to becoming commissioner. Also like me, he played an active role in party politics locally and in the state, and he was very well connected. In 1998, the year before he first ran for Lancaster County commissioner, Shaub worked on the campaigns of state senator Gib Armstrong, Representative John Barley, and Congressman Joseph Pitts.[9]

Shaub announced his bid for the commissioner's seat in November 1998, almost a full year before the election. Standing next to wife, Shendy, and political patrons Representative Barley and Senator Armstrong, Shaub spoke to the assembled reporters at the Republican Committee of Lancaster County party headquarters. "I saw a need for good candidates," he said modestly. "I saw a need for someone with my abilities."[10]

"Pete is uniquely qualified for the job," Barley said, smiling beside Shaub. Also, on hand to show his support was Lancaster city mayor Charlie Smithgall.[11]

It didn't take Shaub long to get attention. In a letter to the *Sunday News* on January 17, 1999, "JUDGEMENT BY SHAUB QUESTIONED," the writer criticized Shaub for "maligning the present county commissioners," led by chairman and Republican opponent Paul Thibault.

Shaub had spoken before an audience of members of Americans for Christian Traditions in Our Nation (ACTION), a conservative

Christian political action group in Lancaster County.[12] In 1999, ACTION represented the most powerful wing of the county's GOP.

ACTION members perceived Paul Thibault to be the worst kind of Republican: a moderate. ACTION opposed Thibault not for his views on gun control or gay marriage; rather, Thibault had violated one of ACTION'S cardinal commandments: Thou Shalt Not Raise Taxes. Thibault's 28 percent property tax raise of 1998 constituted an unforgivable sin.

"There was a promise made [by Thibault] that was totally abandoned, and that's the issue," said ACTION'S president, Bob Kettering. "People are fed up with taxes."[13]

Leading up to the February GOP endorsement vote, local heavyweights Pitts, Barley, Armstrong, and Smithgall all supported and formally endorsed Shaub.

After the Republican Committee endorsement vote in February, the crowded field of seven dwindled to Thibault, Shaub, and Jere Swarr for the May primary.[14] Thibault ran unendorsed by the party.

"You great benefactors, sprinkle our society with thankfulness."
—William Shakespeare, *Timon of Athens*, 1609

As the primary approached, the press seemed to favor Shaub. On March 14, the *Sunday News* featured him in a lengthy, flattering profile. In "SEMPER FI TO IDEAS, ISSUES PETE SHAUB SHUNS POLITICAL BATTLES IN HIS CAMPAIGN FOR COMMISSIONER," Shaub is described as a "man with a mission . . . to unify the battling divisions of the Lancaster County Republican Party."

"I consider Pete Shaub to be a friend," the article quoted Representative John Barley as saying. "He's a good, solid person."

Shaub, the middle-class, college-educated former marine and fast-talking auctioneer, is described in the *Sunday News* article as the "son of a rural, working-class family from southern Lancaster County in which he was the first child to go to college." The piece characterized Shaub as "an intense, carefully prepared candidate who comes to an interview with pages full of notes, and who pauses to write down a thought before it slips away."[15]

Shaub continued to attract important political backing ahead of the May primary. State representatives Katie True and Tom Armstrong both held fundraisers to support Shaub's candidacy. Others raised money for Shaub, too. Representative Barley held multiple fundraisers at his farm estate. Even Peggy Steinman hosted a fundraiser for Pete ahead of the primary. Dale High contributed to Shaub's campaign. Shaub became the candidate of the Lancaster political and business establishment.[16]

Of his impressive list of benefactors, Shaub said to one of Lancaster Newspapers' reporters, "I'm very, very blessed to have such a broad spectrum of support."

As for the hotel room tax, which would be passed in September 1999 and had just become an issue in the campaign, Shaub punted. He said he hadn't studied whether or not it should be imposed.[17] This is a little hard to believe, because his main supporters—Senator Armstrong, Representative Barley, and Mayor Smithgall—had been early proponents of the tax.

"To be effective, you have to be a team player," Shaub said, in another flattering article before the primary. "Citizens (should) feel they can relate to the politician, that politicians aren't detached from them, that politicians are approachable. I think that's something I can really bring." Shaub added that if he became commissioner, he would suffer a significant salary cut. "It's a very big sacrifice—we'll just leave it at that."[18]

As a campaigner, Shaub did a very good job. Physically of medium height, about 5'10", and very fit, he wears his hair in a short brush cut. He is articulate, a fast talker from the auctioneering. He has a particular charisma and physical gracefulness. In the spring of 1999, he was on his best behavior. Pete Shaub wanted to be commissioner very badly.

Shaub pretty much left the other primary candidates alone and went after Thibault frontally. He criticized, among other things, Thibault's inability to build an emergency training facility for police and firefighters. "The emergency training facility is a critical issue that should not have taken 10 years to be built," Shaub said. "It's inexcusable for that facility to be (waiting) for 10 years."[19]

Three weeks before the May primary, confident of a spot on the November ballot, Shaub resigned from Wohlsen Construction. HIs confidence was justified—he won the top spot in the May primary. The unendorsed incumbent, Paul Thibault, came in second, thus ensuring himself a second term as commissioner. Swarr, the other endorsed Republican, was left out.[20]

The primary campaign raised and spent a lot of money. Shaub raised $97,000, and Thibault collected an eye-popping $225,000 through his Friends of Better Government political action committee. Thibault's "Friends" included S. Dale High, Jack Buckwalter, Peggy Steinman, Rufus Fulton, and other top leaders of the Lancaster business establishment.[21]

While Jere Swarr spent only $1.53 per vote and Shaub averaged $2.38 per vote, Thibault forked out $7.79 for each vote cast for him. Although it seemed inconceivable that Republicans wouldn't take two of the three seats on the Lancaster County Board of Commissioners, the GOP candidates still went through the motions of campaigning after the primary. What's more, they continued to raise money. Shaub seemed to have a great time of it.

Pete Shaub was elected Lancaster County commissioner in November 1999. He received 35,064 votes, 913 votes more than Thibault's 34,081.[22] Incumbent Democrat Ron Ford won the minority commissioner's seat.

Storm Watch

"What storm is this that blows so contrary?"
—William Shakespeare, *Romeo and Juliet*, 1594

Within weeks of being sworn into office, Shaub had made headlines. In a *Sunday News* feature on January 16, 2000, "NEW COMMISSIONER VOWS TO SAVE FARMS, FIGHT DRUGS AND 'FURTHER GOD'S KINGDOM,'" Shaub went back to his base. He spoke of his divine mission as Lancaster County commissioner at the quarterly meeting of ACTION in Leola.

"You have given me an opportunity of a lifetime," Shaub told ACTION members. "I get to further God's kingdom. That is what I am called to do to help influence people to change their lives."[23]

Shaub angered Thibault and Ford when he called a meeting with Lancaster Newspapers' reporters in November 2000, in his first year in office, and criticized his commissioner colleagues for their budget. The budget called for a 3.5 percent property tax increase and included the cost of the Barnes Hall juvenile detention facility renovation. Shaub said, "I really think the residents of Lancaster County deserve to have a plan in place that shows us how we're going to pay for things." Shaub met the press on his own without notifying his fellow commissioners.[24] He used this tactic repeatedly during both of his terms in office, to the point of his own undoing.

In "THIBAULT, SHAUB SPAR OVER BUDGET," Shaub said to the *Intelligencer Journal* on November 22, "All I'm saying is that Paul and Ron should pay for all the projects they approved before I came on the board."[25]

Thibault declared Shaub was "carving out what is a destructive precedent. All boards are bound by the decision of previous boards. This is the nature of government. I think he's not aware of how government works."[26] However, Paul Thibault was certainly aware of "how government worked."

Thibault took a patronizing tone with Shaub. "To his credit, Pete is supportive of these things," Thibault said in the *Intelligencer Journal* article. "What is baffling is that he doesn't want to vote to pay for these things."

In the 2001 budget, Shaub designated $16,534 of taxpayer money to buy a Ford Taurus for his exclusive use. The IRS blocked the expenditure, but this story displayed the "loose cannon" tendencies of Pete Shaub.[27] And this wasn't the only time he attempted to use public money for personal items.

Shaub had a particular problem with county administrator Timothea "Timi" Kirchner. Shaub accused Kirchner, the operations officer for county government, of withholding information Shaub had requested to analyze the budget.[28]

When Kirchner, by all accounts a smart and able administrator with excellent job evaluations, came before the County Salary Board for a yearly review and raise, Shaub submitted the lone vote against the pay bump.[29] Shaub carried his feud with Kirchner into my term on the commissioners' board. As with most Pete Shaub feuds, it did not end well for his adversary.

Cleanliness Is Next To . . .

"I'll set thee in a shower of gold, and hail
Rich pearls upon thee."
—William Shakespeare, *Antony and Cleopatra*, 1606

Shaub kept getting headlines into his third year. The *Sunday News* reported on January 27, 2002, that a county employee had been fired for sending copies of an internal memo to the *Sunday News* and WGAL-TV. The memo, authorized by Lancaster Court of Common Pleas president Judge Georgelis, told county probation department staffers that Shaub was prohibited from coming into their office area. Shaub had been using the judge's private shower facilities.[30] He thought he had access to every county office and could make himself at home in all of them. This habit continued into my term with Shaub.

Shaub and the Lancaster County Republican Party were rocked in January 2002, when powerful legislator Representative John Barley announced he was immediately quitting his reelection campaign. In March, citing concerns about his family suffering "considerable harassment," Barley resigned from the most powerful seat in the state legislature.[31] He had been a legislator for almost two decades. Shaub had lost his "good friend" and an important political backer.

Barley didn't reveal precisely why he was leaving politics, other than the vague "harassment" claim. He had been involved in a controversial land sale, in which he netted more than $15 million, but that didn't seem enough to unseat such a powerful man. Ron Harper had also followed Barley around and stung Barley online with his "JohnBarley.com" website and his own, 5thEstate.com.

An aide to House minority leader William DeWeese didn't buy Barley's explanation and had a comment about the Lancaster political culture. "The only story no one is giving any credence to is the one he [Barley] gave," said Mike Manzo, DeWeese's chief of staff. "In Lancaster, it's like blood in the water down there. The sharks are circling. There are lots of stories, but none has been confirmed to my knowledge."[32]

One Good Turn Deserves Another

Shaub stood squarely in the sponsors' corner on the Lancaster hotel and convention center issue. When the hoteliers again took their case to court, Shaub promised, "They are being shortsighted and dragging this out. You have 11 people standing alone who are very agenda-oriented in their approach. But I have no doubt Judge Farina's decision will be upheld."[33]

After Barley left the legislature, he went to work for Arthurs Lestrange, a municipal bond underwriting firm, based in Pittsburgh. Barley's job at the firm was to line up bond agreements.[34] In June, just months after leaving the chairman's seat of the House Appropriations Committee, Barley accompanied two Arthurs Lestrange representatives to meetings inside the county courthouse with commissioners Thibault and Shaub.[35] Barley's support had been key in getting both commissioners their jobs. When the county bond guaranty for the convention center was put together, right before the 2003 election, Thibault and the board voted to hire Arthurs Lestrange to handle the deal.

> "Out of my door, you witch, you hag, you baggage,
> you polecat, you runyon! Out! Out!"
> —William Shakespeare, *Merry Wives of Windsor*, 1600

Shaub simply couldn't avoid negative headlines. When a group of witches applied to have a picnic at a county park as part of the "Lancaster Pagan Pride Festival," Shaub complained he didn't like the fact that the county had to issue the wiccans a permit.

"I don't think it is right that we are required to rent a facility to a group that promotes witchcraft," Shaub said. "I don't think our founding fathers had renting public facilities to witchcraft groups in mind when they made up the laws."[36]

Shaub had his own problems with the parks. One late night in 2002, after Chickie's Rock County Park had closed, park rangers stopped the forty-eight-year-old Shaub with two young women, in their early twenties, in his car. Shaub identified the young women as his daughter and her friend and said that they were conducting a Bible study. The rangers permitted him to leave the park without a citation.[37]

Shaub's Reelection Campaign—2003

When Shaub ran for reelection in 2003, he did so as an unpopular incumbent. It took him no time to start the 2003 campaign off with another misstep. After the holiday break and the unofficial start of the primary race, Shaub invited county department heads and other staff to a campaign kick-off party in support of his reelection. He called them from his office during business hours. This is not only taboo, it is illegal.

Commissioner Ford charged that Shaub used his office improperly and that staff felt "unduly pressured" by Shaub.[38] Ford was right, of course. It demonstrated another instance of Pete abusing his office.

Unlike 1999, when he had been the darling of the party, Shaub did not receive the GOP endorsement in 2003. That went to Dick Shellenberger. The party endorsed only one candidate. This ill-conceived, irresponsible move by the Lancaster GOP allowed Pete Shaub to be reelected based on his name recognition.[39]

The Eye of the Storm

The convention center county bond guaranty put Shaub in a difficult position. He wanted it, but the rest of the field, Republicans and Democrats, including me, all opposed it.

Shaub tried to sidestep the issue. "My job is to listen to all of the information. Once I do that, then I will make my decision," Shaub said of the bond guaranty question.[40] As the campaign progressed, with Clymer pushing the issue to the center of the campaign, Shaub was forced to the same position as the rest of us: to come out in favor of the convention center but against the county bond guaranty (even though he really did support it). He took this public position for purely political reasons.

When the campaign financial reports were made public for the May 2003 primary, a few interesting names and numbers showed up. One $10,000 contribution to Shellenberger's campaign came from

"Responsible Citizens for Economic Progress," the political action committee (PAC) of Stevens & Lee, Attorneys at Law.[41]

Shaub, a sitting commissioner, also got $2,000 from the Stevens & Lee PAC.[42] Stevens & Lee, the county solicitor, was making hundreds of thousands of dollars a year for the firm in special counsel legal work for the county. Also, by this point, 2003, Stevens & Lee had already billed more than $2 million to the Lancaster County Convention Center Authority. That number would more than triple by the time the project was completed.[43]

Storm Warning

"What boded this, but well forewarning wind . . ."
—William Shakespeare, *Henry VI*, Part II, 1590

Dick Shellenberger was a faith-based fellow traveler with Shaub. While Shaub seemed to pander to the fundamentalists for political purposes, Shellenberger appeared to be more of a true believer. I always felt concerned that they would cross the "church-state" line with county government. Those concerns turned out to be justified, especially with the loose cannon Shaub.

In the November 2003 general election, Shellenberger received more votes than Shaub. It didn't matter that Shaub got second place.[44] Shaub was reelected, and he would be the chairman of the Lancaster County Board of Commissioners.

After the election, Shellenberger appeared characteristically modest and deferred immediately to Shaub.

"I was the top vote-getter, but that's only because I wasn't in the spotlight," Shellenberger said to the *Intelligencer Journal*. "I have a

Richard (Dick) Shellenberger
– Chairman, Lancaster County Commissioner, 2004 - 2008

clean slate because I'm not an incumbent. If I were in office, I would have had some people who disagreed with me so I think not being the top vote-getter is normal with incumbency."[45]

For his part, Shaub said the reelection was "very rewarding." After the election, he said,

> I think it's very important that we got a good team in there. Whether I'm chairman or not will be up to the board to decide. We have a lot of issues to talk about. I'm hoping to meet with the other two commissioner candidates, maybe even this week, to find out what's on their minds and what their visions are for the county.[46]

It amounted to another disingenuous statement from Shaub. The chairmanship had already been determined. It was Shaub's board. Hurricane Pete would soon make landfall. We would all be blown away.

Landfall

"We have landed; in ill time: the skies ask grimly
And threaten present blusters."
—William Shakespeare, *A Winter's Tale*, 1610

My first day as commissioner officially began on January 2, 2004. We were administered the oath by Lancaster Court of Common Pleas president, Judge Michael Georgelis in the "Old Court Room."[47] My husband, Alex, and eight-year-old daughter, Leslie, watched as I took the oath of office. Our son, Ander, was away at college in New York City. Everyone felt excited.

On that day, I recalled something my friend and campaign manager Barb Humphrey had advised after I was elected. "You can't do much directly as the minority commissioner," Barb said, "but you can influence things."[48]

I knew I had much to learn, and I wanted to accomplish a few specific things. I wanted to bring more diversity into the government, get more women involved. The Enola Rail Trail also remained high on my priority list. Farmland preservation wasn't just a campaign slogan.

I intended to work to save as much of it as possible. I wanted to steer more benefits to the city. The county had an interest in a thriving city of Lancaster. I knew that from my work as city health director. There was so much to do!

Office Space Assignments

Shaub had already decided the layout of our physical working space. He would keep his office on the right side of the corridor of commissioners' offices. Shellenberger would have the office next to Shaub, the smallest, least desirable office—the one usually occupied by the Democrat.

Shaub assigned me the office traditionally used by the chairman. Located at the end of the hallway, it was the largest and nicest of the three. It had a beautiful burnished wood desk with a lovely bookcase and a credenza of fine craftsmanship. Large windows with a lovely streetscape view covered the north wall. However, the location kept me isolated from the other commissioners and staff, which I soon learned was the point.

Shortly after taking office, the three Lancaster County commissioners attended a breakfast at the Willow Valley Conference Center, sponsored by the Economic Development Company of Lancaster County. With several hundred of Lancaster County's most influential establishment members present, Shaub told the audience how I came to get "the big office."

"Yeah, we gave Molly the big office at the end of the hall. It has its own bathroom," said Commissioner Shaub, "because, you know, women have special needs."[49] The entire room went silent. I looked at my shoes.

"Came there a certain lord, neat, and trimly dress'd . . ."
—William Shakespeare, *Henry IV*, Part I, 1597

It is said that you can tell a lot about a person by how he or she keeps the office. Shaub's commissioner's office was an orderly, meticulous space. His enormous desk had a prominent position, and here Shaub held court in his oversized leather chair. Two small, straight-backed, worn blue cloth and wood chairs sat in front of Shaub's desk, exaggerating the power disparity between the commissioner and those who came to speak with him.

A marine's sword hung on the wall, as did a very large "fire and brimstone" poster of a majestic Moses holding the stone tablets of the Ten Commandments. (Shellenberger had an identical poster in his office.) Behind Shaub's chair were mounted two ten-point buck heads, which stared at you no matter where you were in the room. (One year, Pete brought in the head of a deer his son had shot. It had been mounted poorly, and we kept hearing it crash to the floor. It amused the office staff but annoyed maintenance to no end. To complete the room's motif, Pete displayed two large brass horse trophies, complete with hanging blue ribbons.

Something that further reveals Shaub's self-absorbed personality happened in the summer of 2005, after we had been in office about a year and a half. My family had gone on a horseback-riding trip to Wyoming. For fun, I returned home with a Jackalope. A Jackalope is a fictional creature having a jackrabbit's head with an antelope's antlers. I had a small inscribed brass plaque placed on its wooden base: "Taken in a fair chase by Molly Henderson, Powder River Basin, Wyoming, August, 2005." I mounted the "trophy" behind my desk in my office, much as Shaub had mounted his deer heads. Maintenance loved it. People always laughed and asked about it when entering the room. Oddly, during the next two years, Pete Shaub never noticed. On reflection, Pete rarely laughed.

Jackalope – Taken in a fair chase by Molly Henderson, Powder River Basin, WY, August 2005

Shaub seemed to want people to think he was a tough guy, a *man's man*. Every November, during hunting season, he would grow a scruffy beard and sometimes arrived at work wearing his hunting garb, a flannel shirt and camouflage pants. On another morning, we came in and learned that Shaub had gone to the hospital the previous night for an emergency appendectomy. Yet an hour or so later, there he was, in time for our first meeting of the day.

After Hurricane Katrina hit the Gulf States in August 2005, Shaub traveled to Picayune, Mississippi, for a week to help with construction and aid efforts.[50] Pete took his knowledge and building skills down South to help others. That was to his credit.

The commissioners shared the fifth floor of the courthouse with the Lancaster County District Attorney's office. Donald Totaro had just been reelected to a second term as county DA in 2003.[51] It would not be long before Totaro misplaced the power of his important office. He wouldn't have to travel far to do it.

Department Assignments

Shaub not only dictated office space, but also decreed the areas of the county government where each commissioner would work. Typically, the Democratic commissioner works with the social service departments of the county—mental health, department of aging, and children's services. Considering that I held a degree in public health, had run a municipal health agency, and had hospital experience, it made sense that I would oversee the social service departments.

Nevertheless, Shaub gave social services to Shellenberger. I was to work with the departments of Transportation, the Workforce Investment, Property Assessment, Purchasing, the Public Defender's, Parks and Recreation, and the Lancaster Employment & Training Agency.

I didn't know until later that Shaub and Shellenberger had already planned to sell the Conestoga View nursing home. Conestoga View fell under the social services area of a commissioner's work. I was kept in the dark and down the hall.

In the first week of my term, the commissioners attended a daylong retreat with department heads and staff at the Shuts Environmental Center at Lancaster County Park. The point of the retreat was to give the staff some orientation about the new board. Here, at the Shuts

Center, Shaub announced that Shellenberger would oversee the social and human services of county government.⁵²

The Lancaster Newspapers press covered the retreat. Bernard Harris, a veteran reporter from the *Lancaster New Era*, approached me. Bernie always treated me with professional respect and called me either "Dr." or "Commissioner." He asked why I hadn't been assigned social services, since, he noted, it did usually go to the Democrat. "I guess they don't want a rascally Democrat around all that money," I suggested. Social services took up about half of the county budget. Little did I know what my colleagues were up to.

Lancaster County commissioners sit on several boards. All three commissioners sat on the Retirement Board, along with the controller and the treasurer. We were all on the Salary Board, with several department heads, and all were on the Election Board. With the district attorney, a Lancaster County judge, the county sheriff, and the controller, the three commissioners also made up the Prison Board.

All three commissioners went to monthly meetings at Conestoga View, the county nursing home. A private firm, Complete HealthCare, had managed the facility for ten years, and we were briefed on its operations.

County Staff

The commissioner's job very much depends on the staff. The department heads—competent, professional people—served the taxpayers and citizens of Lancaster County well. Most of them were good people, and it was pleasant seeing them every day.

The county engineer Dave McCudden was a big man with a big booming voice and a strong personality. He had a mop of silver hair and bushy thatches of black eyebrows. He appeared to be an able engineer. McCudden sort of "ruled the roost" in his area of the county government.⁵³

I recall an incident with McCudden during the first weeks of my term. The three commissioners were in a meeting with McCudden, while the county engineer explained something about a county project. I asked if he was describing the "Bernoulli principle," a scientific law that relates to the flow of fluid.[54] (I learned this principle during my studies to be a registered respiratory therapist.)

After I said this, Shaub looked up and snickered, "Well, looks like you're not just another pretty face." Shaub clearly had issues with women. It was a major accomplishment when I finally got him and Dick to stop calling the women administrative staff "the girls".

Yet Pete did surprise me on occasion. Once, during a meeting with all three commissioners and some staff members, I suggested allocating funds to the YWCA and the Sexual Assault Prevention and Counseling Center (SAPCC). Shellenberger chimed in, "You can't tell me an adult woman can be raped." (Quaking in horrified rage, I'm sure I looked just like High at that first meeting.) Pete immediately chastised Dick in a low, harsh tone, saying, "You idiot." The next day, Dick apologized to me and the other women who had been at the meeting.

Beginning in July 2004, Andrea McCue became the chief clerk for Lancaster County. Truth be known, the chief clerk runs the county. Andi McCue replaced Terry Styer, who had resigned in March because of conflicts with Pete Shaub. Andi proved to be a very effective county administrator. A hard worker, organized, and professional, Andrea McCue was named Pennsylvania's Chief County Clerk of the Year in 2015.

Pete and Re-Pete

"I will repeat them, - a, e, i -
—William Shakespeare, *Love's Labour's Lost*, 1594

From the time we took office, in January 2004, Shaub and Shellenberger clearly had plans. In fact, the two stayed in such lockstep that people knew them around the office as "Pete and Re-Pete." At meetings Shellenberger would often add, "I echo that comment."

In the first weeks of 2004, it was apparent that Shaub and Shellenberger intended to reorganize county government. They wanted to run it "more like a business." Pete wanted total control and would clean house to achieve it.

In Shaub's first term, commissioners Thibault and Ford had excluded him. Shaub's unpredictable behavior marginalized him, and they shut him out of the process. Despite being a Republican, Shaub found himself the de facto minority commissioner. Now, however, with Shellenberger following *him*, Shaub had control, and that's just what he wanted. And Shellenberger, pleasant, passive, and inexperienced, happily turned his vote over to Shaub.

After we formally voted Shaub chairman of the commissioners' board, the first motion made was to reappoint Stevens & Lee county solicitor. In discussing the motion, I voiced opposition to the reappointment but, to show unity on the board, voted for the motion. Stevens & Lee once again became the solicitor for the county and the LCCCA and High's lobbyist at the same time.

John Espenshade was the Stevens & Lee solicitor for Lancaster County.[55] I remember looking at Espenshade, an unprepossessing, man, and thinking, *Nice suit*. Espenshade wore beautifully tailored suits that were surely quite expensive. I wondered, *How can he wear such fine clothes on $56,000 a year retainer from the county?* I can't recall him ever actually answering any of my questions in a meeting. The Lancaster Newspapers didn't make a big deal of the fact that Stevens & Lee contributed thousands of dollars to both Shaub's and Shellenberger's campaigns.

Pete created an atmosphere of fear and secrecy among county employees through his self-imposed power. Shaub had specific people he wanted eliminated from county government. The first axe would fall on county administrator Timothea Kirchner. Timi Kirchner, a tall, capable woman, had been county administrator for several years. She clashed repeatedly with Shaub in his first term.

I have one vivid remembrance of Timi Kirchner. Very soon after I started the job, we were sitting in her office, and she cautioned me, "Molly, you're going to be very lonely here. Pete and Dick are going to shut you out, and you can't turn to the assistants." She was right, at least for that first year.

Timi Kirchner announced her resignation in the second week of January 2004. She later went to work for Stevens & Lee in the firm's Government Affairs Division.[56]

Another target in Shaub's early sights was planning director Ronald Bailey. Shaub badgered and berated this highly competent and highly regarded man out of his job. Bailey, a smart and knowledgeable asset to the county, was the brains behind the county's "Smart Growth" plan.[57] Bailey was a good man, serious, interesting, and a licensed locomotive engineer for a short spur in Maryland.

Shaub finally pushed Bailey to resign in November 2004.[58] I would not accept Bailey's resignation and implored him to stay. One of Shaub's real misuses of power was forcing Ron Bailey out the door. It meant a major loss for the county.

Two New Additions

Shaub and Shellenberger replaced Kirchner with not one but two people and created two new jobs: chief services officer and county administrative officer.

They advertised nationally for the chief services officer position, and more than a hundred people from across the country applied. The Human Resources Department, led by Thomas Myers, culled the applicants down to the top twenty and gave those applications to the commissioners.[59]

Shellenberger added one application to the pile of twenty. The twenty-first applicant, I later learned, had an inside track on the chief services officer position. His name was Gary Heinke, and he was a good friend of Dick Shellenberger's. They were both fundamentalist Christians and often held prayer sessions at Shellenberger's restaurant, the Eatery. Human resources did not feel that Heinke's skills and experience qualified him for the position. Shellenberger overrode them.

An Excellent Interview

During the interview process, I didn't know about Heinke's prior relationship with Shellenberger. I first learned of it more than a year later in an article about Heinke in the *Lancaster New Era*.[60] A relationship existed, though, and not just between Shellenberger and Heinke. Prior to Heinke's interview with the full board of commissioners, he had been prepped by Shellenberger, Shaub, and county solicitor Espenshade. They supplied him with the questions and the areas that the interview would cover weeks before the meeting took place. They coached him over the phone and when he came to town. Heinke knew exactly what questions to expect. It amounted to yet another misuse of power in this story, with Stevens & Lee again in the middle of it.[61]

At Heinke's interview, he appeared capable and relaxed. He answered questions confidently and seemed very thoughtful. Heinke was personable. His application suggested he had been an assistant school superintendent in Minnesota, but I didn't think he had the bearing of a school superintendent. I didn't want to hire him. I thought that we'd interviewed much more qualified candidates. It didn't matter, as I learned later; the fix was in.

After Heinke had been hired, Shellenberger seemed especially excited around the office, telling everyone Heinke would get things in shape. Heinke would now oversee the biggest piece of the county budget: social services.

Gary Heinke worked primarily under Shellenberger, so our responsibilities rarely crossed. I recall Heinke as a pleasant coworker, though. He dealt with a delicate personnel matter expertly. We had an underperforming department head, a decidedly incompetent man, who needed to be replaced. Heinke deftly handled it without repercussion. I began to gain confidence in him.

Another Excellent Interview

"Many and hearty thanking to you both.
We have made inquiry of you; and we hear
Such goodness of your justice, that our soul
Cannot but yield you forth to public thanks, . . ."
—William Shakespeare, *Measure for Measure*, 1604

Donald Elliott was hired to be the county administrative officer in the spring of 2004. A county administrator prepares the budget, oversees department heads, and conducts the day-to-day functions of the administration. Shaub brought Elliot into county government. Elliot had an MBA, and he listed none other than Nevin D. Cooley, president of Penn Square Partners and High Associates, as one of his references.[62]

What Elliott did while at the county remains a mystery to me. Elliott quit without notice in 2006, after mismanaging several important county deals, including the sale of the Armstrong Building at 150 N. Queen St.[63] Elliot was not helpful. At one commissioners' meeting, with some sixty people demanding answers to reasonable questions about the upcoming budget, I turned to Elliot, who always sat to my right, and said, "Don, please answer these questions." Elliot said out of the corner of his mouth, "You wouldn't throw gasoline on a fire, would you?" Don Elliot looked good on paper and in a suit. Chalk that one up to Pete.

Row, Row, Row Your Boat

> "But here they come;
> If consequences do but approve my dream,
> My boat sails freely, both with wind and stream."
> —William Shakespeare, *Othello*, 1604

In our first year, 2004, Shaub misbehaved outside of the office, too. Without board approval and using county funds, Shaub coerced the head of Parks and Recreation into purchasing a boat.[64] He said the boat, a smart little skiff, was for the "wayward youth" at the Youth Intervention Center at the Sunnyside quarry. In fact, it was for Shaub's personal use. I found out about this when a city resident called me to ask if he could fish in the quarry. (All sports were prohibited in that extremely dangerous water.) He insisted that he saw a man in a boat fishing in the Sunnyside quarry lake, "And it's Pete Shaub fishin' out there." I confronted Pete in his office, with all of the bucks' eyes blazing at me! He told me nobly that he himself planned to teach the young people how to fish. The boat was brought to dry dock. There was no more fishing at the quarry.

Shaub's true talent lay in berating the staff. With his hawk's stare, Shaub yelled and belittled everyone: secretaries, department heads, row officers, and fellow commissioners. Once, when I challenged him in a meeting with department heads, Pete hollered, "Molly, you're just stupid, stupid, stupid!"

My guess is that Pete rarely even considered me. At other times, though, I'm sure I was a thorn in his side. One time involved firearms.

Through Pete's pressure, the Safety Training Center finally opened in the spring of 2004. It is a fabulous facility devoted to training first responders in the county. Most of these selfless people are volunteers. Prior to the grand opening, the commissioners were invited to "try" the various training exercises. In simulations, we donned firefighters' suits and crawled under beams with a hose to dowse flames. Pete and I rappelled down a three-story tower in harnesses to reenact search-and-rescue procedures. But I had the most fun at the firing range where the police practiced.

At the range, the county sheriff guided us. He gave us ear protection and told us where to stand. An officer handed me a Glock and instructed me on how operate it. The range was divided into lanes like a bowling alley. The objective was to shoot a man's silhouette on a large piece of paper as it moved toward you, suspended on a chain.

Pete and Dick had been avid hunters since childhood. My experience with firearms came through a love of history. My hobby is target shooting with a flintlock rifle. It's a very methodical weapon that requires concentration and patience. As I steadily aimed and slowly shot the Glock, Pete and Dick blazed away. At the end of our session, "the girl" had grouped her shots neatly in the lethal zone. Dick laughed and thought it was great. Pete didn't comment. By the time we returned to the courthouse, word had spread all through the county departments that the sheriff had offered me a job.

Shaub hectored the chief clerk, Terry Styer, out of her job, as he had done with Bailey and Kirchner. In a December 2004 article about Shaub's bad behavior ("A Bully in a China Shop"), former chief clerk Terry Styer described working with Shaub to the *Sunday News*.

"He [Shaub] would get mad at people trying to help him avoid problems," said Styer. "I looked for another job because I felt like I could not effectively do my job as long as Pete was in office."[65]

Another staffer, Dee-Dee McGuire, felt so demeaned after an encounter with Shaub in his office that she filed an official complaint with the Human Resources Department. I then demanded that Pete's office door remain open when he met with employees.

"Why then tonight let us assay our plot."
—William Shakespeare, *All's Well That Ends Well*, 1623

I felt especially concerned about Shaub and Shellenberger's penchant for meeting to discuss county business on their own. They often did this with solicitor Espenshade. I warned them repeatedly that this violated the Sunshine Act, and that if it persisted, I would take the matter to the district attorney.

A "Sunshine Act," or "Open Meetings" law, is a statute found in all fifty states. The law stipulates which meetings by officials must be held in public and which may be held in "executive session," away from the public. Exceptions to the Sunshine Act are the purchase of real estate and personnel matters. In Pennsylvania, the Sunshine Act, 65 Pa. C.S.A. § 701–726, says that public officials may not "deliberate" or take "official action" in private session.[66]

On September 7, 2004, I sent a memo to both commissioners, Shaub and Shellenberger, and copied the county clerk, advising them that the secret meetings would stop or there would be consequences. "Let me very clear," I wrote, "that if I discover that these meetings are continuing, in violation of the Sunshine Act, I will not hesitate to bring the issue to the Office of the Lancaster County District Attorney."[67] I later drafted and had my colleagues sign a commissioners' code of ethics called the "Management Protocol." It didn't do much good with my associates.

Shaub even bit the hand that helped put him into office. He called PSP's president Nevin Cooley to meet with the commissioners to explain why the project's architectural designs had not been completed. Cooley told Shaub the LCCCA had not finalized an agreement with the city's Parking Authority. Shaub reacted with exasperation: "Nevin, I ask you, 'Are you going to draw drawings?'"[68]

When Cooley repeated that the LCCCA parking garage agreement had not been signed, Shaub said, "That is just an excuse. Folks, we have a very short time and very short lives. It's time for Penn Square Partners to fulfill their end of the bargain so we can have those schematic drawings done by September 7. We are behind as it is."[69]

Whether Shaub's histrionics had anything to do with it, in June 2004, the parking agreement between the city and the LCCCA was signed, and PSP authorized the schematic drawings for the hotel and convention center. It still took another five years to build the millstone that will remain around the neck of Lancaster County for years to come.

For all of Shaub's talk about "relationships and team building," he based his leadership on power, intimidation, and control. Like a petulant child, each time Pete entered a room, he carried with him an atmosphere of tension and strain. There was an ever-present anticipation of combat, with calamity to follow.

"Misery acquaints a man with strange bedfellows."
—William Shakespeare, *The Tempest*, 1610

Each day became harder and harder for me to face. I was exhausted. I felt like a character in *Dune* who has her "heart plug" pulled and drains away. If I felt like this now, after one year, how could I keep going? Could Shaub have worn me down this far? Then I got some good news: I had Lyme disease! That was treatable—Shaub was not.

The county government could not operate with Pete Shaub as chairman of the Board of Commissioners. Like a Category 5 hurricane, the strongest measured, Shaub had berated and blown through half of the county staff. The county depended on these people to run the departments, to get things done on behalf of the taxpayers. The situation could not continue.

In our board meetings it was obvious that commissioner Dick Shellenberger was as frustrated and concerned as I was with Shaub's behavior. At the beginning of each year the board of commissioners elect the chairman and vice chairman of the board. I decided to vote for a new chairman of the Board of Commissioners after the first of the year, January 2005. As long as he voted for himself, Shellenberger would be chairman. Shaub would lose his power.

The county department heads made a year-end presentation to the commissioners at the Shuts Environmental Center on December 17, 2004. After the presentation Shellenberger informed Shaub that Shellenberger intended to seek the chairmanship. Shaub immediately lost it. Pacing the room and wildly flailing his arms, Shaub screamed at Shellenberger with pure, raging anger. I feared Shaub might strike Shellenberger. He didn't but instead stormed out of the room. Dick and I had no idea what to expect next. I dreaded what might follow.

Hurricane Shaub–Category 5

> I will have such revenge on you both.
> —William Shakespeare, *King Lear*, 1605

Two days later, on Sunday, just before Christmas, Pete called me at home. He asked if he could come over to talk, and I said fine.

On that mild late December day, Shaub rode his bicycle to my house from his home in Millersville. The two of us sat in my living room, where the Christmas tree waited to be decorated. A fire was burning, and I steadied my nerves, uncertain what Pete would do. I felt glad my husband, Alex, and daughter, Leslie, were home at the time.

Pete Shaub, beside himself, then begged to remain chairman of the Board of Commissioners. Desperate, he promised I could be vice chairman if I would change my mind.

I listened, moved by the melodrama of it all. He truly grieved losing his power. He had worked his entire adult life to be in that position. But I would not change my mind. Impossible. Pete Shaub made my work as a Lancaster County commissioner hellish. I gave him no satisfaction.

Shaub stood up, rubbed his eyes, and gravely muttered, "I will destroy Shellenberger."

Pete Shaub would make good on his words.

Chapter Six

IT'S ALL ABOUT THE HOTEL–REALLY

"... The be-all and end-all ...
—William Shakespeare, *Macbeth,* 1605

"Everything the City Needs" was the original pitch to the public, through Lancaster Newspapers, for the convention center and hotel project in 1999.[1] The "public-private" partnership had a $75 million price tag. The combined project consisted of a $30 million tax-exempt "public," nonprofit convention center, and a $45 million "private," "luxury," "four-star" for-profit hotel. The hotel would pay real estate taxes. Public and private sponsors promised the project would create "hundreds" of jobs, "revitalize" the downtown, and put a smile on every child's face.

Dick Shellenberger replaced Pete Shaub as chairman in January 2005. By that time, the hotel room tax had collected $3 million a year for four years.[2] The Lancaster County Convention Center Authority (LCCCA) had borrowed tens of millions of dollars, guaranteed by the county, and it sat in a bank *losing* money.[3] The LCCCA had spent millions on lawyers and consultants, including companies connected to private partner Dale High.[4] And still, not a spade of dirt had been turned.

Looking for Funds

After blowing through the initial $15 million from the 1999 stadium bill leftovers, the project looked for more money.

In spring 2003, Penn Square Partners (PSP) tried to get tax credits for the Watt & Shand building, based on the site's historic value. However, the Pennsylvania Historical and Museum Commission determined that PSP's plans for the building, a Marriott Hotel, would likely not be eligible for $4 million in tax credits. In a letter to the High Real Estate Group, the commission wrote:

> . . . the proposed project is receiving a substantial amount of public money . . . [and that the plans were] grossly out of scale and character with the historic building, [the state museum commission indicates the project will not be recommended for the tax credits:] Given the extent of development and demolition, it is our opinion that this project as proposed does not meet the Secretary of the Interior's Standards for Rehabilitation & Guidelines for Rehabilitating Historic Buildings and therefore will adversely affect the Lancaster Historic District. In addition, due to the extent of development and demolition, it is our opinion that the National Park Service would not approve the project for federal tax credits. . . . The project will also result in substantial change in character to the Watt & Shand building.[5]

"Eight wild boars roasted whole at a breakfast
and but twelve persons there. Is this true?"
　　　—William Shakespeare, *Antony and Cleopatra*, 1607

In February 2004, PSP announced that the project needed an additional $18.6 million. Nevin Cooley, High's lead man to PSP, said that the partners would turn to the state for funding.[6] By this time, without explanation, the project had quadrupled in size and almost doubled in cost.

By early 2005, the project no longer cost $75 million but $137 million, and I was alarmed at the increase in the "public" portion of the cost. Since 2003, the County of Lancaster had guaranteed half of a $40 million bond issue, exposing county taxpayers to more than $60 million in liability.[7] As a county commissioner, I now followed the project very closely.

> "The game is afoot."
> —William Shakespeare, *King Henry IV, Part I*, 1597

By mid-September of 2004, my growing concern about the project increased my scrutiny. Too much public money had moved, and moved quickly, around this scheme. As commissioner, I had to look after the county's funds. It was my fiscal responsibility—my duty. I went to Clarence Kegel, an attorney with an excellent reputation in contract and business law. Kegel's firm had done work for the county during the construction of the Clipper Magazine baseball stadium. Clutching the convention center's contract files close to my body, I walked in the rain between tight brick buildings from the courthouse to Kegel's office. I delivered the documents to Kegel, who regarded me with the most piercing eyes I have ever encountered. He asked to have a week to review them.

I returned a week later for Kegel's report: "This is either the sloppiest piece of legal work I have ever seen, or something is afoot."

In January 2005, the Brookings Institute published, "Space Available—The Realities of Convention Centers as Economic Development Strategy," by Dr. Heywood Sanders. The Brookings study painted a bleak picture of publicly owned convention centers. The report showed that despite considerable taxpayer investment, these convention centers almost never generated the promised economic development. From the Brookings article:

> The overall convention marketplace is declining in a manner that suggests that a recovery or turnaround is unlikely to yield much increased business for any given community, contrary to repeated industry projections. . . . Nonetheless, localities, sometimes with state assistance, have continued a type of arms race with competing cities to host these events, investing massive

amounts of capital in new convention center construction and expansion of existing facilities.[8]

On March 3, 2005, Dr. Sanders came to Lancaster and gave a presentation to a packed auditorium on the status of convention centers. I attended Dr. Sanders's presentation, where he said,

> I get real numbers and try to assess what happens . . . there is a lot of risk: risk of the local market; risk of the national economy; risk of competition . . . there are fewer large events, fewer attending, a decrease in conventions, people are using the Internet to do their own booking and there is fear in our post 9/11 environment.[9]

Also speaking that evening was Thomas Hazinski, a consultant with HVS International. HVS had been hired by PSP in 2004 to conduct a market study of the project. "Will it make money?" Hazinski asked. He answered, "As a hotel, yes, but not as a convention center."[10]

Despite the grim outlook, taxpayer money kept flowing to project sponsors. In 2003 alone, the LCCCA paid High and Stevens & Lee $2.3 million.[11] The entire hotel room tax revenue coming to the authority that year amounted to about $3 million. The hotel developer (High) and the author of the law that created the room tax (Stevens & Lee) were paid about 75 percent of the hotel tax revenue that came to the LCCCA.

Now, at the end of 2004, PSP clamored for more. The partners wanted to change their financial relationship with the City of Lancaster. PSP asked to be exempt from paying property taxes on their "luxury," "upscale," "four-star" for-profit hotel. And they also requested tens of millions of dollars from the taxpayers of Pennsylvania to build it.

Armstrong Law Change No. 2

On April 1, 2004, the Pennsylvania legislature quietly made an amendment to the Infrastructure and Facilities Improvement Program (IFIP). The amendment—P.L. 200, No. 23, 2004, called "Act 23"—added chapter 34 to the IFIP law of 1990.[12] The 2004 Act 23 amendment was sponsored by Republican friends-of-the-project state senator "Gib" Armstrong and state senator "Chip" Brightbill. (Senator Brightbill joined the Stevens & Lee law firm after leaving the Senate.)[13]

As he did in 1999, when he made a small but consequential change to the 1994 Third-Class County Convention Center Authority Act, Senator Armstrong similarly amended the IFIP legislation. This time, Armstrong added language to the IFIP, naming publicly owned "hotel establishments" and "convention centers" to be eligible "project users" for state grants under IFIP funding.[14] It would not be the last time Armstrong changed legislation to benefit the project.

On December 17, 2004, in a front-page story in the *Intelligencer Journal*, "City Takes Key Role in Hotel and Convention Center Project: Partnership Wants to Sell Hotel to Agency," the newspaper reported a new financial plan proposed by Penn Square Partners.[15]

The article described PSP's proposal to sell the Watt & Shand property to the city's Redevelopment Authority of the City of Lancaster (RACL). With RACL ownership, the partners, through RACL, would apply to the state for a total of $36 million in construction loans for the hotel.

According to the plan, PSP would make "lease payments" to RACL for the use of the hotel for twenty years. The lease payments would be applied to the debt service of two state bonds totaling $36 million:

- The $12 million Act 23 bond;
- And $24 million in "lease revenue bonds."

Bonds are essentially low-interest loans issued by a governmental entity such as RACL. After twenty years, Penn Square Partners, RACL, and the LCCCA would have joint ownership of the hotel, according to the plan.

The *Intell* article addressed the issue of tax immunity and broke down the complicated details of the financing plan for the hotel:

> As part of the proposal, which must be approved by City Council, the hotel would become tax exempt, but Penn Square Partners would continue to pay the equivalent of taxes to the city and the School District of Lancaster during construction.

After construction, the city and school district would receive payments in lieu of taxes and a share in the hotel profits. . . . Each of the city's debt payments toward its $36 million in bonds would be covered by Penn Square Partners hotel lease payments. . . . [S]ince the hotel would become tax exempt because it would be owned by the city, the partnership has agreed to pay the city $100,000 a year for 20 years. Penn Square Partners also has agreed to pay the School District of Lancaster $100,000 a year for 20 years. . . . If the hotel reaches a 12 percent profit margin, Penn Square Partners would give the city 10 percent and the school district 20 percent of the profits. The partnership projects annual payments to both entities could total more than $200,000. . . . Cooley said Penn Square Partners would "protect" the Redevelopment Authority from any litigation related to the hotel. . . .

Project developers said that because the city stands to benefit from new jobs and business development related to the convention center and hotel, making the city a partner is a natural.

We think this is a capitalization project that benefits everybody and spurs economic development," Cooley said. "This project is all about opportunity, and it's right now at the doorstep.

Lancaster mayor Charlie Smithgall said he was convinced the deal between Penn Square Partners and the city would work. "Success is our only option," he said. "Get the shovels in the ground, and get this thing going immediately."[16]

There are two fundamental reasons Penn Square Partners wanted RACL to take title to the hotel:

1. With RACL "ownership," the project would be eligible for Act 23 funding. PSP, a private corporation, did not qualify for the state grants. RACL, a public agency of the city, did qualify for the subsidies; and

2. PSP wanted to transfer title ownership to RACL to avoid paying real estate taxes on its for-profit hotel by sharing RACL's tax immunity. By shifting title ownership of the building to a public entity, PSP would exempt itself from paying property taxes on the hotel it would operate on a for-profit basis.

The Role of a Redevelopment Authority

The Redevelopment Authority of the City of Lancaster (RACL) was created in 1957 as part of Pennsylvania's Urban Redevelopment Law of 1945, P.L. 991, § 1. The Urban Redevelopment Law is an "Act to promote elimination of blighted areas and supply sanitary housing in areas throughout the Commonwealth. . . ."[17]

The Urban Redevelopment Law creates "Redevelopment Authorities, which shall exist and operate for the public purposes of the elimination of blighted areas through economically and socially sound redevelopment of such areas, as provided by this act."[18]

The Urban Redevelopment Law conferred significant power to the redevelopment authorities, two of which—one county, one municipal—could be established in each county within the Commonwealth. Redevelopment authorities were empowered to borrow money, issue bonds, issue credit, purchase, lease, and sell real estate, among other powers, including eminent domain rights.[19]

Although the statutory authority of RACL has a broad reach, a redevelopment authority only has power to act for a "public purpose." The financing plan PSP put forth in December 2004—transferring title ownership to RACL, in order to qualify for state funds and exempt themselves from paying real estate taxes—seemed designed to serve a "private," rather than a "public," purpose.

The Pennsylvania Supreme Court has stated that once a redevelopment authority rehabilitates a blighted property, it has achieved the public purpose of redevelopment. The redevelopment authority should then have the property "re-transferred to private ownership."[20]

"Who lets so fair a house fall to decay . . ."
—William Shakespeare, *Sonnet 13*, circa 1600

The term *blight*, according to the Urban Redevelopment Law, is a zoning designation, characterized as "urban obsolescence beyond salvage by private rehabilitation" (35 P.S. § 1702). A city or county planning commission certifies whether a building or a district is blighted.

Not only was the Watt & Shand building structurally sound, it stood in Lancaster's central, far from "blighted," business district. Similar to the Kleiss Saloon and the home of former congressman Thaddeus Stevens, it also had historical significance.[21]

As for the building being past the point of "private rehabilitation," Greist Building owner and businessman Rob Ecklin had offered the same $1.25 million to buy the building as Penn Square Partners.[22]

The Project Was Really in Trouble by 2005

In the first months of 2005, Nevin Cooley, High executive and president of PSP, set aside the December 2004 financing plans for the hotel. He went looking for support of a different financing proposal for his partnership's "private" hotel.[23]

Cooley still desired to avoid real estate taxes on the hotel the partners intended to build and run for profit. Pursuant to the IFIP Act and Armstrong's Act 23 amendment, Cooley sought approval of another "project plan" between PSP and RACL. It was called a "TIF" plan.

Many Miffed by the TIF

Tax Increment Financing (TIF) is a state-administered financing mechanism designed to encourage real estate development in blighted areas. Launched in 1990 as part of the IFIP law and run by the Pennsylvania Department of Community and Economic Development (DCED), the program provides grants to certain issuers of debt, such as a redevelopment authority, in order to assist with payment of debt service.[24] State grants ranged from $200,000 a year for ten years to $1 million per year for twenty years.

TIF financing establishes a way for a private developer to avoid paying real estate taxes.[25] A public body such as RACL takes title to the property and applies for TIF funds and issues bonds. The bond proceeds are used for construction of the project. The project developer, instead of paying property taxes, has them abated by local taxing bodies, due to the taxing bodies' tax-exempt status, and diverts those tax payments to service the debt on the state bond. When the bond is paid, the tax revenue is diverted back to the taxing bodies.

It's All About the Hotel—Really

So, to summarize the plan at this time:
- PSP transfers the title to the Watt & Shand building to RACL.
- RACL applies for TIF funds of $12 million in Act 23 bonds.
- RACL, being a public body, does not pay property taxes.
- PSP pays debt service on Act 23 bonds.
- PSP makes payments to the city and school district "in lieu" of taxes.
- If the Marriott Hotel profits exceed 12 percent, additional payments to the city and school district will be made.
- None of the local taxing bodies—the school district, the city, or the county—receives property taxes.
- When the debt is paid, tax money will go back to the taxing bodies.[26]

There's More to It

A TIF plan must receive approval by local taxing authorities because they give up their tax revenue on the proposed project. The loss of tax money continues until the debt service on the construction bonds is paid off in twenty years. In the case of the Lancaster hotel project, the local taxing authorities consisted of:
1. The School District of Lancaster (School Board), 65.25 percent of tax revenue;
2. Lancaster City (City Council), 25.08 percent of tax revenue; and
3. Lancaster County (Board of Commissioners), 9.69 percent of tax revenue.[27]

The TIF plan proposed by PSP had the effect of eliminating real estate taxes on the hotel. The taxing authorities approving the partners' TIF plan—the school district, the city, and the county—would receive only the amount of real estate taxes based on the assessed value of the property *before* construction. All additional real estate taxes resulting from an increased assessment on the completed hotel would be applied to fund debt service on bonds used to finance construction of the hotel. Only after completion of debt service on the state bond—twenty years—would the hotel pay full real estate taxes to the school district, the city, and the county. During that entire twenty-year period of time, Penn Square Partners would run the hotel for profit, not pay real estate taxes, and have the option to purchase the hotel building from RACL for $2.25 million, a small fraction of the value of the $60-plus million hotel.[28]

The TIF and the School District of Lancaster, a.k.a. "The Red Tornado"

"Forced to retire by fury of the wind."
—William Shakespeare, *Henry VI*, Part III, 1591

The School District of Lancaster, an urban, grossly underfunded system, would receive the largest percentage of property tax revenue from the hotel. As a top priority, PSP knew it had to convince this governmental body to adopt its proposal.

Penn Square Partners president Nevin Cooley lobbied the nine School District of Lancaster board members intensely. He met individually with each member.[29] Cooley's TIF proposal asked the School District of Lancaster to redirect 90 percent of the real estate tax revenue it was to receive from the hotel to pay down hotel mortgage bonds. The school district would waive that tax revenue for twenty years, and when the bond was paid off, the district would receive the full real estate tax payments due to it. The partners also promised the district cash payments of $100,000 per year and a portion of the Marriott Hotel's profits if these exceeded 12 percent.

Mike Winterstein, a Republican former school board member, recalled Nevin Cooley's lobbying. After leaving the school board, Winterstein said,

> I remember Cooley coming to talk with me about the TIF. After he gave his pitch, I told him the schools needed money, and that I believed economic growth would only come with *taxable* economic growth. I wanted the hotel, which was privately-owned, after all, to be entirely taxed as a private business. We saw the tax revenue as the cornerstone of economic development. We on the School Board simply weren't buying what Penn Square Partners was selling.[30]

It's All About the Hotel—Really

The pressure PSP brought to bear on the school board members was featured in a February 16, 2005, *Intelligencer Journal* article, "A Crossroads for Convention Center." Described by the *Intell* as an "innovative tax-based financing plan," Mark Fitzgerald, of High's real estate group, made the TIF sound like the only financing option for the partners' hotel. He said,

> If the school board would reject the financing plan, it would deliver a serious blow to the project. That [a rejection by the school board] would put a delay on this project that I don't know if it will recover from. . . . The state has said in order to be considered for the $12 million on this project, we must have all our agreements at the local level in place to be able to demonstrate to the state that this project is moving forward.[31]

The school board members bristled at Penn Square Partners' hard sell.

"They thought this was going to be easy for them," said board member Veronica Urdaneta, of the partners' plan in the February 16 *Intell* article. "But they need to prove to the citizens of this city that what they are proposing is actually worthwhile for the city and the district."[32]

The TIF and the County

"Have you, I say, an answer of such fitness for all questions?"
—William Shakespeare, *All's Well That Ends Well*, 1604

The county considered the tax status of the Marriott Hotel a very important issue. The county's $40 million guaranty with the LCCCA (and the associated risk to county taxpayers of more than $60 million) depended on the Marriott Hotel being constructed at Penn Square. The county could not impose its guaranty on taxpayers if the project wasn't built at the Watt & Shand site on Penn Square.[33] The county had a direct and compelling interest in the taxability of the hotel.

Although the county would receive the smallest percentage of property tax revenue from the TIF proposal, our board was

Howard Kelin – Attorney, Kegel, Kelin, Alm and Grimm; Special Counsel to Lancaster County Commissioners

required to vote on the plan if the Lancaster school board passed it. So, we looked at it very closely.

To give us an understanding of how the TIF proposal affected the county, our board hired special legal counsel Howard Kelin, of the Lancaster law firm of Kegel, Kelin, Almy & Grimm.[34] Shellenberger and I each talked with Kelin about our respective concerns. Kelin drafted "Questions and Topics for PSP, LCCCA, and RACL." What came to be known as the "57 Questions" consisted of questions about the TIF proposal and other project issues. Commissioner Shaub did not provide questions.

"I think we have a right to ask for this information, because it's public money," Shellenberger observed after the county issued the 57 Questions.[35] (See Appendix B.)

Regarding convention center financing, we noted in one of our questions that the partners' TIF plan identified $40 million from the 2003 county-guaranteed bond. But the closing statement from the bond sale indicated that only $31.7 million had been placed into a construction account. Where was the other $8.3 million?[36]

We inquired why such an important document concerning the TIF would be delivered to the school board, the city, and the county so late in the process?[37] An "economic feasibility study" that PSP had commissioned would be provided to those taxing bodies on March 11, 2005. This allowed people only one business day to read it before the school district vote on the TIF.

What Penn Square Partners—High Industries, Lancaster Newspapers, and Fulton Bank—attempted to do in early 2005 was to change the financial terms of their investment in their "private" hotel. Now, instead of a "public-private" project, as sold to the public, PSP wanted to turn it into an essentially "public-public" project. As originally planned, the public would have paid for 100 percent of the convention center, but now the public would also pay for more than 80 percent of the "private" hotel.

In 1996, former Lancaster mayor and future LCCCA chairman Art Morris had opposed the Harrisburg Area Community College buying the Watt & Shand building, saying, "I have a number of concerns, but a significant one is the tax base of this city."[38]

The county had the same concern. Yet Morris now supported the TIF, saying nothing of the "tax base of this city" when it came to Penn Square Partners' hotel.

On Friday, March 11, 2005, the "57 Questions" were hand-delivered to the offices of the LCCCA, Penn Square Partners, and RACL. We indicated that the responses should be in writing and would be made public.

"Beware the Ides of March."
—William Shakespeare, *Julius Caesar*, 1605

The school board vote on the Penn Square Partners' TIF proposal was scheduled for Tuesday, March 15, 2005. Despite being a complex piece of municipal finance, the TIF issue became big news in Lancaster County. All three Lancaster Newspapers covered the topic extensively leading up to the school board vote.[39]

Public opinion was strongly opposed to the project and the Partners' TIF plan. The *Intelligencer Journal* published the results of one of its "People Polls" a few days before the school board vote in March, and 93% of respondents were against the TIF.[40] Also in 2005, Fox43-TV reported the results of a poll conducted by Opinion Dynamics Corporation, a leading, Massachusetts-based consultant, specializing in social and behavioral health and market research. The Opinion Dynamics poll surveyed 500 Lancaster County residents on the issue of the hotel and convention project. Sixty-eight percent opposed the county's bond guarantee of the project, the position held by Shellenberger and me.[41]

Interestingly, about three weeks prior to the vote, on February 21, in the middle of the TIF public debate, the *Lancaster New Era* ran a couple-thousand-word profile, "Taking the High Road," about the High family legacy in Lancaster. With Dale High having such a sensitive issue up for a public vote, I thought the timing of the piece—published by Penn Square partner Lancaster Newspapers—was questionable. It seemed designed to make High more sympathetic prior to the pending TIF vote.[42]

As if negotiating a basketball contract, as the vote neared, PSP upped the offer to the school board from $100,000 a year in lieu of taxes to $150,000.[43]

Five days ahead of the school board vote, the board held a special public meeting at the Edward Hand Middle School in Lancaster. At least two hundred people, myself included, filled the Hand auditorium that evening for the three-hour meeting. The format of the meeting called for PSP to present its TIF plan to the board, and then the board would hear comments, but not answer questions, from the audience. First to speak was Dale High.

High began stiffly. "Like Thaddeus Stevens, whose former home sits on the site of this project," he said, "I have a passion for public education."[44]

High spoke for fifteen minutes, but he spent less than two on the TIF proposal. The rest of the time, he focused on recounting the money that he and his partners, the Steinmans and Fulton Bank, had given to the school board over the years. High then turned the microphone over to Nevin Cooley, the president of Penn Square Partners.

Cooley spoke more technically about the TIF proposal, saying the project would bring, in addition to the promised (if deferred) tax revenues, "two to three hundred permanent jobs, and bring almost $10 million into the local economy." He also said something that struck me as odd. Cooley said, "We were asked by our community to develop the full-service luxury hotel this project and community so desperately needs."[45]

I have lived in the Lancaster "community" virtually my entire life, knocked on thousands of doors, and spoken with thousands of people, and I never heard anyone talk about a "desperate need" for a "full-service luxury hotel" in downtown Lancaster. The only people

It's All About the Hotel—Really

who seemed to desperately want the project were those who stood to make money from it.

David Hixson, the LCCCA executive director, spoke in support for the TIF plan, saying, "It is the best plan for the school district." Like Cooley, Hixson spoke of the "hundreds" of jobs and the $10 million cash injection into the Lancaster economy from the hotel.[46]

After Hixson came a line of project supporters, including:
- Jack Howell, director of the Lancaster Alliance, the organization co-founded by High, Buckwalter, and Fulton;
- Tom Baldridge of the Lancaster Campaign, a subsidiary of the Lancaster Alliance;
- Mayor Charlie Smithgall;
- Charles Simms, a Smithgall-appointed RACL chairman; and
- Ted Darcus, the new LCCCA board chairman.

Longtime project supporter Representative Mike Sturla, angry and impatient, harangued the school board members, reminding them that he was a former Lancaster city councilman who had to make tough decisions. Sturla said that if the school board voted down the TIF proposal, there would be no future help from Harrisburg for Lancaster. Sturla closed by harrumphing that the board should just pass the TIF and get on with it.

I remember that at some point during this period, I questioned Sturla directly about the TIF issue. I called him on my cell phone, while sitting in my car in front of the jail after a Prison Board meeting. I told Mike that the project just didn't make sense financially.

"It would be better if it never opened its doors," Sturla said. "These things never make money. But it will do other things for the city."

Most people in the Hand auditorium opposed the TIF proposal, and a line of opponents queued up to speak:
- Peter Chiccarine, an executive with the Eden Resort and a plaintiff in the litigation against the LCCCA, pointed out that the room-night projections by PSP did not apply to the Lancaster market.[47]
- Randolph Carney, who would later sit on the school board, spoke about the bond risk to city taxpayers and the cost to the schools.

- R. B. Campbell, the Republican city controller and a real estate investor, pointed out that under the partners' proposal, the hotel would be tax-free for years and then be sold back to the partners for a small fraction of its market value.[48]

"A hit, a very palpable hit."
         —William Shakespeare, *Hamlet*, 1600

Five days later, on March 15, the School Board of Lancaster voted 7 to 1 against the Penn Square Partners' TIF proposal.[49]

"We are very disappointed. Over the past seven years, we have made our best efforts to bring the Watt & Shand building back to life," said Penn Square partner and Lancaster Newspapers' chairman Jack Buckwalter to the *Lancaster New Era* in the March 17 edition. "It appears that we cannot proceed under the conditions as set by the school board. So, the project very well at this juncture could die."[50]

On March 17, the *Intelligencer Journal* published a statement by Dale High.

> Since you will read and hear speculation about Penn Square Partners' position and potential actions, I want to give you the courtesy of knowing the facts:
>
> We have given the School District of Lancaster our best and final offer, which was based on feedback we received from the School District board last week. We believe our offer addressed their concerns and was a fair compromise to the proposal they presented us. We cannot negotiate further the terms of our offer.
>
> We have an obligation to our shareholders and the hundreds of families we employ throughout our region to operate profitable businesses. Despite our considerable charitable contributions to our community, we are not a charity and we cannot solve all the School District's financial problems with this project.
>
> We have stopped all work on our portion of this project, effective this morning.

We do not know and will not speculate on the actions that the Lancaster County Convention Center Authority will take as the result of last night's decision by the School District's board.

We have not made any decision about alternative uses of the property we own on Penn Square. Rumors, speculation and "informed opinion" to the contrary are inaccurate.

As you know, our state government representatives have made it clear that the School Board's action will result in the loss of more than $46 million dollars that the Commonwealth has invested or has promised to invest in downtown Lancaster. Our representatives have made it equally clear that these funds will not be put "on hold" or returned to our community at some later date. They are lost. As citizens of our community, we are deeply saddened that the project in which our community has invested years, millions of dollars and many of its hopes has been dealt this blow.

Rufus Fulton, Jack Buckwalter and I are grateful for the support of the community including business, political and civic leaders and the many individual citizens who have offered their support. We always will remember your encouragement and willingness to support this project publicly.

—S. Dale High[51]

"Peace, fool! Thy master and his man are here,
And that is false those dost report to us."
—William Shakespeare, *A Comedy of Errors*, 1589

High did "stop work" on the project and instructed his workers to remove "High Construction" signs from the fencing around the Watt & Shand building.

"We made it clear that this is our best offer," said Cooley, after the school board vote. "There is nothing more that we can do. If I could have offered something different, I would have. We can't go forward, and the community and the taxing authority will continue to have a building that is empty and deteriorating and not generating anything in new taxes."[52]

Nevin Cooley may have said, "We have no 'Plan B,'" after Penn Square Partners' TIF defeat, but that wasn't true. PSP had a plan already in place—an even more lucrative deal for the partners than the TIF.

> "As from your graves rise up, and walk like sprites."
> —William Shakespeare, *Macbeth*, 1605

The day after Easter and less than two weeks after taking down signs and pronouncing the project "dead," it was miraculously resurrected. In "Hotel Plan Rescued," the *Lancaster New Era* reported excitedly:

Skip the school board.
 Forget the county commissioners' 57 questions.
 The Lancaster City Redevelopment Authority this morning unveiled a new way to finance—and keep alive—a proposed 300-room convention center hotel on Penn Square. . . . [53]

What the sponsors described as "a new way to finance" the hotel comprised a variation of two proposals that had been floated back in December 2004.[54]

Two major differences existed between PSP's two December 2004 proposals and the one in March 2005.[55] The first difference concerned the ownership of the hotel after the twenty-year bond debt service was retired. In one of the December proposals, Penn Square Partners would sell the Watt & Shand property to RACL, which would lease the hotel to the partners for twenty years. The partners' lease payments would be used to pay the debt service on hotel construction bonds. After twenty years, when the bond debt was retired, RACL would transfer title to Penn Square Partners with no final payment. In the other December proposal, after the twenty-year debt service term had expired, Penn Square Partners, RACL, and the LCCCA would share joint ownership of the hotel.[56]

The following table explains the differences in the three plans for RACL to purchase the Watt & Shand building from Penn Square Partners (PSP):

It's All About the Hotel–Really

December 2004 Plan I	December 2004 Plan II	March 2005 Plan III
PSP sells building to RACL	PSP sells building to RACL	PSP sells building to RACL
RACL applies for $36 million in Pa. state funding	RACL applies for $36 million in Pa. state funding	RACL applies for $36 million in Pa. state funding
PSP guarantees $36 million bonds	PSP guarantees $36 million bonds	City of Lancaster guarantees $36 million bonds
After bonds are paid, hotel transferred to PSP, with no final payment	After bonds are paid, hotel co-owned by RACL, PSP, LCCCA	After bonds are paid, PSP has "purchase option" to buy hotel for $2.25 million

The March 2005 plan called for PSP to sell the Watt & Shand property to RACL for $6.8 million. (The partners had paid $1.25 million in February 1998). The plan then called for RACL to lease the hotel back to the partners, using the lease payments to pay debt service on a $24 million hotel construction bond. After twenty years, Penn Square Partners would have the exclusive purchase option on the hotel for the fee of $2.25 million. The hotel, estimated by the partners to cost $60,300,000, and with an assessment of $28.3 million, would be exempted from paying real estate taxes for the twenty-year period of the bond debt.[57]

The City Holds the Bag Now, Too

"... Too little payment for so great a debt."
—William Shakespeare, *The Taming of the Shrew*, 1593

In the "new" March 2005 financing plan, the City of Lancaster—not PSP—would guarantee the $36 million in hotel construction bonds. The March 2005 PSP proposal now foisted onto the City of Lancaster the risk of any real estate taxes applicable to the Marriott Hotel, with the city also guaranteeing all of RACL's debt payment obligations.[58]

In the new hotel-financing plan, after RACL took ownership of the property, the agency would apply for a $12 million bond under Act 23 through the state's Department of Community and Economic Development (DCED). Based on projections that the hotel would generate at least $1 million a year in state sales, occupancy, and income taxes, the state would rebate the money in the form of grants. After three years, the DCED would review the grant program. If the hotel's sales, occupancy, and income taxes did not cover the debt service, the Act 23 grant allocation could be reduced. The General Assembly could reduce funding, which could also lessen the grant amount funneled to the Marriott Hotel. If PSP did not meet these debt service requirements, the City of Lancaster, as the guarantor, would have to make the $12 million debt payment under this proposal.[59]

Next, according to the March 2005 plan, RACL would issue $24 million in construction bonds (that is, take out loans) from private banks. The debt payments for these bonds were to be covered by "lease" payments from Penn Square Partners to RACL. These lease payments were not real estate tax payments. They would strictly be used for debt service.[60] This plan expressly stipulated that if the partners' "private" hotel (taxable, at this point) was not granted tax immunity, the City of Lancaster, through a guaranty, would be responsible for paying real estate taxes on the hotel.[61]

RACL's $24 million in "Lease Revenue" bonds" and the $12 million Act 23 funds would be used to fund construction costs for the private Marriott Hotel, run for profit by Penn Square Partners. PSP had invested only $10 million of its own money into the hotel. After the Lease Revenue bonds were paid off in twenty years, according to a "Lease-Purchase Agreement" between RACL and Penn Square Partners, RACL would transfer title of the now seventeen-story hotel to the partners at a cost of $2.25 million (two million, two hundred fifty thousand dollars). All $36 million of the borrowed money would be guaranteed by the taxpayers of the City of Lancaster, not by Penn Square Partners.[62]

Clipper Stadium

"We have had pastimes here and pleasant game, . . ."
—William Shakespeare, *Love's Labour's Lost*, 1594

Contrast the PSP/RACL $24 million hotel lease-purchase proposal—a plan that ends with a nominal fee buyout by the tenant after twenty years—with the publicly financed Clipper Magazine Stadium, opening in 2005.[63] The Redevelopment Authority of the *County* of Lancaster, along with our board's help, working in partnership with the city and private sponsors, built the beautiful 6,000-seat Clipper Magazine baseball stadium on the site of a former rail yard, in a formerly downtrodden part of northwest Lancaster city.[64]

The naming rights to Clipper Magazine Stadium were sold to a local coupon magazine company for $2.5 million for ten years (since renewed). The Lancaster Barnstormers, a minor league baseball team from the independent Atlantic League, have been Clipper Magazine Stadium's primary tenant. The Barnstormers have leased the stadium for twenty years but do not have the option to purchase the stadium after the expiration of the lease. The county retains the facility and the equity built up during the twenty years. The county's Redevelopment Authority also reserved rights to use the stadium facility for other community activities.[63] This is in keeping with the mandate of the "public purpose" requirement of redevelopment authorities, pursuant to the Urban Redevelopment Law establishing redevelopment authorities.[65]

Act 23, Real Estate Taxes and Lancaster City

After learning of the new Penn Square Partners hotel-financing plan, the county requested the law firm of Kegel, Kelin, Almy & Grimm provide the county with a legal opinion regarding the taxability of Penn Square Partners' Marriott Hotel.

In April 2005, Howard Kelin concluded that the Marriott Hotel should be subject to real estate taxes and explained the very large, and very real, risk to city taxpayers. If the hotel was exempted from paying real estate taxes, according to Kelin, "city taxpayers stand to lose $14 million" that would be due on the hotel. And that number could have been much higher.[66]

Kelin's legal opinion also pointed out that the project clearly violated Act 23, which required that PSP, as the "project user," sign a contract agreeing "to timely pay all Commonwealth and local taxes and fees."[67] Kelin's analysis suggested that the proposed $36 million city guaranties were illegal.

Four weeks after the school board rejected the TIF proposal (and four weeks after PSP pronounced the project "dead"), Penn Square Partners and RACL rushed their new plan to the Lancaster City Council.

The seven-member Lancaster City Council was scheduled to vote on two ordinances pertaining to the hotel portion of the project—Ordinance Nos. 5 and 10 on April 12. The previous month, on the same day as the Edward Hand TIF public meeting, the council passed Ordinance No. 15, authorizing RACL to take part in the project.[68]

The City's Ordinances

Ordinance No. 5
Ordinance No. 5 was the $12 million Act 23 bond and city guaranty of Penn Square Partners' March 2005 plan.

Ordinance No. 5 provided that the City of Lancaster intended "to incur lease rental debt in the maximum aggregate principal of $12,000,000; to be evidenced by a Guaranty Agreement with respect to a series of bonds to be authorized and issued by the Redevelopment Authority of the City of Lancaster in connection with a redevelopment project in this city."

Ordinance No. 10
Ordinance 10 was the city's guaranty of the $24 million in "lease-revenue" hotel construction bonds. It would appear that the project sponsors were concerned that Kelin's legal opinion about the real estate taxes liability was correct as it is. It is written in Ordinance No. 10, the city's $24 million guaranty that the City of Lancaster explicitly agrees to exempt Penn Square Partners from ever paying property taxes. From page 3 of Ordinance No. 10, the second "Whereas":

"Whereas, The financial feasibility of the Hotel Project as a redevelopment project of the Authority is dependent, in part, on the immunity of the real property comprising the Hotel Project from assessment and payment of property taxes, . . ."[69]

As noted above, according to the "Hotel Tower Lease Agreement" between RACL and Penn Square Partners, after the $24 million lease revenue bonds of Ordinance No. 10 were paid off, Penn Square Partners would have the exclusive option to buy the hotel for $2.25 million (two million, two hundred fifty thousand dollars).[69]

The City Council Vote

The Lancaster City Council passed Ordinances No. 5 and No. 10 on April 12, 2005, both with 6–1 votes. Republican Luis Mendoza cast the dissenting vote. Mendoza complained that he hadn't been given sufficient time and information to review the complex agreements before voting on them.[70]

In the view of many, the potential loss vs. reward to the city did not come close to being worth the gamble. The three main dangers to Lancaster city in this project were: (1) city guaranty of bonds; (2) county guaranty (the city is part of the county); and (3) revenue lost to the school district. Similarly, those in Lancaster Township, as part of the School District of Lancaster and the county, would be exposed twice by the dangers of this project. I am at a loss to understand why the Lancaster City Council voted to put its residents at such risk.

The Controller Catch

"This is my treasurer: let him speak, my lord,
Upon his peril, that I have reserved
To myself nothing. Speak the truth, Seleucus."
—William Shakespeare, *Antony and Cleopatra*, 1606

After the City Council passed Ordinances Nos. 5 and 10, project supporters assumed the city would send the bond application documents, including the city's guaranties, to the Department of Community and Economic Development (DCED) in Harrisburg.

Then PSP could count on $36 million taxpayer dollars to help it build its property tax–free hotel.

Yet there was a slight glitch. Before the loan applications could be sent to the DCED, the Lancaster city controller was required to sign the documents. The controller, Robert B. "RB" Campbell Jr., refused to sign them.[71]

Campbell, a Republican, had read Kelin's legal opinion on the hotel's taxability and was concerned about the legality of the Act 23 application. Campbell, a real estate investor with an accounting degree, sent a letter to Mayor Smithgall, writing that he would not execute the documents until independent legal counsel advised him on the legality of the city's application. Campbell wrote:

> As Controller for the City of Lancaster, I have a fiduciary responsibility to residents of the City and have sworn under oath to uphold the law. Therefore, based on the aforementioned I strongly believe my signing the application may be a violation of both of these duties of my office.[72]

A furious Smithgall filed a lawsuit in the Lancaster County Court of Common Pleas the same day he received Controller Campbell's letter. He wanted to force Campbell to sign the DCED documents. A week later, Judge Paul Allison entered an order authorizing the mayor to sign the documents. In the DCED proceedings filed with the state, Mayor Smithgall signed the debt statement and the borrowing base certificate as attorney-in-fact for Campbell.

Enough Is Enough

"The terms of our estate may not endure
  Hazards so near us as doth hourly grow . . ."
    —William Shakespeare, *Hamlet*, 1600

On May 2, Commissioner Shellenberger issued a lengthy public statement enumerating dozens of significant problems with the project, including:

1. Increased taxpayer funding;

It's All About the Hotel–Really

2. The significant rise in the cost of the project;
3. The failed TIF;
4. The illegal $36 million city guaranties; and
5. The county's $40 million guaranty.

Chairman Shellenberger announced that he would request the Board of Commissioners to take action against the project.[73]

Two days later, our Commissioners Board officially withdrew support for the project and requested that the LCCCA, the RACL, and Penn Square Partners stop spending money on the project. We also asked the LCCCA to repay the county-backed $40 million construction loan.[74]

The county directed counsel to file a complaint with the DCED, seeking a ruling on the Act 23 requirement that the project user "timely pay all local taxes," as well as a ruling on the legality of the $36 million in city guaranties. The complaint, claiming numerous violations of the Pennsylvania Local Government Unit Debt Act, was submitted to the DCED on May 16, 2005.[75] The battle lines had been drawn.

Complex by Design

"This is a strange maze as e're men trod;
And there is in this business more than nature
Was ever conduct of . . ."
—William Shakespeare, *The Tempest*, 1611

That was the situation in early 2005. (See "The Map," page 158). I had been in office a little more than a year. I had weathered Year One of Hurricane Shaub. Now, with my vote, along with that of Commissioner Shellenberger, the county was officially working to stop the entire hotel and convention center project. By the spring of 2005, I stood on the opposite side of the powerful Lancaster establishment, including Dale High and Lancaster Newspapers.

I believed that the private "partners" (PSP) in the project had not negotiated fair deals with the public partners. The result was that the project was now primarily publicly funded and benefited the financial investments of the private Penn Square Partners: High, Lancaster Newspapers, and Fulton Bank. These were the richest, most powerful entities in Lancaster County, yet they had received unfair government assistance, massive public subsidies, and enormous tax breaks the average developer would never dream of getting, all so they could build, and profit from, a hotel.

Penn Square Partners devised this complex, financial design to take advantage of low interest rates from the city's credit rating and to avoid paying real estate taxes on its private hotel. PSP endlessly claimed that it had done this for "the community." In the scheme, the partners called on public officials to do their undertaking. Laws were changed. Tens of millions of dollars flowed through public authorities. In my opinion, each change in the plan increased the partners' profit and decreased the partners' risk. The partners devised the plan with one simple objective: to make money, a lot of money.

And we—two Lancaster County commissioners—stood in the way of that money. Shellenberger and I posed a clear and present danger to the project.

Despite the support of Penn Square partner Lancaster Newspapers and several key public officials, the larger Lancaster County community decidedly opposed the project in the spring of 2005. I don't recall a single supporter for the project when I traveled throughout the county, other than a small, select group of individuals. Many spoke of their opposition to the project. According to Jack Buckwalter's deposition, "Letters to the Editor" in the Lancaster Newspapers were 4 to 1 against the project at this time.

The letters evidently embarrassed the private sponsors, and Peggy Steinman herself stepped in to address it. In the spring of 2005, during the hotel-financing tumult, Ms. Steinman placed a call to Lancaster Newspapers chairman Jack Buckwalter and asked if something could be done to provide some balance to the anti–convention center sentiment appearing in her newspapers. "We need more positive letters to the editor," she told Jack.[76]

Jack did better than that.

Principals Involved with the Lancaster Hotel and Convention Center Project

SEE "THE MAP" – GRAPHIC CONSTRUCT OF THE HOTEL AND CONVENTION CENTER PROJECT OF LANCASTER COUNTY, 2006

Elected Officials
- Gibson Armstrong – PA State Senate, 13th District, 1984-2009; PA House of Representatives, 100th District, 1977-1984; Republican
- P. Michael Sturla – PA House of Representatives, 1991-current; Democrat
- Paul Thibault – Lancaster County Commissioner, 1996-2004; Republican
- Ronald Ford – Lancaster County Commissioner, 1996-2004; Democrat
- H. Pete Shaub – Lancaster County Commissioner, 2000-2006; Republican
- Richard Shellenberger – Lancaster County Commissioner, 2004-2008; Republican
- Molly Henderson – Lancaster County Commissioner, 2004-2008; Democrat
- J. Richard Gray – Mayor, Lancaster City, 2006-2018; Democrat
- Charles Smithgall – Mayor, Lancaster City, 1998-2006; Republican
- Lancaster City Council- seven members, Republicans/Democrats
- School District of Lancaster- Board of Directors, nine members, Democrats/Republicans

Penn Square Partners
- High Industries –2006, 44% ownership of hotel
- Lancaster Newspapers – 2006, 44% ownership of hotel
- Fulton Bank – leaves partnership in 2007 (12%)

Attorneys
- Stevens and Lee Attorneys at Law
    Solicitor for County of Lancaster- John Espenshade, resigns in 2006
    Solicitor for Lancaster County Convention Center Authority- John Espenshade
    Stevens and Lee wrote PA Convention Center Authority Act
    Stevens and Lee - High's Registered Lobbyist
- Kegel, Kelin, Almy and Grimm LLC., Attorneys at Law
    Howard Kelin, Solicitor for County of Lancaster during convention center proceedings.
- Other Attorneys
    Barley, Snyder & Associates
    Richard Sprague

Authority Boards
- Lancaster County Convention Center Authority Board– seven members, alternating number of appointments by the Lancaster County Commissioners and Mayor of Lancaster (City Council), Ted Darcus, chairman.
- Redevelopment Authority Board of the City of Lancaster – (RACL) five members appointed by the mayor of Lancaster (City Council), Charles Simms, chairman.
- Parking Authority of Lancaster City – five members appointed by the mayor of Lancaster (City Council).

Others
- PA Dutch Visitors Bureau - now Discover Lancaster!
- Lancaster County Hoteliers
- Historic Preservation Trust – Stevens/Smith House
- Art Morris – Former Lancaster City Mayor, 1080-1990, Republican; 2008,
    Chairman, Lancaster County Convention Center Authority;
    Columnist for Lancaster Newspapers.

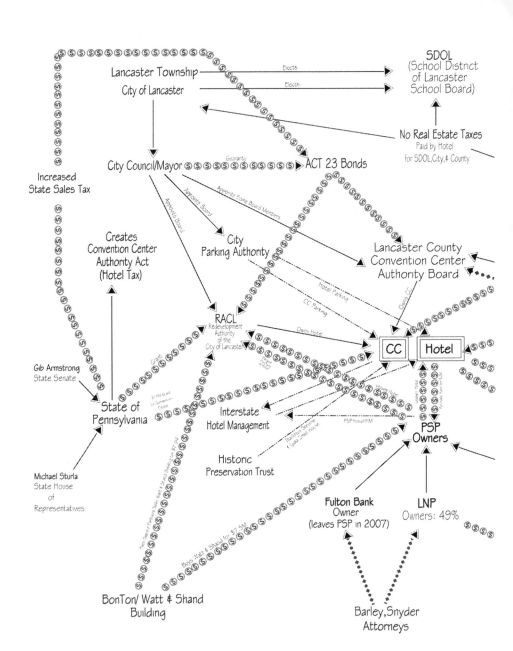

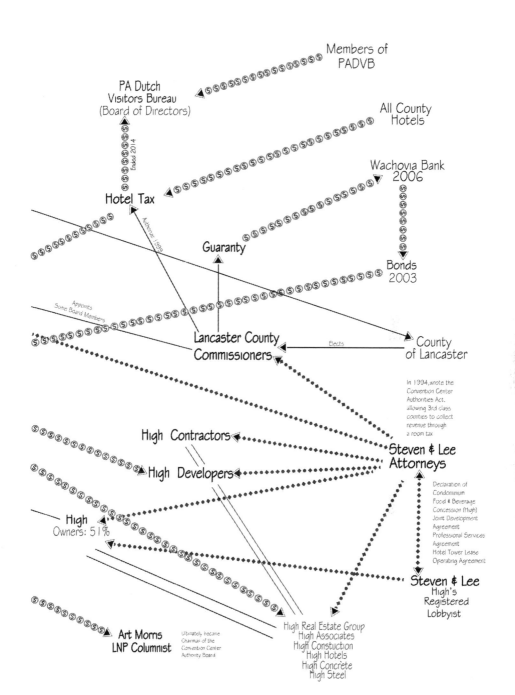

Chapter Seven

"MOLLY IS TOAST"

> "Go fetch me a quart of sack; put a toast in't."
> —William Shakespeare, *Merry Wives of Windsor*, 1600

The project proponents needed a plan to deal with Shellenberger and me. Lancaster Newspapers' chairman Jack Buckwalter took Peggy Steinman's suggestion seriously. Peggy was the boss, and the boss wanted to see more positive letters to the editor about the hotel and convention center project in her newspapers. Jack spoke with his editors.

Until that point, 2005, Lancaster Newspapers' role in the project had been as a cash investor and a publicist. For years, the broadsheets of the *Intell*, the *New Era*, and the *Sunday News* displayed uncritical articles and made glowing promises of jobs and a city transformed by "the convention center."

High ran the project on behalf of Penn Square Partners, and the person running it for High was Nevin Cooley. Rufus Fulton, the president of Fulton Bank and a board member of several High companies, appeared uncomfortable with the bank's minority investment. Fulton had considerably less involvement than High or the newspapers in the project and soon left the partnership entirely.[1]

The TIF debate ignited considerable public opposition to the project. Citizens lined up at meetings to speak against it, and they wrote those letters Peggy Steinman didn't like. By early 2005, Shellenberger and I found ourselves very much in the opposition camp. We represented the majority of the commissioners and now strongly confronted the project. Our concerns were substantive and many:

- PSP and Act 23, taking a "private hotel" off the tax rolls;
- 2003 County Bond Guaranty—the project had changed substantially in just two years;
- The bond proceeds were losing money through negative arbitrage;
- The debt service (paying off the debt) was not prioritized over expenses for convention center operations, making taxpayers responsible for any shortfall;
- No feasibility study had ever been done on the project (only two market studies);
- Poor treatment of the Thaddeus Stevens/Lydia Smith historic property;[2]
- Unfulfilled promises were made concerning women and minority contracts; and
- The promised "luxury" hotel had now transformed into a sub-sized Marriott.[3]

"And with mine eyes I'll drink the words you send,
Though the ink be made of gall."
—William Shakespeare, *Cymbeline*, 1609

Jack Buckwalter and PSP were right to consider Dick Shellenberger and me a serious threat to the project. Based on the growing mountain of evidence, we believed the project was a terrible idea. Furthermore, we intended to look out for the taxpayers' interests and try to stop it.

My press coverage changed dramatically in the spring of 2005. For years, I had been covered fairly by all three Lancaster Newspapers, even the Republican *Lancaster New Era*. Yet from 2005 until I left office in 2008, the coverage was so negative, biased, and false that I later sued Buckwalter and several Lancaster Newspapers editors and reporters for libel.[4]

Although it did not produce ultimate victory, the lawsuit I filed later against Lancaster Newspapers produced important evidence. While preparing for the suit, Buckwalter, Cooley, and the newspapers' editors

"Molly Is Toast"

and reporters were all deposed under oath. These depositions revealed the separation of the business side of Lancaster Newspapers from the editorial side to be nonexistent. Lancaster Newspapers' publishing and editorial sides spoke with one voice. Increasingly it seemed, it was the voice of Penn Square Partners.

During Buckwalter's deposition, he revealed his involvement in the letter-writing campaign prompted by Peggy Steinman. My attorney, George Croner, asked Buckwalter, "So you had a discussion, and there was a suggestion in which you were somehow involved about using Lancaster Newspapers, Inc., to publish letters prepared by an advocacy group in favor of the project, correct?"

Jack Buckwalter: "Yes."[5]

Before Lancaster Newspapers involved itself in the hotel and convention center project, the quality of journalism of its three newspapers had generally been competently professional. The reporting covered the local news, politics, and culture adequately. A Lancastrian generally trusted what he or she read in any of the three major Lancaster Newspapers.

The dailies, the *Intell* and *New Era*, competed against each other for stories as if they had different publishers—which they didn't, of course. Their staff members all worked out of the same offices, even sharing workspaces. Each newspaper had its own staff and political party identity reflected on the editorial pages. The *Sunday News* ostensibly remained politically neutral. The differences among the papers gave Lancaster County readers at least a sense that the coverage was balanced.[6]

The hotel and convention center project changed that for the Steinmans. With the project, they faced a clear conflict of interest. The Steinman family was investing a few million dollars in a major downtown commercial development and would receive tens of millions of taxpayer dollars to do it. They had never done that before—invested in a public-private project that received massive taxpayer subsidies. The hotel was located in the Steinmans' neighborhood. They owned virtually every building on W. King Street, twelve properties in all, leading up to the hotel. This project hit very close to home for the

Steinmans, personally and financially.[7] As a journalistic story, it was ripe for investigation.

In 2005, Lancaster Newspapers generated the most revenue of all of the businesses in the Steinman domain.[8] The coalmines and the television and radio stations had long been sold. Now, the circulation of the two dailies was strong. The morning *Intell* had added readers, to about 47,000, with the *New Era* losing them, slipping to about 42,000 daily. The *Sunday News* had a hefty 96,000 weekly circulation in 2005.

Intelligencer Journal (morning)	47,000, editor, Raymond Shaw
Lancaster New Era (evening)	42,000, editor, Ernest Schreiber
Sunday News	96,000, editor, Marvin Adams[9]

These are very impressive numbers for a market with a total population of 490,000 residents. Practically every adult, and possibly every voter, in Lancaster County read one of the Lancaster Newspapers every single day of the week. In just a couple of years, however, the smartphone would gut the newspaper industry.

The Steinmans had a significant financial investment in the project. "The amount of capital which we [Lancaster Newspapers] put in as our share was $8,225,000," Buckwalter said in his deposition in 2010. "And then the amount of money that we had to put up as collateral for a $12 million loan, we had to put up $18 million, to get $12 million. And then we agreed to build the parking garage which would cost us $11,600,000."[10]

That is a substantial amount of money. The proposed hotel, now costing almost $70 million and massively subsidized with public money, would increase the property value of other nearby commercial properties, including the Steinmans' block on W. King Street.

Understandably, Buckwalter, as the steward of the Steinmans' publishing business, wanted to protect their investment. What is not understandable or acceptable is Buckwalter protecting that investment by misusing the immense power of the press he controlled, which is exactly what he and his editors did.

To handle the letters Peggy Steinman wanted to see in her newspaper, Buckwalter turned to *New Era* editor Ernest J. Schreiber. Buckwalter said it was Schreiber who "suggested that people like [former county

"Molly Is Toast"

commissioner] Terry Kauffman and Art Morris could spearhead something like this [letter writing campaign]."[11]

Arthur Morris was a natural choice to "spearhead" a letter-writing campaign on behalf of the project. Morris, a Republican, had been a popular two-and-a-half-term mayor of the City of Lancaster from 1980 to 1990.[12]

Art Morris had also been a track star at McCaskey High School in the city. In 1963, he set the state record in the most painful of races: the mile. (Morris ran 4:20.3 for the record that year.)[13] He was tenacious and could live with pain, even thrive on it. That's what it takes to be a miler.[14] Art Morris had expressed interest in bringing a convention center to downtown Lancaster, going back to the 1980s. In 1986, while mayor, Morris convened an exploratory "convention center task force committee."[15] Still, no private interest in the idea materialized, so it was tabled.

When the Harrisburg Area Community College (HACC) attempted to move into the Watt & Shand space, Morris took a stance as the most vocal opponent against the college's plans. A primary objection, as he stated many times, was that HACC, a nonprofit, would not pay property taxes.

"I have many concerns [about HACC]," Morris said to Lancaster Newspapers during the HACC debate in 1996, "and a significant one is the tax base of this city."[16]

Yet Morris, an outspoken supporter of both the hotel room tax and the $40 million county bond guaranty, offered not an iota of objection when PSP took its hotel completely off the tax rolls by selling it to RCAL. Morris could live with Dale High and the Steinmans—but not a community college—getting a tax-free hotel.

Arthur Morris – Former Lancaster City Mayor, 1980 – 1990; Former Chairman Lancaster County Convention Center 2008

Art Morris was also a defendant in my libel suit, along with Buckwalter, Schreiber, and others. Morris had supported the current project since day one. He counted among the "pile of people" (his words) who met at High's Greenfield complex right after Charlie Smithgall took office as mayor in 1998.[17] At this meeting, they brainstormed ways that High, Buckwalter, and Fulton could buy the Watt & Shand building.

Morris wrote a twice-monthly column in the "Perspective" section of the *Sunday News*. He had complete freedom in choosing topics for his column. If anyone edited the columns at all, it was for punctuation. Morris wrote it, and the *Sunday News* published it.[18] The publisher didn't kill any of his columns. His picture ran next to his name. Morris also regularly wrote letters to the editors of all three Lancaster Newspapers. It seemed that virtually all of them were published, and most of them prominently, meaning they appeared among the first letters in the section. The former mayor proved to be the ideal person to write letters on behalf of the project.

Buckwalter also enlisted other high-profile people to "write" letters to the editor. One of them was Dennis F. Cox, a well-known advertising executive and a former Steinman Foundation scholarship winner.

Mr. Cox agreed to allow Buckwalter draft a letter in Cox's name. A memo Buckwalter wrote, which was turned over in the discovery process of the libel suit against him, shows the level of fine-tuning that went into this letter campaign.

"Discussed the need for rewording the part of the Dennis Cox 'letter to the editor' about the proposed convention center that cited his belief that the county commissioners had 'lied,'" Buckwalter wrote to *New Era* editor Ernie Schreiber. "That allegation was too broad, should have been narrowed to subject at hand."[19]

The Cross-Ruff

> "Who may, in the ambush of my name, strike home,
> And yet my nature never in the fight
> To do in slander."
> —William Shakespeare, *Measure for Measure*, 1604

Pete Shaub, in his fierce hunger to hurt Shellenberger, had repeatedly made himself available to the newspaper executive. He often dropped by at Buckwalter's fourth-floor W. King Street office. Shaub had done this since his first term as commissioner. Buckwalter considered Shaub a solid supporter of the project in 2005.[20] I'm not sure whether Shaub had a personal problem with me or not. He wanted to destroy Dick Shellenberger for replacing him as chair of the commissioners' board, yet my vote was the deciding one that put me on Shaub's enemies list. I also opposed Buckwalter's project.

In the weeks leading up to, and after, the March 15 vote, when the school board rejected PSP's TIF plan, the newspaper coverage took a sharply negative tone.

On March 23, both dailies reported on a commissioners' meeting from the previous day. During the meeting, Shaub, as he had done on several occasions, turned his sights on me. As always, I didn't respond and just let him rant. But that wasn't how it was reported. The outburst appeared on the front page of both daily publications.

In "Shaub Attacks Henderson Over Center: Accuses Her of Sabotage," the *Intelligencer Journal* led with, "Lancaster County Commissioner Pete Shaub on Tuesday accused fellow Commissioner Molly Henderson of 'sabotage' in trying 'to kill' the downtown convention center/hotel project.

"'Commissioner Henderson has repeatedly put up roadblocks to try to kill this project,' Shaub said."[21]

Hours later, the *Lancaster New Era* ran: "Henderson, Shaub Spar; Big Crowd Backs Hotel/Supporters jam meeting to endorse Penn Square project while commissioners continue to bicker."

The *New Era* article began:

> In the face of Commissioner Molly Henderson's contention that she has not gotten enough information on the $129 million Penn

Square hotel project, Commissioner Pete Shaub leveled a question: "Do you or do you not support a hotel and convention center on Penn Square?" Shaub twice asked Henderson this morning.

"I'd like to know which side of the mouth you are talking out of today," Shaub added. "It's time to stop dancing."[22]

I felt a bit shocked to read about myself in such terms and characterized so falsely. I wasn't about to "spar" or "bicker" with Pete Shaub or "sabotage" or "kill" the project. The Lancaster Newspapers reporters knew who they were talking about. They had covered me for years, and everything about my public demeanor had always been measured and polite. The stories seemed contrived and played for maximum effect in both dailies. These front-page stories were no mere warning shot.

It continued. A week later, on March 30, in the *Intelligencer Journal*'s "Project Divides Officials/ Penn Square Proposal Roils Commissioners," the "dysfunctional commissioners" narrative began to take shape. The article again starts with a Shaub attack: "Lancaster County Commissioner Pete Shaub on Tuesday accused his fellow commissioners of misconduct and obstructionist behavior."[23]

The hits kept coming. A few days later, on April 3, the *Sunday News* got into attack mode by publishing, "Good Golly, Molly! Democrat who had Republican support acts independently/Henderson's questions on downtown project rile her friends in both parties."[24]

The Power of the Press

"Let me be cruel, not unnatural;
I will speak daggers to her but use none,
My tongue and soul in this be hypocrites."
—William Shakespeare, *Hamlet*, 1600

Clearly, at this point Shellenberger and I had become targets of the newspapers because we opposed the project. I still had no idea of the extent to which we would be targeted in spring 2005, but the attacks had begun.

I found it disappointing, certainly, that the Lancaster Newspapers would now engage in such a dirty, misleading campaign. However, they couldn't change what we did regarding the project. As county commissioners, we remained fully within the bounds of our office in asking these questions about the project. It was our duty, in fact. Asking questions infuriated PSP, and the partners struck back through Lancaster Newspapers.

During one of his drop-in visits to Buckwalter's office, Shaub said something that Jack Buckwalter thought important enough to write down.

From page 285 of Jack Buckwalter's deposition, February 3, 2010:

Q. And then the last line is the one that you related to me earlier, where you say Shaub said to you, *"Molly is toast"*?
A. Yes.
Q. And you underlined *toast*?
A. Yes.
Q. But he didn't explain what he meant by that?
A. No.
Q. And you didn't ask him what he meant by that?
A. No.[25]

I knew what he meant.

Buckwalter also met regularly with High's Nevin Cooley. The day after the school board rejected the TIF, the *New Era*'s editorial sounded as if Cooley had written it himself. "It was the brainchild of three local CEOs, S. Dale High, Rufus Fulton, and John M. Buckwalter, who wanted to save downtown Lancaster, their hometown, and they spent hundreds of hours trying to do it," the editorial read.[26] Note the tense: it "was" the brainchild. They were reporting the project dead. Yet reports of the project's demise were greatly exaggerated. Two weeks later, of course, PSP bypassed the school board and sold the building to the city (RACL) for a $6 million more than PSP paid for it, a plan that had been in place for months.

Shellenberger and I voted to directly challenge the project by the spring of 2005. The county asked Special Counsel Kelin to analyze the legality of the Act 23/RACL deal. In April, we released Kelin's analysis. Kelin's report said PSP did not qualify for the property tax exemption under Act 23. RACL technically owned the building, but Penn Square Partners would be its "primary user." A private primary user must pay property taxes, per Kelin's reading of the law.

The response of Lancaster Newspapers to Kelin's report made it very clear that things would get ugly from here on out.

On the day we released Kelin's report, the *Lancaster New Era* editorial published, "County Plan to Kill City Project Will Fail." The first sentence established the tone:

> Today the Lancaster County Commissioners declared financial war on the City of Lancaster.
>
> They crawled from beneath the rock of 57 questions with which they had hoped to sink the city's plans to revitalize the downtown and openly declared themselves opponents of the proposed convention center/hotel on Penn Square.

The editorial continued:

> The commissioners' determined effort to sabotage city redevelopment boggles the mind. . . . But County Commissioners Dick Shellenberger and Molly Henderson say they know better than all of them.
>
> They have declared themselves enemies of the city—a declaration that will be remembered long after the convention center and hotel rise on Penn Square.

When asked under oath, Buckwalter said he could not recall anyone ever being called an "enemy of the city" in his more fifty years with Lancaster Newspapers.[27]

(For a list of the 57 Questions, see Appendix B.)

Despite the name-calling, Shellenberger and I didn't feel as if we had a choice. We had been elected to do a job: protect the interests of the taxpayers and the citizens of Lancaster County. Our counsel had just told us that the project would not be eligible for funds it counted on to build the hotel. The cost of the entire project had skyrocketed. The sponsors couldn't or wouldn't answer basic questions about economic feasibility.

In response to the *New Era* "enemies of the city" editorial, we sent a statement to the *Sunday News*, which it published in the letters section the following Sunday. In the "Statement from Two Commissioners," we reminded the sponsors that as county commissioners, we had demonstrated great commitment to the City of Lancaster. This included millions of dollars to:

Keep county government offices downtown as the courts grew;
Support the Lancaster City Safety Commission;
Invest in the Pennsylvania Academy of Music, (Ware Center);
Invest in the Clipper Magazine Stadium; and
Invest in the Northwest Corridor, among other projects.
(For additional county projects, see Appendix D.)

I had lived in the city, worked in the city, gone to school in the city, and been the head of the city's Public Health Department. My husband's business was downtown, and our children had been students in the School District of Lancaster. These are not the actions of an enemy of the city.

Our statement addressed the accusation that we wanted to "kill" the project. "We are neither taking now, nor planning, any steps to disrupt the project." But, we advised, "As the project evolves, we shall continue to evaluate whether county action should be taken on any issue."

As we closed the statement, we mentioned the undignified tone of the debate and directed it at the private sponsors of the project, High, Lancaster Newspapers, and Fulton.

> A deep disappointment over the past two months is that some whose wisdom we have long respected have acted disrespectfully in response to our call for public discourse. To them, we offer Lincoln's public reply about a harsh critique by the famous publisher Horace Greeley, "If there be perceptible in it an impatient and dictatorial tone, I waive it in deference to an old friend, whose heart I have always supposed to be right."[28]

The deposition testimony in the libel case revealed that these weren't "old friends," and their hearts were not right.

"Tis true indeed' the collusion holds in the exchange."
—William Shakespeare, *Love's Labour's Lost*, 1594

In the campaign against me and Dick Shellenberger, Jack Buckwalter acted as the conduit between Cooley, the president of PSP, and the three Lancaster Newspapers. In memos Buckwalter turned over in discovery of the libel action, along with his deposition testimony, the interrelationship between PSP and the editorial side of Lancaster was exposed under oath. The agreement between its business investment and the three Lancaster Newspapers can be seen when Buckwalter discusses how to respond to the statement Shellenberger and I released to the *Sunday News* on April 17.

In a "file memo" dated April 19, 2005, one week after the "enemies of the city" *New Era* editorial, Buckwalter dictated to his secretary, "Talked to Nevin Cooley today. He is preparing a critique of Henderson and Shellenberger's position statement in the *Sunday News* of April 17. After it's polished, Nevin will send it to Dale and myself for suggestions on how to communicate it." Buckwalter concludes the note with a confident, "Nevin will release at right time."[29]

Buckwalter and Cooley came up with a "get tough" "Shellenberger Strategy," which also included me.[30] "Where is Molly Henderson mentioned in this total situation?" wrote Buckwalter in another handwritten memo. "She is rarely mentioned. She wants to kill the project."[31]

According to Buckwalter, Cooley had a problem with me. "Nevin wanted to go after the commissioners, particularly Molly Henderson," Buckwalter testified.[32]

"To negotiate with Shellenberger gives him credibility," Buckwalter wrote in a file memo from June 10, 2005.[33] From the beginning of the project and on several occasions, Cooley held editorial briefings with the Lancaster Newspapers editors and their staffs on the project at the Lancaster Newspapers' headquarters.[34]

Cooley also had connections inside the courthouse with John Espenshade and Don Elliott, the county administrative officer.[35] Shaub had brought Elliott in, and Elliott had used Cooley as a professional reference on his application to the county.[36] Espenshade was the county solicitor and a solicitor for LCCCA. His firm, Stevens & Lee, operated as the registered lobbyist of High Industries.

The "get tough" response to our April 17 statement came in the form of a 4,000-plus-word "letter" bylined by Nevin Cooley and published in the *Sunday News* on May 22.[37] The long essay gives a strikingly imprecise defense of the many questions Shellenberger and I raised regarding the project.

Writing directly to Shellenberger and me, Cooley stated,

> There is ample and credible evidence that you have used and continue to use misinformation and confrontational rather than collaborative actions to waste our community resources and to stand in the way of this project. . . . You have used repeated threats, charges, claims and legal bullying, to serve a purpose known only to you that has hurt our community's reputation, morale and financial standing.[38]

Location, Location, Location

"What is the city but the people?"
    —William Shakespeare, *Coriolanus*, 1607

Jack Buckwalter looked at a newspaper the way he looked at the City of Lancaster. It had slums, working-class districts, and high-rent neighborhoods. Location, location, location. The front page, Jack used to say, "that's very valuable real estate."[39]

The newspaper's attack had not happened ad hoc. It was planned and executed by Cooley and Buckwalter and several editors and reporters from all three Lancaster Newspapers. It was not journalism. They misused the great power of the press. They did it, mostly, I believe, for financial gain and to protect the investment of High and the Steinman family. Part of their motive, I also believe, centered on the fact that I had the temerity to question the hierarchy of the county, the people "in charge." At that point, during the first half of 2005, Lancaster ceased publishing credible newspapers. Lancaster Newspapers would thenceforth be used as a weapon on behalf of its business interests.

Between April 19 and June 8, 2005, Jack Buckwalter held at least five different meetings with the top editors of the three Lancaster

Newspapers. Buckwalter and his staff discussed how they would cover Shellenberger and me. After Buckwalter got that call from Peggy Steinman in early 2005, the plan began between Buckwalter, PSP (Cooley), and the editors of Lancaster Newspapers. First, they "got tough." When that ploy didn't get traction, Buckwalter, Cooley, and *New Era* editor Ernie Schreiber came up with a "kicking-off point" for a story demanding that Shellenberger and I explain exactly why we opposed the project.[40]

The Editors

> ". . . that which is the strength of their amity
> shall prove the immediate author of their variance."
> —William Shakespeare, *Antony and Cleopatra*, 1606

The top editors of each of the three newspapers met separately with Buckwalter to discuss the project. The editors at the time were:

Ernie Schreiber for the *Lancaster New Era*;
Ray Shaw for the *Intelligencer Journal*; and
Dave Hennigan, then Marv Adams for the *Sunday News*. (Adams took over for Hennigan in the fall of 2005.)[41]

Ernest J. Schreiber

Ernest J. Schreiber was the editor of the *Lancaster New Era* in 2005. I've described people who unquestioningly embraced the project as "blindly following" the Steinman/High development. Schreiber and his *New Era* staff led the over-the-top "coverage" on the project. It was Schreiber who selected the "Everything the City Needs" headline in late August 1999, just weeks before the Thibault board of county commissioners passed the hotel room rental tax.[42]

Schreiber also decided on the daily editorial topics and wrote many of them for the *New Era*. Schreiber knew his boss, Buckwalter, felt displeased with the county commissioners, and the editorials reflected that. Schreiber admitted meeting with Buckwalter "half-a-dozen times" about the hotel and convention center project.

"He [Buckwalter] was disappointed with the leadership that the board of Shellenberger, Shaub and Henderson were providing," Schreiber testified.[43]

During his deposition testimony, Schreiber was asked about a potential conflict of interest with Lancaster Newspapers covering a story in which it had a substantial financial investment. Schreiber recalled one meeting that involved Buckwalter, *Intelligencer Journal* editor-in-chief Raymond Shaw, *Sunday News* editor Marv Adams, and himself.

Ernest Schreiber – Editor, Lancaster Newspaper, Inc., now retired

Schreiber stated under oath in his deposition testimony, "There was a time where Ray Shaw, Marv Adams, and I were with Jack Buckwalter and Ray said something like, 'This certainly is something I feared all along—that there would be this perception of a conflict of interest when we got involved in this.'"[44]

Regarding how the *New Era* would handle the project, Schreiber said, "I and my news editors recognized that there would be a perception of a conflict of interest in our company investing in a civic project."[45]

Schreiber, who said he believed Shellenberger and I were "trying to derail the project," acknowledged that he communicated regularly with PSP's Cooley during 2005. "I may have told Jack that I was talking to Nevin Cooley, or that our reporter was talking to Nevin Cooley," Schreiber said during his deposition.[46]

Buckwalter's notes from this time reveal the close, active relationship between the project's private partner and the top editor of Lancaster Newspapers, Schreiber (EJS). Examples from Buckwalter's handwritten memos:

"EJS to talk wo [sic] Nevin Cooley. (April 15)"

"EJS will do study on taxes and the project. (May 01)"

"EJS to talk wot [sic] Nevin Cooley. (June 10)"
"EJS talked to Nevin Cooley. (July 15)"
"EJS indicated that he would run an editorial on the amount of county risk. (July 15)"
"Spoke to EJS . . . Nevin is to write a letter to Shellenberger. (August 08)"[47]

In responsible print journalism, there should be a rigid "church-state" divide between the business and the editorial operation of a newspaper. Advertising can't dictate what goes on the front page. The editor makes that decision. Buckwalter's memos show that at Lancaster Newspapers, those two sides had fused into one, at least in regard to the hotel and convention center project. The memos reveal an explicit agreement between Penn Square Partners and Lancaster Newspapers. Buckwalter manipulated the power of the press to further their project and destroy duly elected public officials.

Charles Raymond Shaw

Charles Raymond "Ray" Shaw took an opposite role from Ernie Schreiber at the *Intelligencer Journal*, its managing editor. Shaw shared Buckwalter's view that in a newspaper, some sections of the newspaper were more valuable than others. Shaw generally became involved in page-one story decisions, the high-end property of the newspaper.[48] Regarding the hotel and convention center project, Ray Shaw had less direct involvement with Buckwalter and Cooley than *New Era* editor Ernie Schreiber did. The project seemed to make Shaw uncomfortable, and he didn't know much about it.[49]

Shaw reported to Jack Buckwalter, then to Chip Miller, Lancaster Newspapers' president after 2005. As he did with the top editors of each newspaper, Buckwalter met periodically with Shaw and his deputies to discuss events and things that happened in the newspaper.

"Mr. Miller was likely at a luncheon where the commissioners were part of a broader discussion, that I can recall," said Shaw, who was also deposed as a defendant in the libel lawsuit. "There were possibly several times that he [Buckwalter] mentioned the project to me. I think there was some unhappiness that the commissioners were opposing the project."[50]

Marvin I. Adams, Jr.

Helen Colwell Adams – Political reporter for Sunday News and Marvin Adams – Editor of the Sunday News

Marvin I. "Marv" Adams, Jr., was the editor of the third Lancaster Newspaper, the *Sunday News*. Adams had moved up officially to the editor's position in November 2005, replacing David Hennigan, who retired.[51]

Adams began working for Lancaster Newspapers in 1969 as a messenger and became full time in 1972 after graduating from college. He didn't undertake any graduate work or enroll in additional journalism courses.[52]

Describing his role with the *Sunday News*, Adams, said in his deposition: "I write. I edit. I supervise."[53]

The Steinmans considered the *Sunday News* a very important newspaper. It allowed the company to reach its readers seven days a week. The Sunday edition essentially combined the circulations of the two dailies. The *Sunday News*, a couple of pounds of news, opinion, comics, and classifieds, reached nearly 100,000 Lancaster County households every week.[54] And Adams oversaw the whole thing—front page, editorial page, columnists, staffing, and vacations.

During his deposition testimony, Adams said he had misgivings about the newspapers' investment in the hotel and convention center project. Adams, who had been invited to the editorial luncheons since 1984, recalled a discussion with Lancaster Newspapers chairman Jack Buckwalter.

> "I made it clear [to Buckwalter] that I was uncomfortable with the fact that the company was involved in a project like this. Not because I thought that I had a conflict of interest in our reporting, but because of the perception. Perception is not a fact, but perception is what it is."[55]

Their having met at work, Adams happened to be married to the *Sunday News*' "Perspective" section editor and political writer Helen Colwell Adams. I sued Helen Colwell Adams for libel when my term ended.[56]

In 2005, Lancaster Newspapers, Inc., chairman Jack Buckwalter had known editors Ernie Schreiber, Ray Shaw, and Marv Adams for decades. Buckwalter played an integral part in grooming them for their current positions. He was their employer, their boss, as Peggy Steinman was Buckwalter's boss. They all worked in the same building. They saw one another in the halls and the elevators at 8 W. King Street. The men ate lunch together. They wished each other Merry Christmas every year and asked after one another's children. From my perspective, they all played on the same side.

> "O, that a mighty man of such descent,
> Of such possessions, and so high esteem,
> Should be infused with so foul a spirit!"
> —William Shakespeare, *Taming of the Shrew*, 1593

The Steinman family had a very good run in Lancaster County. Part of the establishment since the eighteenth century, the Steinmans monopolized the daily newspaper market for most of a century.

"Molly Is Toast"

Generations of Lancastrians made reading one of the Lancaster Newspapers an ingrained daily habit. By 2005, Lancaster Newspapers—the *Intelligencer Journal*, the *Lancaster New Era*, and the *Sunday News*—had amassed a huge store of goodwill and trust in the minds of their readers. But now they began to misuse that trust.

The articles and the editorials critical of "the commissioners" appeared more frequently in 2005. A negative press campaign had begun. I required Lancaster Newspapers' reporters to send me their questions in writing, so that my responses would also be in writing. Whenever I spoke to reporters from any of the Lancaster Newspapers, I asked them to read back to me what they had written down. I didn't trust them to convey my message accurately.

Chapter Eight

CONESTOGA VIEW

"What chance is this that suddenly hath cross'd us?"
—William Shakespeare, *Henry VI*, Part I, 1591

The plan wasn't working. By spring 2005, Shellenberger and I stood squarely in the crosshairs of Lancaster Newspapers. Cooley and Buckwalter directed the coordination between PSP and Lancaster Newspapers. They, along with certain editors, consulted with each other regularly about the "get tough" strategy targeting the two questioning commissioners.

Despite the "puff pieces" promoting the project, the continued "letters to the editor," and the scathing columns and editorials excoriating "the commissioners," Penn Square Partners was losing the public relations battle. Public opposition to the taxpayer-financed project had grown.[1]

Local developers and those with convention center experience publicly expressed opposition to the project.[2] Other community leaders objected to the lack of promised consultant contracts for minorities and women.[3] Historic preservationists felt rightly concerned about the treatment of the Thaddeus Stevens/Lydia Smith House, as well as the Watt & Shand building itself.

The project still remained years away from completion. Construction had not begun, financing wasn't secured, architectural designs hadn't been completed, and we, the majority of the board of Lancaster County commissioners, openly opposed the project. Penn Square Partners felt apprehensive. Then the partners got a break.

Red Herring No. 1

"Bait the hook well; this fish will bite."
—William Shakespeare, *Much Ado about Nothing*, 1598

Originally built in 1799 as an almshouse to care for the county's elderly indigent, Conestoga View was a 206-year-old nursing home owned by Lancaster County. In 2005, Conestoga View, retaining the original name, was a 35-year-old, 14-story building that housed a 446-bed facility on 39 acres of surrounding land. The main tower had been constructed in 1970, and it had 35-year-old construction issues. Building codes and handicapped regulations would never permit a facility like this today.[4]

The county morgue and Children and Youth Services also occupied the grounds. The morgue—undersized, antiquated, and creepy—was in the basement of the main building. Children and Youth Services had a complex of buildings nearby. About 20 percent of the county government workforce, which included nurses, aides, cooks, and so on, had some connection with Conestoga View.[5]

Until July 2005, if the Lancaster Newspapers ever mentioned Conestoga View, it was in the obituary section. For the next two years, however, Conestoga View made the front pages, the editorial pages, and the "Letters to the Editor" pages almost every day of the week—sometimes several times a day.[6]

Lancaster County commissioners sat on various boards as part of their duties. We were members of the election, prison, and salary boards, among others. The Board of Commissioners also represented the county at monthly business meetings at Conestoga View. These meetings were open to the public. The reporter Bernie Harris is the only person I recall ever attending. He came to our initial meeting in 2004. That was it. Former Lancaster mayor Art Morris, who would soon express profound interest in Conestoga View, never attended a single business meeting from 2004 until 2008.[7]

At these meetings, I learned about the dire financial condition of Conestoga View. The financial statements showed that the facility had lost more than $1 million a year.[8] Every month, the purse grew more and more empty. Parentheses appeared at the bottom line of the budget, month after month. The situation was not sustainable, and, due to federal and state budget cuts, patient care would eventually be compromised, or taxes would have to be dramatically raised throughout the county.

The idea to sell Conestoga View had germinated in the mind of Pete Shaub years earlier.

After Shaub's first term as commissioner, he discussed selling Conestoga View with Lancaster County solicitor and Stevens & Lee partner John Espenshade. Shaub and Shellenberger campaigned on the idea of privatizing county holdings. They believed that the functions of government were better served in private hands—that government should be run more like a business.[9]

As I campaigned for the minority seat during the summer of 2003, Shaub, Shellenberger, and Espenshade decided to sell Conestoga View after Shaub and Shellenberger took office.[10]

Lancaster County voter demographics assured Republicans Shaub and Shellenberger of election in November.[11] They figured they would get a running start on their administration, so prior to taking office they decided to sell Conestoga View.

"Seal up your lips, and give no words but mum:
The business asketh silent secrecy."
    —William Shakespeare, *Henry VI*, Part II, 1590

The meetings between Shaub and Shellenberger in 2003 didn't violate the state "Open Meetings" law or the Sunshine Act because Shellenberger hadn't taken office yet. So the two men didn't make up a voting quorum of at least two county commissioners.[12]

After Shellenberger left office, he said, "Conestoga View was losing money, and Pete and I felt this was the kind of thing that government should not be doing. This was the philosophy I campaigned on. Anything the private sector can do; the government should not be doing."[13]

When Shaub and Shellenberger took office in 2004, they, along with solicitor Espenshade, continued to pursue selling Conestoga View. The three secretly negotiated to sell the facility to Complete Healthcare Resources, which had already successfully operated Conestoga View for more than a decade. Now, when Shellenberger and Shaub—both sitting commissioners—met, they were in violation of the Sunshine Act.

Shaub, Shellenberger, and Espenshade went to great lengths to keep me in the dark about these negotiations to sell Conestoga View (CV), because they thought I would oppose it. They even used a secret code, "Charlie Victor," to refer to Conestoga View on their calendars. A grand jury investigation revealed this a year and a half later.[14]

The deal that Shaub, Shellenberger, and Espenshade secretly negotiated proposed to sell CV and its grounds to Complete Healthcare for a total of $12 million—$8.5 million for the buildings, the balance for compensation and assurances that no job cuts would be made, and no indigent patients denied care.[15]

I had no idea what Shaub, Shellenberger, and Espenshade were doing. Often, they met outside the courthouse, sometimes at the offices of Stevens & Lee. I learned later that they had worked on the Conestoga View deal at the commissioners' offices by means of "walking the halls." When a surrogate for one commissioner meets with another commissioner, then the surrogate "walks the halls" back to the other commissioner's office and briefs him. No one ever walked the halls for me during my term in office.[16]

Due to the deteriorating relationship between Shaub and Shellenberger in 2004, caused by Shaub's abrasive behavior, the two Republican commissioners often employed "walking the halls" to work out issues, including the details of the Conestoga View sale.

Enter Don Elliott and Gary Heinke

The person walking the halls for Shaub was county administrative officer Don Elliott, well-dressed and unmotivated. Chief services officer Gary Heinke walked the halls as Shellenberger's proxy.

As I mentioned earlier, Gary Heinke and Dick Shellenberger were good personal friends. After being sworn into office, Shellenberger, along with Shaub and solicitor John Espenshade, helped Heinke get the new position of chief services officer. The three sent Heinke material and job-related questions in advance of the formal interview and had several phone conversations and meetings with him.¹⁷ My colleagues kept me completely uninformed of the preferential treatment given to Heinke and also to Elliott, in applying for his job.¹⁸

When I reviewed Heinke's résumé and application, I didn't think he was a good fit for the chief services officer position and didn't recommend him for the final interview group. Shellenberger overrode that and had Heinke's application moved to the "to-be-interviewed" pile. Heinke was scheduled to be in the finalists' pool of in-person interviews.

Donald Elliott – Lancaster County Administrator, 2004 – September 2006

Heinke absolutely nailed the interview before the three commissioners and Espenshade. He acted poised and prepared and had a well-considered answer to every question. Yet it's a lot easier to ace an interview if you know which questions you'll be asked.¹⁹ Even so, I didn't feel he had the bearing of an assistant school superintendent, which was mentioned on his résumé.

Gary Heinke was hired as chief services officer and began work at the end of March 2004.²⁰ Despite my objections to his hiring, I didn't have a problem working with Heinke. He was well-read and had a good sense of humor.

April Fool's Day

"Would it be better, madame, than I am?
I wish it might, for now I am your fool."
—William Shakespeare, *Twelfth Night*, 1599

In the last days of March 2005, "Andi" Murphy, the county's communications director, began courting me. One day, Andi asked me to go to lunch. This wasn't unusual. I remained on friendly terms with everyone in the office—even Shaub, for the most part—and I got on fine with Andi.

After we sat down, I clearly saw that Andi had been tasked with an agenda. She gave me a rather "hard sell" to attend a "Core Services Review" presentation by Don Elliott and Gary Heinke, analyzing the county's business and financial operations.[21] I didn't want to go, but Andi persisted and asked me "to just come and listen." Those were her exact words. I relented and said I would attend as a favor to her. It was scheduled for April 1, 2005. April Fool's Day. Perfect!

Long after I left office, when I thought about this meeting, I remembered what former county administrator Timothea Kirchner told me as I began my term: "You won't have any friends here, Molly." She was right. Andi Murphy wasn't a friend, and I shouldn't have gone to that presentation.

The April 1, 2005, Core Services presentation took place at 10:00 a.m. in room 503 of the courthouse, where the commissioners held our regular public work sessions. We called it the "fishbowl," because the curtains remained open, and we could see people walking around

Gary Heinke – Lancaster County Human Services Administrator, resigned 2005

the office, and they could see us. There was nothing "secret" about it. Don Elliott gave a Power Point presentation, part of which focused on the financial health of Conestoga View—staffing, insurance, taxes, debt service. He said he was examining alternatives for the facility, including the possible sale of Conestoga View. The commissioners didn't discuss the subject. We didn't vote or deliberate on anything. I said not a word. I just listened. The presentation ended informally, and Elliott said he would continue his analysis. That presentation changed my life and cost me my job.[22]

After learning that Conestoga View might be sold, I took it upon myself to investigate county-owned nursing homes. I met with Michael Wilt, the executive director of the Pennsylvania Association of County Affiliated Homes.[23] We met for lunch at the end of April 2005 at a pizza restaurant in a strip mall outside of Harrisburg. Wilt, the statewide expert on the subject, said that in the previous four years, thousands of nursing home beds had changed hands throughout the state. He explained that many counties were unable to manage their nursing homes effectively, and many had been sold at a small fraction of their value. Wilt said it was a combination of reduced federal and state funding, along with the need for counties to increase taxes significantly that led to the sale of county homes.

All of the official financial statements I read had reported that Conestoga View lost money every month. Furthermore, the Bush administration had cut federal funds to states, which, in turn, reduced funding for county services. Fewer funds meant a lower level of care for Conestoga View residents. A major funding source known as IGT, Intergovernmental Transfer, was to be halted in 2005. In addition, only county-owned nursing homes are required to pay back to the state 10 percent of the cost of Medicaid residents' care. Private facilities don't have to do this. I wondered, *What would be the best outcome for the residents?*

A county like Lancaster simply found it beyond its capacity to run a nursing home the size of Conestoga View. The facility was too big and losing money. Selling it to the company that had managed it capably for the previous dozen years with its economy of scale, Complete HealthCare Resources, seemed like the responsible thing to do.[24]

No Political Expedience

"... I will rather sue to be despised than to deceive."
—William Shakespeare, *Othello*, 1604

The vote to authorize selling Conestoga View was scheduled for July 6, 2005.[25] I didn't intend to vote for the motion when I awoke that morning. In the car on the way to the courthouse, I still didn't plan to vote for it. The sale made sense from a financial standpoint, and residents' care would improve, but Conestoga View had an emotional hold on many, including me. I truly agonized over the decision. On one hand, I didn't want to go down the path of privatizing county services with Shaub and Shellenberger. On the other, I witnessed ever-growing funding shortages and cutbacks. Future care would be compromised, accompanied by county tax increases. Moving Conestoga View to Complete HealthCare appeared to be the responsible thing to do for the residents, the staff, and the taxpayers of Lancaster County.

When the July 6 public commissioners' meeting began at 9:15 a.m., I made a motion to delay the agreement, in order to allow public review. My motion failed. The agreement was then put up for a vote and was passed, 3 to 0. The resolution indicated that the County of Lancaster intended to finalize the sale at a later date. (See Appendix E)

I could have voted "nay," and the agreement would have passed without my vote, but that would have been against my integrity. My decision to vote "yea" on the agreement was an informed decision. I understood what was happening at Conestoga View:

The situation was not sustainable, and patient care would become compromised;

I had hospital/clinical experience as a respiratory therapist specializing in rehabilitation of elderly infirm patients;

The cutbacks from the federal and state government would continue;

The facility's physical structure needed repair;

The existing building would never be allowed today;

The facility was not keeping pace with the additional demands of an aging population—e.g., a specialized dementia unit;

The patient rooms were antiquated;

It was running more than a $1M a year deficit;

County taxes would have to be increased substantially to cover costs; Other counties faced the same situation (see Appendix F);

Complete Healthcare Resources had administered Conestoga View for more than ten years and knew the home;

Complete Healthcare Resources operated other homes throughout the country; according to *Provider Magazine* as of 2013, Complete Healthcare Resources had thirteen facilities throughout the nation;

Complete Healthcare Resources had an "economy of scale" that afforded tremendous purchasing power, which the county did not have;

Complete Healthcare Resources committed to keeping Conestoga View available to indigent individuals; and

Complete Healthcare Resources committed to maintaining the patient/staff ratio.

Complete Healthcare Resources has honored its agreement to the county made at the sale of Conestoga View in 2005.

In addition, Conestoga View, now privately owned, is on the tax rolls of the School District of Lancaster, Lancaster Township, and the county.

For more information on Conestoga View, visit: www.ConestogaViewNursing.com or www. Pennsylvania Department of Health.gov.

Take the Ball and Run

"Madame, this is a mere distraction."
—William Shakespeare, *Henry VIII*, 1612

Conestoga View had been a county institution for a long, long time, and change is difficult. The necessary and inevitable change was made even more difficult by the newspapers' manipulation of the public's emotional attachment to the nursing home. The purpose of the exploitive and relentless coverage was to take the unpopular hotel and convention center project off the front pages and undermine the credibility of the two commissioners who opposed it. (See Appendix C.) As Lancaster Newspapers did earlier when they promoted the project with articles playing on the public's true affection for the Watt & Shand building, they manipulated readers over Conestoga View. They again employed the tactic of using valuable newspaper "real estate" to further the project.

After the July 6 vote that agreed to sell Conestoga View, the coverage from Lancaster Newspapers became much more antagonistic and personal.

The first shot from Lancaster Newspapers on CV appeared in the next *Sunday News*' "Coffee with Clyde" column, written by then editor Dave Hennigan.[26] The "Clyde" column appeared in the "Perspective" section of the *Sunday News*, opposite the editorial page. This constituted prime broadsheet space in the largest circulation of the Lancaster Newspapers: 100,000 Lancaster County households in 2005.[27]

"Coffee with Clyde" consisted of a popular collection of observations from Hennigan. Hennigan used "Clyde" as a device that he called an alter ego. Hennigan's "Mr. Editor" would have "conversations" with "Clyde," whom he invariably described during this time as his "jogging friend."

Yet "Clyde" may have taken physical form. There are those who believe that, for most of 2005, Clyde frequently represented the views of the very real former mayor and well-known running enthusiast Art Morris.

The July 10 "Coffee with Clyde" column ("Clyde Busts Commissioners for Speeding"), began:

> Good morning, Clyde. What's going on?
> "The county commissioners played a little 'full steam ahead' on Wednesday," my jogging friend said, sipping his coffee.
> Indeed, Clyde. What do you mean?
> "They approved the sale of Conestoga View in record time, Mr. Editor. It took the commissioners only six days from when it became public to unload a piece of Lancaster."
> What's the point, Clyde?
> "What's the rush, Mr. Editor? They pulled this stunt over a holiday weekend, when few people could react, and when a couple did complain, they ignored their request to postpone the vote . . ."[28]

My belief is that "Clyde" became another platform for Art Morris's attacks in the *Sunday News*. By July 2005, Jack Buckwalter had already enlisted Morris to be part of the "get tough" policy against Shellenberger and me, using Lancaster Newspapers. The Clyde column worked in tandem with Morris, who had his own monthly opinion column in the *Sunday News*.[29]

And "Clyde," like Morris, strongly supported the hotel and convention center project. Two days before the critical March 15, 2005, School Board of Lancaster vote on the tax increment financing plan proposed by Penn Square Partners, the "Clyde" column titled "Clyde Backs the Project," defended the partners' TIF proposal. The last line of the column belonged to Clyde. Hennigan's "Mr. Editor" asks the mysterious Clyde his position on Penn Square Partners' TIF proposal:

> And how do you feel, Clyde?
> "I think it's [the TIF is] crucial to the future of the city, Mr. Editor. Downtown has a lot going for it right now, with many new projects either underway or planned. But it needs this catalyst to close the deal."[30]

In the days and weeks following the July 6 vote to sell Conestoga View, letters to the editor appeared daily, criticizing the commissioners for the sale. "Lancaster County is poorer now that Conestoga View has been privatized," began a typical letter, this one published on July 12 in the *Intell*. "I learned that our county commissioners have been in secret negotiations for many months to sell the Conestoga View home," read a *New Era* letter of July 18.[31]

A sameness, a common tone, characterized the letters, suggesting to me orchestration and coordination. And as we have seen, the leadership of Lancaster Newspapers had previously manipulated newspaper coverage, which included writing phony "letters."

Sunshine Law Casts a Shadow

"Vouchsafe to show the sunshine of your face . . ."
—William Shakespeare, *Love's Labour's Lost*, 1594

The *Sunday News* editorial page first addressed the Conestoga View issue on July 17, 2005. "In the Dark" suggested that the Board of

Commissioners had violated the Sunshine Act when it sold the facility. The alleged secrecy of the sale would be the main thrust of the coverage in the weeks and months to come. "In the Dark" concludes: "But did the county explore other companies for comparison? Was there a better deal? We don't know. And neither do you."[32]

Bold headlines and harshly critical articles of the Conestoga View sale proliferated in the Lancaster Newspapers. On the same day—July 21, 2005—both the *Intell* ("Nursing Home Sale Unsettles Employees") and the *New Era* ("Conestoga View Sale Mishandled") ran separate front-page articles about the negative impact of the sale on Conestoga View employees.[33]

The letters kept coming. "I was astounded when I read Lancaster County planned to sell Conestoga View to a for-profit corporation," read another *Intell* letter from July 22.

Hennigan's "Clyde" column stayed on the topic of Conestoga View during the entire month of August. "No Sunshine Keeps Public in the Dark," accused the August 7, 2005 installment, again suggesting Sunshine violations. Two weeks later, on August 21, in, "Clyde Joins in Verbal Beating of Public Officials," Hennigan wrote,

> What else has folks stirred up, Clyde?
> "I'm not sure what can be done about it, Mr. Editor, but the sale of Conestoga View by the county commissioners has a foul taste to it. . . ."[34]

In addition to writing his own column, Art Morris was also featured as the subject of articles about the Conestoga View sale. In yet another front-page article, on August 24, the *Lancaster New Era* published, "Morris: Halt Conestoga View Sale." In the article, former mayor Morris, who had no training in accounting, appraisals, nursing homes, or county government, is quoted at a commissioners' meeting telling the board, "There is absolutely no justification for the speed with which you are moving forward on this sale."[35]

The "coverage" of Conestoga View exceeded by far any story that Lancaster Newspapers reported on during the summer of 2005. For example, on July 7, the day after the commissioners agreed to vote to sell Conestoga View, the Pennsylvania General Assembly, including some members of the Lancaster delegation, voted themselves huge pay raises that ranged from 16 to 34 percent. Lancaster Newspapers published a total of eight articles on the pay raise during the next two months. In that same period, more than twenty articles appeared on the sale of Conestoga View, not including dozens of similar-sounding letters to the editor.[36]

The Board of Commissioners addressed every concern made by Morris and other critics of the sale. Built into the agreement to sell Conestoga View were written assurances that:

- Staff would not be cut;
- Vacation days would be honored;
- Insurance plans kept; and, most important;
- That no indigent patient would be refused admittance and;
- Treatment would be maintained AND it would be improved.[37]

The Pennsylvania County Code required the sale of Conestoga View to have at least two appraisals prior to purchase.[38] The county got two appraisals. Several public meetings took place between the July 6, 2005, commissioners' meeting and the September 28 finalization of the deal.

The Supporting Cast

"The actors are at hand and by their show
You shall know all that you are like to know."
    —William Shakespeare, A Midsummer Night's Dream, 1595

The newspapers' relentless campaign about Conestoga View needed some new dramatic props. During the summer of 2005, a cast of four people dressed for the occasion appeared in the audience, planted there to watch Morris peer over his glasses and lecture the commissioners.

Most weeks, the supporting cast members—Tony Allen, Bill Bonnano, Donna Grady, and Jane Albright—showed up at the 9:15 a.m. Wednesday commissioners' meetings. Each person wore a white T-shirt with "Lost Our Home!" printed on the front and the back. Their "home" was Conestoga View. None of them lived there, and none, including Morris, had ever attended a public meeting at Conestoga View.[39]

Tony Allen, Mrs. Albright, William Banano –
Citizens opposed to the sale of Conestoga View

The quartet usually sat together and stared at the commissioners, as we conducted the meeting. Albright, mayor Charlie Smithgall's mother-in-law, wore a scowl, which she seemed to train on me. I remember her staring at me and saying caustically, "And you, Molly Henderson, just sit there stone-faced."

Allen, a large man, often spoke for the group. "Education should relieve anxiety," Allen said at a commissioners' meeting before the final vote on September 28. "I came here today to be educated, and I think my anxiety has gone up even more than what it was before, because it's obvious that this thing has been totally botched." At another meeting, Allen rose to speak and, pointing his finger at Shellenberger, warned him to "release yourself from the evil clutches of Molly Henderson."[40]

I don't recall Donna Grady speaking. She just sat there next to Mrs. Albright, wearing a matching T-shirt and glaring at us. The last of the four was Bill Bonnano, a bespectacled, mutton-chopped man. Bonnano read his disapproval of us from a prepared script. I have always wondered who wrote them. Some afternoons Bonnano stood guard, pacing on the sidewalk in front of the courthouse with a puppet of Pinocchio perched on his arm and wearing his "Lost Our Home" T-shirt. It was quite a sight.

Other "plants" showed up at these commissioners' meetings before the final Conestoga View vote. At times in the audience, in addition to Morris and the "Lost Our Home" foursome, were former commissioner Paul Thibault, who said, "I've looked at the books, and they are shaky numbers"; Lancaster Chamber of Commerce president and head of the Lancaster Campaign Tom Baldridge, who offered, "We cannot support the sale as presently structured"; and Lancaster mayor Charlie Smithgall, who commented, with his usual delicacy, "This [Conestoga View] is the last and only place that will take ventilator patients, quads, paraplegics, etc."[41] (As of 2018, Conestoga View still accepted patients with more challenging needs. Visit www.ConestogaViewNursing.com.)

On into the Fall

"O yes, an 'twere a cloud in autumn."
—William Shakespeare, *Troilus and Cressida*, 1601

On September 21, in front-page stories in both the *Intelligencer Journal* ("Stuckey Questions Sale") and the *Lancaster New Era* ("Controller: It Doesn't Add Up"), the county controller Dennis Stuckey challenged the county's financial analysis. "We think there was some faulty logic coming up with the numbers," Stuckey said in the *Intell* article. "It's [Conestoga View is] operationally sound at this point."[42]

Yet controller Stuckey chose to ignore that Conestoga View was drawing from the "Home Enterprise Fund" to pay its operating costs. The state and federal government had set up this fund ten years earlier to reimburse Conestoga View for expenses. However, the state and federal government had ceased paying into the Home Enterprise Fund in 1999, while Conestoga View kept drawing on the fund to pay for its operations. In 2001 and 2002 alone, CV had drawn more than $2.5 million from the fund to cover operating expenses, as the balance got lower and lower.[43]

At the end of 2004, the Home Enterprise Fund had just $114,417 in the bank. Conestoga View still had operating losses of more than $659,000, leaving a net loss of more than $540,000 for 2004. Finally, debt service remained on a $1.5 million bond issued by a previous commissioners' board.[44] Conestoga View had sunk into a terrible financial condition and would continue costing the county a lot of money. These facts supported selling the facility. Again, it was absolutely the responsible thing to do.

Day after day, seven days a week, articles, columns, editorials, and letters to the editor about Conestoga View utterly dominated Lancaster County "news." The close and important mayoral election between incumbent Republican Charlie Smithgall and Democratic challenger J. Richard Gray received a small fraction of the newspaper "coverage" that Conestoga View did.[45]

The critics of the Conestoga View sale, the ones quoted in the articles, had a few things in common. None of them, including Morris, had ever expressed any previous concern about the nursing home. The former mayor had never made the elderly a priority during his years in office or after leaving. None of the plants at the commissioners' meetings had ever attended a single Conestoga View business meeting, open to the public, prior to the sale. They had no idea about the facility's financial condition. Even so, they lined up to criticize the sale and the board for making it.

These public critics had one more thing in common: all had come out as strong, early supporters of the hotel and convention center project. Every one of the previous quotes came from published Lancaster Newspapers articles before the final vote on CV. Day after day, Lancaster Newspapers stayed on this story, far out of proportion to its journalistic significance.

CV Headlines

Headlines are very important to a newspaper. They summarize the story. People often read headlines alone and skip the article. We see headlines when someone else reads a newspaper in a doctor's office, on the bus, or at a restaurant. We look across the room and know what the main stories are about. We look at a headline through the window of a newspaper kiosk and decide whether we want to buy the paper. This was how many people bought newspapers before the age of the smartphone. We looked through the window to see the headline, put a coin in a slot and opened the box, and took a newspaper.[46]

A small sample of headlines from front-page stories in the weeks prior to the September 28 Conestoga View vote reveal the story Lancaster Newspapers was spinning:

- "County Urged to Postpone Sale of Conestoga View," *Lancaster New Era*, September 7, 2005
- "Mayor: Keep Conestoga View," *Intelligencer Journal*, September 8, 2005.
- "Conestoga View: Is It Still Home for the Poor?" *Lancaster New Era*, September 14, 2005
- "Controller: It Doesn't Add Up," *Lancaster New Era*, September 21, 2005
- "Leaders: Shellenberger Should Quit," *Lancaster New Era*, September 22, 2005
- "Did County Violate State Law in Drafting Conestoga View Sale?" *Lancaster New Era*, September 24, 2005
- "Opposition to Conestoga View Sale Grows," *Intelligencer Journal*, September 27, 2005

The *Sunday News'* "Clyde" continued to gnaw at Conestoga View. Note the following "Clyde" columns: "Clyde Can't Figure Sale of County Home," September 11, 2005; "County Home Being Sold in Broad Daylight," September 18, 2005; "Opponents of County Home Sell-Off Seethe," September 25, 2005.[47]

The *Lancaster New Era* also kept the issue at a fever pitch. In its September 23 editorial, "County Missteps Hurt City Progress," *New Era* editor Ernie Schreiber wrote of the commissioners, "They decided to sell off Conestoga View to an out-of-town businessman at the bargain price of $13 million, a fraction of what it would cost to build a comparable facility. ... Never before have county leaders made so many missteps so rapidly."[48]

The articles contained quotes from Lancaster "leaders," the same line-up of hotel and convention center sponsors. Consider the *Intell* article of September 22, "Leaders: Shellenberger Should Quit." In it, Senator Gib Armstrong, who'd supported Shellenberger when he ran and went to the same church, said of the mild-mannered commissioner, "The guy [Shellenberger] is out of control."[49]

Former county commissioner Paul Thibault said of Shellenberger, "A lot of people are shaking their heads and asking who is this person in the courthouse? He's [Shellenberger's] there for a year and a half and wants to reshape everything in Lancaster County, while ignoring all the rules. This is not a Republican attitude. This is dictatorship."

Referring to Shellenberger and me, Lancaster city mayor Charlie Smithgall commented, "What the commissioners have done is simply underhanded," adding, "He [Shellenberger] should resign. It is time.... The county commissioners—Shellenberger and Molly Henderson—seem bent on killing any forward movement in the city, especially in downtown."

In "Controller: It Doesn't Add Up," controller Dennis Stuckey said, "From what we see, it's not the money loser they [the commissioners] say."

Even Rick Gray, the Democrat candidate for mayor (an office he would win), piled on the county commissioners. Gray criticized us for our position on the hotel and convention center project. "It is unfortunate that we have gotten to the point where our county commissioners are working against the biggest proactive economic development project in the city," said Gray a few days before the Conestoga View vote.

Two days prior to the vote, Commissioner Pete Shaub, the man who'd conceived and been the driving force behind the sale for more than two years, decided he wasn't going to vote for it. On September 26, the *Intelligencer Journal* ran a page-one item, "Conestoga View Numbers a 'Mistake,'" in which the ever-surprising Shaub announced he no longer supported the sale. Shaub accused Shellenberger and me of disseminating false financial information about Conestoga View. Then he took a typical Shaubian sidestep.

"The most important thing about this deal is that people trust their commissioners," Shaub said. "Our integrity has been contaminated."[50] Shaub had done that all by himself. It had been almost a year since a sobbing Pete Shaub sat in my living room, begging to remain chairman. Shaub had said he would ruin Shellenberger, and he was making good on his word.

On Tuesday, September 27, at the commissioners' regular work session a day prior to the Wednesday public vote, Shaub made a motion to postpone the vote. It was not passed. A financial deadline existed with Complete Healthcare Resources.

The next day, the County of Lancaster voted 2 to 1 to finalize the sale of Conestoga View and its grounds to Complete Healthcare Resources for a total of $13.5 million. Shaub voted no.

On September 30, two days after the sale of Conestoga View, members of the Lancaster City and County Medical Society filed a lawsuit. The Medical Society argued that the county had negotiated a "sweetheart deal" with Complete Healthcare and "the commissioners deprived the residents and taxpayers of Lancaster County of the opportunity to obtain maximum value for Conestoga View through any type of competitive bidding procedure, in gross dereliction of their fiduciary duties."[51]

On the day the suit was filed, Lancaster County judge James Cullen rejected the Medical Society complaint and upheld the sale. In fact, the sale of Conestoga View was perfectly legal. The County Code had required multiple appraisals before the facility was sold. The county got multiple appraisals. Again, it was the responsible thing to do.

The Medical Society story ran on the front page of the *Lancaster New Era*. Clearly, even after the final sale, Lancaster Newspapers would continue to "cover" Conestoga View. It was irresponsible and an egregious misuse of the press.

It Keeps Going and Going . . .

"Please you, repeat their names, . . ."
—William Shakespeare, *Two Gentlemen of Verona*, 1594

On October 2, in the first "Coffee with Clyde" column after the vote, "Clyde Can Only Ask, 'But Why?'" began with:

Good morning, Clyde. You look puzzled.
"Where are they coming from?" my jogging friend said the other day, sipping his coffee.
Who, Clyde?
"Dick Shellenberger and Molly Henderson, the county commissioners. Why are they so strongly opposed to the convention center-hotel project? Why were they so insistent that Conestoga View be sold? Those are questions being asked all over town. Doesn't matter where I go. People bring it up."[52]

The same *Sunday News* editorial, "A Shameful Deal," used particularly disrespectful language in referring to the "commissioners," meaning Shellenberger and me.

> Barring a miracle, by the time you read this, Conestoga View will be the property of Complete HealthCare Resources. The sale was to take effect at 12:01 a.m. Saturday.
>
> We'd hope the Lancaster County commissioners would be ashamed, but they've proven themselves a shameless lot. They did a sloppy deal in secret to sell the county nursing home, sprang it on the public, then whined that the county would lose millions if the commissioners backed out.[53]

These words appeared in the most significant section, on the most important page of the Sunday newspaper, the editorial page. This was the voice of Lancaster Newspapers. These weren't ordinary words.

The person who actually tapped out those carefully selected words was Helen Colwell Adams, the political reporter for the *Sunday News*. Hennigan had only weeks until retirement. Running the newsroom was Helen's husband, Marvin "Marv" Adams, Jr., the *Sunday News'* news editor.

Colwell Adams, the one who called us a "shameless lot," had enrolled in a Master of Divinity degree program at Evangelical Theological Seminary during the 2005 time period.[54] She often used Biblical references to criticize "the commissioners" in her editorials. We'll get to those later. The "Coffee with Clyde" column of October 9, 2005, "Commissioners Are Acting Like Children," really illustrates the level of coordination and cynicism between Art Morris and Lancaster Newspapers.

Several months earlier, as noted, Lancaster Newspapers' Jack Buckwalter had recruited Morris to help with a letters-to-the-editor campaign to offset the negative letters regarding the hotel and convention center project. One of those manufactured letters, revised and edited by Nevin Cooley and Buckwalter, had been penned "by" Dennis Cox, a "prominent," well-known Lancaster businessman.[55] Yet Cox didn't write the letter on his own, and Morris likely knew it.

The October 9 "Coffee with Clyde" column refers to the phony Cox letter:

[Hennigan]: In a letter to the editor this past week, Dennis Cox, former owner of Godfrey Advertising, suggested that both Mr. Shellenberger and Ms. Henderson are voting to "repay some personal and political debts."
[Clyde]: "That's a very serious accusation, Mr. Editor, but you must respect the author of the letter who is one of the most prominent businessmen in the area."[56]

"Repay Some Personal and Political Debts"

There was not the slightest evidence that I had "personal and political debts" I needed to repay, nor did I. Hennigan and "Clyde" knew very well that this letter didn't come from Cox alone. He planted that notion in the newspaper and used the "Clyde" persona to do it. It was pure invention.

In the month following the sale, in October 2005 (according to ProQuest, a database that tracks Lancaster Newspapers articles), 156 separate articles and letters on Conestoga View appeared in the three Lancaster newspapers—thousands of column inches (see Appendix C). Every one of those articles had a negative slant, except one—my published explanation of the sale.

The local citizens felt strong emotional ties to CV. It had been the county home for a long time, and change can be difficult. This needed to be acknowledged and respected. In the *Sunday News* on October 9, 2005, in "Why We Sold Conestoga View," I explained in detail, again, the reasoning behind voting for the sale. (See the letter in Appendix E and also Appendix F, "Pennsylvania County Nursing Homes.")[57] I mentioned that massive Bush administration decreases in federal and state funding had created a crisis in all county-level human services, including nursing home services.

I pointed out that Dauphin County would probably have to close its county nursing home, even after spending $20M to upgrade it two years earlier. The Dauphin County home lost $8 million in 2004, and Dauphin County had raised real estate taxes by 20 percent in each of the previous two years. Dauphin County sold its home in 2006 for $22 million.[58]

Pennsylvania's 67 counties had, at their peak, 54 county nursing homes. Some counties had none, and some, more than one. When Conestoga View was sold in 2005, the state had 33 county homes. By 2016, only 23 remained.[59]

The article explained the impracticality of the county owning a brick-and-mortar nursing home as a means of providing indigent care to the elderly. The trend leaned toward home-based and community-based care. I reassured the readers that the county's agreements with Complete Healthcare Resources provided assurances of continued access to quality care, no matter who owned Conestoga View. Complete Healthcare Resources had access to $1 million a year in government funding not available to the county. This multi-facility owner/operator had far greater operating efficiencies.

After three months of incessant negative "coverage" from Lancaster Newspapers, my 800 words on the topic didn't register in people's minds. The Lancaster County reading public had been bombarded with a daily refrain of "the commissioners are dishonest and incompetent idiots," and 800 words in one article wouldn't change that impression. The well had been poisoned.

My public record demonstrated years of service and support of city endeavors. As commissioner, I'd voted to apportion millions of dollars for important city-based projects, including the Pennsylvania Academy of Music and Clipper Magazine Stadium. I worked tirelessly on the Enola Low Grade Line. Why all of this negative attention?

I knew why. Conestoga View amounted to a $13 million deal. The hotel and convention center project, in 2005, had already topped $140 million, and it hadn't even begun construction yet. The county had guaranteed a $40 million bond for the project. Shellenberger and I were challenging that bond and tens of millions of dollars of state funding for the Steinman and High hotel. We were a clear and present danger to it, and we had to be sidelined.

Conestoga View became a fabulous "red herring" for the sponsors. This gift fell into the lap of Lancaster Newspapers. With Conestoga View, Lancaster Newspapers—a Penn Square partner—had the story to divert public attention away from the beleaguered hotel and convention center project. It was a misuse of their duty. But even the immense power of the press was not enough. It would take more.

Chapter Nine

THE DA INVESTIGATION

"Then we are like to have biting statues,
unless his teeth be pulled out."
—William Shakespeare, *Henry VI*, Part II, 1590

Art Morris did not let it go

He had sunk his teeth into the issue of Conestoga View. The ex-mayor and tenacious former miler was obsessed with the county's sale. Even after the September 28, 2005, vote; even after a judge upheld the sale; even after the commissioners' board answered every concern; and even after the county deposited the check, Morris remained fixated.

Morris attacked the commissioners for hiring the lawyers who handled the sale.[1] He criticized financial details and the "secrecy" of the deal and the speed with which it took place. Art Morris tailed CV shuttle vans around town after the sale, reporting to Lancaster Newspapers that the vans hadn't changed license plates.[2] Morris wanted to know why county-issued gas cards were still being used.[3] He attended almost every commissioners' meeting, braying on about the sale—all after it was a done deal.

None of these were legitimate news stories, but that didn't stop Lancaster Newspapers from publishing them prominently days and weeks after the CV deal was finalized. PSP had to keep the non-story going. The editors of Lancaster newspapers, with Buckwalter's approval, continued to publish often-lengthy articles, maliciously critical of "the commissioners."

The newspapers now used the term "the commissioners" to refer indiscriminately to all three board members, regardless of each person's individual action. Many of the Lancaster Newspapers articles ran with photographs of all three commissioners, even when the subjects of the article were Shaub and Shellenberger.

At one commissioners' meeting, the Lancaster Newspapers' photographer entered abruptly. I recognized him from other events. He took at least twenty-five shots with his clunky camera while moving around the room, then left abruptly. A politician always looks for a "photo-op," but this was ominous. *How is my hair?* I wondered but just kept smiling. Grouping me with the other two commissioners on Conestoga View damaged me politically and injured my reputation in the community. It deliberately discredited me by association.

And Morris operated in the middle of it all, feeding Lancaster Newspapers stories day after day, which appeared in print day after day. Authentic news journalism aims to factually report and investigate issues of importance to the general public. Its role is to provide the public with information they *need* to know, about topics meaningful to their lives.[4] Conestoga View, a legal sale of a county asset, did not merit the amount and prominence of coverage it received. The daily coverage of this non-issue was a terrible misuse of the power of the press. It continued and intensified. It did, however, divert public attention away from the massive amounts of public money flowing to the hotel and convention center.

Print It and They Will Read

"Here 'tis; here's a paper: shall I read it to you?"
—William Shakespeare, *All's Well That Ends Well*, 1602

The readers of Lancaster Newspapers naturally read what was printed. With only one printing press in town, what came off that press was what they read. The newspapers presented Lancaster County readers with the Conestoga View story almost every day of the week. They read that "the commissioners" met in "secret"; "the commissioners" sold out the poor and the elderly; "the commissioners" got a sweet deal. This made up the thread of each story. With nothing countering it, people believed it.

The DA Investigation

By late October 2005, more than 150 Conestoga View–related items had run in the three Lancaster Newspapers in less than four months. According to the database ProQuest, which tracks Lancaster Newspapers' content, the approximate number of articles with the words "Conestoga View" and "county commissioners" found together from 2004 to 2008 was as follows:

Approximate Number of Articles with "County Commissioners" and "Conestoga View

2004	35
2005	223 (99% coming in the last six months of the year)
2006	323 (57 in the month of December)
2007	212
2008	45
2009	22[5]

Meanwhile, Back at the Project

By the fall of 2005, Shellenberger and I had taken several steps to challenge the hotel and convention center project. Together, we:
- Hired special counsel, Howard Kelin, to provide a legal analysis of the taxability of the Penn Square Partners' hotel. The city council was about to vote on two city hotel bond guarantees, totaling $36 million. Kelin concluded that property taxes would still be due on the hotel, and the $36 million in city guarantees on hotel bonds were a violation of Act 23. It said that the "project user" (Penn Square Partners) had "to timely pay all Commonwealth and local taxes and fees." The city guarantees exempted Penn Square Partners from paying real estate taxes.[6]
- Voted to support a demand that LCCCA cease all spending and repay the county bond.[7]
- Requested the Lancaster County Convention Center Authority (LCCCA) to provide a legal opinion on whether the interest paid on the $40 million county-guaranteed bond qualified for exclusion from federal income tax.[8]

- Voted to authorize special counsel Kelin to investigate whether the county's guaranty of interest payments on the LCCCA bonds could be withdrawn.[9]
- Filed a Local Government Unit Debt Act lawsuit with the Department of Community and Economic Development (DCED), arguing that the city of Lancaster's two guaranties totaling $36 million were in violation of Act 23 and therefore illegal.[10]
- Voted to file a Petition for Review in the Nature of a Declaratory Judgment, seeking a judgment as to whether the DCED improperly awarded special grants to RACL for use in the private portion of the Hotel and Convention Center project under the Act 23 program.[11]
- Appointed three new members with hotel/tourism experience to the LCCCA board of directors. The new members asked many of the questions raised by us on the commissioners' board. They demanded accountability and information from the LCCCA board.[12]
- On September 27, 2005, the day Conestoga View was sold, the county voted 2–1 to explore separating the 3.9 percent "bed tax" from the 1.1 percent "excise tax."[13]

I know that list reads like a welding manual, but these were real challenges to the project. Yet instead of addressing our concerns and covering these issues, Penn Square partner Lancaster Newspapers wore out the Conestoga View story for more than two entire years.

"It's Not a Republican or Democrat Issue—It's a Taxpayer Issue."
—Representative Katie True, April 7, 2006

A word on Dick Shellenberger.

Dick Shellenberger did not have to take the stand he did with respect to the hotel and convention center project. He had everything to lose—his job, his standing in his party, his community. Shellenberger came from the conservative wing of the Lancaster County Republican Party. He and Senator Gib Armstrong went to the same church. The heavy-hitters of the Lancaster Republican political establishment, which had endorsed Shellenberger in 2003, stood firmly behind the project. Senator Armstrong, Representative Barley, former commissioners Thibault and Kauffman and now Shaub, and ex-mayor Art Morris and Mayor Smithgall were all staunch, day-one supporters. All had taken steps in their official capacities to help the project.

Shellenberger, to his great credit, thought for himself about the project and concluded it didn't make sense for the people he represented. In the spring of 2005, he said,

> I have become firmly convinced that construction of the hotel/convention center, according to the latest plans and most recently estimated costs, is the wrong direction. What was once a $75 million project funded with 47% public money has mushroomed into a $137 million project funded with 93% public money; and I, in good conscience, can no longer stand by while the taxpayers of Lancaster County foot the bill for a project which I believe has become significantly flawed.[14]

On many levels, Shellenberger and I were as different as two people could be. Shellenberger emerged from the conservative Christian fundamentalist faction of the Republican Party. I remained a "dyed-in-the-wool" Democrat. Think Pat Robertson and Gloria Steinem. However, Dick and I agreed on the hotel and convention center project. We understood it was all about the hotel. We had committed to doing our jobs to serve the best interests of the residents of Lancaster County.

> A grave? O no! A lantern, slaughtered youth.
> For here lies Juliet, and her beauty makes
> This vault a feasting presence full of light.
> —William Shakespeare, *Romeo and Juliet*, 1591

The time I felt most impressed with Dick Shellenberger was during the Nickel Mines tragedy.

We were alerted to the shooting of the Amish children in the southern part of the county over the special speakerphone in the small fifth-floor meeting room. The phone connected to the County Emergency Management Department. Somehow, I *knew* only the girls had been shot. We were all struck dumb. The state police and local emergency authorities took charge and did a good job. Governor Rendell called immediately. When the news broke, Lancaster County came to a standstill. Eight little Amish girls were shot, and five died in their one-room schoolhouse on October 2, 2006.[15]

Within the next few days, the Amish community held services for the girls. As one of the top officials representing the county, I felt unsure how to approach the situation. I didn't want to intrude in the very private lives of the devastated Amish community, nor did I want to appear uncaring. As I wavered, on the verge of choosing noninterference and not attending, Shellenberger came into my office.

"Come on, we're going to the viewings," he said.

I replied, "Won't we be intruding?"

Confidently, he assured me, "No, it's a sign of caring, that we respect the loss. I'll help you." And he did.

In all of my days as Lancaster County commissioner and since, going to express my sorrow to the Amish families on behalf of the county citizens was truly the most humbling and painful experience. Dick and I approached the house of each little girl, where family members had gathered. It was a sunny, cool day in October. Family members rested on the lawn around the dwelling under trees displaying red, yellow, and gold leaves. Inside the house, kindred sat on benches along the walls of the first floor, quietly talking.

As Dick and I went into the homes, Amish relatives and neighbors escorted us to meet the parents of the slain children. They were gracious and acknowledged our presence. At each home, we were taken to a separate room. The room was empty, save for one straight-backed wooden chair and a wee girl, who appeared asleep. The child lay in a tiny plain plank casket, wearing a hand-sewn ivory linen gown trimmed in lace with a matching linen cap. Each little girl had a small round beige Band-Aid on her petite temple. I wept for weeks.

> "Now quick desire hath caught the yielding prey."
> —William Shakespeare, *Venus and Adonis*, 1593

Art Morris still kept sniffing around the fifth floor of the courthouse during October 2005. Then one day Morris cornered his next prey: Gary Heinke. In less than a week, Heinke had become a household name. Morris had delivered the next red herring for the newspaper to the county's front stoop.

I first heard about the Heinke controversy on the afternoon of October 24, when someone brought the *Lancaster New Era* to my attention. On the front page, an above-the-fold article demanded, "Who Is Gary Heinke?"[16] The article, bylined by veteran *New Era* reporter Bernard Harris, credits Art Morris, "a county government watchdog," with discovering discrepancies in Heinke's résumé.

Evidently, during one of Morris's many forages on the fifth floor, he'd obtained a copy of Heinke's application for employment to the county and his accompanying résumé. I don't know how Morris obtained these documents. I believe that Pete Shaub, who was involved in Heinke's hiring, had tipped off Morris, as a way to continue his vendetta against Shellenberger.

Morris reported to the *New Era* that the Ph.D. Heinke claimed to have from Trinity Theological Seminary was not accredited by the U.S. Department of Education. Heinke did have a master's degree in theology from prestigious Duke University but wrote on his résumé that it was in ethics. Finally, on his official county application, Heinke indicated he had been an intern assistant to a school superintendent. However, on his résumé, he said he was "assistant superintendent" in the Minnesota school district.[17]

The next day, the commissioners authorized an immediate internal investigation into Heinke's hiring. With this being a personnel matter, the county directed the head of human resources, Tom Myers, along with Joseph Hofmann, a county attorney, to independently investigate it.[18]

On that day, October 25, the morning *Intelligencer Journal* ran a front-page article, "Heinke Cries Foul over Scrutiny over His Résumé."

"To have somebody [Morris] make a personal attack on a staff person of this county," Heinke said, "that makes every county employee fair game for somebody who's going to run to the press with what they think is some dust in the corner of your life that really doesn't exist."

Blood was in the water—or the ink—and the sharks at the paper were circling. Later that afternoon, the *Lancaster New Era* ran on its front page: "A Question of Credentials."[19]

Heinke had been ambushed. "There is nothing to hide here," he said. "I have been above board with this board of commissioners and with this county from day one and I stand by that. There is nothing there that has been anything of a deceptive nature, whatsoever."

On October 27, the front page of the *Intelligencer Journal* featured this article: "Stuckey: Go Home, Heinke." In it, county controller Dennis Stuckey recommended that Heinke take a leave of absence. "It would provide an opportunity for Heinke to get out of the mix of things here for a little while," Stuckey said.[20]

Gary Heinke resigned as chief services officer for Lancaster County the next day.[21]

Throw the Net a Bit Wider

"Help, master, help! Here's a fish hangs in the net,
like a poor man's right in the law; . . ."
—William Shakespeare, *Pericles*, 1608

Heinke's resignation didn't stop the Myers inquiry or Art Morris's crusade against the county commissioners.

Myers concluded that Heinke had falsified his résumé but *not* his official county application. Had Heinke falsified the application, he would have been in violation of a state law. It was moot, though. Heinke had already resigned more than a week earlier. (see pressedthebook.com for the Myers Report)

The E-Mail

"I am bound to serve,
This letter is mistook, it importeth none here;
It is writ to Jaquenetta."
—William Shakespeare, *Love's Labours Lost*, 1594

The DA Investigation

Yet it wasn't moot to one person. On Monday, November 7, 2005, at 8:14 a.m., District Attorney Donald Totaro sent an e-mail to Lancaster County human resources director Thomas Myers. The "Subject" of the e-mail was "Gary Heinke." In the e-mail, Totaro asked Myers ("Tom") for a copy of Myers's report on Heinke when it was completed. Here is a verbatim transcription of the entire 49-word e-mail that Totaro sent to Myers:

> Tom: I understand you are currently investigating the circumstances surrounding the hiring of Gary Heinke, and a final report is expected later this week. Once you have concluded your investigation, I would appreciate a copy of that report, along with copies of all relevant documentation. Thank you. Don Totaro (See Appendix A).

That is the entirety of Totaro's e-mail. The commissioners did not respond to it. Although the commissioners' names appeared on the "To" line after Myers's, the e-mail was clearly addressed only to Myers. It was not our report. It was Myers's. We did not conduct the investigation. Myers did. We did not have access to the report or "relevant documentation." Myers did.[22]

Totaro addressed "Tom" Myers, not the Lancaster County commissioners. Also note, in the friendly e-mail to "Tom," that Totaro "understand[s]" the investigation is "currently" being investigated by Myers, and that a "final report is expected" at an indeterminate time "later this week." Totaro's genial request divulges no sense of urgency or importance, no threat of action if Myers refuses.

Donald Totaro – Lancaster County District Attorney, 2000 – 2008, currently a Judge of Court of Common Pleas

211

Totaro does not indicate he is conducting his own investigation. He gives no deadline for producing the report.

Totaro concludes his note—not an official demand for documents—with an unpressured: "Once you have concluded your investigation, I would appreciate a copy of that report, along with copies of all relevant documentation."

The next day, Tuesday, the *Lancaster New Era* published "County Completes Report on Heinke." The article, bylined by Jack Brubaker, begins:

> County officials have completed a two-week-long investigation into the hiring of Gary D. Heinke, the human services chief who resigned Oct. 28 following allegations of false representation of his credentials. The Lancaster County commissioners should receive a full report Wednesday. "That's my goal," said J. Thomas Myers, the county's human resources director, who headed the investigation.

The article clearly shows that Myers was in control and possession of the report on Heinke, and Myers's "goal" was to deliver the report to the commissioners on Wednesday. It is inconceivable the district attorney didn't know that Myers, and not the county commissioners, controlled the Myers Report on Gary Heinke.

On Wednesday, November 9, forty-eight hours after Totaro's e-mail, Myers delivered his report to the county commissioners. The next day, Thursday, November 10, Myers gave a copy of the report to Totaro.

Despite having written his e-mail to Myers only seventy-two hours earlier and receiving the report itself, District Attorney Totaro used that interval of time as the cause to petition the Court to authorize a criminal grand jury investigation into the hiring of ex-county employee Gary Heinke.[23]

On the same day that Totaro received the Myers Report, just seventy-two hours after his e-mail to Myers, he filed a "Notice of Submission" with the Lancaster County supervising judge, Louis Farina (see Appendix A). Totaro asked for permission to use a grand jury to investigate Heinke. Farina approved Totaro's petition on the same day.[24] Before the afternoon edition of the *Lancaster New Era* hit the press on that Thursday, November 10, Totaro had applied for, had approved, and made a public comment about a grand jury investigation into the padded résumé of a former county worker.

"Wherever it takes us," said District Attorney Donald R. Totaro to the *Lancaster New Era* on that day, the 10th, when asked about the scope of the Heinke grand jury investigation.[25]

Art Morris was triumphant. "I hope [District Attorney Totaro] expands the investigation to include all aspects of the Conestoga View sale," Morris said to the *Intelligencer Journal* in its November 18 edition. "I certainly hope the process with Gary Heinke is fully reviewed and everybody's role in that."[26]

Art Morris got his wish . . . and more.

Totaro's Oath

"Then, good my lords, bear witness to his oath."
—William Shakespeare, *The Winter's Tale*, 1610

In his "Commonwealth's Affidavit," filed six months later, July 12, 2006, while the grand jury investigation was ongoing, District Attorney Totaro, officially and under oath, stated the reasons for a grand jury investigation into Heinke.[27] (See Appendix A) The district attorney wrote:

"I, Donald R. Totaro, District Attorney of Lancaster County, Pennsylvania, the affiant below, having been duly deposed, represents as follows:
1. "The original Notice of Submission regarding the résumé and hiring of Gary Heinke was prepared and filed after the Lancaster County Board of Commissioners initially failed to comply with a request for production of documents through traditional investigative means. . . .
2. "On November 7, at 8:14 a.m., this affiant [Totaro] emailed then-Lancaster County Director of Human Resources J. Thomas Myers, as well as the entire Board of Commissioners requesting a copy of the Myers Report, which explained the hiring process for Gary Heinke. Although the email was opened by all three County

Commissioners on November 7, 2005, not one Commissioner responded to that email prior to the Notice of Submission."

The affidavit implies that the November 7 e-mail was equally addressed to Myers and all three commissioners. It demonstrably was not.

Totaro directed his e-mail only to Tom Myers and made the request for the report only to him. There was no reason to believe, after the published *Lancaster New Era* article on November 8, that the commissioners had even *received* the report.

The affidavit suggested that Totaro's e-mail to Myers made an official demand of the commissioners to hand over the Myers Report.

> ". . . the Lancaster County Board of Commissioners initially failed to comply with a request for production of documents through traditional investigative means . . ."

In contrast to the affidavit, Totaro's November 7, 2005 e-mail, was a request of Thomas Myers for his, Myers's, report. The 49-word e-mail did not ask the county commissioners for Myers's report. In the e-mail, Totaro asks *Myers* for *Myers's* report. The statement from the affidavit "not one Commissioner responded to that e-mail prior to the Notice of Submission" is technically true but omits to state that the November 7 e-mail *to Myers* did not ask *the commissioners* to respond. The affidavit implies that the commissioners ignored a request when, in fact, no request was made of the commissioners.

The Totaro affidavit continues:

> Because November 11th was Veteran's Day, and County government would be closed for the holiday, a decision was made to prepare a Notice of Submission and present this to the Supervising Judge of the Lancaster County Investigating Grand Jury on November 10, 2005. This decision was made because of a total lack of response from the Board of Commissioners to a request from this office for a copy of the Myers Hoffman report, and because several sources expressed concern that information relevant to the investigation could be displaced or destroyed over the long weekend.

Totaro went further than merely petitioning the Lancaster County Court for a criminal grand jury to investigate an inflated résumé. The DA also filed a "Motion to Prevent Destruction of Evidence during the Investigation by the County Investigating Grand Jury."[28]

Totaro wrote in his affidavit:

> To eliminate the possibility that any evidence could disappear over the long weekend the Notice of Submission would allow this office to file at the same time a Motion to Prevent Destruction of Evidence during the Investigation by the County Investigating Grand Jury. . . . by submitting this investigation to the grand jury, our office could preserve said evidence and then use subpoena powers to receive the necessary information.

Presumably this evidence was evidence that Gary Heinke had puffed his resume. On the very day that he received the Myers Report, November 10, just three days after his genial 49-word e-mail to "Tom" Myers requesting it "later in the week," District Attorney Totaro led a criminal grand jury investigation into the hiring of Gary Heinke. Totaro also seized county records and issued scores of subpoenas to county employees, including the Lancaster County commissioners.[29]

The Grand Jury

"And they have been grand-jury-men since before Noah was a sailor."
—William Shakespeare, *Twelfth Night*, 1601

The grand jury that District Attorney Totaro used to investigate Gary Heinke's hiring was only the third in Lancaster County's history. It had been impaneled earlier in the year, well before the Conestoga View story broke.

Totaro's grand jury request was specific regarding the kinds of cases he wanted to investigate.

Examples of the criminal activity which can best be fully investigated using the resources of the Grand Jury include, but are not limited to, the following: illicit drug enterprises and related activities; racketeering as defined under the Pennsylvania Corrupt Organizations Statute, and unsolved homicides.

In March 2005, a month after Totaro received approval for his investigating grand jury, the *Lancaster New Era* ran an article about the grand jury. In "Target: Unsolved Mysteries/ DA to convene county's third-ever investigating grand jury to tackle stalled murder, drug and racketeering cases," the *New Era* quoted Totaro saying the grand jury was the best way to pursue serious "criminal activity within Lancaster County."[30]

Totaro's grand jury investigation was to identify "those who have committed unsolved murders in Lancaster County." It was that level of case that required "the resources of the Investigating Grand Jury."

Totaro acknowledged the prosecutorial advantages. "An investigating grand jury provides tremendous leverage for law enforcement authorities," he said in the March 2005 *New Era* article.

At the time of Totaro's original request in February 2005, a number of unsolved homicides existed in Lancaster County, including one of a baby in Strasburg.[31] These cases had prompted the request for an investigating grand jury.

Now, in November 2005, before even reading the Myers Report on Heinke, Totaro asked Judge Farina to give him permission to use that same grand jury to investigate a former county employee who had inflated his résumé.

And, based on the affidavit, the president judge of the Lancaster County Courts of Common Pleas, Louis J. Farina, told him to go right ahead.

A Threatening, Powerful Tool

The power of a grand jury is immense. A grand jury is empowered to subpoena witnesses, documents, and records, including banking, business, telephone, and computer records. Failure to comply with a grand jury subpoena can be punishable by imprisonment.[32]

With origins in twelfth-century England, modern U.S. grand juries investigate potential criminal and civil conduct and recommend or don't recommend prosecution.[33] Although the grand jury proceeding often takes place inside a courtroom, a grand jury is not a part of the court, and a judge is not present. A grand jury in the United States usually consists of between 12 and 23 people. Some jurisdictions have as few as 5 citizens seated. Other places have permanent standing grand juries, while some juries are convened as needed.

In Pennsylvania, an "Investigating Grand Jury" is a prosecutorial tool used by a county district attorney or the state attorney general to investigate extremely serious crimes.[34] In 2011, for example, the case of Jerry Sandusky, the convicted pedophile and former Penn State University football coach, had a state grand jury investigation. In 2014, in a high-profile case from Ferguson, Missouri, a grand jury investigated the killing of Michael Brown, an unarmed eighteen-year-old black youth shot to death by a police officer.[35]

After the investigation, if a grand jury believes the evidence presented by the prosecution warrants criminal charges, a "presentment of a true bill" is issued. If the grand jury believes no charges are warranted, a "presentment of no true bill" is issued to the court. If a "true bill" is presented, the individual or individuals investigated are usually indicted and prosecuted criminally.[36]

The grand jury is a secret proceeding, with everything concealed. All grand jury participants, witnesses, jurors, attorneys, stenographers, and bailiffs are sworn to secrecy and subject to prosecution if they disclose information about a case.[37]

It's been said that a grand jury will "indict a ham sandwich," because the proceeding is weighted so heavily in favor of the district attorney that he can make even a ham sandwich seem guilty of a crime.[38] Grand juries are a prosecutor's domain, because:

- A witness has no representation before the grand jury.
- A defense attorney may not object to questioning.
- Only the DA selects the jurors.
- No judge is present to oversee the proceedings.
- A witness may not see the transcript of her testimony.
- A witness may not ask questions.
- A witness is under oath, with the true possibility of perjury if future testimony varies.

- The proceeding is completely run by the prosecutor. The prosecutor in the Heinke grand jury was the Lancaster County district attorney, Donald Totaro.

It is the DA who issues the subpoenas. When a witness appears on the stand, the prosecutor is not required to present evidence to the grand jury in favor of those being investigated. The DA controls the investigation and all information that goes to the grand jury. The DA controls the witnesses, the order in which they testify, the time of day and the date they testify, and what testimony the grand jury will hear. The grand jury hears what the DA wants it to hear. The DA decides when everyone breaks for lunch and when everyone goes home.[39]

Grand jurors are regular citizens selected by the DA's office and screened, according to the DA's criteria. These people are pulled away from their daily lives and asked by the county's top law enforcement official to sit for extended periods of time, hear evidence and testimony, and make decisions that might have a life-changing impact on their fellow citizens.[40]

While impaneled, the grand jurors are dependent on, the DA's office. It is not a requirement that the grand jury be read any instruction on the law. If the DA wants to allow the grand jurors to read the newspaper, he can allow it. The job of a grand jury is solely to judge what the prosecutor produces. The grand jury is a very one-sided process, in favor of the prosecution.

Even after the "ham sandwich" is presented for trial, the person or people are not guilty of a crime. An indictment by a grand jury, a "presentment of a true bill," is not equivalent to a finding of guilt. It is an accusation, not a conviction.

So, grand juries function as powerful prosecutorial tools that can secretly investigate highly sensitive and very serious crimes. District Attorney Donald R. Totaro's original application for a grand jury in February 2005 was to use the "powers of the grand jury" to investigate "illicit drug enterprises and related activities; racketeering as defined under the Pennsylvania Corrupt Organizations Statute, and unsolved homicides."

The DA Investigation

The Stage Is Set

"If this were played upon a stage now, I could
condemn it as an improbable fiction."
—William Shakespeare, *Twelfth Night*, 1599

In 2005, the Lancaster County commissioners shared the fifth floor with the office of the Lancaster County district attorney.[41]

Don Totaro and his staff of assistant district attorneys, detectives, investigators, and various administrators worked right across the hall from the county commissioners and our staff. We waited for the same elevators on our way to lunch, drank from the same hallway drinking fountains, and used the same restrooms.

On November 10, after Judge Farina approved Totaro's request to use the grand jury to investigate the Gary Heinke hiring, members of the DA's staff walked across the hall and hand-delivered more than eighty subpoenas to our fifth-floor offices. Anyone at all connected with the commissioners' office—department heads, administrative staff, and the commissioners—was served. More subpoenas followed.[42]

The working environment at the commissioners' offices before the grand jury investigation had already been chilly. Pete Shaub had waged war on Dick Shellenberger for almost an entire year and had clashed with pretty much everyone in the building. Yet things got frigid after the subpoenas. Speaking with one another or the press about anything related to Heinke was expressly forbidden.[43]

This intimidating exercise of power on the part of the District Attorney thus suitably intimidated the staff. Many felt downright scared. The staff knew that the county had originally convened this grand jury to investigate murder cases. Now the DA would use it on a county personnel matter. In my opinion, it was an insult to of the power and resources of the district attorney's office. And, of course, Lancaster Newspapers kept running daily front-page stories about "the commissioners" and their grand jury investigation.

The editors at Lancaster Newspapers were not satisfied to leave the grand jury investigation in the hands of twenty-three Lancaster County citizens and the DA.[44] They persisted in telling the story, despite the secrecy of the proceedings. Lancaster Newspapers' saturation "coverage" of the Conestoga View sale continued. Reporters wrote the stories in serial form, each day with a new plot twist, a new way to cast "the commissioners" in a more nefarious light. And we could say nothing about it.

The grand jurors were not sequestered or prevented from reading the Lancaster Newspapers. Many of them likely read these stories during the investigation. As for me, I had stopped reading the newspapers by this point. Here's how I would start my day: I'd come into the kitchen, look at Alex, who had read the paper, and ask, "How bad is it?" I could tell just by looking at him what kind of day I would have.

The day after Totaro blanketed the fifth floor with subpoenas, on November 11, the *Lancaster New Era* published "How Heinke Got Inside Track."[45] The article described how commissioners Shellenberger and Shaub and county solicitor John Espenshade had provided Heinke with information and resources about the chief services officer position. No one gave the other applicants the same help. The *New Era* article used the Myers Report as the basis of the story.

Art Stays Busy

Art Morris fed the insatiable Lancaster Newspapers an endless stream of negative stories. In the weeks after the grand jury was launched, the *New Era* ran articles, thousands of words, criticizing the commissioners for the sale. Many of these articles featured Art Morris; for example, "Morris: Review Special Counsel Appointment," from November 29, 2005.[46] Morris chose not to ask questions about the $5 million (and counting) in legal fees that Stevens & Lee received from the LCCCA or the millions the LCCCA paid to consultants who produced little work.[47] Morris focused on Conestoga View because it diverted attention from the hotel and convention center project he championed.

On Sunday, December 11, 2005, in a 2,800-word hit, "Out of Commission," the *Sunday News* painted a picture of the Lancaster County commissioners as bickering buffoons. Political writer and wife of *Sunday News* editor-in-chief Marvin Adams, Helen Colwell Adams, wrote the article.[48]

The DA Investigation

Colwell Adams described the atmosphere at commissioner meetings as

> ... barely concealed hostilities among the three commissioners. ... Most of the visible animosity involves Shaub and Henderson. ... A year's worth of controversies is ending with the district attorney, Don Totaro, hauling the commissioners before a grand jury to investigate possible violations of the law connected with the hiring of Gary Heinke as chief services officer. Some employees say it's embarrassing to be working for the county. Morale is said to be worse than ever.

Throughout the article, Colwell Adams refers to "sources" connected with the grand jury investigation. Example: "Witnesses may begin testifying this week, according to sources." Another example: "Sources said the DA, who is notoriously tight-lipped about investigations, issued 82 subpoenas in one batch and then sent out another batch sometime after that."[49]

Someone at the DA's office wasn't "tight-lipped" enough not to give Colwell Adams these details. And since Totaro didn't launch a separate inquiry into the leak, we might conclude it was someone from the DA's office in "Out of Commission," Colwell Adams surveyed several of the commissioners' most severe critics and project supporters:

- Sen. Gib Armstrong: "I've never seen so many lawsuits,... They break their word.". . . Shellenberger has "lied to me several times. ... I've never seen an elected official, ever, like Molly, who refuses to answer questions. . . . I don't think Don [Totaro] would form a grand jury if he didn't think he had anything."
- William "Bill" Adams, former CEO of Armstrong Industries and founding member, along with High, Buckwalter, and Fulton, of the Lancaster Alliance: "A question for our local historians: Was a board of commissioners in Lancaster County ever under criminal investigation by the district attorney? that is, before 2005?"
- Former mayor Art Morris: "I get a lot of feedback, and there is great discontent across the county. People are upset with the entire collection of commissioners."

Colwell Adams closed the massive article, which ran with unflattering pictures of all three commissioners, by quoting an anonymous "community leader."

> "'Do all three of them remain for the next two years?' one community leader wondered last week. 'That's the million-dollar question. I suspect Don Totaro might have a lot to do with that.'"[50]

I wonder who the mysterious "community leader" could have been . . .

The Facts, Ma'am, Just the Facts

> "What is the reason for this terrible summons?
> What is the matter there?"
> —William Shakespeare, *Othello*, 1604

A county detective named Jan Walters handed me my subpoena. I didn't know Walters well, but I knew that he was a man of good reputation and integrity. He was a nice man, too. Walters seemed embarrassed to be tasked with serving me a summons. I certainly felt the same.

I retained Mark Lovett as my attorney. Lovett was a litigator but not an active criminal defense lawyer.[51] Lovett obtained a proffer letter from the DA's office. A proffer letter explains to the witness the legal basis why she is being interviewed. The DA's office indicated I was not a target of the investigation but didn't say why I would be questioned.[52]

Because the DA gave me no legal basis for testifying, we submitted a "Motion to Quash" the subpoena on June 14, 2006. I was willing to talk, but I had a right to know the basis of the questions. The supervising judge, Louis Farina, denied the motion to quash. Lancaster Newspapers turned this into a story about me "taking the Fifth" to avoid testifying.[53] I testified three times at varying intervals over several months and never invoked the privilege against self-incrimination. It was explained to me that a "classic" prosecutorial tactic where there is no evidence of a crime is to create one by having the target testify – without a lawyer- multiple times over several months in hopes of getting inconsistent testimony to set-up a felony perjury charge. A witness is not allowed to have a transcript or an attorney present during testimony, so her answers of different times are unlikely to be word for word identical. I did not want to be a "ham sandwich."

Chapter Ten

THE GRAND JURY

2005 Recap

"O, I have fed upon this woe already,
And now excess of it will make me surfeit."
—William Shakespeare, *Two Gentlemen of Verona*, 1594

After Shellenberger and I began to seriously question the hotel and convention center project, Lancaster Newspapers negatively featured us in hundreds of articles in 2005.

By the end of 2005, the newspapers had published over 1,200 separate articles, editorials, columns, and letters to the editor. Most of these concerned the sale of the Conestoga View or our actions regarding the project.[1] Lancaster Newspapers provided little coverage of the other work our board did for the county. The newspapers featured no front-page articles about our record of farmland preservation, the successful Clipper Magazine Stadium, or urban enhancement initiatives.[2] Lancaster Newspapers remained virtually silent on anything else going on in the commissioners' office.

The negative narrative about "the commissioners" utterly dominated Lancaster Newspapers' coverage, in wall-to-wall, above-the-fold, seven-days-a-week saturation. The newspaper aimed to have us resign or not seek reelection.

The year 2005 culminated with DA Donald Totaro launching only the third investigative grand jury in Lancaster County history, ostensibly to scrutinize an ex-county staffer's résumé.

The New Mayor

"Mayor, farewell: then dost but what thou mayst."
—William Shakespeare, *Henry VI*, Part I, 1591

On November 8, two days before District Attorney Totaro began his criminal grand jury investigation, the city of Lancaster held a mayoral election. Two-term Republican Charlie Smithgall lost a third-term bid to well-known Lancaster defense attorney J. Richard Gray, a Democrat.[3]

Apart from a $4 million budget deficit, Smithgall's legacy also included the hotel and convention center project. The bellicose Smithgall and former mayor Art Morris had argued against the Harrisburg Area Community College going into the Watt & Shand building. Both Smithgall and Morris had opposed the college, saying it removed the *public* building from the city's property tax rolls. Yet neither said a word years later when Penn Square Partners' privately operated hotel was taken off the same tax rolls. It was Smithgall who first convened High, Buckwalter, and Fulton to buy the Watt & Shand building, and it was Mayor Smithgall who also waived about a million dollars in city construction-related fees for the Partners.[4]

Smithgall ran interference to have the city's redevelopment authority (RACL) purchase, then lease back the Watt & Shand building to PSP. With RACL "owning" the hotel, PSP would not have to pay property taxes. And it was Smithgall (along with his mother-in-law and Art Morris) who showed up at county commissioners' meetings protesting the Conestoga View sale. Smithgall would exit the mayor's office in January 2006.[5]

I knew the man who replaced Smithgall.

J. Richard "Rick" Gray –
Lancaster Mayor 2006 - 2018

J. Richard "Rick" Gray was a large, bow-tie-wearing criminal defense attorney with a reputation of being a bit of a bully, yet he had a good sense of humor, in and out of court. He rode Harley-Davidson motorcycles for recreation. "Job No. 1 is to get our fiscal house in order. Job No. 2 is to get the convention center straightened out. And No. 3, I think, is community policing," Mayor Gray said to WGAL-TV on his first day in office, January 3, 2006.

Gray was elected with an all-Democratic city council. During the campaign for mayor, Gray went back and forth on the hotel and convention center issue. At one public meeting late in the campaign, to an audience of Rotary Club members, Gray seemed to support and not support the project during the same remarks.

"Keeping the county commissioners' concerns in mind," Gray said to the Lancaster Rotary Club members, "if my advisers and I decide it is not what the city needs, we'd have to pull the plug on the project." But, Gray added in the same speech, "Downtown desperately needs a quality hotel, and a convention center can make it work, but it will take aggressive marketing."[6]

I knew Rick, but not well, though our paths had crossed over the years. We were both active Democrats. Rick Gray was the only person in my entire life, before or since, who called me "*Moll*." Prior to taking office as mayor, he said it with a nice, endearing tone. After he took office, the tone changed.

I wanted to work with the mayor on the downtown project. On his second day in office, I sent Gray a letter making several proposals regarding the hotel and convention center. I proposed:

1. A "complete and comprehensive" feasibility study of the project;
2. That funding of the feasibility study come from the county, the city, and the LCCCA;
3. That the sale of the Watt & Shand building to the Redevelopment Authority of the City of Lancaster (RACL) be put on hold until the feasibility study was conducted, and construction bids had been received by the project's developers;
4. That the Watt & Shand building's interior not be demolished until a feasibility study was conducted and the project's construction price had been determined; and
5. That no changes be made on the project's construction bonds or bond guaranties.[7] I was concerned that the Convention Center

Authority was about to enter into a "Swaption Agreement," with the tens of millions of dollars of city- and county-guaranteed bonds.[8]

The sale of the Watt & Shand building from Penn Square Partners to RACL was scheduled for January 31. The historic building, purchased in 1998 for $1.25 million and sitting idle for seven years, was sold to the City Redevelopment Authority for $7.25 million.[9] This was a gain of $6 million for PSP. (The role of RACL was to get blighted properties fixed up and back on the tax rolls. The Watt & Shand building, however, while in need of some work, was not "blighted.")

The Feasibility Study

"May this be possible? May this be true?"
—William Shakespeare, *King John*, 1596

One of the strangest things about the proposed hotel and convention center was that despite now costing more than $140 million, the project never had an economic feasibility study done. The purpose of a feasibility study is to assess the viability of a project. What were the potential problems, and would this project even have a chance of working in the downtown Lancaster market? This absence was odd, considering the level of combined business acumen and experience found in PSP and the other project supporters.

Previous Project Reviews

Market Study #1

Starting in 1999, the private sponsors engaged consulting firms to conduct marketing studies on the proposed project. The Lancaster Campaign, the subsidiary of the Lancaster Alliance, commissioned the first one by Ernst & Young.[10] The alliance had been started by twelve leading Lancaster businessmen, including Dale High, Jack Buckwalter, and Rufus Fulton, representatives of Penn Square Partners.

It did not make a difference to Nevin Cooley and PSP that the Ernst & Young report on the project predicted, at best, tepid results.

And the consultants who drafted the report clearly stated that it was not a thorough feasibility study.

From the Ernst & Young executive summary:

> The financial analyses contained in this report are not considered a "financial forecast" or a "financial projection" as technically defined by the American Institute of Certified Public Accountants. . . .[11]

Market Study #2

As mentioned, the Ernst & Young review was not a certified feasibility study. Then in 2000, the LCCCA commissioned PricewaterhouseCoopers (PwC) to conduct another market study. Pricewaterhouse updated its study in 2002.[12] In both PwC marketing studies, the size and cost of the project rose, which necessitated more public subsidies. The commissioners believed it was well past time for an independent economic feasibility study. This was one of the largest public capital project in Lancaster County's history.

The day after I sent my letter to Mayor Gray, the three LCCCA board members whom Shellenberger and I had appointed—Laura Douglas, Deb Hall, and Jack Craver—held a large public meeting at the cavernous Farm & Home Center.[13]

At regular LCCCA meetings downtown, the public could comment, but the board was not allowed to respond. At this meeting—boycotted by the four city appointees and LCCCA solicitor John Espenshade—the county LCCCA members answered questions from the public.

About two hundred people sitting on folding chairs crowded the large room. The vast majority, regular citizens from around the county, came because they opposed the project. People stood in line and waited to speak. At the microphone, some complained about the burden of the tax on the hotel owners. Others fretted that the project would not benefit or be used by the average citizen. Several worried that the bond guaranties left taxpayers responsible if the project failed to meet its debt obligations.

Then, unannounced, Lancaster mayor Rick Gray marched in, wearing his omnipresent bow tie and a long camel winter coat. He immediately took the microphone. He didn't address the board members up on the stage or the commissioners but pivoted to the audience.

Gray practically sneered as he said, "What do you think is going to happen to this money, if we don't use it for this project? We lose it. It doesn't go anywhere else. You may want to do something else, but this is what we got, folks. This project's gonna get built. Get used to it."[14]

Then the mayor, in office barely twenty-four hours, abruptly turned and left the room, trailed by two scampering aides. Rick Gray had stopped vacillating. I didn't know what had changed his mind, but he now solidly supported the project.

A week later, at a regular commissioners' public meeting, Mayor Rick Gray made another unannounced appearance. Gray learned that our board planned to discuss a feasibility study for the project. He showed up at the fifth-floor commissioners' room, interrupting the meeting already in progress. As he had at the Farm & Home Center, Gray wore his long winter coat and a bow tie. He stood in the back of the room.

Chairman Shellenberger stopped and greeted the mayor pleasantly. "Good morning, Mr. Mayor."

Gray was in no mood for niceties. "If you want a feasibility study so bad," he said with a snarl, "fine, do it. But Pricewaterhouse has to do it, and you have to pay for it yourselves."

Then the bow-tied barrister exited the room. Surprised by the mayor's curt display, everyone in the room fell silent.[15]

Enter Robert Field

Mayor Gray's actions at the commissioners' meeting caught the attention of a new participant in Lancaster's growing civic drama.

Robert Field was a semi-retired real estate developer and investor.[16] Field had grown wealthy developing apartment complexes and hotels in the Middle Atlantic region.[17] He also had holdings in central Europe.

Déjà vu for Field

"Experience is by industry achieved
And perfected by the swift course of time."
—William Shakespeare, *Two Gentlemen of Verona*, 1594

The "East Mountain Inn," at the foothills of the Pennsylvania's Pocono Mountains, first brought convention center issues to Robert Field's attention.[18] The East Mountain Inn is located near Wilkes-Barre in Luzerne County, a "third-class" county, like Lancaster. In 1995, the Luzerne County commissioners considered backing a $22 million bond for a $41 million arena project.

A year earlier, in 1994, Governor Robert Casey had signed the "Pennsylvania Third-Class County Convention Center Authority Act." The act authorized third-class counties to enact a room tax. The Stevens & Lee law firm, Dale High's registered lobbyist, wrote the bill. Stevens & Lee represented the Luzerne County Convention Center Authority, as it would the Lancaster County Convention Center Authority beginning in 1999.[19]

The Luzerne County hotel and motel owners and others objected to the Luzerne County bond guaranty, as their counterparts did later in Lancaster County. Although he lived in Lancaster, Robert Field, owner of the East Mountain Inn, was one of the Luzerne County hotel owners who opposed the bond. In 1996, the Luzerne County commissioners formed the Luzerne County Convention Center Authority. They imposed a room tax, and $44 million later, in November 1999, the Northeastern Pennsylvania Civic Arena and Convention Center was built with taxpayer money.[20]

Returning to 2006

Now, in January 2006, after hearing of Mayor Gray's "offer" to the county, Robert Field pledged $50,000 to support a feasibility study.

Wrote Field to Shellenberger:

> I applaud Mayor Gray's suggestion that the Commissioners order and pay for a feasibility study and his commitment that, if the project will not be feasible, to end his support for the $137 million downtown revitalization initiative. . . . Should funding be an obstacle, I am

prepared to contribute $50,000 towards the cost of a comprehensive feasibility study on the convention center and hotel . . ."[21]

Gray didn't respond to Robert Field but did have a few choice words for Commissioner Shellenberger. The mayor now wavered on the idea of a feasibility study. In a letter sent to Shellenberger, reported on January 14 in both the *Intell* ("Mayor Answers Demands for Study") and the *New Era* ("Mayor: Conditions on Study Delaying Tactic"), Gray called Shellenberger's insistence that an independent firm, one not already affiliated with the project, conduct the feasibility study "disingenuous" and "wasteful" and said that it was "inappropriate" and "smacks of obfuscation and delay."[22]

In the *New Era* article, PSP president Nevin Cooley echoed Gray. "They're [Shellenberger and Henderson are] looking for a way to delay the project, and that is inappropriate," said Cooley.[23]

In addition to having the county pay for the study, Gray now insisted on two conditions:

1. That only PricewaterhouseCoopers perform the study; and
2. That it was to be completed within sixty days.

I defended the need for an independent feasibility study in the *Intell* article. "We're talking about an enormous amount of money," I insisted, "and what we need to find out is the amount of risk that is being placed on the taxpayer." I added that the financial and architectural plans for the project had changed so much in recent years, including a huge leap in costs, that the county owed its constituents a close look at the economic impact of the project.

As for any timeline, I responded, "I certainly want to expedite the process. However, I do not want to compromise quality for expediency. This is a project that will impact the county for a generation or more."[24]

The Previous Pricewaterhouse Studies

At the January 18 commissioners' meeting, the board voted 3–0 to contact Pricewaterhouse about performing a complete feasibility study on the project. We discovered in our research that the previous Pricewaterhouse studies were only "marketing studies," performed for marketing purposes—and those studies were not optimistic about downtown Lancaster as a convention center destination site.

According to the earlier Pricewaterhouse studies, Lancaster had significant "disadvantages" as a location for a hotel and convention center:

- "Air access ('an airport served by major airlines') is important for national and regional events where the majority of attendees fly to the destination. Lancaster's closest major airport is located approximately thirty miles north of the city in Harrisburg.

- "Trade shows are generally located in destinations offering large regional resident populations and large metropolitan area hotel room inventories.

- "[The proposed] facility requires more contiguous exhibit space than can be accommodated in a center city location.

- "Highway access to the center is relevant for statewide and local events since attendees tend to drive to the destination and the venue. Disadvantages or concerns listed by some event organizers included traffic problems getting into downtown, lack of entertainment and evening activity in downtown, and parking issues including availability and the possible lack of free parking."[25]

Pricewaterhouse declined to participate in a new study. The project had become a major local political controversy, and the firm didn't want to be in the middle of it.[26] The firm, in fact, had distanced itself from the project.

In an e-mail sent to LCCCA board member Jack Craver, Robert Canton, the lead consultant for the earlier Pricewaterhouse studies, wrote of the company's serious concerns about how its studies were being used to market the project.

Canton wrote,

We are concerned that PwC's analyses are being used to "promote" the proposed convention center development. I personally wrote a note to [LCCCA executive director] Mr. Hixson requesting that all reference to PwC be removed from the LCCCA website.... Regardless of any review of our prior studies, the physical characteristics of the development that I understand to be proposed are very different from the project I studied (the equivalent of using a study of a 500 room Marriott to evaluate a 300-room Hampton).[27]

Pricewaterhouse's decision not to conduct a feasibility study didn't mean the commissioners would give up. The study had to be done. Too much risk was involved. The project had become too expensive, and we had too many questions and concerns about its economic viability.

On February 8, 2006, the county commissioners voted 2–1 (Shaub voted no) to solicit "Requests for Proposals" to consulting firms to conduct the first actual feasibility study on the hotel and convention center project.[28] Finally, seven years after the project had begun, an economic feasibility study would be done.

PKF

A week later, the county commissioners voted, again with Shaub's dissent, to hire Pannell, Kerr, Forster (PKF) Consulting to do the feasibility study. PKF was a preeminent firm in the field of hospitality consulting. (PKF has since merged its companies with CBRE hotels.)[29]

PKF projected the cost of the feasibility study to be $115,000.[30] Robert Field increased his pledge from $50,000 to $65,000. The commissioners' board asked the LCCCA and the Lancaster City Council to chip in to help pay for the study. All three bodies—the county, the city council, and the LCCCA—had a stake in the project, and we all should have been responsible for paying for the feasibility study.

We, the majority of the commissioners' board, wanted all construction work on the proposed project to halt until PKF had completed the study. The county didn't get any cooperation, financial or otherwise, from the City of Lancaster, four of the seven members of LCCCA, or any other sponsor of the project.

The LCCCA and PSP, through Hixson and Cooley, announced that they would not cooperate in any way with the PKF study. Charles Simms, chairman of the city's redevelopment authority (RACL), also indicated that his agency would not cooperate with PKF.[31]

Ted Darcus—LCCCA Chairman

Rather than communicate directly and professionally with the Lancaster County Board of Commissioners—the very governmental body that had created the LCCCA and enacted the tax that funded it—the chairman of the LCCCA board, C. Ted Darcus, decided to publish an open letter to the "Commissioners" in the February 26 edition of the *Sunday News*. Darcus's 916-word essay took up the entire first page of the Letters-to-the-Editor section of the *Sunday News*. (The normal "letters" word limit was 150 words.)

Dear Commissioners:

We are advised that at your public meeting on Wednesday, Feb. 15, commissioners Shellenberger and Henderson voted in favor of, and announced, the retention of PKF Consulting of Philadelphia by the County of Lancaster to a contract at a price of $115,000. You also announced that $65,000 of the contract price will be funded privately through a local businessman, Robert Field, who is a self-acknowledged opponent of the convention center project.... Specifically, neither the Redevelopment Authority of the City of Lancaster nor Penn Square Partners have expressed any willingness to participate in this further feasibility study by PKF.... Based upon the foregoing, please be advised that the authority views this study to be another example of the two commissioners attempting to usurp the powers of the authority, to diminish, distract and interfere with the ongoing business of the authority in fulfilling its statutory mission, and to bring further focus to the self-interests and competing goals of the project opponents. For these reasons, the authority board and its staff will not participate in the process relating to the consulting services to be provided to the county by PKF Consulting.

Accordingly, the authority places the county and commissioners Shellenberger and Henderson on formal notice that: (1) PKF Consulting and the county are proceeding on your own, independent of the authority; (2) the authority will not be responsive to PKF Consulting's data gathering, other than to continue to respond in conformity with statutory requirements; (3) the authority will not be responsible for any errors in, or misstatements of, data, contractual and/or legal relationships, or other information relating to either the project or the public agencies or private participants; but (4) in the event of any such errors, misstatements, or other dissemination of false or misleading information relating to either the authority, the project, or the public agencies and private participants, the authority will hold the county, commissioners Shellenberger and Henderson, and their consultants, and any public or private group or individual supporting such acts or omissions, financially.
—C. Ted Darcus, chairman,
Lancaster County Convention Center Authority[32]

The voice speaking for the Lancaster County Convention Center Authority board of directors was that of Ted Darcus, the LCCCA's chairman. Darcus was openly hostile to the county's LCCCA board appointees and blatantly discouraged their questions. In one instance, county-appointed board member Deb Hall, executive director of the Ephrata Chamber of Commerce, who ran the Visitor's Center in Ephrata, and a paralegal, made a motion to audit the legal fees of the LCCCA's solicitor, Stevens & Lee.

By this time, the law firm had billed the LCCCA more than $6 million. None of the monthly invoices—many totaling more than $100,000—had details regarding the nature of the work. The bills merely stated: "For professional services rendered on behalf of the Lancaster County Convention Center Authority," followed by the dollar amount. After discussing Hall's motion with the board's solicitor, Stevens & Lee lawyer John Espenshade, Darcus refused to allow it to be voted on by the full board. He cited "attorney-client privilege."[33]

When Hall objected, Darcus blew up. "There is a process in place!" Darcus roared, his voice rising. "I am sick and tired of hearing what you think it is. This meeting is adjourned!" He banged his gavel and stalked off the dais.[34]

After county-appointed board member Jack Craver, retired manager of the famous luxury hotels the Plaza in New York City and Mayflower in Washington, D.C., wrote a letter to the editor of the *Sunday News* supporting the feasibility study, Darcus wanted to put a gag order on the board to prevent its members from speaking to the press.[35]

"We can't have people doing their own thing," said Darcus, doing his own thing. A gag order was never imposed.[36]

Darcus didn't schedule regular convenient meetings. Under Darcus, LCCCA meetings took place at irregular times and intervals. In addition, he often called "executive sessions" in the middle of LCCCA public meetings. During executive sessions, the public had to leave the room, while the board and the solicitor conducted certain types of LCCCA business. Once, when a particularly contentious issue was to be voted on, Darcus called a public meeting for 7:30 in the morning. Right after the meeting began, Darcus ordered that the board go into executive session. This sent members of the audience, who had taken time off work to attend the inconvenient meeting, into the hallway to wait it out.

Harper Surfaces

"Come on, then; I will swear to study so,
To know the thing I am forbid to know;"
—William Shakespeare, *Love's Labour's Lost*, 1594

Sometimes the LCCCA meetings were very entertaining, thanks to Ron Harper, Jr.[37] By 2006, Harper had become well known throughout the county as a kind of independent watchdog for the people. Harper, regardless of the season, always dressed in shorts and a navy-blue T-shirt, with "Official Observer" printed on the back. He might show up anywhere with his video camera. Harper did a great service for the people of Lancaster County with his video recordings because the reporters and the editors at Lancaster Newspapers did not fulfill the job of monitoring public officials.

Many of Harper's greatest hits happened at LCCCA meetings. In 2001, Harper presented former LCCCA chairman Jim Pickard with

Ronald Harper, Jr. – official observer with
"Flat John" portrait (Espenshade)

a chocolate cream pie. The "humble pie," according to Harper, was to teach the imperious Pickard some humility. Pickard flushed crimson, grabbed the pie, and awkwardly flung it back at Harper, showering pie shrapnel on the poor stenographer below. It was hilarious to everyone but Pickard and the stenographer. It made the evening news.[38]

During Darcus's tenure, Harper often stood at the public microphone with his arm around a life-size cardboard photograph of LCCCA solicitor and Stevens & Lee lawyer John Espenshade. Harper called the cutout "Flat John" and had "conversations" with it, mocking the stone-faced, well-dressed solicitor.

After leaving the board in 2008, county-appointed LCCCA board member and international business owner Laura Douglas summed up her time under Darcus:

> Quite simply, the Convention Center Authority was the worst organization I have ever encountered, let alone been a part of. It was very clear that the authority had no regard for the source of

its revenues, the taxpayer. Mr. Darcus was a very strongly divisive force on the board. He was blinded by certain issues, and instead of considering them, would go ahead and move forward on his own.[39]

Darcus could steamroll the LCCCA's seven-member board because he had the votes. The other three city appointees were notable for not being noticed, and they dependably rubber-stamped whatever Darcus wanted. Four beats three every time.

David Hixson—LCCCA Executive Director

Hired in July 2003, David Hixson was the third person to hold the position as the board's executive director, following Pickard and a man named Michael Carper. Hixson had no hospitality or convention center industry experience.[40]

Hixson didn't seem to grasp many of the details concerning the project. During meetings, he appeared lost at times, even as he followed a script. It didn't matter. When either Hixson or Darcus needed direction, they looked to Espenshade at the end of the dais. The Stevens & Lee lawyer told them what to do.[41]

So, while the LCCCA board was divided 4–3, with Hixson and Espenshade, it was more like a 6–3 split. The sponsors controlled the executive director, the chairman, and the solicitor positions.

Now Shellenberger, Shaub, and I had started to attend Consortium meetings about the convention center. These monthly meetings were held on the top floor of the Griest Building, then the highest building in Lancaster. You could see the whole city from up there. Coincidently, C. Emlen Urban, the architect of the Griest Building, had also designed the Watt & Shand building.

The Lancaster Alliance/Campaign had called the Consortium meetings to help prepare the area for the future hotel and convention center. They discussed issues such as transportation, parking, entertainment, and local support. I remember feeling physically ill as I listened to the lack of structure, planning, and coordination involved in this project. I rarely spoke. Shaub did ask good questions, though. After a while the meetings stopped—or, at least, we were not invited anymore.

Conestoga View—2006

David Hixson – Executive Director, Lancaster County Convention Center; resigned 2007

Conestoga View continued to dominate the newspaper coverage the last six months of 2005 and during all of 2006—far, far more than anything related to the convention center project.

In early January 2006, three months after the county sold the nursing home and two months after DA Totaro opened his grand jury investigation into the hiring of a former county employee, Lancaster Newspapers still covered Conestoga View as if it were the story of the century.

The grand jury investigation did not staunch the flow of nonstop Conestoga View stories, and neither did the turn of the new year. The *New Era* opened the year with the January 5, 2006, editorial "Commissioners Need to Let in More Sun," which reads in part:

> The sun isn't shining very brightly on county government these days.
> Commissioners Dick Shellenberger and Pete Shaub's disdain for the state's open-meetings law—the Sunshine Act—is quite evident.
>   Much the same can be said of their colleague, Molly Henderson.
>   This has been especially true about the controversial sale of Conestoga View, the 446-bed nursing home on East King Street. . . . Shaub wanted to open the process, but Shellenberger and Henderson favored continued secrecy. . . . Sadly, to this

day, the commissioners don't seem to think they did anything wrong.

They don't understand that their secrecy generated far more negative reaction than early disclosure would have done.

They don't understand that they did something wrong. They see no need to apologize or promise an end to such secrecy. . . .

For all the public knows, the commissioners will repeat secret meetings whenever they fear that public reaction to their plans might be negative. . . . Most county and local office holders go out of their way to discuss public matters in public. The commissioners should be no different.[42]

Of course, due to the grand jury investigation, the county commissioners could say nothing. I don't think I even spoke the words "Conestoga View" during this time. So, Lancaster Newspapers kept taking free shots at "the commissioners," and we had to remain mute.

Conestoga View provided daily content for Lancaster Newspapers. Shellenberger and I, the majority of the Lancaster County Board of Commissioners, had openly challenged the hotel and convention center project. Lancaster Newspapers held a 44 percent private ownership stake in the hotel portion of the project at this point in 2006.[43]

Conestoga View furnished an ongoing narrative for all three Lancaster Newspapers. That narrative had two basic objectives as it concerned the hotel and convention center project: one, the story and its repeated telling demonized "the commissioners"; and, two, it took the hotel and convention center off the front pages and the editorial pages.

On February 16, 2006, the readers of the *Intelligencer Journal* saw on the front page, "County Broke Law, Morris says."[44] This is what tens of thousands of people saw when they picked up the newspapers from their driveways, brought them inside, and read them over their morning coffee and cereal. This is the headline people saw in newspaper kiosks and in waiting rooms across Lancaster County that day.

The "county" could say nothing in rebuttal. I could say nothing. I guess I could have, but I didn't want to go to jail.

Morris stood up at the February 15 commissioners' meeting and accused the board of violating the Pennsylvania Municipalities Planning Code in selling Conestoga View. "You carried out the sale of Conestoga

View with utter disregard for the law," Morris scolded, peering over his glasses like a cross British headmaster.

"Thank you for your comments, Mr. Morris," was all that board chairman Dick Shellenberger could say in response. Dick didn't want to go jail, either.

By 2006, Bernard Harris had covered the county commissioners for the *Lancaster New Era* for several years. I never had any complaints about Bernie. He seemed to be a responsible journalist covering the county, as far as I was concerned. However, lately Bernie's articles had become less frequent. My belief is that the editors took Harris off the commissioner beat and replaced him with Brubaker. Harris stopped attending the meetings and stopped writing articles.

By early 2006, the most prominent, page-one *New Era* stories involving the Lancaster County commissioners were now written by John H. "Jack" Brubaker, III.[45] After I left office, I sued Brubaker for libel, along with other Lancaster Newspapers employees, who included CEO Jack Buckwalter and *New Era* editor-in-chief, Ernie Schreiber. As a defendant, Brubaker was also deposed. In 2003, *New Era* editor-in-chief Schreiber moved Brubaker from the editorial page to become what he called an "investigative reporter and general assignment reporter."[46] Ernie Schreiber and Brubaker had a very close working relationship for many years. The two of them had collaborated on several editorials in the recent past, lambasting "the commissioners" for our position on the hotel and convention center project and, of course, Conestoga View. Both publicly supported the hotel and convention center project.

"We have sort of an unusual situation in that I work directly with Ernie Schreiber," Brubaker said during his deposition. "I enjoy working with Ernie."[47]

After it was decided that the newspaper's focus would be Conestoga View, Schreiber assigned Brubaker to it. By early 2006, Brubaker had published dozens of items related to the sale.

On a single day, February 17, Brubaker published four separate articles in the *New Era*, each negative and each related to Conestoga

View: "How Did County Decide to Sell Nursing Home?"; "Did County Break Pa. Law?"; "How Does Depreciation Figure in Financial Health?"; and "Accounting Yardsticks Give Different Measures."[48]

The sheer amount of time, space, and resources Lancaster Newspapers devoted to the Conestoga View story was truly amazing, even five months after the sale. This serialized drama in print involved reporters, editors, copy editors, photographers, the president and CEO. To give today's reader a sense of the attention just one of the three Lancaster Newspapers devoted to the Conestoga View issue, following is a list of the headlines, the dates, and the number of words in each article that ran in the *Lancaster New Era* from February 16, 2006, to March 16, 2006. *This is just one newspaper's coverage for thirty days:*

Feb. 16. "New Questions Raised over Conestoga View Sale" (762 words)
Feb. 17. "How Did County Decide to Sell Nursing Home?" (832 words)
Feb. 17. "Did County Break Pa. Law?" (1,431 words)
Feb. 17. "How Does Depreciation Figure in Financial Health?" (248 words)
Feb. 17. "Accounting Yardsticks Give Different Measures" (212 words)
Feb. 22. "Morris Warns of Sale Precedent" (451 words)
Feb. 28. "Law Firm Agrees to Release Records" (728 words)
Mar. 2. "Demo Henderson's Role as GOP Spoiler" (588 words)
Mar. 4. "County Gets Itemized Conestoga View Bills" (395 words)
Mar. 6. "Nursing Home, though Sold, Will Cost County in Future" (567 words)
Mar. 6. "Fair Value for Conestoga View?" (712 words)
Mar. 6. "Value of Sale: $11.3M, Not $13.3M" (499 words)
Mar. 8. "Sunlight Is the Best of Disinfectants . . ." (824 words)
Mar. 14. "Shaub: I Had Role in Sale" (461 words)
Mar. 14 "County to Release Conestoga View Records" (59 words)
Mar. 14. "Shaub Contradicts Earlier Statements" (281 words)
Mar. 15. "Revealed Secrets Spark New Fight" (1,127 words)
Mar. 16. "Commissioners Need an Exit Strategy" (642 words)

One newspaper, thirty days. Eighteen separate articles from one newspaper, not including dozens of letters to the editor. This sample does not include any items from the *Intelligencer Journal* and the

Sunday News, both of which "covered" Conestoga View to a similar extent, often repeating quotes and text.

It was not coverage but a campaign, using the powerful Lancaster Newspapers to squelch "the commissioners." The stories didn't stop on March 16, either. They kept going. On March 21, the *New Era* ran "No Trace of Commissioners' Deal with Lawyers in Any County Files," and on the same date splashed a front-page "Ex-Officials Rip Secret Deal."[49]

In another Brubaker piece on March 29, "They've Got Another Secret, County to Release Records—without Black Marks," the *New Era* reporter suggested that there was another layer of "secrecy" to the sale: the legal work.[50]

Brubaker, or whoever wrote the *New Era* headline on April 29, 2006, got a little carried away with the great Conestoga View caper. The headline stated, "The Perfect Secret, County Officials Kept a Tight Lid on the Sale of Conestoga View until the Deal Was Suddenly Announced. Here's How They Did It."[51]

"Here's How *They* Did It." Who were "they"? I attended a single presentation regarding the *possible* sale of Conestoga View. No deliberation about the sale took place at that presentation. I had no role in helping Gary Heinke get hired. This was an established fact. Of the Myers Report, Brubaker admitted that he "read it very carefully."[52] Still Brubaker, seven months after the sale, grouped me with the other two commissioners by using the pronoun *they*. Brubaker did much worse than that.

The "articles" simply didn't stop. The journalistic value of the sale of Conestoga View had long been exhausted. It was absurd that Art Morris, Ernie Schreiber, Jack Brubaker, and the staffs of all three Lancaster Newspapers still kept pursuing the legal invoices related to the Conestoga View sale—fees that came to less than $300,000—when the legal fees from the same law firm, Stevens & Lee, involving the hotel and convention center project were in the millions of dollars. And 2006 wasn't even halfway finished.

Chapter Eleven

THE RELENTLESS PRESS

"From this time forth I never will speak word."
—William Shakespeare, *Othello,* 1603

The ongoing grand jury investigation put a "gag order" on the county commissioners. We couldn't say anything about the daily Conestoga View stories in Lancaster Newspapers.

During 2006, Art Morris and LNP's editors and staff, including Chairman Jack Buckwalter, worked together to keep Conestoga View in the news. That year, they published more than *five hundred* separate items on Conestoga View, *not* including obituaries.[1]

I believe the strategy of Lancaster Newspapers—44 percent owner of the hotel portion of the project—was to saturate the newspapers with articles and editorials that focused on the county commissioners and Conestoga View.[2] With public attention diverted, PSP could finance and build the hotel and convention center before the Board of Commissioners could stop it.

We tried to counter the published criticisms of the Conestoga View sale. In October 2005, weeks after the sale, I wrote an open letter to the *Sunday News,* "Why We Sold Conestoga View." Speaking for the board, I explained the sale and said that the process should have had more public discussion.[3] The county had hired the unimpeachable accounting firm of Reinsel Kuntz Lesher (RKL) to conduct an independent audit of Conestoga View's books from 2000 through 2004.[4]

The Accountants

"Spare your arithmetic; never count the turns;
Once, and a million."
—William Shakespeare, *Cymbeline*, 1609

RKL found that Conestoga View had lost $4.4 million between 2000 and 2004. The firm also discovered an accounting error from 2001, resulting in another $4 million loss.[5] RKL reported that the error involved Conestoga View recording bond money as income. The county had loaned CV money for capital improvements, and this needed to be paid back. The nursing home had been more than $8 million in the red at the time of the sale. RKL's report supported the county's financial assessment of CV.

Yet even the RKL report was criticized. County controller (and future county commissioner) Dennis Stuckey, whose office provided RKL with Conestoga View's financial information, said he disagreed with the independent report.

"Reinsel Kuntz Lesher took numbers provided by the controller's office and put them together to fit the commissioners' point of view," stated Stuckey to the *Intelligencer Journal* on May 3, in, "Controller, Commissioners at Odds over Report."[6]

Controller Stuckey, who was not an accountant, accused the most established, well-regarded accounting firm in Lancaster County of getting involved in politics. (Stuckey planned to run for county commissioner in 2007. He was elected and has remained commissioner as of this writing in 2018, into his third four-year term.)

RKL partner Robert Simons pointed out the $4.4 million accounting error that the county controller's office had not caught. Simons said it artificially inflated the nursing home's earnings.

Stuckey couldn't admit his error. "Until documents are produced that convince me otherwise, I strongly support my staff and our conclusions regarding Conestoga View," he taunted, oblivious to the fact that *he had already produced those documents.*

I called on Stuckey to show some professional integrity and admit his mistake. Buried in the April 6, 2006, *Intell* article, my quote said, "The report of highly respected regional independent accounting firm

Reinsel Kuntz Lesher unequivocally stated that the controller's office erroneously overstated Conestoga View operating income by over $4 million, and it is past time for Mr. Stuckey, for the good of the county taxpayers, to work to correct, not repeat, this error."

I felt gratified that during this time, the county managed to purge itself of Stevens & Lee. Longtime county solicitor John Espenshade resigned, to be replaced in early 2006 by Don LeFever. The well-regarded, experienced LeFever became the county's "in-house" attorney. LeFever also had a flair for the esthetic. With his keen eye, he observed that some of the paintings hanging throughout the courthouse were exceptionally valuable. These old and significant pieces needed to be preserved. He saw to it that the paintings were saved.

Meanwhile, Back at the Ranch

In the spring of 2006, the county waited for the PKF economic feasibility report on the hotel and convention center project. By early May, PKF submitted the "Executive Summary" of the study. PKF concluded that the project would lose at least $1.3 million per year and recommended that project sponsors consider "downsizing" or "find an alternate use for the site."

> [O]ur findings lead us to conclude that the potential economic benefits are not likely to be sufficient to justify the risks involved, including the potential need to raise the hotel tax to fund operating deficits after several years should the reserves become depleted. We therefore recommend that, prior to proceeding further with this project, the parties involved consider exploring a downsizing of the project or an alternate use for the site.[7]

The hotel project supporters harshly criticized the PKF report. In a May 5, 2006, article, "Gray Rips Negative Report, Mayor Says County Study of Penn Square Project Slanted," the new mayor questioned PKF's impartiality.

"Let me just say that I've tried many cases," the mayor said, "and I know that if you shop hard enough you can find people who can put things in the best light for you when faced with questions and assumptions."[8]

"Is this the party to whom I am speaking?"
—*Ernestine*, Lily Tomlin, circa 1970

"More of your conversation would infect my brain."
—William Shakespeare, *Coriolanus*, 1607

I phoned Mayor Gray to discuss the PKF conclusions. The report painted a very bleak picture of the financial future of the project. Gray was out of town, and I reached him by cell phone. Recently, I had been in Harrisburg to discuss the project with one of Governor Ed Rendell's aides, Lance Simmons. I wanted to talk with Gray about that, too.

The conversation with the mayor was so extraordinary, I transcribed it by hand immediately after we hung up (this is a verbatim, non-edited transcription of my handwritten note):

On Fri. May 5, 06, after visit with Lance Simmons, I call Rick Gray on cell at about 5:15. He says he's in Ohio and back on Sun. I say I'll call him to set up a time to talk/meet. I sent him an email on 5/7/06, Sunday morning about 10:00 am or so. I call at 11am or so on cell and leave a message and later on landline to leave a message at his home. He returns on cell at about 6:10 pm as I am on my way to a Columbia Dems meeting.

Rick comments on his trip to see his son's house. I say nice day for a trip and thank him for getting back to me. I ask when I might meet with him—perhaps tomorrow morning. He says he has early meetings and asks what it is about. I say, "Our favorite real estate project." He says, "Nothing to discuss." I say I have a few items to bring up. He, "Like what?" I told him that I met with the Gov. at the CCAP [County Commissioners Association of Pennsylvania] convention and the Gov. told me he would keep the money for the convention center project in Lancaster County. Rick interrupts me with, "The County not the City?!"

I then go on, after I asked to be allowed to finish, that the feasibility study has come back with less than supportive results. Rick makes disparaging remark about study. I then bring up that I have heard that an alternate "Plan B" for the site may be presented soon. He wanted to know who and when. I did not give who, and

> *I didn't know when. He then said I have betrayed the city and how could I do a 180 on my campaign statement to support the CC?*
>
> *I reminded him I had two caveats: 1) No county guarantee and 2) The CC had to be self-supporting. He said CC's are never self-supporting. I stated that the project had dramatically changed since 2003. He said I was jeopardizing economic development in the city and I didn't know what was at stake. I said I was very concerned about the risk to taxpayers. I said I would like to propose to the Gov. to keep 2M for Central Market and 1M for Bethel AME. He cut me off and said how dare I talk to the Governor about such things and to "Keep your nose the fuck out of City politics."*
>
> *I said I had not contacted the Gov. directly but there were many ideas that I wanted to discuss with him. Rick: "I can't believe the balls you have to see the Gov. What balls you have to do that.!" He complained that County money went to farmland preservation. I said that this Board of Commissioners is the first to divide money for urban revitalization. He then accused me of holding up the project and having things delayed. I asked him how anything I had done to question the project caused a delay.*
>
> *He brought up the TIF and that the school board of Lancaster should have done a TIF. I had no response. Rick is very angry at this point. I ask what do you need to look at another project? He says the finances don't work. I say, "What does that mean?" He says the money doesn't come together, to that effect. He then says if I don't back off this, "I will tear you a new asshole!" I say Rick I hope we can get past this and work together on other projects together. He said nothing else to discuss. I hung up.*[9]

Thus, ended my Sunday evening conversation with the mayor of the City of Lancaster. At the bottom of the two-page, double-sided note, I wrote a rather ominous fragment: *"absolute threat to my political career."*

A "Plan B" alternate proposal to the hotel and convention center project did exist. Three people—a leading out-of-state developer, a building restoration specialist, and a leading Lancaster County realtor—were prepared to buy the Watt & Shand building and develop it as a mixed-use space.[10] The first few floors would be retail business, with the upper floors sold as luxury condominiums. The development would pay property taxes, stimulate the downtown economy, and raise downtown property values.

Yet Plan B was a non-starter after that conversation with Rick Gray. He was wrong when he said I didn't know what was "at stake." I knew exactly what was at stake: the taxpayers' money. No matter how unhappy and uncivil it made Gray and other project sponsors, I wasn't going to back down. My responsibility was to the residents and the taxpayers of Lancaster city and county.

Act 23—2006

The county continued to challenge the state Act 23 funding for the hotel in 2006. On February 22, Kelin filed a lawsuit on behalf of the county commissioners. We wanted the Department of Community and Economic Development to rule on the legality of the project's Act 23 application.[11]

Project developer PSP, through the Redevelopment Authority of the City of Lancaster (RACL), applied for $14 million in Act 23 funds. These funds were to help pay down future construction debt—yet another public subsidy for the "private" PSP project that also relieved them of paying property taxes.

To receive Act 23 money, the project (hotel) needed to be publicly owned. (See Chapter Six: "It's All About the Hotel—Really.") On January 31, 2006, PSP sold Watt & Shand to RACL at a $6 million gain.[12] Act 23 funds were to be used by redevelopment authorities for properties considered "blighted." After rehabilitation, the property would go back on the tax rolls.[13] According to their financing plan, PSP would "lease" the building from RACL, so that RACL could apply for the Act 23 funds.

An original requirement of Act 23, 2004, grants was that the "project user" must "timely pay all Commonwealth and local taxes and fees." According to RACL's application, Penn Square Partners was the "project user." So, the county had petitioned the Court to require the Department of Community and Economic Development—the agency that dispensed the Act 23 funds—to rule on the question of whether PSP should pay "all Commonwealth and local taxes and fees," including property taxes, as stipulated.[14]

About a month later, in March 2006, the Pennsylvania senate approved changes to Act 23. This was Senator Armstrong's third change in the law to help the project. The changes were made in the Senate Appropriations Committee, where Armstrong was a member and soon to be chairman.[15] Through experience, he had learned that all bills go through the Appropriations Committee, but they don't necessarily come out the same way.

Lights, Camera, Action

"One man in his time plays many parts."
—William Shakespeare, *As You Like It*, 1599

The previous year, in March 2005, an obscure bill, HB 983, was introduced to amend the 2004 Act 23 legislation.[16] HB 983 established a film production grant program for movies made in Pennsylvania. When HB 983 left Senator Armstrong's Appropriations committee a year later, the bill retained its original filmmaking language, but Senator Armstrong had added language in the bill that specifically benefited the downtown Lancaster hotel and convention center project.[17]

Act 23: Version 2004 and Version 2006

Armstrong Change in Act 23, Version 2004

In 2004, Senator Armstrong introduced Act 23. It made "hotel establishments" and "convention centers" eligible for funding under the Infrastructure Facilities Improvement Program (IFIP). Originally included in the act was §3406(b) (11), which required PSP, as the "project user" of the hotel, "to timely pay all Commonwealth and local taxes and fees." There is nothing else written in this section in the 2004 version of Act 23.

Still, the project had gotten very expensive by 2006, and PSP needed more help.

Armstrong's amendment to Act 23 in 2006 gave a municipality (i.e., the City of Lancaster) or "issuing authority" the power to "pay, waive, abate, settle, compromise or reimburse any local tax, fee or other costs imposed on the project user by a local government."[18]

When Armstrong sent the bill to the Senate for a vote, it passed resoundingly, 46–1, on March 14, 2006.[19]

When Kelin learned of Armstrong's move, he was livid. "This validates our legal analysis," a disgusted Kelin avowed to the *Intelligencer Journal*. "The only way they can cure the violation is to change Act 23. It's clearly tailored to address the County's challenge."[20]

Misusing his powerful position to benefit the downtown project was a familiar tactic for senior senator Armstrong. Senator Armstrong changed Pennsylvania law three times to specifically benefit the downtown Lancaster hotel and convention center project:

1. In 1999, he changed the PA Third Class County Convention Center Act of 1994 to disqualify an existing facility in Lancaster County as a Convention Center in favor of the downtown project. This made the hoteliers' pending lawsuit invalid.

2. In 2004, he changed Pa. Act 23 law with Infrastructure Facilities Improvement Program (IFIP), which allowed financing of "hotels" and "convention centers." The "project user" had to "timely pay all Commonwealth and local taxes and fees."

3. In 2006, he changed Pa. Act 23 to allow municipalities to waive taxes, fees, and so on, due on the project user by a local government.

The Lancaster Delegation

"We must make a scarecrow of the law,
setting it up to fear the birds of prey
and let it keep one shape till custom make it
their perch and not their terror."
—William Shakespeare, *Measure for Measure,* 1603

The Republican Lancaster County House delegation was furious with Armstrong's move to change Act 23. When the Act 23 bill got to the House in April and Lancaster's representatives learned of Senator Armstrong's changes to the film bill, they were outraged and insulted at Armstrong's maneuver:

- "If it had been a straightforward, good idea, why didn't we know about it?" objected state representative Katie True. "I'm sure those who are party to this (project) knew also, and if there had been any respect for the House members, we would have at least sat down and talked about it. This is not a Republican issue, and this is not a Democratic issue. This is a taxpayer issue. Sen. Armstrong had to go back and change the law. That told me there was something wrong with the way this (project) has been developed."

- "The proposed changes to Act 23 specifically are designed to deal with the Lancaster project," stated Representative Dave Hickernell. "My biggest concern is we are trying to circumvent a court case that is pending by (voting on) a piece of legislation to make that go away. I have a problem with that."

- State representative Gordon Denlinger of Narvon said, "We continue to hear no reasonable explanation, no prospect, that it will carry its own weight or not be a burden on the taxpayers."[21]

The intra-party criticisms of the powerful Senator Armstrong were surprising, and more surprising was that the Lancaster Newspapers published them. However, the editors buried the comments within the newspaper, rather than displaying them on page one. It didn't really constitute "big news," in other words. Still, I commended the House members for standing up to Armstrong.

Because of the Lancaster delegation's reaction to Senator Armstrong's latest change, the amended HB 983 was withdrawn from a House vote on April 7, 2006. Two weeks later, the bill was put before the House for a vote on April 27, and it passed 146–41. Every Lancaster County House Republican voted against the bill. The only House member to vote for the legislation was a hotel project supporter, Democrat representative Mike Sturla.[22]

After the vote, Representative Hickernell said, "I have serious concerns about passing laws to circumvent a court case, which is clearly what we are doing in this case. If this is a viable project, it's time to stop asking the state to do more and more and more. It needs to stand on its own."[23]

The Senate passed HB 983 48–1, and Senator Gib Armstrong couldn't stop himself from gloating.

"Ninety-eight percent of the Senate agrees with me, and 75 percent of the House agrees with me, so I think I'm in pretty good company," Armstrong said after the Senate vote.

Representative Katie True appeared disgusted with Armstrong. "The people Sen. Armstrong represents don't all agree with him, which is much more important than the people in Harrisburg," she said.[24]

Prior to the House vote, I called state representative Katie True to discuss the situation. I stood outside in the morning sunshine on the front porch of a friend's house, using my cell phone. She said the delegation from Lancaster wanted more time to study the bill. She told me she had approached the speaker of the House, John Perzel, and requested more time. Perzel responded, "Let me make a phone call." Speaker Perzel returned in five minutes, reporting to Representative True, "Dale says to vote on it now."

The rejection of House Bill 983 by all Lancaster County Republican state House members demonstrated that Shellenberger and I were in step with most county residents. This wasn't reflected on the pages of project sponsor Lancaster Newspapers or in the actions of the city's mayor, but it supported the notion that we were on the right track for the taxpayers.

On May 12, 2006, Pennsylvania governor Edward G. Rendell signed Armstrong's amended Act 23 bill, allowing the City of Lancaster to waive property taxes for Penn Square Partners' privately-owned hotel. The deal was sealed.

Meanwhile, Back at the Ranch

"For pity is the virtue of the law,
And none but tyrants use it cruelly."
—William Shakespeare, *Timon of Athens*, 1605

The grand jury investigation continued to hang over the hotel and convention center activity. In May 2006, DA Donald Totaro petitioned president judge Louis Farina again. He requested to expand the grand jury investigation of Gary Heinke to include all three county commissioners. Farina approved the request. Now I was a target of a criminal grand jury investigation.

It was as if the Myers Report—the county's independent investigation into the hiring of Gary Heinke—didn't exist and had never happened. At the time when the DA was using the resources of his office—attorneys, investigators, administrative staff—to investigate the county commissioners on a personnel matter, important criminal issues remained to be dealt with in Lancaster County.

In April 2006, a young Lancaster County man was charged with bludgeoning or strangling six relatives, whose bodies were found wrapped in sheets in his grandmother's basement.[25] Another county resident was charged with running a $10 million cocaine operation, bringing several kilos of illegal drugs into the county every week.[26] Yet even with those major cases active, District Attorney Totaro used the resources of his office and a 23-person grand jury to investigate a county employee who had quit six months earlier over an inflated resumé.

The High Hemisphere—Full Speed Ahead

"O, it is excellent to have a giant's strength,
but it is tyrannous to use it like a giant."
—William Shakespeare, *Measure for Measure*, 1603

By January 1, 2006, High Associates—one-half of Penn Square Partners—had been "master developer" of the project for several years.

High Real Estate Group acted as the "construction manager" and received $52,500 per month from the Lancaster County Convention Center Authority (LCCCA) for "advisory services," even though construction had not started.[27] As construction manager, High set criteria and standards for contractors' bids when public offers began.

On March 20, 2006, the LCCCA voted to solicit nineteen construction contracts for public bids.[28] The documents had hundreds of pages and were delivered to the board via e-mail a couple of days prior to the vote—a move that exasperated the county-appointed board members.

"There is not nearly enough time and not enough information to properly review these contracts before voting to send out the bids," fumed Deb Hall to LCCCA chairman Darcus, holding up a thick binder. "It's more of the same thing with this board and its chairman, 'We're going to jam this thing through, no matter what.' This is not the way to run a board funded by the taxpayers. Frankly, I'm getting tired of it, Ted."[29]

Laura Douglas also complained about the lack of time for review of the documents. "It makes it look bad for the public," Douglas said. "There may not be cause for concern, but I think to all appearances the public has a reason to be concerned."[30]

Despite the protests of the three county-appointed board members, the letting of the bids passed with a 4–0 vote. Hall, Douglas, and Craver abstained, saying they had insufficient time to properly review the documents.

I spoke with Laura Douglas about her memory of that time. She remembered the vote quite clearly. She had noted 35 sections in the documents with red tabs that she had questions about. She related to me that Ted Darcus told her, "Sit down, stop grandstanding, and no more comments!" LCCCA member Joe Morales, sitting next to Laura, asked her, "Did you actually read this? I didn't." Then another member, Willy Borden, commented, "I didn't read it either, That's what we have lawyers for."[31]

The bids came back in May. When the bids were opened, the project was at least $13.6 million over budget. The construction budget for the convention center went from $89 million to $102.6 million after the bid opening.[32]

A week later, the *Intelligencer Journal* reported that the bid overage was $25.4 million.[33] Although the *Intell* reported it, county-appointed LCCCA board member Laura Douglas had discovered the nearly $12 million error. She had told the *Intell* of the discrepancy. The "general trades" contract was by far the largest and most expensive bid, at $22 million. The lowest general trades contract was bid by Wohlsen Construction, a large, established Lancaster firm. Yet Wohlsen's bid was twice what had been budgeted for general trades.[34]

> "I can add colour to the chameleon
> Change shapes with Proteus for advantages."
> —William Shakespeare, *Henry VI*, 1591

Because of the substantial cost overage, the bid process went back to square one. Shellenberger and I urged PSP and the LCCCA to halt the costly and risky project.[35] They ignored our call. The bids went out again.

After creating the bidding standards as construction manager for the project, High Construction "resigned" as construction manager on June 8, so that it could bid for the lucrative "general trades" contract on the re-bid. This gave High an obvious competitive advantage.[36]

For the re-bid on July 19, four overbid construction contracts were combined into the general trades bid. There was only one bidder: High Construction. Wohlsen did not re-bid. High companies won other contracts, too. High Concrete Structures received the pre-cast concrete bid. Previously, in 2001, High had been awarded a no-bid twenty-year food and beverage concession.[37] Both of those contracts were, like the general trades contract, contracts awarded by the LCCCA to affiliates of High, a the private partner of the project.

> "O what a crocodile world is this,
> Compose'd of treacheries and ensnaring wiles!"
> —William Shakespeare, *Othello*, 1603

Eight days later, after the re-bid contracts were tallied, the LCCCA announced that a $20 million budget overage existed. High's $37.1 million bid alone was $15.7 million above budget for general trades.

As they did after the School District of Lancaster rejected their TIF proposal, plan sponsors sounded a doomsday knell about the project.

On July 28, in "Bids Doom Center Plans: Penn Square Partners Says $20 Million Gap 'Too Great,'" several key sponsors pronounced the project "dead" . . . again.[38]

"It's a sad day, one could say we are still going to try, but it is very unlikely at this juncture," said Penn Square Partner and Lancaster Newspapers chairman Jack Buckwalter. (A year earlier, after the TIF defeat, Buckwalter sounded equally pessimistic. "It is unlikely that we can organize any combination of resources and strategies that will allow us to move forward with the project as currently designed," Buckwalter had said in March 2005.)[39]

Representative Mike Sturla felt saddened by the overbid and spoke of the project in the past tense. "They [Penn Square Partners and LCCCA] have exhausted their options," said Sturla of the sponsors. "Time is essentially what killed the project."[40]

Mark Fitzgerald, a High Associates executive and vice president of PSP, pointed his finger directly at the county commissioners. "The actions of the county have poisoned the well, and they continue to threaten frivolous lawsuits to delay the project," accused Fitzgerald. "They wanted to kill the project."[41]

My comment to the *Intell* remained consistent with what I'd said for the previous year and a half: "I have always been concerned about the taxpayer risk and the imbalance in the public-private partnership. The risk and the expense have been too great for the project."[42]

"And death's pale flag is not advanced there."
—William Shakespeare, *Romeo and Juliet*, 1593

Reports of the project's demise were greatly exaggerated. In August 2006, with headlines fit for a moon landing, the *Intelligencer Journal* blared across the front page in 72-point type: "CENTER CLOSES FUND GAP."

> Lancaster city Mayor Rick Gray announced a plan Thursday to keep alive a hotel/convention center project by plugging a $20

million funding gap. The funds would come from a variety of sources, including $1 million in additional funding from private hotel developer Penn Square Partners and $2 million for the naming rights to the convention center. It does not include any additional money from the state. . . ."[43]

Nobody asked why Rick Gray was fixing the budget deficit for the Lancaster County Convention Center Authority and Penn Square Partners. In office less than one year, he had his own multimillion-dollar city deficit to be concerned with.[44] This issue involved the LCCCA and construction bids for the project. How did Gray intend to come up with a viable "fund gap" solution in less than two weeks?

"'T'is true: there's magic in the web of it . . ."
—William Shakespeare, *Othello,* 1603

"Gray's plan" would close the $20 million gap by Lancaster Newspapers' using $7 million to build a parking garage and loaning the Lancaster Parking Authority $3 million "interest-free." That amounted to $10 million of the $20 million.

The other $10 million would come from PSP investing another $1 million. The LCCCA would charge $2 million for "naming rights" to the convention center. Another $5.25 million would come from "value engineering," that is, cutting costs, using cheaper materials. The sponsors counted another $1.5 million in projected favorable interest rate loans from a bond to be floated by the Redevelopment Authority of the City of Lancaster (RACL).[45]

Gray's plan was illusory. The $7 million from the parking garage, now to be funded by Lancaster Newspapers, was not part of the LCCCA construction budget. That money could not be counted against the $20 million deficit. There was $3 million pledged by the Historic Preservation Trust. This took money allocated for the Thaddeus Stevens/Lydia Hamilton Smith educational museum. (That museum has still not opened as of 2018.) The $5.25 million in "value engineering" resulted in a substandard facility, not the "luxury" "five-star" hotel promised in the front-page run-up to the hotel room tax.

Finally, the $2 million for the "naming rights" was wishful thinking. Counting on $2 million from someone who might pay to have a name on a brass plate at the Convention Center was a reach. Of course, anyone who wanted to buy naming rights had to go through S. Dale High, who had first naming rights. Neither High nor anyone else has stepped up with the $2 million. Project critics said Gray's plan amounted to "smoke and mirrors."[46]

Four days after Rick Gray solved the great convention center budget deficit, the LCCCA approved thirteen contracts, all with 4–0 votes. The county-appointed LCCCA members, disgusted with the process, refused to vote.[47] Later that evening, the RACL board approved the same contracts.

"Neither a borrower or lender be . . ."
—William Shakespeare, *Hamlet*, 1600

The key to stopping the project, from my perspective, was the county's $40 million bond guaranty. Two outgoing commissioners had passed the guaranty in late October 2003, a week before I was elected.[48] The bond exposed Lancaster County taxpayers to $60 million for the life of the guaranty.[49] In other words, if the LCCCA couldn't pay its debt service on the bond, the average Lancaster County taxpayer had to make the payment. The cost of a Happy Meal had gone up.[50]

I had always opposed the bond guaranty. I campaigned opposing it in 2003, as did all of the candidates in that election. The tax had been passed in 1999, years before I ran for commissioner.[51] There was no repealing that. I took the position that the room tax was the only Lancaster County taxpayer money that should go to the project. I never changed that position.

Because the project had grown tremendously in size, cost, and risk, in 2006 the county wanted to revoke the 2003 $40 million county bond guaranty. On May 10, Shellenberger and I voted to petition the state Department of Community and Economic Development (DCED) to review the 2003 guaranty.[52] After the first round of bids showed that the project had a $25 million deficit, the county voted 2–1 (Shaub, a "nay") to revoke the county guaranty if the LCCCA re-marketed the bond in a risky interest market "swap."[53]

The county challenge to the $40 million guaranty was enough for the LCCCA and project sponsors. In June, the LCCCA board voted 4–3 to sue Shellenberger and me personally as county commissioners for creating "immediate, imminent, and irrevocable" harm to the project. Penn Square Partners and RACL joined the LCCCA suit as plaintiffs. They even wanted the Court to place a gag order on us.[54]

The lawsuit that the LCCCA, RACL, and PSP brought against Shellenberger and me began on July 1, 2006.[55] The case was heard in the Lancaster County Court of Common Pleas by Judge Joseph Madenspacher.[56]

Special Counsel Kelin again represented the county. He argued that we had fulfilled our fiduciary duty by challenging the $40 million bond guaranty passed in the last days of a lame duck board of commissioners.

Complex Issues

"Confusion now hath made his masterpiece."
—William Shakespeare, *Macbeth*, 1605

Kelin argued that the bond guaranty, drafted by the county's bond counsel in 2003, and the "Trust Indenture," drafted by the LCCCA's bond counsel, were in conflict.[57] The Trust Indenture was the bond contract made between a bond issuer (the LCCCA) and the trustee (the county). Like the bond guaranty, a trust indenture describes the rules and responsibilities of each party. The primary legal issue before Judge Madenspacher was the county's challenge to the 2003 $40 million LCCCA bond, half of which was guaranteed by Lancaster County taxpayers.

County Ordinance No. 73 stipulated that the LCCCA must demonstrate it had "sufficient funds" to complete the project before re-marketing the bond, while the LCCCA Trust Indenture said only that the LCCCA had to "deliver complete plans" and a "project budget" to the bank, aka "the Trustee."

The two documents didn't mesh. To the county, it certainly seemed as if the "sufficient funds" provision was in place to protect taxpayers. Judge Madenspacher would sort that out.

The Madenspacher hearings lasted five days in mid-July.[58] On July 25, Judge Madenspacher issued temporary injunctions against

Shellenberger and me. We were prohibited from addressing the county guaranty or county financing of the project. The gag order was denied.[59]

Madenspacher did not rule on the bond guaranty. He announced that he would hold hearings in September to address that issue. After the September hearings, Madenspacher issued permanent injunctions against Shellenberger and me, preventing us from revoking the county's guaranty of the project.

On the substantive legal issue, the conflict between the county bond guaranty and the LCCCA's trust indenture, Judge Madenspacher wrote after the September hearings:

> *In reviewing the documents, the Court looks to the entire context of all of the documents and the surrounding circumstances. Thus, where the ordinance requires that the authority shall have certified to the trustee that it has sufficient funds to complete the construction of the Facilities in full accord with the final plans and specifications, and the indenture requires that the authority deliver to the trustee, complete plans and specifications and a project budget, then both documents have the requirement that the trustee have the assurance that the entire project will be completed.*[60]

Despite these roadblocks, two county commissioners, one Democrat and one Republican, continued to challenge the project. As I had promised during the campaign of 2003, our board of commissioners did indeed hold quarterly public meetings outside the city and during evening hours, when constituents could attend more easily. We wanted to hear what the public thought about the project and other issues.[61]

At an evening meeting in East Donegal Township, we heard from the public on reducing the geographic area of the hotel room tax. "It is time for the county commissioners to reconsider whether or not the entire county is the appropriate area for the bed tax," I said at the meeting.[62] We held another meeting at the Ephrata Public Library. About a hundred people overflowed the main meeting room, almost all of them against the hotel and convention center project.[63]

In the meantime, without funding in place, the sponsors proceeded as if it were. Large portions of the home and business of Thaddeus Stevens and Lydia Hamilton Smith were demolished. Oblender's

Furniture store, a downtown fixture for generations, was flattened, over the objections of the owners.[64]

The Lancaster hotel and convention center project caught the attention of organizations outside of Lancaster County. After learning of the Lancaster project, Barry Kauffman, executive director of Common Cause Pennsylvania, wrote a letter to Governor Rendell, urging him to order the auditor general to investigate the LCCCA. Kauffman wrote:

> The apparent lack of transparency and accountability regarding this project has prompted Common Cause/PA to express these concerns to you, and we ask that you instruct the Secretary of Community and Economic Development to:
> 1) conduct a complete review audit of state funding pertaining to this project;
> 2) ensure that this Project is in full compliance with all state laws regarding grants, contracting public input and oversight; and
> 3) ensure that all public records about this Project be made available in full compliance with state law.[65]

The Common Cause request for an investigation was ignored.

Removing History

"The ruin speaks that sometime
It was a worthy building."
—William Shakespeare, *Cymbeline*, 1609

Early in the project, 2001, PSP president Nevin Cooley spoke at a press conference on Penn Square next to the Soldiers and Sailors Monument. A small group of VIPs, including state senator Gibson Armstrong, Lancaster Newspapers' president Jack Buckwalter, and Lancaster mayor Charlie Smithgall, sat behind Cooley.

"Penn Square Partners was formed for one and only one reason," Cooley said, pausing for effect, "to save this [the Watt & Shand] building."[66]

By 2006, the four-foot-high Watt & Shand letters had been removed from the C. Emlen Urban architectural masterpiece. The next year the Lancaster city landmark was delisted from the National Register of Historic Places.

"The [Watt & Shand] facade no longer represents the architecture and heritage of the building," said Carol Lee, supervisor of the Pennsylvania Bureau for Historic Preservation, which recommended the national delisting.[67]

Still, Penn Square Partners attempted to obtain federal tax credits for the formerly historic building. They were denied. High had anticipated receiving about $4 million in tax credits as they developed the building.

"They [Penn Square Partners] weren't happy with us, but we said a 14-story hotel on top of a four-story building does not qualify for tax credits," observed Bonnie Mark, a tax act coordinator for the Pennsylvania Historic and Museum Commission.[68]

As the historic Lancaster buildings came down, the price of the project went up. In November, LCCCA financial adviser Thomas Beckett announced that the cost of the project had grown to $165.5 million.[69] A month later, Beckett again announced the price had risen an additional $5 million, bringing the 2006 total to $170.5 million.[70]

And during the entire year, the Conestoga View articles kept appearing. Each of the three Lancaster Newspapers took its shots almost daily. It was the story that kept on giving. The *Sunday News* introduced a regular little blurb on its editorial pages, starting in June 2006.[71] It came from Marv Adams. He called it "Countdown: Days until the End of Terms for County Commissioners." When the "Countdown" started, 564 days remained. That was true for only two of the three commissioners. One had an earlier termination date.

Chapter Twelve

FINISHING THE JOB

"The secret is so weighty, 'twill require
A strong faith to conceal it."
—William Shakespeare, *Henry VIII*, 1612

The equity stake of each of the Penn Square partners was first publicly revealed during the Madenspacher hearings in July 2006. For eight and a half years after forming PSP, the partners had kept the ownership percentages of High Real Estate Group, Lancaster Newspapers, Inc., and Fulton Bank from the public.

Penn Square Partners in 2006[1]
High Real Estate Group – 44%
Lancaster Newspapers – 44%
Fulton Financial – 12%

Fulton left the partnership the next year. Now High and Lancaster Newspapers each owned 50 percent of Penn Square Partners. "This was a temporary investment for us," said Rufus A. Fulton, Jr., Fulton's president.[2]

It took Lancaster Newspapers more than eight years to disclose its ownership in a project that involved more than $100 million of public money. This indicates how the company covered the project. The company used the newspapers to promote the project, rather than report on it—and, when necessary, to attack opponents of its downtown hotel project.

265

The Investigation Expands

By the fall of 2006, the newspapers had been attacking "the commissioners" for nearly 18 straight months. The most sustained print attacks focused on the sale of the Conestoga View nursing home. That issue first blew up in Lancaster Newspapers in mid-July 2005 and, incredibly, continued almost daily through 2006 *and* 2007.[3]

"Wherever this takes us," DA Totaro announced to the public, about the investigative grand jury that would be used to probe the fudged résumé of a former county employee.[4]

More than a hundred people received subpoenas from the District Attorney's office. I was one of them and testified three times before the grand jury.[5] The first time occurred under the original scope of the investigation, the hiring of former chief services officer Gary Heinke; the second and third concerned the expanded investigation of the sale of Conestoga View.[6]

On March 31, 2006 all three commissioners jointly issued a Conestoga View statement which became known as "The Apology". In that statement Shaub and Shellenberger admitted to secretly meeting with the County Solicitor to discuss the sale of Conestoga View without my knowledge. After that statement the District Attorney expanded his Grand Jury scope beyond Heinke to Conestoga View. Ironically, after nearly one hundred depositions and countless court employee hours, the main conclusions of the Grand Jury report essentially restated the facts contained in the Myers' Report and the public "Apology" (see Board of Commissioners Statement on Process Leading to Sale of Conestoga View, March 31, 2006 at pressedthebook.com).

On June 14, 2006, my lawyer Mark Lovett moved to quash both the original and the amended subpoenas.[7] I was willing to talk and answer any questions but wanted to know the basis in law before appearing. That's what the motion was: an explanation for why I was being questioned. We had not been provided with any from the DA's office. Judge Louis Farina, the supervising judge, denied the request.

In late 2006, we brought in Thomas McGough, of Reed Smith in Pittsburgh, to join my legal team on the grand jury investigation.[8] This was extremely serious.

During the first week of December 2006, assistant district attorney Kenneth Brown contacted Lovett and asked for a meeting. Brown worked on the investigation and was writing the grand jury report.

> "And there's for twitting me with perjury."
> —William Shakespeare, *Henry VI*, Part III, 1590

Lovett met with DA Totaro and his assistant Brown. The district attorney said they were considering charging me with false swearing under oath—perjury—a felony charge! They weren't talking about any substantive offense that had been listed in the notice of submission or the amended notice of submission. They were talking about testimony under oath. Lovett challenged, "Fine. Show it to me." The prosecutors showed Lovett some excerpts from my testimony. "I reviewed their evidence and concluded they had absolutely no basis to even suggest those things [false swearing]," Lovett remarked after reading the excerpts.[9]

Totaro had nothing, because there was nothing. After thirteen months of investigation—using his staff of lawyers, thousands of taxpayer-paid hours, more than a hundred witnesses, and the time of twenty-three grand jurors—there was nothing!

> "Oh, I am fortune's fool."
> —William Shakespeare, *Romeo and Juliet*, 1591

Brown identified what he believed was a violation of the Sunshine Act by me and the other commissioners.[10] My alleged violation was the April 1, 2005, Power Point presentation I had attended. This was the presentation by Don Elliott, the one I went to as a favor to Andi Murphy, the one on April Fool's Day . . . the presentation I did not want to attend and where no official action on Conestoga View was taken.

McGough said they should leave me out of the entire grand jury report. I clearly had nothing to do with the reasons for the grand jury investigation—the hiring of Heinke and any "secret" negotiations involving Conestoga View. The Myers Report showed that, as did the admissions by commissioner Shellenberger and Shaub in the March 31st, 2006 "Apology" statement. There was nothing worth a grand jury investigation from the DA's office.

Yet by this point, we knew what this was about. This—the use of a grand jury and the Lancaster County District Attorney's office—was part of a nearly two-year commissioner character assassination campaign, played out on the pages of Lancaster Newspapers.

My belief was the barrage by the press was a result of the challenge to the hotel and convention center project. I concluded the plan was too risky and costly for the Lancaster County taxpayers and should be stopped.[11]

Lancaster Newspapers, a significant private investor in that project, with more than a dozen properties within a block of it, stood to make tens of millions of dollars from the project.[12] The "Conestoga View and the terrible commissioners" story appeared prominently in the newspapers every day. In my opinion, the newspapers' campaign aimed to divert attention away from the hotel project and to discredit us. That's what the grand jury investigation was about. It had nothing to do with investigating a crime. It was a red herring.

The DA's office kept talking about the grand jury report soon to be released. They mentioned a Sunshine Act violation, as it concerned me. And we argued why—why waste your time on this? It struck McGough, the former U.S. attorney, as strange that a county district attorney would use a grand jury and the power of his office on a possible summary violation.[13] (Examples of other summary violations in Pennsylvania include §6905, Attaching a nail or tack to a utility pole; §6708, Retention of library property after notice to return, more than 30 days; and §2101, Display of flag at public meetings—while in charge of any public gathering, failing to display publicly and visibly the U.S. flag reasonably clean and in good repair.)

One Ham Sandwich to Go . . .

"Get thee glass eyes,
And like a scurvy politician seem
To see things thou dost not."
—William Shakespeare, *King Lear*, 1606

The DA's office had devoted great resources to the Heinke/Conestoga View grand jury. It would have been embarrassing to come up with no charges. Based on the daily attention the newspapers gave Conestoga View, it was obvious where the Lancaster establishment stood on the issue. The commissioners had to be sidelined.

The DA would not walk away from this situation, at least as far as I was concerned. The DA wasn't willing to do that.

It was very clear in the first week of December 2006 that the grand jury report had already been written. During one phone conversation, assistant district attorney Brown read the report with my attorney, Mark Lovett. Brown read the parts that mentioned me and said, "Well, there's really nothing too critical in there, so you really don't have to worry about it." Then Brown added flippantly, *"I don't hose people."*[14] If this was a game to the DA's office, it wasn't to me.

The DA's office wasn't giving up anything. Although there were no crimes found in the grand jury investigation, the word *criminal* was always kept in play. While the DA mentioned criminal conspiracy, the criminal conspiracy dealt with supposedly underlying offenses, none of which were crimes. Beyond that, according to my attorney, the district attorney's understanding of the law, even of the law that they quoted, seemed to be very mistaken.[15]

The Lancaster County district attorney, who subpoenaed and questioned more than a hundred people and had total control of the grand jury process, couldn't come up with any criminal charges. But the DA made it clear to McGough that if I did not accept a citation to a Sunshine violation about the April 1 Power Point presentation, the grand jury would present the violation in its report.[16]

"There's small choice in rotten apples."
—William Shakespeare, *The Taming of the Shrew*, 1591

On December 13, my husband, Alex, and I attended a holiday dinner with one of his clients. While enjoying our evening, I received a call on my cell phone from Tom McGough. I excused myself from the table and listened to McGough for a few moments, then went back to the table. I didn't have to say anything to Alex. He read my face.

The next morning, December 14, was cold and overcast. I appeared at the Magisterial District Justice Richard Simm's office and accepted a citation for one Sunshine Act violation. The judge seemed almost embarrassed to be put through this.[17]

My attorney, Mark Lovett, submitted a statement with our plea:

> Your Honor, we came here this morning on the understanding that Commissioner Henderson would be pleading guilty to a violation of the Sunshine Act. We cannot agree there was official action taken [i.e., a vote or decision to sell property] at any meeting on April 1st, but we do understand that three commissioners were present. . . ."[18]

That was it. I paid a $100 fine. The whole thing took less than four minutes.

These were among the worst four minutes of my life. Justice Simms allowed us to exit through a side door, so we could avoid the press waiting outside.

My Reasoning

"Strong reasons make strong actions."
—William Shakespeare, *King John,* 1595

People ask me, "If you didn't do anything wrong, why did you accept that citation?" Here's why:

1. The DA's office would have most likely moved forward on the April 1 presentation as a Sunshine violation;
2. The newspapers would have covered all events in depth with headlines and articles, step by step, through the hearings or the appeals;
3. It would have cost a tremendous amount of money;
4. With the climate in the county, I would have lost at the district level;
5. With the climate in the county, I would have lost at the Court of Common Pleas;
6. I felt that I would have won at the state level two years later, after spending a lot of money and losing the 2007 election.

That was what I faced and why I took the citation. The next day, December 15, Judge Farina ordered the grand jury report sealed for twenty days. He gave January 8, 2007, as the release date.[19]

> "Who is it in the press that call on me?
> I hear a tongue, shriller than all the music..."
> —William Shakespeare, *Julius Caesar*, 1599

Newspapers are protected in publishing false statements about "public figures." Not only must the statements be false, but the "public figure" must prove malice. There is a line between publishing negative, even misleading, articles and opinions about a public figure and publishing false and defamatory articles. That line is called libel, and in my opinion, it was crossed on at least five separate occasions, beginning on December 14, 2006. In a series of articles published between December 14, 2006 and November 6, 2007, Lancaster Newspapers crossed that line again and again.[20]

The articles published weeks after December 14, 2006, were particularly vitriolic and attacked me personally. Lancaster Newspapers' editors often ran two and three articles on the same day in the same newspaper.[21]

On December 14, in two-inch, above-the-fold, front-page banner headlines, the *Lancaster New Era* reported, as if it were the end of a world war, "COMMISSIONERS PLEAD GUILTY: All 3 Admit Meeting Secretly in Violation of Sunshine Act," an article written by Jack Brubaker.[22] In it, Brubaker falsely stated that the Sunshine Act violation was a "criminal charge" to convince the public that I had violated the Crimes Code. Yet in fact, the Sunshine Act was not recognized under the Crimes Code. This was a misleading statement, and Brubaker, a thirty-six-year veteran reporter, who did his own investigation of Conestoga View, surely knew or should have known that.[23]

Also, in the "Commissioners Plead Guilty" article, Brubaker stated that "two or more of the Commissioners actually attended at least five separate meetings before the sale, according to investigations by the New Era over the past year." The intent of the words was purposely misleading. I had actually attended only one informational meeting, as had been reported.[24]

These statements were made by a reporter, Brubaker, who clearly knew the facts, yet published the erroneous statements to malign and injure my reputation, sway public opinion against me, and force me to either resign from office or decide not to run for reelection. On December 15, the *Intelligencer Journal* published an editorial, "Time to Resign," which reads, in part: "The charges involve a series of private meetings that were conducted in 2004 and 2005 in which the Commissioners met and initiated action that ultimately lead [sic] to the sale of the County property."[25]

This article is false because the "charges" never asserted that I had participated in a "series of meetings" where I "met and initiated action that ultimately lead [sic] to the sale of county property." I attended a single informational meeting in the courthouse, at which no deliberation occurred and no official action was taken. That was part of the public record. Again, the *Intelligencer Journal* editorial writers knew of these facts and still published false statements.

On December 21, 2005 I personally confronted New Era reporter, Jack Brubaker concerning the article "Behind Closed Doors" where he writes I was involved in secretly hiring Stevens and Lee to represent the County in the Conestoga View sale. Espenshade, along with with Shaub and Shellenberger, had negotiated the deal. Accompanying me was Barbara Achtermann, as a witness. We met upstairs in the public library's children's area. Sitting on half-sized chairs, I presented Brubaker with a written request for a correction to his article. He refused my request. I asked why the request was unreasonable. He responded, "No comment." I continued to press for a printed correction to the story that falsely accused me of "secretly" hiring Stevens & Lee. Brubaker got up from his chair, fled the room crying, "God help us all!"

Another false article appeared on December 31, 2006, in the *Sunday News*, "Seeking an Inside View."[26] Again, the newspaper featured the article on the front page and above the fold. The *Sunday News* now reached more than 96,000 Lancaster County households every week.[27] More than one person per household read the *Sunday News*. It is not an exaggeration to say that almost every literate adult in Lancaster County read the *Sunday News*.

> "Rumor: Upon my tongues continual slanders ride,
> The which in every language I pronounce,
> Stuffing the ears of men with false reports."
> —William Shakespeare, *Henry IV*, Part 2, 1597

Associate editor Gil Smart wrote the December 31 article, "Seeking an Inside View."[28] The article falsely states, "Shaub testified twice, but Shellenberger and Henderson testified only once. . . . Shaub who did not hire a lawyer to represent him during the investigation, has said that Shellenberger and Henderson hired lawyers to prevent them from testifying a second time. The appearance of 'Taking the Fifth,' say observers, could be extremely damaging politically."[29]

Prior to the publication of "Seeking an Inside View," Smart exchanged e-mails with me but never asked whether I asserted the Fifth Amendment about any proceeding. He never asked how many times I had testified or anything about the grand jury proceeding.[30] The fact was that I had testified three separate times and never "took the Fifth" or tried to.

I immediately demanded a correction from the *Sunday News*, and on January 7, 2007, the newspaper made a feeble correction. It read: "In a Page One article last Sunday on the grand jury report regarding the sale of Conestoga View, it was incorrectly reported that Lancaster County Commissioners Dick Shellenberger and Molly Henderson had each testified only once before the grand jury, giving the appearance of 'taking the fifth.'"[31]

That was not a "correction." The "correction/clarification" reinforced the idea that I was the subject of criminal charges and sought the protection of the Fifth Amendment to avoid testifying against myself.

After the grand jury report was unsealed on January 10, 2007, Lancaster Newspapers and the public had access to the report.[32] On January 11th, reporter Anya Litvak wrote in the Lancaster New Era: "The grand jury's much anticipated and sharply critical report may well have ended one county commissioner's political career and given a boost to another's... Democrats say the report exonerated commissioner Molly Henderson."

I was exonerated by the grand jury report. There was no presentment of any "crime". On the substantive issues of the hiring of former county employee Gary Heinke and the sale of Conestoga View, the grand jury concluded, as the Myers Report had fourteen months earlier, that I had done nothing improper concerning the hiring of Heinke. With respect to the sale of Conestoga View, the grand jury report said explicitly that I had been deliberately kept "in the dark" by Shaub, Shellenberger, and Espenshade regarding the nursing home sale.[33]

After the grand jury report came out, even Pete Shaub, whose behavior had caused so much damage, wrote in a public response to the report that I had not been part of any "secret" negotiation to sell Conestoga View. "I believe in my testimony that I acknowledged that I told persons to not discuss the CV [Conestoga View] sale with Commissioner Henderson at the direction of Mr. Espenshade," Shaub wrote.[34]

Commissioner Dick Shellenberger's lawyer, former Pennsylvania Supreme Court justice William Lamb, stated after reading the grand jury report, "I'm surprised that the district attorney would engage in such a lengthy and extensive investigation to address a summary offense. To quote Peggy Lee, 'Is that all there is?'"[35] But an "Is that all there is?" grand jury report did not fit the Conestoga View narrative. Anya Litvak, the reporter who with Jack Brubaker on January 11th dared to suggest that the report exonerated me, was involved in only one other article about me and the grand jury report thereafter.

"I am disgrac'd, impeach'd and baffled here,—
Pierc'd to the soul with slander's venon'd spear."
—William Shakespeare, *Richard II,* 1595

On January 10, in another Jack Brubaker, above-the-fold, *Lancaster New Era* front-page article, "Grand Jury: Commissioners Betrayed Public Trust," Brubaker states, "The grand jury had given the commissioners a choice: plead guilty or face a formal presentment recommending that criminal charges be brought against them." I was never given such a "Hobson's choice"—a "take it or leave it" by the grand jury. The grand jury report simply did not say that. Brubaker read the report. This was false.[36]

The next day, January 11, the *New Era* published another false Brubaker article, "Secrecy, Deceit Crippled Probe." Like the story of the previous day, "Secrecy" was a front-page, above-the-fold article. A photograph of Shellenberger and me, but not Shaub, accompanied the article. The piece came with a sub-headline, "How Did Commissioners Avoid Multiple Criminal Charges?"[37]

The January 11 article had this front-page statement: "The Grand Jury Report makes it clear that the Commissioners and Gary Heinke, the former human services administrator hired to conduct the nursing home sale, avoided other criminal charges only because the Grand Jury lacked sufficient corroborating evidence."[38]

This article was supposed to be Brubaker's analysis of the grand jury report. The subhead, "How Did Commissioners Avoid Multiple Criminal Charges?"—was intentionally misleading as it concerned me. The statement that the grand jury "lacked sufficient corroborating evidence" to file "multiple criminal charges" suggests that the grand jury had some evidence but an insufficient amount of evidence. And running a picture of me next to the statement "How Did Commissioners Avoid Multiple Criminal Charges?" certainly suggests that I had somehow gotten lucky and avoided the "multiple criminal charges."[39] This was nowhere to be found in the grand jury report read by Brubaker. Still, it was published in the most prominent part of the newspaper—above the fold on the front page. The First Amendment protects the right of journalists to be wrong. It does not protect journalists from *knowingly* writing something that is wrong.

Again, I immediately demanded a retraction from the *New Era* over the statements made in the January 11 Brubaker article. In response, on January 12, buried deep within "Local Leaders Urge Commissioners: Step Down Now"—with no marking or emphasis—a "correction" appeared: "The *New Era* reported that the investigating Grand Jury said the Commissioners avoided further criminal charges only because the Grand Jury lacked sufficient evidence. Actually, the Grand Jury Report presents no evidence to support further criminal charges against Henderson."[40]

The January 12 "correction" explicitly acknowledged that the newspaper had published false statements against me. Still, the "correction" continued the false notion that I was the subject of "criminal charges" by stating there was "no evidence to support further charges." Yet there were never *any* "criminal charges."

The *Intelligencer Journal* also published libelous articles after the grand jury report was released. On January 11, in "Grand Jury Blasts

Three Commissioners," *Intell* reporter David Pigeon wrote, "However, the key officials involved in the sale—from the three commissioners to the deposed county administrator who helped conduct the sale—escaped serious criminal charges because the grand jury could not corroborate much of the evidence."[41]

"Grand Jury Blasts Three Commissioners" was also a front-page, above-the-fold article. Pigeon wrote,

> While the report does not recommend criminal charges, it does document how the Commissioners kept the sale 'cloaked in a veil of secrecy'; Orchestrated the hiring of a hand-picked administrator, Gary Heinke, to facilitate the sale; Sought a political contribution from an attorney involved in the sale; Involved administrators to help them maintain their secrecy.[42]

The grand jury report—readily available to Pigeon—made no such allegations against me. Publishing those statements was a malicious attempt to suggest that as one of the "three commissioners," I had "escaped criminal charges." That was false.

Pigeon had another article published in the *Intelligencer Journal* the same day, "Report Details 'Veil of Secrecy' in County." Like the other front-page articles, this article contained a subhead, "Secret Meetings on 'Charlie Victor.'"[43]

Wrote Pigeon, "The report details how the commissioners and their surrogates tried to circumvent the Sunshine Act while discussing this sale, even code-naming the nursing home 'Charlie Victor' to keep their discussions confidential."

Here is a verbatim quote from the grand jury report:

> A constant theme of the off-site meetings was that no one outside of "the team" should know about the plan to, or even the possibility of, selling Conestoga View. Commissioner Shaub specifically told team members that Commissioner Henderson should be kept in the dark.[44]

Yet Pigeon, who had the job of reading that report and analyzing its contents, wrote his article to suggest that I had been privy to the

"Charlie Victor" secret code, when the grand jury report explicitly says just the opposite. Again, I demanded a retraction. The next day, January 12, in a "clarification/corrections" buried deeply within the newspaper, the correction ran: "A story in Thursday's *Intelligencer Journal* grouped Henderson with Commissioners Pete Shaub and Dick Shellenberger when reporting on what the newspaper described as 'serious criminal charges' considered by the Grand Jury. The *Intell* erred by failing to make it clear that Henderson was not mentioned in the grand jury report in relation to these charges."[45]

The correction is an explicit acknowledgment that the *Intell* intentionally published false statements about me. And the placement of the "correction" buried in the newspaper—not on the front page, like the libelous statement—was a conscious editorial decision.

More evidence that Lancaster Newspapers' reporters consciously maligned me can be found in a January 12, 2006, e-mail Jack Brubaker sent to me, soliciting a comment. "I understand your situation is different than Shellenberger's," Brubaker wrote.[46] This shows that Brubaker read the grand jury report and therefore knew I had no role in Heinke's hiring or secretly selling Conestoga View, yet still grouped me with Shellenberger as it concerned those issues. Brubaker had knowledge that what he wrote was false.

The next day, January 13—a Saturday—the *Lancaster New Era* published the front-page story "Citizens: GET OUT!" In the article, Brubaker wrote, "The 37-page report, made public Wednesday, provides details of how the Commissioners secretly manipulated the sale of the county nursing home and the hiring of one of the key administrators responsible."[47]

The use of the term *the commissioners* was intentionally misleading. Any reasonable reader would infer from Brubaker's words that I was part of "the commissioners." The grand jury report, which Brubaker acknowledged reading, said that Shellenberger and Shaub "secretly manipulated the sale of the county nursing home and the hiring of one of the key administrators responsible." The grand jury report said I had been intentionally "kept in the dark" about hiring Heinke and the secret Conestoga View meetings.

"I say put money in thy purse."
—William Shakespeare, *Othello*, 1603

The following day, on January 14, the *Sunday News* editorial stated in "Commissioners Shellenberger and Henderson: Have Grace to Resign":

> It's time for Dick Shellenberger and Molly Henderson to resign. That is the inescapable conclusion that arises from the scathing Grand Jury Report on the hiring of Gary Heinke and the sale the Conestoga View nursing home by the Lancaster County Commissioners. . . .[48]

The grand jury most certainly did not reach any "inescapable conclusion" that I did anything that suggested resignation was appropriate. The editorial, written by Helen Colwell Adams, in collaboration with her husband, *Sunday News* editor Marvin Adams, was another effort by Lancaster Newspapers' staff to injure my reputation.[49]

Helen Colwell Adams's editorial also included this statement about me personally: "She sold the elderly and poor of this county for 30 pieces of silver."[50] Colwell Adams, then studying for a divinity degree, compared me to Judas Iscariot, history's worst traitor, who was paid "30 pieces of silver" for betraying Jesus Christ.[51] The hateful statement by Helen Colwell Adams falsely implies I received financial benefit from the sale of Conestoga View. There was no suggestion of that in the grand jury report or in the farthest reaches of the universe. Helen Colwell Adams wrote this intentionally false and misleading statement to discredit me in the eyes of Lancaster County citizens, most of whom knew who Judas was.

During her deposition, when I sued her for libel, Helen Colwell Adams admitted under oath that she had no proof that I had received any compensation: (Q. Did Ms. Henderson receive money for agreeing to sell Conestoga View? "I don't believe she did," Colwell Adams testified.)[52]

A week later, in the January 21 edition of the *Sunday News*, Helen Colwell Adams wrote,

At the conclusion of the damning report on the way the commissioners pulled the wool over the public's eyes in the hiring of Gary Heinke as Chief Services Officer and the sale of Conestoga View nursing home, the grand jury issued what ought to be required reading not just on the fifth floor of the county courthouse but in the state Capitol.[53]

Colwell Adams acknowledged reading the grand jury report and having knowledge of the Myers Report prior to writing the editorials. Both of those reports concluded that I had done nothing "damning" in regard to Gary Heinke or Conestoga View. I "pulled the wool" over no one's eyes. Still, with knowledge of the falsity, Helen Colwell Adams chose not to write the truth about me. Average readers would include me as one of "the commissioners" after reading Colwell Adams's editorial.

On May 1, 2007, the *Lancaster New Era* said that "the commissioners secretly sold" Conestoga View, in the article "Facade of Almshouse May Be Eased to Preservation Trust."[54] The grand jury report clearly stated that I had nothing to do with any "secret" selling of Conestoga View or anything improper concerning the Heinke hiring. Yet with that knowledge, Lancaster Newspapers persisted in repeating that "the commissioners" had done these things. I had not. They knew it.

Once again, I demanded a retraction. One appeared eight days later, on May 9, buried deep in the interior of the *Lancaster New Era* in section C, page 12:

> A May 1 news story about the county's former almshouse noted that the county commissioners "secretly sold" the county's nursing home, Conestoga View, in fact: the Commissioners in a secret meeting, authorized the county to negotiate a sale with only one buyer. The Commissioners were apprised of these negotiations at two other secret meetings. Then they approved the sales agreement in public.[55]

Not only was this "correction" buried deep within the newspaper, the correction was incorrect. The grand jury did not report that I had attended any meeting that "authorized the county to negotiate a sale with only one buyer." That statement can't be backed up anywhere in the grand jury report.

Again, on September 13, 2007, in the 479th front-page story on Conestoga View, the *Lancaster New Era* ran, "Former Exec Sues County," an article about Gary Heinke now suing the county. The article included the statement "A Grand Jury Report released early this year indicated the County Commissioners secretly manipulated the hiring of Heinke and held secret negotiations prior to selling the nursing home."[56]

The grand jury report, as Jack Brubaker knew when he wrote this article, concluded that I had nothing to do with either of those improprieties. Still, he wrote it. Again, I demanded a retraction, which appeared buried in the September 17 newspaper. The "correction/clarification" read:

> A September 13 news story on a lawsuit filed by Gary Heinke, a former county human services director, against the Lancaster County Commissioners, provided background on a grand jury finding issued last January that the Commissioners had secretly manipulated Heinke's hiring. That grand jury finding applied only to majority Commissioners Dick Shellenberger and Pete Shaub, not to minority Commissioner Molly Henderson.[57]

The "correction" explicitly acknowledged that the *New Era* knowingly published false statements about me. These weren't editorial oversights. Lancaster Newspapers published a series of emphatic but false front-page stories and editorials and later buried the corrections and clarifications that I demanded deep within the newspaper. Hundreds of thousands of readers likely read the false front-page stories. Only a relative few, a tiny fraction, read the buried "corrections." The "corrections" failed to dispel the impression that I had been involved in improperly hiring Heinke and "secretly" selling Conestoga View. Because Lancaster Newspapers' staff—Jack Brubaker and Helen Colwell Adams, for example—knew of the contents of the grand jury report, writing and publishing those false stories was intentional.[58]

Adding his voice to the criticism was the "leading critic of the sale of the county nursing home," former Lancaster mayor Art Morris. After the December 14 plea, Morris said, "The criminal act they [the county commissioners] committed far outweighs the penalty they paid."[59]

In a lengthy "letter" to the editor in the *Sunday News* on December 17, 2006, Morris wrote about me, "How stupid does she think the readers are?" Later, he addressed me directly: "How can you begin to talk about your concern for the citizens of this county, when you did not even allow the citizens to have input into the sale of the home? . . . You met behind closed doors for months, plotting the sale of Conestoga View."[60]

After the grand jury report was released on January 10, 2007, Morris wrote another letter, again directed at me, in which he crossed the bounds of civil discourse. The letter, headlined "Henderson Had More of Role Than She's Letting On," was published in the *Lancaster New Era* on January 15, 2007.[61]

In his regular "Sunday's Guest" column of January 28, 2007, Morris again wrote, saying I'd hired Heinke when I "knew" he was unqualified.[62] Morris, indisputably the moving force behind the Heinke and Conestoga View inquisition, disregarded the conclusions of the Myers Report and the grand jury report, as he made his reckless and false accusations.

"If I lose my honour, I lose myself."
—William Shakespeare, *Antony and Cleopatra*, 1606

After the grand jury report was released on January 10, 2007, it became obvious that I was very damaged, politically. Two solid years of anti–county commissioner articles and editorials, with virtually no counterweight, had taken their toll.

The readers of Lancaster Newspapers were Lancaster County voters. They believed what they read, and they read that the county commissioners were "dysfunctional," that they operated in "chaos," and that they were "criminals" who "secretly sold" the county treasure, Conestoga View. And, it must be said, the well-choreographed campaign to kill "the commissioners" worked. Pete Shaub resigned from office in February 2007, eleven months before the end of his term.[63]

Dick Shellenberger took an advertisement out in the *Merchandiser/Pennysaver* free newspaper and announced he would not seek reelection in the fall.[64]

I had to run for reelection. It was imperative to keep standing and move forward. I could not give in to those who wished to silence my inconvenient voice. If a person with my position and background did not speak up for the taxpayers, who would? Though I did receive the endorsement of the county Democratic committee, I had no illusions about the results. One person could not compete with the presses of Lancaster Newspapers. People believed what they read. I was voted out of office on November 6, 2007.

"The rest is silence."
—William Shakespeare, *Hamlet*, 1600

The $200 million hotel and convention center opened its doors in 2009.

EPILOGUE: WHEN TRUTH DOES NOT MATTER . . .

"Truth is truth to the end of reckoning."
—William Shakespeare, *Measure for Measure*, 1603

". . . truth does not matter as long as there is reiteration. . . . a lie, which if repeated loudly and often enough, becomes accepted by the people."
—Winston Churchill, Brighton, England (1947)[1]

On the same day that I lost the November 2007 election, district attorney Donald Totaro was elected as a judge to the Lancaster County Court of Common Pleas. Totaro was by far the leading vote-getter among the judicial candidates, receiving almost 14,000 more than the next judge elected.[2]

In January 2008, Judge Totaro joined President Judge Louis J. Farina on the Lancaster County bench. It was Judge Farina who had approved DA Totaro's grand jury investigation into the padded résumé of a former county employee. That thirteen-month investigation, which focused on the Lancaster County commissioners, with its massive Lancaster Newspapers press coverage, devastated me politically.

In the commissioners' race, I received 5,000 fewer votes than I did four years earlier, and I lost by about 8,000 votes.[3] Lancaster Newspapers, with its Penn Square Partners, had accomplished its objective. I was no longer a Lancaster County commissioner.

Build it and will they come?

The Lancaster Marriott Hotel opened to the public on June 19, 2009. The Lancaster County Convention Center opened a week later.[4] At the time of the hotel's ribbon cutting, former mayor Arthur E. "Art" Morris was chairman of the board of directors of the Lancaster County Convention Center Authority.[5]

As predicted by PKF in 2006, the convention center's operational losses have been relatively close to the estimated amounts: about $1 million a year loss and about $400,000 a year in LCCCA administrative costs. The single biggest issue is the enormous construction debt for this highly leveraged project, the cost of which far exceeds what was planned publicly. The project was refinanced in 2014.[6]

> "I can get not remedy against this consumption of the purse; borrowing only lingers and lingers it out but the disease is incurable."
> —William Shakespeare, *Henry IV*, Part II, 1597

Because of the higher debt payments on project bonds, there has been no money to keep up with the necessary costs of replacing fixtures, furniture, and equipment (FF&E) as they wear out in the project. To address that shortfall, Penn Square Partners has again tapped funds from a municipal authority: the City Revitalization and Improvement Zone (CRIZ) Authority.

CRIZ is a state program administered by the Department of Community and Economic Development, the Governor's Office of Budget, and the Department of Revenue. Its mission is to revitalize local business communities through redistributed tax revenue. A business in a CRIZ-designated district pays sales and local taxes to the state. Those tax revenues are then returned to the local CRIZ authority. The redirected CRIZ funds may be disbursed by the CRIZ Authority to businesses to offset bond debt service payments or to fund other projects. In July 2016, PSP used the newly created CRIZ Authority in Lancaster to secure funding for the $5.6 million in FF&E costs for the proposed new Marriott Hotel tower.

As predicted, the Lancaster County Board of Commissioners voted in 2014 to increase its guarantee of half of the $40 million LCCCA

Epilogue: When Truth Does Not Matter...

construction bond and back the *entire*, now $63 million, LCCCA bond.[7] The move more than doubled the county taxpayer exposure.

Also, as of 2017, a $39.4 million, 12-story, 110-room expansion to the Marriott Hotel has been approved by the LCCCA and the City of Lancaster and is being pursued by Penn Square Partners. It will also be real estate tax–exempt, using the same deal the original hotel has with RACL.[8] High Real Estate, general partner of PSP, has purchased several properties adjacent to the existing hotel.[9] Penn Square Partners will again pursue the same city-guaranteed state financing used to build the 300-room $75 million hotel. That hotel and the $39.4 million addition will remain, at least until 2029, property tax–free.[10] With the hotel addition, a city block of prime downtown Lancaster real estate will not pay real estate taxes for at least two decades. This amounts to millions of dollars of lost revenue to the city, the county, and Lancaster's school district. How much of this prime real estate will be removed from the tax rolls?

"There have been almost no new real estate tax revenues from downtown Lancaster in the past decade," according to Randolph Carney, a member of the School District of Lancaster Board of Directors.

In 1998, before the room tax was imposed by the Paul Thibault–led Lancaster County Board of Commissioners, state senator Gibson E. "Gib" Armstrong said that the hotel industry must support the tax before he could support it. "It's [the tax has] got to have the support of the hotel industry," Armstrong said back then.[11] That was before Senator Armstrong changed Pennsylvania law three times to help the Lancaster project, including once to undermine the hoteliers' lawsuit. The "hotel industry" never supported the project.

"The project has been a negative, not a positive," said Mark Clossey, president of the Greater Lancaster Hotel and Motel Association. Clossey, who is also general manager of the 300-room Eden Resort & Suites, just outside the city, added, "There has been no overflow from any event that the Marriott has brought in, not from any event."[12]

"To sleep, perhaps to dream."
—William Shakespeare, *Hamlet*, 1600

Clossey also said Penn Square Partners' downtown Marriott Hotel has taken thousands of nightly room rentals from other county hotels, and that one-time events have been taken from competing Lancaster hotels and conference centers, which otherwise could have accommodated those events.

Another Lancaster County hotel owner, Rodney D. Gleiberman former owner of the Continental Inn, also gave his assessment of the Marriott Hotel's economic impact on the county's hotels. Gleiberman's Continental Inn and Clossey's Eden Resort & Suites were both plaintiffs against the LCCCA in a 2000 lawsuit challenging the tax.

"The hotel-convention center project is everything that we [the hotel owners] predicted it would be, and nothing that Penn Square Partners, the LCCCA, and the rest of the project cheerleaders said it would be," said Gleiberman.

"The convention center can't pay its bills," continued Gleiberman. "The losses are far in excess of the projections of Penn Square Partners and the LCCCA, and the hotel tax revenue does not cover debt service and operations."[13]

"For loan oft loses both itself and friend,
And borrowing dulls the edge of husbandry."
—William Shakespeare, *Hamlet*, 1600

Regarding the impact of the hotel-convention center on hotel business, Gleiberman said, "The convention center itself has done *nothing* to move the needle on countywide hotel occupancy to any appreciable degree. What I get, that I can directly link to the convention center, is very minimal. What I have lost from business shifting within the County as a result of the convention center offsets any gain by a wide margin."

Gleiberman also commented on the room tax revenue taken from the Pennsylvania Dutch Convention & Visitors' Bureau (now named Discover Lancaster) and diverted to the LCCCA. "The entire hotel industry and tourist industry is set back significantly by the loss of the 20% of the room tax they [the tourism bureau] no longer get, and the huge burden on the tourism bureau's budget to market the convention center."[14] As of 2017, due to the 2014 Collaborative Agreement, conditional funding from bond reserves over $5.75M, up to an amount equal to 20 percent of the previous year's hotel tax, has been restored.[15]

The convention center has yet to sell the naming rights to the facility. In 2006, as part of Mayor Rick Gray's plan to fill a $25 million budget gap, the LCCCA counted $2 million in future naming rights fees. As of 2018, nine years after opening, no one has paid the $2 million.

The Thaddeus Stevens Museum has not opened as of this writing, mid-2018, despite being extensively promoted prior to the convention center's opening. No scheduled opening date has been announced. Like the former historic Watt & Shand building, the home and the law offices of the great American congressman and social justice champion Thaddeus Stevens have been reduced to an empty façade to make way for a hotel and convention center.[16] (See Appendix G, "Summary of the Current Situation of the Project as of 2017.")

"Take note, take note, O world,
to be direct and honest is not safe."
—William Shakespeare, *Othello*, 1603

In a 1996 profile of himself in the *Intelligencer Journal*, Lancaster Newspapers president and CEO John M. "Jack" Buckwalter said confidently, "I will say with a very high degree of assurance we will continue to have two daily papers in this town. There are those that want an evening paper and there are those that want the morning paper."[17]

Buckwalter's "very high degree of assurance" was misplaced. On June 29, 2009, the afternoon *Lancaster New Era* merged with the morning *Intelligencer Journal* and became a single morning newspaper, with both titles combined and stacked above the front-page headline, forming *Intelligencer Journal/Lancaster New Era*.[18] The merger of the two dailies (the loss of the afternoon paper) cleaved Lancaster Newspapers' daily circulation and eliminated several dozen jobs.[19]

In still another name change, in October 2014, Lancaster Newspapers changed both names of the *Intelligencer Journal/Lancaster New Era* and the *Sunday News* to *LNP: Always Lancaster*.[20]

The print *LNP* publications are now printed outside the city of Lancaster in Cumberland County, Pennsylvania. Since May 2015, all *LNP* publications are printed by the PA Media Group at its Hampden Township facility. PA Media Group is a company that was spun off from the former *Patriot-News* (Harrisburg) and Penn Live, an online Pennsylvania news service.[21]

At least seventy-five Lancaster Newspapers jobs were cut with the *LNP: Always Lancaster* production move outside of Lancaster. It will be interesting to see what happens with the now-unused printing and production facility. It is located directly across the street from the hotel and convention center. In 2015–2016, the Lancaster City Alliance attempted to market six properties near the convention center along S. Queen and W. Vine streets. They included several LNP properties, the Swan Hotel and Southern Market Center. It was unsuccessful, and the idea was abandoned.[22]

The people hurt the most by the hotel and convention center project have been the citizens of the City of Lancaster, especially its schoolchildren. The 11,300 students in the School District of Lancaster have not seen a single cent of tax revenue due them from the more than $75 million private, for-profit hotel operated by Penn Square Partners.[23]

In 2005, using former mayor Charlie Smithgall and a compliant City Council, Penn Square Partners transferred title ownership of its hotel to Lancaster City, using the tax-exempt status of a municipal redevelopment authority (RACL) to borrow $40 million from the state of Pennsylvania for the construction of the Lancaster Marriott Hotel. The City of Lancaster also *guaranteed* that the hotel's owners, Penn Square Partners, would *never* have to pay real estate taxes for the duration of the state hotel bonds.[24] The city guaranteed that no money from the hotel would go to the schools. After being stiffed out of its tax revenue, the School District of Lancaster is even charged for holding its graduation ceremony and senior prom at the hotel-convention center.[25]

It is ironic that due to our opposition to the hotel project, Lancaster Newspapers labeled former commissioner Dick Shellenberger and me "enemies of the city."[26] The fact is that as a direct result of the *publicly financed* $200 million hotel and convention center project—a project in which Lancaster Newspapers is a 50 percent *private* stakeholder in

Epilogue: When Truth Does Not Matter...

the hotel—the City of Lancaster, Pennsylvania, is a measurably poorer, more unemployed, more indebted city than it was before the project was proposed. In a 2015 study published by the Floyd Institute for Public Policy at Franklin and Marshall College—*Lancaster Prospers?*—thirteen of fourteen neighborhood-sized census tracts within the City of Lancaster saw a drop in per capita income from 2002 through 2013.[27] The study, based on U.S. Census data, also showed there was a substantial corresponding spike in unemployment in those thirteen tracts. During that period, black unemployment rose from 14 percent to 31 percent, while Latino unemployment went from 11 percent to 23 percent.[28] One of the many empty promises by Penn Square Partners was that the project would bring jobs to the minority community.

Only one tract, "Tract 1," "Center City," saw an increase in per-capita income in Lancaster from 2002 to 2013. The other thirteen tracts, encompassing the rest of the city, saw per-capita decreases from 5 percent to 28 percent, with an average decrease in income for Lancaster's citizens of more 16.2 percent during that time.[29] Tract 1, which saw a 20 percent per capita income increase, includes the $200 million taxpayer-financed hotel and convention center. The tract includes the Lancaster Newspapers headquarters, Fulton Bank, and the several law offices connected to the project. They—Lancaster's inner circle—are the primary beneficiaries from the project.

The unequal "benefit-burden" of the Lancaster hotel and convention center mirrors economic development projects found all over the United States. In Lancaster, as in countless other U.S. cities, it has been the rich, the connected, "the 1 percent"—the top of the establishment, who manipulated the rules and the people who make the rules, all to build themselves a hotel and convention center no one wanted or needed. It was a project that has burdened the many, for the benefit of the very few.

It is strange to write about the American newspaper as something from the past.

From the time when British colonist James Franklin rolled the *Boston Gazette* off his Ramage press in 1719, until the first decade of the twenty-first century, the newspaper was king.[30] The print newspaper was the most important means of reaching and influencing the American public for more than two hundred years. The newspaper broadsheets and tabloids dominated how Americans received news and opinion. The "Fourth Estate," as the press was known, was an established, powerful force in American culture. The newspaper was part of daily life. It shaped public sentiment, made and destroyed politicians.

That time is gone.

Today, in 2018, the daily broadsheet newspaper is virtually extinct. The rise of the Internet and the development and mass adoption of the smartphone, around 2010, have rendered the newspaper slow and dated and completely obsolete as an information source—and economically untenable as a business.[31] But during my term as Lancaster County commissioner, from 2004 to 2008, the newspaper was still very much alive and writing its own draft of history of Lancaster County.

The power of the Lancaster press during the newspaper age, even at the end of it, was immense. Jack Buckwalter, longtime chairman and fifty-year employee of Lancaster Newspapers, along with others, used that power to choreograph an elaborate plan to promote the financial interests of a few in a downtown hotel. They were certainly aware of that power in Lancaster. By orchestrating and participating in a plan to squelch any opposition to the project, using the newspapers, a monopoly in Lancaster County, Buckwalter exploited the immense power of the press. He did it to serve Penn Square Partners private financial interest in the downtown hotel. It was and still is always "all about the hotel."

"Speak of me as I am. Nothing extenuate,
nor set down aught in malice."
—William Shakespeare, *Othello*, 1603

On January 9, 2008, I filed a defamation lawsuit against Lancaster Newspapers, Inc.[32] Also named as individual defendants were Lancaster Newspapers employees John M. Buckwalter, Ernest J. Schreiber, Marvin I. Adams, Helen Colwell Adams, Charles Raymond Shaw, Arthur E. Morris, Gilbert A. Smart, John H. Brubaker, III, and David Pidgeon.

The complaint, which alleged a deliberate plan, listed seventeen specific published occasions, Lancaster Newspapers acted with actual malice, the legal standard for the defamation of a public figure, in covering my actions as Lancaster County commissioner. In those instances, the complaint alleged that Buckwalter and his editors knowingly published false and defamatory material about me and/or did so with reckless disregard for the truth about what they were publishing. It was libelous, according to the complaint filed by my counsel, George W. Croner, Esq., of Kohn, Swift, & Graf, in Philadelphia.[33]

Given recent history with judges Farina and Madenspacher and now Judge Totaro, and considering the hostile political climate in Lancaster County, the suit was filed in Chester County, next to Lancaster over its eastern border. During the time of the alleged libelous articles, Lancaster Newspapers had a small circulation in Chester County, which was necessary in order to have the case be heard there. (We also had to provide affidavits from Chester County residents who read the articles and formed a negative impression of me after reading them.)[34]

The lawsuit in its preliminary stages, through the discovery and deposition process, was intended to support the complaint's allegations of the hands-on orchestration of Buckwalter and his top editors and Penn Square Partners' president and High Associates executive Nevin Cooley. The complaint alleged that the group worked to discredit me using the pages of all three Lancaster Newspapers. Buckwalter and Cooley represented almost 100 percent of Penn Square Partners at the time.[35]

At various times during 2009 and 2010, in a small room, usually at the law offices of Barley Snyder, Lancaster Newspapers' attorney, the collaboration between Lancaster Newspapers and Penn Square Partners was revealed. In that stuffy, windowless conference room, with a court reporter and counsel on both sides, under sworn testimony, Buckwalter and the other defendants, when questioned by Croner and his associate Christina Saler, recounted conversations and memos that took place at the fourth-floor executive offices of Lancaster Newspapers on 8 West King Street.[36]

Because Commissioner Shellenberger and I were "attempting to derail the project," a project in which Lancaster Newspapers held a substantial ownership stake, we had to be sidelined. The weapons were words and pictures printed on the front pages and editorial pages of Buckwalter's Lancaster Newspapers, day after day ... for years.

"Nevin feels that we find it necessary to go forward with this public relations deal," Lancaster Newspapers Chairman Buckwalter wrote privately to *New Era* editor Schreiber about his and Nevin Cooley's plan to use the newspapers Buckwalter controlled to attack me and Shellenberger.[37]

The day after Christmas in 2006, before the grand jury report was released, Buckwalter admitted he "discussed the release by Judge Farina of the findings of the grand jury's probe in the Lancaster County Commissioners" with his editors.[38] The chairman of Lancaster Newspapers and his editors were deciding how they would publish the grand jury report before they read it. The institution Lancaster Newspapers, considered a guardian of community interests, was skillfully being manipulated to attack a public official who opposed its business investments.

It got personal. Ernie Schreiber, *Lancaster New Era* editor in chief, in a May 2005 editorial, referred to Commissioner Shellenberger as the "angel of death," for Shellenberger's position opposing the hotel and convention center. The "angel of death" was Josef Mengele, the infamous Nazi doctor at Auschwitz.[39]

Art Morris, the former Lancaster city mayor and the public face of the Conestoga View attacks, wrote coarsely of me in Lancaster Newspapers in January 2007: "So, County Commissioner Molly Henderson believes that the grand jury report 'vindicates' her position on the sale process and Gary Heinke's hiring. This kind of spew, while typically produced by cattle, is being delivered far too often by Commissioner Henderson."[40]

Actual malice is a nearly impossible legal hurdle to clear in court, and I was unable to get the case before a jury. My suit was dismissed at the Commonwealth Court level.[41] The plaintiff in an actual malice libel suit has an almost insurmountable burden. She faces defendants who in publishing a newspaper have a right to be wrong, the right not to be fair, the right to carry ill will, the right not to report undisclosed sources, even the right to be negligent.[42] Libel defendants—in this case, Lancaster Newspapers and its staff—have all of that walking into court. Our 47-page complaint was never heard by a jury.[43] It was disappointing, because the discovery and deposition evidence was never heard in court. I believe the evidence would have established the plan that supported the actual malice. I believe Buckwalter, Morris, Schreiber, Colwell Adams, Brubaker,

Epilogue: When Truth Does Not Matter...

and the others clearly, demonstrably, had "knowledge of falsity," the actual malice standard, of their published stories. That was shown in the deposition testimony.[44]

By spending so much time and ink on a relentless, misleading newspaper campaign, Buckwalter and his editors overlooked many important and newsworthy accomplishments from the 2004-2007 Board of Commissioners on which I served. (See Appendix D.) Our board was responsible for saving more farmland than any county *in the United States*. We also managed to get farmland preservation funds partly redirected to Lancaster County's urban centers. We believed that thriving urban centers were key to preserving the farmland. That went virtually unreported.

Our Board of Commissioners directed millions of dollars to important projects in Lancaster city, including the Pennsylvania Academy of Music (now the Ware Center), Clipper Magazine Stadium, and the vital "Northwest Corridor," which has helped economically revitalize an entire section of the city. The Better Lancaster Fund is an ongoing grant program established with some of the proceeds from the sale of Conestoga View. The fund supports projects related to early childhood health and development. The first grant went to the Welsh Mountain Medical Center for children's dental services. Since established grants have gone to the SouthEast Lancaster Health Services; the Lancaster Day Care Center; the YWCA; and others. It is administered by the Lancaster County Community Foundation.[45] In addition, Conestoga View, now privately owned, is on the tax rolls of the School District of Lancaster, Lancaster Township and Lancaster County. These actions by the county commissioners did not fit the Lancaster newspapers' story.[46]

"Well, honor is the subject of my story."
—William Shakespeare, *Julius Caesar*, 1599

One morning late in my term as commissioner, while quietly having some Quaker Oat Squares for breakfast and reading at the kitchen table, I had a tremendously unsettling realization. I was reading the notes of a book about the Civil War Battle of Dranesville and saw that the author was using the local Dranesville newspaper as a primary source for his book.[47]

It occurred to me that future historians looking at the years while I was commissioner would turn to Lancaster Newspapers to learn about Lancaster history during my tenure. The thought that these historians would rely on Lancaster Newspapers to write their drafts of history impelled me write this book.

The preceding pages are my attempt to write the authoritative history of the time and the events of my term in office. The hotel and convention center projects is one of the most expensive public capital projects in Lancaster County's history. At taxpayers' expense, two of Lancaster County's most powerful private entities, its biggest industrialist and its monopoly newspaper, leveraged their power to make tens of millions of dollars from this project.

Along with former Lancaster County commissioner Dick Shellenberger, I stood in the way of that windfall, and, as a punishment for our impertinence, the full force and the power of the Lancaster establishment—the newspapers, the politicians, and the business community—came down on us.

What Lancaster Newspapers published, however, was merely the "first draft" of Lancaster history. In the words of Lancaster Newspapers chairman Jack Buckwalter, it was a "public relations deal." This book is intended to be a corrected "second draft."

In addition to correcting the record about my work as commissioner, the aim of this book has also been to scrutinize and expose the real story of the downtown Lancaster hotel and convention center project. It was a project that few, except the private sponsors, seemed to want and made little sense for Lancaster, Pennsylvania. Nevertheless, at great cost to taxpayers, it was built and is costing taxpayers to this day.[48]

Thomas Ricks, in his Pulitzer Prize–winning book *Churchill and Orwell: The Fight For Freedom*, warns that "Those in power will want to divert people from the hard facts of a given matter . . ." That tactic was used repeatedly throughout history and is now played out here in the Red Rose City. Ricks also professes that one must "work diligently to discern the facts of the matter, and then use your principles to respond" (Ricks, p. 265). It was my duty as a

Epilogue: When Truth Does Not Matter...

commissioner to collect project facts and get through the diversions, deception, and distractions to respond in the interest of the taxpayer. I did. Unfortunately, the public was presented with facts shaped to fit the project promoters' opinions.

Those involved must be congratulated, however, for their ability to shape facts to support their story. Control of the presses made Penn Square Partners safe from examination and analysis. The glorified nonstop publicity meant that the project's facts were kept in the dark.

Perhaps now, with this book, they will be brought into the light.

ENDNOTES

Chapter One: Lights! Camera! and the Bard
Chapter Two: Doing Good So You Can Do Well

[1] *The Steinmans of Lancaster: A Family and Its Enterprises*, by John H. Brubaker, III (Steinman Enterprises, 1984), p. 17. John Frederick Steinman, Jr. (1789–1884), was appointed to the first Lancaster school board, a public office, in 1838. Both his son, Andrew Jackson Steinman (1836–1917), and his grandson, James Hale Steinman (1886–1962), served as chairmen of the Lancaster County Democratic Party. That post is an elected position, chosen among members of the Democratic Party "committee" men and women. I was a voting member of the Lancaster Township Democratic committee for more than twenty years. The Steinmans were Democrats when that party was the more conservative of the two major parties; the Republicans were more progressive in the latter part of the nineteenth century; Abraham Lincoln and Thaddeus Stevens were Republicans; Andrew Jackson and Andrew Johnson were Democrats.

[2] High Industries is the umbrella company for all of the High entities. They include: High Steel Structures, LLC; High Concrete Group, LLC; High Service Center, LLC; High Structural Erectors, LLC; High Transit, LLC; High Real Estate Group, LLC; High Associates, Ltd.; High Construction Company; Greenfield Architects, Ltd.; High Hotels, Ltd.; High Environmental Health & Safety Consulting, Ltd.

[3] Not counting the Marriott Hotel, which it "co-owns", Steinman Enterprises, the umbrella company for all of the Steinman companies, including its newspapers, owns thirteen separate properties in the immediate area of the W. King Street Lancaster Newspapers building at 8-10 W. King Street, according to the Lancaster County Assessor's Office.

[4] Lancaster Heritage Center was, at different times, Lancaster's City Hall, county offices, post office, and, from 1800 to 1812, Pennsylvania's State Capitol. It is now a closed Heritage Center Museum. It is located directly across King Street from 8-10 W. King Street, the headquarters and the former printing press for Lancaster Newspapers, half a block from the hotel and convention center. See *The Steinmans of Lancaster*, p. 178.

[5] See *Lancaster New Era*, "He 'Calvinized' the Company," October 27, 1997. This profile of Calvin G. High mentions the Old Town Lancaster renovation by Calvin and Dale High.

[6] The Greenfield Corporate Center is owned by High and managed by High Real Estate. See http://www.greenfieldcorporatecenter.com/default.aspx.

[7] *The Steinmans of Lancaster* devotes chapters four through nine to Andrew Jackson Steinman. Like his father, John Frederick Steinman, Jr., AJ Steinman was a force of nature who left an indelible mark on Lancaster City and County and beyond its borders.

[8] At the time the *Intelligencer* newspaper was purchased in 1866, a year after the end of the Civil War, AJ Steinman was a leading lawyer, businessman, and chairman of the Lancaster County Democratic Party. Of the newspaper acquisition, Brubaker writes in *The Steinmans of Lancaster*: "[AJ Steinman] reluctantly entered into what would become the central business of the family's enterprises," p. 37.

[9] The *Intelligencer*'s position under AJ Steinman on the "superiority of the race of white men" can be found in *The Steinmans of Lancaster*, p. 40.

[10] *The Steinmans of Lancaster*, quoting AJ Steinman's *Lancaster Intelligencer* after Thaddeus Stevens announced he bought a burial plot at the racially integrated Shreiner-Concord Cemetery, p. 40.

[11] Ibid. From *The Steinmans of Lancaster*: "The *Intelligencer* was not displeased when Stevens died in August of 1868, five days before he won a Republican primary with ease. During the campaign for the general election the paper mocked the Republicans for running a 'Corpse for Congress.' But Stevens's name remained on the ballot, and his ghost defeated a live Democratic opponent in a landslide."

[12] *The Steinmans of Lancaster*, p. 26.

[13] After purchasing 8-10 W. King Street, A. J. Steinman and Charles Foltz moved the *Intelligencer*'s operations to that location. It had been on Penn Square previously. See *The Steinmans of Lancaster*, p. 51.

[14] The New York–based newspaper "wars" between Joseph Pulitzer's *New York World* and William Randolph Hearst's *New York Herald* are often used as examples of the "yellow journalism" of the turn of the twentieth century. Yellow journalism is a phrase that means sensationalistic, often tawdry, "journalism." There is debate as to the origin of the *yellow journalism* term. Evidently, yellow ink was used occasionally by the respective newspapers. Also, a popular comic strip at the time, "Yellow Kid," ran in both publications. After his death, Pulitzer (1847–1911) bequeathed funds to create the Columbia University Graduate School of Journalism. In 1917, the prestigious Pulitzer Prizes were established with money Pulitzer left to Columbia.

William Randolph Hearst (1863–1951) was a California-born mining heir. Like the sons of AJ Steinman, J. F. and James Hale, William Randolph Hearst was born to wealth, established family businesses, and grew them substantially. Hearst's "war" with Pulitzer took place in New York. Hearst is also well known for his opulent lifestyle, including his massive home, San Simeon, also known as "Hearst Castle," on the Central California coast.

[15] Nelly Bly (1864–1922) was an extremely important American investigative journalist. In 1887, working for Pulitzer's *New York World*, Bly (real name Elizabeth Cochrane Seaman) feigned mental illness and was admitted to, and reported about,

the appalling conditions at the Women's Lunatic Asylum at Blackwell's Island. H. L. Menken (1880–1956) was a thinking man's Andy Rooney in the first half of the twentieth century. Irascible, cantankerous, and downright mean, Menken was a valuable critic who was read nationally from his base at the *Baltimore Sun*.

[16] *Census on Population and Housing*, Lancaster, Pa., U.S. Department of the Census.

[17] *The Steinmans of Lancaster*, p. 54.

[18] "The sons treated the newspapers as a manufacturing enterprise instead of the political organ and business liability their father had inherited and never altered," p. 84, *The Steinmans of Lancaster*.

[19] *The Steinmans of Lancaster*, p. 85. Charles Steinman Foltz, AJ Steinman's nephew and partner in buying the *Intelligencer* in 1866, sold his interest to J. F. and James Hale Steinman, AJ's sons, for $75,000 on May 1, 1921.

[20] The J. F. Steinman quote to the linotype and monotype print workers threatening to strike, "The employers must win—must, we say . . ." is from *The Steinmans of Lancaster*, p. 85.

[21] The Lancaster newspaper "war" between the Steinmans and Paul Block, Sr., was a hard-fought victory for the Steinmans over the estimable Block. Paul Block (1877–1941) owned a national advertising firm and several newspapers, including the *Los Angeles Express* and the *Pittsburgh Post-Gazette*, at the time he purchased the *Lancaster New Era* in 1923. He was a personal friend of New York City mayor Jimmy Walker and newspaper publisher William Randolph Hearst.

[22] The final total of the sale, according Brubaker's account, was $950,000. The deal involved Janney & Co of Philadelphia selling $600,000 in bonds; Farmers Trust Company loaned the Steinmans $200,000; and the Canadian Newspaper Company also loaned the Steinmans another $100,000. See *The Steinmans of Lancaster*, p. 101.

[23] "Like my father I was never a newsman—always a businessman. That's what I am now. The newspaper is and always has been a business—nothing more!" This direct quote from John Frederick Steinman very much captures the Steinmans' approach; the newspapers were a business, not a journalistic, enterprise. From p. 135 of *The Steinmans of Lancaster*.

[24] The period covering the Steinmans' entry into the radio business, beginning with the Lancaster Station WGAL, is found in *The Steinmans of Lancaster*, pp. 152–158. The Steinmans made an early link between their radio and print followers by calling WGAL "The Voice of the *Intelligencer*" when they purchased it in 1923; p. 153. The Steinmans' reach extended to the Delmarva network (Delaware-Maryland-Virginia) to the east, and to Phoenix, Arizona, to the west.

[25] *The Steinmans of Lancaster*, Chapter 20, "Television," covers the Steinmans' involvement in television. There were decades when the Steinmans owned the biggest television station in the region and the most powerful radio network and had a print monopoly with Lancaster Newspapers; pp. 159–166.

26 Lancaster Newspapers chairman Jack Buckwalter said that the newspapers were the greatest revenue-generator for the Steinmans. From Buckwalter's deposition, February 3, 2010, p. 50: In the libel lawsuit I brought against Lancaster Newspapers and several of its employees, including chairman Jack M. Buckwalter—*Molly Henderson vs Lancaster Newspapers, Inc., John M. Buckwalter, Ernest J. Schreiber, Marvin I. Adams, Jr., Helen Colwell Adams, Charles Raymond Shaw, Arthur E. Morris, Gilbert A. Smart, John H. Brubaker, III, and David Pidgeon*. No. 0712003—

27 The "Steinman sisters" - Louise (1922–2008), Caroline (1925–2010), and Beverly ("Peggy") (1934–), were well known in Lancaster for years. Caroline "Carrie" Steinman Nunan was a highly regarded local philanthropist and conservationist. From her obituary published in Lancaster Newspapers, July 27, 2010:

> She was a life member of the Lancaster County Conservancy and was given the conservancy's Partnership Award, its most prestigious honor, in 1999. That same year, Franklin & Marshall College named its campus, which is a designated arboretum, the Caroline Steinman Nunan Arboretum at Franklin & Marshall College.
> Carrie's numerous board memberships included the American Red Cross, which she served for 15 years as a Gray Lady volunteer at Lancaster General Hospital. She also served on the boards of the Demuth Foundation, Fulton Bank, where she was the first woman director, Planned Parenthood of the Susquehanna Valley, Hospice of Lancaster County, Lancaster Country Day School and Lancaster Symphony Orchestra. She was a past trustee of Lancaster General Hospital."

See http://lancasteronline.com/obituaries/caroline-steinman-nunan/article_b3ea7598-f93f-5741-950a-5ed4c859316b.html.

28 Besides "We give good measure," the High companies also use "Right the first time," as another of their business sayings. See the High website: http://www.high.net/about/philosophy/index.cfm.

29 High's ranking as an employer in Lancaster County varies from year to year. In 2000, for example, it was the 10th-largest employer in the county; in 2012, it was 24th. But wherever the company is ranked on a "largest employers" roster, there is no question that High is among the most powerful and politically influential businesses in the region.

30 The High company biography is found on the www.High.net website and has been featured many times by Lancaster Newspapers. The timing of the positive articles from the Steinman newspapers was always very interesting to me. For example, less than two weeks after the county commissioners passed the hotel room tax in 1999, on September 26, the *Sunday News*, the Steinmans' largest-circulation newspaper, ran a particularly flattering article of Dale High, "The High Road," which began:

> Inside the office building, prominent business executive S. Dale High sits scanning papers on a table.
>
> Outside, a flock of Canada geese glides prettily past High's picture window. "The whole squadron," High remarks later as he walks outdoors to the lush park that he incorporated into the Greenfield Corporate Center.
>
> The sturdy office complex at his back symbolizes the vibrant Lancaster County he would like to preserve for his three children, two stepchildren and eight grandchildren.
>
> But so do the geese and the park and the beckoning open lands beyond.

"The High Road" article in the *Sunday News* followed months of featured articles about Dale High. In the months leading up to "The High Road" article, Lancaster newspapers featured High repeatedly, on April 7 in the *Intelligencer Journal*, "High Will Get Boy Scouts of America for Citizenship"; on May 8, "The *New Era* Red Rose Is Presented to S. Dale High"; on May 13 in the *Intell*, "Scouts Honor: High Praise. S. Dale High Holds the Distinguished Citizen Award"; on August 25, just over two weeks from the room tax vote, in the Steinmans' *Lancaster New Era*, "Pa. Chamber Names High Top Business Leader of '99." These were very prominent articles that ran before the room tax—which would directly benefit High and the Steinmans. This seemed like a marketing campaign, rather than reporting on a major civic project.

[31] The business history of the High companies, beginning in 1931, is also worthy of a book in itself. Like other brilliant business pioneers and visionaries, Sanford High had a combination of great intelligence, technical understanding, energy, and vision. His business acumen was uncanny, and his timing in the steel industry couldn't have been better, coinciding as it did with the great interstate expansion during the 1960s. See the High history at their website: http://high.net/about/history/index.cfm. Also see "He 'Calvinized' the Company," a profile of S. Dale High's older brother, Calvin G. High, *Lancaster New Era*, October 27, 1997. ("The young Calvin High spent every available hour at the shop, fascinated by the ingenuity he saw in the repair and manufacture of fuel tanks, feed mixers, farm wagons and other equipment.")

[32] There is no question that Sanford H. High was a technological innovator in the field of welding. He was the rare mechanic who could also deal with lawyers and politicians in securing government contracts. For a Lancaster County farmer to land the I-695 "beltway" interchange and other major government contracts was quite a feat. Sanford High was named as one of the nation's top hundred private-sector transportation design and construction professionals of the twentieth century by the American Road and Transportation Builders Association's Transportation Development Foundation. See "Taking the High Road," *Sunday News*, February 21, 2005.

[33] The company changed its name from High Welding to High Steel in 1971, the year after it completed the bridgework spanning the Susquehanna River. See the High website company history: http://high.net/about/history/index.cfm.

34 Nevin D. Cooley, president of High Associates and president of Penn Square Partners, as well as longtime High spokesman and spokesman for the hotel and convention project at the center of this book, succeeded Dale High, who remained chairman of the board of all High entities. Cooley retired in 2014. Cooley was replaced by Michael F. Shirk, who is the High CEO as of 2015. Source: High Industries revenue: http://www.inc.com/profile/high-industries.

35 Formed in 1988, eleven years after Dale High was named president and CEO of High Industries, High Hotels owned thirteen hotels in 2015, including half-ownership in the Lancaster Marriott hotel. The High and the Steinman entities own the downtown Lancaster Marriott which has not paid real taxes since the project began, and they can purchase the hotel outright for a fraction of its market value twenty years after "leasing" the building.

36 High Industries is the umbrella company for all of the High entities. They include High Steel Structures, LLC; High Concrete Group, LLC; High Service Center, LLC; High Structural Erectors, LLC; High Transit, LLC; High Real Estate Group, LLC; High Associates, Ltd.; High Construction Company; Greenfield Architects, Ltd.; High Hotels, Ltd.; and High Environmental Health & Safety Consulting, Ltd.

37 From the Steinman Foundation: "The John Frederick Steinman and James Hale Steinman Foundations were established in 1951 and merged to become The Steinman Foundation in 2014." See http://steinmancommunications.com/the-steinman-foundation/.

38 Penn Square Partners president and longtime High spokesman and executive Nevin D. Cooley replaced Dale High as president and CEO of High Industries in 2011. S. Dale High remained, and remains, chairman of the board of all High companies, including the High Family Council.

39 From the High Industries website, "The High Way: A Family Tradition": "The High Family Council provides current and future ownership direction to the High® companies with support from two Boards of Directors and an Executive Committee." At the time of this writing, 2017, the High Family Council consisted of S. Dale High; his wife, Sadie H. High; and their offspring, Gregory A. High, Suzanne M. High Schenk, and Steven D. High.

40 In his February 3, 2010 deposition, Buckwalter recounted the Lancaster Newspapers' circulation numbers for all of the Steinman publications in 2010: "*Sunday News* [has] about 95–96 thousand, the *Intell* and *New Era* combine for about 81,000; *Lancaster Farming* 54,000; *Ephrata Review* 8,200; *Lititz* [*Record*], about 8 thousand . . ." Buckwalter's deposition, Feb. 3, 2010, pp. 57-60.

The *Intell* and the *New Era* merged in June 2009, after the *New Era* ceased publishing an afternoon newspaper. For five years, until 2014, the two papers, delivered in the morning, carried the cumbersome *Intelligencer Journal/Lancaster New Era* as a single paper with two editorial pages. Today the once-thriving newspaper monopoly is down to one daily, called *LNP*.

From the February 3, 2010, deposition of John M. Buckwalter, a defendant in the libel lawsuit, Number 0712003. *Molly Henderson, Plaintiff, v. Lancaster Newspapers, Inc., John M. Buckwalter, Ernest J. Schreiber, Marvin L. Adams, Jr., Helen Colwell Adams.*

[41] Based on the U.S. Department of the Census statistics for 2010, there were 194,084 households in Lancaster County (average size 2.62). This means that Lancaster newspapers were read by about 50 percent of the county's households. Factoring in the "pass-along" rate of those inside a house and readership in professional (doctors, lawyers, dentists, etc.) offices, and the print dominance of Lancaster Newspapers is even more impressive. Virtually every adult read one of the three major Lancaster newspapers.

[42] From the *Intelligencer Journal*, "Keeping Lancaster County in the News," a profile of Buckwalter, June 17, 1996:

During a seven-year stretch when his and his father's careers overlapped and they both lived in Millersville, they drove to work together. The commuting time served as valuable preparation for Buckwalter, because he learned many lessons from his father about running a newspaper business.

[43] During his deposition, Buckwalter referred to *The Steinmans of Lancaster* on the point of the "church/state" separation between the editorial and the publishing sides of the newspapers. The quoted comments were from the Buckwalter's, February 3, 2010, deposition pp. 119-120.

John M. Buckwalter, was a defendant in the libel lawsuit, Number 0712003. *Molly Henderson, Plaintiff, v. Lancaster Newspapers, Inc., John M. Buckwalter, Ernest J. Schreiber, Marvin L. Adams, Jr., Helen Colwell Adams.*

[44] From Buckwalter's obituary, August 12, 2010, "Jack Buckwalter Dies: Civic Leader, Steinman Exec: Led Fight to Build City Center, Hotel":

> Mueller and Buckwalter eventually were among the 18 businessmen, doctors and lawyers who meet every Monday for lunch at the Hamilton Club in Lancaster. The group calls itself the Wash Day Club and will celebrate its 110th year in November.
>
> The group has 18 members because there are 18 places at the table at which they regularly dine. It is named after a group of professionals who worked downtown and whose wives, on laundry day, told them not to come home for lunch. The men started to meet on those days and have lunch together.

See http://lancasteronline.com/news/jack-buckwalter-dies-civic-leader-steinman-exec/article_dc4f6414-6b2e-5cbb-afbd-8578532bb7e5.html.

[45] Ibid. Buckwalter's obituary, 2010; http://lancasteronline.com/news/jack-buckwalter-dies-civic-leader-steinman-exec/article_dc4f6414-6b2e-5cbb-afbd-8578532bb7e5.html.

⁴⁶ When Buckwalter referred to himself being the "chairman of everything," he meant it. During his deposition, he listed all of the Steinman businesses he oversaw. "They all report to me," Buckwalter testified. From Buckwalter's deposition, February 3, 2010, p.53:21.

John M. Buckwalter, was a defendant in the libel lawsuit, Number 0712003. *Molly Henderson, Plaintiff, v. Lancaster Newspapers, Inc., John M. Buckwalter, Ernest J. Schreiber, Marvin L. Adams, Jr., Helen Colwell Adams.*

⁴⁷ It is difficult to pinpoint the precise date that print newspapers in Lancaster County became obsolete. Personal digital assistants (PDAs) with mobile operating systems were becoming mass adapted in the mid-2000s, but it took until the latter part of the decade for the new devices to catch on with the Lancaster County masses. The Apple iPhone was released in 2007, the last year of my term in office. Until 2008 or so, the print Lancaster Newspapers were the dominant form of supplying the news. It is not so today, but it applied during the four years I served as county commissioner.

⁴⁸ In his deposition, Jack Buckwalter made it very clear that he served as chairman of Steinman Enterprises at the discretion of the "Steinman ladies, . . . Beverly Steinman; Caroline Nunan-Hill; Caroline Nunan; Hale Krasne, daughter of late Louise Steinman Ansberry." From Buckwalter's deposition, February 3, 2010, p. 54:5.

John M. Buckwalter, was a defendant in the libel lawsuit, Number 0712003. *Molly Henderson, Plaintiff, v. Lancaster Newspapers, Inc., John M. Buckwalter, Ernest J. Schreiber, Marvin L. Adams, Jr., Helen Colwell Adams.*

⁴⁹ Ibid. p. 187.2, "And the hotel convention center, obviously, was of interest to them [the "Steinman ladies] and we obviously want to keep them informed. At one point all four ladies and myself went out to High to look at the colors of the hotel . . ."

⁵⁰ The work history of Nevin D. Cooley is found in his retirement announcement, "High Companies CEO to Retire," *LNP*, June 24, 2014. Cooley succeeded S. Dale High, who remained chairman of the board of High companies.

Chapter Three: The Project

¹ Political strategist, James Carville's original 1986 quote is said to be: "Between Paoli [near Philadelphia] and Penn Hills [near Pittsburgh], Pennsylvania is Alabama without the blacks. They didn't film *The Deerhunter* there for nothing—the state has the second-highest concentration of NRA members, behind Texas."

² Howard Means, "The Avenger Takes His Place: Andrew Johnson and the 45 Days That Changed the Nation," From p. 111: "Perhaps no city in the North reflects more starkly the divided attitude toward the [Civil] war than Lancaster, Pennsylvania. Said to be the oldest inland city in the United States, . . ."

³ The cost of the Lancaster County Convention Center and Marriott Hotel project has been a question of debate since its inception. When the Penn Square project began in 1999, it was projected to cost $75 million. When I was elected county commissioner

in 2003, the cost was said to have risen to $129 million. By the time I left office, the cost of the center was estimated at $145 million. When it opened in 2009, Lancaster Newspapers published the cost as $187 million. The last several years have seen major debt service payment problems for the center. The Lancaster County Convention Center Authority has had to restructure the debt several times, due to the shortfall. Despite the financial problems of the center, as of this writing in 2018, a new $23 million addition is being planned for the High-Steinman-owned Marriott Hotel, along with more state and local subsidies. This pushes the total cost of the project to almost a quarter billion dollars, not including the millions in fees waived for the project.

[4] "Third-Class County Convention Center Authority Act; Act of 1994, P.L. 1375, No. 162." According to the act, "the purpose of the convention center should be the promotion, attraction, and stimulation, development and expansion of business industry, commerce, and tourism. . . . the development of the convention center will provide benefits to the hotel industry throughout the entire area of the county where the center is developed. . . ." The funds to build the convention center are raised through the "room rental tax," a fee imposed on every hotel and motel room rented within the third-class county. See the act: http://www.luzernecounty.org/content/File/3rd%20Class%20Convtions%20Ctr%20Auth%20Act%201994.pdf.

[5] From the County Commissioners Association of Pennsylvania (CCCAP). Lancaster County's population has passed 500,000, which would now classify it as a "Second-Class A (2-A)" county with a population of 500,000 to 799,999, along with Bucks, Delaware, and Montgomery counties. But at the time of the Convention Center Authority Act's passage in 1994, Lancaster County's population of 446,254 still classified it as "Third-Class" and thereby qualifying for the room tax enactment. See "Counties by Class": http://www.pacounties.org/PAsCounties/Pages/CountiesByClass.aspx.

[6] United States Department of the Census, 1994; Population Lancaster County, Pa., http://www.census.gov/quickfacts/fact/table/lancastercountypennsylvania.

[7] From "Unconventional Decisions: Challenging the Use of Hotel Taxes in Convention Center Projects," published in the *Journal of Constitutional Law*, Vol. 7: 2 (November 2004): 533–559, by Dionne E. Anthon, MBA, and J.D. candidate at the University of Pennsylvania Law School. "Unconventional Decisions" is an analysis of the constitutionality of hotel room rental taxes and an analysis of the "circuit of economic activity" the tax was supposed to generate. See p. 541 of the study.

[8] Despite the longtime power and influence of the Stevens & Lee law firm, not much has been written about the history of the firm. In its literature and on its website, Stevens & Lee refers to the firm's 1928 launch. See http://www.stevenslee.com/about-us/.

[9] Perennially on the *American Lawyer*'s AmLaw 200 firms (by gross revenue), Stevens & Lee was ranked 187th on the 2015 list, with $108,500,000 in gross revenue in 2014. However, due to its relatively small size in relation to other AmLaw 200 firms, Stevens & Lee ranked 79th in profits-per-partner, and 106th in revenue-per-lawyer. See http://

www.americanlawyer.com/law-firm-profiles-result?firmname=Stevens+%26+Lee&slreturn=20150913181148.

[10] For more on Stevens & Lee's services, see http://www.stevenslee.com/about-us/.

[11] For more on Joseph M. Harenza, see his Stevens & Lee profile: http://www.stevenslee.com/?pro=joseph-m-harenza.

[12] Stevens & Lee's—and managing partner Joseph M. Harenza's—designation as "super lawyers" is found here: http://profiles.superlawyers.com/pennsylvania/philadelphia/lawfirm/stevens-and-lee/5cbef913-d7a4-4494-8523-4048db165c4f.html.

[13] Joseph M. Harenza, Stevens & Lee chairman, was the registered lobbyist for High Industries in the years 2005 and 2006, during my term as Lancaster County commissioner. Harenza, who was registered as a lobbyist from 2003 to 2006, represented thirty-three clients, including Comcast, CitiGroup, and Carnegie Mellon University. For a list of Harenza's lobbying clients, including High Industries, see http://classic.followthemoney.org/database/lobbyist.phtml?l=128795.

[14] Stevens & Lee takes credit for the 1994 Third-Class Counties Convention Center Authority Act in a number of places on the firm's website, stevenslee.com. The excerpt quoted in this chapter may be found here: http://www.stevenslee.com/services/tax-exempt-finance/economic-development/.

[15] "3% Hotel Tax Proposed to Fund Convention Centers," *Lancaster New Era*, March 28, 1994, byline: Tim Buckwalter. The Lancaster County commissioners eventually imposed a 5% tax (actually, two taxes) in 1999 and are likely to increase the tax to its statutory limit of 6%, due to the chronic financial problems of the Lancaster County Convention Center Authority.

[16] "Hotel Room Tax Bill Goes to Pa. House," *Intelligencer Journal*, March 29, 1994. This article is an example of how the two daily papers often reported as one. Much was made about each being independently run. However, on issues that affected the investments of Lancaster Newspapers, Inc., all three newspapers spoke with one voice.

[17] Representative Katie True is quoted from the March 28, 1994, *Lancaster New Era* article (note 15 above). Also expressing skepticism about the "3%" hotel room tax were then chairman of the Lancaster County Board of Commissioners James Huber and Harry Flick, then president of the Pennsylvania Dutch Convention & Visitors Bureau.

[18] See THIRD CLASS COUNTY CONVENTION CENTER AUTHORITY ACT—Act of 1994, P.L. 1375, No. 162, Section 4, "Authority Creation," p. 4:

> The governing bodies of a third-class county and the political subdivision constituting the county seat or the county acting alone may create a body corporate and politic to be named the _____ County Convention Center Authority to be created as a public authority and government instrumentality to have continuing succession until its existence shall be terminated by

> law. If the convention center to be constructed by an authority created under this act shall be located within the jurisdictional limits of the county seat of the county, the authority shall be a joint authority of the county and the county seat. If the convention center shall be located outside the jurisdictional limits of the county seat of the county, the authority may be created solely by the county. The exercise by the authority of the powers conferred by this act is, hereby declared to be and shall for all purposes be deemed and held to be the performance of an essential public function.

[19] For the best analysis of the economic impact of publicly financed convention centers during this period, see Dr. Heywood Sanders's excellent study, published by the Brookings Institute, January 2005, "Space Available: The Realities of Convention Centers as Economic Development Strategy." An excerpt:

> The overall convention marketplace is declining in a manner that suggests that a recovery or turnaround is unlikely to yield much increased business for any given community, contrary to repeated industry projections. Moreover, this decline began prior to the disruptions of 9-11 and is exacerbated by advances in communications technology. Currently, overall attendance at the 200 largest tradeshow events languishes at 1993 levels.
>
> Nonetheless, localities, sometimes with state assistance, have continued a type of arms race with competing cities to host these events, investing massive amounts of capital in new convention center construction and expansion of existing facilities. Over the past decade alone, public capital spending on convention centers has doubled to $2.4 billion annually, increasing convention space by over 50 percent since 1990. Nationwide, 44 new or expanded convention centers are now in planning or construction.
>
> Faced with increased competition, many cities spend more money on additional convention amenities, like publicly-financed hotels to serve as convention "headquarters." Another competitive response has been to offer deep discounts to trade show groups. Despite dedicated taxes to pay off the public bonds issued to build convention centers, many—including Washington, D.C and St. Louis—operate at a loss.

Sanders, Heywood, *Space Available: The Realities of Convention Centers as Economic Strategy; Research Brief: Executive Summary*, (Brookings Institution, 2005), p.1.

[20] See "A City Transformed: Redevelopment, Race, and Suburbanization in Lancaster, Pennsylvania, 1940–1980," by David Schuyler (Pennsylvania University Press, 2002).

[21] Born in Conestoga Township, Lancaster County, the architect Cassius Emlen Urban (February 26, 1863 May 21, 1939) designed much of Lancaster between 1890

and 1920. In addition to the Watt & Shand building, Urban also designed the original Brunswick Hotel, as well as the Hager Building, the Kirk Johnson Building, and the W.W. Griest Building, among others. The Hager, Johnson, and Griest buildings are all listed on the National Register for Historic Places, as was the Watt & Shand until Penn Square Partners destroyed it to build their taxpayer paid-for "private" Marriott Hotel.

[22] "Watt & Shand Stores Are Being Bought by Bon-Ton: Name Will Change at Downtown and Park City Locations," *Lancaster New Era*, February 26, 1992.

From the article:

> Watt & Shand, a Lancaster institution for more than a century, is being sold to a York retailer, it was announced today.
>
> The Bon-Ton Stores Inc. will acquire the Watt & Shand stores on Penn Square and at Park City Center, plus its warehouse on Prestige Lane.

[23] *Lancaster New Era*, January 11, 1995, "Downtown Bon-Ton Shuts March 5, Sales Losses Cited." The article begins:

> It's official: The downtown Bon-Ton department store is closing.
>
> The York-based chain announced this morning that Lancaster City's biggest retailer will close March 4, ending months of speculation concerning the store's fate. "We gave it our best shot and worked very hard to make the downtown store successful but unfortunately . . . we just couldn't make it profitable," said Michael L. Gleim, Bon-Ton's senior executive vice president.

[24] *The Killer Angels*, by Michael Shaara (McKay Publishing, 1974), won the Pulitzer Prize in 1975.

[25] A flintlock rifle uses a flint-striking ignition mechanism to fire a round. The process of pouring the gunpowder and striking the flint is delicate and precise, and there are several difficulties with this gun. It is prone to backfire, and moisture and rain preclude the firing of the firearm. The phrase "flash in the pan" originates with the flintlock firearm. There is a flash from the firing of the priming in the pan of a flintlock weapon (musket or rifle) that sometimes occurs without discharging the bullet. Cabin Creek Muzzleloading specializes in custom-made, historically accurate rifles. The gunsmiths use authentic eighteenth-century techniques to build the muzzles. Cabin Creek Muzzleloading is a local treasure. For more information on Cabin Creek Muzzleloading, please visit their website at: http://cabincreek.net/.

[26] The January 22, 1995, *Sunday News* article "Candidate Holds Thank You Party" was another example of the very positive coverage I was receiving from Lancaster Newspapers. The *Sunday News* does not endorse candidates (or it didn't then), but three large, positive, prominently placed articles in the most-read of the Steinman newspapers as I entered the race were certainly very helpful with getting my name recognized throughout the county.

[27] Paul Thibault was viewed as an upset second-place finisher in the May 1995 Republican primary. *Lancaster New Era*, "Thibault in Upset Win Over Huber," May 17, 1995. Terry Kauffman won the primary with 24,905 votes. Thibault received 21,310 votes, trouncing incumbent James Huber, who finished with 17,128. Source: Lancaster County Voter Registration and Board of Elections.

[28] Thibault's donors were featured often in Lancaster Newspapers; e.g., on March 2, 1999, in the *Lancaster New Era*, which publicized Thibault's close relationship with the Lancaster business establishment. See *Lancaster New Era*, "Top Business Leaders Back Thibault's Re-Election Bid."

From the article:

> He may not have the endorsement of the Lancaster County Republican Committee, but incumbent County Commissioner Paul R. Thibault has the support of some of the county's most prominent business leaders.
>
> At a $125-a-plate fundraiser Monday night in the Quality Inn and Suites on Oregon Pike, Thibault, who is seeking re-election, was joined by some 300 supporters. Among those endorsing Thibault were retired Lancaster AAA executive Herbert C. "Bud" Mearig; Tom Baldrige, chairman of The Lancaster Campaign; William W. Adams, former CEO of Armstrong World Industries Inc.; and R. Scott Smith Jr., chairman and CEO of Fulton Bank. Also supporting Thibault, but unable to attend the dinner, were city Mayor Charlie Smithgall, state Rep. John E. Barley, R-Conestoga, and S. Dale High, president of High Industries Inc.

Everyone in this group—six months before the room tax was imposed—joined behind Thibault for the key county commissioner post. They needed that tax passed to get the project rolling.

[29] The proposed HACC purchase of the Watt & Shand building broke in the *Lancaster New Era* on June 19, 1996: "Community College Picks Downtown Bon-Ton as Site, $12 Million Project Will Be 'Showcase' Sept. 1998 Target."

[30] See the HACC website, www.HACC.edu.

[31] Former Lancaster mayor Art Morris's concern for "the tax base of the city" turned out to be quite selective. It did not extend to the private hotel he championed for the Steinman and High families. While objecting to a college going into the Watt & Shand building, Morris raised no concerns about "the tax base of the city" when it came to the Steinmans and the Highs not paying real estate taxes on their private, for-profit hotel. See *Intelligencer Journal*, "Ex-Mayor Questions Bon-Ton Demolition," November 12, 1996.

[32] Art Morris was interviewed on videotape on July 24, 2001, by Ron Harper, Jr., on Penn Square, Lancaster, PA. The videotape is part of an extensive collection made by Mr. Harper. He permitted me to view the collection prior to writing this book

[33] Morris's role in attempting to bring a convention center to Lancaster in the 1980s is referenced in the August 26, 1999, edition of the *Lancaster New Era*, "Efforts to Build Civic, Conference Centers Here Date Back to '40s," and it is also referenced in the *Lancaster New Era*, March 28, 1994, "3% Hotel Tax Proposed to Fund Convention Centers." The 1994 article was the first about the room tax, published months before it became state law. From the 1994 article: "A committee appointed by former Lancaster Mayor Arthur E. Morris studied the feasibility of building a civic center in the late 1980s. But the idea stalled when no viable funding mechanism emerged. . . ."

[34] The launch of the Lancaster Campaign was announced in the *Lancaster New Era*, July 24, 1996: "Campaign Unveiled to Renew City." Its connection to the Lancaster Alliance is made explicit in the article:

> "This is an organized, broad-based effort, aimed at action," said William W. Adams, chairman of the Lancaster Alliance, the business group that spearheaded plans for the campaign. . . . The origin of the campaign, organizers said, lies in work carried out by the Lancaster Alliance, a group of 15 past and present chief executive officers.
>
> (The alliance had added three other members by 1996, after starting with the original twelve.)

[35] The Winterbottom study came in with a roar and huge publicity. The story announcing the study appeared in the *Lancaster New Era* on July 1, 1997, "'Design Doctor' Hired to Revive City." It was the Lancaster Campaign, the Lancaster Alliance offshoot, that hired Winterbottom. Dale High, Jack Buckwalter, and Rufus Fulton were founding and current members of the Lancaster Alliance at the time. The article begins:

The doctor is in.

> The Lancaster Campaign hired urban designer Bert Winterbottom today to create a diagnosis and prescription for revitalizing Lancaster. Like any doctor, he plans to ask the patient about symptoms and future needs. He will interview government and business leaders and hold forums where everyone—city and county residents—can offer their ideas.
>
> Like any patient, Lancaster must participate if the treatment is to succeed.
>
> "Community buy-in, public and private, is absolutely critical to the success of the plan," said Winterbottom, who heads LDR International Corp. of Columbia, Md. . . .

[36] Smithgall made the statement about living on the same block on Lemon Street his entire life to Chris Hart Nibbrig. Smithgall's background was covered in several Lancaster Newspapers profiles, including in the *Sunday News* on June 4, 1995, "Charles Smithgall: Cannon Collector Has a Real Blast." This article contains a number of biographical details and focuses on Smithgall's cannon and weapons collection. Also

see *Intelligencer Journal*, June 27, 1997, "Smithgall's First Fund-Raiser Will Be a Real Blast." This article also references Smithgall's cannons and his appearance in the film *Gettysburg*.

[37] *Lancaster New Era*, April 19, 1997, "Mayoral Candidates Discuss HACC, Plans for Revitalizing Downtown." The question was what to do with the Watt & Shand building:

> SMITHGALL: We need a good anchor for the city. There is the (retail/exposition center) proposal (businessman) Rob Ecklin is promoting. There could be other things on the horizon. The Downtown Investment District and the state Department of Economic Development could help. I'd like to see a better economic driver than a community college. . . .

[38] Dan Langan, a spokesman for the Department of Education, was quoted in an *Intelligencer Journal* article, "State Denies Finds [sic] for HACC," March 27, 1997: "The problem is that it's a $6 million application for a building worth $1.5 million. The responsibility of the commonwealth would be to work with the $1.5 million figure. The market value is $1.5 million." It may have been "worth" $1.5 million, but the Redevelopment of the City of Lancaster would pay $7 million for the building nine years later. RACL bought it from Penn Square Partners, which paid $1.25 million for the building.

[39] "The LDR study is the biggest thing they [Lancaster Campaign] have accomplished," Smithgall said. "Our plan is to follow that as closely as possible." *Intelligencer Journal*, "Behind the Scenes," January 10, 1998.

[40] Lancaster County's other political heavyweight in Harrisburg was former senator Gibson E. Armstrong (born August 28, 1943–). See Armstrong's archived Senate "profile" here: http://www.legis.state.pa.us/cfdocs/legis/BiosHistory/MemBio.cfm?ID=2528&body=S.

[41] From the *Lancaster New Era*, December 3, 1997, "Bon-Ton Building for Sale on Jan. 1, Highest Bidder Will Get It HACC Is Out":

> The vacant Bon-Ton building in Penn Square will go up for sale to the highest bidder on Jan. 1, a company official said today. "It's time for us to move on," said H. Stephen Evans, who heads real estate development for The Bon-Ton Inc. "The building is for sale again, but this time we will seek and expect to obtain a quick disposition and we look to the community to present prospective qualified and civic-minded buyers to lead the redevelopment effort. . . ."

[42] Smithgall made the comment after he considered having the City of Lancaster purchase the building from Bon Ton. From the *Sunday News*, "A Big 3 Works to Buy Bon-Ton," January 18, 1998:

> After watching two years of work on the HACC plan go down the tubes, Bon-Ton decided to put it up for auction. That idea

worried Smithgall. Anybody could buy it, he thought, picturing some foreign investor sitting on the building—and Lancaster's future—for a decade....

[43] Smithgall's first priority, literally from his first day in office, was to find a local buyer for the Watt & Shand building. Pickard volunteered to be the point man for the city on the sale. Of course, this is the same Pickard who would become the first chairman and executive director of the convention center authority. From the *Lancaster New Era*, "City Seeks Role in Sale of Bon-Ton," January 7, 1998:

> Pickard said there are numerous ways the city might gain control of the building's future. They include outright purchase, purchase of an option to buy the building, or purchase of the "right of first refusal"—a means of allowing the city to step ahead of any other potential buyer....

[44] I brought a libel lawsuit against Lancaster Newspapers and several of its employees, including chairman Jack M. Buckwalter—*Molly Henderson vs Lancaster Newspapers, Inc., John M. Buckwalter, Ernest J. Schreiber, Marvin I. Adams, Jr., Helen Colwell Adams, Charles Raymond Shaw, Arthur E. Morris, Gilbert A. Smart, John H. Brubaker, III, and David Pidgeon*. No. 0712003.

[45] See *Lancaster New Era*, "3 Businesses Buy Watt/Shand Bldg. for $1.25 Million," February 17, 1998:

> Finally, the Watt & Shand Building has new owners.
> A partnership of three local businesses bought the elegant gray marble department store on Penn Square for $1.25 million today. The purchase of what many consider the crown jewel of downtown retail buildings came at mid-morning when Penn Square Partners—a joint venture of High Real Estate Group, Fulton Financial Corp. and Lancaster Newspapers Inc.—took ownership of the building from The Bon-Ton department store chain....

[46] See *Intelligencer Journal*, "Campaign Sees Bright Prospects Ahead for City," February 19, 1998.

[47] The "LDR Plan" mentions the "conference center" on page 47 of the report. An online version of the report may be found here: http://www.newslanc.com/document/ldr_plan.pdf.

[48] Ibid. The Watt & Shand reference and the cryptic prediction of a massive public-private project for the site are found on page 55 of the report. An online version of the report may be found here: http://www.newslanc.com/document/ldr_plan.pdf.

[49] The "Stadium Bill" of 1998 was the dominant issue of the Pennsylvania gubernatorial campaign. It served to activate the electoral base of the major parties in Philadelphia and Pittsburgh. Those cities got their stadiums; Lancaster got its convention center, and the taxpayers got the bill.

[50] Lancaster County representative John E. Barley (R-100th) (born December 6, 1945) was a Pennsylvania political heavyweight. His abrupt resignation under mysterious circumstances in 2002 lost the county a major powerbroker in Harrisburg. See Barley's archived House profile here: http://www.legis.state.pa.us/cfdocs/legis/BiosHistory/MemBio.cfm?ID=206&body=H.

[51] Lancaster County's other political heavyweight in Harrisburg was former senator Gibson E. Armstrong (born August 28, 1943–). See Armstrong's archived Senate "profile" here: http://www.legis.state.pa.us/cfdocs/legis/BiosHistory/MemBio.cfm?ID=2528&body=S.

[52] Senator Armstrong first changed Pennsylvania law in October 1999, when he amended the 1994 Third-Class County Convention Center Authority Act to allow Lancaster to build a publicly financed convention center. Armstrong again changed legislation to allow Act 23 to cover convention centers. He again amended Act 23 in 2005, which allowed the High-Steinman-owned private hotel to avoid paying property taxes. All of these amendments were specifically designed and written to help the downtown Lancaster project get more public taxpayer subsidies for the project. Each change is discussed in detail in the body of this book.

[53] See *Lancaster New Era*, "Lancaster Funds Linked to Pa. Stadiums," November 10, 1998. From the article:

> HARRISBURG—An effort to provide $300 million for new sports stadiums in Philadelphia and Pittsburgh could spur some spinoff help for farm preservation and a conference center in Lancaster, local lawmakers said today.
>
> As legislators returned to the Capitol for a post-election session, Gov. Tom Ridge and pro-stadium advocates were taking a careful look at how they might win the votes for some form of public aid for the stadium projects. One scenario, lawmakers said, would put up additional dollars for farmland preservation, a program important to rural Pennsylvania counties.
>
> Another, of high interest here, could put money into the budget for a downtown conference center.
>
> "Those kind of projects—you could negotiate," said state Rep. John E. Barley, a Conestoga Republican who chairs the House Appropriations Committee.

Also, from the *Lancaster New Era* article, Representative Jere W. Schuler, a Lampeter Republican and former high school baseball coach, said, "If they put that in with bonding for stadiums I still would have to take a negative position on it. When I look at these sports stadiums, I don't believe that they provide the employment that they say they provide."

Schuler, a member of the House Education Committee, said it is more important to help public schools. "I just don't think it's proper that we use taxpayer money to build a sports stadium," he said.

⁵⁴ LDR International ("Winterbottom") Report, page 56. Winterbottom was clearly privy to the plans of Penn Square Partners to use a "public-private" approach to building the hotel and convention center. From the report:

> As this report is being written, the ownership of the Watt and Shand Building is being transferred from the current out-of-town owners to a small group of local owners at a fair price. . . . Local public and private leadership must be prepared to support this project with their influence and their financial resources.

⁵⁵ Note how the project gradually got more expensive, even before official construction began. With the very first introduction of a room tax, in the *Lancaster New Era* on March 28, 1994, in "3% Hotel Tax Proposed to Fund Convention Centers," the rate was 3%. The rate went up to 5% by 1998. The cost went from Winterbottom's "$6–8 million" to more than $200 million . . . and it's still adding costs and debt as of this writing in 2018.

⁵⁶ The disingenuousness of the comments from Barley, Armstrong, and Pickard regarding the support of the "hospitality community" is clear. The Greater Lancaster Hotel and Motel Association (GLHMA) overwhelmingly, almost to a hotel, the Lancaster County "hospitality community" rejected and opposed a tax on their businesses to, in effect, subsidize a competitor. In August, 1999, The Greater Lancaster Hotel and Motel Association conducted a survey, in which 54 of 58 establishments opposed the room tax. The survey results were told to Christiaan Hart Nibbrig by GLHMA – member and then owner of the Continental Inn owner, Rodney Gleiberman. The GLHMA survey is referenced in the article, Long, Michael, "Hotel Tax is Project's Linchpin: County Commissioners Likely to Vote on Levy in Mid-September," Intelligencer Journal, August 20, 1999.

"The Greater Lancaster County Hotel and Motel Association approved a near-unanimous resolution opposing the convention center proposal, based on the information provided by project consultants Ernst & Young LLP." Much of the funds collected by the Lancaster County Convention Center Authority were used to construct "common space" between the convention center and the High and Steinman–owned private hotel. So, it is a fact that the tax dollars remitted by the Lancaster County hoteliers went to assist funding the construction of a competitor's private hotel. It is no wonder that all GLHMA members except a High-owned hotel objected to the hotel and motel room rental tax (three abstained).

⁵⁷ The Stadium Bill was frequently tied to Lancaster during the time it was being lobbied in Harrisburg. All of the Lancaster Newspapers covered the story regularly. It was in the November 24 edition of the *New Era* when Barley opaquely hinted that the project might not be built on Lancaster but on Penn Square. See Buckwalter, Tim, "Stadium Bill Goes Down to the Wire." *Lancaster New Era*, November 24, 1998.

Endnotes

[58] Both quotes from Senator Gib Armstrong and Representative Mike Sturla regarding their support for using Stadium Bill money for a Lancaster "conference center" came from the *Sunday News*, "Barley Plays Center Field," November 22, 1998. Quoted from the article was a long-term Lancaster Republican who opposed the bill. Representative Jere Schuler, R-43rd District, who said, "I don't think the taxpayers *Sunday News*, should be paying for a stadium when the owners pay their ballplayers so much money."

[59] See Wolf, Paula, "Between Philly and Pittsburgh," *Sunday News*, December 13, 1998.

[60] The percentage of ownership of the three Penn Square Partners was disclosed only in July 2006 during a court hearing, discussed in detail in Chapter Twelve of this book. It was reported in the three Lancaster Newspapers that High Associates, Lancaster Newspapers, and Fulton Bank were co-equal stakeholders. This wasn't the case. High and Lancaster Newspapers always had co-equal stakes, even after Fulton left the partnership in 2008. Fulton, represented by Rufus Fulton, was never comfortable with the investment. In his deposition as a witness in the libel action I filed against Lancaster Newspapers and several of its staff members—*Molly Henderson vs Lancaster Newspapers, Inc., John M. Buckwalter, Ernest J. Schreiber, Marvin L. Adams, Jr., Helen Colwell Adams, Charles Raymond Shaw, Arthur E. Morris, Gilbert A. Smart, John H. Brubaker, III, and David Pidgeon. No. 0712003*—Fulton described the bank's position vis-à-vis the project. From page 23 of Fulton's deposition: "This [was] a temporary investment for us. Banks should not be in the real estate business. They should lend to people who have real estate projects."

[61] The Steinmans, in addition to owning most of West King Street, also owned a parking garage and a printing plant on Vine Street and Queen Street. In all, they owned thirteen properties, almost an entire square city block, adjacent to the hotel and convention center project, according to the Lancaster County Assessor's Office. The downtown printing press has shut down, and with it, the Steinmans cut many printing jobs. The newspaper industry was almost entirely gone as of 2016.

[62] Lancaster Newspapers also owns the weeklies *Lancaster Farming*, the *Ephrata Review*, and the *Lititz Record Weekly*. In his deposition Buckwalter summed up Lancaster Newspapers' influence: "The point is, we're basically the main information source in Lancaster County."

[63] P. Michael "Mike" Sturla (1956–) has represented the 96th Pa. Assembly district since 1991. He was, and continues to be, the county's only Democrat in the Pennsylvania legislature. Sturla was a supporter of the hotel and convention center project.

[64] In researching the history of Lancaster County, we looked into the background of Pennsylvania's founder, William Penn, and his origins. Penn (1644–1718), the son of a wealthy British navy admiral (to whom the Crown owed a financial favor), was in his early twenties during the last Great Plague of London (1665–1666). The filth and rat problem of that great city contributed to the spread of the bubonic plague that killed 100,000 people in the city.

⁶⁵ Lancaster city mayor Charles W. "Charlie" Smithgall (R) was elected mayor in November 1997 and assumed office in January 1998. Smithgall served until January 2006, when he was succeeded by J. Richard Gray, a Democrat. Smithgall, a voluble pharmacist and gun enthusiast, and Gray, a Lancaster attorney, would both support the hotel and convention center project, the central issue of this book. That put them on the opposite side of the issue from me.

⁶⁶ My hiring by Mayor Smithgall and the city of Lancaster as director of the Environmental Health and Protection Unit was reported in "City Increases Inspections of Restaurants," *Lancaster New Era*, October 20, 1999. From the article:

> Smithgall, who had promised "radical changes" to the way inspections are done, said this morning that inspections will again be on a regular, twice-a-year schedule, with more frequent inspections when problems are found.
>
> The mayor emphasized that more frequent inspections does not mean more harsh inspections.
>
> He announced the hiring of Molly Henderson, 46, as manager of the reconstituted Environmental Health and Protection Unit.
>
> Henderson holds a doctorate in education policy and Smithgall said it was her experience as a Red Cross and Millersville University instructor that made her his choice for the post.
>
> "Molly is willing to approach this with a helping aspect, rather than a punitive aspect," Smithgall said.
>
> Smithgall had refused to release the inspection records for four months, claiming he didn't want to cause problems for restaurateurs.
>
> This morning, he emphasized education before enforcement.
>
> Henderson agreed.
>
> "This is their livelihood, their business," she said of the establishments. "We want to work with them . . . but not compromise the sanitation requirements. . . ."

⁶⁷ It is difficult to describe the unsanitary conditions of Country Boy Meats. My inspection of the market was in October 29, 1999. As director of the Environmental Health and Protection Unit, I felt it necessary to terminate the meat and milk license of Country Boy Meats for public safety. Harris, Bernard, *City Health Unit Pulls Store's Meat/Milk License*, Lancaster New Era, October, 29, 1999, p.A-1., http://www.proquest.com.

Things hadn't changed fifteen years later. From a December 2014 inspection of Country Boy Meats now located in New Danville, PA (still Lancaster County):

> Based on the violations noted in this inspection report, it is clearly evident that the person in charge is not performing the primary duty of ensuring compliance with the food code to protect public health. Repeat violation from previous year inspection. The person in charge is creating a potential rodent-harborage problem by not

disposing of adulterated meat in an acceptable manner of time. The person in charge is not disposing adulterated and meat unfit for consumption as evidenced by rotting meat in outer cooling unit. The person in charge is not monitoring temperatures of the coolers on the outer premise of the facility on a daily basis. The person in charge must ensure that all areas of the facility are accessible during inspection. Upon complaint inspection on 11/17/2014, all areas were not accessible due to the owner having possession of the keys and not being on premise. Observed visible evidence, such as maggots too numerous to count, inside and outside of cooling unit stored on the outer premise of building. The building is 50 feet from the entrance of the retail side of the store. Repeat violation from previous year.

[68] My comments were reported in "City Health Units Pulls Store's Meat/Milk License," *Lancaster New Era*, October 29, 1999.

[69] The coverage leading up to the Lancaster County commissioners' vote on the room tax in 1999 took up most of the year for Lancaster Newspapers. The coverage began January 18 in the *Lancaster New Era* with, "Task Force Hopes and Prepares For $15 Million Conference Center Grant." And the coverage, like a promotional campaign, continued during the entire year, even after the room tax was passed in September. The convention center coverage was not objective. It was written from the perspective of a private investor in the project trying to sell the public on the idea.

[70] The private investment of Penn Square Partners for the $60.3 million hotel was $10 million in 2005. The rest came from state grants and loans. From the County of Lancaster's complaint to the Department of Community and Economic Development:

Hotel Construction Funding Source	Amount
PSP private equity	$10,000,000
Interest earnings	$ 1,300,000
RACL Act 23 Bonds/state grants	$12,000,000
RACL Bond debt paid by PSP lease payments	$24,000,000
Other unidentified state grants	$12,950,000
Total hotel construction cost	$60,300,000

According to Lancaster Newspapers, Cooley talked about the financial investment of the partners after PSP sold the Watt & Shand building to the Redevelopment Authority of the City of Lancaster. Cooley published a lengthy *Sunday News* comment on May 22, 2005, "Statement by Penn Square Partners: Setting the Record Straight: Myths, Mistakes and Misrepresentations": The partners said they were walking away from the project. Cooley wrote,

> Since purchasing the Watt & Shand Building, we have spent $2.35 million—and counting—to secure, insure, maintain and even decorate the building for the holidays. We have spent $3 million

(and counting) for architecture/engineering plans, development and legal fees, keeping our promise to work with the public sector to develop the headquarters hotel. We have committed $35 million to the project: $10 million in cash, $1 million in interest income and lease payments to repay a $24 million bond that will be used to build the hotel shell, which we will convert into the Lancaster Marriott at Penn Square.

[71] The question of whether there was even demand for another downtown hotel was very much open. The Brunswick (134 rooms) on Lancaster Square had low occupancy rates. Another hotel, Lancaster Arts Hotel (68 rooms), opened in 2006, but it is not downtown and is much smaller than either the Brunswick or the Marriott on Penn Square. All of the research shows that most people visit Lancaster County for the shopping outlets, the Sight & Sound Millennium Theater, and the Amish countryside. They stay at the hotels outside the city. The majority don't come to downtown Lancaster. The best source for where tourism dollars are spent in Lancaster County is a study released by "Discover Lancaster" formerly known as the Pennsylvania Dutch and Convention Visitors Bureau. In their 2016 study, "Tourism Economics: The Economic Impact of Tourism in Lancaster County", shows that in 2015 Lancaster County visitors spent more than $400 million in retail sales. In 2010, that amount was $332.3 million. The 2016 study may be found here: http://www.discoverlancaster.com/Uploads/files/TE-DLEEconImpact 2015-2016-05-24.pdf

[72] The "Hotel Room Rental Tax" is defined in Section 23, Subsection (e) of the Third-Class County Convention Center Authority Act of 1994:

> Imposition of Tax—"The County in which the convention center is located is hereby authorized to impose an excise tax on the consideration received by each operator of a hotel within the market area of each transaction of renting a room or rooms to accommodate transients. The tax shall be collected by the operator from the patron of the room and paid over to the county. . . ."

[73] The two "hotel" taxes in Lancaster County were passed September 15, 1999. They were Ordinance 45 and 46. Ordinance 45 refers to the part of the 5% tax that goes to the LCCCA, and Ordinance 46 refers to the part of the tax that goes to the Pennsylvania Dutch Convention Visitors Bureau (PDCVB). As of July 2014 and through 2019, 100% of the hotel room tax goes to the LCCCA. None will go to the PDCVB. This is a result of a default of the LCCCA to "maintain certain minimum balances in the funds held in the Trustee Bank." See Lancaster County Convention Center Authority Financial Statements with Supplementary Information, Years Ended 31 December 2014 and 2013, with Independent Auditor's Report, by Maher-Deussel, Certified Public Accountants, p. 24, n. 13: http://www.lccca.com/wp-content/uploads/2012/04/LCCCA-2014-Audit.pdf. As of 2017, conditional funding from bond reserves over $5.75M, up to an amount equal to 20% of the previous year's hotel tax, has been restored.

Endnotes

[74] In addition to the August 1999 Greater Lancaster Hotel and Motel Association survey, in which 54 of 58 establishments opposed the room tax, GLHMA members attended several commissioners' meetings and spoke against the tax. The *Sunday News* on September 12, 1999, three days before the vote, ran, "Hotel Execs Not Ready to Check Out on Room Tax." The article begins,

> Their strategy is simple. Members of the Greater Lancaster Hotel and Motel Association plan to mount a last-ditch effort to delay a room tax from being levied by the Lancaster County Commissioners. A spokesman for the group said the hoteliers will ask the commissioners at their Tuesday work session to postpone a vote on a tax to fund and support a downtown conference/convention center. . . .

[75] Attorney Christopher C. Connor's letter to the commissioners was presented to them at the September 14, 1999, commissioners' work session. It was covered by the *Lancaster New Era* that afternoon in "Hotel Owners Threaten Lawsuit If County Pushes for Room Tax."

[76] Senator Brightbill's statement that the convention center act was to be limited to Berks and Luzerne counties was made into the legislative record during debate on the bill. It was quoted from "Unconventional Decisions: Challenging the Use of Hotel Taxes in Convention Center Projects," published in the *Journal of Constitutional Law*, Vol. 7:2 (November 2004): 533–559, by Dionne E. Anthon, MBA, and J.D. candidate at the University of Pennsylvania Law School. "Unconventional Decisions" is an analysis of the constitutionality of hotel room rental taxes and an analysis of the "circuit of economic activity" the tax was supposed to generate. See p. 553 of the study; https://www.law.upenn.edu/journals/conlaw/articles/volume7/issue2/Anthon7U.Pa.J.Const.L.533(2004).pdf.

[77] Smithgall made his "no-brainer" comment to the *Intelligencer Journal* on August 25, 1999, three weeks before the vote. The comment was made in the article "Smithgall Selects 3 to Serve on Authority." The county commissioners had yet to pass the room tax and create the convention center authority. But that didn't stop Smithgall (and Lancaster Newspapers) from treating it as a done deal, a fait accompli. There was little doubt the tax would pass.

[78] *Intelligencer Journal*, editorial, September 15, 1999.

[79] Thibault's quote came from the *Lancaster New Era*, September 15, 1999, "To Applause, Hotel Tax Passes." Paul Thibault was clearly the chosen Republican county commissioner of the Lancaster leading business establishment. Unendorsed by the county GOP, Thibault nonetheless raised the most money by far. Among his leading supporters were Dale High, Rufus Fulton, William Adams, and the bulk of the movers-and-shakers.

[80] Ibid. At the end of the article, after the self-congratulation from supporters of the room tax, Michael Gleiberman, owner of the Continental Inn, one of the hotel

establishments that would now be taxed for every room rented, said, "I'm disappointed that [the commissioners] did not take the time . . . to look at this issue further. I don't want to rain on a parade. I want downtown to thrive." But, he added, "I firmly do not believe that the whole project is viable."

Chapter Four: The Project Grows

[1] At the time of the Lancaster County Convention Center Authority's (LCCCA's) establishment, the county, led by Commissioner Paul Thibault, and the city, led by Mayor Charlie Smithgall, were both day-one, strong supporters of the hotel and convention center project. Both selected members to the board who reflected his support of the project and who would vote accordingly. This changed during my term on the county commissioners' board. Dick Shellenberger and I were able to use the county picks to choose people with hotel, convention center, and relevant business experience.

[2] Stevens & Lee was not doing all of this legal work for free. Although not an unusually large law firm, in terms of number of attorneys, Stevens & Lee has long been one of the most profitable law firms in the country, perennially ranking on the *American Lawyer* AmLaw top 200 in revenues-per-partner and profits-per-partner. With the Third-Class County Convention Center Authority Act of 1994, which was authored by the firm, Stevens & Lee essentially set itself up with a number of high-paying clients. In addition to representing the Lancaster County Convention Center Authority, the firm also represented the Berks County and Luzerne County Convention Center Authorities.

[3] At the time of Armstrong's Amendment, another facility was used for conventions, which also measured larger than 40,000 square feet—the 53,000-square-foot Alumni & Fitness on the Franklin & Marshall College campus. Franklin & Marshall is a private institution. The Franklin & Marshall administration did not object to the project, however.

[4] The "Armstrong Amendment" is found in Pennsylvania Statutes, Title 16; Section C (1):

> (c)(1) This subdivision shall not apply to a county which has an existing convention center owned by, leased by or operated by an existing authority or the Commonwealth which covers an area of more than forty thousand square feet.

See more at http//codes.findlaw.com/pa/title-16-ps-counties/pa-st-sect-2399-2.html#sthash.9W96PGCS.dpuf.

[5] Senator Armstrong's legislative maneuver, which produced the "Armstrong Amendment," wasn't reported until after the bill was passed by both houses. The Republican House delegation was clearly perturbed by the underhandedness of Armstrong's little trick. Reported the *Intelligencer Journal* on October 27, 1999, after the bill had passed:

> "I have no recollection of anyone talking to me about it," said Rep. Jere Schuler of Lampeter. "You put a 47-page amendment on my desk and ask me to vote for it in a minute, I can't do that." . . .

Peter Chiccarine, whose management company oversees a number of hotels, including the Eden Resort in Lancaster, said the bill was anticipated but still disappointing.

"What Sen. Armstrong and (Rep.) John Barley did was change the legislation to suit their needs so they could accomplish their goal to build a conference center in downtown Lancaster," he said.

Barley said the convention center project will be good for all of Lancaster County, and he didn't want it to be delayed by "frivolous lawsuits."

[6] See *Lancaster New Era*, November 5, 1999, "Ridge Signs Check—and Key Law." The article begins,

> Standing before nearly 500 cheering people on South Queen Street, Gov. Tom Ridge Thursday made a very public display of support for a proposed downtown convention center in Lancaster. But the oversized posterboard check for $15 million to fund half of the convention center's construction was only the governor's most visible act on behalf of Lancaster's downtown plan this week. On Wednesday, Ridge signed a law that would prevent a threatened legal challenge by opponents of plans for the proposed center and adjacent luxury hotel in the former Watt & Shand department store.

[7] The lawsuit filed by Lancaster County hotel and motel owners was *Bold Corp vs the City of Lancaster, County of Lancaster, and Lancaster County Convention Center Authority*. It was filed on March 24, 2000. The hoteliers' lawsuit was reported in the *Intelligencer Journal*, March 25, 2000: "County Sued Over Hotel Room Taxes." The article begins,

> Firing a legal salvo to block construction of a $30 million downtown Lancaster convention center, 37 Lancaster County hotel and motel operators Friday sued the city and county for taxing hotel rooms countywide to help operate a convention center. . . .

[8] Judge Louis J. Farina (b. 1943–) was first elected to the Lancaster County bench in 1995 and began serving in 1996. He retired in 2016.

[9] The "benefit-burden" question was at the heart of the hoteliers' lawsuit. They were being required to pay a tax that would be partially used to build a convention center and a hotel—a direct competitor. That was the "burden." The "benefit" was much less clear. As a convention location, the city of Lancaster has significant limitations. There is no airport that serves major airlines, so a conventioneer can't fly directly into Lancaster. Traffic congestion is a chronic problem in downtown Lancaster, a major liability for those who would have to drive to Lancaster, where the center was to be located. There are no golf courses close by, which are often cited by conventioneers as desirable in a convention location. And the weather in Lancaster is often inclement, making it an undesirable as a winter convention location. The notion that a Lancaster convention center would suddenly,

upon opening its doors, attract enough convention business to fill up a 300-room hotel and provide meaningful spillover business for the other hotel owners was preposterous on its face. The best study on the impact of publicly financed convention centers was done by Dr. Heywood Sanders in *Space Available: The Reality of Convention Centers as Economic Development Strategy*, published in January 2005 by the Brookings Institute. See http://www.brookings.edu/research/reports/2005/01/01cities-sanders.

[10] The reality show *Hoarders* was first aired in 2009 on the A&E cable television channel. In was then aired under the name *Hoarders: Family Secret* in 2016. Each episode documents a family's struggle with "compulsive hoarding disorder."

[11] The case involving the elderly siblings shows the interplay between my job as the city of Lancaster's director of the Environmental Health and Protection Unit and work with county organizations. I felt that this experience working with county agencies would help me as a Lancaster County commissioner, and it proved to be the case. For more information on the Lancaster County Office of Aging, please see its website at http://www.lancoaging.org/.

[12] The tagline for the great City of Lancaster trash cleanup—"It's city cleanup day, and that's no April fool"—was reported in, "Can't Bag It? City Will Haul It April 1," *Lancaster New Era*, March 22, 2000.

[13] My trash proposal was discussed in some detail in "Trash Plan Questions and Answers," *Lancaster New Era*, June 30, 2000.

[14] Mayor's Smithgall's comment, "We can't be ready. We can't implement it," may be found in "City Delay's Trash Plan Start until Jan. 2002," *Lancaster New Era*, December 23, 2000.

[15] The *Sunday News* editorial "City Restaurants: Well Done" appeared on October 29, 2000.

[16] The eleven plaintiffs in *Bold vs County, City of Lancaster and LCCCA* were the Host Resort and Conference Center; the Eden Resort Inn and Conference Center; the Ramada Inn, on Route 30; Continental Inn; Historic Strasburg Inn; Hershey Farm Restaurant & Motor Inn; Your Place Country Inn; Quality Inn & Suites; Best Western Revere; Italian Villa Motel; and ARA Motel.

[17] In his opinion against the hoteliers, Judge Farina sounded positive about the project. On page 14, paragraph 65, Judge Farina wrote of the coming convention center: "The contemplated convention center will be a facility unlike any currently in Lancaster County, and it will be able to attract conventions and meetings that would not currently come to the Lancaster County market." Judge Farina's decision in *Bold vs County of Lancaster, City of Lancaster, and Lancaster County Convention Center Authority* may be found here: http://prothonotary.co.lancaster.pa.us/civilcourt.public/(S(a4hy1azjyga5otu4csb34kv3))/Handlers/DocumentHandler.ashx?vid=1030286.

[18] Appellate statement of Plaintiff Lancaster County hoteliers to Commonwealth Court of Pennsylvania, *Bold Corp vs the City of Lancaster, County of Lancaster, and Lancaster County Convention Center Authority*.

[19] Commonwealth Court opinion remanding case back to Lancaster County Court, January 23, 2002: http://law.justia.com/cases/pennsylvania/commonwealth-court/2002/1227cd01.html.

[20] Pennsylvania State Supreme Court opinion by Judge Stephen Zappella for *Bold Corp vs County of Lancaster, City of Lancaster, and Lancaster County Convention Center Authority*, July 16, 2002, upholding Judge Farina's original ruling against the hoteliers: https://casetext.com/case/bold-corp-v-lancaster.

[21] Pickard wasn't exactly the picture of magnanimity with his "they are the clear losers" comments. They were made in the October 4, 2002, *Lancaster New Era*, "Convention Center Wins in Court: Officials Planning Hotel and Convention Center Call Unanimous Ruling a Total Victory That Should Pave Way for Construction of the Project."

[22] The issue of "common space" between the hotel and the convention center was a major legal issue for the hoteliers. The two entities would be physically joined, and there were lobbies, bathrooms, staircases, and a large, restaurant-equipped kitchen that would be jointly used by both the "private" hotel and the "public convention center. In this very direct sense, the hoteliers were absolutely directly subsidizing the "private" hotel, their competition. They were taxing their customers 5% and handing 80% of that money over to the convention center authority. The authority was using those funds to build a kitchen for the hotel, lobbies, stairways, and so on. There is something fundamentally unfair about that. Randolph J. Carney, a member of the School District of Lancaster as of this writing in 2018, compiled several contracts between the LCCCA and Penn Square Partners. The "Declaration of Condominium" agreements spell out the "common space" division between the two entities. See pressedthebook.com under "Convention Center Documents."

[23] The Rodney Gleiberman quote was obtained by Christiaan A. Hart Nibbrig, who interviewed Gleiberman in connection with a series Mr. Hart Nibbrig wrote on the hotel and convention center project for Newslanc.com. The series can be found on the homepage of Newslanc.com.

[24] The convention center was hyped like a coming attraction in 1999, especially in the weeks leading up to the September 15 vote. It was the event of the year! As they would later do with the Conestoga View story, the three Lancaster Newspapers were used to help their business concern—this time to promote it. The "Everything the City Needs" *Lancaster New Era* article of August 26, 1999, began:

> In a display that united old foes and bridged city-county and Republican-Democrat differences, county leaders have embraced plans for a $75 million downtown hotel and convention center with almost religious zeal.
> The first public presentation of the project brought nearly 300 people to the standing-room-only meeting in the city's Southern Market Center Wednesday night. The crowd—a Who's Who of county political, business and civic leaders—seemed to seize on the plan which pledges salvation for downtown.

> "I think this is exactly the right thing for the community. This is superb. This is everything the city needs," said former city Mayor Richard Scott, a Republican who two years ago opposed plans to locate Harrisburg Area Community College at the same site. "My sense is that this is a once-in-a-lifetime opportunity," agreed P. Michael Sturla, the city's House representative, a Democrat.

[25] See "Authority Sends Letter Threatening to Sue Hoteliers," *Sunday News*, December 22, 2002.

[26] Ibid.

[27] Mayor's Smithgall's comments, calling local hoteliers "economic terrorists," were referenced in the *Intelligencer Journal*, February 28, 2002, in an article about the mayor's wife threatening a critic of her husband's. From the article:

> Manheim resident Bernie Schriver, known in GOP circles as a political gadfly, filed a complaint last week accusing Debbie Smithgall of telling her husband, "I'll take that gun out of your pocket and blow that son of a bitch away."
> The incident allegedly occurred when Schriver handed Mrs. Smithgall literature calling the mayor a "cannon-mouth" for referring to local hoteliers as "economic terrorists" after they refused to drop a lawsuit against the city, the county and the Lancaster County Convention Center Authority.

Note how close Smithgall's comments were to the 9/11/01 disaster, still fresh in the minds of Americans. Smithgall likened Lancaster County businessmen and women—the hoteliers—to the "terrorists" who knocked down the World Trade Center and attacked the Pentagon. The rhetoric was out of control.

[28] See *Intelligencer Journal*, March 27, 2002, "City Council Wants Lawsuit by Hoteliers Quickly Quashed." The article begins:

> Lancaster City Council officially joined with Penn Square Partners on Tuesday in urging the Pennsylvania Supreme Court to move quickly on the case of the proposed downtown convention center. The resolution, written by councilman John Graupera, asks the Supreme Court to "expedite this case and make a decision, soon, to enable our revitalization."
> It further states that council believes "the actions of the hoteliers are not defensible and we urge them to act constructively for broader community objectives. . . ."

[29] The LCCCA real estate acquisitions were first reported in the *Lancaster New Era*, March 21, 2000, in "Convention Center Panel Purchases 4 Buildings." The home and business of Thaddeus Stevens didn't seem to matter much to the LCCCA's Pickard. From the article:

> Among the buildings being purchased by the authority is the former home of Thaddeus Stevens, Lancaster's leading statesman during the Civil War period. Stevens lived at 47 S. Queen St. from 1843 until his death in 1868.
>
> Pickard said the buildings likely will be razed, but their facades probably will be saved. The facades were deeded to the Historic Preservation Trust of Lancaster County in the 1980s, ensuring their preservation.
>
> He does not yet know what—if anything—will be built on the site. The authority simply wants to have control of the property.

[30] Pickard's statement regarding the LCCCA's "Public Comment" policy was published in the *Intelligencer Journal*, "Authority Says It Will Answer Some Questions," in the May 24, 2000, edition. The headline is misleading; Pickard does not agree to answer questions.

[31] Dale High's construction company, High Construction, received the $52,000 a month from the LCCCA for the first few years until the project went out for construction bids in 2006. Then High resigned as construction manager and bid for the $37 million "General Trades" contract, which it won in 2006 as the sole bidder. High profited in other ways. Another High company received a no-bid, lucrative Food & Beverage concession contract. And, of course, High and Steinman, as the two owners of Penn Square Partners, will have the option of buying the Watt & Shand building at a fixed, and far under market rate of $2.5 million in 2026. The hotel financing is discussed in detail in Chapter Six of this book: "It's All about the Hotel—Really."

[32] The Requests for Proposals for managing the convention center were reported on January 24, 2001, in the *Lancaster New Era* in "Convention Center Authority Will Quiz Possible Operators." The article begins:

> "Tell us what you can do." That is what the Lancaster County Convention Center Authority is asking potential operators of the yet-to-be-built downtown convention center in a letter to be mailed out next week. The center is not expected to become a reality for at least another year. A 10-page request for operating proposals will be mailed to 15 to 20 companies. . . .

[33] Which firm represented the convention center was important to the county's hoteliers, as that firm would be booking the conventions for the facility. The hoteliers were concerned that the events that were booked would use their hotels when they came to Lancaster. Penn Square Partners wanted to select a manager for both the hotel and the convention center, which would put the manager in a position of choosing conventions that benefited the county's hoteliers or the High/Steinman-owned downtown Marriott Hotel. Having a single manager placed the manager in a clear conflict of interest: Does he serve the county hoteliers or the private High and Steinman hotel? High and Steinman, as always, got their wish, and a single manager was selected.

[34] Spectacor was clearly the premium manager of convention centers in Pennsylvania. As noted in the *Intelligencer Journal* on May 10, 2001, in "Authority Narrows Convention Center Companies to Three," Spectacor was impeccably credentialed for the job. From the article:

> Spectacor Management Group operated 21 convention centers, 18 arenas, six stadiums and 10 auditoriums in 1994, including Three Rivers Stadium, Philadelphia Civic Center, Pittsburgh Civic Arena and the CoreStates Complex in Philadelphia.. . . .

[35] Penn Square Partners' announcement that they had selected Interstate Hotels to manage their Marriott Hotel was first made on July 25, 2001, in the *Lancaster New Era*, "Same Boss for Marriott and Center?" From the article:

> On Tuesday, Penn Square Partners announced that Pittsburgh-based Interstate Hotels would manage the Penn Square hotel. The downtown hotel will have a Marriott name under a franchise agreement.
> This morning, Cooley strongly urged the Convention Center board to choose Interstate to operate the center. . . .

[36] The "Tourism Advisory Task Force," appointed by the LCCCA in the spring of 2000, underscored who really ran the project. When the Task Force, originally charged with "solicit[ing] guidance from members of the tourist industry in determining the size, design and market of a downtown convention center," came back with a Spectacor, not an Interstate, recommendation, Pickard and the majority of the board still voted for Interstate at the insistence of Penn Square Partners, who threatened to walk away from the project if Interstate wasn't chosen. It was.

[37] The Tourism Task Force asked three recognized experts on convention centers to consult with them on the manager search. They were Harvey Owen, a retired trade show and convention producer with thirty years of industry experience; Myles McGrane, vice president of operations for the Jacob K. Javits Convention Center in New York City; and Robert Butera, president and CEO of Philadelphia's Pennsylvania Convention Center. See *Intelligencer Journal*, "Consultants Back Separate Managers," August 23, 2001. All three consultants recommended Spectacor.

> Along with the consultants, the Task Force included Blaise Holzbauer, president of hospitality for Willow Valley Resort, which opposed common management; Glenn Redcay, owner of Black Horse Lodge and Suites and Black Horse Restaurant and Tavern, Denver; Lisa Campbell, marketing director for Rockvale Square outlets; chairman and authority member E. Bradley Clark (a vice president of Earl Realty, the parent company of Dutch Wonderland); Al Duncan, chief executive officer of Thomas E. Strauss Inc., parent company of Miller's Smorgasbord and Plain & Fancy Farm Restaurant; Deidre Simmons, Fulton

Endnotes

Opera House director of theater advancement; Jack Howell, Lancaster Alliance president; Brad W. Brubaker, visitors bureau president; and Monica Thomas, the visitors bureau's group tour and travel director. Simmons and Howell were the only votes against SMG. The Lancaster Alliance is the group co-founded by Dale High, Rufus Fulton, and Jack Buckwalter and nine other leading businessmen.

[38] The August 19, 2001, *Sunday News* article "Downtown Hotel Teeters on Brink // Partners in Watt & Shand Building Will Pull Out If Convention Center Authority Takes Advice of Tourism Task Force for Separate Management and Facilities"—was a 2,000-plus-word story on the front page of the Sunday paper. This page is the most-read part of any newspaper.

[39] On the same day as the above story, August 19, 2001, Penn Square Partners president Nevin D. Cooley wrote his 1,000-plus-word "letter" regarding the common manager question. These two items, taking up almost 3,500 words, made up a large part of the *Sunday News* that Sunday. It was another example of Lancaster Newspapers, a private partner in the project, using its presses to further its business interests, rather than using them to inform the public. A normal member of the general public had a 250-word limit for letters.

[40] Smithgall's comments regarding his support for Interstate can be found in the *Sunday News*, August 19, 2001, "Downtown Hotel Teeters on the Brink: Partners in Watt & Shand Building Will Pull Out If Convention Center Authority Takes Advice of Tourism Task Force for Separate Management and Facilities."

[41] Knight-Ridder had been covering the common manager debate. In addition to the September 11, 2001, article, the news service ran items on September 6, 2001, "Compromise on Lancaster, Pa., Convention Center Management Falls Short," and on September 12, 2001, after the board hired Interstate, "Lancaster, Pa., Convention Authority Hires Hotel Operator." Knight-Ridder also picked up the hoteliers' lawsuits.

[42] Dale High's comments comparing the convention center project to the World Trade Center coming down the previous day may be found here: https://www.youtube.com/watch?v=905G-by2WpU.

> Ron Harper, Jr., as he did on a number of important occasions during the development of the hotel and convention center project, was there to video and audio record the meeting. High makes the comparison in the last 45 seconds of the clip.

[43] The LCCCA vote to hire Interstate Hotels to manage both the convention center and the hotel was announced publicly in the *Lancaster New Era* on the same day, September 12, 2001, "Single Operator for Hotel, Center."

[44] The *Sunday News* reported that the city restaurant inspections would be made public in "The Public Wins: Publicizing Restaurant Inspections in the City and County Makes Sense," March 11, 2001.

[45] See "Ron Ford Will Retire Next Year, Demo Commissioner Has Been Community Leader for Three Decades," *Lancaster New Era*, April 13, 2002. It was Ford's minority seat on the Lancaster County Board of Commissioners that I would take in 2003.

[46] The "friendship quilt" theme was not only something I like personally, but it also proved to be good public relations for the campaign. It was unusual, and the newspapers picked up on it. The *Sunday News*, which, as noted, was very positive in its coverage of me until I opposed the hotel and convention center project, ran a major feature on my campaign and its friendship quilt theme. See *Sunday News*, January 12, 2003, "Democrat Uses Quilts as Symbol." From the article:

> Molly Henderson's campaign team was having trouble deciding on a logo. Conestoga wagons? Nope. Red roses? Nah. Stars? Flags? No and no.
> Quilts?
> Well, if you fly over Lancaster County, Henderson pointed out, you see a patchwork of farms and houses. Quilts are a collection of different colors and pieces, symbolizing the county's diversity. They take a lot of time and energy to assemble, just as countians are hard-working.
> "And quilts are for warmth," Henderson said. "They're for safety, for a feeling of home.
> "I don't want this to sound maudlin, but it's true."
> All of which explains why in Henderson's run for county commissioner, quilts are prominent on signs and fliers.

[47] Helen M. Moyer (1918–2011) was a dear friend to me and to Lancaster County. My daughter, Helen Leslie Henderson, is named after her. Helen Moyer was one of the most treasured and influential people in my life, and I miss her very much.

[48] The leadership and the rank-and-file of the Lancaster County Democratic Party were fully behind my candidacy. With Ford and Sturla publicly backing my campaign, I had the support of the top elected Democrats. Both Ford and Sturla were strong supporters of the hotel and convention center project.

[49] Barbara J. Hopkins Humphrey (1951–2014) was one of my very closest friends and absolutely a key player on my campaign team. Barb passed in September 2014, after a short courageous battle with cancer;

http://lancasteronline.com/obituaries/barbara-j-hopkins-humphrey/article_9674068b-852b-5366-919d-6137671f65d2.html.

[50] An article in the *Sunday News* reached virtually all of the Lancaster Newspapers' readership, combining the *Intelligencer Journal*'s and the *Lancaster New Era*'s audiences. This article, a prominently placed 800-word piece that ended with a quote from me, "It's a labor of love," demonstrates that Lancaster Newspapers viewed me favorably prior to my taking a position against their hotel and convention center project.

Endnotes

[51] The Lancaster County Republicans endorsed only Shellenberger in February 2003. From the *Intelligencer Journal*, February 21, 2003:

> Incumbent Lancaster County Commissioner Pete Shaub failed to capture the GOP endorsement early this morning after nine ballots and a week of intense political pressure.
>
> The balloting ended about 1:30 a.m. On the ninth ballot, Shaub captured 186 votes, and county controller Dennis Stuckey received 141. There were 327 votes cast, meaning 218 were needed for endorsement. The 359 members present at the Lancaster County Republican Committee's endorsement convention were unable to endorse two candidates in the hotly contested race for county commissioner but did endorse one: Manheim resident Richard Shellenberger, 57, owner of The Eatery at Granite Run.
>
> Shellenberger captured 292 votes, surpassing the 240 votes needed to win the endorsement. . . .

[52] Chapter Five of this book, "Hurricane Shaub—Category 5," is dedicated to former Lancaster county commissioner Howard "Pete" Shaub, Jr., who was backed by the entire Lancaster County Republican Party in 1999. Shaub began generating unfavorable headlines almost as soon as he got inaugurated. Fewer than two weeks after taking office, Shaub was in the middle of a controversy after he told a group of Christian activists that he was in office "to further God's Kingdom." See *Sunday News*, "New Commissioner Vows to Save Farms, Fight Drugs and 'Further God's Kingdom.'//Shaub's Action Plan," January 16, 2000. On April 29, 2000, the *Intelligencer Journal* ran an article about Shaub and a fundraising controversy, "Shaub Reception Invites Irks [sic] Some, Commissioner Offers a Letter of Apology." The controversies continued during his first year in office. Shaub was at the center of a voter fraud scandal in October. See "Democrats Charge GOP with Illegal Sign-Up of Voters Here," on October 2, 2000. The next month the *New Era* ran, "Thibault, Shaub Spar Over Budget." These headlines followed Shaub during his entire first term until his resignation in his second term.

[53] Richard "Dick" Shellenberger plays a major and complicated role in this story. As described in Chapter Six of this book, Shellenberger joined me on the commissioners' board in opposing and trying to block the hotel and convention center. We were a political odd couple (think John McCain and Gloria Steinem), but we agreed that the hotel project was too risky, too expensive, and not helpful to Lancaster County taxpayers and citizens. As of 2016, Dick Shellenberger was a committee person in Manheim Central, Penn Township Lancaster County. Dick passed away from cancer in January 2019.

[54] The quote, "The community accepted this project years ago. Dozens of revitalization projects—public and private—are based upon its completion," was made in a variety of places and on the record. In this instance, I was quoted in the *Lancaster New Era*, May 1, 2003, "Candidates Weigh in on Convention Center, Hotel Tax," at a forum.

55 The issue of the convention center consultants' exorbitant fees was a major reason I began to oppose the project after I assumed office. I reviewed the "Pay the Bills" documents from the Lancaster County Convention Center Authority and was astounded at the money that was going to these consultants every month. For example, a firm called "Bulls Advisory Group" billed about $40,000 per month, about half a million dollars a year, for "executive consulting services." Another firm, "Growth Business Development," invoiced about $20,000 per month. Ron Harper, Jr., and Chris Hart Nibbrig investigated and could find only one poorly researched report by Dan Logan, the only employee of Growth Business Development. Lawyers were billing in the tens of thousands of dollars every month, including Stevens & Lee (more than $100,000 in several months); Fenningham, Stevens, & Dempster billed more than $50,000 for many months. Finally, there were several months when one of Dale High's companies—High Associates; High Construction; High Concrete, and so on—would combine to bill more than $100,000 in a month. These high fees were paid for many years prior to the project being built.

56 The LCCCA county bond guaranty was my principal objection to the convention center project. The LCCCA was asking the county to guarantee half of the $40 million bond issue. The bond actually exposed Lancaster County taxpayers to $60 million in debt liability over the life of the bond. Lancaster County taxpayers were exposed to more than $60 million in liability because, according to the "Guaranty Agreement" signed by the Board of Commissioners in December 2003, weeks before I took office, the agreement provided that during the 40-year lifetime of the bond, the county would guarantee up to $1,506,960 per year. Multiplying that amount by 40 years is $60,278,400.

57 The financial architecture of the hotel and convention center project was extremely complex and difficult to understand. Whether by design or necessity, the Stevens & Lee–authored law (the 1994 Third-Class County Convention Center Authority Act) created an intricate project that required great financial and legal expertise to understand. In his September 4, 2009, deposition in the libel suit I filed against him and several Lancaster Newspapers employees—*Molly Henderson vs Lancaster Newspapers, Inc., John M. Buckwalter, Ernest J. Schreiber, Marvin L. Adams, Jr., Helen Colwell Adams, Charles Raymond Shaw, Arthur E. Morris, Gilbert A. Smart, John H. Brubaker, III, and David Pidgeon.* No. 0712003—chairman Jack Buckwalter said of the project: "This is one of the most complicated financial situations I have ever seen. And others have said that." Buckwalter held an MBA from the Harvard Business School, so if it was "one of the most complicated financial situations [he'd] ever seen," then it was way over the heads of most "regular" Lancaster citizens not trained in the law or finance.

58 At the time of the LCCCA $40 million bond issue, Lancaster County had a AAA rating by Moody's. Today, in part due to the debt service problems with the convention center bond, Lancaster County has been downgraded to an A1 rating. According to Moody's, "The A1 rating captures a satisfactory financial position, a moderately-sized tax base, weak socioeconomic indicators and an elevated debt burden."

[59] The primary elections are the most important elections in counties such as Lancaster. They determine who goes on the November ballot. A 21% voter turnout on a picture-perfect May spring day is sad, to say the least. Source: Lancaster County Voter Registration and Board of Elections.

[60] May 20, 2003, primary election results may be found at the Lancaster County Office of Voter Registration and Board of Elections, 150 N Queen St #117, Lancaster, PA 17603 (717) 299-8293. See http://www.co.lancaster.pa.us/elections.

[61] Jim Clymer became an unofficial candidate for Lancaster County commissioner about a week after the primary election, in which Shaub, Shellenberger, Saylor, and I received enough votes to appear on the November ballot. With Clymer, it would essentially be a three-person race for the minority seat. See "Clymer Weighing Run for Top County Post," *Intelligencer Journal*, May 28, 2003. From the article:

> Jim Clymer, a former Republican and current Constitution Party national chairman, said he is considering a run for county commissioner in the fall election and will seek the endorsement of the ultra-conservative political action committee Lancaster County ACTION. Constitution Party National Chairman Jim Clymer says he's testing the waters for a run at Lancaster County commissioner. Clymer, of Millersville, a former Republican, picked up his nominating papers from the Lancaster County office of Voter Registration and Board of Elections. . . .

> Also see "Constitution Party Leader Weighs Campaign For County Commissioner," *Lancaster New Era*, May 28, 2003.

[62] Clymer officially qualified to run for Lancaster County commissioner when he submitted the required number of registered voters who signed his petition. The news broke on July 31, 2003, in the *Intelligencer Journal*, "Clymer Gets the Signatures/ Joins Race to Become County Commissioner."

[63] Clymer was a leading figure in the Constitution Party and influential on the Christian right (he was past president of the Religious Roundtable of Pennsylvania). Political background on Clymer as a candidate for state office was derived the Harrisburg Patriot-News, "About James N. Clymer," October 26, 1998.

[64] The comments by Clymer were made at a candidates' debate at Franklin & Marshall College a little over a week before the election. See "Commissioner Hopefuls Debate at F&M," *Intelligencer Journal*, October 23, 2003. My position remained the same regarding the project at the debate: "I am very much in favor of the convention center," I said in my closing statement. "But I do not support the county backing of the bond. The convention center must be self-supporting."

[65] Ron Harper, Jr., kept files on dozens of Lancaster's movers-and-shakers. It was Harper who in late 2003 and early 2004 investigated the superintendent of schools, Ricardo Curry, for handing out high-paying jobs to friends and family members,

including a $1,500-a-day job to an ex-con relative. Curry was eventually charged by the FBI, pled guilty, and went to prison on "honest services fraud" charges.

[66] In an interview with Chris Hart Nibbrig for an article about Harper for the NewsLanc.com website, Clymer said of Harper, "Ron wasn't an official part of my campaign staff, but he was very helpful to it."

[67] For more information on the annual "Millersville Community Parade," please see its website: http://www.parade.millersville.edu/about.html.

[68] The quotes from the commissioner candidates, including my oft-repeated position opposing the county bond guaranty, were from the Franklin & Marshall College debate, "Commissioner Hopefuls Debate at F&M," *Intelligencer Journal*, October 23, 2003.

[69] Charlie Smithgall was always good for an interesting quote. The mayor made his "Happy Meal" comments after the "Midnight" vote on the bond on October 29, 2003, just days before the election. See *Lancaster New Era*, "County Backs Center/ Commissioners Give Planned Downtown Convention Center a Major Boost by Agreeing to Guarantee a $40-Million Bond Issue for the $55-Million Project."

[70] Shaub made it very clear to Republican Party members that he supported the convention center bond, but because of the politics of the commissioners' race and Clymer's serious candidacy, he would vote against the bond, although he was for it. It was classic Pete Shaub.

Chapter Five: Hurricane Shaub- Category 5

[1] My term as Lancaster County commissioner officially began on January 2, 2004. See "New Commissioners Push Team Approach/ County's Top Officials/DA/Row Officers Take Oaths in Formal Ceremony," *Lancaster New Era*, January 2, 2004.

[2] The 2004 Lancaster County budget was $246,681,103. The 2015 Lancaster County budget was $277,767,299. Information regarding the county budget was sourced at the Lancaster County Budget and Financial Information page. See http://www.co.lancaster.pa.us/591/Budget-Financial-Information.

[3] According to the Lancaster County Office of Human Resources, there are "approximately 1,600 full-time employees and 300 part-time employees within the County of Lancaster Government." See http://web.co.lancaster.pa.us/144/Human-Resources.

[4] The meeting with outgoing commissioners Thibault and Ford at the Bird's Nest, while focused on the problem of Pete Shaub, was otherwise pleasant and civil. My opposition to the convention center bond was never personalized. During the campaign, I did not criticize Thibault or Ford for their support of the bond they'd passed. I stated my position and moved on to other issues.

[5] Whether Shaub's views were authentic or intended to capture a constituency, I do not know. But his stated views on social issues came from the far fundamentalist

right. I was concerned from day one in office that Shaub and Shellenberger would cross "church-state" lines and introduce "faith-based" programs into county public policy. Shaub worked on faith-based programs since early in his first term. While he was a candidate, those views were featured in the *Sunday News*, "Common Mission," October 17, 1999. From the article:

> Pete Shaub compares the work of faith-based organizations to the spokes of a wagon wheel. The problem, the county commissioner candidate said, is that the spokes aren't connected. If he's elected on Nov. 2, Shaub, a Republican, wants to change that. He believes county government can complete the circle, drawing faith-based organizations into the social-service system and sharing a vision....

[6] The Shaubs' business was called "Shaub Family Auctioneers." It is now called "Shaub Real Estate Services Group." The auction business was acquired and renamed by Shaub's sister, Jessica Shaub Meyers. The company still provides auction services. See *Sunday News*, April 25, 1999, "Experience as Auctioneer Helps Shaub Sell Himself."

[7] The biographical information about Shaub was aggregated from several profiles of Shaub as he ran for commissioner in 1999, his first term, including the *Sunday News*, March 14, 1999, "Semper Fi to Ideas, Issues/ Pete Shaub Shuns Political Battles in His Campaign for Commissioner." At this point, prior to taking office, Shaub enjoyed the support of the Lancaster political establishment, which included Lancaster Newspapers. See *Lancaster New Era*, January 21, 1999, "After Cheering Thibault, Smithgall Also Backs Shaub as Friend of City," and *Intelligencer Journal*, February 24, 1999, "GOP Backs Swarr, Shaub, Can't Decide on DA Choice, Thibault Says He'll Still Run," and *Lancaster New Era*, April 16, 1999, "Shaub Endorsed by Reps. True and Armstrong, Raises $5,000."

[8] Wohlsen Construction Company was founded in 1877 by Herman F. Wohlsen, a German immigrant. For more on Wohlsen, please see the company's website: http://www.wohlsenconstruction.com/.

[9] *Sunday News*, March 14, 1999, "Semper Fi to Ideas, Issues/ Pete Shaub Shuns Political Battles in His Campaign for Commissioner."

[10] The message from Shaub's announcement was that Shaub had the support of the top Republican establishment. This was in stark contrast to incumbent and fellow Republican Thibault, who was persona non grata within the party and was not endorsed by it. See *Lancaster New Era*, November 19, 1999, "Shaub Joins Commissioner Race, Attracts GOP Backing."

[11] Ibid. *Lancaster New Era*, November 19, 1999, "Shaub Joins Commissioner Race, Attracts GOP Backing."

[12] ACTION—Americans for Christian Traditions in Our Nation—was much more influential in Lancaster County in this time period than it is today. In 1999, ACTION members were about one in four in the Republican Committee. The Christian Coalition and Pat Robertson were also strong at this time. In Lancaster County, the group was

resolutely anti-taxes. Thibault broke that cardinal covenant with them. See *Lancaster New Era*, "Thibault vs. the Religious Right: What the Split Means to Voters," February 18, 1999.

[13] Bob Kettering's comments can be found in a *Sunday News* article, "Judge Keeps Ten Commandments/ Defiant Jurist Who Kept Replica on Alabama Courtroom Wall Tells Conservative Christians U.S. Must Remain 'Under God,'" February 7, 1999. This article described an Alabama judge brought to Lancaster County by ACTION to speak to its members. Also see *Sunday News*, January 31, 1999, "Interviews Can Be Upsetting—and Produce Upsets." This article describes the Republican Committee, including ACTION members, interviewing GOP candidates.

Other comments made by ACTION president Bob Kettering regarding Paul Thibault and Kettering's group may be found in the *Lancaster New Era*, "Thibault Vs. the Religious Right: What the Split Means to Voters," February 18, 1999. From the article:

> "Thibault's great mistake," says ACTION president Kettering, was to promise no new taxes, then vote for a 28-percent real-estate tax increase.
>
> "There was a promise made that was totally abandoned, and that's the issue," Kettering said. "People are fed up with taxes."
>
> While the letter questioning Thibault's record has drawn criticism for its negative tone, Kettering makes no apology for it.
>
> "There were questions that were not being addressed," he said. "I'm not sorry we put the issues on the table."

[14] Shaub and Swarr collected enough votes from the area Republican committees (Penn Manor, Ephrata, Lancaster city, Columbia, Elizabethtown, Warwick, et al.) and secured the endorsement of the party. Endorsement, as in this case, doesn't secure victory in the primary. It does, however, give a candidate resources of the party—signs, stickers, mailings, volunteers—for which other candidates must pay out of pocket. Endorsement also provides greater name recognition, often the key determinant in who gets the vote. For a look into the Republican endorsement process in the 1999 GOP Lancaster County races, see "Grassroots Power Grows with Endorsement Process," *Sunday News*, February 14, 1999. From the article:

> "It makes me proud as an American citizen to be able to participate in this," says Dan Gotshall, a Republican committeeman in the Hempfield area's Farmdale District. "I just feel really, really honored to do it for my community," says East Petersburg South District committeewoman Bonnie Stebbins. Hempfield chairman Dave Dumeyer knows of one committeeman who interviewed every judge candidate at his house for an hour each. Call it the democratization of the Republican Party.

[15] Considering the pariah Shaub became after he assumed office, these early articles about him are really striking for their complimentary tone. This one in the *Sunday News*, written by Helen Colwell Adams and published March 14, 1999, "Semper Fi to Ideas, Issues/ Pete Shaub Shuns Political Battles in His Campaign for Commissioner," begins with:

Howard "Pete" Shaub, former Marine, is a man with a mission. He wants to unify the battling divisions of the Lancaster County Republican Party.

It might take a whole corps of Marines to win that objective, but Shaub is undeterred: If he's elected county commissioner, he says, he will use his position to start peace talks between the party's social conservatives and moderates.

Mostly, Shaub would rather talk about ideas than politics. Ask him about the challenges (he prefers that word to "problems") of running in a three-way race with incumbent Paul Thibault, and he replies, "My emphasis is going to be focusing on the issues and presenting those issues to the voters." and ends with: "Running for commissioner poses another challenge for Shaub—a career change. And it will not be a profitable change, at least financially.

"It's a very big sacrifice—we'll just leave it at that," Shaub says. But there's a reason for doing it.

"We've been blessed with a wonderful quality of life here," Shaub says, "and I want to maintain that quality of life for my children and my grandchildren."

[16] Shaub was not only raising money and getting high-profile endorsements prior to and after the May 18, 1999, primary, he was also getting press with each fundraiser, each endorsement. See *Intelligencer Journal*, April 16, 1999, "Shaub and Thibault Each Pick Up 2 Endorsements, Shaub Fund-Raiser Draws Nearly 60 People"; *Lancaster New Era*, April 16, 1999, "Shaub Endorsed by Reps. True and Armstrong, Raises $5,000"; *Lancaster New Era*, April 30, 1999, "4 Veterans Back Ex-Marine Shaub for County Office"; and *Lancaster New Era*, June 19, 1999, "Shaub Surge: Late Donations Spur Victory Candidate Collects $35,475 in Final 2 Weeks of Campaign."

[17] Shaub's position on the proposed hotel room tax in 1999 may be found in the *Sunday News*, March 14, 1999, "Semper Fi to Ideas, Issues/ Pete Shaub Shuns Political Battles in His Campaign for Commissioner," From the article: "A hotel tax: Shaub says he hasn't studied whether a hotel room tax should be imposed to pay for the local share of a convention center downtown. The state is expected to provide $15 million, but that money needs to be matched."

For Shaub on other issues in the 1999 campaign, see *Lancaster New Era*, "Would-Be Commissioners on Farmland, Taxes, Teen Jail, 3 Candidates Offer Varied Backgrounds," March 12, 1999.

[18] Ibid. *Sunday News*, March 14, 1999.

[19] See *Lancaster New Era*, April 21, 1999, "Shaub Raps Lack of Emergency Training Facility Calls Commissioners' Failure to Come Up with Site 'Inexcusable.'"

[20] The source for the May 18, 1999, Republican primary results was the Lancaster County Office of Voter Registration and Board of Elections.

[21] Thibault's money came from the top Lancaster business establishment, including S. Dale High and other sponsors of the hotel and convention center project. See: "Top Business Leaders Back Thibault's Re-Election Bid," *Lancaster New Era*, March 2, 1999. From the article:

> He may not have the endorsement of the Lancaster County Republican Committee, but incumbent County Commissioner Paul R. Thibault has the support of some of the county's most prominent business leaders.
>
> At a $125-a-plate fund-raiser Monday night in the Quality Inn and Suites on Oregon Pike, Thibault, who is seeking re-election, was joined by some 300 supporters. Among those endorsing Thibault were retired Lancaster AAA executive Herbert C. "Bud" Mearig; Tom Baldrige, chairman of The Lancaster Campaign; William W. Adams, former CEO of Armstrong World Industries Inc.; and R. Scott Smith Jr., chairman and CEO of Fulton Bank. . . . Also supporting Thibault but unable to attend the dinner were city Mayor Charlie Smithgall, state Rep. John E. Barley, R-Conestoga, and S. Dale High, president of High Industries Inc. . . .

For GOP campaign spending for the May 18, 1999, primary, see "$600,000 Spent in GOP Primary," *Intelligencer Journal*, June 19, 1999.

[22] Source for November 2, 1999 Lancaster County commissioners' election results: Lancaster County Office of Voter Registration & Board of Elections. See http://www.co.lancaster.pa.us/elections.

[23] Immediately after having just taken public office in January 2000—the highest elected office in Lancaster County government—Commissioner Shaub told a Christian group that "I get to further God's kingdom. That is what I am called to do to help influence people to change their lives." I knew when I took office on the same Board of Commissioners that Shaub was interested in crossing the line of separation between church and state, and I was alert to stop these efforts. *Sunday News*, "New Commissioner Vows to Save Farms, Fight Drugs and 'Further God's Kingdom.' // Shaub's Action Plan," January 16, 2000.

[24] Shaub made his comments about the other two commissioners and their budget in "Thibault, Shaub Spar over Budget, Proposed Tax Hike Sparks Debate," *Intelligencer Journal*, November 22, 2000.

[25] Shaub's open clashes with fellow Republican Paul Thibault were hard to understand. Shaub needed Thibault on the three-person board. In this case, Shaub was saying he didn't believe the board should abide by a duly passed tax increase, enacted prior to Shaub joining the Board of Commissioners. See "Thibault, Shaub Spar Over Budget," *Intelligencer Journal*, November 22, 2000.

[26] Ibid. "Thibault, Shaub Spar Over Budget," *Intelligencer Journal*, November 22, 2000.

[27] The news of Shaub's county-purchased car broke on December 7, 2000. He had been in office less than one year, had countless controversies and scandals, and wanted

a new car for his private use. See "Commissioners Hear Growth Fund Requests, Shaub Questioned on Proposed Car," *Lancaster New Era*, December 7, 2000. The car was actually on the 2001 budget until the IRS pointed out that it broke regulations. See "Tax Sinks County Plan to Buy Car for Shaub," *Lancaster New Era*, April 27, 2001.

[28] As with many of Pete Shaub's agendas, the accusations by Shaub of county administrator Timothea Kirchner made their way to the front pages of Lancaster Newspapers. See "Shaub Tells County to Come Clean about Debt. But Other Officials Say He's Just Playing Politics," *Intelligencer Journal*, November 11, 2002; and "Shaub: Says County Must Be Up Front about Debt," *Lancaster New Era*, November 12, 2002.

[29] Shaub's was the lone dissenting vote on the pay raise for county administrator Timothea Kirchner. A public record of the vote was "County Administrator Gets 6% Pay Hike in 3–1 Vote," *Lancaster New Era*, June 4, 2001.

[30] Shaub is the only one who could get headlines for using a judge's shower. "Courthouse Turf Tiff Costs Him Job/ Employee, who sent info to media about judge-commissioner scrap, is fired for using e-mail and fax for personal use, breach of confidence." *Sunday News*, January 27, 2002. From the article:

> A 16-year veteran of county government lost his job Thursday because he sent copies of a controversial memo to the *Sunday News* and WGAL-TV. Robert Widmark, a parole program coordinator for the adult probation department, said he was fired after admitting that he provided the memo, which told probation staffers to keep county Commissioner Pete Shaub out of their offices, to the news organizations.

[31] The source of Barley's "harassment" was none other than Ron Harper, Jr. Harper had been hounding Barley for more than a year when Barley announced he wasn't seeking reelection in January 2002. He resigned abruptly in March. More than a year before Barley resigned, on December 17, 2000, Harper's campaign against Barley was featured in the *Sunday News*, "On the Web, Ron Harper Jr. Mercilessly Chides Rep. Barley and Other Political Foes. They Say He's a Publicity Hound. Others Call Him an Effective Watchdog. // He Rattles Barley's Cage." About two weeks prior to Barley's announcement, Harper said he was delivering 3,000 copies of a videotape, *The Politics of John Barley*, to every voter in his district and every lawmaker. See "Rep. Barley Video; Will Be Distributed in New 100th District," *Intelligencer Journal*, January 2, 2002. Also see "Barley Exits 100th Race," *Intelligencer Journal*, January 12, 2002.

[32] John Barley's sudden resignation from office made headlines all over the state. See "Capitol Abuzz Over Powerful Republican Barley's Abrupt Exit," *Pittsburgh Post-Gazette*, March 28, 2002.

[33] Shaub's comments against the hoteliers were made in the *Intelligencer Journal*, May 22, 2001, "County Hoteliers Lodge Appeal in Convention Center Tax Suit // Costly Legal Battle Now Goes before Commonwealth Court."

[34] Barley's association with bond underwriters Arthurs Lestrange was mentioned in the *Sunday News* on May 18, 2003, in an article about large contributors to local campaigns, "Lawyers, Financial Pros Most Generous." From the article: "Shaub picked up $2,500 from the PAC run by Arthurs Lestrange, a bond underwriting company for which former state legislator John Barley works. . . ."

[35] The connection between ex-representative Barley, Arthurs Lestrange, and the county commissioners Thibault and Shaub was made in a *Sunday News* editorial, "A Tainted Move," September 21, four weeks before the bond was to be voted on by the Board of Commissioners. From the editorial: "The resigned state legislator [Barley] works for Arthurs Lestrange, helping to line up bond jobs. Last year he accompanied two company representatives to meetings in the courthouse with Republican commissioners Shaub and Paul Thibault. . . ."

[36] Shaub's comments on the Lancaster Pagan Pride Festival are found in the article "Pagans Picnic, Much to Commissioner's Chagrin," *Sunday News*, September 8, 2002. Also see "Pagans Say Their Piece," *Intelligencer Journal*, September 24, 2002. Although he was unsuccessful in preventing the legal gathering, it was another example of Shaub crossing the line between church and state. In this case, Shaub wanted to decide which groups could use county facilities, according to his beliefs.

[37] Shaub was stopped after hours at the county park Chickie's Rock, in August 2002, just weeks before he wanted to prevent another group, Lancaster Pagan Pride, from holding a lawful gathering in another county park. Shaub's late night at Chickie's Rock was referred to in "A Shaub Constant: Changing His Mind. The Commissioner Has History of Flip-Flopping on Controversial Issues," *Lancaster New Era*, December 27, 2006. The article is a partial recap of some of Shaub's bad behavior in office. From the article: "In August 2002, park rangers found Shaub and two females in Chickie's Rock County Park after hours. Shaub said the women were his daughter and his daughter's friend."

[38] Shaub's using his commissioner's office as a campaign office—and Commissioner Ford's strong objection—was reported in "Ford Accuses Shaub of Abusing Office, Commissioner Seeks Support at Courthouse," *Intelligencer Journal*, January 7, 2003

[39] Frankly, in my opinion, the word for the Republicans endorsing only one candidate is *careless*. After nine nominating ballots with no conclusion, it was clear that the party did not want Shaub reelected. But by the GOP not giving the electorate another endorsed candidate, Shaub's name was most recognizable and as an incumbent he had a huge advantage. Leading up to the GOP endorsement, Shaub and Shellenberger were the top vote getters in the "straw polls" of the various county districts. County controller Dennis Stuckey also did well in the straw polls. Despite his strong position, Shaub was working desperately to secure the endorsement. He tried to persuade four other candidates in the seven-candidate field to drop out. That move made headlines. See "Commissioner Hopefuls: Shaub Urging Us to Quit/ Complaint Filed against Incumbent," *Intelligencer Journal*, February 12, 2003. From the article:

Endnotes

> Three Republican candidates for Lancaster County commissioner are accusing incumbent Pete Shaub of trying to orchestrate the GOP endorsement by pressuring them to withdraw from the race. Former county commissioner Jim Huber, Recorder of Deeds Steve McDonald and county Youth Intervention Center employee Scott Martin all say Shaub pressured them to withdraw. The pressure was so intense, Martin said, that he filed a complaint against Shaub Tuesday with the county ethics commission.

Also see "Candidates Say Shaub Urges Them To Drop Out," *Lancaster New Era*, February 12, 2003.

Two days later, Shaub attempted to get a voting rule change for the GOP endorsement vote on February 20, "Row Officer: Shaub Wants Rule Change/Would Alter Voting Protocol at Convention." The endorsement itself began the evening of February 20 and finished in the early hours of February 21. See "Shellenberger Gets Republican Endorsement / GOP Backs Workman Judge, Ives for Coroner," *Intelligencer Journal*, February 21, 2003. From the article:

> Incumbent Lancaster County Commissioner Pete Shaub failed to capture the GOP endorsement early this morning after nine ballots and a week of intense political pressure. The balloting ended about 1:30 a.m. On the ninth ballot, Shaub captured 186 votes and county controller Dennis Stuckey received 141. There were 327 votes cast, meaning 218 were needed for endorsement. The 359 members present at the Lancaster County Republican Committee's endorsement convention were unable to endorse two candidates in the hotly contested race for county commissioner, but did endorse one: Manheim resident Richard Shellenberger, 57, owner of The Eatery at Granite Run. Shellenberger captured 292 votes, surpassing the 240 votes needed to win the endorsement."

Also see "GOP Nod to Shellenberger, Not Shaub. Newcomer endorsed for commissioner on 4th ballot, but incumbent and five others fail to receive needed two-thirds support. The result: likely 6 candidates on Republican ballot for top county post. Among other contests, Workman backed for judge, Ives for coroner." *Lancaster New Era*, February 21, 2003.

[40] Shaub's noncommittal comments regarding support of the county bond guaranty were made before and after the May primary, including in "County Chiefs Weigh Role in City Project," *Intelligencer Journal*, October 16, 2003. The article references Shaub's support of the project but reluctance to vote for the bond for political reasons. From the article:

> Commissioner Pete Shaub, the only current commissioner who is seeking re-election, refused to answer questions regarding the bond guarantee on Monday. He read from a prepared statement:

"My job is to listen to all of the information. Once I do that, then I will make my decision."

However, at a meet-the-candidates event Tuesday at Willow Valley Resort and Conference Center, Shaub reportedly told the audience he is in favor of the convention center but would vote against a bond guarantee proposed by the authority.

Another commissioner candidate now is accusing Shaub of changing his stance on the issue for political gain.

Jim Clymer, the Constitution Party candidate, said he believes Shaub plans to vote against a guarantee because he believes Thibault and Ford will vote for it, ensuring the project would continue as planned without Shaub alienating voters who don't want a county commitment to the convention center.

[41] The Reading-based Stevens & Lee law firm was all over the state of Pennsylvania. See "Lawyers, Financial Pros Most Generous," *Sunday News*, May 18, 2003. From the article:

> As it develops, Responsible Citizens isn't its full name; that would be Responsible Citizens for Economic Progress. It's one of a handful of political action committees formed by the statewide powerhouse Stevens & Lee law firm.

[42] Ibid. "Lawyers, Financial Pros Most Generous," *Sunday News*, May 18, 2003. From the article:

> Shaub picked up $2,500 from the PAC run by Arthurs Lestrange, a bond underwriting company for which former state legislator John Barley works. Arthurs Lestrange was one of the bond firms that supported Shaub's argument last year that a bond deal being planned by the commissioners would cost taxpayers too much in interest.

[43] The amount of money Stevens & Lee was paid by the Lancaster County Convention Center Authority certainly seemed excessive and was one of my major issues for opposing the project. By September 2006, after the firm had billed more than $7 million to the LCCCA, the three LCCCA board members whom Commissioner Shellenberger and I appointed—Deb Hall, Laura Douglas, and Jack Craver —wrote a letter to District Attorney Totaro, asking the DA to investigate the billings. From the letter:

> Our specific concern here is that we have become aware that almost $7 million in legal fees have been paid to the law firm of Stevens & Lee over several years on the basis of over two-hundred invoices with no additional information attached than "For professional services rendered on behalf of the Lancaster County Convention Center Authority."

The letter is available at pressedthebook.com

[44] The official results for the November 2003 general election for Lancaster County commissioner were Shellenberger, 41,674; Shaub, 37,066; Henderson, 21,713; Saylor, 19,658; Clymer, 17,850; and Kender, 2,182. Source: Lancaster County Voter Registration & Board of Elections. See http://vr.co.lancaster.pa.us/ElectionReturns/November_4,_2003_-_Municipal_Election/a07ae9516d88dca8e8366eb1a3fd1447.asp.

[45] Shellenberger's gracious post-election quotes came from "Democrat Henderson Wins, Joins Two from GOP as Commissioners," *Intelligencer Journal*, November 5, 2003. For my part, I was mentioned in the article as follows:

> Henderson, 50, former city health director, said she first plans to become "fully acquainted with the position and the departments."
>
> "I want to see what the needs of the departments are," she said. "As far as a particular issue, I'd really like to see some consensus there. I really want to work with Mr. Shellenberger and Mr. Shaub to move the county in a positive forward direction. I want to discuss their ideas, too, and see what we come up with."

[46] Because of Clymer's entrance into the race, no one, including the Republicans, was absolutely sure of election, so Shaub was probably genuinely relieved to know he had been reelected to the commissioners' board. Shaub's comments come from "Democrat Henderson Wins, Joins Two from GOP as Commissioners," *Intelligencer Journal*, November 5, 2003.

[47] Judge Michael A. Georgelis (b. 1939–) served on the Lancaster bench for twenty-one years. He retired at the end of 2006. During the last six years of his career, the distinguished Georgelis had several clashes with Shaub.

[48] Barbara J. Humphrey (November 29, 1951–September 1, 2014) was not just a dear friend, she was a brilliant Lancaster political organizer, a Democrat who worked on my staff for all of my runs for commissioner. Barb knew the political players in each district in the county. She was especially attuned to city politics. A lot of good Democrats were elected in major part because of Barb's important work. Barb was co-president of the Lancaster Women's Alliance at the time of her passing. She held several leadership posts with the Lancaster County Democratic Committee. Barb was elected vice chair during the 2006–2010 term and served as chair in 2009. She was a district leader in Lancaster Township. In addition to the invaluable help in my campaigns, Barb was instrumental in electing the first two Lancaster Township Democratic supervisors. This turned Lancaster Township to a Democratic majority. In 2010, Barbara was awarded "Democrat of the Year." As a friend, she was kind and loyal, funny and intelligent.

[49] Shaub made this remark at the Economic Development Company's annual breakfast at the Willow Valley resort, January 9, 2004. The event, minus Shaub's comments, was reported the same day in "County Must Work to Lure Outside Firms, Says EDC Chief," *Lancaster New Era*, January 9, 2004.

⁵⁰ The county's effort to aid the town of Picayune, Mississippi, was reported in "County's Hurricane Relief Effort to Focus on Small Miss. Town," *Lancaster New Era*, October 26, 2005.

⁵¹ Totaro ran unopposed for DA in 2003 and ended up with 52,516 votes. Source: Lancaster County Voter Registration & Board of Elections. See http://vr.co.lancaster.pa.us/ElectionReturns/November_4,_2003_-_Municipal_Election/b482080443832bbc538313a3aab7a7e4.asp.

⁵² The *New Era*'s Bernard Harris reported of Shaub's distribution of assignments in "Commissioners Redistribute County Workload/In an attempt to operate more like a business, the administrator's job will be divided and a human services director will be hired," *Lancaster New Era*, January 6, 2004. From the article:

> The new board, led by chairman Pete Shaub, began the process of dividing the county administrator's job and hiring a new human services director. With the new position, to be called chief services officer, the commissioners will have three chiefs reporting directly to them. Timothea M. Kirchner, who has been the county administrator for nearly eight years.

⁵³ Dave McCudden had been county engineer since 1989. Like many in the courthouse, McCudden found himself in Shaub's crosshairs. In August 2006, Shaub took public issue with how the veteran McCudden chose architects for county jobs. In "Shaub Takes Engineer's Office to Task," Shaub was quoted in the *Intelligencer Journal* article. "If we have local firms that are qualified, we should go out of our way to allow them to submit a proposal to do work for us," Shaub said. "After we evaluate that, we can decide who maybe is the best. We should not just arbitrarily exclude our local people."

The problem with Shaub's analysis was that McCudden's office did include local firms in the selection process for an architect of the $3.5 million forensic center and morgue.

⁵⁴ From *Merriam-Webster*: "BERNOULLI'S PRINCIPLE: a principle in hydrodynamics: the pressure in a stream of fluid is reduced as the speed of the flow is increased."

See http://www.merriam-webster.com/dictionary/bernoulli's%20principle.

⁵⁵ It was the quiet, well-dressed Espenshade who essentially ran the hotel and convention center on the ground for the project sponsors. At the county, where he was solicitor for seventeen years, it was Espenshade who navigated the legal issues for the hotel room rental tax in 1999 and the county bond guaranty of 2003. His Stevens & Lee firm, authored the Third-Class County Convention Center Authority Act of 1994, the enabling legislation on which the room tax was enacted. Espenshade holds degrees from Elizabethtown College, Penn State University, Marburg Universitat (Germany), London Centre for Legal Studies, and the University of Notre Dame Law School.

⁵⁶ Timothea Kirchner resigned fewer than two weeks after our Board of Commissioners took office. Her last day in office was February 17, 2004. See "County OKs Kirchner's Severance MH/MR Chief Likely Will Fill in Temporarily," *Intelligencer Journal*, January 28, 2004." Kirchner's LinkedIn account in 2015 indicates she works as a government

affairs consultant for Stevens & Lee. She does not appear, however, through a search of the law firm's website. See https://www.linkedin.com/in/timothea-kirchner-87393011.

[57] The Lancaster County "Smart Growth" plan was a comprehensive plan that encompassed a broad range of economic, housing, transportation, and financial planning issues. Ron Bailey was the architect of Lancaster's plan, which worked with some of Lancaster County's major institutions, such as Lancaster General Health, the region's main health center and hospital. In Lancaster County, the Smart Growth plan always prioritized the preservation of Lancaster County's rich farmland. The county could not have had a better person than Ron Bailey as head of the Planning Commission.

[58] Bailey's resignation was reported in "County's Top Planner Quits, Cites Differences with Shaub," *Lancaster New Era*, November 23, 2004. From the article:

> Lancaster County's top planner, Ronald Bailey, abruptly resigned his position after 16 years today. The 54-year-old Lancaster Township resident, who makes more than $100,000 a year, said he quit during a morning meeting with the commissioners about the county's 2005 budget. Bailey, who is the director of the planning commission, said he and commissioners Chairman Pete Shaub disagreed over the future of the nationally recognized program. "The chairman of the board and I don't share priorities, is a fair way to describe it," Bailey said.

[59] J. Thomas Myers was the director of the county's human resources department and Ashworth his next in line. Ashworth was acting director after Myers resigned in February 2006—three months after his report on the hiring of Gary Heinke and in the middle of a grand jury investigation into Heinke's hiring. Myers was another Shaub casualty. Both of these people were capable, professional civil servants.

[60] The first attack on Heinke appeared in the afternoon *Lancaster New Era* on October 24, 2005, "Who Is Gary Heinke?" In the article, former Lancaster city mayor Art Morris is labeled a "county government watchdog" who discovered discrepancies in Heinke's résumé. This fudged résumé was the pretext for a grand jury investigation that took more than a year and an abundance of the district attorney's office time, money, and resources. "I'm seeking a full investigation by the county in an open fashion," said Morris in the *New Era* article.

[61] The details of Shaub, Shellenberger, and Espenshade's help to Heinke were investigated and revealed in J. Thomas Myers's report into Heinke's hiring. The ensuing grand jury investigation took thirteen months to reach the same conclusions Myers reached and reported in November 2005. It is interesting that although Lancaster Newspapers ran hundreds of stories about "the commissioners," which meant Shaub and Shellenberger, but the public thought included me, John Espenshade's name was never in them. According to the Myer's Report, Espenshade worked closely with Shaub and Shellenberger, coming up with questions and coaching Heinke.

[62] Don Elliott dated his application for the county administrative officer February 19, 2004 and indicated he could begin work on April 1, 2004. Nevin Cooley, president of Penn Square Partners, was one of three professional references used by Elliot and was referred to as a "colleague". The Elliott application may be found at: Pressedthebook.com under "Official Lancaster county Convention Center and Marriott Hotel Documents".

[63] In December 2004, the Board of Lancaster County Commissioners, faced with a lack of space for county offices, acquired the Armstrong Building on 150 N. Queen St. by eminent domain from its private owner.

[64] The story about Shaub and the boat did not make the newspapers. It happened during my term on the commissioners' board. The Parks Department head at the time was James Hackett, who was strong-armed by Shaub into making the boat purchase. As liaison to Parks, I approached Hackett based on some "office discussion" and got the full story. It appeared that Shaub believed the rules did not apply to him.

[65] "A Bully in a China Shop," was a huge blow to Shaub. After years of Shaub's bad behavior inside the courthouse, the entire county of Lancaster now was aware of his erratic and difficult behavior. The 1,377-word article was published by the *Sunday News*, December 14, 2004, at the end of our first year on the commissioners' board. It was also right around the time Shaub was deposed as chairman of the board. That made Shaub even more disruptive.

[66] The Pennsylvania Open Meetings, "Sunshine Act," may be found online here: http://www.legis.state.pa.us/WU01/LI/LI/CT/HTM/65/65.htm.

[67] The memo I wrote to Shaub and Shellenberger was dated September 7, 2004. These secret meetings between Shaub, Shellenberger, and Espenshade infuriated me. My memos grew increasingly threatening, with the one cited saying I was prepared to go to the district attorney if the meetings persisted.

[68] Shaub's comments imploring Penn Square Partners' president Nevin D. Cooley to produce architectural drawings were published in "Brunswick Added to City Center Plan," *Intelligencer Journal*, June 3, 2004.

[69] Ibid. See "Brunswick Added to City Center Plan," *Intelligencer Journal*, June 3, 2004.

Chapter Six: It's All about the Hotel—Really

[1] "Penn Square Complex Is Hailed as 'Everything the City Needs' Strong Praise from Crowd of Nearly 300," *Lancaster New Era*, August 26, 1999. The front-page article ran three weeks prior to the vote on the hotel room rental tax. Support for a convention center had been stoked to a fever pitch by this time. The article begins:

> In a display that united old foes and bridged city-county and Republican- Democrat differences, county leaders have embraced plans for a $75 million downtown hotel and convention center with almost religious zeal. The first public presentation of the project brought nearly 300 people to the standing-room-only

meeting in the city's Southern Market Center Wednesday night. The crowd—a Who's Who of county political, business and civic leaders—seemed to seize on the plan which pledges salvation for downtown. "I think this is exactly the right thing for the community. This is superb. This is everything the city needs," said former city Mayor Richard Scott, a Republican who two years ago opposed plans to locate Harrisburg Area Community College at the same site. "My sense is that this is a once-in-a-lifetime opportunity," agreed P. Michael Sturla, the city's House representative, a Democrat. . . .

[2] Commissioner Dick Shellenberger was voted chairman of the Lancaster County Board of Commissioners, December 22, 2004, at a regular commissioners' meeting. I voted for Shellenberger.

The "coup" replacing Shaub as chairman of the board was reported three days before the vote on December 19, 2004, in the *Sunday News*: "Shellenberger Takes Charge." Noteworthy are the tone and content of the article, which are highly respectful of Shellenberger and me. The commissioners are differentiated from one another. Later, we were grouped as one, "the commissioners." Underscoring the positive way Shellenberger and I were covered, the article notes several members of the political establishment at Shellenberger's press conference announcing he would be running for chairman of the Board of Commissioners. From the article:

> Some of those moderates were at the press conference—Anne Gardner, vice chairman of the Thibault-founded Friends of Better Government PAC; Ted Darcus, chairman of the Lancaster County Convention Center Authority; Hourglass Foundation board members; and Democratic Party leaders Ken and Judi Ralph and Bill Saylor.
>
> There were also conservatives like former commissioner Jim Huber and other Republican Party committee members from the influential social-conservative wing.

[3] The hotel room rental tax went into effect on January 1, 2000. The room tax revenue going to the Lancaster County Convention Center Authority (LCCCA) averaged $2.857 million per year for the first four years of the project, according to the LCCCA's "Operating Account Ledger." The $40 million county-guaranteed bond was losing money each month, due to negative arbitrage. The amount of interest LCCCA was paying on the $40 million bond sale from 2003 exceeded by .55% the amount of interest LCCCA was receiving on investments of its proceeds from that bond sale. This negative arbitrage situation created an overall loss to the LCCCA of approximately $220,000 a year.

[4] In 2003, the Stevens & Lee law firm received more than $1.4 million from the Lancaster County Convention Center Authority (LCCCA), while High Real Estate was paid $940,000, both for "professional services." This was about 75% of the hotel

tax revenue the LCCCA took in from its portion of the room tax. The LCCCA tax revenue was remitted primarily to two entities; one, an investor in the project; the other, the law firm that was the lobbyist of the investor and that wrote the law to collect the tax revenue. These figures come from the LCCCA Operating Account Ledger for 2003. During the course of the project, including the years when the project remained dormant, with no work being done on the site, each was paid several million dollars, with Stevens & Lee—the firm that wrote the Third-Class County Convention Center Authority Act—eventually being paid more than $7 million on the project, according to the LCCCA billing documents from 1998 to 2007.

[5] The April 24, 2003, letter sent from the Pennsylvania Historical & Museum Commission, Bureau for Historic Preservation to Thomas D. Smithgall of the High Real Estate Group was signed by Kurt W. Carr, chief, Division of Archaeology & Protection. The "building" (it was just a façade by now) was officially delisted from the National Register of Historic Places in 2007. "The façade no longer represents the architecture and heritage of the building," said Carol Lee, supervisor of the Pennsylvania Bureau for Historic Preservation, as she was quoted in "Watt & Shand to Be De-Listed as Historic Place," *Lancaster New Era*, July 20, 2007. The Bureau of Historic Preservation also commented on Penn Square Partners' reaction after learning they wouldn't be receiving tax credits. From the *New Era* article: "'They [Penn Square Partners] weren't happy with us, but we said a 14-story hotel on top of a four-story building does not qualify for tax credits,' explains Bonnie Mark, tax act coordinator for the bureau, a division of the Pennsylvania Historic and Museum Commission."

[6] Penn Square Partners president Nevin Cooley's announcement that the project needed $18.6 million was made during a meeting with our board of county commissioners on February 25, 2004. The meeting was reported in "Penn Sq. Project Leaders Unite, but Seek $18M More from Pa.," *Lancaster New Era*, February 25, 2004, and in "Convention Center Needs $18.6 Million," *Intelligencer Journal*, February 26, 2004. Of the nearly $20 million more in state funds the project sponsors were seeking, project supporter Senator Gibson E. "Gib" Armstrong, who attended the commissioners' meeting, said, "If they [Penn Square Partners] don't get the $18.6 million we don't have a project."

[7] Lancaster County taxpayers were exposed to more than $60 million in liability because of the 2003 bond guaranty. According to the "Guaranty Agreement" signed by the Board of Commissioners in December 2003, weeks before I took office, the agreement provides that during the 40-year lifetime of the bond, the county will guarantee up to $1,506,960 per year. Multiplying that amount by 40 years is $60,278,400. As I said, the project was a bad deal for Lancaster County taxpayers, and that's why I opposed it.

[8] The Brookings Institute published "Space Available: The Realities of Convention Centers as Economic Development Strategy," by Dr. Heywood T. Sanders, in January 2005.

From the article:

> The overall convention marketplace is declining in a manner that suggests that a recovery or turnaround is unlikely to yield

much increased business for any given community, contrary to repeated industry projections. Moreover, this decline began prior to the disruptions of 9-11 and is exacerbated by advances in communications technology. Currently, overall attendance at the 200 largest tradeshow events languishes at 1993 levels.

Nonetheless, localities, sometimes with state assistance, have continued a type of arms race with competing cities to host these events, investing massive amounts of capital in new convention center construction and expansion of existing facilities. Over the past decade alone, public capital spending on convention centers has doubled to $2.4 billion annually, increasing convention space by over 50 percent since 1990. Nationwide, 44 new or expanded convention centers are now in planning or construction.

Faced with increased competition, many cities spend more money on additional convention amenities, like publicly financed hotels to serve as convention "headquarters." Another competitive response has been to offer deep discounts to trade show groups. Despite dedicated taxes to pay off the public bonds issued to build convention centers, many—including Washington, D.C and St. Louis—operate at a loss.

This analysis should give local leaders pause as they consider calls for ever more public investment into the convention business, while weighing simultaneously where else scarce public funds could be spent to boost the urban economy.

The Brookings study can be found here: http://www.brookings.edu/research/reports/2005/01/01cities-sanders.

[9] Dr. Sanders's remarks at Liberty Place, March 3, 2005, were reported in "Convention Experts Debate City Project's Potential for Success," *Intelligencer Journal*, March 4, 2005.

[10] Ibid. Thomas Hazinski's remarks at Liberty Place, March 3, 2005, were reported in "Convention Experts Debate City Project's Potential for Success," *Intelligencer Journal*, March 4, 2005.

[11] According to the Lancaster County Convention Center Authority's Operating Account Ledger, in 2003, Stevens & Lee received more than $1.4 million from the Lancaster County Convention Center Authority (LCCCA), while High Real Estate was paid $940,000, both for "professional services." Hundreds of thousands of additional dollars were paid to other consultants and lawyers, but High and Stevens & Lee were paid most of the hotel tax revenue.

[12] "Act 23" of April 1, 2004, P.L. 200, No. 23, 2004, amended the Infrastructure and Facilities Improvement Program (IFIP) of 1990 to include "convention centers" and "hotel establishments" as "project users" eligible for IFIP grant funding. See §3402(iii) of the law:

"Project user." An industrial enterprise, retail enterprise, manufacturer, hospital, convention center or hotel establishment, which owns, leases or uses all or any part of a project."

Senator Armstrong's Act 23 amendment may be found online here: http://www.legis.state.pa.us/WU01/LI/LI/US/HTM/2004/0/0023..htm.

The Infrastructure and Facilities Improvement Program (IFIP) was intended to enhance economic development by providing financial assistance in the form of multi-year grants to redevelopment authorities for the payment of debt service on projects. The IFIP of 1990 is found here: http://www.legis.state.pa.us/cfdocs/legis/LI/consCheck.cfm?txtType=HTM&ttl=12&div=0&chpt=34.

[13] Former Pennsylvania state senator David J. "Chip" Brightbill is of Counsel at Stevens & Lee, working out of the firm's Harrisburg Government Affairs office. From his profile on the Stevens & Lee website:

> David J. "Chip" Brightbill concentrates his practice in governmental and regulatory matters at all levels of government, particularly involving issues of health care, transportation, energy and the environment. . . . He also served 24 years in the Pennsylvania General Assembly, including six as the Senate Leader and six as the Chair of the Environmental Resources and Energy Committee.

See http://www.stevenslee.com/?pro=david-j-brightbill.

[14] From §3402(iii) of P.L. 200, No. 23, 2004, "Act 23":

> "Project user." An industrial enterprise, retail enterprise, manufacturer, hospital, convention center or hotel establishment, which owns, leases or uses all or any part of a project."

See Act 23 online here: http://www.legis.state.pa.us/WU01/LI/LI/US/HTM/2004/0/0023..htm.

[15] The December 17, 2004, *Intelligencer Journal* article "City Takes Key Role in Hotel at Convention Center Project, Partnership Wants to Sell Hotel to Agency" was remarkable in its detail. The article, published by Penn Square Partner Lancaster Newspapers, is quite specific in how the private hotel would be "sold" to the Redevelopment Authority and then re-sold back to the partners after the bonds borrowed by the Redevelopment Authority were paid off. This took great orchestration between the partners and city and state agencies and involved tens of millions of dollars. Shellenberger and I stood in the way of that project.

[16] Ibid.

[17] The Pennsylvania Urban Redevelopment Act of May 24, 1945, P.L. 991, No. 385 may be found here: http://www.redevelophbg.org/downloads/Urban%20Redevelopment%20Law.pdf.

It's clear from reading the act that its principal objective was to redevelop "blighted" properties, housing, or districts within a city. The Watt & Shand building, on Penn Square in the middle of the downtown shopping district, next to Central Market, several banks and law firms, and the headquarters of Lancaster Newspapers, Inc., was hardly "blighted."

[18] The "public purpose" requirement for Redevelopment Authorities is a fundamental part of the mandate of the authorities, per the Urban Redevelopment Act of 1945. In the case of the Lancaster County project, the Redevelopment Authority for the City of Lancaster was borrowing tens of millions of dollars solely to benefit the private interests of Penn Square Partners. This point was made by the county's attorney, Howard Kelin, in our complaint to the Pennsylvania Department of Community and Economic Development, May 16, 2005. From the Pennsylvania Urban Redevelopment Act of May 24, 1945, P.L. 991, No. 385, Section 4, Formation of Authorities:

http://www.redevelophbg.org/downloads/Urban%20Redevelopment%20Law.pdf.

[19] The "Powers of an Authority" are found Section 9 of the Pennsylvania Urban Redevelopment Act of 1945. From Section 9:

". . . the following powers in addition to those herein otherwise granted:

(a) To procure from the planning commission the designation of areas in need of redevelopment and its recommendations for such redevelopment; (b) To study the recommendations of the planning commission for redevelopment of any area and to make its own additional investigations and recommendations thereon; to initiate preliminary studies of possible redevelopment areas to make and assist in implementing (1) plans for carrying out a program of voluntary repair, rehabilitation and conservation of real property, buildings and improvements, (2) plans for the enforcement of laws, codes and regulations relating to the use of land and the use and occupancy of buildings and improvements, (3) plans for the relocation of persons (including families, business concerns and others) displaced by any other Government activities related to the purposes of this act or any activities of the Authority, (4) preliminary plans outlining redevelopment activities for neighborhoods to embrace two or more redevelopment areas, and (5) preliminary surveys to determine if the undertaking and carrying out of a redevelopment project are feasible. ((b) amended June 26, 1968, P.L.263, No.125) (c) To cooperate with any government, school district or municipality; ((c) amended June 26, 1968, P.L.263, No.125) (d) To act as agent of the State or Federal Government or any of its instrumentalities or agencies for the public purposes set out in this act; (e) To arrange or contract with any municipality located, in whole or in part, within the Authority's field of operation, or with the State or Federal Government for the furnishing, planning, replanning, constructing, installing, opening or closing of streets, roads, roadways, alleys, sidewalks or other places or facilities, or for the acquisition by such municipality, or State or Federal Government of property options or property rights or for the furnishing of property or services in connection with a redevelopment area; (f) To arrange or contract with the Commonwealth, its agencies, and any municipality to the extent that it is within the scope of their respective functions--(1) to cause the services customarily provided by each of them to be rendered for the benefits of such Authority or the occupants of any redevelopment area; and (2) to provide and maintain parks, recreational centers, schools, sewerage, transportation, water and other municipal facilities adjacent to or in connection with redevelopment areas; and (3) to plan, replan, zone or rezone any part of the municipality in connection with any redevelopment proposal of the Authority; (g) To enter upon any building or property in order to make surveys or soundings; (h) To assemble, purchase, obtain options upon, acquire by gift, grant, bequest, devise or otherwise any real or personal property or any interest therein from any person, firm, corporation, municipality or government: Provided, That no real property, located outside of a redevelopment area, which is not necessary to the corporate purposes of the Authority nor necessary to the successful redevelopment of a redevelopment area, shall be purchased by the Authority. ((h) amended June 26, 1968, P.L.263, No.125) (i) To acquire by eminent domain any real property, including improvements and fixtures for the public purposes set forth in this act, in the manner hereinafter provided, except real property located outside a redevelopment area; ((i) amended Dec. 1, 1959, P.L.1637, No.603) (j) To own, hold, clear, improve and manage real property; (k) To sell, lease or otherwise transfer any real property located outside of a redevelopment area and, subject to approval by the local governing body, any real property in a redevelopment area: Provided, That with respect to a redevelopment area the Authority finds that the sale, lease or other transfer of any part will not be prejudicial to the sale or lease of the other parts of the redevelopment area, nor be in any other way prejudicial to the realization of the redevelopment proposal approved by the governing body. ((k) amended May 27, 1957, P.L.197, No.98) (l) To reimburse for their reasonable expenses of removal, any persons (including families, business concerns and others), who have been displaced as a result of any other Government activities related to the purposes of this act or any activities of the Authority; ((l) amended June 26, 1968, P.L.263, No.125) (m) To insure or provide for the insurance of any property or operations of the Authority against any risks or hazards; (n) To procure or agree to the procural of insurance or guaranties from the State or Federal Government of the payment of any debts or parts thereof incurred by the Authority, and to pay premiums in connection therewith; (o) To borrow from private lenders or from the State or Federal Government funds, as may be necessary, for the operation and work of the Authority; (p) To invest any funds held in reserves or sinking funds or any funds not required for immediate disbursement, in such investments as may be lawful for executors, administrators, guardians, trustees and other fiduciaries under the laws of this Commonwealth; (q) To sue and be sued; (r) To adopt a seal and to alter the same at pleasure; (s) To have perpetual succession; (t) To make and execute contracts and other instruments necessary or convenient to the exercise of the powers of the Authority; and any contract or instrument when signed by the chairman or vice-chairman of the Authority, or by an authorized use of their facsimile signatures, and by the secretary or assistant secretary, or, treasurer or assistant treasurer of the Authority, or by an authorized use of their facsimile signatures, shall be held to have been properly executed for and on its behalf; ((t) amended June 6, 1963, P.L.79, No.54) (u) To make and from time to time to amend and repeal by-laws, rules, regulations and resolutions; (v) To conduct examinations and investigations and to hear testimony and take proof, under oath or affirmation, at public or private hearings, on any matter material for its information; (w) To authorize any member or members of the Authority to conduct hearings and to administer oaths, take affidavits and issue subpoenas; (x) To issue subpoenas requiring the attendance of witnesses and the production of books and papers pertinent to any hearing before the Authority, or before one or more members of the Authority appointed by it to conduct such hearing; (y) To apply to any court having territorial jurisdiction of the offense to have punished for contempt any witness, who refuses to obey a subpoena, or who refuses to be sworn or affirmed, or to testify, or, who is guilty of any contempt after summons to appear; (z) To make available to the government or municipality or any appropriate agency, board or commission, the recommendations of the Authority affecting any area in its field of operation or property therein, which it may deem likely to promote the public health, morals, safety or welfare; ((z) amended Mar. 30, 1988, P.L.304, No.39) (aa) To make, directly or indirectly, secured or unsecured loans to any purchaser or owner of a residential housing or a commercial or an industrial project for the purpose of financing the purchase, construction, rehabilitation, demolition or equipping of a residential housing or a commercial and industrial redevelopment program; ((aa) added Mar. 30, 1988, P.L.304, No.39) (bb) To make loans to or deposits with, at the option of the Authority, without requiring collateral security therefor, any financial institution, in order to enable that financial institution to finance the acquisition, construction, rehabilitation or equipping of a residential housing or a commercial and industrial redevelopment program. For such purposes, an Authority may make such loans as the Authority may determine; receive interest on such deposits as may be agreed to with the financial institution; purchase and hold notes or other obligations secured by mortgages, deeds of trust or security interests in residential housing, commercial or industrial projects or property used as additional security, notwithstanding anything to the contrary elsewhere contained in this act; sell, assign, pledge or encumber any security, including mortgages or other security agreements, held by or granted to the Authority or received in connection with the financing of residential housing or commercial or industrial projects and grant to any trustee, in addition to any other rights or remedies contained therein or in any documents granting such security, such other rights and remedies as may be approved by the Authority. ((bb) added Mar. 30, 1988, P.L.304, No. 39.)

[20] The provision known as the "public purpose requirement" is found in the Pennsylvania Constitution, Article IX § 9. The provision prohibits a municipality from loaning its credit for a private purpose. Article IX § 9 states as follows:

> **The General Assembly shall not authorize any municipality or incorporated district to become a stockholder in any company, association or corporation, or to loan its credit to any corporation, association, institution or individual.**
>
> **The General Assembly may provide standards by which municipalities or school districts may give financial assistance**

> or lease property to public service, industrial or commercial enterprises if it shall find that such assistance or leasing is necessary to the health, safety or welfare of the Commonwealth or any municipality or school district. (Emphasis added.)

This Pennsylvania constitutional requirement means a municipality may not lend its credit to a purely private enterprise, which is exactly what RACL did when it guaranteed $36 million in loans for the construction of the hotel.

The leading case regarding the public purpose requirement is *Belovsky v. Redevelopment Authority of City of Philadelphia*, 357 Pa. 329, 54 A.2d 277 (1947). In *Belovksy*, the Court held that the Urban Redevelopment Law is constitutional, and that Redevelopment Authorities may acquire, develop, and transfer property for the purpose of restoring blighted areas. However, the Supreme Court cautioned that once a Redevelopment Authority has improved a blighted property, the public purpose of redevelopment has been achieved, and the authority should then transfer the property to private, taxable ownership. The Supreme Court emphasized that a Redevelopment Authority should transfer property to a private, taxable interest promptly after the public interest of redevelopment has been achieved:

> [P]laintiff misconceives the nature and extent of the public purpose which is the object of this [Urban Redevelopment Law] legislation. That purpose . . . is not one requiring a continuing ownership of the property as it is in the case of the Housing Authorities Law . . . but is directed solely to the clearance, reconstruction and rehabilitation of the blighted area, and after that is accomplished the public purpose is completely realized.
>
> When, therefore, the need for public ownership has terminated, it is proper that the land be re-transferred to private ownership." *Belovsky*, 357 Pa. at 340, 54 A.2d at 282. (Emphasis added.)

The above legal analysis was developed by Howard Kelin, then special counsel for the county, and a partner with Kegel, Kelin, Almy & Grimm. It was part of the official May 16, 2005, complaint by the county to the two city guaranties worth $36 million. The entire $36 million was to be used to build the for-profit Marriott Hotel, owned by Penn Square Partners.

[21] The monetary value of the formerly historic downtown Lancaster district is incalculable. What is the value of 150-year-old American history? The majestic Watt & Shand department store building, designed by the great C. Emlen Urban, was one of the last buildings in Urban's trademark Beaux Artes design style in the country. High Construction tore it down and built a 19-story hotel in its place. The Watt & Shand was listed on the National Register of Historic Places. After the Lancaster Marriott Hotel was built, it was taken off that list.

Thaddeus Stevens was one the greatest congressman who has served the people of the United States—the moving force behind the Reconstruction amendments, 13th,

Endnotes

14th, 15th, giving African Americans constitutional civil rights in the United States. In the course of building the Lancaster Marriott hotel and convention center project, the former home and business of Thaddeus Stevens, including the Kleiss Saloon around the corner, were almost completely demolished. An "educational and interpretive complex" was supposed to be built where Stevens's house once stood. As of the writing of this book, in 2018, nine years after the project opened, the Stevens "educational and interpretive complex" has not opened. Penn Square Partners is, however, seeking more than $20 million in additional public funds.

[22] After the proposal to have the Harrisburg Area Community College buy the Watt & Shand building was killed in 1997 (thanks to the efforts of people such as these future convention center supporters, former mayor Arthur E. "Art" Morris, and future mayor Charlie Smithgall), the owners of the Bon Ton company, which owned the Watt & Shand, decided to put the building up for auction. Smithgall, who was running for mayor, made local ownership of the Watt & Shand a cornerstone of his campaign. In early 1998, it emerged there were two competing local bids to purchase the Watt & Shand—one from the newly formed Penn Square Partners alliance; the other from Robert L. "Rob" Ecklin, Jr., of the Ecklin Group, a real estate development company that owned several properties, including the city's tallest building, the Greist Building on Penn Square. For reasons not publicly disclosed, Ecklin's identical offer of $1.25 million was rejected by Bon Ton. From "A Big 3 Works to Buy Bon-Ton," *Sunday News*, January 18, 1998:

> The investors [Penn Square Partners] would not reveal the purchase price of the building, but Ecklin said he had offered $1.25 million in cash, which Bon-Ton rejected.
> "It's very important that building turns into a use that's vibrant and exciting. I would be a little discouraged that the building is being purchased without a plan," he said.

[23] Nevin D. Cooley, president of Penn Square Partners, was Dale High's point man and principal spokesman regarding the hotel and convention center project. It was Cooley, first hired by High in 1986, who was most often quoted by Lancaster Newspapers as president of Penn Square Partners. It was also Cooley who attended most of the public meetings and spoke on behalf of the partners. Cooley was the High representative working with Lancaster Newspapers' Jack Buckwalter and his editors in their effort to discredit me. Nevin Cooley was deposed in my libel lawsuit against Lancaster Newspapers, Inc., and several of its staff members, *Molly Henderson vs Lancaster Newspapers, Inc., John M. Buckwalter, Ernest J. Schreiber, Marvin L. Adams, Jr., Helen Colwell Adams, Charles Raymond Shaw, Arthur E. Morris, Gilbert A. Smart, John H. Brubaker, III, and David Pidgeon*. No. 0712003. Cooley was deposed on December 3, 2009.

[24] The Tax Increment Financing (TIF) Act of July 11, 1990, P.L. 465, No. 113, may be found online here:
http://www.bluemtpreservation.org/images/act_113_of_1990.pdf.

[25] The March 16, 1991, *Lancaster New Era* article "Sturla Eyes 'Tax Increment District' Here" did not mention a convention center, but Representative Sturla, a Democrat, in 2005, was one of the most outspoken supporters of the Penn Square Partners' TIF plan. I never understood what Sturla derived from supporting the hotel and convention center project with such enthusiasm.

[26] Each Lancaster County taxing authority—the School District of Lancaster, the city of Lancaster, and the County of Lancaster—receives a different percentage of property taxes. So, 65.25% went to the school district, 25.08% to the city, and 9.69% to the county. Still, all three taxing bodies were required to sign off on Penn Square Partners' TIF plan.

[27] The "participation payments" from Penn Square Partners to the School District and the City of Lancaster were a very nebulous provision. These payments depended on Penn Square Partners earning above 12 percent in profits from hotel operations. The payments would thus require Penn Square Partners to open their books, something they, like most private companies, were loath to do. Therefore, when those profit targets were reached and how much would be paid were essentially up to the private Penn Square Partners to disclose. It was hard to count on that money.

[28] The cost of construction of the private hotel owned by Penn Square Partners in 2006 was $60.3 million, according to the budget provided by Penn Square Partners. The following table does not include the city's subsidy of real estate taxes, which would amount to approximately $14 million over the 20-year term of the lease purchase agreement, or the estimated $1 million in city construction fee waivers the project sponsors received. The amount of public financing for the private hotel at this time was $50,030,000, or 83% of the total hotel cost. Penn Square Partners was paying only 17% to build their "luxury" for-profit hotel and zero percent of the convention center.

A breakdown of the sources of funding for the hotel at this time, 2005, according to Penn Square Partners, is as follows:

Hotel Construction Funding Source	Amount
PSP private equity	$10,000,000
Interest earnings	$1,300,000
RACL Act 23 Bonds/state grants	$12,000,000
RACL Bond debt paid by PSP lease payments	$24,000,000
Other unidentified state grants	$12,950,000
Total hotel construction cost	$60,300,000

The foregoing was derived from the legal complaint the county made to the Department of Community and Economic Development, May 16, 2006. The complaint, written by the county's special counsel, Howard Kelin, of Kegel, Kelin, Almy, & Grimm, raised arguments showing the illegality of the two city guarantees, which totaled $36 million.

[29] On March 7, 2005, one week prior to the school board vote, Nevin Cooley, on behalf of Penn Square Partners, wrote to School Board of Lancaster president Patrice Dixon, urging her to vote for the Partners' TIF plan. In the letter, Cooley referred five separate times to a "feasibility study" that he said showed the economic viability of the project. What we knew, and later corrected, was that no true "feasibility study" was ever performed on the project, only market studies that pointed out as many weaknesses as strengths for the downtown Lancaster market.

[30] Former School Board of Lancaster member Mike Winterstein was interviewed by Christiaan A. Hart Nibbrig.

[31] Rarely has a school board vote on an obscure tax-abatement plan created front-page, above-the-fold headlines. But the Penn Square Partners Tax Increment Financing (TIF) plan, to be voted on by the School District of Lancaster, March 15, 2005, did indeed garner the over-the-top coverage. In the *Lancaster New Era* article of February 16, 2005, "A Crossroads for Convention Center," the school board was cast as the only thing standing between the completed project and an abandoned one. The lengthy sub-headline for the article—"Major Funding for Penn Square Project Hinges on Whether the City School Board, City Council and County Commissioners Can Be Convinced the Proposal Would Yield a Profit and Have a Low Risk of Failure. For Now, the Decision Rests with the School Board"—needed all six columns across the front page. Mark Fitzgerald, the High executive quoted in the article, was, after Cooley, the most visible Penn Square Partners spokesperson.

[32] Ibid. School Board of Lancaster board member Veronica Urdaneta was quoted in "Major Funding for Penn Square Project Hinges on Whether the City School Board, City Council and County Commissioners Can Be Convinced the Proposal Would Yield a Profit and Have a Low Risk of Failure. For Now, the Decision Rests with the School Board," *Lancaster New Era*, February 16, 2005.

[33] The $40-million county-backed LCCCA bond—Ordinance No. 73—was enacted by the Lancaster County Board of Commissioners on Wednesday, October 29, 2003—six days before I was elected commissioner. One section of Ordinance No. 73 was part of the basis for our board's motion rescinding the county bond in 2006. Section 7, Subsection (i), of Ordinance No. 73 states a requirement for bond issuance was "That the Authority has sufficient funds to complete the construction of the Facilities in full accord with the final plans and specifications prepared by the architect for the Facilities, and approved by the Authority, . . ." At the time of our resolution—No. 36 of 2006—"sufficient funds" were not secured "to complete construction" of the hotel and convention center project.

Ordinance No. 73 of 2003 may be found online here:

http://lccca.accountsupport.com/wp-content/uploads/2012/04/Tab29B-County-Debt-Act-Proceedings-County-Ordinance.pdf.

[34] The firm Kegel, Kelin, Almy & Grimm is today known as Kegel, Kelin, Almy & Lord, LLC. The firm, with a decades-long reputation for high-quality legal work, was

involved in our board's successful effort in 2004 to build Clipper Magazine Stadium. The founder of the firm, Clarence C. Kegel, Jr., negotiated the legal work on behalf of the county in that case. Howard L. Kelin, chair of the firm's Litigation Group, worked on convention center–related litigation on behalf of the county.

A brief profile of Mr. Kegel may be found here:

http://www.kkallaw.com/?page_id=42.

A brief profile of Mr. Kelin may be found here:

http://www.kkallaw.com/?page_id=45%3E%3Cspan%20style=.

[35] Shellenberger's comments, often repeated during this time period, are found in "Now, County Wants Answers/ Commissioners Shellenberger and Henderson Have 57 Questions; New Feasibility Study May Hold Some Answers," *Sunday News*, March 13, 2005. Also see Appendix B for a list of the 57 Questions.

[36] Question 2 of the "57 Questions" reads, in part:

> 2. 2003 County Guarantee of Financing. Exhibit 7 of the Project Plan identifies $40 million from the 2003 Hotel Tax Revenue Bonds as part of the LCCCA's contribution toward funding of the Convention Center.
>
> However, according to the Closing Statement from the 2003 bond sale (Tab 1), only $31,649,932 from the $40 million bond sale was placed into the Construction Account generated by the bond sale, with the balance of the bond proceeds going to pay for closing costs and other accounts. Why does Exhibit 7 show that $40 million from the bond sale is available for project funding, if the Closing Statement from the bond sale says that only $31,649,932 is available in the Construction Account?

[37] The question from the county commissioners asking Penn Square Partners about the late-in-the-day timing of the TIF proposal was the first of the "57 Questions." The question read:

Timing of the TIF Application and Supporting Information

> 1. You explained that Interstate Hotels Group is working on updated financial projections for the Convention Center and Hotel. We assume this report will be a component of the "economic feasibility study" required by the TIF Act. Unfortunately, you do not expect to receive Interstate's report until the close of business on Friday, March 11. That means the County Commissioners, City Council and the School Board will receive the report just one business day—Monday, March 14—before you expect the School Board to vote on the proposed TIF at its meeting March 15.
>
> Given the importance of the economic feasibility study to the consideration of this project by the Commissioners, City Council

and the School Board, why is this information from Interstate being provided at such a late date?

The County's "57 Questions" may be found online here: http://www.scribd.com/doc/27797238/Lancaster-County-Project-Questions. Also see Appendix B.

[38] Former Lancaster mayor Arthur E. "Art" Morris was arguably the most vocal opponent of the Harrisburg Area Community College (HACC) proposal to buy and move into the Watt & Shand building. It was Morris, along with soon-to-be-mayor Charlie Smithgall, who appeared at public meetings and spoke most often against HACC moving into the building. Morris objected that HACC would be exempt from paying real estate taxes. Morris had no such objection when the Penn Square Partners' hotel was exempted from paying property taxes. Morris's quote comes from "Ex-Mayor Questions Bon Ton Demolition," *Intelligencer Journal*, November 12, 1996.

[39] Beginning on February 16, 2005, with the *Intelligencer Journal*'s "SDL to Decide Center Fate, School Board Skeptical of Tax Agreement," until the school board vote on March 15, there were dozens of articles, editorials, and columns on the TIF. There were polls and letters, all weighing in on the Penn Square Partners' proposal. The TIF coverage continued for weeks after the vote.

[40] The "People Poll" was a weekly Saturday feature of the *Intelligencer Journal*. The poll "Do you favor a TIF for the hotel-center?" was published March 12, 2005, three days prior to the school board vote. From the poll:

> An overwhelming majority of readers responding to this week's People Poll oppose the creation of a Tax Increment Financing district that would allow Penn Square Partners to borrow $22 million from the state to build the hotel and convention center. Poll results were: 45, or, 6.3 percent of the 711 callers favor the creation of the TIF district, or 93 percent oppose the creation of the TIF, 0.5, or 0.7 percent are unsure. . . .

[41] The Opinion Dynamics-Fox43-TV poll was conducted in October, 2005. Five-hundred Lancaster County adults were contacted by phone and asked eight questions pertaining to the hotel and convention center project. Seventy-nine percent of the respondents were aware of the project, the cost of which was $134 million at the time of the poll. Fifty-five percent (55%) of respondents believed the project was "too risky to spend over one hundred and eleven million dollars of taxpayer money in grants, loans and loan guarantees for the convention center project when there is no certainty it will be a success." Thirty (30%) of respondents felt the "convention center project is a good investment of state and local dollars that will help revitalize downtown Lancaster and stimulate the economy." The Opinion Dynamics poll was underwritten by Robert E. Field, a Lancaster businessman.

[42] Lancaster Newspapers regularly ran positive profiles of High or a Steinman around the time an important and/or controversial matter concerning the hotel-convention

center was being voted on. Other than the *New Era*'s "Taking the High Road," published February 21, 2005, three weeks prior to the school board vote where High had a proposal to be voted on by the board, were, "A Sense of Place for All of Us," a complimentary profile of Carrie Steinman Nunan and her philanthropy; "A Sense of Place," published on September 11, 1999, in the *Intelligencer Journal*, four days before the vote on the room tax; and "The High Road," an obsequious profile of S. Dale High, published in the *Sunday News*, September 26, 1999, a week and a half after the room tax was passed, and right before Senator Armstrong changed the Convention Center Act, a move that neutered the hotel owners' pending lawsuit against the project.

[43] S. Dale High was chairman and chief executive officer of High Industries, as well as general partner of Penn Square Partners, during this period, March 2005, when he disclosed that Penn Square Partners had upped the promised annual payments to the School District of Lancaster from $100,000 annually in lieu of taxes to $150,000. High revealed that this occurred in "Statement of S. Dale High regarding action by School District of Lancaster," *Intelligencer Journal*, March 17, 2005. This statement was published two days after the school district voted down High's Penn Square Partners TIF proposal.

From High's *Intelligencer Journal* "Statement": "Last week we responded when the School District board asked for greater security and more revenue from this project. We modified our proposal to increase our voluntary priority payments from $100,000 to $150,000 per year...."

[44] High's comments at the March 10, 2005, public meeting at Edward Hand Middle School were videotaped and posted on youtube.com by Ron Harper, Jr. They may be found here: https://www.youtube.com/watch?v=fXr1J3tV-xA and here, https://www.youtube.com/watch?v=4Xf0UhcSMtk.

[45] Quoted from the comments of Nevin D. Cooley, Edward Hand Middle School, March 10, 2005.

[46] Ibid. LCCCA executive director David M. Hixson's comments at the Edward Hand Middle School on March 10, 2005, came right after High's and Cooley's. Hixson did not address the TIF proposal directly; instead, he talked about how the project would revitalize the downtown Lancaster economy and provide jobs.

[47] Peter Chiccarine, a top executive with the 300-room Eden Resort hotel, was the principal spokesman for the group of hotel and motel owners who sued Lancaster County for enacting the hotel room rental tax in *Bold Corp vs the City of Lancaster, County of Lancaster, and Lancaster County Convention Center Authority*, 77 Lancaster L. Rev. 171 (Ct. C.P. 2000). Two noteworthy facts about the *Bold Corp* lawsuit are that, first, Senator Gibson E. "Gib" Armstrong amended the Pennsylvania Third-Class County Convention Center Authority Act to undermine the hotel owners' lawsuit, and, second, the case was adjudicated locally by Judge Louis J. Farina. Farina, who ruled against the hotel owners, would later approve a criminal grand jury investigation into a minor county personnel matter.

Endnotes

[48] Both Randolph J. Carney and Robert B. "RB" Campbell were Lancaster city residents with backgrounds that allowed them to understand the complex financing plan that was being proposed. Campbell, the city controller with an accounting degree, was perplexed at how all of the benefits of the project seemed to flow to Penn Square Partners, with the public paying the bill.

[49] The final School Board of Lancaster vote on the Penn Square Partners Tax Increment Financing (TIF) proposal was held at J.P. McCaskey High School on March 15, 2005. Again, as had happened at the Edward Hand Middle School, more than a hundred people attended the McCaskey vote.

[50] Lancaster Newspapers chairman Jack Buckwalter's comments were excerpted from "'We Don't Have a Plan B,' After Losing Dramatic Vote, Supporters Concede: Penn Sq. Project Now Appears to Be Dead," *Lancaster New Era*, March 17, 2005.

[51] See "Statement by S. Dale High," *Intelligencer Journal*, March 17, 2005.

[52] It wasn't only Nevin Cooley, Dale High, and Jack Buckwalter declaring the project "dead" or "killed" after the School Board of Lancaster vote. In the article "'We Don't Have a Plan B,' After Losing Dramatic Vote, Supporters Concede: Penn Sq. Project Now Appears to Be Dead" (*Lancaster New Era*, March 17, 2005), other supporters of the project such as Tom Baldrige, president of the Lancaster Chamber of Commerce & Industry, said he was "not optimistic" the hotel and convention center would be built. "This project has been on the ropes many times before, so it's difficult to even count it out. But I think this is a blow that will be particularly difficult to overcome," Baldridge was quoted as saying. And state senator Gib Armstrong weighed in: "It's ironic that the people that would probably benefit the most—the school district—are the ones to kill it."

[53] During this project's entire history, Lancaster Newspapers has played a critical and central role. Lancaster Newspapers was not only a founding stakeholder (50% today) in Penn Square Partners, the "private" partner of the hotel, but also the monopoly publisher of the main source of local news and information in Lancaster County. The three newspapers, at various times, were used to uncritically promote the project and to discredit critics of it. After the TIF vote, the school board was criticized harshly on the pages of Lancaster Newspapers. At the time in question, after the TIF vote, when the "miracle" plan was found for the project, the "news" was trumpeted—the day after Easter—as a project risen from the dead. The front-page, banner-headlined *Lancaster New Era* article "Hotel Plan Rescued" of March 28, 2005, was part of this over-the-top promotion of the project.

[54] The plan proposed by "Hotel Plan Rescued" was a modification of the plan reported on December 17, 2004, in the *Intelligencer Journal* article "City Takes Key Role in Hotel at Convention Center Project, Partnership Wants to Sell Hotel to Agency."

[55] Despite being virtually identical to the plans of December 2004, the March 28, 2005, "Hotel Plan Rescued" still describes a plan for Penn Square Partners to sell the Watt & Shand building to the Redevelopment Authority of the City of Lancaster

(RACL) as a "new" plan. It wasn't new. Lancaster Newspapers had reported it three months earlier. It has always puzzled me why the partners were so adamant (and dramatic) about the TIF proposal when they already had publicly disclosed plans for RACL to buy the building. High even went through the histrionics of removing his signs from the project after the TIF vote and prior to the miracle "rescue." The "new" plan was also reported by the *Intelligencer Journal*, "City to Buy W&S Building," March 29, 2005.

56 The analysis of the differences between the two December 2004 Penn Square Partners proposals to have the Redevelopment Authority of the City of Lancaster (RACL) purchase the Watt & Shand building was derived from the county's complaint to the Department of Community and Economic Development regarding the City of Lancaster's two guaranties (Nos. 5 and 10, of 2005) for hotel bonds, totaling $36 million. The complaint was prepared by the county's special counsel, Howard L. Kelin, of Kegel Kelin Almy, & Grimm.

57 This analysis of the structure of the Penn Square Partners/RACL financing is derived from the county's complaint to the Department of Community and Economic Development. County special counsel Howard L. Kelin, Esq., argued that the two City of Lancaster guaranties—Ordinances Nos. 5 and 10, of April 2005—were illegal for a number of reasons. The tax exemption issue was central to the county's argument. The county argued that providing tax exemption to Penn Square Partners, using RACL title ownership, violated the "public purpose" requirement of the Redevelopment Authority, according to Pennsylvania Urban Redevelopment Act of 1945. The complicated financing scheme was for the benefit of only one private party—Penn Square Partners. The taxpayers of Lancaster were literally co-signing—and guaranteeing—a loan for Penn Square Partners, a private corporation.

58 Ibid. Analysis regarding the debt service guaranties for the state bond was derived from the county's May 16, 2005 complaint to the Department of Community and Economic Development. What was being proposed was extremely difficult for the average citizen to understand. This is very heady municipal finance. Penn Square Partners wanted RACL to borrow $36 million in construction loans to build a Penn Square Partners hotel. Penn Square Partners would then pay the debt service on those loans. If Penn Square Partners could not make the debt payments, they were asking that the City of Lancaster taxpayers make the payments. They were also explicitly asking that in the event the hotel was deemed taxable, the City of Lancaster would guarantee that real estate tax payments would be made on the hotel. The fine print details of the financial structure were lopsided in favor of Penn Square Partners.

59 This analysis of the financing of the $12 million Act 23 bond is derived from the county's complaint to the Department of Community and Economic Development, May 16, 2005. The $12 million Act 23 bond was even more complicated and difficult to understand than the $24 million construction bonds that RACL would float to local banks. The Act 23 bonds were based on projections of hotel sales and occupancy taxes, which would be rebated by the state. The Act 23 grants would be reviewed after three

years, and the grant amount could be reduced, based on a number of factors. The $12 million Act 23 bond is found in City of Lancaster Ordinance No. 5, April 2005.

[60] As with the $12 million Act 23 City of Lancaster–guaranteed bond, this understanding of the $24 million "Lease Revenue" bonds is based on the county's complaint to the Department of Community and Economic Development, May 16, 2005. The county's brief was prepared by special counsel Howard L. Kelin, Esq., of Kegel, Kelin, Almy, & Grimm.

[61] The $24 million city guaranty is included in City Ordinance No. 10, April 2005.

[62] The details of the Lease Purchase agreement between the Redevelopment of the City of Lancaster (RACL) and Penn Square Partners are found in the "Hotel Tower Lease Agreement" of 2005. In Article XIII, "Lessor Covenants," the "Lessor," RACL, agrees to pay the real estate taxes in the event the hotel is determined to be taxable. From Section 13.1, "Payment of Real Estate Taxes":

> In the event that it is determined that the tax immunity of Lessor does not extend to the Condominium Unit, Lessor [RACL] covenants to pay or cause to be paid when due all real property taxes, ad valorem on real property, or any other real estate tax adopted as a total or partial substitute in lieu thereof payable to any taxing authority without reimbursement of any kind whatsoever from the Lessee [Penn Square Partners.]
> See: Pressedthebook.com, for *Hotel Tower Lease Agreement*, 2005

The section of the Hotel Tower Lease Agreement that addresses the $2.25 million purchase option for Penn Square Partners to buy the hotel "condominium," operated for profit for twenty years but exempt from property taxes, is found in Article XXI, Section 21.1, "Purchase Option."

[63] Clipper Magazine Stadium is a successful "public-private" investment that benefits the general public, not a single private entity. The County of Lancaster's Redevelopment Authority, along with city authorities, was able to redevelop a blighted section of the city of Lancaster and build the beautiful Clipper Magazine Stadium. The naming rights to the stadium and the tenants are Lessees only. After twenty years, the county still owns the stadium, unlike the hotel "condominium," which, after a property tax–free twenty years, transfers title back to the private operators of the hotel for a below-market nominal fee.

[64] Located in the "Northwest Corridor" of the city of Lancaster, Clipper Magazine Stadium is an example of a sensible public-private partnership. The 6,000-capacity baseball stadium, with Major League field dimensions, broke ground in April 2004 and opened in May 2005. This was during my term as commissioner, and it was our board that hired Clarence Kegel, of Kegel, Kelin, Almy & Grimm (now Kegel, Kelin, Almy & Lord) to review the county bond guaranty for the $23 million project. Clipper Magazine Stadium is owned by the Redevelopment Authority of the County of Lancaster. This agency is different from the owner of the downtown hotel, the Redevelopment Authority of the City of Lancaster.

The stadium has been a huge success for Lancaster. The Atlantic League minor league professional baseball team, the Lancaster Barnstormers, plays its home games at the stadium, and the venue hosts other events. The facility is used year-round and is available for ice-skating and private rentals.

[65] Much of the legal work on behalf of the county in the Clipper Magazine Stadium project was done by the law firm of Kegel, Kelin, Almy, & Grimm. In the case of Clipper Stadium, the firm's founder, Clarence C. Kegel, Jr., Esq., handled the legal work.

[66] Howard L. Kelin's legal opinion regarding the "Taxability of the Marriott Hotel," dated April 11, 2005, was submitted to the commissioners at the same time the Lancaster City Council was preparing to vote on Ordinances 5 and 10, the two guaranties totaling $36 million. Kelin details how the city loses a minimum of $14 million during the course of the twenty-year bond in Section "2," "Potential Loss Summary." Kelin notes that the amount of property taxes due on the hotel might be higher if the assessed value of $28.3 million were increased. Penn Square Partners valued the hotel at $28.3 million for each of the twenty years. Kelin's analysis pointed out that the building was currently taxable and could be granted immunity only by being brought before the Lancaster County Assessment Board.

[67] Act 23—coauthored by Senator Gibson E. "Gib" Armstrong in 2004—states unambiguously in §3406 (b) (11) that Penn Square Partners (the "project user") would have to pay real estate taxes. The relevant section of the act reads:

"Require the project user to timely pay all Commonwealth and local taxes and fees."

[68] City Council Ordinance Number 15, March 10, 2005, essentially designated the physical area for the project "The Strategic Economic Development Area" and authorized the Redevelopment Authority of the City of Lancaster (RACL) to take part in the project.

[69] City Council Ordinances Nos. 5 and 10 were the basis of the county's formal complaint to the Department of Community and Economic Development against the City of Lancaster's two guaranties, totaling $36 million. Howard L. Kelin, Esq., the county's special counsel, had shown in the complaint that not only was Penn Square Partners, as the "project user" of the hotel, required to pay real estate taxes pursuant to Act 23, but that there were multiple violations of the "Local Government Unit Debt Act." From the county's complaint, Section IV:

The City's two guaranties submitted to DCED for approval violate multiple legal requirements of the Local Government Unit Debt Act, including the following:

A. Both guaranties are illegal because they violate the requirement in Act 23 that the project user pay all local taxes.

B. Both guaranties are illegal because they violate the Pennsylvania Constitution "public purpose requirement."

Endnotes

C. Both guarantees are illegal because they do not evidence the acquisition of a capital asset by a government agency.

D. Both guarantees are illegal because they do not guarantee debt incurred for a project the City is authorized to own.

E. The guarantees are illegal because the City does not have realistic cost estimates for the project.

F. The guarantees are illegal because the debt statement and borrowing base certificate is not signed by the City Controller as required by Ordinances No. 5 and No. 10.

G. The $24 million guarantee is illegal because it is not a guarantee of RACL's bonds; in reality, it is an agreement to pay real estate taxes owed on the Marriott Hotel.

H. The $24 million guarantee is illegal because it is unlawful for a city to agree to pay real estate taxes owed to another taxing authority by another government agency or private party.

I. The $24 million guarantee is illegal because it is unlawful for a city to agree to waive real estate taxes owed to the City of Lancaster.

See Hotel Tower Lease Agreement, Article XXI, Section 21.1 "Purchase Option."

[70] Former Lancaster city councilman Luis A. Mendoza was a consistent opponent of the hotel and convention center project. The Republican Mendoza also spoke out against the high legal bills being paid to the law firm of Stevens & Lee, the solicitor for the Lancaster County Convention Center Authority (and High Industries' lobbyist). Mendoza was interviewed by Christiaan A. Hart Nibbrig for the Newslanc.com "Convention Center Series."

[71] Robert B. "RB" Campbell, the Lancaster city controller, came into office in 1998, having won election in the same cycle as fellow Republican mayor Charlie Smithgall. Both were elected in November 1997. Campbell, while not an opponent of the project, was not a supporter of it, either. Campbell, a reserved, serious man, did not mesh well with the impulsive, garrulous Smithgall.

[72] Mayor Smithgall did not respond to Controller Campbell's letter of April 22, 2005, which only requested that an independent legal review of the guaranties be performed.

[73] Commissioner Shellenberger's statement of May 2, 2005, was published in the *Intelligencer Journal*, "Shellenberger's Statement on Downtown Project."

[74] On May 4, 2005, Commissioner Shellenberger and I voted on motions to demand that the LCCCA cease all spending on the project and repay the entire $40 million county-backed loan. Shellenberger and I also authorized special counsel to investigate whether the county's guaranty of interest payments could be withdrawn.

[75] The county's May 16, 2005, complaint to the Department of Community and Economic Development was made to Steven Fishman, Esq., Office of Chief Counsel, Department of Community and Economic Development. The complaint, written by special counsel Howard L. Kelin, Esq., was based on Mr. Kelin's legal opinion of April 11, 2005.

[76] From a "file memo," part of the discovery evidence from Lancaster Newspapers chairman Jack Buckwalter's deposition: "BRS [Beverly R. Steinman] called and said that we need more positive letters to the editor." Also, from the discovery is a note from Buckwalter to Nevin Cooley, Penn Square Partners president: "The bottom line is that the newspaper, being Penn Square Partners, cannot be as effective as an organized group writing letters of support for the hotel convention center in sufficient number to balance the letters of opposition, which lead four-to-one."

Chapter Seven: "Molly Is Toast"

[1] Fulton Bank president and CEO Rufus Fulton was not a defendant in the libel suit against Lancaster Newspapers, Jack Buckwalter, and several of Lancaster Newspapers staff members: *Molly Henderson vs Lancaster Newspapers, Inc., John M. Buckwalter, Ernest J. Schreiber, Marvin I. Adams, Jr., Helen Colwell Adams, Charles Raymond Shaw, Arthur E. Morris, Gilbert A. Smart, John H. Brubaker, III, and David Pidgeon.* No. 0712003. Fulton was, however, deposed under oath in the case. Fulton, the largest bank in the county, always held a much smaller stake in Penn Square Partners than High and Lancaster Newspapers, and Rufus Fulton took an almost invisible, symbolic role in the partnership. From the deposition, Fulton describes how the partners decided to buy the Watt & Shand building and his discomfort in the partnership:

> Three men are in a room. They decide to buy a building. And the lead in it is High, and they come up with how this thing should be structured. . . . I paid no attention at all [to Penn Square Partners.] . . . The Fulton part of this, we said this is a temporary investment for us. Banks should not be in the real estate business. They should lend to people who have real estate projects. . . . And we also lent money to this project. And you could easily conceive a conflict of interest between owning a piece of real estate and lending money to it, and so that was another reason to get out of it [Penn Square Partners] as an owner.

Fulton left Penn Square Partners in 2007. At the time of his deposition, Fulton was sitting on several High-affiliated boards, including the Penn Square General Corp, High Hotels, and High Real Estate boards of directors. Deposition conducted July 14, 2009, 126 E. King St. Lancaster, PA, pp. 17-18.

[2] It was a travesty how the home and business and legacy of former congressman Thaddeus Stevens were treated in the development of the hotel-convention center project. As noted in Chapter Two of this book, the Steinman family had great antipathy toward the abolitionist Stevens in the nineteenth century. Andrew Jackson Steinman used the *Intelligencer* newspaper he bought in 1866 to criticize Stevens for his politics and his lifestyle. The home and business of Thaddeus Stevens and his companion, Lydia Hamilton Smith, an African American, occupied a corner where the convention center

would be built. It was national historic home next to the "Kleiss Saloon," another historic landmark. At various times, the sponsors tried leveraging the property to get subsidies for the project, considered demolishing the building, and at one point wanted to physically uproot Stevens's home and office and move it to another location (*Intelligencer Journal*, "Authority Decides to Move Three Historic Buildings," April 12, 2001). The hotel and convention center opened in 2009. The Thaddeus Stevens Museum, as of 2018, has yet to open. No opening has been scheduled.

[3] The terms *luxury* was used often, especially in the early Lancaster Newspaper articles promoting the hotel part of the project. Yet the terms were used misleadingly. According to the American Automobile Association, a "luxury" hotel is actually a "five-star" (five diamond) hotel. A luxury hotel has specific amenities: reception is open 24 hours; the staff is multilingual; doorman-service is 24 hours, as is valet parking; a full-time concierge is on staff; there is a personalized greeting for each guest; fresh flowers are in every room; and food and beverage are offered via room service 24 hours. An example, of many, of how the term *luxury* was thrown around is found in the August 19, 1999, *Lancaster New Era* article "Convention Center, Hotel Proposed at Penn Square $75 Million Plan Turns Ex-Watt & Shand into Luxury Hotel and Shops, with 14-Story Tower." The *New Era* article was published about three weeks prior to the county commissioners' vote to impose the room rental tax on Lancaster County hotels and motels. The article begins:

> The former Watt & Shand building, the crown jewel of Lancaster's revitalization plan, would be turned into a luxury hotel with a landmark 14-story tower rising above it, according to a plan unveiled today. . . .The hotel will also house a four-star restaurant, which will cater to the community, rather than hotel guests, he said. The hotel would likely have bell hops and 24-hour room service. The average cost of the rooms would be between $107 and $130 a night.

In 2017, the room rates for the downtown Marriott ranged between $138 and $254. What was promised was a "luxury" hotel; while very nice, is a tier or two beneath that with a triple diamond rating by AAA.

[4] The lawsuit against Lancaster Newspapers and staff members was *Molly Henderson vs Lancaster Newspapers, Inc., John M. Buckwalter, Ernest J. Schreiber, Marvin I. Adams, Jr., Helen Colwell Adams, Charles Raymond Shaw, Arthur E. Morris, Gilbert A. Smart, John H. Brubaker, III, and David Pidgeon*. No. 0712003. The lawsuit is discussed in Chapter Twelve of this book.

[5] Lancaster Newspapers chairman Jack Buckwalter was deposed on two occasions in connection with the libel lawsuit against him, Lancaster Newspapers, Arthur Morris, and several Lancaster Newspapers staff members. Buckwalter was deposed on Wednesday, February 3, 2010, and Friday, February 12, 2010. Both depositions were held at the law offices of Barley Snyder, the newspapers' counsel, at 126 East King Street, Lancaster. Buckwalter stated at several points in his examination by my attorney George Croner that

Beverly R. "Peggy" Steinman called him and explicitly asked Buckwalter to manufacture positive letters to the editor regarding the hotel and convention center project. This example is from page 250 of Buckwalter's February 3, 2010, deposition testimony. Croner is questioning Buckwalter about one of Buckwalter's "file memos," memos written by Buckwalter or dictated by him to his secretary, Kris Trainer, after a meeting:

Q. You will see in the first paragraph under, with number one, the last sentence of that paragraph says, BRS called. Can you tell me who that is?
A. That is Peggy Steinman.
Q. And you say BRS called and said that we need to send more positive letters to the editor. Do you see that?
A. Yes.
Q. Positive letters about what?
A. About the hotel convention center.

And another from pages 256 and 257 of Buckwalter's February 3, 2010 deposition:
Q. All right. And then you say: Out of the blue, Peggy Steinman called and talked about sending more positive letters to the editor. Right?
A. She did call.
Q. And you understood the letters she was talking about referred to the hotel convention center project; right?
A. Yes.
Q. Because that's the subject of this whole memo, right?
A. Yes.

Buckwalter also said that Peggy Steinman asked specifically that Nevin Cooley be involved in the positive letter-writing campaign. From page 251 of Buckwalter's deposition testimony:

Buckwalter: And what, as I recall, what Peggy was saying, that in addition to maybe a letter to the editor being sent by Nevin Cooley, that he ought to get some other people to send them.

[6] With the exception of the convention center issue, and later Conestoga View, the two daily Lancaster Newspapers, the *Intell* and the *New Era*, did compete with each other. The respective papers went to great lengths to "scoop" the other. In 2007, for example, five *Intelligencer Journal* reporters—Brett Lovelace, P. J. Reilly, Paula Holzman, Carrie Caldwell Cassidy, and Madelyn Pennino—invoked the 5th Amendment to avoid incriminating themselves for illegally accessing the county police emergency services website. The reporters broke the law by logging in to the secure site in order to scoop their *New Era* competitors. The reporters were given the password to the site by the Lancaster County coroner Gary Kirchner. Kirchner was indicted by the Pennsylvania attorney general Tom Corbett. For more on this story, see http://lancasteronline.com/news/pa-charges-coroner-with-breach-of-secret-police-files/article_a933eba8-f5bb-5fcd-8235-87734e13486d.html.

[7] At the time the Marriott hotel was built, the Steinmans had been a presence on W. King Street since the eighteenth century. John Frederick Steinman, Sr., took over

Heyne Hardware in 1785. The family, under John Frederick Steinman, Jr., and his sons George Michael and Andrew Jackson Steinman, gradually bought up most of the remaining properties and developed the block, including Steinman Park, a quiet, lovely oasis in the middle of the block. They currently own thirteen properties within a two-block radius of the project. Source: Lancaster County Tax Assessor's office.

[8] Lancaster Newspapers chairman Jack Buckwalter said that the newspapers were the greatest revenue-generator for the Steinmans. From Buckwalter's deposition, February 3, 2010, page 50:

Q. "All right. Of the companies that are part of Steinman Enterprises, which generates the largest amount of revenue for Steinman Enterprises?"

A. Buckwalter: "Lancaster Newspapers, Inc."

[9] The circulation statistics were taken from Buckwalter's deposition, February 3, 2010, pp. 57–59:

"The *New Era* was about 40,000 . . . The *Intell* would've been around 46,000, 47,000. The trend was that the evening paper was declining and the morning paper was gradually increasing. *Sunday News* was about 95,000, 96,000 . . ."

[10] Ibid. Buckwalter discusses Lancaster Newspapers' financial investment in the hotel portion of the project from pages 77–82 of Buckwalter's deposition, February 3, 2010: "The amount of capital which we put in as our share was $8,225,000. . . ."

[11] It is clear from the depositions of Buckwalter, Ernie Schreiber, Jack Brubaker, and the other defendants that the *New Era*, through Schreiber, was the most active in working with Penn Square Partners to "get tough" on me and Shellenberger using the Lancaster Newspapers. This exchange refers to recruiting former mayor Art Morris to form a group supporting the project and is from Buckwalter's deposition, February 3, 2010, pages 298–299. My attorney George Croner is reviewing a memo written by Buckwalter in 2005:

Q. Okay. In your second sentence in paragraph five you say: It is suggested that we develop an advocacy group to organize support of the project. Suggested by whom?

Buckwalter: I'm not sure whether it was—I don't recall exactly who suggested it, but it ties in with that discussion we had about letters to the editor to counteract the many negative letters that we published again and again. . . .

Q. You then go on to say: It was suggested that people like Terry Kauffman and Art Morris could spearhead something like this, as well as Tom Baldridge.

A. Yes.

[12] Morris's two and a half terms were remembered in the *Lancaster New Era* on December 29, 1989, as Morris was leaving office, "Morris Reflects on Highs, Lows of His Decade as Mayor." Morris and the reporter do not mention any work with the elderly or nursing homes.

In his deposition, on pages 21–22, Morris describes his two and a half terms:

Q. And you just indicated to me that you served for a period of 10 years; is that right?

A. I did.
Q. And could you explain to me how that came about?
A. Well, do you want the short version?
Q. Well, let's start with that.
A. Okay. The mayor resigned to become Adjutant Attorney General of the State of Pennsylvania, Dick Scott. And he—that was shortly into his second term. The city council selected an interim mayor for 10 months and scheduled a special meeting. And I ran for mayor for the last two years of that term—a special election, I should say.
Q. And then ran for two terms on your own?
A. I did.
Q. All right.
A. And I ran on my own initially, too. I mean, it was— actually I ran three terms, but it was a two-year and two full terms.
Q. Were you precluded from running for re-election in 1990, or did you choose not to run?
A. 1989 I decided I would not run again.

Biographical information about Art Morris, a defendant in my lawsuit against Lancaster Newspapers, Inc., Jack Buckwalter, and several staff members of LNP, including Morris, was derived from several sources. In the *New Era* article of December 29, 1989, "Morris Reflects on Highs, Lows of His Decade as Mayor." Morris's early background is mentioned. From the article:

> A British native who moved to Lancaster at age 14, went on to become a track star at McCaskey High School and moved up through the ranks of city government after graduating from Penn State University, Morris said he initially found it difficult to make the transition from city employee to a chief executive speaking to leaders of Armstrong and other large corporate establishments.

Another source was a profile of Morris that appeared on the Penn Manor High School website. At the time, Morris was the cross-country running coach at Penn Manor. The article, "A Passion to Run, a Passion to Serve," also recounts Morris emigrating to the United States from England at the age of fourteen. From the Penn Manor article: "Morris sailed from England to America at the age of 14, and landed at J.P. McCaskey High School, a school that has always had competitive track and field athletes." The Penn Manor article may be found here:

http://www.pennpoints.net/2012/02/13/a-passion-to-run-a-passion-to-serve/

Also, biographical information about Morris, including his middle name, was taken from his deposition in my lawsuit against him: *Molly Henderson, Plaintiff, V. Lancaster Newspapers, Inc., John M. Buckwalter, Ernest J. Schreiber, Marvin I. Adams, Jr., Helen Colwell Adams, Charles Raymond Shaw, Arthur E. Morris, Gilbert A. Smart, John H. Brubaker, Iii, David Pidgeon, Defendants.* No. 0712003. The deposition was held January 28, 2010.

From page 4 of his deposition:

Q. Would you state your full name for the record, spelling your last name, please.
A. Arthur E. Morris, E standing for Elmer, M-O-R-R-I-S.
 And from pages 6–7 of Morris's deposition:
Q. How long have you lived in Lancaster County?
A. Since 1960.
Q. Where did you live prior to coming to Lancaster County?
A. In England.
Q. And what were the circumstances that prompted you to relocate into Lancaster County?
A. My brother-in-law, Elmer Ellsworth Stoe, married my sister in 1945 in England, and he's from Lancaster. So, we have a large family and people emigrated in '51, '53, '57. And we came over in 1960, my brother and I, with my mother.
Q. How old were you when you arrived in the United States?
A. 14.

 Morris is listed on the Pennsylvania I Athletic Association Boys Track and Field Championships for his 4 minute 20.3 second mile in 1963. Please see http://www.rodfrisco.com/wp-content/uploads/2010/08/PIAA-BOYS-TRACK-REX-ALL-TIME1.pdf.

[13] In virtually every profile of Morris, his running background is mentioned. When Morris was the Pennsylvania High School mile champion, 1963, he was a classmate of another future mayor, Charlie Smithgall, who also graduated in 1963. According to the Penn Manor profile from 2012, Morris began running competitively prior to coming to the United States in 1960. On May 6, 1954, six years prior to Morris's emigration, fellow Briton Roger Bannister (now knighted) became the first man to break the four-minute barrier in the mile. Bannister was an enormous hero to England's youth during Morris's childhood.

[14] Morris's college educational background—he received a B.S. in civil engineering from Penn State in 1968; no graduate degrees—and work history are recounted by him in his deposition of January 28, 2010 on pages 13–41.

 Interestingly, at this point in the deposition, my attorney George Croner establishes that Morris, although he criticized the Board of Commissioners for its sale of Conestoga View, knew very little about nursing homes, accounting practices, or appraisals, all areas for which he harshly criticized us. From pages 15–16 of his January 28, 2010, deposition:
Q. Do you, Mr. Morris, hold a degree in accounting?
A. No.
Q. Are you a certified public accountant?
A. No.
Q. Have you taken any part of the certified public accountant examination?
A. No.
Q. Do you know or have any idea whether Generally Accepted Accounting Principles apply the same criteria, for example, for auditing a nursing home, as they do for a hotel?

A. I would not know that.
Q. Or I take it, a hospital?
A. I would not know that.
Q. Or an office building; fair to say?
A. It is fair to say that I would not know the standards of general accounting requirements for each and every one of those.
Q. Have you ever read, GAAP, the Generally Accepted Accounting Principles?
A. I read summaries on it, but many moons ago when it first came out.
Q. Do you have any familiarity with GAAS, Generally Accepted Auditing Standards?
A. No.
Q. So I take it, it's fair to say that you would not know what auditing standards were applied to a nursing home as opposed to any other type of business or facility; fair to say?
A. Well, any auditing standards? That's a little broad maybe. But I would not suggest that I understand auditing standards the way a CPA would understand them.
Q. Do you know whether there's any distinction between the auditing standards used, for example, with a nursing home and oh, say, a hotel?
A. I think I answered that.
Q. I asked you about accounting principles. Now I'm asking about auditing standards.
A. I do not.
Q. Are you, Mr. Morris, a member of the Appraisal Institute?
A. I am not, sir.
Q. Do you hold any sort of qualifications or certifications as an appraiser?
A. Again, not understanding what is all encompassing there, do I have any qualifications as simply to be an appraiser? The answer would be no. Could I assist an appraiser in certain aspects of it? I believe I probably could. If it involves engineering, for instance.
Q. All right. But whether or not any engineering assistance was required to actually perform an appraisal, I take it, is something that you wouldn't know, you would rely on an appraiser to tell you?
A. That's true.

 Then, later in the deposition, on pages 66–67, Morris admits his interest in the elderly and nursing homes is recent and not something he was interested in during his decade as mayor:

Q. During the time that you were mayor of Lancaster City, Mr. Morris, did the city own a nursing home? [Morris did not answer the question.]
Q. While you were the mayor of Lancaster City, was any nursing home operated by employees of Lancaster City?
A. Not that I'm aware of.
Q. Can you tell me, during the time that you served as mayor of Lancaster City, for what part of the operating budget of Conestoga View was the city responsible?
A. We weren't responsible. So, I guess the answer is zero.
Q. So I take it, as mayor, you never had any responsibility for any part of the operating budget at Conestoga View; fair to say?

A. I believe that's true.

Q. Have you, sir, ever held yourself out as having any particular expertise in caring for the elderly?

A. I really have a hard time answering that because I'm not sure I understand. Have I held myself out in, with expertise for caring?

Q. Yes.

A. Meaning, have I offered services to people? In that capacity the answer would be no. But if you're asking me, do I feel that I understand the problems of the elderly, and issues associated with that? Since I cared for my mother for many years, then I would not agree with that.

Q. Do you hold yourself as having, hold yourself out as having any particular expertise in operating a nursing home?

A. No, I don't.

Q. How about a continuing care facility?

A. No, I don't.

Q. Or a senior living facility?

A. No, I don't.

[15] Art Morris's 1986 effort as mayor of Lancaster to explore bringing a convention center to downtown Lancaster was mentioned in one of the many articles promoting the project in the weeks leading up to the room tax vote by the Lancaster County commissioners, September 15, 1999. From "Efforts to Build Civic, Conference Centers Here Date Back to '40s," *Lancaster New Era*, August 26, 1999:

> Discussions of a civic, conference or convention center here date to at least the 1940s, newspaper records show, and some say the efforts go back much further than that. Prior to the current proposal, the most recent discussion took place in the 1980s, when then mayor Arthur E. Morris hired a consultant and appointed a committee to oversee a feasibility study.
>
> In 1988, the consultant recommended that a 100,000-square-foot, $17 million civic center be built along Harrisburg Avenue, across from Franklin & Marshall College.
>
> The study committee decided such a project was feasible but said the city could not build and operate a civic center by itself. The effort stalled when no other help was found.
>
> "Somebody had to step up to the plate and nobody stepped up to the plate," recalled Elaine Ewing Holden, who chaired the panel appointed by Morris.

[16] Morris made his quote "I have a number of concerns, but a significant one is the tax base of this city" in the *Intelligencer Journal*, "Ex-Mayor Questions Bon-Ton Demolition," published on November 12, 1996. This quote, one of many opposing the community college moving into the Watt & Shand building, exposes Morris's support of the hotel-convention center project. In 2005, when Penn Square Partners sold the Watt & Shand

building to the Redevelopment Authority of the City of Lancaster (for a profit of about $6 million), they did so to remove the hotel—privately run by Penn Square Partners—from the property tax rolls. Morris's "significant" concern about "the tax base of this city" evidently did not extend to buildings owned by Dale High and the Steinmans.

[17] Arthur E. Morris was a defendant in my libel lawsuit against Lancaster Newspapers, Inc., and several of its staff members—*Molly Henderson vs Lancaster Newspapers, Inc., John M. Buckwalter, Ernest J. Schreiber, Marvin I. Adams, Jr., Helen Colwell Adams, Charles Raymond Shaw, Arthur E. Morris, Gilbert A. Smart, John H. Brubaker, III, and David Pidgeon.* No. 0712003. Morris was deposed on January 28, 2010.

The meeting on January 5, 1998, the day Charlie Smithgall took office as mayor of the City of Lancaster, is very significant in the history of the hotel-convention center project. It was at this meeting—attended by Dale High, Rufus Fulton, Jack Buckwalter, Smithgall, Art Morris, and a few others of that stature and influence at High's Greenfield complex—that it was decided that High, Lancaster Newspapers, and Fulton Bank would buy the Watt & Shand and develop it. This was the beginning of Penn Square Partners, which was formed in the weeks after this meeting.

Morris is asked about the meeting on pages 106–107 of his deposition:

Q. Do you remember if Mr. Buckwalter was at that meeting?
A. I don't know if he was at that meeting or not. There were a lot people in this room. And it was kind of circular, I think people sitting in it, and there was a pile of people. And there were discussions about what to do with the building. But precisely, other than that, I don't have a real good recollection of the meeting. The only reason I really remember it is because I bumped into the new mayor, the new mayor on his first day of office, and I bumped into him.
Q. And how did it come to be that you were at that meeting?
A. I have no idea.

Jack Buckwalter, incidentally, remembered seeing Morris at that meeting, and so testified:
Q. Do you remember whether Arthur Morris was at that meeting?
Buckwalter. I think he was.

So, Morris's presence at that meeting is fundamental to understanding his position on the project: he was, quite literally, a day-one supporter of Penn Square Partners. And he never deviated from that support: from the tax to the bond to the TIF to any aspect on behalf of Penn Square Partners, Art Morris was a high-profile public supporter.

[18] From page 85 of Morris's deposition regarding any editing that was done to his columns:

> Q. Do you recall ever submitting columns for publication that were reduced from what you had submitted?
> A. Only usually grammatically, or to cut out superfluous words. If I submit something for 725 words and they really need to get down to 700, they may take a few words out here and there, but

superfluous. I mean, I asked them never, ever to cut anything out that changed the content without talking to me. And I don't remember them ever talking to me about that.

Q. So I take it that there was never an occasion where you wrote on a topic that they refused to publish?

A. I don't recall—again, we're talking about this situation, not letters to the editor. Correct?

Q. Yes.

A. I don't recall them ever refusing to publish my articles.

[19] Buckwalter's personal copy editing of Dennis Cox's "letter" shows that the line between the publishing and editorial sides of the newspaper did not apply when it came to attacking the county commissioners. From page 275 of Buckwalter's deposition:

Q. Okay. You will see on your calendar for 2005 there is an editorial meeting listed, I don't know whether that was noon or 12:30, on the 4th of October?

A. It's always 12:30.

Q. 12:30?

A. Um-hum.

Q. And in these notes, paragraph two is the one that's left. And it says: "Discussed the need for rewording the part of the Dennis Cox, quote, letter to the editor, close quote, about the proposed convention center that cited his belief that the county commissioners had, quote, lied, close quote. That allegation was too broad. Should have been narrowed to the subject at hand.

[20] Pete Shaub, who burned many bridges he crossed, managed to stay in the good graces of Jack Buckwalter for Shaub's almost two terms as a Lancaster County commissioner.

Here, from Buckwalter's February, 3, 2010, deposition, pages 170–171, Buckwalter speaks about Shaub's office visits:

Q. All right. Did you ever discuss, Mr. Buckwalter, the hotel and convention center project with Pete Shaub?

A. Yes.

Q. On how many occasions?

A. I don't recall the number.

Q. More than one?

A. Yes.

Q. Less than 10?

A. Yes.

Q. All right. And tell me what you remember about having your discussions with Mr. Shaub about the project.

A. He would have his secretary call and ask if it was okay if he would stop in. Other times it would be maybe a telephone call. But most of the time, I recall he stopped in my office and I agreed to talk to him.

Q. Can you tell me, Mr. Buckwalter, from a time standpoint, did this occur during Mr. Shaub's first term as a commissioner from 1999 to 2003? Or during the second term?

MS. GINENSKY: Or both?
BY MR. CRONER:
Q. And if it's both, I mean, yeah, if you can just clarify for me.
A. It could be both. Because I remember his first term, I discussed with him at one point about the fact that Lancaster Alliance would hopefully get the support of the commissioners on our efforts to reduce crime. And he seemed very interested in that.
Q. Who wouldn't want to stop crime?
A. That's right.
Q. There you go. So, Mr.—and I take it that Mr. Shaub always initiated these meetings?
A. Yes. Yes.

... and from page 176, Buckwalter characterizes Shaub's position on the hotel-convention center:
Q. Did you view Shaub as a supporter of the project?
A. Yes.

[21] Also, from the March 23, 2005, *Intelligencer Journal* article "Shaub Attacks Henderson Over Center/Accuses Her of Sabotage," Shaub shot another broadside. "I am appalled that you continually have been against this project ever since this topic has come up, Commissioner Henderson," Shaub said. "Every time there's progress by the community, you continue to throw up roadblocks."

[22] The March 23 coverage from both the *Intell* (above) and the *Lancaster New Era*, "Henderson, Shaub Spar; Big Crowd Backs Hotel. Supporters jam meeting to endorse Penn Square project while commissioners continue to bicker," was not random. Shaub's attacks were aimed at me, by name. The attacks coincided with the "Get tough" strategy that Buckwalter, Cooley, and Schreiber were now executing. And, of course, as shown above, Shaub was on good terms and met many times with Lancaster Newspapers chairman Jack Buckwalter. Shaub's drama was staged, planned, in other words. Finally, the verb *bicker* suggests more than one person was involved. I never engaged with Shaub.

[23] In the March 30 *Intelligencer Journal* article "Project Divides Officials, Penn Square Proposal Roils Commissioners," the subject of the article was Commissioner Shaub's objections to Commissioner Shellenberger and me retaining Howard L. Kelin, Esq., to represent the county in actions we were now taking against the project. Shaub is quoted in the article as saying: "Sounds to me like this board is continually asking Mr. Kelin to work on things that are obstructionist toward construction. Why are you continuing to push this to undermine city revitalization?" I was also quoted in the article. "It's very quixotic," Henderson said about project's financing. "It changes almost daily. That being the case, the county needs to be informed and have counsel on this. These are very complex issues. We need to have clarification. It is important—because we are a major player in this process—that we have a seat at the table, and that we speak for our constituency."

[24] The *Sunday News*'s "Good Golly, Molly" article appeared on April 3, 2005, in the Perspective section of the newspaper. This is a very high-profile spot in the

paper, and the article was enormous, more than 1,400 words. There was absolutely no substance to the article, no sense at all that I was "roiling" the Democratic Party by my position on the convention center. Die-hard Republican project supporters—Gib Armstrong, Charlie Smithgall, Paul Thibault, and Thibault's former campaign manager, Jess Yescalis—were quoted. Yescalis said, "Right now there is a huge sense of disappointment. People thought Molly would be leading the charge for this kind of project." The only ones with a "huge sense of disappointment" were his former boss and his patrons. The public was never behind the project. It was another hit job, and its significance was that they were coming very frequently at this point.

[25] Shaub's quote "Molly is toast," which Buckwalter noted and was produced as evidence in the discovery phase of my lawsuit against Buckwalter and Lancaster Newspapers, was discussed at several points of Buckwalter's deposition, in addition to page 285.

From page 175:

Buckwalter: He [Shaub] did mention the one time about Molly.
Q. What did he mention about Commissioner Henderson?
A. He said, and this was at the end of a conversation. Out of the blue. That "Molly is toast." And I, you know.
Q. And were you alone when he said that, just you and Mr. Shaub?
A. Yes.
Q. In your office?
A. Yes.
Q. Do you remember making a written record of your meeting?
A. Yes, I always do.

From page 184:

Q. Okay. When he [Shaub] made the comment: Molly is toast, could you describe the context? What were you talking about?
A. We were talking about, maybe his legacy or something. And at the end of the meeting he said, "Molly is toast." And I thought, where did that come from?
Q. Sort of the last thing he said before he . . .
A. Yeah. At the end of the conversation. He might have said good-bye, you know. But I mean, that was the, that was the tail end of the meeting.
Q. All right. So, for example, you said that was the tail end of the meeting. Now if I said to you, "Molly is toast," that's how it came up? Literally that spontaneously?
A. (Pause.)
Q. Did it seem germane to you; to what you'd been talking about?
A. No.
Q. Did you ask him, what do you mean?
A. No.

[26] The project was the "brainchild" of many. Included was the law firm of Stevens & Lee. The firm, High's lobbyist, solicitor for the LCCCA and Lancaster County,

wrote the legislation—the 1999 Third-Class County Convention Center Authority Ac—that allowed High, Buckwalter, and Fulton, through politicians they supported, to have the taxpayers of Pennsylvania and Lancaster pay for and guarantee the construction of their private hotel.

[27] The editorial, so malicious. really signaled a level of seriousness on the part of Lancaster Newspapers and Penn Square Partners. The editorial pages of the Steinmans' newspapers were considered sacrosanct by Lancaster Newspapers' readers. This was the voice of the Steinmans and had been for generations of Lancastrians. Even the title suggested a level of personal anger toward Shellenberger and me, "County Plan to Kill City Project Will Fail."

"Kill"? As commissioners, we were acting as the representatives of the voters, and we owed it to them to ask our questions. For having the temerity to ask questions, we were called "enemies of the city." From pages 248–249 of Buckwalter's February 3, 2010, deposition, Buckwalter is asked about the April 12, 2005, *New Era* editorial:

Q. Okay. Did anyone discuss with you, Mr. Buckwalter, before this particular piece was published on April 12th, 2005, that the newspaper was going to call Commissioners Shellenberger and Henderson enemies of the city?
A. No, I didn't.
Q. Do you remember reading that, the last paragraph on the second page?
A. I'm reminded of it. I mean, I'm reminded of it, that I read it.

Q. Okay. And when you read it, or even, frankly as you sit here today, Mr. Buckwalter, do you have a personal recollection of any other occasion when you can recall an article in the Lancaster—any Lancaster Newspapers, Inc., newspaper labeling anyone an enemy of anything?
THE WITNESS: I have no recollection.

[28] Shellenberger's and my statement was published in the *Sunday News*, April 17, 2005. It was troublesome that our basic questions about the project and the recent deal Penn Square Partners and RACL would go unanswered. From our statement:

> In particular, we are very concerned at the proposal that Penn Square Partners receive an immediate $6.8 million that includes reimbursement of all its development costs, and that demolition of the Watt & Shand building may begin in June, six months in advance of receipt of construction bids (which are not expected until late 2005 at the earliest). We believe both those actions would be grievously premature. Building demolition and complete reimbursement to Penn Square Partners should not proceed absent confirmation that funding is available to pay for the actual (not estimated) construction costs.

See http://www.nytimes.com/1862/08/24/news/letter-president-lincoln-reply-horace-greeley-slavery-union-restoration-union.html.

The letter from President Abraham Lincoln to publisher Horace Greeley was written on August 22, 1862.

[29] During Buckwalter's deposition, the exchange around his April 19, 2005, memo was extraordinary. In Buckwalter's own words, the memo describes the involvement of Peggy Steinman, Nevin Cooley, Buckwalter, and *New Era* editor Ernie Schreiber in a coordinated plan to support the project—and attack Shellenberger and me—using the pages of Lancaster Newspapers, Inc.

The following exchange comes from Buckwalter's February 3, 2010, deposition, pages 249–252. Kris Trainer is Buckwalter's longtime secretary ("She can type as fast as I can talk," Buckwalter said in his testimony):

Q. Now let me show you what we marked earlier in the deposition as Exhibit Number 3. And you can keep it there with Exhibit Number 2. Do you recognize Deposition Exhibit Number 3 as another file memo that was typed by Kris Trainer from dictation of your recollection of events that you provided to her?
A. Buckwalter. Yes.
Q. And I take it that would have been on April 19th, 2005; fair to say?
A. Yes.
Q. And the subject here is hotel convention center. Do you see that?
A. Yes.
Q. And you say that you talked to Nevin Cooley today. Do you see that?
A. Yes.

Q. You will see in the first paragraph under, with number one, the last sentence of that paragraph says, BRS called.
Q. Can you tell me who that is?
A. That is Peggy Steinman.
Q. And you say BRS called and said that we need to send more positive letters to the editor. Do you see that?
A. Yes.
Q. Positive letters about what?
A. About the hotel convention center. Because we were getting so many letters to the editor which we published. And this was a suggestion, which I didn't follow.
Q. Okay. And when you wrote here: Called and said that we need to send. Did you have an understanding of what we, she meant? Was that Penn Square Partners or Lancaster Newspapers, Inc. or both?
A. It could refer to we at Lancaster Newspapers, or we meaning, Penn Square Partners.
Q. It could be either one?
A. Yes. But most likely it would have been that, since the [sic] Nevin Cooley is in charge of this, that it would—I would guess it would more likely mean that, as this is being worked on—and that it would be appropriate to somehow balance out the letters, more positive letters to the editor, because Ernie Schreiber was asked for suggestions on how to communicate it. And he said that he felt that the best way is to, is for a letter to the editor. And what, as I recall what Peggy was saying, that in addition to maybe a letter to the editor being sent by Nevin Cooley, that he ought to get some other people to send them.

Q. Ernie Schreiber said that?
A. He felt that—he, in fact, it says here, he said that he felt that a letter to the editor would be the right avenue to do, to communicate this information because of the misinformation that was being sent around. And that, and then Peggy, out of the blue, called and said we need to send more positive letters to the editor. And that just followed through. And the best way to communicate it is a letter to the editor. And so, she said we ought to get more positive letters because so many negative letters were sent out.
Q. Why did you bring Ernie Schreiber into the loop in a hotel and convention center matter?
A. Because he's an editor. And this is talking about *Sunday News*. But generally speaking, under these circumstances, what's the best way to communicate it? And Ernie Schreiber said he felt the best way would be, the right avenue would be a letter to the editor. . . .

[30] The "get tough" and "Shellenberger Strategy," discussed by Buckwalter from pages 258–264 of his February 3, 2010, deposition, again shows the complicity of Penn Square Partners and Lancaster Newspapers in an operation to impugn Shellenberger and me. This was done because of our efforts to stop the hotel-convention center project. It is important to note that this campaign by Penn Square Partners and Lancaster Newspapers and its editors got underway in early 2005 and was maintained until I left office. What was striking to me in reading these depositions was the level of coordinated planning, the back and forth, that went into the newspaper campaign to discredit "the commissioners," i.e., Shellenberger and me. Buckwalter in one afternoon is shown to be consulting with both Penn Square Partners president Nevin Cooley and *Lancaster New Era* editor Ernie Schreiber.

The "file memo" from Buckwalter, discussed below, is dated June 8, 2005.

Q. In the first line of this particular file memo, Mr. Buckwalter, it says: "It is apparent"—I take it that means to you; correct?
A. Yes.
Q. That "we"—is the we, Penn Square Partners?
A. Yes.
Q. "Are not coming out on top with this Shellenberger strategy." Did you come up with the term describing that as the Shellenberger strategy?
A. I don't recall that I came up with it.
Q. Okay. But you use it here in your memo; right?
A. Yes.
Q. Do you remember whether you discussed the Shellenberger strategy with anyone at Penn Square Partners?
A. I don't recall. I probably did, yes. I would say, yes.
Q. Item number three says: Our public relations position was not enhanced by our, quote, get tough, close quote, policy. Do you see that?
A. Yes.
Q. And I take it when you dictated this to Kris Trainer, you told her to put, get tough, in quotes; correct?

A. Um-hum.

Q. Tell me about that. What is the get-tough policy that you are referring to here?

A. I would think that it was Nevin Cooley, and some of these exhibits that you showed me, that they were, that they were seemingly tough. And I don't have, I mean, I have all these ones, I'm not sure which one. But the—obviously what Nevin Cooley was communicating, I deemed it to be a tough approach.

Q. And do you remember whether you told Nevin Cooley you thought his approach was a get-tough policy?

A. I don't recall.

Q. Do you remember whether you discussed that with Peggy Steinman?

A. I don't recall.

Q. How about with any of the editors in any of the newspapers?

A. I don't recall.

Q. In the fifth, item number five, you say: Where is Molly Henderson in this total situation? Question mark. She is rarely mentioned. Do you see that?

A. Yes.

Q. And obviously, you dictated this to Kris Trainer; is that right?

A. Yes.

Q. And then underneath that there's a handwritten entry. Do you see that?

A. Yes.

Q. Can you read that for me?

A. Yes. She wants to kill project and move to North Queen, second block.

Q. Is that your handwriting?

A. Yes.

Q. Can you tell me why that didn't end up as part of the typewritten memo?

A. I thought of it afterwards.

Q. You thought of it afterwards?

A. Yes.

Q. Okay. So, you write, 6/8/05, again, the same date as the date of the memo, EJS—is that Ernie Schreiber?

A. Yes.

Q. To talk to Nevin Cooley?

A. Yes.

Q. Do you see that?

A. Yes.

Q. How did you know that Ernie Schreiber was to talk to Nevin Cooley?

A. I don't recall.

Q. Did you ask him to?

A. I don't recall.

Q. You don't know whether he told you or you asked him?

A. I don't recall.

   (From p. 265)

Q. Okay. And then underneath that you write, EJS will do study on taxes and the—what is the last word there?
A. Project.
Q. Project?
A. Yes.
Q. Meaning the hotel and convention center project?
A. Yes.

(From page 266, but regarding same memo)

Q. By the way, on this Exhibit 3—I'm sorry, I will just give you my copy, no secrets here—this little handwriting here on Exhibit 3, Mr. Buckwalter.
A. Yes.
Q. Can you tell me whose handwriting that is?
A. It looks like mine, but it's so small.
Q. And what does it say?
A. Nevin will release at right time.

[31] Buckwalter deposition, February 3, 2010, pp. 260–261:

Q. In the fifth item, number five, you say: Where is Molly Henderson in this total situation? Question mark. She is rarely mentioned. Do you see that?
A. Yes.
Q. And obviously, you dictated this to Kris Trainer; is that right?
A. Yes.
Q. And then underneath that there's a handwritten entry. Do you see that?
A. Yes.
Q. Can you read that for me?
A. Yes. She wants to kill project and move to North Queen, second block.
Q. Is that your handwriting?
A. Yes.

[32] I don't recall having any issues with Nevin Cooley during the few years we both worked at Lancaster General Hospital in the early 1980s. Cooley was an administrator there from 1981 to 1986. His grudge against me was most likely based on my position regarding the project. However, the problem came about, by early 2005, Nevin Cooley, according to Jack Buckwalter, regarded me as a foe and wanted Lancaster Newspapers to "go after" me. From Buckwalter's deposition, February 3, 2010: "Nevin wanted to go after the commissioners, particularly Molly Henderson."

[33] From Buckwalter's February 3, 2010, deposition testimony, page 264:

Q. And then you write: To negotiate with Shellenberger gives him credibility. Do you see that?
A. Yes.

Endnotes

[34] The communication between Penn Square Partners and Lancaster Newspapers' editors was particularly intensive in the weeks before and after the March 15, 2005, school board vote on PSP's TIF proposal. In addition to Cooley's multiple briefings to editors during this time, between April 19, 2005, and June 8, 2005, Buckwalter himself had at least five scheduled meetings with Lancaster Newspapers' editors to discuss the hotel-convention center project. See page 257 of Buckwalter's February 3, 2010, deposition.

[35] Don Elliott was ineffective as the county's chief administrative officer. On his application to the county, dated February 19, 2004, Elliott used Nevin D. Cooley, of "High Real Estate," as a reference, and characterized Cooley as a "colleague." The Elliott job application may be found at: pressedthebook.com under "Official Lancaster County Convention Center and Marriott Hotel Documents". This website has collected a valuable archive of hotel and convention center–related documents.

[36] Elliot used Nevin Cooley, of High Industries, as a reference on his application for the county administrator position.

[37] The 4,000-word *Sunday News* "Statement by Penn Square Partners," on May 22, 2005, is another example of how the line between Lancaster Newspapers as a business and Lancaster Newspapers as a journalistic enterprise evaporated. This was a case of Buckwalter—wearing the hats of both Penn Square Partner and Lancaster Newspapers' publisher—prioritizing and protecting his private investment over the quality of newspapers he was publishing.

[38] Ibid. "Statement by Penn Square Partners," *Sunday News*, May 22, 2005.

[39] On page 203 of Buckwalter's February 3, 2010, deposition testimony, Buckwalter was asked by my attorney George W. Croner about his meetings as chairman of Lancaster Newspapers with the editors at Lancaster Newspapers. Again, the line between the business/publishing side and the editorial side is blurred at Lancaster Newspapers under Buckwalter. From the deposition: "[T]here were times when we might have said that the front-page has too much of, like a picture of a duck. And I comment [to the editors] on the fact that that's very valuable real estate, so to speak."

[40] The deposition testimony Lancaster Newspapers chairman Jack Buckwalter, made under oath, continues to show the coordinated plan to use the pages of Lancaster Newspapers to attack me and Commissioner Shellenberger. Along with the "get tough" approach, Buckwalter, Cooley, and *New Era* editor Ernie Schreiber tried publicly questioning Shellenberger and me on our opposition to the project. From pages 269–270 of Buckwalter's deposition:

Q. And can you tell me why you were talking to Ernie Schreiber about a kicking-off point story for S & H [Shellenberger & Henderson] to explain exactly why they oppose?
A. I don't recall.
Q. And when you talk about why they oppose, you are referring to the hotel and convention center project; correct?
A. Yes.

Q. And to Shellenberger and Henderson's opposition to that project?
A. I have the word *commissioners* there.
Q. Yes. And you are referring to their opposition to the hotel and convention center project; aren't you?
A. Yes.
Q. And Commissioners Shellenberger and Henderson's opposition to the project was a problem for the project; wasn't it, Mr. Buckwalter?
A. Explain problem.
Q. Well, it was posing a problem in terms of moving the project forward towards completion; was it not?
A. Yes.

[41] Dave Hennigan had been the *Sunday News* editor for twenty-one years before retiring in October 2005. Hennigan's "Coffee with Clyde" column first made the Conestoga View sale a public issue. Hennigan died in July 2015 at the age of seventy-five.

[42] The newspaper coverage in the weeks prior to the September 15, 1999, vote on the hotel room tax was beyond over the top. The *Lancaster New Era* front-page "Penn Square Complex Is Hailed as 'Everything the City Needs,' Strong Praise from Crowd of Nearly 300," August 26, 1999, was one of dozens of "articles" about the proposed project. The pro-project tone of the article is set in the first paragraph:

> In a display that united old foes and bridged city-county and Republican-Democrat differences, county leaders have embraced plans for a $75 million downtown hotel and convention center with almost religious zeal. . . .

Lancaster New Era editor Ernest J. Schreiber was a defendant in the libel lawsuit I brought against Lancaster Newspapers, *Molly Henderson vs Lancaster Newspapers, Inc., John M. Buckwalter, Ernest J. Schreiber, Marvin I. Adams, Jr., Helen Colwell Adams, Charles Raymond Shaw, Arthur E. Morris, Gilbert A. Smart, John H. Brubaker, III, and David Pidgeon.* No. 0712003. Schreiber was deposed under oath on December 9, 2009, at 126 E. King Street, at the offices of Barley Snyder, Lancaster Newspapers' counsel. The biographical and professional/career information was stated by Schreiber under questioning from my attorney George Croner. See pages 10–13 of Schreiber's deposition. Other biographical/professional background on Schreiber was taken from his retirement announcement article in June 2011. See:

http://lancasteronline.com/news/ernest-schreiber-retiring-as-new-era-editor/article_02db82ce-eb22-5cdc-a6a6-67f9decd4759.html.

[43] Schreiber deposition, December 9, 2009, page 31.

[44] From page 35 of Schreiber's deposition, editor Schreiber describes a conversation with Lancaster Newspapers, Inc., chairman Jack Buckwalter about the conflict of interest in having the newspaper report on a project in which it had a private investment:

"I don't have a specific recollection of the time or place. But I do believe that there were, there was a time where [*Intelligencer Journal* editor] Ray Shaw and I were with Jack Buckwalter and Ray said something like, this certainly is, you know, this is something that I feared all along, that there would be this perception of a conflict of interest when we got involved in this."

[45] Ibid. Schreiber deposition, page 36:

Schreiber: I will say that I and my news editors recognized that there would be a perception of a conflict of interest in our company investing in a civic project.
Q. And you recognized that right from the start?
A. Yes.
Q. And did you talk to your editors about it right from the start?
A. Yes.

[46] Schreiber's comment that he told Jack Buckwalter that he was speaking with Nevin Cooley occurs on page 180 of Schreiber's December 9, 2009, deposition. Schreiber acknowledges the Cooley contact as my attorney George Croner questions him about a Buckwalter file memo from June 8, 2005.

Q. Okay. Do you remember being told by anyone, on or about June 8, 2005, to talk to Nevin Cooley?
A. I may have told Jack that I was talking to Nevin Cooley, or that our reporter was talking to Nevin Cooley.

[47] Jack Buckwalter's habit of memorializing every meeting with a written memo was valuable in showing the union between Penn Square Partners and the editors and reporters of Lancaster Newspapers, in this case *New Era* editor Ernie Schreiber. From Buckwalter's deposition of February 3, 2010, beginning on page 229, my attorney George W. Croner questions Buckwalter about the memos from the year 2005 noted in the chapter. This time period was around the controversial School Board of Lancaster vote on Penn Square Partners Tax Increment Financing (TIF) plan on March 15, 2005. The school board rejected the partners' plan. It was the TIF issue, and its aftermath, that produced this series of memos. Buckwalter's memos revealed that even prior to the TIF vote, Buckwalter, Cooley, and Schreiber were coordinating among themselves with a public relations strategy, using Lancaster Newspapers to help their project and discredit Shellenberger and me:

> "EJS to talk to Nevin Cooley. (April 15), "EJS will do study on taxes and the project (May 01), deposition page 265; "EJS is to talk to Nevin Cooley. (June 08), deposition page 262"; "EJS talked to Nevin Cooley. (July 15), "EJS indicated that he would run an editorial on the amount of county risk (July 20), "Spoke to EJS . . . Nevin is to write a letter to Shellenberger. (August 08), deposition page 263."

[48] If a newspaper's sections were looked at like real estate, Shaw worked only the high-end neighborhood: the front page. From his October 29, 2009, deposition, page 25, Shaw describes his primary function with the *Intelligencer Journal*: "On most days I was responsible for choosing the stories that would appear on page one and laying out the look or the design of page one."

⁴⁹ *Intelligencer Journal* editor, Ray Shaw's discomfort and lack of information about the project and its private ownership structure were displayed during an exchange during his October 29, 2009, deposition. On pages 31–32 of his deposition, Shaw, after stating that Lancaster Newspapers chairman Jack Buckwalter was unhappy with Shellenberger and me for our positions on the hotel and convention center project, answers questions from my attorney George Croner about Penn Square Partners:

Q. And tell me about any other occasion where Mr. Buckwalter voiced views on the project aside from what you just described for me.
A. Well, at the very initiation of it when he told me that Lancaster Newspapers was going to become part of the project.
Q. At the very beginning?
A. At the very beginning.
Q. Before Penn Square Partners was formed?
A. I don't know when Penn Square Partners was formed.
Q. All right. Well, let's put it this way. At the time Mr. Buckwalter told you that Lancaster Newspapers was going to participate in—and what did he tell you they were going to participate in?
A. In the hotel part of the convention center project.
Q. And when he told you that, and I take it that you don't remember when that was?
A. No.
Q. You don't know whether, whether Penn Square Partners had been formed or not?
A. I don't know.

⁵⁰ Ibid. Ray Shaw deposition, October 29, 2009, pages 29, 30.

⁵¹ Marvin Adams's promotion from news editor to editor of the *Sunday News* was announced on October 29, 2005 in the *Sunday News*.

See http://lancasteronline.com/news/adams-is-sunday-news-editor/article_46fa65b3-2c70-50fb-b366-baafe7affd49.html.

Adams retired as "print editor" of the combined *Intelligencer Journal/Lancaster New Era*" in April 2013.

⁵² Former *Sunday News* editor Marv Adams was a defendant in the libel lawsuit I brought against Lancaster Newspapers, Inc., and several of its employees, *Molly Henderson vs Lancaster Newspapers, Inc., John M. Buckwalter, Ernest J. Schreiber, Marvin I. Adams, Jr., Helen Colwell Adams, Charles Raymond Shaw, Arthur E. Morris, Gilbert A. Smart, John H. Brubaker, III, and David Pidgeon.* No. 0712003. Adams was deposed on the same day as *Intelligencer Journal* editor Ray Shaw, October 29, 2009. Both were deposed separately at the offices of Barley Snyder, counsel for Lancaster Newspapers, Inc. The educational and professional background information was derived from Adams's deposition testimony, pages 8–22.

⁵³ From the deposition testimony of Marvin I. Adams, October 29, 2009, page 11.

Q. And as the editor of the *Sunday News* what are your responsibilities?

A. My responsibility is getting out the Sunday paper every Sunday. I write. I edit. I supervise.

And from page 24 of Adams's deposition:

Q. Okay. Looking at the time frame from 2005 to 2007, can you tell me who decides what appears as content in the *Sunday News*?
A. I do.
Q. And who decides what appears on the front page?
A. I do.
Q. Who decides what the headline will be on the front page?
A. In most cases, I do.
Q. Who decides who gets printed on the editorial?
A. I do.
Q. Who decides what columnist gets published on any particular Sunday?
A. I do.

[54] The circulation statistics were derived from the deposition testimony of Lancaster Newspapers chairman John M. Buckwalter, February 3, 2010, pp. 57–59: "The *New Era* was about 40,000 . . . The *Intell* would've been around 46,000, 47,000. The trend was that the evening paper was declining and the morning paper was gradually increasing. *Sunday News* was about 95,000, 96,000 . . ."

[55] From page 29 of the deposition testimony of Marvin I. Adams, October 29, 2009:

Q. Did you ever discuss with anyone at Lancaster Newspapers, Inc. whether Lancaster Newspapers, Inc.'s participation in Penn Square Partners posed a conflict of interest with respect to the newspapers' reporting on the project?
A. Yes, I did.
Q. And with whom did you have that discussion?
A. Many people.
Q. Can you tell me any of them?
A. I've had that discussion with Jack Buckwalter. I've had it informally with people on my staff.
Q. Well, when you say informally with people on your staff, is that as opposed to some sort of formal discussion with Mr. Buckwalter?
A. Well, the discussion with Mr. Buckwalter was not what I would call a formal discussion.
Q. Okay. Tell me about that one. Was it more than one conversation?
A. I think I made it clear over a period of time that I was uncomfortable with the fact that the company was involved in a project like this. Not because I thought that I had a conflict of interest in our reporting, but because of the perception. Perception is not fact, but perception is what it is.

[56] Helen Colwell Adams of the *Sunday News* was one of the ten defendants sued for libel by me, in *Molly Henderson vs Lancaster Newspapers, Inc., John M. Buckwalter, Ernest J. Schreiber, Marvin I. Adams, Jr., Helen Colwell Adams, Charles Raymond Shaw, Arthur E. Morris, Gilbert A. Smart, John H. Brubaker, III, and David Pidgeon*. No. 0712003. Ms. Colwell Adams was deposed on October 5, 2009.

Chapter Eight: Conestoga View

[1] It was the TIF (tax increment financing) plan, introduced by Penn Square Partners in early 2005, that ignited public opposition to the project (see Chapter Six: "It's All about the Hotel—Really"). It was that plan to have the School Board of Lancaster waive property taxes from the private hotel that also, in large part, raised my concerns about the project. But the public was clearly opposed to the project at this time, five-plus years after the hotel tax went into effect. In addition to the letters to the editor opposing the project, on March 12, 2005, the *Intelligencer Journal* published a "People Poll" showing that 93% of respondents opposed the Penn Square Partners TIF proposal. See "People Poll: Do you favor a TIF for the hotel/cc center?" *Intelligencer Journal*, March 12, 2005. From the article:

> An overwhelming majority of readers responding to this week's People Poll oppose the creation of a Tax Increment Financing district that would allow Penn Square Partners to borrow $22 million from the state to build the hotel and convention center. Poll results were: 45, or, 6.3 percent of the 711 callers favor the creation of the TIF district.661, or 93 percent oppose the creation of the TIF.5, or 0.7 percent are unsure.

[2] Victor Capecce wrote an open letter in 2004 that was originally published on Ron Harper, Jr.'s website, 5thestate.com (now defunct). Mr. Capecce's letter was featured in the *Intelligencer Journal*, "Convention Center Wisdom Found on Both Sides of Debate," March 12, 2004.

Thomas Despard, a successful Lancaster developer, was both incensed and incredulous that the sponsors of the hotel-convention center project were proposing to demolish the home and building of Thaddeus Stevens and Lydia Hamilton-Smith. Like Capecce, instead of going home after work, Despard would sit through LCCCA meetings in order to speak regarding the folly of the project. Both Capecce and Despard were quoted in the article "Critics Hammer Penn Sq. Project; Large Crowd's Harsh Questions Go Unanswered. Developers Absent," *Lancaster New Era*, March 31, 2005. The article begins:

> Victor Capecce, a Lancaster man experienced in trade show exhibits, called the planned $129 million downtown hotel and meeting center "an economic catastrophe" waiting to happen.
>
> Dr. Philip Taylor labeled it a "runaway train" and urged the county commissioners to stop it.
>
> And city resident Randolph Carney said he was concerned that the hotel developer, Penn Square Partners, was hiding information about the project.
>
> "I ask you to start a formal investigation into this matter," he implored to the Lancaster County Commissioners on Wednesday evening.
>
> The three men and 19 others took a turn at the microphone at the county Farm & Home Center, all to criticize the long-planned, controversial economic development project.

Endnotes

Some had spoken against it frequently in the six years since plans were first announced. Others were newcomers to the issue.

But all thanked Commissioner Chairman Dick Shellenberger and Commissioner Molly Henderson, who presided over the session, for the opportunity to voice their opinion. . . .

Developer Tom Despard, who has pushed an office and residential condominium plan for the former department store, said a convention center simply isn't right for Lancaster.

It will not, he said, create "the buzz" to bring people downtown. He said that buzz comes from having parking, housing, offices and attractions. . . .

And, he added, "I'm not a nay-sayer. Sometimes people say I am. But I'm very much for the city. I just want to see it done right."

[3] Reverend Forbes worked with businessman Lenwood Jackson and Reverend Earl Harris and Reggie Guy out of Harrisburg to pressure the LCCCA board to hire African-American consultants. I shared the reverends' concern for the underrepresentation of minorities and women in receiving contracts from the LCCCA board. There were vague promises of "hundreds of good jobs," but those had not materialized. And the lucrative contracts seemed to go to the High Companies.

[4] The land that became Conestoga View was purchased November 27, 1798, in an agreement between the directors of the Poor and House of Employment and Matthias Slough. The agreement included ninety acres south of the turnpike road leading from the borough of Lancaster to Abraham Witmer's bridge, according to Lancasterhistory.org; see Folder 31, http://www.lancasterhistory.org/index.php?option=com_content&view=article&id=825:lancaster-county-almshouse-and-hospital-collection&catid=37:manuscript-groups&Itemid=57.

[5] In 2004, there were more than 600 county employees working for Conestoga View. The facility had 442 residents. According to the agreement of sale our board made with Complete HealthCare services in 2005, staffing levels were to remain stable for two years. In 2007, we passed a motion to remove the two-year limit. "We will sustain those [staffing] levels forever," said Peter Licari, president of Complete Healthcare, to the *Lancaster New Era*. See "Conestoga View Staff Levels May Be Locked; County Discusses Fixed-Ratio Personnel Requirement for Ex-County Nursing Home," *Lancaster New Era*, April 24, 2007.

[6] According to ProQuest, a data base that tracks Lancaster Newspapers articles, from July 10, 2005, until December 31, 2007—almost 2½ years—there were approximately 1,237 separate items, consisting of articles, columns, editorials, and letters, regarding "the commissioners" and Conestoga View published in the three Lancaster Newspapers.

[7] Former Lancaster city mayor and *Sunday News* columnist Arthur E. "Art" Morris was a defendant in my lawsuit against Lancaster Newspapers: *Molly Henderson vs Lancaster Newspapers, Inc., John M. Buckwalter, Ernest J. Schreiber, Marvin I. Adams,*

Jr., Helen Colwell Adams, Charles Raymond Shaw, Arthur E. Morris, Gilbert A. Smart, John H. Brubaker, III, and David Pidgeon. No. 0712003.

During Morris's deposition on January 10, 2010, my attorney George W. Croner exposed Morris's ignorance in the very areas he was professing expertise: nursing homes, accounting practices, and appraisals, all areas for which he harshly criticized our board.

From pages 15–16 of his January 28, 2010, deposition:

Q. Do you, Mr. Morris, hold a degree in accounting?
A. No.
Q. Are you a certified public accountant?
A. No.
Q. Have you taken any part of the certified public accountant examination?
A. No.
Q. Do you know or have any idea whether Generally Accepted Accounting Principles apply the same criteria, for example, for auditing a nursing home, as they do for a hotel?
A. I would not know that.
Q. Or I take it, a hospital?
A. I would not know that.
Q. Or an office building; fair to say?
A. It is fair to say that I would not know the standards of general accounting requirements for each and every one of those.
Q. Have you ever read, GAAP, the Generally Accepted Accounting Principles?
A. I read summaries on it, but many moons ago when it first came out.
Q. Do you have any familiarity with GAAS, Generally Accepted Auditing Standards?
A. No.
Q. So I take it, it's fair to say that you would not know what auditing standards were applied to a nursing home as opposed to any other type of business or facility; fair to say?
A. Well, any auditing standards? That's a little broad maybe. But I would not suggest that I understand auditing standards the way a CPA would understand them.
Q. Do you know whether there's any distinction between the auditing standards used, for example, with a nursing home and oh, say, a hotel?
A. I think I answered that.
Q. I asked you about accounting principles. Now I'm asking about auditing standards.
A. I do not.
Q. Are you, Mr. Morris, a member of the Appraisal Institute?
A. I am not, sir.
Q. Do you hold any sort of qualifications or certifications as an appraiser?
A. Again, not understanding what is all encompassing there, do I have any qualifications as simply to be an appraiser? The answer would be no. Could I assist an appraiser in certain aspects of it? I believe I probably could. If it involves engineering, for instance.
Q. All right. But whether or not any engineering assistance was required to actually perform an appraisal, I take it, is something that you wouldn't know, you would rely on an appraiser to tell you?
A. That's true.

Endnotes

Then, later in the deposition, on pages 66–67, Morris admits his interest in the elderly and nursing homes is recent and not something he was interested in during his decade as mayor:

Q. During the time that you were mayor of Lancaster City, Mr. Morris, did the city own a nursing home?
[Morris did not answer the question.]
Q. While you were the mayor of Lancaster City, was any nursing home operated by employees of Lancaster City?
A. Not that I'm aware of.
Q. Can you tell me, during the time that you served as mayor of Lancaster City, for what part of the operating budget of Conestoga View was the city responsible?
A. We weren't responsible. So, I guess the answer is zero.
Q. So I take it, as mayor, you never had any responsibility for any part of the operating budget at Conestoga View; fair to say?
A. I believe that's true.
Q. Have you, sir, ever held yourself out as having any particular expertise in caring for the elderly?
A. I really have a hard time answering that because I'm not sure I understand. Have I held myself out in, with expertise for caring?
Q. Yes.
A. Meaning, have I offered services to people? In that capacity the answer would be no. But if you're asking me, do I feel that I understand the problems of the elderly, and issues associated with that?
Since I cared for my mother for many years, then I would not agree with that.
Q. Do you hold yourself as having, hold yourself out as having any particular expertise in operating a nursing home?
A. No, I don't.
Q. How about a continuing care facility?
A. No, I don't.
Q. Or a senior living facility?
A. No, I don't.

And Art Morris, as mayor of Lancaster for ten years, did not have any noteworthy initiatives to help the city's elderly, including those at the county-owned Conestoga View nursing home, during his decade in office. In fact, in late 1989, as Morris was leaving office, the *Lancaster New Era* ran a 2,000-plus word, two-part article, "Morris Reflects on Highs, Lows of His Decade as City's Mayor," and "Morris Cared about People," on December 29 and 30, 1989. There is no mention of the elderly in the recap of the Morris years.

[8] It was very clear when I assumed office that Conestoga View was losing money. As commissioners, we reviewed the balance sheets during the monthly public business meetings and found the facility was losing about $1 million per year. And the trend of reduced state and federal spending would only increase the losses. Despite the poor

financial condition of Conestoga View, people such as Art Morris, who knew next to nothing about accounting or nursing homes (see note 7, above), and Lancaster County controller Dennis Stuckey insisted Conestoga View was not losing money. In 2006, our board hired the accounting firm of Reinsel Kuntz Lesher, with its impeccable reputation regionally, to audit Conestoga View. The firm confirmed the losses and was reported in the *Lancaster New Era* on April 18, 2006, in "Audit Pegs Conestoga View Losses." From the article:

> An accounting firm hired by the Lancaster County Commissioners has concluded that Conestoga View nursing home lost considerably more money during its last five years under county control than the Controller's Office had estimated.
>
> The firm's numbers essentially split the difference between Stevens & Lee's results and the controller's, estimating that Conestoga View lost an average of $900,000 a year from 2000 to 2004.
>
> The accountants found what they termed a "significant understatement of operating expenses and overstatement of operating results" in the controller's numbers, resulting in more than $4 million in additional losses over the five-year period.

[9] My term in office, from 2004 to 2008, coincided with the second presidential term of George W. Bush. Bush ran on a platform of "smaller government," which translated into fewer federal dollars to the states. Of course, Bush wasn't talking about making the federal budget deficit smaller or shrinking military spending. But his policies did affect how much money was going to the states. And in Harrisburg, belts were tightened. Lancaster County received less federal and state money, and it affected our ability to maintain Conestoga View.

[10] The details of the sale of Conestoga View are found in "Report Number 1" of the Investigating Grand Jury II, 2005. As noted in the grand jury report, Commissioner Shaub and soon-to-be commissioner Dick Shellenberger secretly discussed the sale of the facility well before Shellenberger took office, in January 2004. From page 20, footnote 20:

> 20. The grand jury finds as a fact that Commissioner Shaub had begun discussing the possible sale of Conestoga View prior to being re-elected for his second term as a county commissioner. Commissioner Shaub discussed this plan with candidate Shellenberger as early as September of 2003, which was before the general election in which Mr. Shellenberger was elected as a county commissioner. Commissioner Shaub coined the term 'Core Services Review."

The grand jury report is found here: http://panewsmedia.org/docs/default-source/government-affairs-documents-2013/lancaster-county-grand-jury-report-sunshine-act.pdf?sfvrsn=0.

Endnotes

[11] Voters in Lancaster County may vote for up to two members for the three-person commissioners' board. Two candidates from each major party appear on the ballot and any other candidate who has qualified for the ballot. The top three vote getters make up the Board of Commissioners. The composition of the County Board of Commissioners is stipulated in the Pennsylvania General Assembly, County Code, Act of Aug. 9, 1955, P.L. 323, No. 130, Article V, Section 501. See http://www.legis.state.pa.us/WU01/LI/LI/US/HTM/1955/0/0130.htm.

[12] Pennsylvania Sunshine Act, Title 65, Chapter 7, § 704:

§ 704. Open meetings.
Official action and deliberations by a quorum of the members of an agency shall take place at a meeting open to the public unless closed under section 707 (relating to exceptions to open meetings), 708 (relating to executive sessions) or 712 (relating to General Assembly meetings covered).

See: http://www.legis.state.pa.us/WU01/LI/LI/CT/HTM/65/65.htm.

[13] Shellenberger made the comment to Newslanc.com. See "Convention Center Series."

[14] The revelation that the term *Charlie Victor* was used to hide the Conestoga View secret meetings between Shaub, Shellenberger, and Espenshade was made in testimony during the grand jury investigation. From pages 19 and 20 of the grand jury report:

> A constant theme of the off-site meetings was that no one outside of "the team" should know about the plan to, or even the possibility of, selling Conestoga View. Commissioner Shaub specifically told the team members that Commissioner Henderson should be kept in the dark. Each of the team members was told not to put the off-site meetings on to their calendars. Some team members referred to the sale of Conestoga View as "the project" or as "Charlie Victor," so as to further hide the purpose of their meetings. . . .

[15] The final price for Conestoga View was $12 million, according to an audit of the sale by the large Lancaster accounting firm Reinsel Kuntz Lesher (RKL). Our Board of Commissioners hired RKL in early 2006 to allay public concern about the sale. The *Lancaster New Era* reported on the RKL audit on April 18, 2006. From the article: "Their [RKL] study also found that the county received a total of $12 million from the sale of Conestoga View, including $8.5 million in cash and another $3.5 million in non-cash benefits and assets."

[16] Regarding the practice of commissioners Shaub and Shellenberger using surrogates to conduct meetings on Conestoga View, the grand jury report reads on pages 20–21:

> In addition to off-site secret meetings where Commissioners Shellenberger and Shaub were physically present, there were a number (the exact number could not be determined with certainty by the grand jurors) of meetings that occurred where the two commissioners participated in the meetings by sending Mr.

Heinke and Mr. Elliot in their stead. The two commissioners then would question Mr. Heinke and Mr. Elliott in detail about what occurred at the meetings when they returned to the courthouse. Mr. Heinke referred to these interrogations as "back briefs," where he would be asked to brief the secret meetings in detail, usually to Commissioner Shaub. A constant theme of the off-site meetings was that no one outside of "the team" should know about the plan to, or even the possibility of, selling Conestoga View. Commissioner Shaub specifically told the team members that Commissioner Henderson should be kept in the dark.

And from page 32 of the grand jury report:

In "walking the halls," either Mr. Heinke or Mr. Elliot would walk into a single Commissioner's office and ask for that commissioner's opinion or vote on a particular subject. After receiving the information, either Mr. Heinke or Mr. Elliott would repeat the same procedure with each of the other two commissioners individually....

[17] The secret work that Shellenberger, Shaub, and Espenshade did on behalf of Heinke was indefensible. They created an unfair playing field for the other legitimate applicants. As the grand jury reported, I was completely unaware of the pre-interview preparation and coaching the three provided to Heinke. The grand jury report describes this advance preparation between the four men on pages 5–8.

[18] The grand jury report noted that county administrative officer Don Elliott, also received pre-interview questions ahead of his interview on page 11, note 11:

(11) Mr. Heinke was not the only applicant to be given preferential treatment during the current board's hiring process. Mr. Elliott, before he was interviewed for the CAO position, received the topics of the interview questions from Commissioner Shaub.

[19] The grand jury describes Heinke's interview before the commissioners' board on page 12 of its report:

When [human resources staff member] Ms. [Bonnie] Ashworth introduced Mr. Heinke to the board at the beginning of the interview, there were no signs that any of the commissioners recognized him or had had an ongoing relationship with him prior to that interview. Mr. Heinke interviewed flawlessly—he never had to stop to think of a response to a question or to keep himself from answering incorrectly. As one grand jury witness noted, "These answers were just rolling off his tongue, and he'd throw up these examples and he had examples for everything, and writing down things and taking notes. And by the time he was finished, I couldn't even speak. I had never seen such a perfect, flawless interview."

Endnotes

[20] The date of Heinke's hiring and his start date were mentioned by the grand jury on pages 12, 13 of the grand jury report.

[21] The "Core Services Review," I later learned, was a "team" of Shaub, Shellenberger, Espenshade, Elliott, Heinke, and a few others. This was the group that was secretly conspiring to sell Conestoga View out of the public eye. From page 18, footnote 20:

> (20) The grand jury finds as a fact that Commissioner Shaub had begun discussing the possible sale of Conestoga View prior to being re-elected for his second term as a county commissioner. Commissioner Shaub discussed this plan with candidate Shellenberger as early as September of 2003, which was before the general election in which Mr. Shellenberger was elected as a county commissioner. Commissioner Shaub coined the term "Core Services Review."

[22] It was this innocuous informational meeting on April 1 to which I accepted a citation to violating the Sunshine Law. This plea is one of the biggest regrets of my life. As I explain in this book, it was clear that I would be charged with this violation. If I challenged it, I would lose at the local judicial level, then probably win on appeal. In the meantime, I would have spent more than $100,000 and lost the election. So, I decided to take that plea and move on with my job as commissioner. That was a mistake. The April 1 meeting, as described in the chapter, did not involve any deliberation or official action; it was an informational meeting. It was therefore not a violation of the Sunshine Law. I never should have pled guilty.

[23] The organization Pennsylvania Association of County Affiliated Homes now goes by the name "Pennsylvania Coalition of Affiliated Healthcare & Living Communities."

[24] As the Reinsel Kuntz Lesher audit of 2006 proved, Conestoga View was unsustainable, losing almost $1 million per year. The county not only received a market-value price for Conestoga View, the patient care has improved across the board. No jobs were lost, and the facility is thriving, with no indigent patients turned away.

[25] One of the most interesting details from the grand jury report is that evidently Commissioner Shaub, who had gone to extreme lengths to conceal the sale of Conestoga View, leaked the impending sale to Lancaster Newspapers. It was as if he were kicking off a campaign. The campaign lasted the next eighteen months. From the grand jury report, page 26:

> Towards the end of June, 2005, Commissioner Shaub leaked news of the impending sale of Conestoga View to the *Lancaster New Era* newspaper; soon thereafter, the impending sale of Conestoga View was publicized in that newspaper.

[26] *Sunday News* editor David Hennigan came to Lancaster Newspapers in 1968 as a reporter for the *Intelligencer Journal*. Hennigan switched to the *Sunday News* in the 1970s and rose to the editor position in 1984, from which he retired in November 2005. Mr. Hennigan died in 2015. His *LNP* obituary may be found here. http://

lancasteronline.com/news/local/former-sunday-news-editor-david-hennigan-dies/article_9c2f1080-2fe7-11e5-b568-bfc2e9e42a27.html.

[27] The circulation statistics were taken from the deposition of Lancaster Newspaper's chairman John M. Buckwalter during his deposition, February 3, 2010, pp. 57–59:

"The *New Era* was about 40,000 . . . The *Intell* would've been around 46,000, 47,000. The trend was that the evening paper was declining and the morning paper was gradually increasing. *Sunday News* was about 95,000, 96,000."

Buckwalter was one of several Lancaster Newspapers employees sued in the libel action: *Molly Henderson vs Lancaster Newspapers, Inc., John M. Buckwalter, Ernest J. Schreiber, Marvin I. Adams, Jr., Helen Colwell Adams, Charles Raymond Shaw, Arthur E. Morris, Gilbert A. Smart, John H. Brubaker, III, and David Pidgeon*. No. 0712003.

[28] The July 10, 2005, "Coffee with Clyde" column kicked off the Conestoga View "coverage." It was clear from the outset that former mayor Arthur E. Morris would be the point man for the attacks. Morris attended every commissioners meeting, berating the board for the sale. As we have established through his own testimony in the lawsuit brought against him, Morris knew virtually nothing about accounting, nursing homes, or county government. Morris had no experience in nursing homes or county government or the appraisal of real estate.

[29] Morris began writing his twice-monthly *Sunday News* column in July 2003. He discusses the agreement, payment ($75 per column), and circumstances of agreeing to write the column (he was asked by editor Dave Hennigan) on pages 78–88 of his deposition. Morris was a defendant in the libel lawsuit *Molly Henderson vs Lancaster Newspapers, Inc., John M. Buckwalter, Ernest J. Schreiber, Marvin I. Adams, Jr., Helen Colwell Adams, Charles Raymond Shaw, Arthur E. Morris, Gilbert A. Smart, John H. Brubaker, III, and David Pidgeon*. No. 0712003.

[30] See "Clyde Backs the Project," *Sunday News*, March 13, 2005.

[31] I have shown that a letters-to-the-editor campaign against Shellenberger and me had begun prior to the agreement to sell Conestoga View. After the July 6, 2005, vote, the campaign became more aggressive and personal and singularly aimed at the Conestoga View issue. At no point was the intention to reduce services to the elderly residents of the facility or to cut jobs for county residents. The hysteria over Conestoga View was, I believe, entirely orchestrated, and the conductor was former mayor Arthur E. "Art" Morris.

[32] As the "In the Dark" editorial acknowledged, "[T]he county took steps to safeguard the staff and residents and to ensure the needy always will have a home at Conestoga View." There was no legal problem with the sale of Conestoga View. It was a good deal for the county, for the staff, and for the residents of Conestoga View. But the editorial is clearly trying to raise questions of propriety and integrity about the sale. This is the beginning of that narrative. See "In the Dark," *Sunday News*, July 18, 2005.

[33] From a journalistic perspective, it is hard to see the justification for devoting front-page "real estate" to the pending vote over the sale of Conestoga View. That both the

Intell and the *New Era*, supposedly independent newspapers, would, on the same day, two months before the final vote, run anti-commissioners articles on the sale of Conestoga View speaks to the coordination between the "separate" newspapers. The story's news value simply wasn't as big as it was being played. Buckwalter and Lancaster Newspapers' editors manufactured the content on a daily basis. See "Nursing Home Sale Unsettles Employees" and the *New Era* "Conestoga View Sale Mishandled," July 21, 2005.

[34] The August 21, 2005, *Sunday News* "Coffee with Clyde" column, "Clyde Joins in Verbal Beating of Public Officials," also criticized the Pennsylvania General Assembly for their 2 a.m. pay raise for themselves.

[35] In the August 24, 2005, *Lancaster New Era* article "Morris: Halt the Sale," Art Morris describes our board as "dictatorial" and very authoritatively lays out all that is wrong with the Conestoga View sale.

The article begins:

> Former Mayor Arthur E. Morris today asked the Lancaster County Commissioners to stop the sale of Conestoga View and challenged the commissioners on their "dictatorial" decision to sell the county nursing home to the private sector. Morris, addressing the commissioners this morning during the public comment period of their weekly meeting, flatly declared that Conestoga View is not a big money-loser once indirect reimbursements paid for county services and a bottom-line $7 million in assets are considered. Over 15 years, those reimbursements alone would exceed the sales price of $8.7 million, Morris said. Beyond that, he said official county financial records show the county has not lost gobs of money in recent years as commissioners assert.

As shown during his deposition testimony, under oath in the libel suit against him, Art Morris did not know the first thing about nursing homes, public or private; did not know anything about accounting methods or appraisals or anything about county government and how it financed nursing homes.

From pages 15–16 of his deposition:

Q. Do you, Mr. Morris, hold a degree in accounting?
A. No.
Q. Are you a certified public accountant?
A. No.
Q. Have you taken any part of the certified public accountant examination?
A. No.
Q. Do you know or have any idea whether Generally Accepted Accounting Principles apply the same criteria, for example, for auditing a nursing home, as they do for a hotel?
A. I would not know that.

Q. Or I take it, a hospital?
A. I would not know that.
Q. Or an office building; fair to say?
A. It is fair to say that I would not know the standards of general accounting requirements for each and every one of those.
Q. Have you ever read, GAAP, the Generally Accepted Accounting Principles?
A. I read summaries on it, but many moons ago when it first came out.
Q. Do you have any familiarity with GAAS, Generally Accepted Auditing Standards?
A. No.
Q. So I take it, it's fair to say that you would not know what auditing standards were applied to a nursing home as opposed to any other type of business or facility; fair to say?
A. Well, any auditing standards? That's a little broad maybe. But I would not suggest that I understand auditing standards the way a CPA would understand them.
Q. Do you know whether there's any distinction between the auditing standards used, for example, with a nursing home and oh, say, a hotel?
A. I think I answered that.
Q. I asked you about accounting principles. Now I'm asking about auditing standards.
A. I do not.
Q. Are you, Mr. Morris, a member of the Appraisal Institute?
A. I am not, sir.
Q. Do you hold any sort of qualifications or certifications as an appraiser?
A. Again, not understanding what is all encompassing there, do I have any qualifications as simply to be an appraiser? The answer would be no. Could I assist an appraiser in certain aspects of it? I believe I probably could. If it involves engineering, for instance.
Q. All right. But whether or not any engineering assistance was required to actually perform an appraisal, I take it, is something that you wouldn't know, you would rely on an appraiser to tell you?
A. That's true.

[Then, later in the deposition, on pages 66–67, Morris admits his interest in the elderly and nursing homes is recent and not something he was interested in during his decade as mayor]:

Q. During the time that you were mayor of Lancaster City, Mr. Morris, did the city own a nursing home?
A No.
Q. While you were the mayor of Lancaster City, was any nursing home operated by employees of Lancaster City
A. Not that I'm aware of.
Q. Can you tell me, during the time that you served as mayor of Lancaster City, for what part of the operating budget of Conestoga View was the city responsible?
A. We weren't responsible. So, I guess the answer is zero.
Q. So I take it, as mayor, you never had any responsibility for any part of the operating budget at Conestoga View; fair to say?

A. I believe that's true.

Q. Have you, sir, ever held yourself out as having any particular expertise in caring for the elderly?

A. I really have a hard time answering that because I'm not sure I understand. Have I held myself out in, with expertise for caring?

Q. Yes

A. Meaning, have I offered services to people? In that capacity the answer would be no. But if you're asking me, do I feel that I understand the problems of the elderly, and issues associated with that? Since I cared for my mother for many years, then I would not agree with that.

Q. Do you hold yourself as having, hold yourself out as having any particular expertise in operating a nursing home?

A. No, I don't.

Q. How about a continuing care facility?

A. No, I don't.

Q. Or a senior living facility?

A. No, I don't.

[36] Many, if not most, of these dozens of Conestoga View articles had Art Morris and his criticisms of the commissioners at the center. These included a half-dozen *Sunday News* "Coffee with Clyde" columns, including the column that kicked off the "coverage," the July 10 "Clyde Busts Commissioners for Speeding." Morris, of course, had never shown any interest in Conestoga View, yet was suddenly cast as the fearless protector of the elderly poor and an authority on the county-owned nursing home. As shown in note 36, Art Morris had absolutely no professional expertise in areas in which he held himself as an authority—accounting, auditing, appraisal. He did, however, present his ideas with a great deal of confidence.

[37] The county addressed and answered each and every question and concern regarding the sale, and yet the "coverage" continued to be overwhelmingly negative, shows the artificial, manufactured nature of the story. No jobs would be cut. Care would be improved. It was shown the facility was costing the county about $1 million per year. It did not seem to matter that the sale made sense.

[38] The statute governing the sale and acquisition of county-owned real property may be found in the Pennsylvania County Code, Article XXIII. Grounds and Buildings. (b) Acquisition, Use, Leasing and Disposing of Real Property for County, Sections 2305-2311.

The County Code may be found online here:

http://www.legis.state.pa.us/WU01/LI/LI/US/HTM/1955/0/0130..HTM.

[39] The "Lost Our Home!" foursome of Allen, Bonnano, Grady, and Albright not only appeared at commissioners meetings, but did so before and after the meetings with signs that also read, "Save Our Home!" The "street performances" were part of an additional campaign as well, the making of a "story" against "the commissioners."

⁴⁰ At the time he was wearing the "Lost Our Home!" T-shirt and reviling our board, Tony Allen, a Republican, was a Lancaster Township supervisor. Allen was voted out of office in 2009 and faced an investigation into his actions alleging that he had impersonated a poll watcher on election night, 2009. See http://lancasteronline.com/news/tony-allen-is-focus-of-complaints/article_83368937-9432-50bc-b2a6-2773654da9b1.html.

⁴¹ Former commissioner Thibault was actually someone who could speak to the financial condition of Conestoga View. But, as we have argued, the Conestoga View "story" was a red herring, a diversion from the troubled hotel and convention center project. And on that subject, Thibault, who as commissioner had passed the room tax and guaranteed the $40 million county bond for the project, fell behind Art Morris and criticized the Conestoga View sale. Mayor Smithgall's comments (and Thibault's, above) were quoted in "Mayor: Keep Conestoga View," *Intelligencer Journal*, September 8, 2005. Smithgall never attended a single Conestoga View business meeting, open to the public, during this time.

⁴² Controller Stuckey's actions concerning the sale of Conestoga View were disingenuous. Stuckey, as controller, had all of Conestoga View's financial information in his office and was in a position to publicly confirm Conestoga View's dire condition. Instead, as shown in the two September 21, 2005, front-page articles referenced in the chapter, the *Intell*'s "Stuckey Questions Sale," and the *New Era*'s, " Controller: It Doesn't Add Up," Stuckey questioned the numbers from his own office. Later, in 2006, he questioned the audit by the independent accounting firm Reinsel Kuntz Lesher. The accounting firm, one of the largest in the region, with an impeccable reputation, used the controller's numbers to show Conestoga View was losing even more than the county said. Stuckey never admitted his error. He chose to say, "Reinsel Kuntz Lesher took numbers provided by the controller's office and put them together to fit the commissioners' point of view," *Intelligencer Journal*, "Controller, Commissioners at Odds Over Report," May 3, 2006.

⁴³ I became aware of the Conestoga View draw from the county's "Home Enterprise Fund" soon after taking office in 2004. Our Board of Commissioners attended monthly public Conestoga View business meetings. Reading the financials of the facility, I could see that the nursing home was costing the county a lot of money.

⁴⁴ The numbers regarding the Home Enterprise Fund came from the county controller's office. It was the same financial data used in the Reinsel Kuntz Lesher audit of 2006, which confirmed the county's analysis of the facility's financial health.

⁴⁵ When Lancaster Newspapers did turn its attention away from Conestoga View, the focus was still on attacking Commissioner Shellenberger and me. In this article, "Leaders: Shellenberger Should Quit," *Lancaster New Era*, September 22, 2005, both mayoral candidates, Smithgall and Gray, join with Senator Gib Armstrong, Paul Thibault, and others condemning Shellenberger. Their anger was prompted by the county, per our prerogative, choosing our own appointee to the Lancaster County Convention Center board of directors. The comments from the mayoral candidates are interesting because

they reveal the real source of the attacks—the county's opposition to the downtown hotel-convention center project. Here is Mayor Smithgall in the *New Era* article: "The county commissioners—Shellenberger and Molly Henderson—seem bent on killing any forward movement in the city, especially in downtown." And here is candidate Gray: "It is unfortunate that we have gotten to the point where our county commissioners are working against the biggest proactive economic development project in the city."

[46] A good, succinct headline primer is posted by the Columbia University Graduate School of Journalism: http://www.columbia.edu/itc/journalism/isaacs/client_edit/Headlines.html. Stephen Isaacs, who put the primer together, was associate dean of academic affairs and professor at the school. He became an emeritus professor in 2012. Dean Isaacs died in 2014.

[47] Each of the *Sunday News*'s "Coffee with Clyde" columns—September 11, 18, and 25—began with Hennigan's "jogging friend" providing the details. These were the columns leading up to the September 28, 2005, commissioners' vote to finalize the sale of Conestoga View.

[48] *Lancaster New Era*, September 23, 2005, "County Missteps Hurt City Progress." After listing several revitalization efforts in the city but neglecting to credit the county, the editorial names Commissioner Shellenberger and me as roadblocks to city progress. From the editorial:

> The only blot on this picture lies in the well-intentioned, but seriously flawed missteps that County Commissioners Dick Shellenberger and Molly Henderson have made as they move from one city project to the next."

[49] Both Senator Armstrong and Commissioner Shellenberger were longtime Calvary Church members, located just north of Lancaster city. Shellenberger recalled that during his term, Armstrong visited him at his house. The two were standing in Shellenberger's driveway, and Shellenberger asked Armstrong, "Why are you doing all this stuff for the convention center project?" By then, Armstrong had changed the law a couple of times to enable the project and was an outspoken supporter. "Time to pay Dale back," was Armstrong's response. Shellenberger told that story to Chris Hart Nibbrig after Shellenberger left office.

[50] Pete Shaub's sudden reversal on selling Conestoga View was classic Shaub. After spending more than two years first arranging, then executing the sale, Shaub, days before the final vote, came out against the sale he'd orchestrated. It was Shaub who said the words, "Molly is toast," to Jack Buckwalter in a meeting between the two. The phrase was written down by Buckwalter. After the intensely negative newspaper coverage of the Conestoga View sale, Shaub now left Shellenberger and me alone to absorb the criticism of the sale.

[51] The Lancaster City and County Medical Society's filing of an injunction against the Conestoga View sale was reported in "Injunction Is Denied," *Intelligencer Journal*, October 1, 2005.

⁵² The October 2, 2005, *Sunday News* "Coffee with Clyde" column, the first after the September 28 sale, was the column in which "Clyde" talks about the "letter to the editor" from Dennis Cox. This was the same Dennis Cox whose "letter" Jack Buckwalter was copy editing. And, of course, it was Art Morris who was recruited by Buckwalter to spearhead the pro–convention center "letters"-to-the-editor campaign.

⁵³ Both Helen Colwell Adams and her husband, Marvin I. "Marv" Adams, were defendants in the libel suit I brought against Lancaster Newspapers and several of its staff members, including columnist and former mayor Arthur E. "Art" Morris, *Molly Henderson vs Lancaster Newspapers, Inc., John M. Buckwalter, Ernest J. Schreiber, Marvin I. Adams, Jr., Helen Colwell Adams, Charles Raymond Shaw, Arthur E. Morris, Gilbert A. Smart, John H. Brubaker, III, and David Pidgeon*. No. 0712003. Helen and Marv Adams were deposed in connection with the libel suit. Helen Adams was deposed October 5, 2009, and Marv Adams was deposed October 29, 2009.

⁵⁴ Helen Colwell Adams discusses her Master of Divinity degree work on pages 10–11 of her October 5, 2009 deposition. Ms. Adams began coursework in 2005 and finished in December 2009.

⁵⁵ Dennis F. Cox was an extremely well-known person among Lancastrians in the 2005-time period. Cox, whose father was the first news director and anchor for the Steinman's WGAL television station, was an early recipient of a Steinman Foundation scholarship. In addition to owning Godfrey Advertising and many buildings along "Gallery Row" on Prince Street, Dennis Cox was active in civic organizations, including serving on the boards of the Lancaster Alliance-backed Lancaster City Safety Coalition, Boys & Girls Clubs, and the Downtown Investment District. So, a letter from Dennis Cox was not an average letter to the editor.

⁵⁶ Ibid.

⁵⁷ My *Sunday News* piece from October 9, 2005, "Why We Sold Conestoga View," had absolutely no effect on the coverage. (See the letter in Appendix E and also Appendix F, "Pennsylvania County Nursing Homes.") Mark Twain once said, "Never get into a fight with someone who buys ink by the barrel." That's what it felt like fighting Lancaster Newspapers. Eight hundred words wasn't very much ink.

⁵⁸ Mark Gilger, Jr., "Schuylkill County Commissioners Face Tough Decision on Rest Haven," *Republican Herald*, August 16, 2014.

⁵⁹ Kelly Andrisano, executive director, Pennsylvania Coalition of Affiliated Healthcare and Living Communities, September 30, 2016.

Chapter Nine: The DA Investigation

¹ Art Morris made a public issue of the hiring of lawyers connected with the Conestoga View sale and also how much they were paid. Morris was aware that by 2005, several million dollars had been spent on legal fees by the Lancaster County Convention Center Authority (LCCCA), yet instead chose to focus on the $288,000 in fees,

completely legitimate, spent on the Conestoga View transaction. Morris's interest in the legal fees was mentioned in "Deal Looks Like a Steal," *Sunday News*, November 6, 2005. In the beginning of the article, Morris is held as an authority on nursing home financing. Yet, as he revealed during his deposition, Morris knew nothing about nursing homes, public or private, nothing of accounting or appraisal methods. Yet over and over, he was held by Lancaster Newspapers, and himself, as an expert on the subject. The article begins:

Art Morris propped up two hand-drawn charts and started talking.

The charts showed the impact of the sale of Conestoga View on the county's budget and on Complete HealthCare Resources' bottom line.

"This was a sweetheart deal for these people," Morris, the former mayor of Lancaster, charged at the Wednesday county commissioners' meeting....

Morris has also questioned why the sales agreement was dated July 6, the same day the commissioners voted to hire Stevens & Lee attorney Joanne Judge as special counsel on the transaction.

Stevens & Lee billed about $288,000 for fees associated with the sale, while the law firm of Kegel, Kelin, Almy & Grimm received about $13,000 for reviewing the contract, according to Stuckey's office....

[2] Each time Art Morris came up with a "problem" with the Conestoga View sale, one of the Lancaster Newspapers immediately, and without investigating, reported it. The issue with the county license plates was reported in "County Plates Now Off Conestoga View Vans," *Lancaster New Era*, October 13, 2005. Like many of the Art Morris–prompted articles, "County Plates Now Off Conestoga View Vans" begins with the words *Art Morris*:

Art Morris has maintained for months that Lancaster County officials were ignoring small, but important, details in the sale of its Conestoga View nursing home. Late last week, he saw evidence of his claims driving by on Broad Street near the former county home....

With respect to the license plates, they were in the process of being replaced when Morris "broke" the non-story. There was nothing improper about the timing.

[3] In yet another example of Art Morris making up a story where none existed—and Lancaster Newspapers unquestioningly publishing it—Morris made an issue out of the gas purchased for Conestoga View vans. Morris argued that the public was paying for the gas after the sale to Complete HealthCare Resources, the new owners of the facility. He failed to understand that Complete Healthcare had agreed to pay for the gas during the transfer of ownership. See http://lancasteronline.com/news/gas-card-use-newest-flap-at-conestoga-view/article_1f428808-d4f1-523d-a602-0f6ec711322e.html.

[4] According to the American Press Institute: "The purpose of journalism is thus to provide citizens with the information they need to make the best possible decisions about their lives, their communities, their societies, and their governments." See

https://www.americanpressinstitute.org/journalism-essentials/what-is-journalism/purpose-journalism/.

Using this definition, the "coverage" of Conestoga View far exceeded its importance as a news story to the community. It was a big focus on a story that wasn't a big story. Conestoga View was losing money. The county assured people that no one would be turned away and that good-quality care would still be available. No jobs would be lost. These were the important issues around Conestoga View, and they had been resolved and reported. Now, conversely, the hotel and convention center project was, in fact, important to the lives of Lancaster County's citizens. In that case, Lancaster Newspapers' "coverage" alternated between raw promotion of the project in which LNP was a partner and attacking anyone who questioned it. In both cases, it was a misuse of the journalistic role of the press.

[5] In addition to searching the Proquest.com archives, we also cross-checked with Newslibrary.com. In both, we used the search terms "Conestoga View" and "County Commissioners" to arrive at the numbers in the chapter.

[6] Howard Kelin's legal opinion for the county regarding the taxability of the hotel was dated April 11, 2005, one day before the Lancaster City Council passed the two city guaranties, City Ordinances Nos. 5 and 10. Kelin showed that the "project user," Penn Square Partners, was required to "to timely pay all Commonwealth and local taxes and fees," pursuant to 12 Pa. C.S.A.§ 3406(b) (11). Kelin also showed that if the guaranties stood and Penn Square Partners was exempted from paying real estate taxes, the city would lose, conservatively, $14 million (fourteen million dollars) in real estate taxes during the life of the bonds.

[7] Following a public letter to the LCCCA written by Commissioner Shellenberger, "Shellenberger's Statement on Downtown Project," published in the *Intelligencer Journal*, May 2, 2005, the county voted 2–1 on May 4, 2005, to support a demand that the LCCCA cease all spending and repay the county bond. From Shellenberger's letter:

> The simple fact is that Penn Square Partners and the Convention Center Authority have abandoned the project that had initially received substantial public support. As the project is now proposed, all but a very small amount of the cost and risk will involve taxpayer money. Moreover, the cost and risk to taxpayers have increased dramatically. Many community members have said they supported the project as initially conceived; however, the project is now at a point where the cost and risk of public funds are too high to be justified. As stewards of the public trust, I believe the Commissioners must conclude the line of acceptable public funding and taxpayer risk has been crossed far beyond what is prudent to support. . . .

[8] The county voted 2–1 (Shaub against) on April 19, 2005, to ask the LCCCA to provide a legal opinion on whether the interest paid on the $40 million county-guaranteed bond qualified for exclusion from federal income tax.

Endnotes

⁹ Also during the May 4, 2005, regular county commissioners meeting, the county voted (2–1; Shaub against) to authorize special counsel Kelin to investigate whether the county's guaranty of interest payments on the LCCCA bonds could be withdrawn.

¹⁰ The county's special counsel Howard Kelin, of Kegel Kelin Almy & Grimm, was authorized to file the complaint regarding the two city guaranties (city Ordinances Nos. 5 and 10) with the Department of Community and Economic Development (DCED). The complaint argued that the guaranties violated Act 23 and several provisions of the Local Government Unit Debt Act. The complaint was filed with the DCED on May 16, 2005. The complaint argued the city guaranties were illegal for the following reasons:

- Both guaranties are illegal because they violate the requirement in Act 23 that the project user pay all local taxes.
- Both guaranties are illegal because they violate the Pennsylvania Constitution "public purpose requirement."
- Both guaranties are illegal because they do not evidence the acquisition of a capital asset by a government agency.
- Both guaranties are illegal because they do not guarantee debt incurred for a project the City is authorized to own.
- The guaranties are illegal because the City does not have realistic cost estimates for the project.
- The guaranties are illegal because the debt statement and borrowing base certificate are not signed by the City Controller as required by Ordinances No. 5 and No. 10.
- The $24 million guaranty is illegal because it is not a guarantee of RACL's bonds; in reality, it is an agreement to pay real estate taxes owed on the Marriott Hotel.
- The $24 million guaranty is illegal because it is unlawful for a city to agree to pay real estate taxes owed to another taxing authority by another government agency or private party.
- The $24 million guaranty is illegal because it is unlawful for a city to agree to waive real estate taxes owed to the City of Lancaster.

¹¹ On July 20, the county voted (2–1; Shaub against) to file a Petition for Review in the Nature of a Declaratory Judgment seeking a judgment as to whether the DCED improperly awarded special grants to RACL for use in the private portion of the Hotel and Convention Center project under the Act 23 program. This petition was in reference to Ordinance No. 5, the $12 million Act 23 bond, which the City of Lancaster guaranteed. The county's petition argued that RACL was violating its mission in serving a private, rather than a public, interest in applying for the annual Act 23 grants that would fund the private Marriott Hotel owned by Penn Square Partners.

¹² The county appointed three new members to the LCCCA board of directors with hotel, tourism, and business experience. The new members—businesswoman Laura Douglas, Ephrata Chamber of Commerce executive director Deb Hall, and former Plaza Hotel general manager Jack Craver—asked many of the questions raised by us

on the commissioners' board. They demanded accountability and information from the LCCCA board.

[13] On September 27, 2005, the day before Conestoga View was sold, during the commissioners' public work session, the county voted 2–1 to explore separating the 3.9% "room rental tax" from the 1.1% "excise tax." The coverage by Lancaster Newspapers after this action, in which no action against the tax was passed, made the vote seem fatal to the project. On September 27, 2005, the *Lancaster New Era*, in, "Senator: Proposal May Kill Center," uses the words *kill* and *death* throughout the article. The article begins:

They found a way to kill the convention center, state Sen. Gibson E. Armstrong charged today.

County Commissioners Molly Henderson and Dick Shellenberger want to separate the hotel and excise taxes, which Armstrong says could easily lead to the death of the $134 million downtown convention center project.

Such a move could also sink farmland preservation and possibly plunge the county into depression, Armstrong said.

My comment was published in the *New Era* on the "de-coupling" of the taxes. "Why these are two distinct, separate entities [the convention center and the visitor's bureau] and why they are together has always puzzled me," said Henderson.

[14] Former commissioner Shellenberger's quote was excerpted from his "Shellenberger's Statement on the Downtown Project," *Intelligencer Journal*, May 2, 2005. (Notice how the *Intell* editors chose not to use Shellenberger's title, "Commissioner," in the headline.) Shellenberger's 3,400-plus word statement was a detailed analysis of the problems, questions, and issues associated with the project. Shellenberger turned his cheek and struck a magnanimous tone toward his name-calling detractors:

> Senator Armstrong, Mayor Smithgall, and Representative Sturla are dedicated public officials who have invested significant time and energy in Lancaster City revitalization. Similarly, Convention Center Authority members have spent enormous time fulfilling their duties—as volunteers and a matter of public service. We are fortunate to have individuals who care so deeply about Lancaster City.
> Fulton Bank, Lancaster Newspapers, and High Industries stepped forward seven years ago, spent $1.2 million of their own money to acquire the Watt & Shand building, and presented a hotel/convention center plan as a major step towards Lancaster City revitalization. These companies are good corporate citizens. Entirely aside from the hotel/convention center plan, they have made many contributions over many years to the Lancaster community, and I trust they will continue to do so for many years to come.
> I appreciate the hard work of Dale High, Jack Buckwalter, Rufus Fulton, Gib Armstrong, Mike Sturla, Pete Shaub, Charlie Smithgall, Convention Center Authority members, and many others.

Endnotes

[15] The Nickel Mines shootings of October 2, 2006, garnered international attention. The grace and dignity of the Plain population were shown to the world. In that evil incident, 8 of 10 little girls, ages 6 to 13, were shot. Five died.

[16] The "Who Is Gary Heinke?" *Lancaster New Era* article of October 24, 2005, reflected extensive investigation on the part of Lancaster Newspapers. There were several out-of-state interviews and inquiries that went into the reporting of the piece. Every quote was aimed at hurting Heinke. Art Morris is credited in the *New Era* with uncovering the résumé discrepancies.

Arthur Morris, a former Lancaster City mayor, says Heinke's resume doesn't wash.

He delivered a letter to the commissioners today calling for an official inquiry into Heinke's credentials.

"I'm seeking a full investigation by the county in an open fashion," said Morris.

[17] Heinke's entire work history and the process he underwent when hired by the county was detailed in the report by county human resources director J. Thomas Myers, November 10, 2005, then by the grand jury report of December 2006. Heinke was clearly a personnel matter, and the county appropriately and immediately turned it over to the county's Human Resources Department to investigate it. That such a small matter as an inflated résumé would be given a full grand jury investigation conducted by the Lancaster County district attorney, as discussed in this book, is a complete misuse of the grand jury system and the office of the district attorney. The Lancaster *New Era* reported on Heinke's background, October 28, 2005, in "Heinke." Again, Art Morris was credited with digging up Heinke's work history. From the article:

> Former Lancaster City Mayor Arthur Morris prompted that review when he pointed to several discrepancies between Heinke's resume and what employers and colleagues told Morris.
> Morris began examining Heinke's credentials because he believes the administrator seriously bungled the sale of Conestoga View county nursing home to a private operator.

[18] October 25, 2005, is an important date because that is when the county commissioners directed the head of the Human Resources Department, J. Thomas Myers, to conduct an investigation into the hiring of Gary Heinke. The commissioners turned the matter over to Myers and had nothing to do with the investigation. This was a matter of public record. It was reported in the October 28, 2005, *New Era* article "Heinke": "The Lancaster County Commissioners early this week asked J. Thomas Myers, the county's human resources director, to conduct an in-house review of how Heinke was hired in March 2004."

District Attorney Donald R. Totaro—whose offices were located on the same floor as the county commissioners—was certainly aware that Myers, not the commissioners, would be conducting the investigation. Eight days later, the district attorney would write an e-mail to Myers, asking for a copy of Myers's report when completed. Later, District Attorney Totaro reported to the Court that he asked the county commissioners for the report. That misleading statement by DA Totaro was the basis for the grand jury investigation.

[19] It was a full-court press on the Heinke story. On the 25th of October, between the *Intell*'s "Heinke Cries Foul Over Scrutiny Over His Résumé" and the *New Era*'s "A Question of Credentials," an issue about a fudged résumé dominated the front pages of both Lancaster daily newspapers.

[20] Controller Dennis Stuckey was unhelpful during the Conestoga View process. He accused the commissioners of misrepresenting Conestoga View's financial condition, although our analysis was based on numbers from the controller's office. Then, on the Heinke matter, Stuckey involved himself by asking that Heinke be given a leave of absence. "Stuckey: 'Heinke, Go Home,'" on October 27, 2005, was another front-page story in Lancaster Newspapers, this one in the *Intelligencer Journal*. Stuckey became a county commissioner in 2008 and was in his third term in 2018. In the five days from "Who Is Gary Heinke?" on October 24, 2005, to "Heinke: A Pattern of Error," on October 28, Lancaster Newspapers published six separate front-page articles about Heinke.

[21] Both the *Intelligencer Journal* and the *Lancaster New Era* reported Heinke's October 25, 2005, resignation on October 29, 2005. Heinke submitted his resignation late in the day on Friday the 25. The *Intell* ran, "Under Fire, Heinke Quits," and the *New Era* ran "Probe to Go on as Heinke Quits Top County Job." It is important to note that both articles refer to the investigation by human resources director "Tom Myers." From the *Intell* article: "Heinke's resignation came as Tom Myers, the county's human resources director, was investigating the accuracy of credentials listed on the resume Heinke submitted." And from the *New Era*: "Top county officials today said they expect the investigation into the hiring of Gary Heinke as Lancaster County's human services chief will continue despite his abrupt resignation Friday evening." This demonstrates that it was well-known public knowledge that "Tom" Myers, not the county commissioners, was conducting the Heinke investigation. District Attorney Totaro represented in his affidavit to the Court, requesting a grand jury to investigate Heinke that he asked the commissioners for the report. He asked Myers for his report, not the commissioners.

[22] It is not clear why District Attorney Totaro included the county commissioners in the "To" line of the Myers e-mail. Totaro addressed entire contents of the e-mail to "Tom" and referred specifically to Myers's investigation: "you are currently investigating" . . . "Once you have concluded your investigation" . . . "Thank you . . ." Totaro is obviously aware Myers is conducting the investigation and addressing him, not the county commissioners. The function of including the commissioners in the e-mail is to copy them, not make the request of them. But having the commissioners' names on the "To" line did allow Totaro to claim he asked the commissioners for the report. Yet Totaro knew it was not in our possession and that we did not conduct the investigation..

[23] Again, the timing is important here. District Attorney Totaro wrote the e-mail to Myers on Monday, November 7, 2005. The next day the *New Era*, in "County

Endnotes

Completes Report on Heinke," quotes Myers as saying that his "goal" was to get the county commissioners the report by Wednesday. On Thursday—just 72 hours after sending the November 7th e-mail and less than 24 hours since the commissioners were given the report.

[24] This is one of the central themes of power and influence shown in this book. District Attorney Donald R. Totaro requested a copy of a report from a personnel investigation by the human resources director on Monday "when it [was] completed." On Thursday morning, one day after the report was handed to the Lancaster County commissioners, District Attorney Totaro filed a request with the Court, approved by the Court, to use a sitting grand jury to investigate the commissioners. Totaro did not even wait to read the Myers Report, which was delivered to him before noon on November 10. This course of action by the district attorney's office is difficult to comprehend.

[25] Just three days after his informal e-mail request for the Myers Report, District Attorney Totaro began his grand jury investigation. It was reported in the *Lancaster New Era*, "DA Launches Heinke Probe," November 10, 2005. Myers was baffled by the investigation into the Heinke hiring, the very issue he just investigated. "I don't know totally what he's asking for," Myers said.

[26] Art Morris was quoted in "Grand Jury Investigates Heinke's Hiring," *Intelligencer Journal*, November 18, 2005. Once again, Morris is credited with originally investigating the Heinke hiring. From the article:

> Former Lancaster city Mayor Art Morris said he was pleased an investigation has begun.
> "I certainly hope the process with Gary Heinke is fully reviewed and everybody's role in that," Morris said.
> "I hope it gets broadened to include the entire Conestoga View deal."
> Morris first brought the allegations against Heinke to light weeks ago after his own investigation of Heinke's resume discovered several discrepancies in his educational and employment background.

[27] The "Commonwealth Affidavit," submitted to the Court in July 2006, was a sworn, under oath, statement of the facts from the district attorney, representing the Commonwealth of Pennsylvania. Totaro's affidavit relied on the allegation that the county commissioners refused to turn over material to the district attorney. As his own e-mail shows, Totaro made the request of "Tom" Myers, not the county commissioners. Even though the official affidavit did not present the accurate sequence of events, a grand jury investigation was still launched. (See Appendix A)

[28] The "Motion to Prevent Destruction of Evidence during the Investigation by the County Investigating Grand Jury" was submitted by District Attorney Totaro to the Court on November 10, 2005, along with the "Notice of Submission" request for a grand jury investigation. It added to the deep chill that fell over the commissioners' offices after the subpoenas were delivered.

[29] All three county commissioners received subpoenas from Totaro's office on November 10, 2005.

[30] The March 15, 2005, "Target: Unsolved Mysteries / DA to Convene County's Third-Ever Investigating Grand Jury to Tackle Stalled Murder, Drug and Racketeering Cases" was a very prominent article in the *Lancaster New Era*. And the main thrust of the article was how the grand jury would be used for the most serious of criminal cases. The article begins:

> For the third time in local history, an investigating grand jury has been convened in Lancaster County.
> Its mission: to compel witnesses to tell what they know about unsolved murders, drugs, racketeering and other serious crimes.
> District Attorney Donald Totaro said today he received President Judge Louis J. Farina's permission to convene an investigating grand jury in February, believing it is the best way to pursue certain "criminal activity within Lancaster County."

[31] Other unsolved murders at the time of District Attorney Totaro's February 14, 2005, application for a grand jury investigation included the homicide of Cortney Fry, a young woman from the Columbia borough, the remains of whom were discovered in January 2005, and Heather Nunn, a city resident killed in her home in October 2004. The baby was "Baby Allison," whose body was found dead in the trash near an Amish school in the southern part of the county in December 2003.

[32] The grand jury is found in Pennsylvania Law, Title 42, Chapter 45, "Juries and Jurors," Subchapters (A-F). See: http://www.legis.state.pa.us/WU01/LI/LI/CT/HTM/42/00.045..HTM.

[33] Historians date the beginning of the grand jury to 1166, when, in England, Henry II enacted the "Assize of Clarendon," a decree explaining how the courts would be administered throughout the Kingdom. The Assize (Latin: assidēre ("to assist in the office of a judge") provided that a group of important men in each shire (county-sized district) bring indictments to the royal justices. The justices traveled the realm in a circuit each year adjudicating cases, criminal and civil, brought before them by these grand jury precursors. The grand jury was codified further in 1215 by King John in the Magna Carta, Article 61:

> ... the barons shall choose any twenty-five barons of the kingdom they wish, who with all their might are to observe, maintain and secure the observance of the peace and rights which we have conceded and confirmed to them by this present charter of ours; in this manner, that if we or our chief Justiciar or our bailiffs or any of our servants in any way do wrong to anyone, or transgress any of the articles of peace or security, and the wrong doing has been demonstrated to four of the aforesaid twenty-five barons, those four barons shall come to us or our chief Justiciar, (if we are

out of the kingdom), and laying before us the grievance, shall ask that we will have it redressed without delay.

[34] The rules for a Pennsylvania Investigating Grand Jury are found in the Pennsylvania Code, Chapter Two, Part (B) (1,2), Rules 220-244. See http://www.pacode.com/secure/data/234/chapter2/chap2toc.html.

Also, Pennsylvania Law, Title 42, Chapter 45, "Juries and Jurors," Subchapters (D), "Investigating Grand Juries." See http://www.legis.state.pa.us/WU01/LI/LI/CT/HTM/42/00.045..HTM.

[35] The Sandusky and Michael Brown cases underscore the serious nature of crimes usually investigated by grand juries. Often grand jury investigations involve highly sensitive or high-profile cases. In Lancaster, District Attorney Totaro's original request for an investigating grand jury in February 2005 was in line with other grand juries. He wanted to investigate the serious crimes of racketeering, large-scale drug dealing, and unsolved homicides. Gary Heinke's résumé didn't merit this type of investigation.

[36] A grand jury presentment of a "true bill" (Latin: Billa Vera) is the written opinion of a grand jury certifying that sufficient evidence has been heard, and that the grand jury believes it is probable that a crime has been committed by a specific person or persons and recommends the accused be tried in Court. The grand jury foreperson signs the true bill statement.

[37] The secrecy clause of the grand jury proceedings is found in P.L., Chapter 45, Title 42, (b), "Disclosure of proceedings by participants other than witnesses":

> . . . a juror, attorney, interpreter, stenographer, operator of a recording device, or any typist who transcribes recorded testimony may disclose matters occurring before the grand jury only when so directed by the court. All such persons shall be sworn to secrecy, and shall be in contempt of court if they reveal any information which they are sworn to keep secret.

[38] Sol Wachtler, former chief judge of the New York state courts, made his famous "ham sandwich" comment in an interview with the *New York Daily News*, January 31, 1985. From the article "New Top State Judge: Abolish Grand Juries & Let Us Decide":

> In a bid to make prosecutors more accountable for their actions, Chief Judge Sol Wachtler has proposed that the state scrap the grand jury system of bringing criminal indictments.
>
> Wachtler, who became the state's top judge earlier this month, said district attorneys now have so much influence on grand juries that "by and large" they could get them to "indict a ham sandwich."

See http://www.nydailynews.com/news/politics/chief-judge-wanted-abolish-grand-juries-article-1.2025208..

[39] The powers, composition, and rules of Pennsylvania grand jury proceedings are found in P.L. Chapter 45, Title 42, Subchapter (D) "Investigating Grand Juries," § 4545-4549. See http://www.legis.state.pa.us/WU01/LI/LI/CT/HTM/42/00.045..HTM.

40 "Composition of an Investigating Grand Jury" is found at P.L. Chapter 42, Subchapter (D) § 4545. See http://www.legis.state.pa.us/WU01/LI/LI/CT/HTM/42/00.045..HTM.

41 In 2017, the offices of the Lancaster County Board of Commissioners are located at 150 N. Queen Street, 7th Floor, Suite 715, Lancaster, Pa. 17603. The Office of the District Attorney is still located on the fifth floor of the County Courthouse, 50 N. Duke Street, Lancaster, Pa. 17608.

42 The *Lancaster New Era*, on November 18, 2005, reported on the courthouse subpoenas. "Subpoenas Rock Courthouse." This was another above-the-fold, front-page story. The article begins:

> The county's district attorney has ordered the commissioners and dozens of county employees to testify before an investigative grand jury probing the case of Gary D. Heinke, the county official who handled the sale of Conestoga View nursing home.
> Lancaster County Courthouse employees say the documents have blanketed the courthouse since Tuesday.
> "It's awful for the whole staff," one employee commented.

43 The only people whom grand jury witnesses are permitted to speak with about the grand jury proceedings are legal counsel. From P.L. Chapter 45, Title 42, Subchapter (D)," Investigating Grand Juries," § 4549. "Investigating Grand Jury Proceedings," subsection (d).

See http://www.legis.state.pa.us/WU01/LI/LI/CT/HTM/42/00.045..HTM.

44 The "Selection and Custody of Jurors" is found in P.L. Chapter 45, Title 42, § 4524. SUBCHAPTER B.

45 The November 11, 2005, *Lancaster New Era* article "How Heinke Got on Inside Track [sic]" was based on the Myers Report. The Myers Report, like the grand jury report, concluded that I knew nothing about and had no part in helping Heinke in the hiring process. The *New Era* article reads:

> Compiled by J. Thomas Myers, the county's human resources director, the report says Heinke conferred repeatedly with Shellenberger for at least 10 months before the county commissioners named him to the post.
> He also conferred with Commissioner Pete Shaub and county solicitor John Espenshade for at least seven months before he got the job.
> Shellenberger, Shaub and Espenshade concealed these communications from the other county commissioner, Molly Henderson, and from the county's Human Resources Department, according to the report.

Despite reporting what Myers said about my non-involvement with the Heinke hiring, the *New Era* and the other Lancaster Newspapers repeatedly conflated me with the other two commissioners.

[46] There was simply no aspect of the sale of Conestoga View about which Art Morris did not consider himself an expert. An engineer, not an attorney or an accountant, Morris deemed himself also a legal expert. From "Morris: Review Special Counsel Appointment," *Lancaster New Era*, November 29, 2005:

> The lawyers should give back the money. That's what former Mayor Art Morris believes attorneys who served as special counsel on the Conestoga View nursing home sale should do if they performed their work without legal authorization. In a letter to Lancaster County Controller Dennis Stuckey, delivered this morning, Morris asked for a full review of the appointment of special counsel. . . .

[47] The legal fees paid to the law firm of Stevens & Lee totaled almost $5,350,000 by the end of 2005. By 2009, when the project opened, the firm that wrote the Third-Class County Convention Center Authority Act had been paid more than $8,000,000. The consultants hired by the LCCCA were paid in the millions of dollars. For example, Maurice Walker, a business consultant, was hired to essentially do the job of the executive director, David M. Hixson. Mr. Walker was paid in excess of $300,000 per year for his consulting work. Hixson was paid $90,000, in addition. Dale High's real estate, construction, and food and beverage businesses receive millions from the LCCCA.

[48] The December 11, 2005, *Sunday News* article "Out of Commission" was a major attack on the Board of Commissioners. Several high-profile leaders harshly criticized the entire board. Senator Gib Armstrong, who belonged to Shellenberger's church, said Shellenberger "lied to me several times." I wasn't spared. The *Sunday News* quoted from Paul Thibault's PAC website, "The word 'lame' does not begin to describe Molly Henderson's nervous attempts to distance herself from the disaster that is The Great Conestoga View Fiasco, . . . "

[49] In journalism, anonymous "sources" should be treated with great circumspection and should be avoided, if possible. Helen Colwell Adams uses them repeatedly in the December 11, 2005, *Sunday News* "Out of Commission" article and others. Here's a brief section of the almost 3,000-word article where Colwell Adams uses unnamed sources:

> The divisive political atmosphere surrounds Henderson too.
> Other Democrats have expressed frustration at what they perceive as her willingness to vote with Shellenberger even on issues that Democrats expected her to view in a different light; Conestoga View, for instance.
> She has split with key party officials, in particular state Rep. Mike Sturla and former commissioner Ron Ford, on the convention center project.

[50] The sheer weight of the "Out of Commission" article was extremely heavy. Timed two weeks before Christmas, in the Lancaster Newspapers' largest circulation newspaper, the *Sunday News*, and quoting most of the Lancaster establishment as they scathingly criticized us, it was clear that Lancaster Newspapers and Penn Square Partners would hold nothing back against Shellenberger and me. And this was still the beginning.

⁵¹ Mark E. Lovett, Esq., is currently (2018) a partner at the Lancaster law firm Brubaker Connaughton Goss & Lucarelli LLC.

⁵² The primary contact for us at the district attorney's office was K. Kenneth Brown, II. Brown, as of 2015, was chief counsel to the inspector general of Pennsylvania.

⁵³ The suggestion that I had "taken the Fifth" was one of the statements that we believed was libelous. This was published in the *Sunday News*, December 31, 2006, days before the grand jury report was publicly released. The article, "Seeking an Inside View," written by Gilbert A. Smart, read in part:

> Shaub, who did not hire a lawyer during the investigation, has said that Shellenberger and Henderson had hired lawyers to help them avoid testifying a second time. The appearance of "Taking the Fifth," say observers, could be extremely damaging politically.

As stated in the chapter, I testified three times before the grand jury and never asserted Fifth Amendment privilege. And, again, a *Sunday News* reporter relies on unnamed sources, "say observers." This was reckless journalism and highly damaging. I had exchanged e-mails with Smart, the reporter. He never asked about "taking the Fifth." It was part of my libel lawsuit against Lancaster Newspapers, Inc., and several of its staff members. Each libelous statement contained in the lawsuit is discussed in Chapter Twelve of this book. Also see *Molly Henderson vs Lancaster Newspapers, Inc., John M. Buckwalter, Ernest J. Schreiber, Marvin I. Adams, Jr., Helen Colwell Adams, Charles Raymond Shaw, Arthur E. Morris, Gilbert A. Smart, John H. Brubaker, III, and David Pidgeon.* No. 0712003.

Chapter Ten – The Grand Jury

¹ It is difficult to quantify the precise number of negative articles concerning "the commissioners" and me during this period, from 2005 thru 2007. I used the database ProQuest to count the number of articles. ProQuest is a Michigan-based global information and content technology company that, among other services, electronically archives newspapers. ProQuest has more than 125 billion digital pages in its database. When we put the search terms "Molly Henderson" and "County Commissioners" into the ProQuest search engine for 2005, it turned out 399 articles. During the time I was in office, from 2004 to 2008, there were a total of 1,653 articles published with "Molly Henderson" and "County Commissioners. (See Appendix C) The ProQuest numbers do not include letters to the editor, which also numbered in the hundreds. The letter-writing campaign instigated by Lancaster Newspapers owner Peggy Steinman and carried about by chairman Jack Buckwalter, with the help of Art Morris and others (see Chapter Seven of this book), was responsible for many of these letters.

² One of worst consequences of Lancaster Newspapers solely focusing its "coverage" of Conestoga View and its negative articles on "the commissioners" and the convention center was that it ignored the real work our board did on behalf of the people of Lancaster County. Apart from our record of being ranked number one in the United

States in farmland preservation in 2007 (and number one in Pennsylvania), our board guaranteed a $10 million bond for Clipper Magazine Stadium and "bridged" a $1 million shortfall for the stadium. Working with the Career and Technology Center, the county commissioners completed the state-of-the-art Lancaster County Public Safety Training Center (http://www.lcpstc.org/). Our board provided $1.2 million to the Lancaster City Safety Coalition, an auxiliary of the Lancaster Alliance, cofounded by the three Penn Square Partners and nine others. The County Commissioners Board on which I served also provided another $1 million for development of the Northwest Corridor section of the city. The Pennsylvania Academy of Music (now the Ware Center) received $1 million from the county commissioners. Outside the city, our board assisted the Columbia Borough "River Park," as well as the Northwest Lancaster County River trail. Our board completed a downtown intersection Improvement & Design plan in Elizabethtown and opened Freedom Memorial Park in Millersville. The county awarded the Lancaster County Conservancy a $1 million grant. (See Appendix D for a table of projects of our board from 2004 to 2008.)

[3] Democrat Rick Gray received 5,051 votes to Charlie Smithgall's 3,718 votes on November 8, 2005. Gray, who completed his third term in 2018, assumed office on January 3, 2006. Source: Lancaster County Voter Registration and Board of Elections.

[4] The extent of the subsidies given to Penn Square Partners went beyond the millions saved from the Partners' property tax exemption through Act 23. According an article in the *Intelligencer Journal*, August 11, 2005, "County: Offer to Waive Fees Violates Act 23," "an estimated $1 million in fees associated with the project" had been waived by Mayor Smithgall. The lost fees could only be estimated because the city planning department hadn't been tasked with adding up the lost revenue from "development plans, zoning applications, utility hookups, sidewalk improvements." Paula Jackson, the city of Lancaster's chief planner, said in the *Intelligencer Journal* article that she didn't know exactly how much money the Partners saved from the fee waivers. "We haven't been calculating because we haven't had to," Jackson was quoted in the article. "We haven't been told how much we're not getting." Also see "Planners: Center Still Costs $134 Million," John M. Spidaliere, October 22, 2005, *Lancaster New Era*; and "Pa. House Gives Boost to Plans For City Center/Hotel," *Lancaster New Era*, April 27, 2006 (no byline given).

[5] Former City of Lancaster mayor Charlie Smithgall was one of the most important public officials in bringing the hotel-convention center project to downtown Lancaster. Apart from being an extremely outspoken opponent of the Harrisburg Area Community College moving into the Watt & Shand building prior to his election as mayor, Smithgall made his number-one priority from his first day in office landing a local tenant for the Watt & Shand. It was Smithgall who brought in James O. Pickard to find a buyer for the building. It was Smithgall who waived more than a million in fees for the construction of the project. Smithgall showed up at all of the major meetings, advocating for the project, whether it was the room tax in 1999, the $40 million county bond in 2003, or the TIF in 2005. Smithgall, a friend of former senator

Gibson E. "Gib" Armstrong, played an essential role in "running interference" for the project from the city's mayor's office. Smithgall chose Convention Center Authority board members who reflected his support of the project and Penn Square Partners. He backed the city's guaranties of $36 million for the hotel. Charlie Smithgall was a very good friend of the project developers. But as of January 3, 2006, he was gone. Now, it was Rick Gray's turn.

[6] Gray's comments to the Rotary Club came from "Mayoral Hopefuls Lay Out Agendas," *Lancaster New Era*, October 13, 2005. Smithgall was less equivocal than Gray in his support for the project. From the article:

> Smithgall, who has served two terms as mayor, said he has never wavered in his support of the convention center project and still believes it will be the keystone of a downtown economic boom.
> "We'll move forward with it," said Smithgall.

[7] My proposals, which were sent to Mayor Gray, were introduced at a regular county commissioners meeting on January 4, 2006. I introduced a motion asking the board to vote on the proposals at its January 11, 2006, meeting the following week. The proposals were reported in "Commissioner Asked to Consider Proposals," January 4, 2006, *Lancaster New Era* (PA).

[8] The Convention Center Authority's intention to enter into a "swaption" agreement with its county- and city-backed bonds was picked up by a periodical: *The Bond Buyer*, "Pennsylvania County Authority Proceeding with Swap Plans," January 20, 2006. From the *Bond Buyer* article:

> Plans by the Lancaster County, Pa., Convention Center Authority to enter into a forward-starting swap are progressing despite its postponement of two board meetings that led some to wonder whether plans had stalled, the agency's financial adviser said yesterday.
> The swap would hedge interest rate risk on a future issue, slated for about $50 million, to help finance a long-disputed, $137 million hotel and convention center complex in the tourist area about 90 minutes west of Philadelphia. Supporters say the project will revitalize downtown Lancaster and the surrounding region. Opponents have challenged many aspects of the development, including its financing....

[9] The January 31, 2006, date was the consummation of the deal that was originally brought to the public in December 2004. This was prior to Penn Square Partners' unsuccessful attempt to receive real estate tax abatement through a Tax Increment Financing (TIF) proposal. The sale of the Watt & Shand building by Penn Square Partners to the Redevelopment Authority of the City of Lancaster (RACL) for $7.25 million was reported on February 9, 2006 in "Watt & Shand Building Sold," *Lancaster New Era*. Although pleased with the sale, Mayor Gray appeared impatient with the pace of the project, based on his comments:

"It's another step forward to completing this long-standing project," Lancaster Mayor Rick Gray said of the transaction.

"We're moving forward to bring closure to a project that has dominated debate and consumed our public interest for far too long," the mayor said today.

Although no construction or development had taken place on the Watt & Shand site, and the building stood just as it had the day of purchase in 1998, the partners received a gain of $6 million on the sale to RACL. They attributed $4.6 million of the price to "development costs, heat, taxes, placing Christmas ornaments, and other expenses" since Penn Square Partners bought the building. Incidentally, during that time, Penn Square Partner High Industries was paid millions of dollars from the LCCCA for "Developer's Fees." And, again, no work was done from a construction standpoint during these years.

[10] The Ernst & Young "Market Study, Cash Flow Estimates, and Economic Impact Analysis" was delivered to the Lancaster Alliance auxiliary, Lancaster Campaign, on July 19, 1999. A digital version may be found under "Convention Center Documents," at pressedthebook.com

[11] Ibid. From the Ernst & Young "Market Study, Cash Flow Estimates, and Economic Impact Analysis," executive summary.

[12] The first Pricewaterhouse Coopers (PwC) market study, "Market & Economic Analysis for the Proposed Convention Center in Downtown Lancaster," was delivered to the Lancaster County Convention Center Authority on November 7, 2000. In 2002, PwC was asked by the LCCCA to provide an "Update" to its 2000 study. It was in the update where the physical size of the project grew substantially from its original size of 61,000 square feet to 183,917 square feet, which included 66,745 square feet of "shared space" between the "private" hotel and the "public" convention center. In 2005, PwC wrote a letter to LCCCA executive director David Hixson, demanding that all references to PwC be immediately removed from the LCCCA website. Robert Canton, author of the letter and principal author of both PwC studies, was alarmed at how the project had changed since its 2002 "Update." Canton wrote that comparing the project in 2005 to the project he evaluated in 2002 was "the equivalent of using a study of a 500 room Marriott to evaluate a 300-room Hampton." See: pressedthebook.com; *Pricewaterhouse Coopers, Market Study, 2002*

[13] The meeting called by the county-appointed LCCCA board members—Laura Douglas, Deb Hall, and Jack Craver—was covered by both of Lancaster Newspapers daily newspapers. The meeting was held in the Farm & Home Center on Manheim Pike on the night of January 4, 2006. Both the *Intelligencer Journal* ("Convention Authority Forum Full of Complaints"), and the *Lancaster New Era* ("Center Foes Get No Satisfaction from New Mayor") reported on the meeting the next day, January 5.

[14] Chris Hart Nibbrig was at the Farm & Home Center meeting on January 4, 2005, and commented on Mayor Rick Gray's remarks. "It was a star turn by the new mayor," said Hart Nibbrig. "Rick didn't remove his coat. He just strode up to the microphone,

ignored the board members, and spoke directly to the audience. He seemed angry and spoke condescendingly. And after he finished, he just spun around and marched out, with a couple of aides scuttling after him. The room was stunned."

[15] Gray had been in office for eight days at the time he interrupted the Board of County Commissioners meeting on January 11, 2006. There was no professional courtesy displayed by Mayor Gray.

[16] The background material on Robert Edwin Field (February 25, 1937–) came from Chris Hart Nibbrig. Hart Nibbrig, an alumnus of the Columbia University Graduate School of Journalism, with magazine and newspaper experience, covered the hotel and convention center project for Field's Newslanc.com website from 2006 to 2007.

[17] Robert Field's company, the Manor Group, owns eight apartment complexes in three states (PA, NJ, WV) and four hotels, two in Pennsylvania and two in New Jersey, according to its website, themanorgroup.com.

[18] Field became a center of controversy in Luzerne County when he contributed $35,000 to a group opposing a Luzerne County–backed bond guaranty for a new convention center. The *Times Leader* of Wilkes-Barre, Pa., reported of Field's involvement on June 23, 2005, in "Property Owner's $35,000 Campaign Contribution Helped Finance Group's Push to Relieve County Taxpayers of Guaranteed Bond for Arena."

> WILKES-BARRE—A Lancaster-based property owner with significant local ties contributed $35,000 to Taxes No—or more than 90 percent of the group's total fund drive—to help defeat the arena ballot question last month, according to expense reports.
>
> Both Taxes No and Arena Yes, along with most candidates, filed their second campaign expense report on June 15. The reports show Taxes No raised $36,234.50 during the second filing period. Arena Yes collected $55,403 on top of the $211,000 it had raised by May 1.
>
> The May 16 ballot question was defeated by 48 votes. The question asked voters to let the county guarantee a maximum $22 million bond for the $41.2 million project. Arena Yes has challenged the outcome in county court because of alleged vote tampering.

It was property owner Robert Edwin Field's donation that helped put a dent in the better-financed Arena Yes's media onslaught.

Without Field, the group opposed to public funding for the arena/convention center project could not have afforded about $17,000 in television and radio spots in the race's final turn. See http://www.luzernecounty.org/county/boards-authorities/luzerne-county-convention-center-authority.

[19] In addition to the Luzerne County Convention Center Authority (and later Lancaster County Convention Center Authority), the law firm of Stevens & Lee—the authors of the Third-Class County Convention Center Authorities Act—represented the Berks County Convention Center Authority.

Endnotes

[20] Today, the Northeastern Pennsylvania Civic Arena and Convention Center is named the Mohegan Sun Arena at Casey Plaza. The naming rights are connected with the Mohegan Sun Pocono, Racetrack, and Casino, also located in Wilkes-Barre, Pa.

[21] Robert Field made his offer of a $50,000 subsidy for a feasibility study on the day Gray interrupted the county commissioners meeting, January 11, 2006. The *Intelligencer Journal* reported Field's offer the next day: "Field Offers $50,000 for Center Study," January 12, 2006. The article begins:

> For local businessman Robert Field, the price of learning whether his dire predictions for the proposed downtown hotel/convention center would come true will cost $50,000. Field Wednesday night offered $50,000 to Lancaster Mayor Rick Gray and the Lancaster County commissioners to pay for a feasibility study on the downtown project. "It is my belief that the report would enable the parties to make an informed decision and . . . that harmony and comity will be restored to our community," Field wrote.

[22] See "Mayor Answers Demands for Study," *Intelligencer Journal*, January 14, 2006, and "Mayor: Conditions on Study Delaying Tactic," *Lancaster New Era*, January 14, 2006. Again, the new mayor's attitude (despite his being in office less than two weeks) derisive and personal.

[23] Ibid. *Lancaster New Era*, January 14, 2006, "Mayor: Conditions on Study Delaying Tactic." In this case, instead of addressing the issue and get an independent, non-affiliated firm to conduct the feasibility study—Penn Square Partners, through Nevin Cooley personalized an attack on Shellenberger and me. Remember, a true feasibility study had never been performed on the project by this point, February 2006.

[24] The issue of getting a feasibility study performed on the project was possible because Shellenberger and I represented the majority of the Board of Commissioners. This is what vexed Penn Square Partners, including Lancaster Newspapers. We were in a position, by virtue of the office we held, to seriously challenge the project and perhaps stop it. Calling for an independent feasibility study was well within our purview as county commissioners. After all, the county had guaranteed half of a $40 million bond for the project. We had a right to see if the money was being properly spent. But we were definitely viewed as a threat and were treated as "enemies" of the city and of progress by Lancaster Newspapers. See "Mayor Answers Demands for Study" *Intelligencer Journal*, January 14, 2006.

[25] It did not take a six-figure market study to see the inherent drawbacks to building a 200,000-square-foot convention center and a 19-story hotel in the middle of the worst traffic congestion in Lancaster city or county. Apart from the extremely dubious financing, a burden that overwhelmingly and increasingly fell on the public sector, the very idea of a project of this size going into the center of the city made no sense. Downtown Lancaster, Pennsylvania, was simply not a good convention destination. It is hard to access, the traffic was (and is) terrible, and there's not much to do for entertainment. See: pressedthebook.

com; Pricewaterhouse Coopers, "Market & Economic Analysis for the Proposed Convention Center in Downtown Lancaster, 'Update,' 2002," pp. 31–38.

26 The commissioners acceded to Mayor Gray's demand that only Pricewaterhouse Coopers conduct the feasibility study, but that gesture was moot when Pricewaterhouse declined to engage with the project again. "Consultant Won't Do New Study of Center," *Lancaster New Era*, January 28, 2006. Also online, see http://lancasteronline.com/news/consultant-won-t-do-new-study-of-center/article_55f98948-ca6f-5d11-a4b1-92857d23c8b8.html.

27 The e-mail from Pricewaterhouse Coopers consultant Robert V. Canton was originally sent to county-appointed board member Jack Craver in November 2005. Craver, our appointment to the LCCCA board, had decades of hospitality business experience, including working as general manager of the Plaza Hotel in New York City and the Mayflower Hotel in Washington, D.C. So, he knew the business. Pricewaterhouse Coopers consultant Robert Canton's e-mail to LCCCA board member Jack Craver may be found at pressedthebook.com in the November 2005 entries. The e-mail is also quoted in "Consultant Won't Do New Study of Center," *Lancaster New Era*, January 28, 2006.

28 The February 8, 2006, decision by the county commissioners to issue Requests for Proposals for a feasibility study was embarrassingly late for the project. But at least it was going to get done. The commissioners' action was reported in "County Seeks Study of Center Finances," *Lancaster New Era*, February 8, 2006.

29 The county hired Pannell Kerr Forster (PKF) to conduct the first-ever true feasibility study of the hotel and convention center project. The firm, an international giant in the consulting field, would not "play politics" with a hundred-thousand-dollar report in Lancaster, Pennsylvania. PKF's hiring was reported in "County OKs New Study of Center," *Intelligencer Journal*, February 16, 2006. PKF, now CBRE Hotels, may be found here: http://www.cbrehotels.com/EN/services/valuation-services/PKF-Consulting-and-Research/Pages/default.aspx.

30 Ibid. "County OKs New Study of Center," *Intelligencer Journal*, February 16, 2006.

31 LCCCA chairman C. Ted Darcus's 916-word "Letter Sent by Authority," to the *Sunday News*, February 26, 2006, was another example of the Lancaster Newspapers' animosity toward the commissioners. In this case, Darcus exceeded the letters word limit by five times. The absence of cooperation from the other entities involved in the project—Penn Square Partners, LCCCA, and RACL—is another example of disregarding the public's representatives in this project. The Lancaster County commissioners had imposed the room rental tax (the revenue of which went mostly to the LCCCA) and guaranteed tens of millions of dollars in construction bonds. The county commissioners had established the LCCCA, and still we could not get cooperation from these entities. In this case, it was their inaction that was the misuse of power. It showed a complete lack of regard for the people of Lancaster County, who were financially guaranteeing the project.

Endnotes

[32] Ibid. "Letter Sent by Authority," *Sunday News*, February 26, 2006.

[33] LCCCA board member Deb Hall's motion to have the LCCCA board conduct a legal audit of the fees from Stevens & Lee was made on June 8, 2006. Darcus spoke for the board in not allowing a vote. The contentiousness of the meeting was captured in a June 11, 2006, *Sunday News* headline, "Fight Night." Hall's motion is referenced below:

> Absent from the seven-member board were Willie Borden, a city-appointed member, and Jack Craver, a county-appointed representative.
>
> That kept the board weighted in favor of the project's public-private financing deals and enabled the board to vote down a proposal by board member Deb Hall to have an independent audit of the authority's payments to its legal firm, Stevens & Lee. . . .
>
> The authority receives a monthly invoice from Stevens & Lee that gives the fees and costs for "professional services rendered on behalf of Lancaster County Convention Center Authority." No itemized bill is provided to the authority or its board members, although they can schedule an appointment with the law office to review a detailed invoice.

The *Sunday News* published a statement from Hall on June 11, 2006. From the statement:

> In response to our memorandum requesting a legal audit of the Stevens & Lee law firm, Lancaster County Convention Center Authority Chairman Ted Darcus stated at the June 8 public meeting that such a review should not take place because of "attorney-client privilege." He advised the convention-center authority board to vote down a motion requesting the audit.

Mr. Darcus was misleading by implying the audit would violate attorney-client confidentiality. Showing how to avert any possible "attorney-client" confidentiality problem was the main purpose of the proposal.

[34] Ibid.

[35] Craver's letter to the editor was published in the *Sunday News*, February 26, 2006. In his letter, Craver drew on his decades of experience managing a large luxury hotel, giving a cogent analysis of the importance of having a proper economic feasibility study conducted on the project. From Craver's letter:

> Since late in 2000, the estimated cost of the Lancaster County Convention Center project has increased from $70 million to $145 million [including the proposed parking garage], and yet not one bid has been opened.
>
> Not one study has been completed that addresses economic feasibility and estimates cash flow from the center project.

Since Sept. 11, 2001, the group-travel and convention market has changed significantly, making markets like Lancaster County less attractive.

Why should anyone care about this? Both Lancaster County and the city have guaranteed millions of dollars on bond issues, and the economic feasibility of this project is crucial for taxpayers.

But what about several reports that the Lancaster County Convention Center Authority commissioned previously? Not one addresses the economic feasibility of the project.

The report that the authority refers to most frequently in support of the project is one done for the trial on the hotel-tax challenge in December 2000.

That report, really a market study, was done by PricewaterhouseCoopers. . . .

This PKF report will analyze the current economic viability and/or the associated economic risk of this disputed project.

Unfortunately, as of this date, Penn Square Partners, the private developer of the hotel has refused to participate with PKF in this study and the authority has not yet said whether it will participate.

As a new member of the authority, I do not want this project to fail.

However, more importantly, I do not want the county and the city to be funding, via bond guarantees, a project that lacks current data to support its viability.

That would mean that not only will the hotel owner pay more through a higher hotel tax, but the taxpayers will be asked to step in via higher real-estate taxes to fund the guarantees created by the shortfalls.

—Jack Craver,
Lancaster County Convention Center Authority

Jack Craver was a fine gentleman. The Cornell-educated, majoring in the Hospitality Industry, Craver passed away in May of 2008. He was seventy-seven.

[36] See the previously mentioned June 11, 2006, *Sunday News* article "Fight Night."

[37] Any history of the hotel and convention center is incomplete without mention of Ronald Preston Harper, Jr. A gifted investigator, Harper was a clever and effective agitator of the Lancaster establishment. Through his 5thestate.com website, Harper recorded and posted some of the misdeeds of the sponsors of the project.

[38] The Pickard pie episode was reported in the *Intelligencer Journal*, May 10, 2001. The pie toss happened the previous night, on May 9. The main subject of the LCCCA meeting that evening was the selection of a manager for the convention center. This

was a particularly contentious debate. From "Authority Narrows Convention Center Companies to Three":

> James O. Pickard didn't have a taste for humble pie Wednesday.
>
> The chairman of Lancaster County Convention Center Authority was presented with a chocolate cream pie by self-appointed political watchdog Ron Harper Jr., who appeared at the authority's meeting to criticize Pickard for "bulldozing people and properties" with his politics during the planning of a proposed downtown convention center. As Harper pulled out a "beautiful and delicious pie disguised as humble pie" to make his point to Pickard, he suggested to Pickard, "Don't be so prideful.. . . . Stop and get a humble attitude."
>
> That's when the pie hit the fan.
>
> Pickard hurled the pie, pan and all, across City Council chambers, where it splattered across a carved wooden table bearing the city's seal.
>
> Pickard said Wednesday it was the third time Harper approached him with "items that pose a threat," referring to the pie, and a copy of Dale Carnegie's book, "How to Win Friends and Influence People" and a painted gold plunger, both presented to Pickard last June.
>
> The Golden Plunger Award is Harper's gift to politicians who, he believes, "trash the public's trust."
>
> Pickard also tossed Carnegie's book, like the pie, into the air.
>
> Harper, not appreciating Pickard's suggestion that his pie, book and plunger posed threats, countered that Pickard's comments were slanderous and demanded an apology.
>
> "You are not royalty," Harper told Pickard as an audience of about 20 silently watched the drama unfold and the pie go stale.
>
> Pickard responded with a threat to have Harper removed by a police officer.
>
> "The whole community is getting tired of you and your act," Pickard said to Harper, who caught the action on a digital video camera. "You'll get no apology from this chair."

[39] LCCCA board member Laura Douglas made her comments about Ted Darcus to Newslanc.com, Robert Field's website.

[40] David M. Hixson's hiring as executive director of the LCCCA was reported in "Ex-Schweiker Aide Executive Director of Convention Center," *Lancaster New Era*, July 9, 2003. Hixson's background information used in this chapter was derived from this article.

[41] John Espenshade, a partner at Stevens & Lee—the authors of the 1994 Third-Class County Authority Act, the enabling legislation for the project—had been the solicitor

of record for the LCCCA since its inception in 1999. The firm had billed more than $6 million at this point, 2006.

[42] The rather benign headline of the *Lancaster New Era* editorial, "Commissioners Need to Let in More Sun," on January 5, 2006, belied an assault on all three commissioners. The attacks regarding the Conestoga View sale, made after the Myers Report went public, were damaging to me in many ways, including politically. The editors and the reporters at the *New Era* were aware that I had not participated in any "secret" meetings, nor did I do anything improper with respect to the Gary Heinke hiring. Yet they persisted in suggesting, and sometimes saying outright, that I was engaged in the secrecy.

[43] The ownership breakdown of Penn Square Partners was not made public until the summer of 2006. It was disclosed in a courtroom during a legal action brought against the Lancaster County commissioners by the Lancaster County Convention Center Authority. The commissioners were being sued for our actions (County Resolutions Nos. 36 and 37) revoking the county's $40 million bond guaranty and shrinking the area from which the room tax could be collected. The LCCCA was also asking the Court to place a gag order on Commissioner Shellenberger and me. During testimony, it was revealed that general partner High Industries held a 44 percent share; Lancaster Newspapers held 44 percent; and Fulton Bank, 12 percent. See *Penn Square General Corporation and the Redevelopment Authority of the City of Lancaster v. County of Lancaster, et al.*

[44] The *Intelligencer Journal* article "County Broke Law, Morris Says" was published on the same day, February 16, 2006, as "County OKs New Study of City Center," which reported on the hiring of PKF to perform the first-ever feasibility study of the hotel-convention center project. The "County Broke Law" article about Conestoga View was page A-1; the one about hiring PKF, B-2+.

See the article online at:

http://lancasteronline.com/news/county-broke-law-morris-says/article_9e0a4e4a-8b87-5a96-b6fa-9326b1d1e52a.html.

[45] John H. "Jack" Brubaker III was a defendant in the libel action I filed against Lancaster Newspapers and several of its staff members, *Molly Henderson vs Lancaster Newspapers, Inc., John M. Buckwalter, Ernest J. Schreiber, Marvin I. Adams, Jr., Helen Colwell Adams, Charles Raymond Shaw, Arthur E. Morris, Gilbert A. Smart, John H. Brubaker, III, and David Pidgeon.* No. 0712003. The switch from *New Era* reporter Bernard Harris (not a defendant) to Brubaker covering the county commissioners was made after the Conestoga View story turned into the grand jury story. *New Era* editor Ernest J. "Ernie" Schreiber, another defendant in the legal action against Lancaster Newspapers, discussed assigning Brubaker, a more experienced reporter, to the county beat. From pages 54–56 of Schreiber's deposition:

Q. And who had that county beat in the 2005 to 2007 period?
A. Would have been Bernie Harris, John Spidaliere and Anya Litvak . . .
Q. During this same time period was there another reporter by the name of Jack Brubaker?
A. Yes.

Q. That worked at the *New Era*?
A. That's right.
Q. And what was his assignment during this period?
A. He was our in-depth projects reporter. Everyone else in the *New Era* was really devoted to day-to-day coverage. When there was something that required ongoing multiple day reporting and writing, we turned to Jack
Q. And who appointed him to that particular position?
A. I did. . . .
Q. All right. And who at the *New Era* was assigned to report on that [the grand jury proceedings]?
A. Jack Brubaker.
Q. And did you make that assignment?
A. At some point, yes.

[46] The move from the editorial page to investigative and special assignments reporter was made by *New Era* editor Ernie Schreiber. (See note number 42, above.) From pages 11–12 of the deposition of defendant John H. Brubaker, III, in the action *Molly Henderson vs Lancaster Newspapers, Inc., John M. Buckwalter, Ernest J. Schreiber, Marvin I. Adams, Jr., Helen Colwell Adams, Charles Raymond Shaw, Arthur E. Morris, Gilbert A. Smart, John H. Brubaker, III, and David Pidgeon*. No. 0712003:

Brubaker: "In 2003 I switched roles off the editorial page and I became an investigative reporter and general assignment reporter, as well as columnist."
Q. "What precipitated that switch?"
A. "It is something that I wanted to do for sometime. And the opportunity became available and the editor at that time, Ernie Schreiber, wanted to make the switch. And so we did."

[47] From pages 70–71 of the deposition of defendant John H. Brubaker, III, in the action *Molly Henderson vs Lancaster Newspapers, Inc., John M. Buckwalter, Ernest J. Schreiber, Marvin I. Adams, Jr., Helen Colwell Adams, Charles Raymond Shaw, Arthur E. Morris, Gilbert A. Smart, John H. Brubaker, III, and David Pidgeon*. No. 0712003.

[48] The four articles published in the *Lancaster New Era*, bylined by Jack Brubaker on February 21, 2006—"How Did County Decide to Sell Nursing Home?"; "Did County Break Pa. Law?"; "How Does Depreciation Figure in Financial Health?"; and "Accounting Yardsticks Give Different Measures"—were for one newspaper on a single day. The day prior, in the other Steinman daily, the *Intelligencer Journal*, the headline of the day was, "County Broke Law, Morris Says." This illustrates the constant coverage by Lancaster Newspapers over the sale of a county asset five months earlier. It wasn't "coverage" in any professional journalistic sense of the word. These "articles" were hardly providing the public with information.

[49] "Ex-Officials Rip Secret Deal," published in the *Lancaster New Era*, March 21, 2006, was another Jack Brubaker above-the-fold, front-page, article. The article, published a full six months after the sale of Conestoga View, was an example of the planning between the sponsors of the convention center project and Lancaster Newspapers. In the article,

Brubaker brings back former county commissioner Paul Thibault, who chaired the board when it passed both the room tax and the $40 million county guaranty. Thibault, a former history professor, said of the Conestoga View sale, "I don't see a shred of legality here."

http://lancasteronline.com/news/ex-officials-rip-secret-deal/article_b529ee42-00b8-5582-9582-f1481b5d63ec.html.

50 The Jack Brubaker *Lancaster New Era* article "They've Got Another Secret, County to Release Records—without Black Marks," March 29, 2006, was part of an ironic "investigation" into the legal billing connected with the Conestoga View sale. All three Lancaster Newspapers devoted considerable attention and space to the billings of the Stevens & Lee law firm. The total legal fees to Stevens & Lee for the Conestoga View transaction were $288,000. By 2006, Stevens & Lee had been paid more than $6 million by the Lancaster County Convention Center Authority, but Brubaker and Lancaster Newspapers, along with Paul Thibault, and Art Morris, said nothing about that. This is an example of how Conestoga View was used as a red herring, a diversion from the much more costly, risky, and perhaps verboten (according to our lawsuit with the DCED) hotel-convention center.

Jack Brubaker's article "The Perfect Secret, County Officials Kept a Tight Lid on the Sale of Conestoga View until the Deal Was Suddenly Announced. Here's How They Did It," *Lancaster New Era*, April 29, 2006, is a good example of how Lancaster Newspapers had merged together, all three of the commissioners into one group. While it was true and established that Shaub and Shellenberger secretly met to sell Conestoga View, it was also true and established that I was kept completely in the dark and out of the loop regarding the sale. Having read the November Myers Report, Brubaker knew this. But Lancaster Newspapers did not present it that way. This was a decision made and/or okayed by editor Ernie Schreiber.

52 Under oath, as a defendant in the libel action against him, John H. Brubaker, III, testified regarding the Myers Report. From Brubaker's deposition testimony, September 4, 2009: "Tom Myers, who was the chief author of it, called a news conference in his office and basically took us through this. And then I went back to the office and read it carefully, whenever this was released. [November 10, 2005]"

And regarding the Heinke hiring, Brubaker testified," [M]y recollection is that she [Molly Henderson] was not impressed with Gary Heinke and, in fact, did not favor him for the position."

Brubaker's apparent knowledge of the falsity of what he was writing was the basis of my lawsuit against him and Lancaster Newspapers.

Chapter Eleven: The Relentless Press

1 The red herring coverage of Conestoga View continued during 2006, when more than 500 articles deriding "the commissioners" were published. The database ProQuest. com was used to count the number of articles. ProQuest, a Michigan-based global information and content technology company, electronically archives newspapers.

Proquest.com has more than 125 billion digital pages in its database. When placing the terms "Molly Henderson" and "County Commissioners" into the Proquest.com search engine for 2006, indicates 521 articles. During my in office, from 2004 to 2008, there were approximately 1,653 articles published with "Molly Henderson" and "County Commissioners," This does not include letters to the editor. (See Appendix C)

[2] In 2006, Lancaster Newspapers, Inc., under the name Penn Square Limited, LLC, was a 44 percent limited partner in Penn Square Partners. High Real Estate Group, under the name of Penn Square General Corp., owned 44 percent as general partner, and Fulton Bank owned 12 percent as a limited partner. It took eight years from the formation of Penn Square Partners, and a lawsuit, for Lancaster Newspapers to disclose its 44 percent ownership stake in the project. The ownership percentages of Penn Square Partners were disclosed by Penn Square Partners vice president and High executive Mark Fitzgerald in court under questioning by the county's attorney Howard Kelin, in July 2006. The *Lancaster New Era*, in, "Newspaper's Stake in Project Surprises Foes," July 18, 2006, begins:

> There were few surprises last week at the Lancaster Convention Center hearing. But in one of them, the public learned for the first time what stake each of the investors in the hotel part of the project holds.
>
> According to testimony by Mark Fitzgerald, a Penn Square Partners executive: Penn Square Limited, which is owned by Lancaster Newspapers, owns 44 percent. Penn Square General Corp., which is owned by High Real Estate Group, owns 44 percent. And Fulton Bank owns 12 percent.
>
> The disclosure of the newspaper company's previously undisclosed level of investment prompted gasps of surprise from project opponents who were observing the two days of testimony. . . .

See the article online: http://lancasteronline.com/news/newspaper-s-stake-in-project-surprises-foes/article_df947a78-7255-5364-860f-c569ca982f50.html.

Jack Buckwalter, chairman of Lancaster Newspapers, Inc., was a defendant in the lawsuit *Molly Henderson v. Lancaster Newspapers, Inc., John M. Buckwalter, Ernest J. Schreiber, Marvin I. Adams, Jr., Helen Colwell Adams, Charles Raymond Shaw, Arthur E. Morris, Gilbert A. Smart, John H. Brubaker, Iii, David Pidgeon*. Buckwalter discussed the ownership changes in Penn Square Partners during his deposition on February 3, 2010. At this point in the deposition, Buckwalter is confronted with documents that show that Lancaster Newspapers actually had a higher equity stake in Penn Square Partners. From the deposition, pp. 162–163:

Buckwalter: ". . . it started out where it was, as I recall, it was 50, 25, 25. Or something like that. Oh, wait a minute. No, it wasn't that either. Because we [High, LNP, Fulton] all went in—it was—I'm not sure whether it was one-third, one-third, one-third. And then it evolved   the final one, the final position, and when Fulton Bank was out, it was 50/50. 50 percent general partnership of High, and 50 percent Lancaster Newspapers, as the Penn Square Limited. . . .

Q. So at least in terms of percentage interest, Lancaster Newspapers, Inc. at that point was an equal partner [to High]; fair to say?
A. At what point?
Q. At the point when it was 50/50, that you just described for me, when Fulton went out.
A. Oh, yes.
Q. Yes. And for example, in January of 2005, Lancaster Newspapers, Inc. actually had a higher percentage of interest, ownership interest in the partnership than any other partner; did it not?
[Buckwalter is handed exhibit 26, a statement showing Penn Square Partners ownership interest.]
A. That's strange. Yeah, I don't know why that—I mean, I can't explain that. But Fulton Bank is still in it. So that the, that—why the interest at that juncture? We had 46.34. General partner, 41.46. And Fulton, 12.20. I cannot explain that.
Q. But that's what it shows on Exhibit 26; does it not?
A. Yes, it does.

[3] In my open letter in the *Sunday News*, "Why We Sold Conestoga View," October 9, 2005, I wrote regarding the public process of the sale:

> The commissioners should have made sure the county educated the public about the reasons for this change. That is why, when the sales agreement was presented in July, I made a motion to delay signing the binding sales agreement to allow public review. My motion did not succeed. The failure to properly educate the public before signing was a mistake. . . .

(See the letter in Appendix E and also Appendix F, "Pennsylvania County Nursing Homes.")

[4] Reinsel Kuntz Lesher (RKL) is one of the most established and highly regarded accounting and business consulting firms in Pennsylvania. With more than 300 employees and offices in Lancaster, Reading, York, and Harrisburg, RKL is a recognized authority in its field. It is, by far, the largest accounting firm in Lancaster County. In 2014, RKL was rated number 72 in a ranking of national accounting firms by Accounting Today, and number 70 in 2015. It is important to understand the impeccable credentials and reputation of RKL because, as described in this chapter, Controller Dennis Stuckey accused this firm of adjusting its analysis for political reasons.

Reinsel Kuntz Lesher's website may be found here: http://www.rklcpa.com/.

The county's hiring of RKL occurred at a regular commissioners meeting, January 24, 2006. The *Intelligencer Journal*, in, "Firm to Figure Financial Bottom Line of Conestoga View Sale," January 25, 2006, reported the decision by the Board of Commissioners to hire RKL. My quote in the article was: "There is so much going on here, it's imperative to get this close-out done accurately."

[5] The Reinsel Kuntz Lesher "close-out" report on Conestoga View was written up in the *Lancaster New Era*, "Audit Pegs Conestoga View Losses," April 18, 2006.

> An accounting firm hired by the Lancaster County Commissioners has concluded that Conestoga View nursing home lost considerably more money during its last five years under county control than the Controller's Office had estimated.
>
> The accountants found what they termed a "significant understatement of operating expenses and overstatement of operating results" in the controller's numbers, resulting in more than $4 million in additional losses over the five-year period. . . .

[6] Controller Dennis Stuckey's accusation that Reinsel Kuntz Lesher "took numbers provided by the controller's office and put them together to fit the commissioners' point of view" is one of the most outrageous aspects of this story. The headline should have been, "Controller Charges RKL with Malpractice." The controller for Lancaster County, Stuckey, was charging that one of the most highly regarded accounting firms in the United States would risk its reputation for a $75,000 study.

[7] Pannell Kerr Forster submitted its "Market Feasibility Study, Proposed Hotel/Convention Center, Lancaster, Pa.," to the Board of Commissioners, May 12, 2006. The report is available under "Convention Center Documents" at pressedthebook.com website. The quote that sponsors should "consider exploring a downsizing of the project or an alternate use for the site" may be found on page 11-13 of the study.

[8] At the point of the May 5, 2006, *Intelligencer Journal* article "Gray Rips Negative Report, Mayor Says County Study of Penn Square Project Slanted," Mayor Rick Gray, in office about a year and a half, had established himself as an adversary of the county and a strong supporter of the convention center project. In responding to the PKF study, Gray was dismissive and questioned PKF's impartiality. PKF, a nationally recognized authority, examined the data before it and concluded that the Penn Square Partners plan wouldn't work; it recommended that sponsors should "consider exploring a downsizing of the project or an alternate use for the site" (from page 11-13 of PKF feasibility study).

[9] I took notes after some meetings. But even if I never took notes, I still would have transcribed the conversation with Mayor Rick Gray on May 7, 2006. It was that extraordinary.

[10] The out-of-state developer, the York-based restoration specialist, and the Lancaster real estate broker who had a plan, "Plan B," to redevelop the Watt & Shand building into a mixed-use—property tax–paying—project were very successful, well-known, and highly regarded in their respective areas. Their plan, to have the lower levels of the building retail and the upper floors luxury condominiums, would have truly revitalized downtown.

[11] The county's February 22, 2006, complaint to the Department of Community and Economic Development (DCED) regarding the city's $14 million guaranty

pursuant to Act 23 grant funding, was similar to the complaint of May 16, 2005, which objected to the $12 million city guaranty of Ordinance No. 5 of 2005. The city guaranty had grown by $2 million. The county was objecting that the guaranty violated several provisions of the Local Government Unit Debt Act, including violating the act by using the funds for a "private," not "public," purpose and that the "project user," Penn Square Partners, had been exempted from paying property taxes.

[12] The final sale of the Watt & Shand building by Penn Square Partners to the Redevelopment Authority of the City of Lancaster occurred on January 31, 2006. This was the culmination of the plan that was first disclosed to the public in December 2004. Penn Square Partners would sell the building to RACL, which would lease it back to the partners for twenty years, avoiding real estate taxes and allowing the partners to purchase the building after twenty years at a very inexpensive $2.25 million. The building would cost more than $60 million to build. The $2.25 million price was a true bargain. At the time of the sale to RACL, the Watt & Shand, owned by Penn Square Partners for the previous eight years, was virtually unchanged. No demolition or construction work had taken place. The building was essentially as it stood the day Bon Ton sold the building to the partners in February 1998. The sale was reported in, "Watt & Shand Building Is Sold," *Lancaster New Era*, February 9, 2006. Of the disparity between the price RACL paid for the building, $7.25 million in cash and loan forgiveness, and what Penn Square Partners paid for the building, $1.25 million, the *New Era* wrote:

> The purchase price [of the Watt & Shand] covers $4.6 million the partners have paid for development costs, heat, taxes, placing Christmas ornaments, and other expenses since they bought the building.

By this point, 2006, Penn Square Partner High Real Estate had been paid more than $50,000 per month in "developer's fees" by the LCCCA for several years. So, with the profit from selling the Watt & Shand and the consulting fees and the contracts and owning half the hotel, High was making money at every point in the development.

[13] It was clear from the legislation creating redevelopment authorities in the state of Pennsylvania—the Pa. Urban Redevelopment Law of 1945, P.L. 991, § 1—that their purpose "shall exist and operate for the public purposes of the elimination of blighted areas through economically and socially sound redevelopment of such areas, as provided by this act." Nowhere in the act is it suggested that the purpose of a redevelopment authority is to take a property off the tax rolls, develop a for-profit "private" hotel, and sell it to the operator of the hotel for a small fraction of its market value after twenty years.

[14] The county believed that the city guarantee to pay real estate taxes on the Marriott Hotel violated Act 23, 12 Pa. C.S.A. §3406(b) (11), which required Penn Square Partners (as the "project user") to sign a contract agreeing "to timely pay all Commonwealth and local taxes and fees." It was difficult to argue that Penn Square Partners, operating the Marriott Hotel for profit, was not the "project user."

Endnotes

[15] Senator Gibson E. "Gib" Armstrong, who amended both Act 23 and the Third-Class County Convention Authority Act in 2004 and 1999, became chairman of the Senate Appropriations committee in 2007. He retired from the Senate in 2008.

[16] House Bill 983, from March 2005, amending Title 12 (Commerce and Trade) of Pennsylvania statutes, originally establishing a film production grant program, and the legislative history of the bill may be found online here: http://www.legis.state.pa.us/CFDOCS/billInfo/bill_history.cfm?syear=2005&sind=0&body=H&type=B&bn=983.

[17] The final May 11, 2006, Act 23 amendment of House Bill 983 may be found here: http://www.legis.state.pa.us/WU01/LI/LI/US/PDF/2006/0/0042..PDF.

[18] A comparison of the two versions, 2004 and 2006, of the referenced section of Act 23 in—§3406(b) (11)—is as follows:

2004 version:
§ 3406. Approval.
(b) Grant approval. . . .The contract shall include provisions which do all of the following:
... §3406(b) (11) "Require the project user to timely pay all Commonwealth and local taxes and fees."
There is nothing else written under this clause.

2006 version

§ 3406. Approval.
(b) Grant approval. . . . The contract shall include provisions which do all of the following:

§ 3406 (b)(11) Require the project user to timely pay all
Commonwealth and local taxes and fees that are then due and
owing. <u>A local government unit</u> as defined under 53 Pa.C.S.
Pt. VII Subpt. B (relating to indebtedness and borrowing) <u>or
an issuing authority may enter into an agreement or adopt an
ordinance or resolution to permit the local government unit
or issuing authority to pay, waive, abate, settle, compromise
or reimburse any local tax, fee or other imposition
applicable to a project user imposed by any local government
unit or issuing authority.</u> The agreement, ordinance or
resolution shall not affect the eligibility of an applicant
or a project to receive a grant under this chapter. [Underline added.]

[19] The 46 to 1 Senate vote for HB 983, after Senator Gib Armstrong amended the legislation, was held on March 14, 2006. The history of HB 983—originally a filmmaking bill—may be found here:

http://www.legis.state.pa.us/CFDOCS/billInfo/bill_history.cfm?syear=2005&sind=0&body=H&type=B&bn=983.

[20] County special counsel Howard Kelin's comments regarding Senator Armstrong's amendments to Act 23 were published in "Senate Approves Changes to Act 23," *Intelligencer Journal*, March 21, 2006. Senator Armstrong, when asked by the newspaper for a comment on his amendment, said, "Whether it makes (the county's legal opposition) moot or not, I don't know. I'm sure there will be attorneys suing on anything."

[21] The comments from the Lancaster County House Republican delegation after hearing of Senator Armstrong's changes to Act 23 were found in "Convention Center Bill Withdrawn," *Intelligencer Journal*, April 7, 2006. The delegation's reaction was also covered by the *Lancaster New Era*, in "Protests Erupt over Tactics," April 6, 2006.

[22] The 146-41 House vote passing Senator Armstrong's amendment to Act 23 was recorded in the *House Legislative Journal*, 2006, page 979. Every Lancaster County Republican House member, including Senator Armstrong's son, Representative Gibson C. Armstrong, voted against the amendment. The vote, including the names of the legislators and how they voted, may be found online here: http://www.legis.state.pa.us/WU01/LI/HJ/2006/0/20060426.pdf#page=42.

[23] Representative David Hickernell's comments following the April 26, 2006, House vote on Senator Armstrong's Act 23 amendment are from "House OKs Convention Center Bill," *Intelligencer Journal*, April 27, 2006.

[24] Ibid. Both Representative Katie True's and Senator Gib Armstrong's comments are from "House OKs Convention Center Bill," *Intelligencer Journal*, April 27, 2006. Representative Hickernell was particularly incensed. "How many laws are we going to need to pass here in Harrisburg to continue to prop up this convention center project? It's time, after seven or eight years, the state needs to step back," Representative Hickernell added in the *Intelligencer Journal* article.

[25] On April 4, 2006, Jesse Dee Wise, Jr., twenty-one, killed six family members in Leola, Lancaster County. At the time of the mass murder, District Attorney Totaro was in the fifth month of his criminal grand jury investigation into the padded résumé of Gary Heinke. The *Philadelphia Inquirer* reported the story, which was national news, on April 14, 2006. See http://articles.philly.com/2006-04-14/news/25394358_1_strangling-family-house-bodies.

[26] The $10 million cocaine conspiracy case was reported in the *Lancaster New Era*, "$10M Coke Ring Busted Here, Eleven Alleged Dealers, 100 Kilos of Cocaine Seized in Undercover and Wiretap Operation," April 20, 2006, and the *Intelligencer Journal*, "Officials: $10 Million Cocaine Ring Shut Down, Eleven people have been charged in connection with a drug operation officials said was bringing several pounds of cocaine into Lancaster County every seven to 10 days from The Bronx, N.Y.," April 21, 2006.

[27] Subsidiaries of High Industries were directly paid by the Lancaster County Convention Center Authority beginning October 25, 2000, when High Associates was paid $750 for "advisory services," with check number 1082. (See "Firm Hired to Guide Convention Center Approvals," *Intelligencer Journal*, September 14, 2000. From the article "Backers of a proposed $30 million downtown convention center Wednesday inked a $600,000-plus

Endnotes

deal with High Real Estate Group to manage early development of the project. . . .") The agreement called for High to be paid 2% (two percent) of the overall construction costs. Two weeks later, High Real Estate Group was paid $10,000 for "advisory services," with check number 1084. The $10,000 monthly payments to High Real Estate Group continued until March 13, 2002, when High Associates began to be paid a much higher fee, as the cost of the project had grown substantially. The first check written by the LCCCA (check number 2049) to High Associates reflecting the increase in payment was dated March 13, 2002, in the amount of $67,635.21. The next month, on April 10, 2002, High Associates was paid $52,647.49, with check number 2062. High Associates continued to receive the $52,500 monthly "advisory" and "developer" fees until 2006. Source: Lancaster County Convention Center Authority Operating Account Ledger—For Period September 1, 1999, to December 31, 2003; and Lancaster County Convention Center Authority Balance Detail Sheet through December 31, 2005. These documents were referred to as the "Pay the Bills" ledger for the LCCCA. Other High companies received contracts (e.g., High Concrete) from the LCCCA. And, as noted several times in the body of this book, the firm of the LCCCA's solicitor, Stevens & Lee, was paid several million dollars for various "professional services rendered on behalf of the Lancaster County Convention Center Authority." Stevens & Lee, the authors of the Third-Class County Convention Center Authority Act, was also the registered lobbyist for High Industries during this period.

[28] The news that bids would be let by the Lancaster County Convention Center Authority was reported in the *Intelligencer Journal*, "Officials to Seek Construction Bids," March 20, 2006.

[29] Deb Hall's comments at the March 20, 2006, Lancaster County Convention Center Authority board meeting were noted by Christiaan A. Hart Nibbrig. They were also reported in the *Intelligencer Journal*, "Officials to Seek Construction Bids," March 20, 2006. Mr. Hart Nibbrig regularly attended LCCCA and Lancaster County commissioners' meetings in 2006 and 2007.

[30] LCCCA board member Laura Douglas's comments were reported in the *Intelligencer Journal*, "Officials to Seek Construction Bids," March 20, 2006.

[31] Interview with Laura C. Douglas, March 14, 2016, Lancaster, PA.

[32] The LCCCA bids were actually opened in two stages; the smaller contracts were opened May 9, 2006. Those bids were for precast concrete, laundry service, food service, and fire protection. High Construction was the only bidder for the precast concrete contract and won the job with a bid of $2,554,000. See *Intelligencer Journal*, "Officials Unseal 1st Bids for City Center," May 10, 2006. The $13.6 million LCCCA bid overage was reported by the *Intelligencer Journal*, "City Center Officials Open Bids," May 18, 2006. The bids were opened at a public meeting on May 17, 2006, at Southern Market Center.

[33] The $25.4 million LCCCA bid overage was reported in the *Intelligencer Journal*, "Center Developers Tackle $25M Funding Gap," May 24, 2006. This was reported after Laura Douglas, a county appointment to the LCCCA board, discovered that the bids were more than $25 million over budget.

34 Wohlsen Construction, the low March 17 general trades bid, had no prior connection to the project.

35 My comments are found in "Center Project in Jeopardy," *Lancaster New Era*, May 24, 2006. "'The risk at this time is inordinately high for the county taxpayer,' said Henderson, in explaining why she opposes the project. 'This has become almost a 100 percent taxpayer risk.'" Also, see *Intelligencer Journal*, "Center Developers Tackle $25M Funding Gap," May 24, 2006. Commissioner Shellenberger commented in the *Intell*. "'It's time to move on,' Shellenberger said. 'Is the center worth this much fuss or aggravation or divisiveness? Is this project worth spending this kind of tax dollars? I'm here to say my answer is 'No.'"

Also, on May 24, 2006, Commissioner Shellenberger and I passed a resolution revoking the $40 million county bond guarantee if the LCCCA remarketed the bond.

36 As noted, High Real Estate had been "Master Developer" for the hotel and convention center project since 2000. From that point, High Real Estate was paid more than $1 million by the Lancaster County Convention Center Authority (LCCCA) for "advisory services" in the development of the project. By June 2006, as the project was sent out to bid, in addition to all of the planning in which High was involved as master developer and construction manager, multiple High companies had been already contracted with the LCCCA. There is little doubt S. Dale High's team knew the construction specifications of the project better than anyone else and were thus in an advantageous position to bid on the general trades contracts when it went out for re-bid.

The announcement that High would bid on the general trade contract is found in the *Intelligencer Journal*, "High Plans to Bid on Contract for Center Project," June 9, 2006. In the article, county-appointed LCCCA board member Deb Hall said what many of us were thinking: "This is just another revenue source for them [High]."

37 High Concrete won the precast concrete contract from the LCCCA as a single bidder in May 2006. In December 2001, the LCCCA signed the twenty-year "Food and Beverage Agreement between the Lancaster County Convention Center Authority and Penn Square Partners." The food and beverage contract stipulates that in exchange for full catering rights for the convention center, Penn Square Partners must pay 5% (and up to 10%) of revenues to the LCCCA.

The food and beverage contract may be found online here: https://www.scribd.com/doc/27796646/Food-Beverage-2001.

38 The article "Bids Doom Center Plans," *Intelligencer Journal*, July 27, 2006, begins with the announcement that the project has been "killed":

> Skyrocketing construction costs and determined opposition to a hotel and convention center proposed for downtown Lancaster likely have killed the project after nearly eight years of planning, developer Penn Square Partners announced Wednesday. . . .

39 Lancaster Newspapers chairman Jack Buckwalter's comments after Penn Square Partners' 2005 TIF defeat by the School District of Lancaster are found in "'We Don't

Have a Plan B,' After Losing Dramatic Vote, Supporters Concede: Penn Sq. Project Now Appears to Be Dead," *Lancaster New Era*, March 17, 2005.

[40] Ibid. Representative Sturla's comments are found in "Bids Doom Center Plans," *Intelligencer Journal*, July 27, 2006.

[41] Ibid. "Bids Doom Center Plans," *Intelligencer Journal*, July 27, 2006. It was absurd for High executive Mark Fitzgerald to blame the county commissioners, meaning Shellenberger and me, for the bid overages. That was a function of the market and the price of materials. The fact was, that project was going to cost over $25 million more than budgeted. It should have ended there.

[42] Ibid. I must say that I did think the $25.4 million bid overage was too much for project sponsors to overcome. This was the re-bid, so it did seem like the gap was insurmountable. I thought this was the end of the project.

[43] One peculiar thing about the saving of the project announced in the *Intelligencer Journal*, in "Center Closes Fund Gap," August 11, 2006, was that this was evidently coordinated by Lancaster mayor Rick Gray. Gray had been equivocal in support for the project as he ran for office in 2005. After assuming office in January 2006, Gray became a fierce defender of the project. How did Gray, a defense lawyer in office only seven months, solve the financing of a then $140 million hotel and convention center project?

[44] Regarding the budget deficit Smithgall left Gray, see the November 23, 2005, *Intelligencer Journal*, "Smithgall Proposes No Tax-Hike in '06 Budget," which refers to the $7 million budget deficit.

From the article:

> Mayor Charlie Smithgall unveiled the proposed $40.7 million budget at a City Council meeting Tuesday in Southern Market Center.
> "It's a fair budget," Smithgall said. "It's a workable budget. If it was mine, I would get through the year with it."
> Next year will be the city's first with Mayor-elect Rick Gray, who two weeks ago defeated Smithgall in the general election.
> Gray said he has concerns about the increase in spending and a $7 million budget deficit that Smithgall wants to plug by dipping into the city's reserve fund.

The article may be found online here: http://lancasteronline.com/news/smithgall-proposes-no-tax-hike-budget/article_985a044e-6869-54fe-8a21-6afeaff50fa8.html.

[45] A breakdown of the "Gray Plan"—including the "value engineering" component—is found in "Center Closes Fund Gap," *Intelligencer Journal*, August 11, 2006.

[46] This analysis was derived from "Smoke and Mirrors," an online post at Lancasterfirst.org. The post is attributed to Thomas Despard and Bruce L. Clark. Lancasterfirst.org was an online repository for many official project-related documents. The website Lancasterfirst.org was an invaluable resource in the research for this book.

47 The approved bids of August 14, 2006, were reported in the *Intelligencer Journal*, "Center Contracts Approved," August 15, 2006. At the LCCCA meeting that approved the contracts (4–0, three county abstentions), April Koppenhaver, a city art gallery owner, said to the board, "If you vote for these contracts, you are hijacking the city and county."

48 The $40 million Lancaster County–backed guaranty was Resolution No. 73, passed October 2003, one week prior to my election to the commissioners' board. It passed 2 to 1, with Commissioner Shaub voting against the resolution.

49 Lancaster County taxpayers were exposed to more than $60 million in liability because of the 2003 bond guaranty. According to the "Guaranty Agreement" entered by the county in December 2003, weeks before I took office, the agreement provides that during the 40-year lifetime of the bond, the county will guarantee up to $1,506,960 per year. Multiplying that amount by 40 years is $60,278,400.

50 Leading up to the October 29, 2003, Lancaster County commissioners' vote on the $40 million LCCCA bond guaranty, emotions were high on both sides of the issue. Lancaster mayor Charlie Smithgall downplayed risk to taxpayers. From the article "County Backs Center," October 29, 2003:

> Lancaster Mayor Charlie Smithgall was more blunt on Tuesday, but he turned his attention to the project's detractors.
>
> Smithgall challenged opponents of the bond guarantee to look into the faces of the county's unemployed—about 70 percent of whom live within a few blocks from the planned convention center and hotel.
>
> "I'd be happy to set up a meeting," the mayor said.
>
> He challenged them to tell city residents, many of whom live at or below the poverty line, that the $2.66 a year the county taxpayer would have to pay if the project failed was more important than them having work and feeding their children.
>
> "That $2.66 is less than a Happy Meal. This project will change lives," Smithgall said.

51 On September 15, 1999 the Lancaster County Board of Commissioners passed three resolutions—Nos. 44, 45, 46—establishing the Lancaster County Convention Center Authority (No. 44) and enacting the room rental (No. 45) and excise taxes (No. 46). The taxes commenced on January 1, 2000.

52 The county's petition to the Department of Community and Economic Development (DCED) in 2006 concerned the $40 million bond guaranty agreement (from Resolution No. 36 of 2003). The county's position was that the guaranty was a party to funding a project that did not have secure financing, and that was a different project than the one guaranteed in 2003. As he did in 2005, when he filed a complaint against the two City of Lancaster Act 23 guaranties, Howard L. Kelin filed the complaint with the DCED on behalf of the County of Lancaster. That case was decided against the county on May

Endnotes

3, 2006. Senator Gibson E. "Gib" Armstrong's amended Act 23—circumventing the county's case—was passed into law by the House and the Senate on May 2, 2006.

[53] The county commissioners' vote on May 24, 2006, to rescind the county $40 million guaranty if the Lancaster County Convention Center Authority (LCCCA) remarketed the bond (now depleted to about $31 million) was reported in the *Lancaster New Era*, "Center Project in Jeopardy," May 24, 2006. The process of an issuer (the LCCCA) remarketing a bond (loan) at a different interest rate is called a "swaption." The county wanted the LCCCA to take no such action, in light of the uncertain financing of the project. A swaption is a binding agreement that, in this case, would be part of the financing of the project for almost forty years. The bids had just come in $25.4 million over budget. The county had been concerned with the idea of a swaption for months. The idea had been introduced in late 2004 by the LCCCA's financial adviser, Thomas Beckett of Fairmont Capital. The *Bond Buyer* covered the issue in January 2006, in "Pennsylvania County Authority Proceeding with Swap Plans," January 20, 2006.

[54] The Lancaster County Convention Center Authority (LCCCA) vote to sue the Lancaster County Board of Commissioners, with Commissioner Shellenberger and me named individually, was reported in the *Intelligencer Journal*, "Developers of Center/Hotel Sue Officials," June 14, 2006. One of the LCCCA's attorneys, John Fenningham, said that Shellenberger and I were "creating a chilling effect on the authority's ability to advance the project. We had no choice."

The lawsuit—an authority suing the governmental body that formed it—also asked the Court to prevent the county from appointing new members to the LCCCA board. And the LCCCA brief asked the Court for a gag order on the commissioners, preventing us from "communicating an intent to, or taking actions that are . . . adverse to the project."

[55] The lawsuit filed by Penn Square Partners and the Lancaster County Convention Center Authority, June 2006, was *PENN SQUARE GENERAL CORPORATION, the General Partner of Penn Square Partners, a Pennsylvania Limited Partnership, and the Redevelopment Authority of the City of Lancaster v. COUNTY OF LANCASTER, Board of County Commissioners of the County of Lancaster, Molly Henderson, Commissioner, and, Richard Shellenberger, Commissioner.*

Lancaster County Convention Center Authority v. County of Lancaster, Board of County Commissioners of the County of Lancaster, Molly Henderson, Commissioner, and, Richard Shellenberger, Commissioner.

[56] Joseph C. Madenspacher was elected to the Lancaster County Court of Common Pleas in 1999. Prior to joining the Court, Judge Madenspacher was Lancaster County district attorney. Madenspacher's successor as Lancaster County district attorney was Donald Totaro, an assistant district attorney. Totaro followed Madenspacher on to the Court in 2007. Madenspacher succeeded Judge Louis J. Farina as president judge of the Lancaster courts. Judge Farina presided over the hotel and motel owners' lawsuit (*Bold Corp vs the city of Lancaster, County of Lancaster, and Lancaster County*

Convention Center Authority, filed March 24, 2000; see Chapter Four) and approved a criminal grand jury investigation request from District Attorney Totaro in 2005. (See Chapter Ten.)

[57] What the county was arguing, specifically, was that the 2003 County Guaranty agreement, pursuant to Resolution 73 of 2003, required the LCCCA and Penn Square Partners to have "sufficient funds to complete the construction of the Facilities in full accord with the final plans and specifications prepared by the architect for the Facilities and approved by the Authority." Yet the "Trust Indenture," the agreement between the LCCCA and M&T Bank, only stipulated that LCCCA submit a "project budget which shall include a detailed itemization of all construction costs to be incurred in connection with the Convention Center including (without limitation) all architectural, engineering and consulting fees, and a detailed itemization of all non-construction costs to be incurred by the Issuer in connection therewith." The discrepancy, the county argued through Howard L. Kelin, then interim county solicitor, rendered the guaranty invalid. The county's position was reported in the *Intelligencer Journal*, "Center Bond Guarantee Questioned," June 27, 2006.

[58] The "Madenspacher hearings" were open to the public and covered by Lancaster Newspapers. The first day of the hearings, July 12, 2006, was reported in the *Intelligencer Journal*, "Battle Over City Project Moves to Courtroom," July 13, 2006. Both the *Intelligencer Journal* and the *Lancaster New Era* covered the hearings during the five days they were held.

[59] Although Judge Madenspacher did not finally rule on the primary issue of the validity of the $40 million LCCCA, county-guaranteed bond, and the gag order request was ignored entirely, the *Intelligencer Journal* portrayed the preliminary ruling as a defeat for the "commissioners." See "Ruling Rejects Commissioners," *Intelligencer Journal*, July 24, 2006.

[60] Judge Joseph C. Madenspacher's October 23, 2006, ruling may be found online here: http://lancasteronline.com/news/convention-center-court-case-decision/article_f10fc0f1-391e-5ea0-b602-9aec05e71a47.html.

The *Intelligencer Journal* covered the decision in "Court Sides with City Center Supporters," October 24, 2006.

[61] Our board was not the first Board of Commissioners to hold evening meetings. In April 2003, the county commissioners, chaired by Paul Thibault, held the first evening meeting at the county courthouse. The meeting began at 7:00 p.m. See "Commissioners First Evening Meeting Is Tonight," *Intelligencer Journal*, April 8, 2003.

[62] The hotel room rental tax, enacted in September 1999 and commencing on January 1, 2000, was collected monthly from every hotel and motel within 984-square-mile Lancaster County. That tax revenue was paid to the county treasurer and remitted to the LCCCA to subsidize the cost of the Marriott Hotel, a direct competitor. My comments at the evening East Donegal meeting in regard to shrinking the area from which the hotel room rental tax could be collected was reported in "Henderson

Targets Tax, Commissioner Wants to Look at Funding Source for Proposed Center," *Intelligencer Journal*, June 1, 2006.

[63] The evening county commissioners meeting at the Ephrata Public Library was held on June 22, 2006. The meeting was reported in "Great Divide Laid Bare at Convention Center Mtg., Opponents, Supporters Air Views in Ephrata," *Intelligencer Journal*, June 23, 2006. Although the headline suggested a divided crowd, the audience was overwhelmingly opposed to the project.

[64] Rick Atwater was co-owner and manager of Oblender's Furniture Store. Oblender's great-grandfather, Christopher W. Oblender, had founded the business. The business, along with four other buildings, was purchased by the LCCCA under the threat of eminent domain. Oblender felt forced to sell and commented about the price in "Convention Center Panel Purchases Four Properties," *Lancaster New Era*, March 21. "It's all too low. The only reason we're selling is because of the threat of eminent domain," said Atwater.

[65] The letter written to Governor Edward G. Rendell by Common Cause Pa. executive director Barry L. Kauffman is dated May 4, 2006. Copied in the letter to the governor was Dennis Yablonsky, secretary of the Pennsylvania Department of Community and Economic Development. From the Common Cause letter:

> We have watched as the Project has ballooned from a $70 million private-public project initiative, to one for which the public is now financially responsible, and which has an estimated cost of over $140 million dollars. We have noted with interest the many questions asked by Lancaster County taxpayers about the project. The questions that most deeply concern us are those that speak to the lack of accountability and transparency in the administration of this project.

[66] Penn Square Partners president Nevin D. Cooley made his remarks about the partnership buying the Watt & Shand building "for one and only one reason . . . to save this [Watt & Shand] building," at a press conference on Penn Square, July 24, 2001. The reason for the press conference was to announce that the hotel Penn Square Partners was going to own would be a Marriott hotel. The press conference was videotaped by Ron Harper, Jr., and posted on youtube.com. Because Harper used a copyrighted soundtrack, the audio to Cooley's remarks has been removed by youtube.com. The press conference, which included Senator Gib Armstrong, Mayor Charlie Smithgall, Commissioner Paul Thibault, and Congressman Joe Pitts making statements, was also reported in the *Lancaster New Era* in a front-page, above-the-fold article, "Downtown Goes 'Upscale' // Marriott to Open Hotel in Watt & Shand Building in 2004 // Announcement Called 'Great News.'" The *New Era* article included this projection: "The hotel and convention center are expected to employ 300 to 400 full-time jobs and also trigger spending of tens of millions of dollars annually here."

[67] The delisting of the Watt & Shand building was reported in the *Lancaster New Era*, "Watt & Shand to Be Delisted as Historic Place / State Says Keeping the Facade of

the Venerable Lancaster Site Is Not Enough to Keep It on the National Register," July 20, 2007. The comments from Carol Lee, supervisor of the Pennsylvania Bureau for Historic Preservation, are in the article.

[68] Ibid. Bonnie Mark, tax act coordinator for the Pennsylvania Historic and Museum Commission, was quoted in the *Lancaster New Era*, "Watt & Shand to Be Delisted as Historic Place / State Says Keeping the Facade of the Venerable Lancaster Site Is Not Enough to Keep It on the National Register," July 20, 2007.

[69] LCCCA financial adviser Thomas Beckett announced the $10 million cost increase for the project at an LCCCA meeting November 16, 2006. It was reported in "Convention Center Cost Up $10M," November 17, 2006.

[70] The second cost increase in a month, bringing the project budget to $170.5 million, was announced at a LCCCA Finance Committee meeting, December 13, 2006. It was reported in "Center Price Tag Increases by $5M," *Intelligencer Journal*, December 14, 2006.

[71] Former *Sunday News* editor Marvin I. Adams, who originated the "Countdown," was a defendant in the libel lawsuit I brought against Lancaster Newspapers, Inc., and several of its employees, *Molly Henderson vs Lancaster Newspapers, Inc., John M. Buckwalter, Ernest J. Schreiber, Marvin I. Adams, Jr., Helen Colwell Adams, Charles Raymond Shaw, Arthur E. Morris, Gilbert A. Smart, John H. Brubaker, III, and David Pidgeon*. No. 0712003. Adams was deposed on October 29, 2009. Reference to the "Countdown" is found on page 96 of Adams's deposition.

Q (GW Croner). What countdown are you referring to there?
A (M. Adams). There was a countdown on the editorial page that ran, not every Sunday, but most Sundays, that told how many days were left in the terms of—at first it was three commissioners, and then after Shaub resigned it became the two commissioners.
Q. And who initiated that countdown?
A. I did, sir.
Q. And when did you begin it?
A. It was about 500 and some days, 550 days left in their [Shellenberger and Henderson] terms. That would have been some time, I think it was June of 2005, I believe.

Chapter Twelve: Finishing the Job

[1] The ownership breakdown of Penn Square Partners—High Industries; Lancaster Newspapers, Inc.; and Fulton Financial Corp (Fulton Bank)—was disclosed to the public in 2006 in a courtroom more than eight years after the founding of the partnership in January 1998. Until the disclosure by High and Penn Square Partners executive Mark Fitzgerald during questioning in the Madenspacher hearings of July 13–15, 2006, the only statement regarding the ownership breakdown was a sentence usually placed at the end of Lancaster Newspapers articles related to the project:

> Penn Square Partners includes general partner Penn Square General Corp., a High Industries affiliate, and limited partners

Fulton Bank and Lancaster Newspapers Inc., publisher of the *Intelligencer Journal, New Era* and *Sunday News*.

Lancaster Newspapers staff, including chairman John M. "Jack" Buckwalter, said that the above disclaimer was sufficient disclosure of Lancaster Newspapers' ownership interest in Penn Square Partners, and that their newspapers reported on the story as if it were just another news story. The Lancaster County Convention Center project was one of the most expensive public capital projects in the city's and the county's history. It involved almost $200 million, most of them public dollars. A newspaper with the staffs and resources of the *Intelligencer Journal*, the *Lancaster New Era*, and the *Sunday News* should have investigated and reported the ownership interests of the private partners in such a project from its very beginning. But it took eight years, and under court testimony, for the disclosure to be reported in only one of the Lancaster Newspapers.

The Penn Square Partners ownership disclosure was not reported during the hearings, but a few days after they concluded, on July 18 in the *Lancaster New Era*, "Newspaper's [sic] Stake in Project Surprises Foes." The article may be found online here: http://lancasteronline.com/news/newspaper-s-stake-in-project-surprises-foes/article_df947a78-7255-5364-860f-c569ca982f50.html.

There was a point when Lancaster Newspapers actually had a higher equity stake in Penn Square Partners than High. Lancaster Newspapers chairman Jack Buckwalter was a defendant in my libel lawsuit against Lancaster Newspapers and some of its staff, *Molly Henderson vs Lancaster Newspapers, Inc., John M. Buckwalter, Ernest J. Schreiber, Marvin L. Adams, Jr., Helen Colwell Adams, Charles Raymond Shaw, Arthur E. Morris, Gilbert A. Smart, John H. Brubaker, III, and David Pidgeon*. No. 0712003.

Buckwalter, a defendant in the suit, was deposed September 4, 2009. In the course of the deposition, Buckwalter was presented by my attorney George W. Croner with an official document, an exhibit in the case, that showed in January 2005, Lancaster Newspapers had a larger equity stake than High.

From pages 162–163 of Buckwalter's deposition:

Q. Yes. And for example, in January of 2005, Lancaster Newspapers, Inc. actually had a higher percentage of interest, ownership interest in the partnership than any other partner; did it not?

[Mr. Croner points to a line of the document.]

Buckwalter. That's strange. Yeah, I don't know why that—I mean, I can't explain that. But Fulton Bank is still in it. So that the, that—why the interest at that juncture? We had 46.34. General partner [High], 41.46. And Fulton, 12.20. I cannot explain that.
Q. But that's what it shows on Exhibit 26; does it not?
A. Yes, it does.
Q. All right. And in fact, in July of 2006, during the course of the litigation that was taking place over the convention center authority, if you remember I showed you this article which we marked as Exhibit 546.

And the public disclosure in the article was that the High entity, which was Penn Square Partners executive I'm sorry, Penn Square Partners, Limited, had 44 percent.

Penn Square General had 44 percent. And Fulton had 12. In July of '06; is that correct? A. That's what it says. ...

From page 165 of the Buckwalter deposition:

Q. At no point in time did the High entity have a higher percentage ownership interest in the partnership than Lancaster Newspapers; correct?

Buckwalter. It is my understanding that that is true.

[2] Rufus A. Fulton, Jr., then president and CEO of Fulton Financial Corp. (Bank), was not a defendant in my libel lawsuit against Lancaster Newspapers and several of its staff members. Fulton was a witness in the case, however, and was deposed on July 14, 2009. Fulton's comments about the project being a "temporary investment for us," may be found on page 23 of his deposition:

From page 23:

Rufus Fulton. "[E]arly on we, the Fulton part of this, said this is a temporary investment for us. Banks should not be in the real estate business. They should lend to people who have real estate projects.

But from the very beginning we said that we were not interested in remaining in this for the long term, and at some point we wanted to be taken out. And we were.

And I can't tell you when that was. But it's probably four, five years ago now. It might be less than that, actually, because—I'm really not sure. Maybe three years."

[3] The anti-commissioners' coverage from all three Lancaster Newspapers began in early 2005. This was after the "coup" of December 2004, when Commissioner Shellenberger and I voted to replace Commissioner Pete Shaub as chairman of the Lancaster County Board of Commissioners. Shellenberger and I started to challenge the hotel and convention center project. This is when the negative articles began appearing. This was the "get tough" strategy Lancaster Newspapers used, and that is discussed in Chapter Seven: "Molly Is Toast." According to the database ProQuest, which tracks many publications, including Lancaster Newspapers, the approximate number of articles with the search terms "Conestoga View" and "County Commissioners" from 2004 through 2008 was as follows:

Year	Approximate Number of Articles
2004	35
2005	223 (99% coming in last six months of year)
2006	323 (with 57 in the month of December)
2007	212
2008	45
2009	22

[4] District Attorney Donald R. Totaro's "wherever this takes us" comments were published in the *Lancaster New Era*, "DA Launches Heinke Probe," November 10, 2005. One can only wonder why the district attorney used a criminal grand jury to

investigate a padded résumé of an employee who had resigned months earlier and been previously examined by human resources in the Myers Report.

[5] I testified three times before the grand jury: on April 13, 2006, under the original scope of the Heinke hiring; and twice more on July 17 and September 28, 2006, after the scope was enlarged to include the sale of the Conestoga View nursing home. I believe the dates of testimony were spaced far apart so that I might forget earlier testimony or answer a similarly phrased question differently, opening myself up to perjury charges.

[6] The original "Notice of Submission" to use a criminal grand jury to investigate the Gary Heinke hiring was presented by District Attorney Totaro to—and approved by—the Supervising Judge of the Lancaster County Court of Common Pleas, Judge Louis J on November 10, 2005. The "Amended Notice of Submission" was submitted by Totaro and approved by Farina on May 1, 2006. The use of the court system to probe what was essentially a county personnel matter was, I believe, a misuse of the of the judiciary.

[7] The first motion to quash the subpoena was filed my lawyer Mark E. Lovett, Esq., on June 13, 2006, and the second motion to quash was filed on June 15, 2006. At the time, Lovett was a partner and a litigator at the law firm of Hartman, Underhill & Brubaker (HUB). While at HUB, Lovett worked with the city of Lancaster during the Smithgall administration, enforcing municipal ordinances. Mr. Lovett is currently a partner at the law firm of Brubaker Connaughton Goss & Lucarelli LLC.

[8] W. Thomas McGough, Jr., Esq., was brought in by my attorney Mark E. Lovett, Esq., toward the end of the grand jury investigation. Mr. McGough was also deposed as a witness in my libel lawsuit against Lancaster Newspapers and several staff members, *Molly Henderson vs Lancaster Newspapers, Inc., John M. Buckwalter, Ernest J. Schreiber, Marvin L. Adams, Jr., Helen Colwell Adams, Charles Raymond Shaw, Arthur E. Morris, Gilbert A. Smart, John H. Brubaker, III, and David Pidgeon.* No. 0712003. Mr. McGough was deposed on January 26, 2010. McGough, an experienced litigator and a partner at the top Pittsburgh-based law firm of Reed Smith, was involved in discussions with the district attorney's office as they were writing the grand jury report. Today, Mr. McGough is executive vice president and chief legal officer for the University of Pittsburgh Medical Center.

[9] My attorney Mark E. Lovett, Esq., was deposed as a witness in my libel lawsuit against Lancaster Newspapers and several of its staff members: *Molly Henderson vs Lancaster Newspapers, Inc., John M. Buckwalter, Ernest J. Schreiber, Marvin L. Adams, Jr., Helen Colwell Adams, Charles Raymond Shaw, Arthur E. Morris, Gilbert A. Smart, John H. Brubaker, III, and David Pidgeon.* No. 0712003. Lovett's comments regarding his conversations with Kenneth Brown, assistant Lancaster County district attorney, come from his deposition testimony, January 12, 2010.

[10] Ibid. From the deposition testimony of Mark E. Lovett, Esq., January 12, 2010.

[11] The cost of the project in late 2006 was $170.5 million, nearly $100 million more than when it was promoted as "Everything the City Needs," in 1999. Then, the private partners were to pay more than 60 percent of the cost of the project. In 2006, after the guaranties, the grants, the loans, the bonds, and the taxes, Penn Square Partners was paying less than 10 percent of the total costs.

[12] According the Lancaster County Tax Assessor's office, Lancaster Newspapers, Inc., owns thirteen separate properties in the area immediately surrounding the site of the hotel and convention center. Those properties would likely appreciate in value with the addition of a Marriott Hotel and a new convention center. Moreover, as discussed in detail in Chapter Six: "It's All about the Hotel—Really," Penn Square Partners (High Industries and Lancaster Newspapers) has the option to purchase the hotel from the Redevelopment Authority for the City of Lancaster for a below-market price of $2.25 million. This is after operating the hotel (which cost more than $60 million to build) at a profit for twenty years, while not paying real estate taxes.

[13] W. Thomas McGough, Jr., Esq., seemed baffled that I was included in a grand jury investigation. McGough described an exchange with Assistant District Attorney Brown in his deposition of January 26, 2010:

> I told him [Brown] I think you should leave Molly out of the whole thing; that it didn't sound to me like there was anything worth pursuing from his standpoint. He never suggested that there were criminal charges in the offing against Molly. He never threatened that sort of thing and he kept talking about this report that was going to come out. And he kept talking about the Sunshine Act violation. And I argued to him, why,—why waste your time, basically. . . . He didn't believe that walking away, at least as far as Molly was concerned, from this situation, was viable—he wasn't willing to do that.

[14] The comments from Kenneth Brown, saying he doesn't "hose" people, were recounted by my attorney Mark E. Lovett during his deposition testimony, January 12, 2010. The exchanges revealed the one-sided, pro-prosecutor nature of the grand jury process. After the thirteen-month investigation, there were no grounds for presentment of a true bill against me. Yet it was the district attorney's office that, after conducting the investigation without any defense cross-examination, wrote the grand jury report summarizing the investigation.

[15] Ibid. Testimony of Mark E. Lovett, Esq., January 12, 2010. I had no intent to violate the Sunshine Act on April 1, 2005.

[16] The April 1, 2005, PowerPoint presentation is discussed in Chapter Eight: "Conestoga View." That was the meeting county staffer Andi Murphy coaxed me into attending. The meeting was not a Sunshine violation. No official action or deliberation—which must take place for there to be a Sunshine violation—was taken. I could have fought it, but the violation would have been presented regardless of any action I took. This was the dilemma I faced.

Endnotes

[17] The date that I accepted the citation to a Sunshine Act violation was December 14, 2006.

[18] At the time, I felt that taking the violation was the best way to resolve the situation. I believed if I did not take that plea, I would be charged with the Sunshine violation. If I challenged it in a Lancaster court, I believed I would lose. Perhaps I could have prevailed on appeal, but that would have taken the rest of my term (and $100,000 in legal fees). Still, in retrospect, I wish I had not taken that plea. It is a decision I regret.

[19] Judge Louis J. Farina's order sealing the grand jury report until January 8, 2007, was reported in the *Lancaster New Era*, "Judge Seals Grand Jury Report," December 19, 2006. Commissioner Shellenberger's attorney commented in the *New Era* article:

> William H. Lamb, a West Chester attorney and former Pennsylvania Supreme Court justice who represents Commissioner Dick Shellenberger, said he would have to discuss the matter with his client.
>
> "But I don't know what's proved by releasing the report," he said.
>
> Lamb sent out a press release following the guilty pleadings last Thursday. He downplayed the offenses, noting that he was "surprised that the district attorney would engage in such a lengthy and extensive investigation to address a summary offense."
>
> He further emphasized that comment this morning, noting that the 13-month grand jury process has cost "tens of thousands of dollars" and resulted in "parking tickets."
>
> "To quote Peggy Lee," he said, "Is that all there is?"

[20] Libel, as it concerns a "public figure," is an extremely high legal bar to clear. The 1964 landmark legal case *New York Times Co. v. Sullivan*, 376 U.S. 25, established the "actual malice" standard for the libel of public figures. Actual malice requires that the victim of the libelous statement(s) must prove that the reporter or the writer of the alleged libel had "knowledge that it was false or [wrote it] with reckless disregard for the truth." in writing the statement(s).

According to *New York Times v. Sullivan*, libel of a public figure, such as an elected county commissioner, must not only contain false statements and, as noted, be written with the knowledge of the falsity of those statements, but the statements have to be demonstrably damaging.

In the case of the five Lancaster Newspapers articles that are cited in my case, the false articles, written with knowledge that they were false, had the intended effect of damaging my political reputation, rendering me unelectable.

The *New York Times v Sullivan* decision may be found online here: https://supreme.justia.com/cases/federal/us/376/254/case.html.

[21] In the first week after the December 14 pleading, there were a total of fourteen separate articles published about "the commissioners" and the "secret sale" of Conestoga View. Most of the articles were above-the-fold, front-page articles and also included editorials. Several of the articles were more than 1,200 words in length. The following list below does not include letters to the editor (e.g., "Shocked by Arrogance of Commissioners"):

1. "Commissioners Plead Guilty: All 3 Admit Meeting Secretly in Violation of Sunshine Act," *Lancaster New Era*, December 14, 2006.
2. "Commissioners Guilty of Violating State Law: Pleas Roil County's Political Waters," *Intelligencer Journal*, December 15, 2006.
3. "Time to Resign," *Intelligencer Journal*, December 15, 2006.
4. "Commissioners Guilty of Violating State Law: Grand Jury Concludes Year-Long Probe," *Intelligencer Journal*, December 15, 2006.
5. "Guilty," *Lancaster New Era*, December 15, 2006.
6. "Guilty Pleas: Political Fallout Debated: Are Commissioners on Way Out?" *Lancaster New Era*, December 15, 2006.
7. "Grand Jury: Report Coming," *Lancaster New Era*, December 15, 2006.
8. "Sunshine Act: Grand Jury Usually Not Involved," *Lancaster New Era*, December 15, 2006.
9. "County Home: What's Next? After Guilty Pleas by Commissioners for Illegal Meetings, a Civil Challenge Could Be Tried to Reopen Sale. Acting in Secret 'Flawed' Sale," *Sunday News*, December 17, 2006.
10. "Humbugs! Countdown of the Days Left in County Commissioners' Terms: 385. The Commissioners' Guilty Pleas for Violating the Sunshine Act in the Sale of Conestoga View Is an Early Christmas Present for Us," *Sunday News*, December 17, 2006.
11. "Judge Seals Grand Jury Report. Findings in Investigation of Conestoga View Sale Ordered to Remain Secret for 20 Days, So Those Criticized in Report Have Chance to Respond," *Lancaster New Era*, December 20, 2006.
12. "Report Exposed Secret Conestoga View Meetings; Finds Flaws in Handling of Legal Fees," *Intelligencer Journal*, December 20, 2006.
13. "County Judge Seals Grand Jury Report," *Intelligencer Journal*, December 20, 2006.
14. "Secret Process Preceded Election, Special Report Reveals Roots of Conestoga View Sale," *Lancaster New Era*, December 20, 2006.

[22] The December 14 *Lancaster New Era* article "Commissioners Plead Guilty: All 3 Admit Meeting Secretly in Violation of Sunshine Act," dominated the front page of the newspaper that day. The article was accompanied by an unflattering photograph of all three county commissioners.

[23] In 2006, John H. "Jack" Brubaker, III, had been a professional journalist for thirty-six years. After beginning his career as an education reporter for the *Danville (Va.) Register* in 1970, Brubaker was hired by the *Lancaster New Era* in 1973. He moved from being an editorial writer in 2003 to working as an investigative reporter. Brubaker had been covering the Conestoga View issue almost exclusively for many months, with dozens of bylined articles. It was, therefore, libelously reckless to suggest a Sunshine Act summary violation as cognizable under the Crimes Code. It was not. Brubaker knew that or should have, and by publishing that error libeled me.

[24] The one meeting I attended—to which I accepted a citation for a Sunshine Act violation—was the April 1, 2005, informational "presentation," in which no deliberation, vote, or official action was taken, and in which I said not a word. To suggest that I, as one of "the commissioners," was secretly meeting to sell Conestoga View was provably false. Again, reporter Brubaker was aware of the falsity of the statement, yet wrote and published it without regard for its truthfulness.

[25] It is important to understand that these articles were appearing daily and in the most prominent places in all three Lancaster Newspapers. The December 15, 2006, *Intelligencer Journal* editorial "Time to Resign" further reinforced the false idea that I was involved a series of secret meetings to sell Conestoga View. The reading public was being given knowingly false information. the intent of which was to damage my reputation and drive me from office.

[26] The article in question, "Seeking an Inside View," by associate editor Gilbert A. Smart, was published by the *Sunday News* on December 31, 2006. The grand jury report had not been released.

[27] The circulation statistics were derived from the deposition testimony of Lancaster Newspapers chairman John M. Buckwalter, February 3, 2010, pp. 57–59: "The *New Era* was about 40,000 . . . The *Intell* would've been around 46,000, 47,000. The trend was that the evening paper was declining and the morning paper was gradually increasing. *Sunday News* was about 95,000, 96,000 . . ."

[28] Gilbert A. Smart, former associate editor of the *Sunday News* (LNP), was a defendant in my libel lawsuit against Lancaster Newspapers and several of its staff members: *Molly Henderson vs Lancaster Newspapers, Inc., John M. Buckwalter, Ernest J. Schreiber, Marvin I. Adams, Jr., Helen Colwell Adams, Charles Raymond Shaw, Arthur E. Morris, Gilbert A. Smart, John H. Brubaker, III, and David Pidgeon*. No. 0712003.

[29] "Taking the Fifth" ("No person . . . shall be compelled in any criminal case to be a witness against himself), while a right of all U.S. citizens under the Constitution, has been associated with guilt in the public mind since the McCarthy hearings of the early 1950s. This was demonstrated in an interview with Senator Joseph McCarthy (R-Wisconsin), conducted by Edward R. Murrow on CBS-TV, March 9, 1954. The interview was one month prior to Senator McCarthy's infamous Senate Subcommittee on Investigations hearings. Senator McCarthy talked about certain witnesses he expected to see at the hearings: *"And wait till you hear the bleeding hearts scream and cry about our methods of trying to drag the truth from those who know, or should know, who covered up a Fifth Amendment Communist . . ."* (Italics added.)

For a transcript of the Murrow-McCarthy interview online, please see "Edward R. Murrow: A Report on Senator Joseph R. McCarthy (CBS-TV, March 9, 1954)": http://www.lib.berkeley.edu/MRC/murrowmccarthy.html.

[30] From page 125 of Gilbert A. Smart's deposition of September 3, 2009:

Smart. "I don't believe I ever asked Commissioner Henderson whether she ever took the Fifth Amendment."

³¹ The "correction" made by the *Sunday News* on January 7, 2007, appeared on page A-2, on the inside of the front page, on the left side of the newspaper. The false statement appeared on the front page the previous week. There is a considerable difference between the front page and an interior page, especially an interior page on the left side of the newspaper, such as page A-2. Apart from the placement, the "correction" failed to correct the error of the statement.

³² The grand jury report was unsealed on January 10, 2007. As with other stories pertaining to Conestoga View and the grand jury, the unsealing of the grand jury report was on the front-page, with above-the-fold, banner headlines, "Grand Jury: Commissioners Betrayed Public's Trust/Judge Unseals Investigative Panel's Report, which Blasts County Officials' Secretive Handling of Conestoga View Sale," *Lancaster New Era*, January 10, 2007.

The article begins:

> The Lancaster County Commissioners secretly manipulated the sale of the county nursing home, including the hiring of one of the key administrators responsible, a grand jury report revealed today. "The grand jury clearly documents a betrayal of public trust by those who were elected to represent the citizens of Lancaster County," said District Attorney Donald Totaro, who coordinated the grand jury probe.

³³ From pages 20–21 of the grand jury report:

> A constant theme of the off-site meetings was that no one outside of "the team" should know about the plan to, or even the possibility of, selling Conestoga View. Commissioner Shaub specifically told the team members that Commissioner Henderson should be kept in the dark.

The LANCASTER COUNTY INVESTIGATING GRAND JURY II, 2005 Report No. 1, may be found online here: http://panewsmedia.org/docs/default-source/government-affairs-documents-2013/lancaster-county-grand-jury-report-sunshine-act.pdf?sfvrsn=0.

³⁴ Former commissioner Pete Shaub's written comments, in which he "acknowledged that I told persons to not discuss the CV [Conestoga View] sale with Commissioner Henderson at the direction of Mr. Espenshade," were published in the *Sunday News*, January 14, 2007.

³⁵ Former Pennsylvania Supreme Court justice William H. Lamb's comments about the grand jury report, "'Is that all there is?" appeared in "Grand Jury: Commissioners Betrayed Public's Trust/Judge Unseals Investigative Panel's Report, which Blasts County Officials' Secretive Handling of Conestoga View Sale," *Lancaster New Era*, January 10, 2007.

³⁶ *Lancaster New Era*, January 10, 2007. The libelous statement made by John H. "Jack" Brubaker, a defendant in my lawsuit against Lancaster Newspapers and several of its staff members, appeared in "Grand Jury: Commissioners Betrayed

Public's Trust/Judge Unseals Investigative Panel's Report, which Blasts County Officials' Secretive Handling of Conestoga View Sale," *Lancaster New Era*, January 10, 2007. The statement is discussed on page 29 of my complaint against Brubaker and Lancaster Newspapers, in *Molly Henderson vs Lancaster Newspapers, Inc., John M. Buckwalter, Ernest J. Schreiber, Marvin L. Adams, Jr., Helen Colwell Adams, Charles Raymond Shaw, Arthur E. Morris, Gilbert A. Smart, John H. Brubaker, III, and David Pidgeon.* No. 0712003.

[37] The biased nature of the "coverage" was demonstrated in the days after the grand jury report was released in such articles as Brubaker's "Secrecy, Deceit Crippled Probe: How Did Commissioners Avoid Multiple Criminal Charges?" *Lancaster New Era* article of January 11, 2007.

[38] *Lancaster New Era* reporter John H. "Jack" Brubaker knew, because he had read the grand jury report, that there was no factual basis for an inference that I "avoided further criminal charges" only because the grand jury lacked "sufficient corroborating evidence." There isn't even a suggestion of this in the grand jury report. Yet Brubaker wrote it, and Lancaster Newspapers published it. That appears to be an example of the knowledge of falsity required under libel law. See *New York Times v. Sullivan*, 376 U.S. 254 (1964).

[39] The libelous statement made by John H. "Jack" Brubaker in the January 11, 2007, *Lancaster New Era* article "Secrecy, Deceit Crippled Probe: How Did Commissioners Avoid Multiple Criminal Charges?" is discussed on page 30 of my complaint against Lancaster Newspapers and several of its staff members, *Molly Henderson vs Lancaster Newspapers, Inc., John M. Buckwalter, Ernest J. Schreiber, Marvin L. Adams, Jr., Helen Colwell Adams, Charles Raymond Shaw, Arthur E. Morris, Gilbert A. Smart, John H. Brubaker, III, and David Pidgeon.* No. 0712003.

[40] The "correction" of *Lancaster New Era* reporter Jack Brubaker's January 11 article, "Secrecy, Deceit Crippled Probe," appeared in "Local Leaders Urge Commissioners: Step Down Now," January 12, 2007. "Local Leaders" was co-bylined by Brubaker and former *New Era* reporter Anya Litwak.

The "correction" (there was no indication it was a "correction" in the article; just two sentences in the middle) only compounded the original libel by using the word *further* criminal charges. As stated in the body of the chapter, there weren't any "criminal charges" against me contained in the grand jury report.

The article itself, "Local Leaders Urge Commissioners: Step Down Now," is an extraordinary example of the newspaper's organized campaign using Conestoga View. In the article, virtually the entire Lancaster political establishment, from both parties, called for the resignation of our entire Board of Commissioners.

The article begins:

> Several present and former public officials today called for the resignation of all county commissioners in the wake of an investigating grand jury report detailing widespread secrecy and deceit in county government. Even those who did not call

for resignations said it will be difficult, if not impossible, for the commissioners to function in office through the end of their terms next January. . . . Former U.S. Rep. Bob Walker, former County Commissioner Jim Huber and former Lancaster Mayor Art Morris, all Republicans, also called for the commissioners to resign. . . . State Sen. Gibson Armstrong, a Republican who has previously and publicly urged Commissioner Dick Shellenberger to resign, reiterated the message this morning. "He should do the right thing," Armstrong said. . . . Former Democratic County Commissioner Ron Ford said Shellenberger and Henderson have lost the trust of the public and will find it nearly impossible to govern in that environment.

"I think they've probably reached that point," Ford said today. Ford advised that the commissioners should evaluate if they can still be effective in office. "Part of that is acknowledging the volume and seriousness of public criticism," he said, "which the current board "does not completely comprehend." It's almost a somewhat delusional aspect" of this board," Ford said. . . . Lancaster Mayor Rick Gray, a Democrat, said, "I don't think it's to the benefit of the county to continue the animosity and lack of trust." Gray said the credibility beating the commissioners have suffered, culminating in the grand jury report, "should prod them to reconsider their strategy for the remainder of their terms," although he stopped short of calling on them to resign. The mayor reserved his harshest words for Henderson, calling her a "dismal failure as a minority commissioner," who defied her watchdog role and became complicit in the secrecy surrounding the sale of Conestoga View. To call the grand jury report a vindication, which Henderson has done, betrays a "Nixonian standard of ethics," Gray said. "If your standard is 'I didn't violate criminal law,' that's no standard at all." . . .

Morris said the commissioners "can continue in office, but not effectively, because they have lost all credibility. Even county employees cannot trust them now," he said. Every week these people stay in office is one less week recovering from this mess and digs a deeper hole for us," he noted. "If they believe they were elected to serve the county for good, the best way they can do that now is to leave."" He said, "the damage done to county government "has been a team effort on behalf of the commissioners."

My published comment in the article took aim at Lancaster Newspapers:

Those who do not realize that the grand jury report has confirmed and vindicated my position, have likely been misled by the incorrect statements about the grand jury report in the *Intell* and the *New Era*.

The article may be viewed online here: http://lancasteronline.com/news/local-leaders-urge-commissioners-step-down-now/article_79f1aed1-1ff9-5f72-bf55-313f077ec0fe.html.

[41] The *Intelligencer Journal* article "Grand Jury Blasts Three Commissioners," by David Pidgeon, January 11, 2007, began by generalizing the three commissioners, without differentiating between us:

> A grand jury report released Wednesday harshly criticizes the Lancaster County commissioners for secretly agreeing to sell the Conestoga View nursing home in 2005. . . .

There is no place in the grand jury report in which I was "harshly" criticized in any manner.

David Pidgeon was a defendant in my libel lawsuit against Lancaster Newspapers and several of its staff members, *Molly Henderson vs Lancaster Newspapers, Inc., John M. Buckwalter, Ernest J. Schreiber, Marvin L. Adams, Jr., Helen Colwell Adams, Charles Raymond Shaw, Arthur E. Morris, Gilbert A. Smart, John H. Brubaker, III, and David Pidgeon.* No. 0712003.

[42] Ibid.

[43] The two *Intelligencer Journal* articles published on January 11, 2007, both written by David Pidgeon—"Grand Jury Blasts Commissioners" and "Report Details 'Veil of Secrecy in County/ Secret Meetings on 'Charlie Victor'"—took up most of the *Intell*'s front page, above and below the fold. The articles were also accompanied by a large picture of the three commissioners. This is what tens of thousands of Lancastrians saw first thing in the morning on January 11.

[44] After thirteen months and a huge waste of the district attorney's resources and taxpayer money, the grand jury concluded exactly as the Myers Report had: that Shaub and Shellenberger met secretly to hire Heinke and sell Conestoga View. Molly Henderson—according to the Myers Report and the grand jury—had absolutely nothing to do with it.

The reference in the chapter about keeping me "in the dark" about the secret meetings appears on pages 20 and 21 of the grand jury report. Lancaster County Investigating Grand Jury II, 2005, Report No. 1.

[45] The "correction/clarification" that appeared buried in the *Intelligencer Journal* on January 12, 2007, demonstrates just how damaging a statement can be. The previous day, two front-page *Intell* articles written by David Pidgeon said that I was one of "three commissioners" who "escaped serious criminal charges," according to the grand jury report, on which the articles were based. The two articles, with a picture of all three commissioners, covered the front page of the newspaper. The impression of the front-page articles with photographs has far more impact than two sentences buried in the interior of the paper.

[46] The e-mail that *Lancaster New Era* Jack Brubaker wrote to me was dated January 12, 2007, and is Exhibit U in my complaint against Brubaker and Lancaster Newspapers,

Molly Henderson vs Lancaster Newspapers, Inc., John M. Buckwalter, Ernest J. Schreiber, Marvin L. Adams, Jr., Helen Colwell Adams, Charles Raymond Shaw, Arthur E. Morris, Gilbert A. Smart, John H. Brubaker, III, and David Pidgeon. No. 0712003.

Jack Brubaker had covered the grand jury investigation for more than one year. It was the thirty-six-year veteran reporter's beat and investigative assignment at the time the grand jury report was released After January 10, 2007, he would have been expected to read the unsealed grand jury report. In fact, Brubaker testified on page 154 of his deposition that he read the grand jury report as soon as it was released. *[Brubaker: "May I see the article?" Christina Donato Saler, attorney deposing defendant: "I actually don't have a copy of the article with me, unfortunately."]. http://panewsmedia.org/docs/default-source/government-affairs-documents-2013/lancaster-county-grand-jury-report-sunshine-act.pdf?sfvrsn=0. Also see, Brubaker, Jack, "County Completes Report on Heinke", Lancaster New Era, November 8, 2006..

[47] The waves of articles condemning "the commissioners" in the days and weeks after the grand jury report continued with the *Lancaster New Era*'s January 13, 2007, "Citizens: GET OUT!" The report had led the news all week, with article after article attacking "the commissioners," including "Local Leaders Urge Commissioners: Step Down Now," on January 11, 2007, where the Lancaster political establishment collectively called for our board's resignation.

"Citizens: GET OUT!" was an attempt to drive all three commissioners from office. Note that "about three dozen people" are said to have been polled, and that the "informal poll" followed several days of anti-commissioner front pages.

The article, bylined by Tom Murse and Jane Holahan, begins:

> Note to the County Commissioners: The public wants you to resign. Right now. An informal survey today shows they have lost trust in you and don't think you can govern effectively. A few believe you should go to jail and just about everyone wants a fresh start in county government. The *New Era* asked about three dozen people whether the commissioners should resign in light of this week's grand jury findings and a long history of controversy....

[48] The theme for Lancaster Newspapers the first week after the grand jury report came out was to force the two commissioners to resign. (Shaub announced on December 26, 2006, that he would resign on February 4, 2007.) The *Sunday News*'s editorial of January 14, 2007, "Commissioners Shellenberger and Henderson: Have Grace to Resign," was extremely damaging. The *Sunday News* had a circulation of almost 100,000, most of that subscription home delivery. It was the newspaper, supposedly nonpartisan, that was read by the whole family.

[49] *Sunday News* editorial writer and religion reporter Helen Colwell Adams was a defendant in my libel lawsuit against Lancaster Newspapers and several of its staff members, *Molly Henderson vs Lancaster Newspapers, Inc., John M. Buckwalter, Ernest J. Schreiber, Marvin L. Adams, Jr., Helen Colwell Adams, Charles Raymond Shaw, Arthur E. Morris, Gilbert A. Smart, John H. Brubaker, III, and David Pidgeon.* No. 0712003.

Endnotes

Describing the editorial writing relationship between his wife and himself, former *Sunday News* editor Marvin I. "Marv" Adams said in his deposition, "I am the music and she's the lyrics," meaning Marv came up with the ideas and Helen tapped them out on the keyboard. Marv Adams was a defendant in the libel lawsuit I brought against Lancaster Newspapers, Inc. and several of its employees, *Molly Henderson vs Lancaster Newspapers, Inc., John M. Buckwalter, Ernest J. Schreiber, Marvin I. Adams, Jr., Helen Colwell Adams, Charles Raymond Shaw, Arthur E. Morris, Gilbert A. Smart, John H. Brubaker, III, and David Pidgeon*. No. 0712003. Adams was deposed on October 29, 2009.

[50] *Sunday News* editorial writer, editor, and religion reporter Helen Colwell Adams, a defendant in my libel lawsuit against Lancaster Newspapers and several of its staff members, was deposed on October 5, 2009.

The editorial written by Colwell Adams on January 14, 2007, "Commissioners Shellenberger and Henderson: Have Grace to Resign," was among the most damaging items published by Lancaster Newspapers. This was the first Sunday after the grand jury report was released. It followed several days of scathing criticism of "the commissioners" for our role in the hiring of Gary Heinke and the "secret" sale of Conestoga View.

In addition to naming me in the title of the editorial ("Commissioners Shellenberger and Henderson: Have Grace to Resign"), the editorial strongly suggests that I personally was more involved than the grand jury concluded. Colwell Adams's editorial:

> Ms. Henderson, the Democrat, definitely knew by April 2005 about the CV plan, and Mr. Heinke told the grand jury that she admitted to him she had known about the deal in 2004. Yet she did not oppose the sale or alert the public. She sold the elderly and poor of this county for 30 pieces of silver. . . . We're not sure which is more horrifying: that Mr. Shellenberger and Ms. Henderson would be trying to spin this to survive politically, or that key Democrats would be willing to give up any claim to moral high ground by helping Ms. Henderson salvage her career. At least the county GOP is backing away from Mr. Shellenberger."

The editorial ended by comparing Shellenberger and me unfavorably to Richard Nixon: "Even Richard Nixon had the grace to resign."

Ms. Colwell Adams indicated she was a divinity student at "Evangelical Theological Seminary" on pages 10–11 of her deposition of October 5, 2009.

The Biblical (*King James Version*) reference to "thirty pieces of silver" is found in Matthew 26, verses 14–16:

> Then one of the twelve, named Judas Iscariot, went to the chief priests and said, "What are you willing to give me to betray Him to you?" And they weighed out thirty pieces of silver to him. From then on he began looking for a good opportunity to betray Jesus.

[52] *Sunday News* editorial writer Helen Colwell Adams admitted in her deposition that she had read the grand jury report prior to writing the editorial. And regarding my

involvement in the Gary Heinke hiring, Colwell Adams testified on pages 49–50 of her deposition in response from a question from my attorney Christina Donato Saler:

Attorney Saler. "When you read the grand jury report, do you recall the grand jury concluding that Molly Henderson had any role in assisting Mr. Heinke with his hiring process?"

Helen Colwell Adams: "Not to my knowledge, no."

Attorney Saler: "And do you recall, when you read the grand jury report, did you take from it that only Commissioners Shellenberger and Shaub were involved in assisting Gary Heinke in the hiring process?"

Helen Colwell Adams: "They [Commissioners Shellenberger and Shaub] were the ones, according to the grand jury report, who provided him information in advance of interviews and so forth."

. . . and from pages 54–61 of Colwell Adams's deposition:

Q. So in your reading of the grand jury report then there is no mention of Ms. Henderson having secret meetings with Commissioners Shellenberger or Shaub prior to April 1st, 2005?
A. To the best of my knowledge.
Q. In reading the grand jury report, is it your understanding that Commissioners Shellenberger and Shaub had other meetings, non-public meetings, in addition to the April 1st, 2005 meeting with Ms. Henderson?
A. Yes.

This proves that Colwell Adams had knowledge of the falsity of what she was writing by including me with commissioners Shaub and Shellenberger.

On pages 59–61 of the deposition:

Q. Okay. And the last sentence: "Yet she [Commissioner Henderson] did not oppose the sale or alert the public. She sold the elderly and the poor of this county for 30 pieces of silver." What exactly do you mean by that sentence, "She sold the elderly and the poor of this county for 30 pieces of silver"?
A. That is a reference to a biblical story about the betrayal of Jesus by Judas. And that is what that sentence is a referral to, a betrayal.
Q. For 30 pieces of silver?
A. That's a part of the metaphor.
Q. All right. So, when you were making this reference to Ms. Henderson, you were intending it to mean that she betrayed the poor of Conestoga View, the residents of Conestoga View?
A. And the poor of the whole county of Lancaster, yeah.
Q. And were you also suggesting that she received some form of personal financial gain by her betrayal?
A. No, that was not intended.
Q. After reading this sentence, though, you do understand that this is a suggestion it makes?

THE WITNESS: I don't think it does make that.

Q. You don't think that 30 pieces of silver can be equated to Ms. Henderson receiving a financial gain?
A. No. The important thing in the story of the betrayal of Jesus by Judas is not the money he received, but the betrayal.
Q. But in fact he did receive money; correct?
A. He gave it back.
Q. Did Ms. Henderson receive money for agreeing to sell Conestoga View?
A. I do not know that. I don't believe she did.

[53] The *Sunday News* editorial of January 21, 2007, was titled, "Sunny Side Up." The editorial, written by Helen Colwell Adams, was accompanied by editor Marv Adams's "Countdown: Days Left in Terms of Commissioners Shellenberger and Henderson: 351." The "Countdown" appeared every week on the editorial page and amounted to an editorial itself. This item appeared in the Sunday newspaper for more than a year and a half.

[54] The *Lancaster New Era* article "Facade of Almshouse May Be Eased to Preservation Trust," was bylined by Jack Brubaker, a defendant in my libel lawsuit against Lancaster Newspapers and several of its staff members, *Molly Henderson vs Lancaster Newspapers, Inc., John M. Buckwalter, Ernest J. Schreiber, Marvin L. Adams, Jr., Helen Colwell Adams, Charles Raymond Shaw, Arthur E. Morris, Gilbert A. Smart, John H. Brubaker, III, and David Pidgeon*. No. 0712003.

The statement was made in the first paragraph of Brubaker's article. It appeared four months after the grand jury report was released and was read by Brubaker. Nowhere in the grand jury report is it suggested that I was part of the "secret sale." Yet once again, Brubaker wrote and Lancaster Newspapers published the libelous statement.

[55] Setting aside the inaccurate "correction/clarification," its placement in an interior section of the *New Era*, eight days after the false front-page story, demonstrates the pattern and practice of Lancaster Newspapers. As shown, reporter Jack Brubaker was very familiar with the contents of the grand jury and the Myers reports, both of which independently found I had nothing to do with a "secret sale." And, once again, Brubaker, under editor Ernie Schreiber, knowingly wrote and published the false suggestion that I was involved in a "secret sale." The May 1, 2007, *Lancaster New Era* article in question, "Facade of Almshouse May Be 'Eased' to Preservation Trust," may be found here:

http://lancasteronline.com/news/facade-of-almshouse-may-be-eased-to-preservation-trust/article_f73a5d73-56fa-5396-a96e-8281b89966ab.html.

[56] The September 13, 2007, article "Former Exec Sues County," was another *Lancaster New Era* front-page article bylined by Jack Brubaker, along with Cindy Stauffer. The article was accompanied by photographs of Shaub, Shellenberger, Heinke, and me. Since the first story about Conestoga View and the county commissioners, in July 2005, there were 479 separate articles about the topic. We used the database ProQuest to count the number of articles. ProQuest is a Michigan-based global information

and content technology company that, among other services, electronically archives newspapers. ProQuest has more than 125 billion digital pages in its database. When we put the search terms "Molly Henderson" and "County Commissioners" and "Conestoga View" into the ProQuest search engine for 2005, it turned out 399 articles. During the time I was in office, from 2004 to 2008, there were a total of 1,653 articles published with "Molly Henderson" and "County Commissioners. (See Appendix C) The ProQuest numbers do not include letters to the editor, which also numbered in the hundreds.

[57] The *Lancaster New Era* "correction/clarification" of the false September 13, 2007, article "Former Exec Sues County" appeared on page C-8 in the September 17, 2007, *Lancaster New Era*. Still again, we see a front-page, above-the-fold false statement, against a buried, downplayed "correction" somewhere in the interior of the newspaper.

[58] The intentionality—the knowledge of falsity—in publishing the false statements about me was a component in my libel lawsuit against Lancaster Newspapers and several of its staff members, *Molly Henderson vs Lancaster Newspapers, Inc., John M. Buckwalter, Ernest J. Schreiber, Marvin L. Adams, Jr., Helen Colwell Adams, Charles Raymond Shaw, Arthur E. Morris, Gilbert A. Smart, John H. Brubaker, III, and David Pidgeon.* No. 0712003. Jack Brubaker and Helen Colwell Adams, prominent reporters for the *Lancaster New Era* and the *Sunday News*, respectively, had closely read the grand jury and knew of the Myers reports. Yet with the knowledge of the contents of those reports, which they acknowledged revealed that I was unaware of any impropriety in Heinke's hiring and that the sale of Conestoga View was not secret both Brubaker and Colwell Adams wrote and published statements to the contrary.

[59] Former Lancaster mayor Arthur E. "Art" Morris's quote, "The criminal act they [the county commissioners] committed far outweighs the penalty they paid," may be found in the *Intelligencer Journal*, "Grand Jury Concludes Year-Long Probe; Commissioners Guilty of Violating State Law," December 15, 2006. This was an above-the-fold, six-column banner, front-page article, complete with photographs of all three county commissioners. Morris, a columnist with the *Sunday News*, was a defendant in my libel lawsuit against Lancaster Newspaper and several of its staff members, *Molly Henderson vs Lancaster Newspapers, Inc., John M. Buckwalter, Ernest J. Schreiber, Marvin L. Adams, Jr., Helen Colwell Adams, Charles Raymond Shaw, Arthur E. Morris, Gilbert A. Smart, John H. Brubaker, III, and David Pidgeon.* No. 0712003.

[60] A letter to the editor from former mayor Art Morris was not like a typical letter to the editor. Mr. Morris, a two-and-a-half term ex-mayor of the city, was the primary source for Lancaster Newspapers, the recognized "expert," on the Heinke and Conestoga View stories. So, when Morris leveled his opprobrium at someone, it carried a lot of weight. Morris's published letter of December 17, 2007 (which exceeded the 200-word limit), appeared in the *Sunday News*.

[61] Former Lancaster mayor Art Morris's letter "Henderson Had More of Role Than She's Letting On," *Lancaster New Era*, January 15, 2007, appeared on page A-13. This is the letter where Morris says my defense of the grand jury report exonerating me

from the Heinke hiring and the "secret sale" of Conestoga View was compared to "spew which is produced by cattle."

[62] Art Morris's 900-plus word "Sunday's Guest" column "Missed Opportunities, Unmet Expectations," was published in the *Sunday News*, January 28, 2007, and entirely dedicated to attacking me. Morris's statement that I "knew beforehand" of Heinke's background was knowingly false. The grand jury report was released January 10, 2007, and it clearly concluded I did not know "beforehand" anything about the Heinke hiring process. Creating this false impression was intentional on Morris's part.

[63] Commissioner Pete Shaub, the ex-marine who created chaos throughout the courthouse in seven years as a Lancaster County commissioner, officially quit his job February 14, 2007. See: Reilly, P.J., "Storm Steals Shaub's Final Act," *Intelligencer Journal*, February 14, 2007.

[64] Former Lancaster County commissioner Richard "Dick" Shellenberger did not give Lancaster Newspapers the scoop on his announcement not to seek a second term, instead taking out a display advertisement in the *Pennysaver/Merchandiser* newspaper. This is a controlled circulation (free) newspaper directly mailed to Lancaster County households. Commissioner Shellenberger, although improperly involved in the Heinke hiring and sale of Conestoga View, was also victimized by the anti-commissioners Lancaster Newspapers campaign. Conestoga View became the red herring because of Shellenberger's and my opposition to the hotel and convention center project. Shellenberger's decision not to run for reelection was reported in Pidgeon, Dave, "Shellenberger Won't Seek Second Term," *Intelligencer Journal*, January 17, 2007, and Brubaker, Jack, "Shellenberger Out of the Race: What It Means," the *Lancaster New Era*, January 17, 2007, http://www.proquest.com.

Epilogue

[1] Winston Churchill's quote is found in the foreword of *Brighton Conference Resolutions*, by the National Union of Conservative and Unionist Associations (St. Clements Press, 1947). The Brighton Resolutions memorialized motions passed at the 1947 annual Conservative Party conference in Brighton, England, September 1947.

Here is the full Churchill quote:

> The Bolsheviks have discovered that truth does not matter so long as there is reiteration. They have no difficulty whatever in countering a fact by a lie which, if repeated often enough and loudly enough, becomes accepted by the people.

[2] District attorney Donald R. Totaro, a Republican, received 51,613 votes for judge to the Lancaster County Court of Common Pleas. The second-leading vote getter, Margaret C. Miller, received 38,025.

Source: Lancaster County Voter Registration and Board of Elections.

[3] In the November 2007 Lancaster County commissioner's election, I received 17,021 votes, while the other endorsed Democrat, Craig Lehman, received 25,113 votes. Republicans Scott Martin and Dennis Stuckey received 37,843 and 35,518 votes, respectively; Jere Swarr, a Rapho Township, Republican supervisor, was also on the ballot, and received 13,900 votes

Source: Lancaster County Voter Registration and Board of Elections.

[4] There were several opening dates for the finished hotel and convention center project. It was announced in 2008—"Marriott Lancaster on Schedule for March," *Sunday News*, July 20, 2008—the project would open in March 2009. Then, in November 2008, the opening date was pushed back to April 2009: "Convention Center Opening Set for April 21, Firmed-Up Timeframe Allows Event Planners to Move Ahead with Bookings," *Lancaster New Era*, November 21, 2008. Then, again, it was moved back another month to May, "A Look Inside Downtown Marriott Prices & Features, as Grand Opening Is Pushed Back Today to Week of May 11, We Take You on a Tour of the $170M Hotel and Convention Center," *Lancaster New Era*, March 25, 2009. When May arrived, another delay was announced but with no clear opening, "Delays Costing Center Money, Revenue Lost as Events Cancel, Move," *Intelligencer Journal*, May 1, 2009. The hotel opened on June 19, 2009, and the convention center opened on June 24, 2009.

[5] Former mayor and hotel-convention center project supporter, as well as leading the attack on Conestoga View, Art Morris, was named to the LCCCA board in April 2007. He resigned from the board in 2010.

[6] The Lancaster County Board of Commissioners voted for the $63 million convention center bond guaranty on July 1, 2014. The 2 to 1 vote (Lehman against) was reported in "It's Official, Commissioners Vote to Approve Convention Center Guarantee," *LNP*, July 1, 2014.

See http://lancasteronline.com/news/local/it-s-official-commissioners-vote---to-approve-convention/article_01d1a08e-013a-11e4-8520-001a4bcf6878.html.

[7] Ibid.

[8] The $23 million hotel expansion will use the same funding mechanism that was used to build the existing Marriott Hotel. This means the Redevelopment Authority of the City of Lancaster (RACL) will have property title for the hotel expansion, thereby exempting the hotel expansion from paying property tax rolls, as it did with the existing Marriott. Also, as part of the funding for the expansion, Penn Square Partners will use RACL to borrow funds from the state to build the expansion. The partners will pay the debt service on the state bonds but, again, will pay no local property taxes. See "LCCC Authority Approves Marriott Expansion," *Central Penn Business Journal*," February 6, 2015; http://www.cpbj.com/article/20150206/CPBJ01/150209838/lccc-authority-approves-marriott-expansion

> If the financing of the hotel expansion is the same as the existing Marriott Hotel, then the real estate acquisitions of High Real Estate—14, 16, and 18 E. King Street—will be "sold" to RACL,

which will then apply for the state bonds to be used to build the $23 million Penn Square Partners' hotel expansion. The title transfer to RACL also exempts Penn Square Partners' hotel expansion from paying real estate taxes. So, once again, High will buy a taxable city property, transfer ownership to the city, borrow money and take advantage of low interest rates due to city "ownership," develop the hotel and operate it for profit, and pay exactly zero dollars and zero cents in real estate taxes to the City of Lancaster, the School District for the City of Lancaster, and the County of Lancaster. When we say the project is "All about the Hotel," this is what we mean. The major beneficiaries of the hotel and convention center project were the two owners of the hotel—High and Steinman.

See "From High Real Estate Buys 3rd Small Parcel on East King Street," *LNP*, January 9, 2015.

Note the timing. Although, in the article, Penn Square Partners president Mark Fitzgerald says the properties may be developed as "an office building . . . . . as well as other possible uses that may involve replacing the existing structures," in just four weeks, the $23 million hotel expansion was announced.

[9] An article on the last High Real Estate acquisition on E. King Street may be found here: http://lancasteronline.com/business/local_business/high-real-estate-buys-rd-small-parcel-on-east-king/article_ba68df2e-9828-11e4-bf7e-9b951a51021f.html

[10] "PILOT Deal on Penn Square Marriott Expansion Holds Good, Despite Project Cost Hike, Council Told," Tim Stuhldreher, July 4, 2017, LancasterOnline.

[11] Senator Gibson E. "Gib" Armstrong's full comment after the hotel room rental tax was first proposed in Lancaster in 1998 was: "Let's check it out with some of the people in the hospitality industry. The hospitality industry has to be reassured." See the *Intelligencer Journal*, in "Local Leaders Consider Taxing Tourists to Help City," April 2, 1998.

[12] Mark Clossey, former general manager of the Lancaster Host hotel and longtime general manager of the Eden Resort hotel, has been one of the most active of the Lancaster County hoteliers questioning the Lancaster hotel and convention center project. The Eden was one of the original 37 plaintiffs challenging the room tax in 2000. Mr. Clossey's comments were derived from "Lancaster County Convention Center: Economic Impact So Far; Report Finds Convention Center Has Boosted Economic Activity Here, but Hotel Group Contends It's Hurt Them," *LNP*, December 22, 2013.

See http://lancasteronline.com/business/local_business/lancaster-county-convention-center-economic-impact-so-far/article_de7734ac-0484-11e4-a17a-001a4bcf6878.html.

[13] Rodney D. Gleiberman, former owner of the Continental Inn, was also one of the original 37 hotel owner plaintiffs who sued the Lancaster County commissioners for

imposing the hotel room rental tax. In addition to being a plaintiff, Gleiberman, was also a sharp critic of the project through his blogspot. Gleiberman's comments were made in a written exchange with Christiaan A. Hart Nibbrig.

[14] Ibid

[15] For the original Collaboration Agreement, see http://www.lccca.com/wp-content/uploads/2014/09/Tab-3-Collaboration-Agreement-Issuer-County-City-RACL-and-PDCVB1.pdf/. And for the updated agreement, see http://www.lccca.com/2017/01/13/collaboration-agreement-30-month-update/.

[16] More than eight years after the opening of the hotel and convention center, the Thaddeus Stevens museum sits unopened and empty. The buildings that once housed the great civil rights congressman and his companion, Lydia Hamilton-Smith, are completely torn down, except for a partial façade. The sponsors of the project, Penn Square Partners, repeatedly touted the Stevens Museum as being an important part of the project.

[17] Former Lancaster Newspapers, Inc., chairman John M. "Jack" Buckwalter's comments are found in a profile of Buckwalter in 1996, "Keeping Lancaster in the News," *Intelligencer Journal*, June 17, 1996.

[18] The merger between the *Intelligencer Journal* and the *Lancaster New Era* was announced in "A New Beginning for *Lancaster New Era*; Starting Monday, the *New Era* Becomes Part of a New And Improved Morning Newspaper. Today, We Look Ahead at a Future Filled with Promise and Back at a History Filled with Achievement," *Lancaster New Era*, June 26, 2009. The article was written by longtime *New Era* staff writer Jack Brubaker, a defendant in my libel lawsuit against Lancaster Newspapers and several of its staff.

[19] Another defendant in the libel suit, *Intelligencer Journal* editor Charles Raymond "Ray" Shaw, confirmed the Lancaster Newspapers' job losses. From page 18 of Shaw's October 29, 2009, deposition:

Q. So is the total number of employees for the *Intelligencer Journal/New Era* fewer than the individual sums that worked for those two papers prior to the consolidation?
A. Yes.
Q. By what order of magnitude?
A. By approximately 40 percent.

See http://lancasteronline.com/news/a-new-beginning-for-lancaster-new-era/article_f78a163c-0c0b-5554-90d3-28938aab3541.html.

[20] In 2014, the "merged" print newspaper, *Intelligencer Journal/Lancaster New Era* was renamed again, "*LNP*," evidently, and anachronistically, short for "Lancaster Newspapers." See: http://www.washingtontimes.com/news/2014/oct/16/lancaster-newspaper-has-new-name-lnp/.

[21] In 2015, Lancaster Newspapers moved its printing operations out of downtown, taking with it 40 full-time and 35 part-time jobs. See:http://abc27.com/2015/01/14/lnp-to-move-newspaper-printing-out-of-lancaster/.

[22] "Lancaster City Alliance Marketing Properties Near Convention Center," March 4, 2016, Dan Naphin, *LNP*.

[23] Owners of real estate in the City of Lancaster are required to pay property taxes. Property owners must pay a property tax to each of the three taxing bodies in Lancaster County: the city, the county, and the School District of Lancaster. Each taxing body has a separate millage rate. A mill is equal to $1 in taxation for every $1,000 of assessed value of the property. The current rate for the School District of Lancaster is currently 26.6793; the city, 14.02; the county, 3.735. If the $75 million Marriott Hotel, operated for profit by Penn Square Partners, was taxed at current millage rates, Penn Square Partners would be paying approximately $2 million *per year* to the school district; more than $1 million to the city of Lancaster, and more than $250,000 to the county. For Lancaster millage rates, see http://cityoflancasterpa.com/tax-fees-faq.

[24] As discussed in the book, it became clear to me after I began to look into the project that it was "all about the hotel." This meant that most of the benefits (and money) were going to the private owners of the Marriott Hotel, Penn Square Partners, currently made up of High Real Estate and Lancaster Newspapers, Inc. For a detailed analysis of the hotel's role in the overall project, please see Chapter Six of this book, "It's All about the Hotel—Really."

[25] In 2015, the School District of Lancaster paid Penn Square Partners $14,054 for a high school graduation ceremony and paid an additional $21,978 to the Lancaster County Convention Center Authority for its senior prom. Source: School District of Lancaster Graduation Prom Cost Comparison, 2014–2016.

[26] It was in an April 12, 2005, *Lancaster New Era* editorial, "County Plan to Kill City Project Will Fail," where former Lancaster County commissioner Dick Shellenberger and I were labeled "enemies of the city." The editorial is discussed in Chapter Seven of this book.

[27] The Floyd Institute report—*Lancaster Prospers? An Analysis of Census Data on Economic Opportunities and Outcomes*—is very important in analyzing the impact of the $200 million hotel and convention center project. The report roughly covers the time period from the pre-construction planning of the project through its construction, public opening, and four years of operation, from 2002 to 2013. The report was researched and written by Antonio Callari, the Sigmund M. and Mary B. Hyman Professor of Economics at Franklin & Marshall College; Evan Gentry, research specialist and economics lab assistant, Floyd Institute for Public Policy; and Berwood Yost, director, Floyd Institute for Public Policy.

[28] In the report's conclusions, the researchers sharply criticize the City of Lancaster for "farming out" city economic development to private entities, such as the Lancaster Alliance. Three of the founding members of the Lancaster Alliance later formed Penn Square Partners.

From the *Lancaster Prospers?* report:

> While a narrative has emerged about the urban renewal success of the City, mostly focused on Center City and the Arts, the

reality is that the economic conditions of many City residents have largely grown worse in terms of opportunities and outcomes. . . . We conclude from our findings that the City's economic growth has not delivered on its implied promises. Areas of the City (Tracts 1, 8, and 4) which have received explicit attention and investments from City officials, or civic groups (SACA), or private stakeholders (Lancaster General Health), have benefitted significantly from these investments. But the remaining areas of the City, not supported by specific policy initiatives, show a deterioration of general economic conditions and a worsening of the conditions that support a healthy social fabric. . . . What we are criticizing is that the City seems to have outsourced their responsibility to guide the community toward an inclusive and sustainable vision of economic development.

[29] See *Lancaster Prospers? An Analysis of Census Data on Economic Opportunities and Outcomes*, Floyd Institute for Public Policy, Franklin & Marshall College, 2015, page 10.

[30] The *Boston Gazette* was published from 1719 to 1798 and is considered the first independent press in the British colonies. The *Boston News-Letter* (1704–1776) is considered the first continuously published newspaper printed in the British colonies. The *Boston News-Letter* was funded by the Crown and approved by the colonial governor. The *Boston Gazette* was published by James Franklin (1697–1735), Benjamin's older brother. Benjamin Franklin (1706–1790) was a legally indentured servant to older brother James and also worked on the *Boston Gazette*. James Franklin began publishing the *New England Courant* in 1721. Benjamin also contributed to the *Courant*, anonymously publishing letters under the female nom de plume Silence Dogood. James had rejected Benjamin's submissions to the *Courant,* and Benjamin, still James's apprentice, left the letters, which were very popular with readers, under the *Courant*'s door every two weeks. When James discovered the ruse, he reacted angrily toward his younger brother, with whom he already had a poor relationship that included physical mistreatment. It was after Mrs. Dogood's identity was discovered and James's hostile reaction that Benjamin left his brother and the *Courant* and moved to Philadelphia, where he made history.

[31] A postmortem on the print newspaper has yet to be written. Lancaster Newspapers is among the thousands of print publications to either cease publication or drastically reduce circulation and downsize staff. It is also a global trend. In 2016, the British *Independent*, which once had a daily circulation of 400,000, announced it was ceasing the print newspaper. At the time of the announcement, circulation of the *Independent* had fallen to 56,000. See:http://www.telegraph.co.uk/finance/newsbysector/mediatechnologyandtelecoms/12153947/The-Independent-newspaper-confirms-an-end-to-print-production.html.

Endnotes

[32] The lawsuit—*Molly Henderson vs Lancaster Newspapers, Inc., John M. Buckwalter, Ernest J. Schreiber, Marvin I. Adams, Jr., Helen Colwell Adams, Charles Raymond Shaw, Arthur E. Morris, Gilbert A. Smart, John H. Brubaker, III, and David Pidgeon. No. 0712003*—was filed with the Chester County, Pennsylvania, Court of Common Pleas on January 8, 2008.

[33] George W. Croner, Esq., of the Philadelphia firm Kohn, Swift, & Graf, was the lead attorney in my lawsuit. Mr. Croner graduated with distinction from the U.S. Naval Academy and received his J.D., cum laude, from the University of Pennsylvania law school. Prior to joining Kohn, Swift, & Graf, Mr. Croner served as member of the Judge Advocate General Corps of the U.S. Navy. For more on George W. Croner, please see http://kohnswift.com/attorneys/croner/.

[34] The change of venue rule may be found at 231 Pa. Code Rule 1006: http://www.pacode.com/secure/data/231/chapter1000/s1006.html.

[35] During the time I was in office, High Real Estate and Lancaster Newspapers represented 88 percent of Penn Square Partners, each holding a 44 percent stake. Today, Penn Square Partners consists of general partners Penn Square General Corp., a High Real Estate Group affiliate, and Penn Square Ltd., an affiliate of Lancaster Newspapers Inc. In 2007, Fulton Financial, Corp.—which held a 12 percent share of the partnership—divested from the project.

[36] The depositions of all of the defendants in *Molly Henderson vs Lancaster Newspapers, Inc., John M. Buckwalter, Ernest J. Schreiber, Marvin I. Adams, Jr., Helen Colwell Adams, Charles Raymond Shaw, Arthur E. Morris, Gilbert A. Smart, John H. Brubaker, III, and David Pidgeon. No. 0712003*, as well as several witnesses, including Penn Square Partners president Nevin D. Cooley and Fulton Financial Corp. president and CEO Rufus A. Fulton, were used extensively in writing this book. In those depositions, in their own words and under oath, the defendants and Cooley acknowledged and described how they colluded, using the pages of Lancaster Newspapers, to ruin me politically.

[37] Buckwalter's "public relations" quote comes from his February 10, 2010, deposition in the lawsuit *Molly Henderson vs Lancaster Newspapers, Inc., John M. Buckwalter, Ernest J. Schreiber, Marvin I. Adams, Jr., Helen Colwell Adams, Charles Raymond Shaw, Arthur E. Morris, Gilbert A. Smart, John H. Brubaker, III, and David Pidgeon. No. 0712003*. Mr. Buckwalter testified twice, on February 3 and 10, 2010.

[38] Ibid., Buckwalter deposition.

[39] Likening commissioner Dick Shellenberger to Josef Mengele, one of the most vile and notorious Nazis, only underscored the viciousness of the newspaper character assassination campaign. Shellenberger's "crime" was the same as mine—we opposed the Lancaster Newspapers hotel project, and for that we were called the worst names imaginable in print.

[40] Former Lancaster mayor Art Morris's comments were made in a letter to the editor, "Henderson Had More of a Role Than She's Letting On," *Lancaster New Era*, January 15, 2007.

[41] The 30-page Commonwealth Court opinion may be found here: http://bloximages.newyork1.vip.townnews.com/lancasteronline.com/content/tncms/assets/v3/editorial/a/4f/a4f11d5e-af33-59ac-980d-a384789c8759/523282c99c78c.pdf.pdf.

[42] The actual malice standard for the libel of a public figure is deliberately set exceedingly high. The standard was set in 1964 in the landmark *New York Times Co. vs. Sullivan* lawsuit, 376 U.S. 254 (1964). All of the protection is on the side of the journalist. Actual malice requires that the plaintiff prove that he *knew* that what he was publishing was false. Without an admission of the knowledge of falsity, making a case for it is clearly very difficult. We believed we could have made that case to a jury, given the opportunity to present the facts as they were revealed in deposition testimony and other evidence we had gathered, much of which has been discussed in this book.

For an online version of the *New York Times Co. v Sullivan*, 376 U.S. 254 (1964), please see https://supreme.justia.com/cases/federal/us/376/254/.

[43] An online version of our complaint, *Molly Henderson vs Lancaster Newspapers, Inc., John M. Buckwalter, Ernest J. Schreiber, Marvin I. Adams, Jr., Helen Colwell Adams, Charles Raymond Shaw, Arthur E. Morris, Gilbert A. Smart, John H. Brubaker, III, and David Pidgeon. No. 0712003*, may be found here: http://www.newslanc.com/document/215159Henderson_suit.pdf.

[44] What the deposition testimony attempted to show was that the Lancaster Newspapers top leadership, planned to publish "news" articles that they knew were false. The grand jury report, released January 10, 2007, discharged me of misconduct regarding the subjects of the grand jury investigation: the hiring of Gary Heinke and the sale of Conestoga View. Concerning the hiring of ex-county employee Gary Heinke, the grand jury report reads:

> The September 2, 2003 fax [contacting Heinke prior to his hiring] was not revealed to Commissioner Henderson. . . . " (p. 6) . . . "Commissioner Henderson did not vote to interview Mr. Heinke" (p. 9)... "The vote behind closed doors [to hire Heinke] was again two votes for Mr. Heinke (Commissioners Shellenberger and Shaub) and one against (Commissioner Henderson) . . . (p. 12)

And regarding the "secret" sale of Conestoga View, the grand jury report reads on pages 20–21:

> A constant theme of the off-site meetings was that no one outside of "the team" should know about the plan to, or even the possibility of, selling Conestoga View. Commissioner Shaub specifically told the team members that Commissioner Henderson should be kept in the dark.

An online version of the grand jury report may be found here: http://panewsmedia.org/docs/default-source/government-affairs-documents-2013/lancaster-county-grand-jury-report-sunshine-act.pdf?sfvrsn=0.

Endnotes

[45] Melody Keim, V.P. of Programs and Initiatives, Lancaster County Community Foundation, e-mail, February 12, 2016, Lancaster, PA.

[46] Please see Appendix D for a table of the projects of the 2004–2008 Lancaster County Board of Commissioners.

[47] I have been an avid reader of Civil War history for many years. The Battle of Dranesville took place on December 20, 1861, in Fairfax County, Virginia. The Union, under Brigadier General Edward O.C. Ord, met the Confederate army under the common of Brigadier General J.E.B. Stuart. The battle's significance is that it was one of the first Union victories in the eastern theater. The Confederacy lost 230 men, while the Union had 70 killed, while driving away Stuart and his Confederates. See John S. Salmon, *The Official Virginia Civil War Battlefield Guide* (Mechanicsburg, PA: Stackpole Books, 2001.

[48] The costs of the Lancaster Marriott hotel and Lancaster County Convention Center go well beyond the more than $200 million that will be spent on it. More than 95 percent of the cost of that $200 million is paid for by taxpayers. Each year, the School District of Lancaster and the City and County of Lancaster are collectively deprived of millions of dollars in property taxes due them because the Marriott Hotel—run for profit by Penn Square Partners—has been exempted from paying property taxes. The money spent on this project could have been used for much more deserving, and public-serving, uses. The library system needed modernization. Areas outside of "Center City" needed infrastructure investment. And, most of all, the schools needed teachers, books, and repair. Instead, the most public money ever spent on a single project in the history of Lancaster County was spent on a private hotel and a financially insolvent convention center. It is a shame.

END

Appendix A
Totaro's Request for a Grand Jury

On February 14th, 2005, District Attorney Totaro formally requested an investigating grand jury. He made the request to Lancaster County president judge Louis J. Farina. Judge Farina approved the request:

IN THE COURT OF COMMON PLEAS OF LANCASTER COUNTY, PENNSYLVANIA
CRIMINAL DIVISION

IN RE: APPLICATION OF DONALD R. TOTARO :
DISTRICT ATTORNEY OF LANCASTER COUNTY :
REQUESTING AN ORDER DIRECTING THAT AN :
INVESTIGATING GRAND JURY BE SUMMONED :
APPLICATION REQUESTING AN ORDER DIRECTING
THAT A COUNTY INVESTIGATING GRAND JURY BE SUMMONED
TO THE HONORABLE LOUIS J. FARINA, PRESIDENT JUDGE OF THE COURT OF
COMMON PLEAS OF LANCASTER COUNTY:

Donald R. Totaro, District Attorney of Lancaster County, Pennsylvania, hereby makes application for the summoning of an Investigating Grand Jury and respectfully represents as follows:

1. Applicant is the duly elected District Attorney of Lancaster County.
2. The convening of an Investigative Grand Jury is necessary because of the existence of criminal activity within Lancaster County which can best be fully investigated using the investigative resources of the Grand Jury. This conclusion has been reached after appropriate investigation and consideration by the District Attorney and law enforcement personnel.
3. The applicant has identified particular investigations which are now in progress, or which are contemplated in the near future, which can best be fully investigated using the resources of the Grand Jury.
4. Examples of the criminal activity which can best be fully investigated using the resources of the Grand Jury include, but are not limited to, the following: illicit drug enterprises and related activities; racketeering as defined under the Pennsylvania Corrupt Organizations Statute, and unsolved homicides.
5. Should the Court grant this application, matters which require the resources of the Investigating Grand Jury for adequate and proper investigation will also be submitted as authorized by 42 Pa.C.S.A. & 4541 et. seq.

Appendix A

WHEREFORE, pursuant to 42 Pa.C.S.A. & 4543(b), the District Attorney of Lancaster County respectfully requests that the President Judge of the Court of Common Pleas of Lancaster County issue an order directing that an Investigating Grand Jury be summoned and convened, and that a supervising judge thereof be appointed.
Respectfully submitted,

OFFICE OF THE DISTRICT ATTORNEY

Donald R. Totaro
District Attorney

IN THE COURT OF COMMON PLEAS OF LANCASTER COUNTY, PENNSYLVANIA
CRIMINAL DIVISION
IN RE: APPLICATION OF DONALD R. TOTARO :
DISTRICT ATTORNEY OF LANCASTER COUNTY :
REQUESTING AN ORDER DIRECTING THAT AN :
INVESTIGATING GRAND JURY BE SUMMONED :

ORDER

AND NOW, this 14th day of February, 2005, pursuant to and based upon the application of the District Attorney, it is hereby ORDERED that an Investigating Grand Jury be summoned to be designated Grand Jury II. The Court finds that the facts set forth in the District Attorney's Petition requesting an Investigating Grand Jury adequately demonstrate the need for the summoning of a County Investigating Grand Jury.

The Honorable Louis J. Farina, President Judge of the Court of Common Pleas of Lancaster County, is designated as the Supervising Judge of this Grand Jury.
BY THE COURT: Hon. Louis J. Farina, President Judge (31)

Pressed

IN THE COURT OF COMMON PLEAS OF LANCASTER COUNTY, PENNSYLVANIA

CRIMINAL DIVISION

IN RE   :
                                                :
LANCASTER COUNTY INVESTIGATING   :   Investigation No:
GRAND JURY II, 2005   :

ORDER

AND NOW, this 10 day of November, 2005, pursuant to and based upon the Notice of Submission of the District Attorney of Lancaster County, the Court hereby finds that the facts set forth in the District Attorney's Submission requesting an Investigating Grand Jury to investigate the circumstances surrounding the hiring of Gary Heinke as Lancaster County Human Services Administrator, do adequately demonstrate that investigative resources of the Lancaster County Investigating Grand Jury are required in order to adequately investigate this legitimate law enforcement and investigative inquiry.

BY THE COURT:

Appendix A

Henderson, Molly

From: Totaro, Donald (County)
Sent: Monday, November 07, 2005 8:14 AM
To: Myers, Thomas; Shaub, Howard "Pete"; Shellenberger, Dick; Henderson, Molly
Cc: Stuckey, Dennis
Subject: Gary Heinke

Tom, I understand you are currently investigating the circumstances surrounding the hiring of Gary Heinke, and a final report is expected later this week. Once you have concluded your investigation, I would appreciate a copy of that report, along with copies of all relevant documentation. Thank you. Don Totaro.

Donald R. Totaro
Lancaster County District Attorney

*** INTERNET EMAIL CONFIDENTIALITY NOTICE ***
The information transmitted in this email is intended only for the person or entity to whom it is addressed, and contains confidential and/or privileged material that may be subject to protection under the law. If you are not the intended recipient, you are hereby notified that any review, retransmission, dissemination, distribution, disclosure, copying, or other use of this transmission, or taking of any action in reliance upon this information, without the express written approval of the Office of the District Attorney of Lancaster County, is strictly prohibited and may subject you to criminal or civil penalties. If you received this message in error, please contact the sender immediately by replying to this e-mail, and delete this message from your computer.

Pressed

IN THE COURT OF COMMON PLEAS OF LANCASTER COUNTY, PENNSYLVANIA
CRIMINAL

IN RE   :
                                                  :
LANCASTER COUNTY INVESTIGATING   :   Investigation No:
GRAND JURY II, 2005   :

NOTICE OF SUBMISSION

TO THE HONORABLE LOUIS J. FARINA, PRESIDENT JUDGE:

AND NOW, this 10th day of November, 2005, Donald R. Totaro, District Attorney of Lancaster County, files the following Notice of Submission of Investigation:

Pursuant to 42 Pa.C.S. § 4550(a), notice is hereby given that the matter described below should be brought to the attention of the Lancaster County Investigating Grand Jury, because investigative resources of the Grand Jury are required in order to adequately investigate the matter. Those resources include, but are not limited to, the power to compel the attendance of witnesses, the power to require the production of documents, records and other evidence, as well as the other investigative resources of the grand jury.

The matter to be submitted to the Grand Jury for investigation involves the hiring of Gary Heinke as Lancaster County Human Services Administrator, and the following information is obtained from a 13 page report submitted by J. Thomas Myers, Lancaster County Human Resource Director, who conducted an internal investigation of this matter.

According to the Myers report, over 100 individuals applied for the position of Lancaster County Human Services Administrator. Gary Heinke was one of those applicants. Although Human Resources did not recommend Mr. Heinke for the position, Lancaster County Commissioner Richard Shellenberger requested that Mr. Heinke be considered for an interview. Mr. Heinke was subsequently offered the position on March 24, 2004.

Appendix A

According to the Myers report, during the interview in March of 2004, the Board of Commissioners was encouraged to take notes. However, only Commissioner Howard "Pete" Shaub kept his notes. The notes of Commissioners Shellenberger and Molly Henderson are apparently no longer available. At no time did any Commissioner indicate they had a prior relationship with Mr. Heinke, or in any way communicate with him about the vacant position. At no time did any Commissioner acknowledge they had provided Mr. Heinke with information about the position or the County before the position was posted.

According to the Myers report, on October 26, 2005, Commissioner Shaub delivered to Human Resources a copy of a cover letter and resume from Mr. Heinke that was dated May 27, 2003 and was addressed to the residence of Commissioner Shellenberger. The letter and resume are distinctive in that they are printed on the back of a letter from the Shellenberger primary campaign. This letter suggests it was a follow-up to earlier correspondence with Mr. Shellenberger about working for the county. The letter also included a resume that was different from the resume submitted on January 13, 2004 that was used during the hiring process.

According to the Myers report, upon further investigation, it was determined that Mr. Heinke exchanged a number of e-mails with Commissioners Shaub and Shellenberger prior to the actual interview. Some were sent to the Lancaster County address and some to the residence of each commissioner. Mr. Myers was unable to determine what, if any responses were made by Shellenberger or Shaub because the e-mails sent to the county address were not archived. Phone records also list a 32 minute call on February 27, 2004 from the Commissioners Office to Mr. Heinke from a line in a vacant office. None of the commissioners remember placing the call or contacting Mr. Heinke.

According to the Myers report, upon comparing the information listed on the original resume with the resume that was submitted as part of the Application for Employment, a number of "noticeable differences" were observed by Mr. Myers. However, Human Resources was unable to reach any conclusion regarding the extent of assistance or guidance Mr. Heinke may have received from any of the commissioners.

According to the Myers report, it was also noted that some information on the application was not accurate. While not listed in their entirety, some erroneous information can be characterized as follows:

a) The degrees and major course work in the resume parallel the transcripts, except one. The resume lists his major course work at Bethel Theological Seminary as "Pastoral Ministries, Human Resource Development." Pastoral Ministries is appropriate, but Human Resource Development is a questionable assertion. Mr. Myers found this to be an inaccurate characterization.

b) On his employment application, Mr. Heinke listed he worked as an Assistant Superintendent, without stating it was an internship. According to Mr. Myers, "this is a misrepresentation of his volunteer (unpaid) activities."

c) Under "Additional Experiences," Mr. Heinke claimed he served on the Arden Hills City Council. It was determined that this listing was "fictional."

In conclusion, the report by Mr. Myers states that some of the changes between resumes and the information listed on the application were "misrepresentations" or "falsehoods," although there was no evidence to prove that Mr. Heinke received any inappropriate assistance from County representatives in crafting his second resume.

Appendix A

The application signed by Mr. Heinke clearly states as follows: "I understand that any false answers, statements or representations made by me in this application shall constitute sufficient cause for dismissal and/or penalties under 18PA Cons.Stat., Section 4904 related to the Unsworn Falsification to Authorities."

The Commonwealth submits there is sufficient information to ultimately determine whether criminal laws were violated by Mr. Heinke and/or other individuals with regard to the submission of his application containing fictitious information. However, this can only be accomplished by utilizing the resources of the Investigating Grand Jury. Witnesses cannot refuse to cooperate, as the Investigating Grand Jury will compel attendance and cooperation. The Investigating Grand Jury will require truthful testimony, under consequence of perjury, and this powerful mechanism can be used to decipher inconsistent statements or refresh recollection. Further, the Commonwealth believes there are additional witnesses to this incident who have personal knowledge of the circumstance surrounding the manner in which Mr. Heinke's resume was drafted and presented to the Lancaster County Board of Commissioners for consideration. The Commonwealth may be prepared to offer immunity to those individuals in exchange for their testimony, which can only be done through the Investigative Grand Jury.

Therefore, the Lancaster County District Attorney's Office requests the utilization of the resources of the Investigating Grand Jury in order to determine the extent of knowledge and information all witnesses possess in connection with this legitimate law enforcement and investigative inquiry.

11/10/05
Date

Donald R. Totaro
District Attorney

IN THE COURT OF COMMON PLEAS OF LANCASTER COUNTY, PENNSYLVANIA

CRIMINAL DIVISION

IN RE: :
            :
LANCASTER COUNTY INVESTIGATING : INVESTIGATION NO.
GRAND JURY II, 2005 :

COMMONWEALTH'S AFFIDAVIT

I, Donald R. Totaro, District Attorney of Lancaster County, Pennsylvania, the affiant below, having been duly deposed, represents as follows:

1. The original Notice of Submission regarding the resume and hiring of Gary Heinke was prepared and filed after the Lancaster County Board of Commissioners initially failed to comply with a request for production of documents through traditional investigative means. This request was made based upon specific allegations of criminal conduct by Mr. Heinke (Unsworn Falsification to Authorities), and questions as to whether any members of the Board of Commissioners assisted in the fabrication of Mr. Heinke's resume.

2. On November 7, 2005, at 8:14 a.m., this affiant emailed then-Lancaster County Director of Human Resources J. Thomas Myers as well as the entire Board of Commissioners requesting a copy of the Myers report, which explained the hiring process for Gary Heinke. Although the email was opened by all three county commissioners on November 7, 2005, not one commissioner responded to that email prior to filing of the Notice of Submission.

3. On November 9, 2005, the completed Myers report was presented to the Board of Commissioners. Despite the fact that the report had been completed and presented to the Commissioners, there was still no reply from Mr. Myers or any of the Commissioners to

this affiant's email of November 7, 2005 requesting a copy of the report. This office also did not receive a copy of that report.

4. Because November 11, 2005 was Veteran's Day, and county government would be closed for the holiday, a decision was made to prepare a Notice of Submission and present this matter to the Supervising Judge of the Lancaster County Investigating Grand Jury on November 10, 2005. This decision was made because of the total lack of response from the Board of Commissioners to a request from this office for a copy of the report, and because several sources expressed concern that information relevant to the investigation could be misplaced or destroyed over the long holiday weekend.

5. To eliminate the possibility that any evidence could disappear over the long weekend, the Notice of Submission would then allow this office to file at the same time a Motion to Prevent Destruction of Evidence During the Investigation by the County Investigating Grand Jury. Absent probable cause, the District Attorney's office could not obtain a search warrant to seize computers or other documents. However, by submitting this investigation to the Grand Jury, our office could preserve said evidence and then utilize subpoena powers to receive the necessary information.

6. During the afternoon hours of November 10, 2005, while the Notice of Submission and Motion to Prevent Destruction of Evidence were being prepared, a copy of the Myers report was finally served on the District Attorney's Office. Nevertheless, the failure of the commissioners to respond to this affiant's email of November 7, 2005, and the substantial delay in providing this office with the completed Myers report remained a concern regarding the extent to which the commissioners or Mr. Myers would voluntarily

cooperate with our investigation. Furthermore, the content of the report contained information indicating important emails were not archived, none of the commissioners recalled engaging in a 32 minute conversation with Mr. Heinke from the commissioners office during the time period Heinke fabricated his resume, and interview notes with Mr. Heinke were "no longer available" for at least two of the commissioners. These factors were significant in concluding that sufficient information to ultimately determine whether criminal laws were violated by Mr. Heinke and/or other individuals could only be accomplished through the identified resources of the investigating grand jury. They also showed that immediate action had to be taken to preserve any remaining evidence.

7. In addition to allowing for retrieval of any and all documents relevant to the investigation through the use of subpoena *duces tecum*, the grand jury now provided this office with the legal authority to compel testimony from witnesses who were unwilling to cooperate outside the grand jury investigation. For example, while Mr. Myers was unwilling to cooperate under normal investigative measures and retained an attorney, he agreed to talk to members of this office in a proffer setting made possible through the Grand Jury.

8. Once our investigation into the Heinke hiring began, several witnesses while testifying began to delve into the sale of Conestoga View. Those witnesses were reminded and the grand jury was admonished by Assistant District Attorney K. Kenneth Brown that such testimony was not relevant to the matter before the Investigating Grand Jury. However, because statements made by some of those individuals alleged possible violations of the law with regard to the sale of Conestoga View, this affiant made a decision to

Appendix A

independently begin a traditional investigation into the sale of Conestoga View Nursing Home by the Lancaster County Board of Commissioners and other individuals.

9. When members of this office began interviewing witnesses in regard to the sale of Conestoga View Nursing Home, many inconsistencies arose that could only be remedied by taking those witnesses before the Investigating Grand Jury and allowing the grand jury to make determinations as to credibility. This fact was clearly stated in the Amended Notice of Submission.

10. In addition to allowing the Grand Jury to make credibility determinations with regard to the aforementioned inconsistencies, this affiant determined it was necessary to place those witnesses under oath before the grand jury, with the understanding that they would face charges of perjury if they continued to be dishonest or deceptive.

11. In her Motion to Quash Subpoena, Commissioner Henderson makes an inflammatory and unsupported allegation that the Commonwealth is using the grand jury for improper political purposes, while proceeding at "a snail's pace" that will affect the spring 2007 Commissioner primary election. Counsel for Commissioner Shellenberger made a related allegation when he stated in a letter dated April 18, 2006 to this affiant that "the overtones and subsequent damage to the public trust of a grand jury investigation when none is warranted can be catastrophic." Both commissioners ignore the fact that by putting these issues before the Investigating Grand Jury and allowing the grand jury to operate in secrecy and without public scrutiny, the investigation into these matters should remain outside the public eye. They also fail to recognize that this grand jury investigation could exculpate as much as inculpate any person of interest.

12. Commissioners Henderson and Shellenberger also ignore the fact that the Commonwealth has in no way acknowledged the existence of an Investigating Grand Jury with regard to these specific issues or discussed this matter with any other entity. Rather, due to the direct and intentional actions taken by at least two county commissioners, including making statements immediately following appearances before the Grand Jury and issuing a public plea in the Lancaster Newspapers to speed up the investigation, the existence of this grand jury investigation and specific details have been disclosed to the news media.

13. To reiterate, the Grand Jury continues to operate under a cloak of secrecy and outside of the political arena. The only exceptions involve communication to the news media from county commissioners. The District Attorney's Office has never leaked any information to any source.

14. The District Attorney's Office has also not slowed the process in an effort to draw it out into the political season, as suggested by Commissioner Henderson. To the contrary, our office added one day in June and one day in July to the Grand Jury's normal schedule in an attempt to finish the investigation by July of 2006. There is no grand jury session scheduled for August, and our office clearly wanted to submit this investigation to the Grand Jury for a resolution prior to the political calendar. This affiant made that intent very clear to the Grand Jury Supervising Judge when the request was made to add the additional dates. With the added dates, the commissioners would have testified during the June session of the Grand Jury. Unfortunately, when Commissioners Shellenberger

Appendix A

and Henderson filed their Motions to Quash Subpoena, the process was delayed by at least one month and is now likely to extend into the political season due to their actions.

15. In conclusion, the county commissioners are clearly to blame for publicly acknowledging the fact that there is a grand jury investigation into the hiring of Gary Heinke; the county commissioners are clearly to blame for publicly acknowledging the fact that the sale of Conestoga View is also before the grand jury; the county commissioners are clearly to blame for any grand jury information that has been made public through the news media; and the county commissioners are clearly to blame for delaying the progress of this investigation into the upcoming political season.

Date: 7/12/06

Donald R. Totaro
Lancaster County District Attorney
50 North Duke Street
P.O. Box 83480
Lancaster, PA 17608-3480
(717) 299-8100
Attorney I.D. No. 49810

Sworn to and subscribed before me this 12th day of July, 2006

Michelle M. Reed
Notary Public

My commission expires:

Commonwealth of Pennsylvania
NOTARIAL SEAL
MICHELLE M. REED, Notary Public
Lancaster, Lancaster County, PA
My Commission Expires April 17, 2010

Appendix B

THE 57 QUESTIONS: QUESTIONS AND TOPICS FOR PSP, LCCCA, AND RACL

QUESTIONS AND TOPICS FOR PSP, LCCCA AND RACL

The Board of Commissioners for Lancaster County requests that Penn Square Partners ("PSP"), the Lancaster County Convention Center Authority ("LCCCA") and the Redevelopment Authority of the City of Lancaster ("RACL") – as a part of their presentation of information to the Commissioners regarding the TIF Act application for the combined convention center and hotel in downtown Lancaster – address the following questions and topics.

The Commissioners may ask additional questions and raise additional topics as they continue to analyze the TIF Act application and further information is provided to them. The Commissioners have a responsibility to protect the interests of Lancaster County taxpayers. In 2003, the County guaranteed one-half of a $40 million bond sale, which exposes taxpayers to a total potential liability in excess of $60 million.

Commissioner Shaub has not presented any of these questions. He believes the information he needs to evaluate the TIF Act application has either already been provided or will be provided in the upcoming presentation to the Commissioners.

1. **Timing of the TIF Application and Supporting Information**

    - You explained that Interstate Hotels Group is working on updated financial projections for the Convention Center and Hotel. We assume this report will be a component of the "economic feasibility study" required by the TIF Act.

        Unfortunately, you do not expect to receive Interstate's report until the close of business on Friday, March 11. That means the County Commissioners, City Council and the School Board will receive the report just one business day – Monday, March 14 – before you expect the School Board to vote on the proposed TIF at its meeting March 15.

        Given the importance of the economic feasibility study to the consideration of this project by the Commissioners, City Council and the School Board, why is this information from Interstate being provided at such a late date?

    - Why did you not initiate the TIF process in mid-December 2004, at the same time you decided to transfer ownership of the hotel property to RACL? Did you believe then that a for-profit hotel operation can avoid local real estate tax if the property is leased from RACL? What happened since mid-December 2004 to lead you to change your mind and propose the TIF?

Appendix B

2. **2003 County Guarantee of Financing**

   - Exhibit 7 of the Project Plan identifies $40 million from the 2003 Hotel Tax Revenue Bonds as part of the LCCCA's contribution toward funding of the Convention Center.

     However, according to the Closing Statement from the 2003 bond sale (Tab 1), only $31,649,932 from the $40 million bond sale was placed into the Construction Account generated by the bond sale, with the balance of the bond proceeds going to pay for closing costs and other accounts.

     Why does Exhibit 7 show that $40 million from the bond sale is available for project funding, if the Closing Statement from the bond sale says that only $31,649,932 is available in the Construction Account?

   - Further, it appears that no money from the 2003 bond sale can be used directly to fund construction of the Convention Center.

     Section 5.02(c) of the Trust Indenture between LCCCA and Manufacturers and Traders Trust Company, dated December 15, 2003 (Tab 2), states that no construction funds from the bond sale may be disbursed until the initial $40 million bond is converted to $40 million in tax-exempt bonds. Only the proceeds from the tax-exempt bond sale will be available to fund construction costs.

     Thus, the funds to be used for construction of the Convention Center will come not from the proceeds of the initial 2003 bond sale, but rather from the proceeds of the subsequent tax-exempt bond sale.

     If the initial 2003 bond sale did not generate funds that could be used for construction of the Convention Center, why was it held?

   - According to the Closing Statement from the 2003 bond sale (Tab 1), there were $423,674 in closing costs associated with that sale.

     Further, as reflected in both the Closing Statement (Tab 1) and Section 5.02(a) of the Trust Indenture (Tab 2), $2,000,000 from the 2003 bond sale was set aside to pay for closing costs that will be associated with the conversion of the 2003 bond sale to tax-exempt bonds, at the time funds are actually needed for construction of the Convention Center.

     Also, pursuant to Section 202(i) of the Trust Indenture (Tab 3), the amount of interest LCCCA is paying on the $40 million bond sale from 2003 exceeds by .55% the amount of interest LCCCA is receiving on investments of its proceeds from that bond sale. This "negative arbitrage" situation appears to create an overall cost to LCCCA of approximately $220,000 a year.

The $423,674 in closing costs associated with the 2003 bond sale (most of which will need to be repeated, and paid for out of the $2 million set aside for closing costs on the future tax-exempt bond sale), plus the $220,000 per year negative arbitrage costs associated with the 2003 bond sale (approximately $275,000 over 15 months since December 2003), total approximately $700,000 to date since the 2003 bond sale.

What was the purpose of spending this $700,000 in taxpayer money (plus additional interest at $220,000 per year until the tax-exempt bonds are sold), if the funds from the 2003 bond sale could not be used to fund construction of the Convention Center?

Why not wait until construction funds are actually needed, and then generate the funds necessary for construction of the Convention Center through a traditional tax-exempt bond sale?

- Why does PSP's website (Tab 4) say that the 2003 bond sale was to finance construction of the Convention Center, when the bond sale documents state that no money from that sale can be used for construction, and that funding of construction must await the sale of traditional tax-exempt bonds?

- Was the reason for the 2003 bond sale to create a $40 million borrowing vehicle to which the then-existing Board of Commissioners could adhere the County's guarantee (as they did by a 2-1 vote), which guarantee is then transferred under the documents to the tax-exempt bond when construction funds are actually needed, all as a means to preclude the Board of Commissioners at the time such funds are actually needed from voting on whether to have the County guarantee the $40 million borrowing?

If so, were you aware it would cost $700,000 (and counting) of taxpayer money to accomplish the goal of avoiding such a vote by a future Board of Commissioners?

If so, why was this justification not explained publicly at the time of the 2003 bond sale or at the time of the 2003 County guarantee? Why has the public explanation instead been that the 2003 bond sale will finance construction of the Convention Center, when the reality is such funds cannot be used for that purpose?

- Page 2 of the Guaranty Agreement entered by the County in December 2003 (Tab 5) provides that during the 40 year lifetime of the bond (unless

3

Appendix B

it is refinanced earlier to tax-exempt bonds), the County will guarantee up to $1,506,960 per year. Multiplying 40 times that annual guarantee maximum amount equals $60,278,400. Are County taxpayers therefore exposed to a potential liability under the 2003 bond sale of $60,278,400?

3. **Interaction of Hotel, Convention Center and "Common Elements"**

    - The cost allocation provided to the Commissioners on March 2, 2005 (Tab 6), states that the Convention Center will cost $68.7 million and the hotel will cost $60.3 million. How much of those costs cover the "common elements" to be shared by both facilities?

    - What is the square footage allocation between the Convention Center, the hotel and the common elements?

    - Please specify all arrangements or agreements between the Hotel (PSP) and Convention Center (LCCCA) regarding use of the common elements and of each other's facilities. If such details are not yet established, please identify whether such arrangements or agreements will be "arms length" transactions or some other kind of transactions.

    - To the extent not already identified in the Project Plan, please identify (a) any payments made or anticipated to be made from LCCCA or RACL to PSP, and (b) any expenditures made by LCCCA or RACL that will benefit PSP or the hotel operation.

4. **Convention Center**

    - Page 8 of the Project Plan identifies three "market feasibility studies" concerning the Convention Center (two by Pricewaterhouse Coopers LLC in 2000 and 2003, and one by C.H. Johnson in 2003), and one additional report concerning parking by Cagley & Harman in 2003.

        Given the changes in the convention industry since 2003, how much reliance do you believe the Commissioners, City Council and the School District should place on these reports?

    - The initial Pricewaterhouse Coopers report from 2000 projected the market demand for a downtown Lancaster convention center based in large part on written surveys completed by state and regional associations.

        According to page 43 of the 2000 report (Tab 7), where an association responded to the survey indicating that it might "possibly" use a downtown Lancaster convention center, Pricewaterhouse Coopers characterized that response as indicating the association was a "likely" user of a Lancaster convention center. Then, in evaluating the market

4

demand for the convention center, Pricewaterhouse Coopers relied heavily on such "likely" users of the proposed facility.

Are you concerned that by characterizing an association which indicated it would "possibly" use the convention center as a "likely" user of the convention center, Pricewaterhouse Coopers may have overestimated the market demand for the convention center?

Please provide copies of all completed surveys received by Pricewaterhouse Coopers in its 2000 evaluation of the market demand for a downtown Lancaster convention center.

- At page 31 of its 2003 report (Tab 8), Pricewaterhouse Coopers acknowledges that of the "likely" users of a downtown Lancaster convention center from its 2000 survey (including those who had indicated they might "possibly" use the facility), only about 80% would consider using the convention center.

If only 80% of the former "likely" users from 2000 remained willing to consider using the facility in 2003, was that not an indication of decreased market interest in the downtown Lancaster convention center?

Please provide copies of all completed surveys received by Pricewaterhouse Coopers in its 2003 evaluation of the continuing market demand for a downtown Lancaster convention center.

- The C.H. Johnson report from 2003 (Tab 9) provides absolutely no backup data or analysis to support its projected usage of the convention center and related financial assumptions concerning operation of the convention center.

Did you receive any backup data or analysis to accompany this report? If so, please provide it.

5. **Hotel**

- Page 1 of the Project Plan describes the proposed hotel as a "full service" hotel. Previously, project consultants had described the facility as a "four-star hotel" (PricewaterhouseCoopers, Robert V. Canton, November 6, 2000) (Tab 10), and an "upscale, full-service hotel" (Ernst & Young, LLP, April 28, 1999) (Tab 11).

Is the Marriot Hotel going to be designed and constructed to a "four-star" or "upscale" quality, so that it obtains a higher ranking in the hospitality industry than the five local "competitive" hotels identified in the 2005

Appendix B

Smith Travel Report (Willow Valley, Best Western Eden Resort, Holiday Inn Lancaster, Hampton Inn and Hilton Garden Inn)?

If not, what justifies your assumption that the Marriot Hotel will be able to charge the premiums in average daily hotel rate you have projected, as compared to the rates you have projected for the "competitive" hotels ($130.50 as opposed to $117.40 in 2007, and $142.50 as opposed to $125.75 in 2009)?

If not, what justifies your assumption that at these premium rates, the occupancy rate at the Marriot Hotel will equal the occupancy rate you project for the "competitive" hotels (68% by 2009)?

Does your analysis take into account that parking at the "competitive" hotels is free, and parking at the Marriot Hotel will be for a fee? Doesn't the existence of a parking fee at the Marriot increase the effective daily rate to patrons as compared to the daily rate at "competitive" hotels? Won't parking fee information be readily available and relied upon by convention planners and the traveling public?

What was the basis for selecting the five "competitive" hotels from among those in the Lancaster market? Why is the Lancaster Host not included in your "competitive" set of hotels?

- Pages 24-25 of the HVS Market Study issued in 2003 (Tab 12), provide that in projecting demand for the hotel, HVS relied upon a "recent" study commissioned by the LCCCA. However, the data relied upon is from the PricewaterhouseCoopers 2000 report, which was three years old at the time HVS relied upon such projections. In addition, the projections of PricewaterhouseCoopers (as stated above) relied upon its characterization of convention planners who might "possibly" use the downtown Lancaster convention center as "likely" users of the facility.

  Do you believe that such reliance on the 2000 PricewaterhouseCoopers study undermines the credibility of HVS's projection of hotel rooms attributable to Convention Center attendance?

- HVS projects that total attendance of 10,000 at conventions and trade shows hosted by the Convention Center will translate to 22,500 room nights at the hotel, that total attendance of 70,000 at consumer shows hosted by the Convention Center will translate to 18,750 room nights at the hotel, and that total attendance of 24,000 at other events hosted by the Convention Center will translate to 3,900 room nights at the hotel, for a total of 45,150 room nights at the hotel generated from the Convention Center.

- Can you provide statistical data from other combined convention centers and hotels to support your projected ratios between uses of the proposed convention center and hotel room nights in Lancaster?

- Do you dispute Heywood Sanders' contention that currently in the industry, the trend is approximately a 1-to-1 ratio of convention and trade show attendance to room nights, and that the ratio of room nights being generated by consumer shows and other events is lower than your projections?

- Please provide a copy of the lease for the hotel (or the latest draft version of the proposed lease) between RACL and PSP that is referenced on page 1 of the Project Plan.

6. **Parking**

- Page 5 of the Project Plan states that the Lancaster City Parking Authority will lease a "portion" of the King Street garage to the LCCCA, and that LCCCA and the Parking Authority will build a new parking garage with 300 spaces to augment the King Street garage. What will be the cost to the LCCCA and the Parking Authority, respectively, for this new parking garage?

    How many spaces in the King Street garage will be leased to the LCCCA? The same number of new spaces being created in the new garage (300)?

- The 2003 Cagley & Harman report states at page I-2 (Tab 13) that the Convention Center will create a total parking demand of 1058 spaces. Taking into account some parking availability outside of a parking garage, the Cagley & Harman report concludes that the "parking structure servicing the LCCC should have a minimum capacity of 846 spaces."

    If there are only 300 spaces available for the Convention Center at the King Street garage, where are the additional 546 spaces that Cagley & Harman says are needed?

    Do you believe the parking plan identified at page 5 of the Project Plan reflects a feasible approach for the project?

- Who is paying for the improvements to the King Street garage identified on page 5 of the Project Plan, and at what cost?

- What is the projected parking cost for patrons of the Convention Center and the Marriott? As asked earlier, won't the existence of a parking fee impact the room rate and occupancy factors at the Marriott?

Appendix B

- Please provide copies of any agreements between the LCCCA and the Parking Authority.

7. **Project Costs**

    - As required by the TIF Act, please provide a "detailed list" of all the estimated project costs that are shown on Exhibit 6 of the Project Plan. Also, please identify who prepared such detailed information, and when.

    - Do your current cost projections take into consideration cost escalation likely to occur between now and the time contractors submit bids on the construction contracts? If the TIF is approved, when will bids be submitted?

    - What happens to the project if the TIF is approved, but the construction bids exceed the construction budget? What is the specific impact under such circumstances to the County's 2003 guarantee?

    - Regarding site acquisition costs of $5,290,000, who paid or owes this amount, to whom, and for what site? As part of this, please include any payments made or owed to PSP for the Convention Center site.

    - Please provide the most recent detailed estimate of "hard costs" projected in the amount of $77,946,045, identifying when the estimate was prepared and by whom.

    - Regarding furniture, fixtures and equipment costs of $14,421,000, please provide a detailed list identifying what items are to be purchased, by whom, at what projected cost, and who will retain ownership of such items.

    - Regarding professional fees and soft costs of $14,980,000, please provide a detailed list identifying the nature of such costs and to whom they are to be paid.

    - Please provide a detailed list of the projected financing costs of $11,768,844.

    - What is the purpose of the "Reserve for Future Eligible Project Cost" account in the amount of $5,200,000?

8. **Project Financing**

    - Regarding the three state grants RACL has secured in the aggregate amount of $7,250,000 (page 10 of the Project Plan), have any express limitations been imposed on the use of those funds. If so, what limitations

8

have been imposed, by whom and through what written document? Please provide copies of any such documents.

- Has RACL received any of the funds from such grants? If so, how much and when was the money received? If not, what is the funding source from which RACL has loaned PSP $3.2 million, as indicated on page 10 of the Project Plan?

- With regard to the $3.2 million loan from RACL to PSP (page 10 of the Project Plan), please specify all uses of the loan proceeds and the amount of each use. What is the interest rate on the loan? Will the loan be repaid if the project does not go forward? Please provide a copy of the loan agreement.

- Please identify the additional $12 million state grant RACL intents to seek, referred on page 10 of the Project Plan. What verbal or written assurances have been made that such grant will be approved, and by whom? Please provide a copy of any written assurances.

- The annual state grant expected to support a $12 million bond offering over 20-years (page 10 of the Project Plan) is subject to review by DCED and the Pennsylvania Department of Revenue after three years. It will be renewed beyond three years only if you establish that the incremental sales, uses & occupancy and personnel income taxes generated by the project equal the amount of the grant paid during the first three years.

  As depicted in the March 2003 Financial Projections provided by PSP, the vast majority of the projected incremental taxes generated by the project come from sales and use tax paid at the Marriot Hotel. If the amount of such incremental taxes attributable to the sales and use paid at the Marriot are substantially lower because your projected premium hotel rates and your projected occupancy rate are not fulfilled, does that place at risk the receipt of the state grant for the final 17 years of the 20-year grant?

  If the state grant is terminated after 3 years because the projected sales and use taxes paid at the Marriot Hotel do not materialize, what is the amount of potential liability to the City of Lancaster, which must guarantee the bonds?

- Exhibit 7 of the Project Plan states that Penn Square Partners is contributing $35.3 million of "private sector" funding toward the project.

  However, this amount includes $10 million in TIF note payments, which is money that but for the TIF would be paid in real estate taxes to Lancaster County, the City of Lancaster and the School District of Lancaster. Because it is the three taxing authorities that would be

Appendix B

agreeing to relinquish their right to $10 million in tax revenue, is it not more accurate to portray this $10 million as a public sector contribution by those three taxing authorities, rather than as a contribution by PSP?

- Does PSP or any of its affiliates intend to seek federal income tax credit for the $10 million in private investment? If so, and if such credit is provided, to what extent will that likely reduce the true cost of such investment?

- Is PSP's financial risk in this project limited to its $10 million investment? If not, please explain any other financial risk to PSP?

- Is PSP's $10 million contribution allocated to any specific purchase or cost?

- Has PSP, LCCCA or RACL received any written assurance from legal counsel that the $40 million bonds that ultimately will be issued to finance construction of the Convention Center will be entitled to tax-exempt status pursuant to the Internal Revenue Code provisions distinguishing between "governmental issues" and "private activity bonds"?

Will the bonds be a governmental issue or a private activity bond?

If the latter, will the bonds qualify for an exclusion of interest from federal income tax pursuant to Section 141 of the Internal Revenue Code?

If the bonds do not qualify for tax-exempt status pursuant to the Internal Revenue Code, what would be the ramifications on the project? On the County's 2003 guarantee?

9. **Operating Costs and Income**

- Please provide detailed line item lists of all projected operating costs and income for both the convention center and hotel. Please identify who prepared the lists and when they were prepared.

10. **External Economic Impact**

- Page 2 of the Project Plan states that after construction is completed, the convention center and hotel will generate up to 250 full-time equivalent permanent jobs. In contrast, financial projection materials PSP provided the Commissioners dated March 2005 state that the convention center and hotel will generate 207 full-time equivalent permanent jobs. Which number should the Commissioners, City Council and the School Board rely upon in evaluating the external economic impact of the project?

10

- What is the projected hourly wage rate for the "service" positions anticipated for the hotel and convention center?

- The allocation of project costs provided on March 2, 2005 (Tab 6) allocates $60.3 million to the construction of the hotel. At page 2 of the Project Plan, you state that the assessed value of the hotel (which equates to fair market value) immediately upon completion of construction will be $28.3 million.

  What is the basis for your assertion that the fair market value of the hotel immediately upon construction will be less than half of the construction cost?

  Please provide a copy of any appraisal you have received from a Pennsylvania certified appraiser supporting this determination.

- Based on current real estate tax rates for Lancaster County, the City of Lancaster and the School District of Lancaster, the totals mills of 30.582 is allocated 9.69% to the County (2.962 mills), 25.08% to the City (7.67 mills) and 65.23% to the School District (19.950 mills).

  Given these percentages, why does PSP offer the City a larger amount of "PSP Priority" payments than it offers to the School District? (In the March 2005 financial projections provided by PSP, see the "Summary" page for the 20 year period.)

  Why does PSP offer no "PSP Priority" payments or "PSP Participation" payments to the County?

  Why are the PSP Priority payments and the PSP Participation payment not allocated among the three taxing authorities on a percentage basis that is consistent with their respective millage rates?

  Why is the City singled out for preferential treatment, and the County singled out to receive no additional payments whatsoever?

- Does Exhibit 5 of the Project Plan reflect that if PSP's projections prove accurate, the three taxing authorities over 20 years will have relinquished over $7 million in tax revenues ($19,059,700 minus $12,019,800 = $7,039,900), all of which will become profit to PSP?

11. **Miscellaneous**

- The Project Plan at page 1 identifies "Penn Square Partners" as a Pennsylvania limited partnership consisting of Penn Square General Corporation, Penn Square Limited, LLC, and Fulton Bank. There is no

Appendix B

mention of Lancaster Newspapers, Inc., High Industries, Inc., or any of their affiliates.

Please identify the percentage ownership of Penn Square Partners, Penn Square General Corporation and Penn Square Limited, LLC.

- Page 3 of the Project Plan states that LCCCA will enter a purchase agreement with the condominium association for the Convention Center, but does not state that RACL will also enter a purchase agreement with the condominium association for the hotel. Will RACL do so? Please provide copies of all such purchase agreements to the Commissioners.

- Please provide copies of any agreements between the LCCCA and the Historic Preservation Trust regarding the proposed interpretive museum referenced at page 7 of the Project Plan.

- Although the TIF Act requires the host municipality (City of Lancaster) to sponsor the TIF, it does not require the School District and the County to opt into the TIF. That is, from a legal standpoint, the TIF program is permissible even if the School District or the County opts out of participating in the TIF. Taxing authorities that opt out of the TIF would levy real estate taxes based on future tax assessments, including any incremental assessments attributable to the project.

  Because the County's share of real estate taxes is relatively low (currently less than 10% of the combined millage of all three taxing authorities), does the economic feasibility of the project fail if only the County opts out of the TIF?

- What do you believe are the five most significant concerns and risks associated with this project?

- What do you believe are the five most significant benefits that can be achieved with this project?

Appendix C

NEWSPAPER HEADLINE EXAMPLES AND ARTICLE COUNT 2004–2007

Newspaper Headline Examples And Article Count 2004–2007

LANCASTER, PA. THURSDAY, JANUARY 11, 2007

Report details 'veil of secrecy' in county

Secret meetings on 'Charlie Victor'

BY DAVE PIDGEON
Intelligencer Journal Staff

The 37-page grand jury report on the sale of Conestoga View and the hiring of former county administrator Gary Heinke contains damning evidence of how the county commissioners secretly orchestrated the sale and manipulated Heinke's hiring.

The report describes how the commissioners and their surrogates tried to circumvent the Sunshine Act while discussing the sale, even code-naming the nursing home "Charlie Victor," to keep their discussions confidential.

The following are witness quotes and grand jury observations from the report:

♦♦♦

"Many (if not most) of the witnesses who testified regarding the secret and nonpublic meetings were found by the grand jurors to be either less than forthcoming or actively deceitful ...."

"In the words of one grand juror, 'It seems to be they studied the art of deception real well; now she "doesn't know this," or "I don't remember.'"

Please see MEETINGS, page A7

Molly Henderson   Dick Shellenberger   Pete Shaub

LANCASTER NEW ERA

THURSDAY, JANUARY 11, 2007

Pennsylvania's Largest-Circulation and Most-Honored Afternoon Newspaper

Secrecy, deceit crippled probe

■ How did county commissioners escape multiple criminal charges? Local grand jurors blame inconsistent testimony and lack of records.

By JACK BRUBAKER
New Era Staff Writer

the grand jury lacked sufficient corroborating evidence.
The jurors' frustration at

Commissioners Dick Shel-

Newspaper Headline Examples And Article Count 2004-2007

NCASTER NEW ERA
FRIDAY, JANUARY 12, 2007

Pennsylvania's Largest-Circulation and Most-Honored Afternoon Newspaper

Local leaders urge commissioners:
STEP DOWN NOW

■ Concern is growing that county government will struggle to function in aftermath of damaging report from investigative grand jury.

By JACK BRUBAKER and ANYA LITVAK
New Era Staff Writers

Several present and former public officials today called for the resignation of all county commissioners in the wake of an investigating grand jury report detailing widespread secrecy and deceit in county government.

Even those who did not call for resignations said it will be difficult, if not impossible, for the commissioners to function in office through the end of their terms next January.

The critical officials said their concern is not political or philosophical, but practical.

"There comes a time when you have to put the interest of the county above everything else," said state Rep. Katie True, a Republican. "This is a huge distraction and they need to move on for the good of the county."

Former U.S. Rep. Bob Walker, former County Commissioner Jim Huber and former Lancaster Mayor Art Morris, all Republicans, also called for the commissioners to resign.

State Sen. Gibson Armstrong, a Republican who has previously and publicly urged Commissioner Dick Shellen-

True Walker Armstrong Morris

berger to resign, reiterated the message this morning. "He should do the right thing," Armstrong said.

Republican Commissioner Pete Shaub, who will resign next month to take a job in the private sector, declined to comment.

Shellenberger, a Republi-

Please see RESIGN page A3

LANCASTER NEW ERA
SATURDAY, JANUARY 13, 2007

www.LancasterOnline.com
Pennsylvania's Largest-Circulation and Most-Honored Afternoon Newspaper

Inside
SATURDAY
Tonight
Clouds, rain, 43°
Tomorrow
Rain, drizzle, 48°
THE WEATHER MAP, B4

Citizens: GET OUT

Countians irate with commissioners, informal poll finds

■ Grand jurors cited officials' secrecy, deceit, ineptitude. Public wants them out of office now.

By JANE HOLAHAN and TOM MURSE
New Era Staff Writers

Note to the County Commissioners: The public wants you to resign.

Right now!

An informal survey today shows they have lost trust in you and don't think you can govern effectively. A few believe you should go to jail

and just about everyone wants a fresh start in county government.

The New Era asked about three dozen people whether the commissioners should resign in light of this week's grand jury findings and a long history of controversy.

The 37-page report, made public Wednesday, provides details of how commissioners secretly manipulated the sale

of the county nursing home, Conestoga View, and the hiring of one of the key administrators responsible. All three have pleaded guilty to violating the Sunshine Act.

Today's survey, held at Central Market and the Apple Tree Restaurant in Manor Township, found an overwhelmingly negative response toward the commissioners. Plenty of people were eager to express their frustration, anger and disgust with Dick Shellenberger, Molly Henderson and Pete Shaub (who announced last week that

Please see STREET page A4

Bon Klos, 71, expresses his opinion at Central Market this morning.
Andrew P. Blackburn/New E

> **EDITORIALS**
>
> **Commissioners Shellenberger and Henderson:**
>
> # Have grace to resign
>
> It's time for Dick Shellenberger and Molly Henderson to resign. That is the inescapable conclusion that arises from the scathing grand jury report on the hiring of Gary Heinke and the sale of Conestoga View by the Lancaster County commissioners.
>
> We knew the situation on the fifth floor of the courthouse was bad. The grand jury report makes it clear that things were worse than we imagined.
>
> We would include Pete Shaub with his colleagues, but he already had the sense to quit, effective Feb. 16.
>
> According to the grand jury, the Conestoga View sale. According to the grand jury, which noted pointedly that Mr. Espenshade's testimony was believable, Mr. Shellenberger said, "Look, we just paid you $300,000, I think you can afford $20."
>
> Wait, there's more.
>
> Far from being shamed or saddened, Mr. Shellenberger has begun attacking the grand jury and District Attorney Don Totaro, not to mention Lancaster Newspapers. And Ms. Henderson has actually issued a statement saying the report "vindicates" her. And some Democratic leaders seem to agree.

According to ***ProQuest***, a database that catalogs newspaper publications, Lancaster Newspapers had 1,653 articles in which my name appeared from January 1, 2004, to December 31, 2007. This four-year span was very close to my term as county commissioner. If one puts "Molly Henderson" and "county commissioner" in the search block, 1,653 references surface.

Total articles with "Molly Henderson" and "county commissioner": 1,653 (2004–2007)

2004—324 articles
2005—399 articles
2006—521 articles
2007—409 articles

Newspaper Headline Examples And Article Count 2004–2007

	2004	**2005**	**2006**	**2007**
January	25	23	38	75
February	20	14	31	53
March	24	36	38	39
April	36	37	40	29
May	15	43	44	26
	2004	**2005**	**2006**	**2007**
June	22	04	61	10
July	18	33	58	15
August	21	32	30	08
September	22	43	49	38
October	34	47	28	60
November	24	40	37	41
December	63	47	67	15

Intelligencer Journal—682
Lancaster New Era—629
Sunday News—342

The most numerous articles were on Friday, Dec. 15, 2006, 9 articles; 5 in the *New Era* and 4 in the *Intelligencer Journal*; 2. The second most numerous day was Sunday, Dec. 24, 2006, with 8 articles in the *Sunday News*.

There is no space in this Appendix to print the headlines from over 1,650 articles published over four years. As examples, this Appendix includes seven front page, top-of-the-fold headlines published during one 30-day period.

Appendix D

LANCASTER COUNTY BOARD OF COMMISSIONERS 2004-2007

Projects Assumed, Initiated and/or Completed

$280M budget, 27 departments and agencies, 2,500 employees

Projects in and with the City of Lancaster

- Northwest Corridor with Franklin & Marshall College and Lancaster General Health, $1M
- Lancaster Academy of Music –becomes the Ware Center through Millersville University, $1M
- YMCA Capital Campaign - $120.000
- YWCA Capital Campaign - $110,000
- Weed and Seed (anti-drug program) $175,000
- Lancaster Crime Coalition $1.2M
- Central Market Study
- Threshold Foundation - agricultural education for children in an urban setting (Dig It Project)

Lancaster County Board of Commissioners 2004-2007

- Safe Communities $120,000
- Clipper Stadium $1.1M ($500,000 loan)
- Downtown Investment District - $79,000 (06-07)
- Roberto Clemente Park – brownfield rehabilitation, previous board of commissioners
- San Juan Bautista Center $94,000, begun by previous board of commissioners
- Churchtown Underground Railroad Project - $150,000
- Brightside Opportunity Project - $50,000
- Sunnyside Residential Development – exploratory, ongoing
- Urban Enhancements Funds
    Lancaster Square Revitalization - $150,000
    Parks and Open Space Master Plan - $100,000
- Through the Metropolitan Planning Organization (Transportation/Penn Dot), permanent
    Bridge projects: Dillerville Road, Fruitville Pike
    Amtrak Station Renovations
    S. Duke Street Corridor Enhancements
    Buck Intersection

Countywide Projects

- Open and make operational the County Public Safety Training Center for first responder training for county and out of state personnel, begun by previous commissioners
- Sell Conestoga View Nursing Home, to Complete Health Care Resources which had been managing it the previous 10 years for $12+M.
- Conestoga View is now on the tax rolls of the School District of Lancaster and Lancaster Township and Lancaster County
- *Establish Better Lancaster Fund* from proceeds of Conestoga View sale $942,500. An ongoing endowment managed by the Lancaster County Community Foundation. First recipient was Welsh Mountain Medical Center for childhood dental care in 2007. According to Melody Keim, V.P. of Programs and Initiatives at the Lancaster County Community Foundation the *Better Lancaster Fund*, designated to

focus on children ages zero through 5 in Lancaster has distributed funds to the following grant applicants:

- 2009 – Lancaster Day Care Center, $6,605, literacy promotion
- 2010 – SouthEast Lancaster Health Services, $22,395, Baby's First Doctor Initiative
- 2010 – YWCA, $20,000, Children of Teen Mothers; Lancaster Day Care Center, $5,670, literacy; S. June Smith Center, $19,500, adaptive technologies; Fulton Opera House, $10,808, preschool arts education for low income children preparing for literacy
- 2011 – Fulton Opera House, $10,000, pre-school arts education for low income children preparing for literacy; Lancaster Day Care Center, $10,000, parent-child literacy program; Ephrata Area Education Foundation, $4,707, with Ephrata Area School District learning for those at risk
- 2012 – SouthEast Lancaster Health Services, $20,000, pediatric check-ups; Fulton Opera House, $10,000, preschool arts education for low income children preparing for literacy
- 2013 – Fulton Opera House, $27,000, pre-school arts education for low income children preparing for literacy.
- 2014 – Clinic for Special Children, $23,000, child development program within the Plain community.
- 2015 – Water Street Ministries, $28,700, relocation funding.

From Urban Enhancement Funds

- Northwest Lancaster County River Trail – E. Donegal Township, $330,000
- Downtown Intersection Improvement and Design- Elizabethtown, $202,000
- Comprehensive Wayfinding Project – Ephrata, $83,000
- Downtown Redevelopment Project- Denver, $250,000
- Grandview Acquisition and Site Development – Mount Joy, $250,000
- River Park Expansion – Columbia, $125,000
- Freedom Memorial Park – Millersville, $150,000
- Community Center – Mountville, $250,000
- Visitor's' Center and Historic Theater – Marietta, $75,000

Environmental

- Lancaster Farmland Trust - $500,000 to stimulate matching grants. Awarded Boyd Award for Distinguished Service to Agriculture
- Agricultural Preservation Board - $8.8 M, from County, State and Federal sources. $5.5M Bond. #1 in PA for farmland preservation in 2005
- Lancaster Farmland Trust - $1M – to work with Plain sects to preserve farms
- Urban Enhancement Funds - $2.7M first time use of bond money to assist urban projects rather than all agriculture projects, see above projects
- Blue Ribbon Commission on Lancaster County Agriculture – to keep farmers farming in Lancaster. Co.
- Lancaster County Conservancy- $1M, to save open and natural areas in the county.
- Further development of:
    a. Money Rocks Park in East Earl Township
    b. Conewago Rail Trail, 5.1 miles long in West Donegal Township
    c. Lancaster Junction Trail, 2.2 miles between Rapho and Donegal townships
    d. Chickies Rock Park, bridge underway for the NW Trail, second largest Lancaster County Park
    e. Master Plan for County Central Park underway
- Conestoga Greenway Trail at Sunnyside Peninsula – links Lancaster City and Lancaster Township underway, now complete

Administrative

- State mandated County Comprehensive Plan entitled Envision is completed. It deals with Smart Growth; grow management; housing; heritage; rural strategies;
- Management Protocol developed for commissioner/staff interaction.
- Ban cigarette smoking on county property.
- Evening quarterly meeting throughout the county at municipal offices for example Fulton Twp.; Strasburg Borough; Columbia Borough, E. Cocalico and others.

- Implement Help America to Vote Act (HAVA) mandated by Congress after 2004 election. New voting system and new voting machines. Insist on verifiable paper trail
- Retain fulltime in-house attorney
- Minority and Women Owned Task Force established to review bidding for County contracts
- Puppy Mill task force established – review state Agricultural Regulations
- Reentry Management for Prison Reform and Needs
    Support Drug Court development
    Support Job Court development
- Additional space used for Children and Youth Department
- Offer housing at the Youth Intervention Center to other counties which are overcrowded.
- Transfer prison medical care to a private concern through the Prison Board
- Purchase/eminent domain 150 N. Queen Street to meet the needs of the growing court system
- Reorganize Reassessment Appeals Board – put in place parameters for director's membership and qualifications
- First total in-house countywide real estate reassessment completed saving the county hundreds of thousands of dollars.
- Set-up challenge grants to county townships to help fund local libraries
- Begin digitization of courthouse records for faster, clearer, more organized access.

Appendix E

WHY WE SOLD CONESTOGA VIEW

NewsBank NewsLibrary
NewsLibrary

Paper: Sunday News (Lancaster, PA)
Title: Why we sold Conestoga View
Date: October 9, 2005

Molly Henderson
Lancaster County Commissioner

The Conestoga View Nursing Home is now owned by Complete Healthcare Resources, the private company that has operated Conestoga View for the last 12 years. There have been many questions about this transaction. They deserve answers.

If county government does not plan for the future now, the massive Bush administration decreases in federal and state funding will create a crisis in all county-level human services.

For that reason, the county's chief administrator and chief of human services have been conducting a core services review for the last year and a half.

Making sure the indigent have quality nursing care is one of many important human service responsibilities of our county. We did not want to find ourselves in the position of our neighbor, Dauphin County, which will probably have to close its county home even after spending $20 million to upgrade its nursing home two years ago, losing $8 million on its nursing home this year, and raising Dauphin County real estate taxes by 20 percent in each of the last two years.

The county must and will continue to ensure that all our indigent receive proper care. County ownership of bricks and mortar is not the best way of providing indigent care in today's world. The trend to home-based and community-based care will continue.

The county's agreements with Complete Healthcare Resources provide assurances of continued access to quality care no matter who is the owner of Conestoga View

With the oversupply of nursing home beds in excellent for-profit and non-profit facilities, the county can provide any necessary support without owning a building.

In discussions, the executive director of the Pennsylvania. Association of County Affiliated Homes stated that in the last four years, 2,000 nursing home beds have changed hands throughout the state for these reasons.

What would the future of Conestoga View operations have been?

Conestoga View is 35 years old, and depreciation, repair and replacement costs would be ever increasing.

Conestoga View represented a large part of the county's management expense. Overhead is real.

Complete Healthcare Resources has access to a million dollars a year in government funding not available to the county and, as a multi-facility owner/operator, has far greater operating efficiencies.

Without a change in ownership, the county's losses would have increased year by year in multi-million dollar amounts.

Without a sale, the School District of Lancaster would have continued to subsidize Conestoga View by lost real estate taxes estimated at more than $200,000 per year.

State law specifically provides for the manner of sale of the county home and requires a fair market sale supported by multiple independent appraisals, which is what the county did.

Why We Sold Conestoga View

State law does not require bids for the sale of a county home because that is not the way to the best deal. Lawrence County sold Hill View Manor this year at auction for less than 10 percent of the amount offered years ago in a sale negotiation.

Not only did the county receive a fair price, the staff, residents and families affected by the sale obtained the reassurance of a known 12-year owner/manager.

Since taking office, the commissioners have attended monthly Conestoga View meetings (open to the public) and educated themselves about Conestoga View

Some people are concerned that the sales agreement was drafted "behind closed doors." The county solicitor, and later special counsel, along with county staff, conducted negotiations. The job of the commissioners, like all other elected officials, is not to write agreements, but to approve or disapprove the documents drafted by the professionals.

The commissioners should have made sure the county educated the public about the reasons for this change. That is why, when the sales agreement was presented in July, I made a motion to delay signing the binding sales agreement to allow public review. My motion did not succeed. The failure to properly educate the public before signing was a mistake.

The comments of the public were very helpful, and were used, in enhancing the Complete Healthcare Resources agreement concerning indigent care provisions, the most critical part.

The fact that the sale went through does not mean that the commissioners disregarded those who opposed the sale. Their concerns were legitimate and understandable.

Sometimes the board of commissioners must disappoint those who desire the county to fund an important and desirable program.

The county's resources are limited and come primarily from real estate taxes, in many cases falling upon senior citizens who want to remain in their homes.

The county must first fund mandated services and then those services that only the county can perform.

I am confident that board of commissioners' decision will enable the county to provide the best array of human services, including continued assurance of nursing home care for the indigent.

Appendix F

PENNSYLVANIA COUNTY NURSING HOMES

The county-run nursing homes in Pennsylvania are nearly a thing of the past. At one time Pennsylvania mandated its 67 counties to provide care for its indigent, elderly residents. The requirement was dropped in the 1960s. At its peak, there were 54 county related nursing homes. Some counties shared facilities and some counties had more than one home. By 2017 only 23 remained.

The decrease in county owned homes continues to this day, and is caused by many factors, most of them a result of deep financial distress at the county, state and federal funding sources.

The trend toward "age in place" care (getting care at home), the reality of growing operational costs, tax increases, and the looming decline in quality high quality care prompted the need for alternative administration for the nursing homes. To maintain care at a facility, many counties opted to privatize their homes. Strict parameters on such sales are codified by the state of Pennsylvania County Code.

Some counties place contractual measures within the agreements made with the purchasing entity. Some of those measures include: maintaining the existing number of "beds" for indigent and Medicare/Medicaid residents; medical and staff to resident ratios, retention of existing staff and other site-specific demands. This was done in Lancaster County, Pennsylvania, in 2005, when the County sold Conestoga view to the private firm that had run the facility for more than ten years. After the sale, Lancaster County, the School District of Lancaster and Lancaster Township could realize property tax revenues from the private owner.

Pennsylvania County Nursing Homes

Below is a list some of the Pennsylvania county nursing homes sold in last decade. Others were sold earlier. The size and condition of the homes vary tremendously resulting in differing prices. Some had existing debt at the time of sale. Others had significant future and ongoing debt or pending tax increases which advanced the transaction.

County	Year Sold	Beds	Cost
Adams County	2011	135 beds	$6.1M
Beaver County	2013	600 beds	$37.5M
Blair County	2013	240 beds	$16.5M
Butler County	2014	220 beds	$20.4M
Cambria County	2010	370 beds	$14.3M
Carbon County	2010	200 beds	$11.M
Dauphin County	2006	404 beds	$22M
Franklin County	2013	186 beds	$11M
Lackawanna County	2010	272 beds	$13.4M
Lancaster County	2005	446 beds	$8.5M + $4.8M
Lebanon County	2014	324 beds	$25.5M
Luzerne County	2005	353 beds	$2M
Mercer County	2009	100 beds	$5M
Montgomery County	2014	467 beds	$41M
Northumberland Co.	2009	271 beds	$16.5M
Schuylkill County	2015	142 beds	$11M
Warren County	2014	80 beds	$2.3M

Source: Mark Gilger, Jr., Schuylkill County commissioners face tough decision on Rest Haven., *Republican Herald*, Aug. 16, 2014.

Lancaster County's care of the indigent began in 1799 with an almshouse. Almost 200 years later, in 1970, the high-rise Conestoga View Nursing Home was built. As society and medical care evolve how attention is given to those in need changes. Change is inevitable and can be difficult. It is unfamiliar. This is particularly true when traditional models are shifted. By accepting the eventuality of change and preparing for it there can be a smooth transition.

Appendix G
STATUS OF THE LANCASTER COUNTY CONVENTION CENTER AND MARRIOTT HOTEL PROJECT AS OF 2018

The ever-increasing public funding of the "private" hotel described in this book did not end when the hotel was built. A detailed analysis of the subsequent events is beyond the scope of this book. A few highlights are listed below.

- The County of Lancaster now guarantees a $63 million dollar convention center bond, an increase of more than $20 million from the original $40 million bond (a bond for which the County only had 50% exposure.) The $63 million bond guarantee, for which the county has 100% exposure, is a temporary fix, only until 2019, when an increase in the countywide hotel tax is expected.

- A $30 million, 12-story, 110-room expansion to the Penn Square Partners' Marriott Hotel has been approved by LCCCA and the City of Lancaster. The expansion will also be property tax-exempt.

- High Real Estate, a 50% stakeholder in Penn Square Partners, the private entity that leases and operates — but does not pay property taxes on — the Marriott Hotel, has purchased properties around the hotel/convention center. These properties will be developed into a $30 million hotel "expansion." The expansion will have the same property tax-free status as the main hotel. This means that no real estate taxes will be paid on the hotel, including the expansion, for two decades to the school district, the city, or the county, amounting to millions of dollars of lost revenue.

- CRIZ—the City Revitalization and Improvement Zone—has been utilized for the project. State and local taxes collected within the CRIZ geographic area are used to repay debt service and to stimulate economic development within the CRIZ. Penn Square Partners was approved in July 2016 for $5.6 million in CRIZ financing.

- Reminiscent of the many statutory changes to benefit the project described in this book, the CRIZ legislation was amended in 2016 to provide further special benefits to the hotel operated by Penn Square Partners.

- Buried in the "library" section of the Lancaster County Convention Center website are a number of interesting documents.

    - The December 31, 2018 audited financial statement reveal an operating loss of $4,350,943, up from 2017. Interest expense is another $2,382,348. Those figures exceed the net $5,365,425 hotel room rental tax revenues. The LCCCA liabilities exceed its assets by $5,599,265.

    - 2018 audit Note 2 reveals that the 20% of the hotel room rental tax which was to go to Lancaster's Tourism Bureau (Discover Lancaster!) after being taken by the LCCCA until 2015 will be kept by the LCCCA at least until the end of 2023 under a 2018 Memorandum of Understanding, also disclosed on the website.

    - Note 8 of the 2018 audit reveals that the LCCCA's Interest Rate Swap, which I opposed, was $17,729,546 underwater.

The Lancaster County Convention Center and Marriott Hotel Project... by the numbers

The cost of the overall convention center and hotel project has risen from $75 million, when introduced in 1999, to more than $200 million in 2018. When the project began, it was proposed as a 55/45 split, public/private. The public sector, the taxpayers, would pay for the $30 million public convention center, and Penn Square Partners, the private investors, would pay for the for-profit $45 million hotel. As the project evolved, and expanded in size, scope, and cost, the percentage of private financing for the hotel dwindled. When the project finally opened in 2009, at a total cost of $177.6 million, the percentage of the overall cost of the project borne by Penn Square Partners was less than 5%. For the privately-owned hotel only, with a cash investment of $11 million for the hotel, Penn Square Partners invested less than 15% of the cost.

Timeline	Cost
1999	$75 Million
2004	$89 Million
2006	$102.6 Million
2006	$129 Million
2006	$134 Million
2007	$135 Million
2009	$177.6 Million
2018	$208 Million

Status of the Lancaster County Convention Center

Overall Cost Lancaster County Convention Center and Marriott Hotel 1999

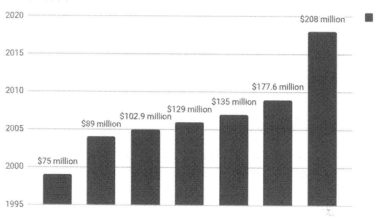

Cost of hotel and convention center project (Sources: LCCCA; Penn Sq. Partners; Lancaster Newspapers

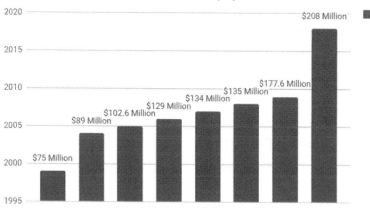

Percentage Public vs. Private Investment Hotel-Convention Center project — 1999

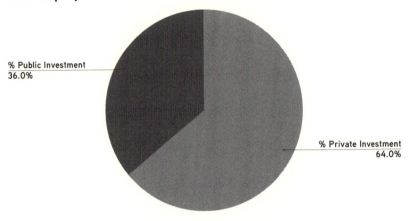

Percentage Public vs Private Investment Hotel-Convention Center Project — 2018

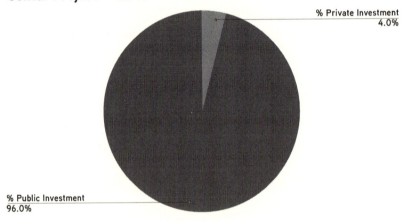

Sources: Lancaster County Convention Center Authority; Penn Square Partners; Lancaster Newspapers, Inc.]

Appendix H

DOCUMENTS FOUND ON PRESSED THE BOOK WEBSITE

PRESSEDTHEBOOK.COM

The documents listed below correlate with the text of the book *Pressed* by Molly Henderson

Please note that there will be additions to the website from time to time as documents become available.

Acronyms found at the website:

LCCCA - Lancaster County Convention Center Authority
PSP - Penn Square Partners (Lancaster Newspapers and High Industries)
RCAL - Redevelopment Authority of the City of Lancaster
TIF - Tax Increment Financing
DCED - PA Department of Community and Economic Development
PDCVB - PA Dutch convention and Visitors Bureau, (Discover Lancaster!)

1994
- Pennsylvania Third-Class County Convention Center Authority Act

1999
- July- Commonwealth of PA Department of Community and Economic Development – Community Revitalization Assistance Program(DCED) – Redevelopment Authority of City of Lancaster(RCAL), $2M.

- September 3, Hotel Tax Proposal – Letter from Lancaster Campaign to Lancaster County commissioner Paul Thibault encouraging a hotel room tax for Lancaster county
- September 15 – Lancaster County Ordinances 44, 45. These establish the Lancaster County Convention Center Authority(LCCCA) and proposed Hotel Room Rental Tax on all Lancaster County hotels and motels
- Ernst & Young Market Study for hotel and convention center
- October 19 - Pennsylvania Senate – Amended House Bill 148 (Armstrong Amendment)
- Outline of Booking Policy & Room Block Agreement. - PA Dutch and Convention Visitors Bureau (now Discover Lancaster!)(PDCVB), Outline of Booking Policy & Room. Block Agreement for Lancaster County convention Center.

2000
February
- Redevelopment Loan Agreement between Penn Square Partners(PSP) and the Redevelopment Authority of the City of Lancaster(RACL).

March
- Contract for Community Revitalization Assistance Program, Commonwealth of Pennsylvania Department of Community and Economic Development(DCED)

November
- Pricewaterhouse Coopers Market and Economic Analysis for the Proposed Convention Center in Downtown Lancaster

2001
November
- Stevens/Smith House elements retained or re-used

December
- Booking Room block Agreement -LCCCA and PSP Agreement with letter

December 20
- Governing Letter from PSP to LCCCA
- Professional Services Development Agreement- LCCCA and PSP
- Food and Beverage Concession Agreement – LCCCA and PSP
- Reciprocal, Easement, Operating and Use Agreement – LCCCA and PSP
- 2001 Joint Development Agreement – LCCCA and PSP

2002
- Pricewaterhouse Coopers Update

June 23
- Qualified Convention Center Management Agreement – LCCCA and Interstates Hotels Company
- Lease Agreement PSP and LCCCA

September
- Wachovia Bank commitment to provide financing in the amount of $25,000,000 to the Lancaster County Convention Center Authority

December 2002
- Hoteliers Complaint to Commonwealth Court Against County of Lancaster, RCAL, LCCCA Commonwealth of Pennsylvania DCED and PSP.

2003
April 23
- Pennsylvania Historical and Museum Commission, Bureau for Historic Preservation letter to PSP

August 7
- C/H. Johnson Consulting draft analysis of the Lancaster Convention Center Project Summary

December 2003
- Manufacturers and Traders Trust Company Hotel Tax Revenue Bonds at $40,000,000, by the County of Lancaster

2004
March 31
- Act 23 of 2004, Senator Gibson Armstrong's #2 to assist the project.

June 17
- Agreement for Development of Parking Facility, LCCCA and City of Lancaster Parking Authority

2005
February 24, 2005
- Redevelopment Authority of the City of Lancaster(RACL) Request for an Infrastructure and Facilities Improvement Program Grant for the Lancaster County Convention Center/Hotel Project
- Financial Projection for Lancaster Marriott at Penn Square by PSP (power point)

Tax Increment Financing - TIF
February 24
- RCAL, School District of Lancaster, and PSP Tax Increment Financing Agreement (draft)

March
- PSP's Response to the School District of Lancaster's Critical Questions
- Lancaster County Convention Center Misconceptions Dispelled (PowerPoint PSP/LCCCA)
- School District of Lancaster Tax Increment Financing (TIF) Analysis

March 11
- County of Lancaster (Commissioner) TIF Act Application/Questions

March 15
- School District of Lancaster Statement Regarding TIF- Downtown Hotel and Convention Center Project

April 2005
- Tax Increment Financing School District of Lancaster Resolution- unsigned

April 11, 2005
- Taxability of Marriott Hotel – Legal Opinion, Kegel Kelin Almy & Grimm

May 16, 2005
- Local Government Unit Debt Act/Complaint by County of Lancaster
- Declaration of Condominium of the Penn Square Hotel and Convention Center

October 2005
- Purchase Option Agreement between RACL and LCCCA

November 2005
- Rob Canton email from Pricewaterhouse Cooper regarding use of PwC in the project's promotion
- Tom Myers Report

November 9, 2005
- Professional Services Development Agreement- LCCCA and High Associates, LDT
- Joint Development Agreement – LCCCA, RACL and PSP.
- Transfer Agreement – PSP and RACL, move Watt & Shand Building to RACL.
- Hotel Tower Lease Agreement – RCAL and PSP.

2006

January 2006
- Joint Development Agreement between LCCCA and RCAL

January 30, 2006
- Easement Agreement between Lancaster Historic Preservation Trust and LCCCA concerning the Thaddeus Stevens/Lydia Smith property.

February 1, 2006
- Amended and Restated Open-End Leasehold Agreement between PSP and RCAL

March 31, 2006
- Board of Commissioners' statement on process leading to sale of Conestoga View

May 2006
- Public letter on the Project from Dick Shellenberger

May 12, 2006
- PKF Feasibility Study on hotel/convention center project

July 12 & 14
- Transcripts of PSP, RCAL & City of Lancaster v. Lancaster County Board of Commissioners (Henderson and Shellenberger). Part I – July 12, Part II–July14.

July 26, 2006
- PSP Statement on project construction bid overage from WGAL-TV release 2007

December 2006
- Grand Jury Report

2007

March 2007
- Lancaster Convention Center Authority and Marriott Hotel – Phase I & II -Sources and Uses

March 27, 2007
- Declaration of Condominium Agreement between LCCCA and RCAL – This conveys the hotel to RACL and leases it back to PSP. The Convention Center is conveyed to LCCCA.
- Amended Lease Agreement between PSP and LCCCA

March 28, 2007
- First Amendments to Booking Room Block Agreement between LCCCA and PSP
- First Amendment to Food and Beverage Concession Agreement between LCCCA and PSP
- PaDCVB (Discover Lancaster!) First Amendment to Outline of Booking Policy and Room Block Agreement Lancaster County Convention Center First Amendment to Joint Development Agreement between LCCCA, RCAL and PSP.

June 2007
- House Bill 1589,Capital Budget Project, Senator Gibson Armstrong's third law change to the help the Convention Center project. (see page 160 of the bill) Funds were also steered toward the Stevens/Smith House, County Rail/Trail and surveillance cameras.

2010

May 27, 2010
- Global Food and Beverage Agreements - Second Amendments to the Joint Development Agreement, the Professional Services Development Agreement and the Food and Beverage Concession Agreement, and Agreement Regarding Payment for Contractor Overtime and Resolution of Claims

2011
- Fiscal Impact and Recovery of the LCCCA from Lancaster County PADCVB (DiscoverLancaster)

2014
June 19, 2014
- 2014 Lancaster County Convention Center Collaboration Agreement between County of Lancaster, Lancaster City, RACL, LCCCA, Lancaster City Revitalization and Improvement Zone Authority and PDCVB.

July 2014
- County Ordinance No. 111, Amending and Restating Hotel Room Tax revenue bonds...". County of Lancaster now guarantying up to $63,590.000 in Hotel Tax Revenue Bonds.

August 1, 2014
- Guaranty Agreement between Lancaster County and Manufacturers Traders Trust company and LCCCA. County now guarantees full amount of bonds.

2016
July 2016
- Amended and Restated Declaration of Condominium for Penn Square July 2016 between LCCCA and RCAL.
- Indemnity Agreement between PSP,LCCCA and RCAL concerning the tower addition to the hotel.

Tab 17b County Ordinance

Audits of Lancaster County Convention Center Authority
  2001
  2002
  2003
  2004
  2005
  2006
Miscellaneous – Shuttle Marketing

TIMELINE RELATED TO LANCASTER COUNTY HOTEL AND CONVENTION CENTER PROJECT

1729 — May 10. Lancaster County established.

1734 — City of Lancaster established.

1744 — Christian and Anna Steinman, arrive in the North American British colonies.

1752 — John Frederick Steinman, Sr.(1752- 1823), born, only child of Christian and Anna Steinman, Lititz, Pennsylvania.

1760 — Christian Steinman dies.

1764 — Anna Steinman re-marries Christopher Heyne, a successful Lancaster hardware merchant, who owned "Heyne's Hardware" on W. King Street.

1777 — September 27th, the city of Lancaster functions as the new nation's capital.

1787 — Pennsylvania becomes the 2nd state of the United States, December 12th.

1789 — John Frederick Steinman, Jr. (1879-1884) born.

1791 — James Buchanan (1791–1868), 15th U.S. President, born in Lancaster.

1792 — Thaddeus Stevens (1792-1868) born April 4th in Vermont. Moved to Lancaster at age 50.

1790 — The population of Lancaster County is approximately 36,000; the population of the city of Lancaster is 3,800.

1794 — Lancaster Journal newspaper founded.

1799-1812 — With the population of Lancaster County about 36,000, and the city 4,200, the city of Lancaster was officially Pennsylvania's state capital.

1800 — The population of Lancaster County is approximately 43,000; the population of the city of Lancaster is about 4,200.

1810 — The population of Lancaster County is approximately 53,000; the population of the city of Lancaster is about 5,400.

1818 — City of Lancaster incorporated as a city.

1820 — The population of Lancaster County is approximately 68,000; the population of the city of Lancaster is about 6,700.

1830 — The population of Lancaster County is approximately 77,000; the population of the city of Lancaster is about 7,700.

1836 — Andrew Jackson "AJ" Steinman born, October 10th.

1836 — School District of Lancaster established.

1840 — The population of Lancaster County is approximately 84,000; the population of the city of Lancaster is about 8,400.

1850 — The population of Lancaster County is approximately 100,000.

1851 — Christiana Riot.

1860 — The population of Lancaster County is approximately 116,000; the population of the city of Lancaster is about 17,600.

1866 — Andrew Jackson Steinman (1836-1917) acquires Lancaster *Intelligencer*.

1870 — The population of Lancaster County is approximately 121,000; the population of the city of Lancaster is about 20,200.

1877 — Lancaster New Era established.

1880 — The population of Lancaster County is approximately 139,000; the population of the city of Lancaster is about 25,800.

1884 — John Frederick Steinman, Jr. (1789-1884), dies at 94.

1884 — John Frederick Steinman (1884-1980), son of AJ Steinman, grandson of John Frederick Steinman, Jr., born.

1886 — James Hale Steinman (1886-1962), Publisher, Lancaster Newspapers, born.

Timeline

1890 — The population in Lancaster County is approximately 149,000; the city of Lancaster was about 32,000.

1900 — The population in Lancaster County is approximately 159,000; the city of Lancaster, about 32,000.

1905 — AJ Steinman and his partner, Charles Foltz, purchase the buildings at 8-10 West King Street, a few doors from Steinman Hardware.

1909 — July. AJ Steinman and Charles Foltz start the *Lancaster Morning Journal* to pair with their afternoon *Intelligencer*.

1910 — The population in Lancaster County is approximately 159,000; the city of Lancaster, about 47,200.

1917 — Andrew Jackson "AJ" Steinman (1836-1917) dies, age 81.

1920 — The population in Lancaster County is approximately 173,800; the city of Lancaster, about 53,200.

1921 — In May of 1921, the Steinman brothers buy-out Charles Steinman Foltz's 50% interest in the *Intelligencer* newspaper.

1923 — New York-based publisher and advertising executive Paul Block, Sr. purchases the afternoon Lancaster New Era.

1928 — Lancaster Newspapers controls all three Lancaster newspapers, the morning Intelligencer-Journal, the afternoon *Lancaster New Era*, and the Sunday News.

1928 — Berks County judge John Bergen Stevens opens the Stevens & Lee law firm in Reading, Pa., April 1st, 1928.

1930 — The population in Lancaster County is approximately 196,900; the city of Lancaster, about 59,900.

1931 — High Welding established by Sanford H. High and his older brother, Benjamin.

1940 — The population in Lancaster County is approximately 212,500; the city of Lancaster, about 61,300.

1942 — Sanford Dale "Dale" High (1942- present) born.

1949 — The first broadcast of Steinman-owned WGAL television is made to a Lancaster audience, March, 1949.

1950 — The population in Lancaster County is approximately 234,700; the city of Lancaster, about 63,800.

1954 — WGAL broadcasts its first show in color, the Tournament of Roses Parade from Pasadena, California.

1960 — The population in Lancaster County is approximately 278,400; the city of Lancaster, about 61,100.

1962 — Lancaster Newspapers Publisher, James Hale Steinman (1886-1962), dies, age 76.

1963 — Dale High graduates from Elizabethtown College with a degree in Business Administration.

1970 — The population in Lancaster County is approximately 319,700; the city of Lancaster, about 57,700.

1971 — September 28. Park City shopping mall opens.

1978 — The Steinmans are forced by the FCC to sell WGAL-TV in Lancaster on anti-trust grounds.

1977 — Sanford H. High turns his company, now called "High Steel," and subsidiaries, over to youngest son, S. Dale High, 35, names him President and CEO.

1980 — The population in Lancaster County is approximately 362,300; the city of Lancaster, about 54,700.

1980-1990 — Arthur Elmer Morris is mayor, city of Lancaster.

1980 — John Frederick Steinman (1884-1980), Publisher, Lancaster Newspapers, dies, age 90.

1983 — John M. "Jack" Buckwalter (1931-2010) is promoted from executive vice-president of Lancaster Newspapers to President and CEO.

1983 — Sanford H. High, dies in December at age 76.

1985 — Gibson E. "Gib" Armstrong is elected to Pennsylvania State Senate representing the 13th district.

1986 — Nevin Donald Cooley, Jr. joins the High companies as vice-president of development and acquisitions for High Associates, a commercial real estate development company.

1990 — The population in Lancaster County is approximately 422,800; the city of Lancaster, about 55,600.

1991 — P. Michael Sturla (b. 1956) is elected to the Pennsylvania Assembly, representing the 96th District, which includes the City of Lancaster.

Timeline

1992 —February. The 115 year-old historic Watt & Shand department store, built in 1895 and designed by C. Emlen Urban, is sold to the York-based Bon-Ton Stores, Inc. Three years later the landmark downtown store is closed.

1993 — The Lancaster Alliance is formed.

1994 — March 28. The downtown Lancaster hotel and convention center project is first introduced to the readers of Lancaster Newspapers.

1994 — December. The Pennsylvania Third Class Convention Center Act is signed into law by Governor Robert P. Casey.

1995 — March. The Bon Ton company closes its downtown Penn Square store.

1995 — March. Paul R. Thibault, an unendorsed Republican, upsets incumbent Lancaster County Commissioner James Huber in the March Republican primary, secures place on November ballot.

1995 — November. Paul R. Thibault is elected Lancaster County Commissioner.

1996 — July. Harrisburg Area Community College (HACC) trustees vote to purchase the Watt & Shand building. HACC applies for more than $8 million in state funding.

1996 — Lancaster Campaign, a private subsidiary of the Lancaster Alliance, is formed.

1997 — March 27. HACC application is denied by state department of education on March 27, ending the move of the community college downtown.

1997 July — The Lancaster Campaign hires LDR, International to *"create a diagnosis and prescription for revitalizing Lancaster."*

1997 — November 4 . Lancaster pharmacist, and Civil War-era cannon gun collector, Republican Charlie Smithgall, is elected mayor.

1998 — January 4. Mayor Charlie Smithgall takes office.

1998 — January. The partnership of Penn Square Partners is formed.

1998 — February. The Watt & Shand building is purchased by Penn Square Partners.

1998 — April 2. The *Intelligencer Journal* in *"Local Leaders Consider Taxing Tourists to Help City"* introduce the idea of levying a 5% hotel room rental tax in Lancaster County.

1998 — November — Pennsylvania Governor Tom Ridge is re-elected.

1999 — Molly Henderson is named by Mayor Charlie Smithgall as director of the Environmental Health and Protection Unit in Lancaster city, from October, 1999, to June, 2002.

1999 — February. Pennsylvania Governor Tom Ridge, who took office in 1995, signs $750 million Stadium Bill.

1999 — August 26. All summer, all three Lancaster Newspapers devote extensive coverage to a convention center and hotel on Penn Square.

1999 — October 19. Sen. Gib Armstrong introduces an amendment to House Bill 148.

1999 — November 3. Pennsylvania Governor Tom Ridge signs the Sen. Armstrong-amended Convention Center Act legislation.

2000 — The population in Lancaster County is approximately 470,700; the city of Lancaster, about 56,300.

2000 — January 01, 2000. Hotel and room rental tax begins.

2000 — February. Ron Harper, Jr. launches website, 5thestate.com.

2000 — March 24. Thirty-seven Lancaster County hoteliers file a civil lawsuit in the Court of Common Pleas in downtown Lancaster.

2000 — July. A "Tourism Task Force," appointed by the Lancaster County Convention Center Authority, and comprised of some of its members, recommends the size of the convention center expaned from 61,000 square feet to at least 100,000 square feet.

2001 — February. Sen. Gib Armstrong leads a Lancaster delegation to Washington, D.C., requests up to $25 million in federal funds to revitalize downtown Lancaster.

2001 — July 24. Penn Square Partners announces its private hotel will carry the Marriott 'flag.'

2001 — August 15, In a 7-2 vote, the Tourism Task Force recommends that Spectacor, not Interstate, manage the convention center.

Timeline

2001 — September 12. The Lancaster County Convention Center Authority disregards its own Task Force's recommendation, and the objection of the county's hoteliers, and votes to hire Interstate Hotels to manage both the hotel and convention center.

2002 — January. Lancaster Judge Louis Farina decides against the hoteliers on all counts.

2002 — January 24. The Commonwealth Court remands hoteleliers' case back to the Lancaster Court.

2002 — April 20. Lancaster businessman, Chris Kunzler, in a letter to the editor of the Sunday News raises the issue that a county-guaranteed bond.

2003 — May. Molly Henderson is the top Democrat vote-getter in the county commissioner primary, putting her on the November ballot.

2003 — June. Attorney Jim Clymer enters the County Commissioner race.

2003 — July. David M. Hixson is hired as Executive Director of the Lancaster County Convention Center Authority (LCCCA).

2003 — July/August. Lancaster County Commissioner Pete Shaub and Republican Commissioner-candidate, Dick Shellenberger, begin to meet with Lancaster County solicitor, John Espenshade, a Stevens & Lee partner, to discuss selling the county-owned nursing home, "Conestoga View."

2003 — October 29. The Lancaster County Board of Commissioners vote 2-1 (Shaub votes no) to guarantee half of a $40 million convention center construction bond.

2003 — November 6. Dick Shellenberger, Pete Shaub, and Molly Henderson are elected Lancaster County Commissioners.

2004 — January 8. Lancaster County Commissioners Dick Shellenberger, Pete Shaub, and Molly Henderson are sworn into office.

2004 — March. Gary Heinke is hired as Chief Services Officer for Lancaster County.

2004 — The amendment known as 'Act 23' is passed in the Pennsylvania legislature.

2005 — January. Dick Shellenberger takes over as chairman of commissioners board.

2005 — The Brookings Institute publishes study, "Space Available – The Realities of Convention Centers as Economic Development Strategy," by University of Texas professor, Dr. Heywood Sanders.

2005 — March. The Lancaster Group conducts a study of 25,808 people in eleven locations around Lancaster City and County, asking them whether they support or oppose this project. More than 89% of those polled do not want to see the project built.

2005 — March 11. Commissioners Shellenberger and Henderson send "57 Questions" to Penn Square Partners, the Redevelopment Authority of the City of Lancaster (RACL), and the Lancaster County Convention Center Authority (LCCCA).

2005 — March 12. The *Intelligencer Journal* publishes a poll, three days before the School Board TIF vote, the results of which show 93% of respondents oppose the Penn Square Partners' financing plan.

2005 — March 15. In a 7-1 vote (with one abstention), the School Board of Lancaster refuses to back Penn Square Partners' Tax Increment Financing (TIF) proposal.

2005 — April 12. The Lancaster City Council votes to apply for $36 million in Act 23 state funding.

2005 — July 6. At a regular Lancaster County Commissioners' board meeting, County Commissioners Dick Shellenberger, Pete Shaub, and Molly Henderson vote unanimously to enter into an agreement to sell Conestoga View, the county-owned nursing home.

2005 — September. Senator Gib Armstrong and Lancaster Mayor Charlie Smithgall publicly call for Commissioner Shellenberger's resignation.

2005 — September 28. The sale of Conestoga View is voted on by the Lancaster County. Commissioners. Shellenberger and Henderson vote to sell the facility; Shaub votes no.

2005 — October 24. Gary Heinke, hired as Chief Services Officer for the county in 2004, is first mentioned as a target of Lancaster Newspaper investigation.

2005 — October 25. Heinke assures the commissioners the information on his resume is accurate.

Timeline

2005 — October 28. Gary Heinke resigns as Lancaster County's Chief Services Officer.

2005 — November 6. Democrat Rick Gray defeats Smithgall to become Lancaster's new mayor.

2005 — November 10. Lancaster County District Attorney, Donald Totaro, begins a grand jury investigation into the hiring of Gary Heinke.

2006 — January 4. County Commissioner Molly Henderson sends letter to LCCCA and Mayor-elect Gray making four proposals regarding project.

2006 — January 11. Mayor Rick Gray appears at a regular county commissioners meeting and tells commissioners if they want a feasibility study, they need to pay for it themselves, and not ask the city for funds.

2006 — January 31. The Redevelopment Authority of the City of Lancaster (RACL) buys the Watt & Shand building from Penn Square Partners for $7.25 million.

2006 — January 31. The Lancaster Historic Preservation Trust approves development of an historic Thaddeus Stevens interactive museum on site of Stevens' former home and office.

2006 — February 15. The Lancaster County Commissioners hire consulting giant Pannell, Kerr, Forster (PKF) to perform the first feasibility study on the hotel and convention center project.

2006 — February 22. Lancaster County Commissioners Henderson and Shellenberger file lawsuit challenging ACT 23 state funding of project.

2006 — February 23. David M. Hixson, Lancaster County Convention Center Authority executive director, states his board will not cooperate with the PKF study.

2006 — February 25. County commissioner Pete Shaub publicly criticizes selection of PKF to perform feasibility study.

2006 — February 28. Commissioners Henderson and Shellenberger's challenge to ACT 23 is heard in Commonwealth Court.

2006 — March 4. Asbestos and hazardous debris is removed from Watt & Shand building in preparation for demolition.

2006 — March 20. The Lancaster County Convention Center Authority (LCCCA) seeks construction contracts for project.

2006 — March 21. State Senate passes Act 23 amendment.

2006 — April 6. Sen. Armstrong's bill is withdrawn from a House vote due to heavy protest from Lancaster lawmakers.

2006 — April 25. The Redevelopment Authority for the city of Lancaster (RACL) announces it will float an additional $2 million hotel construction bond, increasing the city's exposure from $12 million to $14 million on the bond.

2006 — April 26. The Pennsylvania State Assembly passes Armstrong's amendment, 146 to 41.

2006 — May 5. The PKF "Executive Summary" of its feasibility study is released.

2006 — May 10. County Commissioners Henderson and Shellenberger vote to petition the state Department of Community and Economic Development to review the county's 2003 $40 million bond guaranty.

2006 — May 12. Pennsylvania Governor Ed Rendell signs the Sen. Armstrong-amended Act 23 bill. Rendell's signature means that Penn Square Partners will not pay property taxes on its Marriott Hotel, although it will be the "primary user" of the hotel.

2006 — May 17. The Lancaster County Convention Center Authority (LCCCA) board opens the remaining construction bids.

2006 — May 24. The Intelligencer Journal reports that the construction bids submitted to the LCCCA actually put the project $25.4 million over budget, not the reported $13.6 million overage.

2006 — May 24. Commissioners Henderson and Shellenberger vote to revoke the $40 million county bond if the LCCCA re-markets the bonds.

2006 — May 31. Commissioner Henderson publicly questions whether the geographic area from which the hotel and motel room rental tax was drawn is legal.

2006 — June 1. Demolition on the project site resumes after sponsors acquire permit.

Timeline

2006 — June 8. County-appointed LCCCA board member, Deb Hall, introduces a motion to have a "legal audit" of legal fees paid by the Convention Center Authority.

2006 — June 8. High Construction Company resigns as "Construction Manager" of the project.

2006 — June 8. Sunday News editor Marvin "Marv" Adams begins "countdown" until the ends of the terms of Commissioners Shaub, Shellenberger and Henderson.

2006 — July 12. The courtroom hearings begin on the lawsuit against Commissioners Shellenberger and Henderson.

2006 — July 12. The Lancaster-based Horst Hotels, LLC and Ephrata Motels Partners sue Penn Square Partners, the Lancaster County Convention Center Authority, and the Redevelopment Authority of the City of Lancaster, arguing the hotel room rental tax is unconstitutional.

2006 — July 17. Madenspacher hearings end.

2006 — July 25. Judge Madenspacher issues temporary injunctions against Commissioners Henderson and Shellenberger.

2006 — July 27. The last of the convention center construction bids is opened. High Construction is the only bidder for the General Trades contract.

2006 — August 4. The lawsuit brought by Commissioners Henderson and Shellenberger challenging Act 23 funding is defeated in Commonwealth Court.

2006 — August 11. Lancaster Mayor Rick Gray introduces a plan to deal with the $20 million bid overage by shifting money between accounts, demanding over $5 million in concessions from contractors, and soliciting $3 million in to purchase an "easement" for the facade of the Watt & Shand building.

2006 — August 24. Judge Madenspacher announces hearings scheduled for September 28, 29, 2006, to address the $40 million county bond guaranty.

2006 — August 29. Commissioners Henderson and Shellenberger vote to appeal the Commonwealth Court Act 23 ruling.

2006 —September 15. Lancaster-based Horst Hotels and Ephrata Motel Partners withdraw their joint lawsuit against Penn Square Partners, the Lancaster County Convention Center Authority, and the Redevelopment Authority of the City of Lancaster.

2006 — September 28, 29. The Madenspacher hearings begin again.

2006 — October 13. The Four-foot high Watt & Shand letters are removed from the historic building.

2006 — October 24. Judge Joseph Madenspacher issues permanent injunctions against Commissioners Henderson and Shellenberger.

2006 — October 31. Commissioners Henderson and Shellenberger vote to appeal the Madenspacher decision in Commonwealth Court.

2006 — November 8. Lancaster County commissioners Henderson and Shellenberger write a letter to M&T Bank, which holds the construction bond.

2006 — November 16. The cost of the hotel and convention center project has increased $10.1 million.

2006 — November 22. The State Supreme Court rejects appeal from Commissioners Henderson and Shellenberger without hearing the case.

2006 — December 13. The hotel and convention center project will cost an additional $5 million, increasing the total to $170.5 million.

2006 — December 14. Commissioners Dick Shellenberger and Pete Shaub accepted citations for two violations of the state's Sunshine Act related to the sale of Conestoga View. Molly Henderson accepted one citation with a statement.

2006 —December 14. The Lancaster County Convention Center Authority board votes to increase borrowing limit from $47 million to $64 million.

2006 — December 15. After the grand jury investigation is complete, a report is submitted to Lancaster president judge Louis J. Farina.

2006 — December 26. Commissioner Pete Shaub announces he will resign his office, effective February 4, 2007.

2007 — January 8. Grand Jury report unsealed and publicly released.

2007 — January 17. Lancaster County Commissioner Richard "Dick" Shellenberger announces he will not seek re-election.

Timeline

2007 — February. Lancaster County Commissioner, Howard "Pete" Shaub, resigns from office.

2007 — March 30. Fulton Bank divests from Penn Square Partners.

2007 — April 24. Art Morris is named to the Lancaster County Convention Center Authority (LCCCA) board of directors by Lancaster Mayor Rick Gray.

2007 — April 27 Ted Darcus steps down as chairman of LCCCA board.

2007 — May 4. Art Morris is voted chairman of the LCCCA board

2007 — July. With only a portion of the façade remaining after extensive demolition, the Watt & Shand Building is de-listed from the National Register of Historic Places.

2007 — July 27. LCCCA Executive Director, David M. Hixson, resigns. Art Morris, on the board less than three months, is now chairman and acting-executive director of the LCCCA.

2007 — Molly Henderson loses re-election for Lancaster County Commissioner.

2008 — January 8. Molly Henderson sues Lancaster Newspapers, Inc. and individual defendants John M. Buckwalter, Ernest J. Schreiber, Marvin L. Adams, Jr., Helen Colwell Adams, Charles Raymond Shaw, Arthur E. Morris, Gilbert A. Smart, John H. Brubaker, III, and David Pidgeon for libel.

2008 — February. Art Morris is re-elected chairman of LCCCA board of directors.

2008 — August 31. The Lancaster County Convention Center Authority votes to collect $500,000 in state money targeted for the convention center.

2008 — October 31. Sen. Gibson E. Armstrong pledges another $3 million in state funds for the project.

2008 — November 4. Sen. Armstrong's seat in the Senate is taken by Lloyd Smucker after Armstrong's retirement.

2009 — June. After months of delays, and many event cancellations, the Lancaster County Convention Center and Marriott Hotel opens to the public.

2009 — June 26. The Lancaster New Era publishes for the last time.

2009 — November. Convention Center faces nearly $1 million deficit for operating budget for 2010.

2009 — December 31. Intelligencer Journal names the convention center and Conestoga View as part of its "Top Ten stories of the decade."

2010 — February. The Sunday News reports that, according to Lancaster County Treasurer, Craig Ebersole, hotel tax revenues in the county are down 8%, from $5.8 million to $5.4 million for 2009.

2010 — August 11. John M. Buckwalter, former chairman of Lancaster Newspapers, dies, age 79.

2010 — The population in Lancaster County is approximately 519,400; the city of Lancaster, about 59,300.

2011 — February. The Sunday News reports that, according to Lancaster County Treasurer, Craig Ebersole, hotel tax revenues in the county were up 10% $5.4 million in 2009 to $5.9 million in 2010.

2011 — August. Lancaster County Convention Center Authority board votes to refinance $63.9 million construction bond debt.

2012 — April 2. LCCCA takes all 5% of the hotel room rental tax.

2012 — June 7. The Lancaster tourism bureau the Pennsylvania Dutch Convention and Visitors Bureau (PDCVB) releases study on convention center financial problems, and suggests restructuring the debt.

2012 —June 10. The convention center's financial problems — predicted by Commissioners Molly Henderson and Dick Shellenberger — is now front page news.

2012 — August 23. The "Martin Plan" is introduced by Lancaster County Commissioner, Scott Martin.

2012 —September. Mayor Rick Gray proposes raising the room tax rate to cover debt service gap.

2013 — February. Wells Fargo, the bond debt holder, gives the LCCCA a three-month extension to restructure its $64 million bond debt.

2013 — March 4. Four years after the hotel and convention center opens, and 14 years after the project is introduced to the Lancaster public, the Lancaster Historical Society applies for funding to plan the Thaddeus Stevens Museum.

Timeline

2013 — April. The Pennsylvania Dutch Convention and Visitors Bureau is again forced to give up its 20% share of room tax revenue so that the Lancaster County Convention Center Authority can make its bond debt payments.

2013 — August 23. The deadline for the refinancing of the Lancaster County Convention Center's $64 million debt is extended for the third time.

2013 — September 5. Lancaster County Commissioner, Scott Martin, announces he has reached a tentative agreement for his six-party plan to re-finance the convention center debt.

2013 — December 24. The Lancaster County Convention Center Authority authorizes its officers to act on an extension of the bond debt payment terms if offered by Wells Fargo.

2014 — January 4. Commissioner Scott Martin announces six-party plan has been agreed to by all six parties.

2014 — June 11. Commissioner Scott Martin's plan is still not signed, and is opposed by fellow commissioner, Craig Lehman.

2014 — June 19. Commissioner Scott Martin announces his plan has been adopted by all parties except Penn Square Partners.

2014 — June 25. The Pennsylvania Dutch Convention and Visitors Bureau, one of the six parties — declines to support the Martin Plan.

2014 — June 25. Nevin Cooley retires as CEO of High companies.

2014 — July 2. By a 2-1 vote (Lehman votes no), the Lancaster County Board of Commissioners pass Martin's plan.

2014 — October. Lancaster Newspapers, Inc. changes the name of the Intelligencer Journal/Lancaster New Era and Sunday News to LNP: Always Lancaster.

2014 — December. Along with Bethlehem, Lancaster is selected as one of the first two cities to participate in the Pennsylvania City Revitalization & Improvement Zone (CRIZ) program.

2015 — January 11. High Real Estate Group purchases third East King Street parcel next to the Marriott Hotel for "possible future development."

2015 — January 31 Penn Square Partners announce plans for a $23 million expansion for the Marriott Hotel.

2015 — February 1. The Lancaster County Convention Center Authority approves Marriott Hotel $23 million expansion plan for the Lancaster Marriott at Penn Square.

2015 — August. "Lancaster Prospers? An Analysis of Census Data on Economic Opportunities and Outcomes," a study published by the Floyd Institute for Public Policy, Franklin & Marshall College, is published.

2016 — February 16. The Lancaster Historical Commission approves High Associates' plans to demolish three buildings on East King Street..

2016 — February 25. The Lancaster City Council approves Marriott hotel expansion plan.

2016 — July 27. The $30 million expansion of the Marriott hotel receives approval to finance some costs using CRIZ program revenue to pay debt service on a $5.6 million bond.

2016 — September 9. The Lancaster city Planning Commission approves of the city Redevelopment Authority's proposal for the $30 million, 110-room Marriott hotel expansion.

2016 — October 12. Lancaster City Council approves $30 million Marriott hotel plan.

2016 — November 25. LNP reports the the Lancaster County Convention Center Authority will receive $700,000 from the CRIZ program.

2017 — July 20. Penn Square Partners challenge $52.3M Marriott assessment.

2017 — September 2. Appeals Board Hearing is held to determine the assessed value of the Penn Square Partners-operated Marriott Hotel.

2017 — October 16. The Thaddeus Stevens Museum is still not open.

2018 — Construction of Marriott expansion underway.

BIBLIOGRAPHY

AAA Tour Book Pennsylvania, AAA Publishing, Heathrow, FL, 2017.

Abrams, Floyd, *Speaking Freely: Trials of the First Amendment*, Penguin Publishing, 2006.

Anthon, Dionne E, "Unconventional Decisions: Challenging the Use of Hotel Taxes in Convention Center Projects," published in the Journal of Constitutional Law, Vol. 7: 2, November, 2004.

Ballenger, Janice, *Addicted to Life and Death*, Masthof Press, Morgantown, PA, 2008.

Bly, Nellie, *The Collected Works of Nellie Bly,* Golgotha Press, 2015.

Brubaker, Jack, *Remembering Lancaster County*, The History Press, Charleston, SC, 2010.

Brubaker, John H. III, *The Steinmans of Lancaster, A Family and its Enterprises,"* Steinman Enterprises, 1983.

Buck, William J., *William Penn in America; or an account of his life from the time he received the grant of Pennsylvania in 1681, until his final return to England,"* Library of Congress, 1888. The book may be found online here: https://archive.org/details/williampenninam00buckgoog

Callari, Antonio, Evan Gentry and Berwood Yost, *"Lancaster Prospers? An Analysis of Census Data on Economic Opportunities and Outcomes,"* Franklin & Marshall College, Floyd Institute of Public Policy, 2015.

Callender, Edward Belcher, *Thaddeus Stevens: Commoner,* originally published 1882.

Churchill, Winston, *Brighton Conference Resolutions, [foreword],* by the National Union of Conservative and Unionist Associations, St. Clements Press, 1947.

Clark, LeRoy D, *The Grand Jury: The Use and Abuse of Political Power,* HarperCollins, 1975.

Collazzo, Sonia G., Camille L. Ryan, Kurt J. Bauman, "Profile of the Puerto Rican Population in the United States and Puerto Rico, 2008," U. S. Census Bureau, Housing and Household Economic Statistics Division. See online here: https://www.census.gov/hhes/socdemo/education/data/acs/paa2010/Collazo_Ryan_Bauman_PAA2010_Paper.pdf

County of Lancaster, Pennsylvania, "History of the Lancaster County Courthouse," at the Lancaster County government website: http://web.co.lancaster.pa.us/DocumentCenter/Home/View/328.

Eastman, Frank Marshall, Courts and Lawyers of Pennsylvania: *A History, 1623-1923, Volume 4, American Historical Society, 1922.* A digital version of this book may be found here: *https://books.google.com/books?id=CXAmAQAAMAAJ&printsec=frontcover&source=gbs_ge_summary_r&cad=0#v=onepage&q&f=fals*

Ellis, Franklin, and Samuel Evans, *History of Lancaster County, with Sketches of many its pioneers and prominent men,* Everts & Peck,1883. The book may be found online here:

https://books.google.com/books?id=WsQxAQAAMAAJ&printsec=frontcover&source=gbs_ge_summary_r&cad=0#v=onepage&q&f=false

Forest, Tuomi J., *William Penn: Visionary Proprietor,* University of Virginia Press, A digitized version may be found here: http://xroads.virginia.edu/~cap/penn/pnind.html

Haresta, Joseph M, *The Amish—A People of Preservation and Profitability: A Look at the Amish Industry in Lancaster County, Pennsylvania,* Journal of Amish and Plain Anabaptist Studies" vol 2, issue 1, 2014.

Harris, Alexander, *A Biographical History of Lancaster County,"* E. Barr & Company, 1872. A digitized version of the book may be found here: https://books.google.com/books?id=0EwOAAAAIAAJ&printsec=frontcover&source=gbs_ge_summary_r&cad=0#v=onepage&q&f=false

Henriques, Diana B., *The Machinery of Greed,* Lexington Books, 1986

Historical Papers and Addresses of Lancaster County, Vols. 4-6. Lancaster County Historical Society, 1896.

Kearns Goodwin, Doris, *Team of Rivals: The Political Genius of Abraham Lincoln,* Simon & Schuster, 2005.

Kirk, Andrew, "*Desperation, Zeal, Murder: The Paxton Boys,*" Penn State University, 2009. Article may be found online here: http://pabook2.libraries.psu.edu/palitmap/PaxtonBoys.html.

Kraybill, Donald B., *Concise Encyclopedia of Amish, Brethren, Hutterites, and Mennonites,* Johns Hopkins University Press, 2010.

Kraybill, Donald B., *Who Are the Anabaptists: Amish, Brethren, Hutterites, and Mennonites,* Herald Press. 2003.

Lancaster County Planning Commission, "Agricultural District Zoning District Guidelines for Lancaster County, Pennsylvania," 2010, See: http://www.lancastercountyplanning.org/DocumentCenter/Home/View/107

Landis, David H., *John Wright: Historical Papers and Addresses of Lancaster County,* Lancaster County Historical Society, originally published by the Library of the University of California, 1910.

Lehman, James O., and Steven M. Nolt, "*Mennonites, Amish and the Civil War,* Johns Hopkins University Press, 2007.

Lewis, Anthony, *Make No Law: The Sullivan Case and the First Amendment,* Vintage Books, 1992.

Mapes, Mary, *Truth and Duty,* St. Martin's Press, New York, NY, 2005.

Mayer, Brantz, *Memoir and Genealogy of the Maryland and Pennsylvanian Family of Mayer,* WK Boyle & Son, 1878.

Means, Howard B., *The Avenger Takes His Place: Andrew Johnson and the 45 Days that Changed the Nation,* Houghton Mifflin Harcourt, 2006.

Members of Congress, "Memorial addresses on the life and character of Thaddeus Stevens delivered in the House of Representatives, Washington, D.C. December 17, 1868," Government Printing Office, 1869. Available online here: *https://books.google.com/books?id=WGsFAAAAQAAJ&printsec=frontcover&source=gbs_ge_summary_r&cad=0#v=onepage&q&f=false*

Menken, H.L., *My Life as an Author and Editor,* Knopf Doubleday Publishing Group, 1995.

Mintz, Steven, (ed.) *Native American Voices: A History and Anthology,* Brandywine Press, 2000.

Mosier, John, *Hitler vs. Stalin: The Eastern Front,* Simon & Schuster, New York, NY, 2010.

O'Neill, Tip, *All Politics is Local,* Adams Media Corp., 1994.

Penn Family Papers. Historical Society of Pennsylvania, "Indian Affairs, Vol I., University of Virginia. A digital version of the Penn Family Papers may be found here: http://www2.hsp.org/collections/manuscripts/p/Penn0485A.html

Pennsylvania Bureau of Labor Statistics, Occupational Employment and Wages in Lancaster. http://www.bls.gov/regions/mid-atlantic/news-release/occupationalemploymentandwages_lancaster.htm

Pennsylvania Department of Agriculture's "Food Safety Inspections Database": http://www.agriculture.pa.gov/Protect/FoodSafety/Food%20Safety%20Inspection%20Reports/Pages/default.aspx#.V1eLArsrLIU

Ricks, Thomas, *Churchill & Orwell, The Fight for Freedom,* Penguin Press, NY, NY, 2017

Salmon, John S., *The Official Virginia Civil War Battlefield Guide,* Stackpole Books; Mechanicsburg, Pa. 2001.

Sanders, Heywood, *Convention Center Follies,* University of Pennsylvania Press, Philadelphia, PA, 2014.

Schuyler, David, A City Transformed: Redevelopment, Race, and Suburbanization in Lancaster, Pennsylvania, 1940-1980, Pennsylvania University Press, 2002.

Shaara, Michael, *The Killer Angels,* McKay Publishing, 1974.

Singer, Allen J. "*New York and Slavery: Time to Teach the Truth,* SUNY Press, 2008.

Slaughter, Thomas P., *Bloody Dawn: The Christiana Riot and Racial Violence in the Antebellum North,* Oxford University Press, 1991.

Smith, Calvin E., *Stevens & Lee, a Memoir,"* Stevens & Lee, 1978; (found at the special collections section of the Alvernia College Library in Reading, Pennsylvania.)

Bibliography

Stevens, Thaddeus, (Beverly Wilson Palmer, Beverly [ed.]), *The Selected Papers of Thaddeus Stevens Vol. 1, 1865-1868,* University of Pittsburgh Press, 1998.

U.S. Census Bureau, *Federal Spending to states,* See: http://www.census.gov/prod/www/governments.html

U.S. Department of Agriculture. Soil Conservation Service, Soil Survey of Lancaster County, Pennsylvania, in connection with Pennsylvania State University College of Agriculture and the Pennsylvania State Environmental Resources State Conservation Commission

Warren, Christian, *Brush with Death: A Social History of Lead Poisoning,* Johns Hopkins University Press, 2001

Winpenny, Thomas R. *"Bending is Not Breaking: Adaptation and Persistence Among 19th Century Lancaster Artisans,"* University of America Press, 1990.

INDEX

A

Act 23 134-136, 138-139, 150-152, 154-155, 162, 169-170, 205-206, 250-254, 313, 317, 347-348, 354, 360, 362, 403, 413, 428-430, 434-435, 513, 523-527

Adams, Helen Colwell 95, 177-178, 200, 220, 278-280, 290, 300, 303-304, 312, 315, 330, 334, 353, 364-365, 368, 372, 382, 384-385, 388, 394, 400, 411-412, 422-423, 425, 438-439, 441, 445, 447, 449-454, 461-462, 529

Adams, Marvin 164, 177, 220, 278, 384

Armstrong, Gibson 60, 64, 157, 263, 448, 512, 515

B

Bailey, Ron 123, 343

Barley, John 60, 65, 68, 101, 107-108, 112, 321, 337-338, 340

Block, Paul 32, 299, 519

Brown, Kenneth 266, 412, 441-442

Brubaker, John 32

Buckwalter, John, "Jack" 24, 37, 41-44, 57, 61, 110, 146-147, 156, 161-163, 169, 172-173, 175-176, 178, 190, 200, 228, 242, 245, 258, 263, 290, 294, 300, 303-304, 310, 327, 330, 353, 359, 363-365, 367-368, 372-374, 380-385, 399-400, 404, 412, 425, 432, 439

C

Campbell, R. B. 146

Clossey, Mark 285, 457

Clymer, James 99

Complete Healthcare Resources 19, 184, 187, 189, 198, 200, 202, 401, 501-503

Conestoga View 16-17, 19, 119-120, 181-184, 187-206, 213, 215, 220, 225, 240-247, 264, 266-268, 271-274, 276-281, 292-293, 366, 369-370, 382, 386-387, 389-402, 404-406, 410-412, 422-424, 426, 427, 440-449,

451-456, 462, 497, 501-505, 514, 523-524, 528, 530

Cooley, Nevin 44, 72, 127, 132, 138, 140, 144, 148, 161, 169, 172-173, 175-176, 200, 228, 232, 263, 291-292, 344, 346, 353, 355, 359, 363, 366, 377-381, 383, 417, 531

Cox, Dennis 166, 200-201, 373, 400

Craver, Jack 229, 233, 237, 340, 403, 415, 418-420

CRIZ 19, 284, 507, 531, 532

D

Darcus, Ted 145, 157, 235-236, 256, 345, 418-419, 421, 529

Douglas, Laura 229, 238, 256-257, 340, 403, 415, 421, 431

E

Elliott, Don 172, 184, 186, 267, 344, 381, 392

Espenshade, John 75, 78, 122, 157, 172, 183, 185, 220, 229, 236, 238, 247, 343, 410, 421, 523

F

Farina, Judge Louis 80, 212, 222, 255, 266, 523

Feasibility Study 20, 142, 162, 227-232, 234-235, 237, 248, 355-356, 371, 417-419, 422, 427, 515, 525-526

Field, Robert 230-235, 416-417, 421

Foltz, Charles 30-31, 298, 519

Ford, Commissioner Ron 56, 69, 88, 95, 103, 106, 110, 328, 411, 448

G

Gleiberman, Rodney 87, 314, 323

grand jury 17, 45, 184, 212-213, 215-221, 240-241, 245, 255, 266-270, 273-274, 276-277, 279, 281, 283, 292, 343, 358, 391-393, 405-407, 409, 412, 423, 430, 440-443, 445-448,

450-453, 455, 462, 525, 528

Grand Jury 214, 225, 275, 278, 280, 390, 408, 410, 444, 449, 454, 515, 534

Gray, Mayor J. Richard 60, 157, 196, 198, 226-227, 229, 230, 248, 250, 258, 260, 287, 316, 413-415, 417, 427, 433, 448, 525, 527, 529-530

Greater Lancaster Hotel and Motel Association 73, 285, 314, 319

H

Hall, Deb 229, 236, 256, 340, 403, 415, 419, 431-432, 527

Harper, Ron 112, 237, 309, 327, 330-331, 337, 358, 386, 421, 437, 522

Harris, Bernie 182, 422

Harrisburg Area Community College 57, 61, 143, 165, 226, 324, 345, 353, 357, 413, 521

Heinke, Gary 45, 123-124, 184-186, 209-213, 215, 219, 221, 244, 255, 266, 273, 275-276, 278-280, 292, 343, 405, 406-407, 409, 422, 424, 430, 441, 451, 452, 462, 523-525

Henderson, Commissioner Molly 12, 23, 55, 84, 96, 118, 157, 167, 170, 172, 194, 198-199, 240, 273, 278, 280, 292, 300, 303-304, 312, 315-316, 328, 330, 353, 364-365, 368, 372, 379-380, 382, 384-385, 387, 394, 399, 400, 404, 410, 411-412, 422-425, 435, 438-439, 441, 445, 447, 449-454, 461-462, 494, 501, 510, 522-525, 528-530

Hennigan, Dave 174, 190, 382, 394

High, Sanford 37-39, 43, 301

High, S. Dale 17, 23-24, 26, 28, 39-40, 43, 52, 54, 61-62, 67, 93, 109-110, 131, 144, 146, 147, 155, 165, 169, 228, 231, 260, 297, 300-302, 304, 309-310, 319, 325, 327, 330, 336, 353, 358-359, 372, 404, 411, 432, 520

hoteliers 72, 78, 80, 85-89, 92, 113, 157, 252, 285, 314, 319, 321-325, 327, 337, 457, 512, 522-523

hotel tax 50-51, 75, 77, 85, 134, 247, 286-287, 305-306, 310, 314, 318-319, 329, 335, 345, 347, 356, 386, 420, 506, 512-513, 516, 530, 533

K

Kegel, Clarence 133, 361

Kelin, Howard 142, 151, 157, 205, 349, 352, 354, 402-403, 425, 430

Kirchner, Timothea 49, 122, 186, 337, 342

L

Lancaster Alliance 42, 54-55, 58, 60, 62, 145, 221, 228, 239, 310, 327, 374, 400, 413, 415, 459, 521

Lancaster Campaign 42, 58, 60, 74, 90, 145, 195, 228, 309-311, 336, 415, 512-521

Lancaster County Convention Center Authority 19, 50, 77-78, 93, 115, 131, 147, 157, 205, 231, 236, 256, 259, 284, 305-306, 314, 318, 320-325, 330, 340, 345, 347, 358, 363, 400, 415-416, 419-422, 424, 430-432, 434-435, 459, 509-513, 516, 522-532

Lancaster Newspapers 12, 16-17, 20, 23-24, 28, 32-33, 40-41, 43, 50-51, 54, 56-58, 61, 67-70, 78, 84, 87-88, 94, 109, 111, 120, 122, 131, 142-144, 146, 155-157, 161-166, 168-179, 181-182,

189-193, 196, 199-206, 219-220, 222, 225, 237, 240-245, 253-254, 258-259, 263-266, 268, 271, 273, 277-283, 287-294, 297, 299-305, 308-310, 312, 314-315, 317, 319, 323, 327-328, 330, 333, 337, 343, 348-349, 353, 357, 359, 363-368, 372, 374-378, 380-385, 387, 393-395, 398, 400-402, 404-406, 410-412, 415, 417-418, 422-426, 432, 436, 438-443, 445-451, 453-455, 458-462, 494, 509-510, 515-522, 529-531

Lancaster Prospers 14, 289, 459-460, 532-533

libel suit 166, 292, 330, 364, 395, 400, 458

Litvak, Anya 273-274, 422

Lovett, Mark 222, 266, 269-270

M

Madenspacher, Joseph 261, 528

Market Study 134, 228-229, 415, 417, 420, 496, 512

Marriott hotel 302, 353, 366, 437, 463

Marriott Hotel 12-13, 17, 28, 48, 132, 139-141, 149-151, 284-286, 288, 297, 304-305, 308, 325-326, 344, 352, 362-363, 381, 403, 428, 436, 442, 456, 459, 506-507, 514-515, 526, 529, 531, 532

McCudden, Dave 120, 342

McCue, Andrea 121

McGough, Thomas 266, 441-442

Morris, Mayor Art 60-61, 74, 143, 157, 165-166, 182, 190, 192, 200, 203, 207, 209-210, 213, 220-221, 226, 244-245, 280, 292, 309, 343, 367-368, 371-372, 389-390, 395, 397-398, 400-401, 405, 407, 411-412, 424, 448, 454-456, 461, 529

Murphy, Andi 186, 267, 442

Myers, Tom 45, 209, 214, 406, 424, 514

N

Nickel Mines 207, 405

November 2003 general election 115, 341

Nursing Homes 187, 192, 201-202, 367, 369-370, 388, 390, 394-396, 400-401, 426, 504, 505

P

Penn Square Partners 53, 61-62, 68, 79, 90-93, 124, 127, 132, 135-136, 138, 140-144, 146, 148-153, 155-157, 161, 163, 170, 176, 181, 191, 205, 226, 228, 235, 250, 254-255, 258-259, 261, 263-265, 283-286, 288-291, 295, 302, 308, 311-312, 314-315, 317, 323-327, 344,

INDEX

346, 349, 352-364, 367, 371-372, 376-378, 381, 383-386, 402-403, 411, 413-415, 417-418, 420, 422, 425-426, 428, 432, 435-439, 442, 456-459, 461, 463, 506-507, 509-511, 521-522, 524-527, 529, 531-532

Pennsylvania Dutch & Convention Center Visitors Bureau 91

Pickard, James 61

Pidgeon, David 290, 300, 312, 315, 330, 353, 364-365, 368, 372, 382, 384-385, 388, 394, 400, 412, 422-423, 425, 438-439, 441, 445, 447, 449-451, 453-454, 461-462, 529

PKF 20, 234-236, 247-248, 284, 418, 420, 422, 427, 515, 525-526

Pricewaterhouse 229-230, 232-234, 415, 418, 420, 512, 514

ProQuest 201, 205, 316, 387, 402, 412, 424-425, 440, 453-455, 494

PSP, see Penn Square Partners

Q

Questions 142-143, 148, 170, 356-357, 478, 524

R

Redevelopment Authority of the City of Lancaster 317, 359-362, 371, 414, 422, 428, 435, 456, 510-512, 524-525, 527-528

Reinsel Kuntz Lesher 20, 245-247, 390-391, 393, 398, 426-427

Ricks, Thomas 294

Ridge, Governor Tom 63, 313, 321, 522

S

Sanders, Heywood 133, 307, 322, 524

Schreiber, Ernie 166, 174, 176, 178, 197, 242, 244, 292, 367, 377-379, 381, 383, 423-424, 453

Schuyler, David 53, 307

Shaub, Commissioner Howard, "Pete" 23, 106, 108-111, 114, 118, 121, 125, 128-129, 131, 157, 167, 168, 183, 198, 209, 219, 240, 274, 277, 280-281, 329, 332-335, 337, 339, 342-343, 373, 399, 404, 410, 440, 446, 455, 523-525, 528

Shaw, Ray 174-176, 178, 382, 384

Shellenberger, Dick 16, 23, 97, 114-115, 123, 128, 131, 162, 167, 170, 172, 184, 199, 206-207, 219, 240, 242, 273-274, 277-278, 280, 282, 288, 294, 320, 329, 345, 387, 390, 399, 404, 443, 448, 459, 461, 514, 523-524, 528, 530

Smart, Gil 273

Smithgall, Mayor, Charlie 59, 60-61, 66, 71, 74, 79, 84, 88, 103, 107, 136, 145, 166, 194-196, 198, 226, 263, 288, 309, 320, 332, 336, 353, 357, 363, 369,

372, 375, 404, 413-414, 433-434, 437, 521-522, 524

Smith, Lydia Hamilton 259, 262, 364

Stadium Bill 63-65, 67-69, 73, 101, 132, 312, 314-315, 522

Steinman, Andrew Jackson 29, 31-32, 42, 297-298, 364, 366, 518

Steinman, Beverly, "Peggy" 34-35, 37, 109-110, 156, 161, 163-164, 174, 178, 366, 377, 379, 412

Steinman, Caroline Nunan 29, 35-36, 43, 300

Steinman, Christian and Anna 29, 517

Steinman, James Hale 31, 43, 297, 299, 302, 518, 520

Steinman, John Frederick 34, 297-299, 302, 366, 517-518, 520

Stevens & Lee 48-50, 65, 73, 75, 77-78, 115, 122, 124, 134-135, 172, 183-184,

220, 231, 236, 238-239, 244, 247, 272, 305-306, 320, 330, 340, 342-343, 345-346, 347, 348, 363, 375, 390, 401, 411, 416, 419, 421, 424, 431, 519, 523, 536

Stevens, Thaddeus 30, 89, 138, 144, 162, 181, 259, 262, 287, 297-298, 324-325, 352-353, 364-365, 386, 458, 514, 517, 525, 530, 532, 535, 537

Stuckey, Dennis 195, 198, 210, 246, 329, 338, 339, 390, 406, 411, 426-427, 456

Styer, Terry 121, 126

Sunshine Act 89, 127, 183-184, 192, 240, 267-271, 276, 344, 391, 442-444, 528

T

Thibault, Commissioner Paul 56-57, 60, 69, 74, 79, 96, 103, 106-108, 110-111, 157, 195, 197, 285, 309, 319-320,

334-336, 338, 375, 398, 411, 424, 436-437, 512

Tax Increment Financing, see TIF

TIF 20, 138, 139-146, 148, 152, 155, 161, 167, 169, 191, 249, 258, 353-359, 372, 381, 383, 386, 413-414, 432, 510, 513-514, 524

Totaro, Donald 45, 119, 211, 218, 225, 255, 283, 408, 435, 446, 525

True, Katie 51, 109, 206, 253-254, 306, 430

U

Urban, C. Emlen 53-54, 239, 263, 352, 521

W

Watt & Shand 54-55, 57, 60-62, 67, 89, 132, 135, 138-139, 141, 143, 146-149, 165-166, 181, 189, 226-228, 239, 249-250, 263-264, 287, 308-309, 311-312, 317, 321, 325, 327,

346, 348, 352-353, 357, 359-360, 364-365, 371-372, 376, 404, 413-415, 427-428, 437-438, 514, 521, 525, 527-528, 529

Made in the USA
Middletown, DE
22 August 2019